W9-CIF-824

Also by Gershom Gorenberg

The End of Days:
Fundamentalism and the Struggle
for the Temple Mount

Shalom, Friend:
The Life and Legacy of Yitzhak Rabin (coauthor)

THE ACCIDENTAL EMPIRE

THE
ACCIDENTAL
EMPIRE

ISRAEL AND THE BIRTH OF
THE SETTLEMENTS, 1967–1977

GERSHOM GORENBERG

TIMES BOOKS

HENRY HOLT AND COMPANY · NEW YORK

Times Books
Henry Holt and Company, LLC
Publishers since 1866
175 Fifth Avenue
New York, New York 10010
www.henryholt.com

Copyright © 2006 by Gershom Gorenberg
All rights reserved.
Distributed in Canada by H. B. Fenn and Company Ltd.

Library of Congress Cataloging-in-Publication Data

Gorenberg, Gershom.
  The accidental empire : Israel and the birth of settlements, 1967–1977 /
Gershom Gorenberg.—1st ed.
    p. cm.
  Includes bibliographical references and index.
  ISBN-13: 978-0-8050-7564-9
  ISBN-10: 0-8050-7564-X
  1. Land settlement—West Bank—Governmental policy—Israel.
2. Land settlement—Gaza Strip—Governmental policy—Israel. 3. Jews—
Colonization—West Bank. 4. Jews—Colonization—Gaza Strip. 5. Israel—
Politics and government—1967–1993. I. Title.

HD850.5.Z63G67 2006
956.9405'3—dc22   2005052988

First Edition 2006

Designed by Victoria Hartman

Map © 2006, Anita Karl and Jim Kemp

Printed in the United States of America

5 7 9 10 8 6 4

For Myra

Our only trouble is that we haven't land enough. If I had plenty of land, I shouldn't fear the Devil himself!

—Lev Nikolayevich Tolstoy,
"How Much Land Does a Man Need?"

Mere anarchy is loosed upon the world . . .
Surely some revelation is at hand

—William Butler Yeats, "The Second Coming"

Contents

Cast of Characters

GOLDA MEIR, Labor Party secretary-general, prime minister 1969–1974 (Mapai)

THEODOR MERON, legal counsel to the Foreign Ministry

MOSHE NETZER, Defense Ministry official, head of Nahal under Dayan, adviser on settlement under Peres (Rafi)

SHIMON PERES, Dayan loyalist, Knesset member, defense minister (Rafi)

YAAKOV PERRY, Shin Bet agent in Nablus

YITZHAK RABIN, army chief of staff, ambassador to the United States, prime minister 1974–1977 (Labor)

PINHAS SAPIR, finance minister (Mapai)

MEIR SHAMIR, head of the Galilee office of the Jewish Agency's Settlement Department

HAIM MOSHE SHAPIRA, interior minister (National Religious Party)

YAAKOV SHIMSHON SHAPIRA, justice minister (Mapai)

ZORACH WARHAFTIG, religious affairs minister (National Religious Party)

RA'ANAN WEITZ, head of the Jewish Agency's Settlement Department (Mapai)

Note: The Labor Party was formed in 1968 as a union of the Mapai, Rafi, and Ahdut Ha'avodah parties. It contested the elections of 1969, 1974, and 1977 in the Alignment with the left-wing Mapam Party.

The United Kibbutz Movement and the Merom Golan Settlement

CARMEL BAR, army veteran, settler

RAFAEL BEN-YEHUDAH, organizer

YEHUDAH HAREL, organizer, settler

KOBI RABINOVICH, army tank veteran, settler

EYTAN SAT, organizer

YITZHAK TABENKIN, socialist theoretician and ideological leader of the movement

The Religious Settler Movement

YOEL BIN-NUN, student at Merkaz Harav, Gush Emunim ideologue

YEHUDAH ETZION, student at Har Etzion yeshivah, founder of Ofrah settlement

MENACHEM FELIX, settler in Hebron and Kiryat Arba, organizer of Sebastia settlement bids

BENNY KATZOVER, settler at Hebron and Kiryat Arba, organizer of Sebastia settlement bids

TZVI YEHUDAH KOOK, rabbi, spiritual leader and head of the Merkaz Harav yeshivah

MOSHE LEVINGER, rabbi, founder of the Hebron settlement and Kiryat Arba, a leader of Gush Emunim

MOSHE MOSKOVIC, activist in reestablishment of Etzion Bloc settlements

HANAN PORAT, student at Merkaz Harav, settler at Kfar Etzion, a leader of Gush Emunim

ELIEZER WALDMAN, rabbi, settler in Hebron and Kiryat Arba, Gush Emunim activist

Israel Defense Forces

DAVID ELAZAR, head of Northern Command in 1967, chief of staff in Yom Kippur War

SHLOMO GAZIT, Dayan's coordinator of Israeli government activities in the occupied territories

MORDECHAI GUR, head of paratroopers in 1967, chief of staff following Yom Kippur War

MORDECHAI HOD, commander of Israel Air Force in 1967

UZI NARKISS, head of Central Command in 1967

ARIEL SHARON, head of Southern Command, later a Knesset member and adviser to Prime Minister Rabin

Israeli Writers

NATHAN ALTERMAN, poet, founder of the Movement for the Whole Land of Israel

HAIM GOURI, poet and journalist, veteran of the Palmah pre-state militia

YISRAEL HAREL, Orthodox journalist, activist in the Movement for the Whole Land of Israel

CHAIM SABBATO, memoirist of the Yom Kippur War

MOSHE SHAMIR, novelist, former leftist turned supporter of the Whole Land of Israel

NAOMI SHEMER, popular songwriter, creator of "Jerusalem of Gold," Whole Land advocate

Settlement Opponents and Critics

LATIF DORI, Mapam party activist

ARIE ELIAV, Labor Party secretary-general

ODED LIFSHITZ, member of Kibbutz Nir Oz, organizer of Mapam kibbutzim against expulsion of Sinai Bedouin

AMOS OZ, novelist, kibbutz member

YOSSI SARID, protégé of Pinchas Sapir, Knesset member

Arab Political and Cultural Figures

SULEIMAN HUSSEIN UDAH ABU HILU, sheikh of a Bedouin tribe in northeastern Sinai

YASSER ARAFAT, leader of Fatah and the Palestine Liberation Organization

HAFIZ AL-ASAD, president of Syria

HUSSEIN IBN TALAL, king of Jordan

MUHAMMAD ALI AL-JABARI, mayor of Hebron

GAMAL ABDEL NASSER, president of Egypt

ZAID AL-RIFAI, adviser to King Hussein, prime minister of Jordan

ANWAR AL-SADAT, president of Egypt, succeeding Nasser

AZIZ SHEHADEH, Ramallah lawyer, formerly from Jaffa, advocate for a Palestinian state alongside Israel

RAJA SHEHADEH, son of Aziz Shehadeh; memoirist

FADWA TUQAN, Palestinian poet

United States Officials

McGEORGE BUNDY, former national security adviser, special coordinator for Mideast policy (Johnson administration)

GERALD R. FORD, president of the United States 1974–1977

LYNDON B. JOHNSON, president of the United States 1963–1969

HENRY KISSINGER, national security adviser, secretary of state (Nixon and Ford administrations)

RICHARD M. NIXON, president of the United States 1969–1974

WILLIAM ROGERS, secretary of state (Nixon administration)

WALT W. ROSTOW, national security adviser (Johnson administration)

DEAN RUSK, secretary of state (Johnson administration)

HAROLD SAUNDERS, National Security Council and State Department expert on the Middle East (Johnson, Nixon, and Ford administrations)

JOSEPH SISCO, assistant secretary of state (Johnson, Nixon, and Ford administrations)

THE ACCIDENTAL EMPIRE

Israel, the Occupied Territories, and Key Early Settlement Sites

Main map labels:

LEBANON
SYRIA
Merom Golan
Quneitrah
DMZ
Aalleiqa
Katzrin
GOLAN HEIGHTS
Haifa
Sea of Galilee
Ramat Magshimim
DMZ
Jordan River
Jenin
Mebolab
SAMARIA
Sebastia
Nablus
Kaddum
Argaman
Tel Aviv
WEST BANK
Gilgal
JORDAN RIFT
Ramallah
Ofrah
Jericho
Ma'aleb Adumim
JERUSALEM
Bethlehem
Kalyah
Alon Shvut
Kfar Etzion
Kiryat Arba
Hebron
JUDEA
JORDAN
Dead Sea
GAZA STRIP
Netzarim
Gaza
Kfar Darom
Yamit
Khan Yunis
Beersheba
Diklah
Sadot
Al-Arish
SINAI
ISRAEL
Mediterranean Sea

Top-left inset:

— — — June 4, 1967 lines

☐ Areas occupied by Israel after June 10, 1967

LEBANON
SYRIA
ISRAEL
JORDAN
EGYPT
SINAI
SAUDI ARABIA
Di-Zahav
Ofirah (Sharm al-Sheikh)
Red Sea

Left inset:

Border of Israeli-annexed East Jerusalem

WEST BANK
JERUSALEM
Old City

Legend (bottom):

— — — June 4, 1967 lines

☐ Areas occupied by Israel after June 10, 1967

■ Early Settlement Sites

☐ No Man's Land

Kms.
0   30
Miles
0   30

DECEMBER 1975:
NORTH FROM JERUSALEM

"We are divided," Haim Gouri's mother had taught him, "between those with meager spirits and those with torn souls." That night, more than ever, Gouri counted himself as one of the raggedly ripped souls, and he envied the other sort.[1]

A solitary Israeli army jeep growled north from Jerusalem on the road winding through the dark hills of the West Bank. A soldier drove, another carried a gun to protect Gouri and his wife, Aliza, who had insisted on coming along though she could not understand how he had thrust himself into this madness.

The moon, only a narrow crescent, an accidental pencil stroke of light on the December sky, had already set when the jeep pulled out of its Jerusalem base near midnight. They rode though Ramallah and past the shadowed Arab villages strung out along the mountain ridge, and on through Nablus, where by daylight Palestinian demonstrators had littered the road with burning tires, and headed on. Yitzhak Rabin, the prime minister, had insisted that Gouri—a poet and journalist turned negotiator on a moment's whim—could not go this way at night in his own car to carry a message from the government.[2]

Fifty-two years old, Gouri had a face made of sharp angles: sharp chin and nose, sharp brows above deep-set eyes. Eight and a half years before, on the third day of the Six-Day War of 1967, he had worn a uniform himself as he drove north in a convoy from Jerusalem toward newly conquered Ramallah, a platoon commander in the reserves called up for duty in a sudden conflict. That time, a June sun had drenched the hills. The land he passed through had been part of the British-ruled Palestine of his youth, but had lain, unreachable, beyond the frontier since Israel's establishment in 1948. "It seemed to me I'd died and was waking up, resurrected," he had written in June 1967. "All that I loved was cast at my feet, stunningly ownerless, landscapes revealed as in a dream. The old Land of Israel, the homeland of my youth, the other half of my cleft country. And their land, the land of the unseen ones, hiding behind their walls."³

The memory still shone, incandescent, whenever he came this way, though he had since concluded that the war had "liberated the land but torn the nation"—deeply dividing Israelis about whether the land taken in the battles against Jordan, Egypt, and Syria was liberated or occupied, about whether Israel must hold some or all or none of it, about how to see the "unseen ones"—the Arabs who lived there. On this cold night, Gouri feared the nation was on verge of brother fighting brother.⁴

North of Nablus, next to the village of Sebastia, the jeep turned onto a dirt road lined with pines and cypresses. A two-story stone building, an abandoned train station at which passengers had last alighted when the British ruled Palestine, overlooked a narrow valley splotched with the glow of campfires.

"The scene was surrealistic," Gouri would recall. Thousands of people waited in freezing cold. Most were Orthodox Jews, young men and women and teenagers, the armies of the night, camped out here in defiance of Rabin's government, aflame themselves with the passion of demonstrators anywhere who are many and certain. They were there demanding that Rabin allow Jews to settle on the outskirts of Nablus, to stake a claim that would keep Israel from giving up part of the ancient homeland in return for peace. They sought to shatter a policy that said the hill country should be set aside, to be conceded when the time came, in order to avoid permanent Israeli rule over its Arab population. For a week, the crowd in the valley had grown and shrunk and grown, tense with the possibility of confrontation and the improbable hope of victory. Around them waited soldiers, ready for orders to pull them, struggling, onto buses and—as Gouri noticed with sardonic fury—meanwhile protecting the law-defying settlement supporters from the Palestinians demonstrating against their presence.[5]

Gouri had come earlier that day as a journalist, to look and write. The would-be settlers conjured up passions he remembered from his own days in a socialist youth movement intoxicated with the land; and they conjured up fear of anarchy, the collapse of the state.

"Happy are the whole, and woe to the torn . . ." he wrote that week, describing his visit. "In my life, too, there have been times when I've been at one with a deed. Today, too, I'm utterly at one with a few principles. But this time I wander torn among people swept up in messianic fervor."[6] He wanted this confrontation to end peacefully, within the rules; he feared the shock waves in a fractured nation if one pregnant woman were to miscarry as she was pulled to the buses. So he had stepped out of the role of journalistic witness and into the role of actor, proposing a compromise—to his old comrades-in-arms who now ruled the country, and now, with their approval, the handwritten terms scrawled by a senior cabinet minister, to the organizers at Sebastia. Inside the train station, the leaders of the Gush Emunim, Israel's most successful protest movement, argued through the night about whether Gouri's compromise meant victory, as Gouri and his wife shivered outside.

IN THE UNCERTAIN memory of many Israelis and Israel-watchers, the issue of settlement in occupied land began in the struggle between Yitzhak Rabin's first government in the mid-1970s and the young radicals of Gush Emunim. The story therefore becomes a simple one: On one side are the secular pragmatists of the left; on the other, the religious fanatics of the right. Or—in another telling that changes the labels without drastically changing the script—on one side are uninspired defeatists; on the other, the truest patriots.

In either telling, the confrontation at the Sebastia train station in the first week of December 1975 marks the point of departure for a long and contentious journey. Gush Emunim and its successors have gone on to build communities throughout the territories Israel overran in June 1967. Settlers have benefited from government support, especially after Israel's Labor Party lost power to the right-wing Likud bloc in 1977—and yet, again and again, some have also clashed with the state, at times violently. The question of whether the settlement imperative or democracy takes precedence has threatened to rip Israel apart.

In accounts of Mideast diplomacy as well, the settlements first appear in the mid-1970s, as if from nowhere, with no explanation of how they appeared on the landscape.[7] Since then, Israel's settlements have seized an ever more prominent place on the international agenda. The most accepted approach to ending the entanglement of Israelis and Palestinians requires dividing the land that both consider their home. And the very purpose of settlements is to stand in the way of Israel forfeiting the land it took in 1967, or at the very least, to ensure that it will retain as much of that land as possible.

In his eighties, one of the most renowned poets in a country where poets achieve popular stardom, Haim Gouri says today that getting involved at Sebastia was "the greatest foolishness of my life." His hope that a compromise would restore "the rules of the game" of civil discourse and law has proven vain. Long after Sebastia, he has watched Israeli soldiers struggle with defiant settlers. He has been accused, he says with pain, of being "the father of the settlements," as if he will be remembered for that and his poems will be forgotten.[8] The charge is unjust, and not only because he was badly used at the time, his compromise quickly twisted by politicians—particularly by Rabin's defense minister and chief rival, who was then known for his pro-settlement views, Shimon Peres.

In fact, Sebastia was not the beginning of settlement, but the *end* of the beginning. It was the culmination of a story that began even before the guns of the Six-Day War cooled. Religious radicals, convinced they were fulfilling God's plan for history, indeed played a central role—but alongside of, or even as understudies to, secularists identified with Israel's political left. Some had torn souls. Some were certain of what they were doing, were "made of exclamation points," in Gouri's phrase. Without intending to do so, they helped beget the religious settler movement, and then were stunned by it.

There are ironies inside ironies. Those who began the process of settlement beyond Israel's prewar borders believed passionately in the Jewish state. The older ones had helped create it. Yet they were inspired by the glory of their youth, the fervor of times before the state existed, when they were rebels, not officials. Now, impossibly, they tried to play both roles. The victory of 1967 represented a triumph of the state they had built. Yet it also yielded unplanned conquests, an accidental empire.

The process of settlement, of taking ownership of that empire, led to the state's gradual unraveling, blurring its borders, undercutting its authority. It pulled Jews and Arabs back into an older kind of conflict—instead of a battle between states, a struggle between two ethnic groups struggling for control of the same undivided land—the conflict that existed before the partition of Palestine and Israel's establishment. Victory faded into a tragedy of unending struggles, internal and external.

Sebastia was a crossroads, but the journey had begun years earlier, before anyone could drive north on the road from Jerusalem.

1

THE AVALANCHE

One day in early May 1967, General Uzi Narkiss stood in the shade of pine trees on the breeze-stroked hilltop of Kibbutz Ramat Rachel, at the edge of Israeli West Jerusalem, and looked out past the armistice line at Bethlehem and the Judean Desert in the Jordanian-held West Bank. With him stood journalist Haim Gouri and a young intelligence officer. It was a clear day in the brief Israeli spring, after the rains have stopped, before the dry heat scorches the last pale green from the hillsides and leaves them yellow-brown. Still, when Gouri wrote of his day with the general for his newspaper, his tone would be overcast, melancholy with nostalgia. He and Narkiss were looking at the territory of memory—as unreachable as one's youth.[1]

Narkiss, forty-two years old and the head of the Israeli Defense Forces' Central Command, turned his binoculars to a flat-topped mountain to the southeast, site of a ruined fortress built by King Herod of Judea two millennia ago. Narkiss had hidden there for a day, he told the intelligence officer, back in 1946: His unit of the underground Haganah had attacked the Allenby Bridge over the Jordan River, as part of an operation aimed at driving the British from Palestine. Afterward they escaped by boat across the Dead Sea and climbed the desert cliffs to the ancient fortress, took cover there through daylight, then hiked through the hills to Ramat Rachel.

The young officer looked at Narkiss and mapped the line between Israeli generations: "You've passed through those places," he said. "Our experiences are different." He added, in the vague wish of someone with many years ahead of him, "Still, we'd like to go one day—let's hope in a time of peace."

On maps, the armistice line between Israel and Jordan was drawn in green. The line wrapped around West Jerusalem as if it were a peninsula of Israel surrounded by a sea of Jordanian territory. Ramat Rachel was a tinier peninsula, a promontory pointed southward toward Bethlehem and, beyond that, Hebron. After curling around the kibbutz, the Green Line sliced through Jerusalem, cleaving neighborhoods. Splotches of land were designated as demilitarized zones by the armistice agreement signed in April 1949, at the end of Israel's war of independence. The agreement looked forward to a permanent peace settlement, but that never came, so the Green Line remained the border, temporary in perpetuity.[2] Israel's parliament, the Knesset, stood just over a mile from the frontier; the prime minister's house, two-thirds of a mile. On the Jordanian side, the walled Old City nuzzled up against the border.

Gouri was accompanying Narkiss for a tour of the urban frontier. The two were friends, members of an aristocracy of old fighters. They had met in pre-state days as young recruits to the Palmah, the elite force of the Haganah. The Palmah had been closely tied to a pro-Soviet movement of farm communes, kibbutzim, known as Hakibbutz Hame'uhad, the United Kibbutz, whose original goal had been turning all of Jewish Palestine into a single collective. Some people had called the Palmah "the Red Army of the United Kibbutz."[3] Now Gouri wrote for the daily newspaper of the party tied to that movement.

"It's so quiet here," Narkiss said, looking at the hills. "It seems like you're allowed to just get up and walk over there."

How long, Gouri asked, could the strange situation continue in Jerusalem? "We should be prepared to live like this for years and years," Narkiss answered. "It might last forever, and it could change any day. We know this is the border, and that's that."

* * *

READING NARKISS'S words from the standpoint of history, looking back through the smoke of burning Egyptian tanks in the Sinai sands, one might suspect he was being disingenuous, that behind blank words he hid plans of war and conquest. But history can mislead us: It tells how things turned out. That is precisely what people living not-yet-history, looking forward into uncertainty, cannot know. What appears inevitable, even intentional, in retrospect, is often a series of accidents in real life.

Narkiss was being forthright: The top brass of the Israel Defense Forces (IDF) did not expect war. Earlier in 1967, Colonel Shlomo Gazit, the head of Military Intelligence's research department, had presented Armored Corps commander General Yisrael Tal with a report on the atrocious level of training of Egyptian tank crews. "If you are right," Tal replied, "they have no possibility of contending with us militarily." Tal's response only reinforced Military Intelligence's repeated evaluations that, even though the Arab countries aspired to destroy Israel, war was unlikely.[4] In March 1967, at a briefing for top commanders, General Aharon Yariv, the head of Military Intelligence, declared there was no chance of war in the Middle East in the next eight years. Egypt, the most powerful Arab country, was tied down in a civil war in Yemen; other Arab countries would not fight Israel on their own.[5]

That hardly meant that Israel was ready to convert tanks into tractors. Indeed, one reason for confidence was Israel's deterrent power. Through the mid-1960s, Prime Minister Levi Eshkol and military Chief of Staff Yitzhak Rabin had worked to acquire new arms, especially for the air force and armored corps, to convince Arab leaders they should not attack.

Still, tensions had been growing since 1964 on the eastern border. To cripple the Jewish state, Syria had tried to divert the headwaters of its main water supply, the Jordan River; Israel foiled that plan by bombing the earthworks.[6] Syria sponsored Palestinian groups, particularly the Fatah movement, that aimed at reclaiming Palestine from the "Zionist entity" via "armed struggle" and that launched terror attacks from both

Syrian and Jordanian territory. The Israeli army responded with cross-border retaliation raids. A de facto peace between Israel and Jordan—including secret meetings between top Israeli officials and the young King Hussein—evaporated.[7]

Along the 1949 armistice line with Syria—on the eastern shore of the Sea of Galilee and along the deep, humid valley of the Jordan River—were demilitarized zones that Israel regarded as its territory, a claim Syria rejected. On the ground, each side held part of these zones. Each time Israel sent tractors to farm disputed land, Syria answered with gunfire, sometimes shelling kibbutzim in the valley from the Syrian heights that rose steeply to the east. Recent Israeli histories argue that the Israeli generals deliberately initiated some such incidents: Syrian fire provided a pretext for a stronger Israeli response, really intended as retaliation for Palestinian attacks.[8] The clashes grew worse. On April 7, 1967, Syria answered a foray by two Israeli tractors with mortar and cannon fire, to which Israeli warplanes retorted by strafing and bombing Syrian positions. Israeli jets downed Syrian planes in dogfights over Damascus; Syrian shells leveled Kibbutz Gadot, inside a demilitarized zone on the Jordan River bank, north of the Sea of Galilee.[9]

Yet as Gazit has admitted, "Israeli intelligence erred in not drawing conclusions from the escalation, and did not warn that it could lead to a major conflagration."[10] Rather than being a deliberate prelude to war, the sparring testified to Israel's confidence that it could punish Syria without risking all-out conflict.

Nor was conquest on the Israeli military agenda. The army's five-year development plan, put together under Eshkol and Rabin, presumed that Israel could "realize fully its national goals" within the armistice lines.[11]

That reflected the position of Eshkol's ruling Mapai party. Mapai—the Workers Party of the Land of Israel—was established in 1930. Its founders were Jewish immigrants from places such as Minsk, Kiev, Warsaw, and Lvov, who had abandoned traditional Judaism as outmoded. Facing two shining secular ideas of utopia, they chose both: socialism along with Zionism, the belief that Jews must return to their homeland to build their own nation. In the Jewish community of British-ruled Palestine, where everything from unions to health clinics to sports teams belonged to parties, Mapai dominated.

In 1937, when a British government panel called the Peel Commission first proposed solving the ethnic conflict between Jews and Arabs over Palestine by dividing the land into two states, Mapai leader David Ben-Gurion failed to win his party's unqualified support for the plan. The Arabs rejected the Peel plan completely, and the British abandoned it. But ten years later, when the United Nations voted to split Palestine into Jewish and Arab states, Mapai endorsed partition, which promised immediate independence for a state with a Jewish majority.[12]

The U.N., though, did nothing to enforce its own decision. First Palestine's Arabs took up arms against the Jews and partition. When the British pulled out and Ben-Gurion led the Jews to declare Israel's independence on May 14, 1948, the neighboring Arab countries invaded—so that the moment of statehood marked a graduation from ethnic conflict to a war between sovereign nations.

By the war's end, Israel's forces had pushed back the Arab armies and won land beyond the U.N. partition lines, and as many as 750,000 Palestinian Arabs had fled from their villages and cities in the new Jewish state or had been expelled by Jewish forces, becoming refugees. Six thousand Jews were killed, out of the 650,000 Jews in Palestine when the war began. No Palestinian Arab state arose. The kingdom of Transjordan annexed the piece of Palestine its army had seized, on the West Bank of the Jordan River, and the kingdom's name became Jordan. The Gaza Strip, a sliver of Palestine packed with refugees on the Mediterranean coast, remained under Egyptian military rule. Parts of Israel's borders matched the old internationally recognized boundary of British Palestine, but elsewhere the country's territory was defined only by the armistice lines, which meandered crazily through the countryside, defying topography. North of Tel Aviv, Israel narrowed to a coastal strip just nine miles wide, beneath Jordanian-ruled hill country. Though Israel had a natural port on the Red Sea at its southern tip, Eilat, Egypt imposed a blockade farther south, at the Straits of Tiran.[13]

If there were diplomatic openings for peace, they were missed; the armistice led not to permanent peace but to permanent conflict. After Arab nationalist Gamal Abdel Nasser came to power in Egypt in 1953, that country sponsored a campaign of attacks on Israel, from both Gaza and the West Bank, by Palestinian "self-sacrificers." Israel answered with retaliation raids, killing civilians as well as soldiers. In one particularly gruesome raid, led by a young officer named Ariel Sharon, commandos killed over sixty civilians in the West Bank village of Qibyah.

The border battles, Nasser's deal to buy a new army's worth of Eastern Bloc weaponry via Czechoslovakia, his support for Algerian revolutionaries, his nationalization of the Suez Canal—all combined to make allies of Israel, Britain, and France. At the end of October 1956, Israeli prime minister David Ben-Gurion won his cabinet's approval for an invasion of Egypt's Sinai Desert, in collusion with the two European powers. Ben-Gurion hoped to shatter the Egyptian army and end the Palestinian attacks—and to acquire at least a piece of the Sinai, including Sharm al-Sheikh, the cape controlling the Straits of Tiran.[14] Under Chief of Staff Moshe Dayan, the Israel Defense Forces seized the entire Sinai Peninsula in just three days. Politically, though, it was a meager victory. Facing immense pressure from U.S. president Dwight Eisenhower, Israel withdrew to the armistice lines, and Nasser assumed mythic stature among Arab nationalists as the man who stood up to imperialists. But the U.N. Emergency Force (UNEF) took up positions on the Egyptian border and at Sharm al-Sheikh; the straits did stay open; and for a few quiet years Palestinian raids ceased, until the Fatah campaign began.[15]

And in Israel, irredentism—claims to territory beyond the borders—receded from political debate. In 1963, Eshkol replaced Ben-Gurion as Mapai leader and prime minister. When President Lyndon Johnson invited Eshkol to America in 1964, the visit ended with a joint statement calling for maintaining the territorial integrity of all Mideast countries—implying that both the United States and Israel regarded the armistice lines as final borders.[16] In the 1965 election campaign Mapai's platform—in an era when Israeli parties worried out their platforms with theological seriousness—called for pursuing every opportunity for peace "based on respect for the political independence and territorial integrity of all states in the region."[17]

Like middle-aged movements that had led revolutions in other countries, Mapai steadily shed its ideology. The Mapai method, as Israeli philosopher Moshe Halbertal puts it, was that "every big problem had a small solution."[18] The campaign of 1965 revolved mainly around a feud within the ruling camp: Ben-Gurion split with Eshkol and led a group of young acolytes, including Moshe Dayan and Shimon Peres, to form a new party—the Worker's List of Israel, known by its Hebrew acronym Rafi. The rebels did poorly, winning only ten seats in the 120-member Knesset, and found themselves on the opposition benches.

Even the militant Herut party of Menachem Begin, with its roots in the radical nationalism of the European right between the world wars,[19] softened its irredentist claims in return for respectability. In 1965 it ran for parliament on a joint ticket called Gahal with the mainstream Liberal Party ("liberal" in the European sense of capitalism and small government). Herut agreed that "integrity of the homeland"—meaning the claim to territory beyond the Green Line—would not be part of their joint platform.[20]

The shift went beyond political programs. A growing number of Israelis had grown up or arrived in the country after independence. In the Hebrew literature created by young writers of that time, notes Israeli historian Anita Shapira, there was "no hankering for some ancient historical agenda with Biblical sites and vistas. . . . Tel Aviv, the new Jerusalem, the kibbutzim—these were the foci of the new Hebrew literature."[21] For the post-independence generation, Shapira argues, Arabs were not extras in a romantic vision of the biblical past but hostile strangers across the border or dangerous infiltrators crossing it. Even the term "Land of Israel," the Jewish homeland, shifted meaning: In pre-state days, it meant at least all of British Palestine, or could include the East Bank of the Jordan or stretch farther, depending on one's reading of the Bible and history, or on how much one compensated for present Jewish weakness with the grandeur of myth. After independence, in the Hebrew of at least some young Israelis, "Land of Israel" was virtually a synonym for "State of Israel."

So at Ramat Rachel, General Narkiss told Gouri that the border was established fact. "It's our fate to live like this, and so we live," he said, adding, "A generation has arisen that has never known the land beyond the border."

From the kibbutz, they headed into the city, following the border. Narkiss told of a nun at the Notre Dame convent, which faced the armistice line, who once coughed while standing at her window. Her false teeth fell into no-man's-land, and U.N. observers searched for hours among ruins and trash to find them. In Abu Tor, a neighborhood divided in two, Gouri's photographer snapped a small boy and girl, holding hands, in an alleyway ending in barbed wire. "They were born here," Gouri wrote. "Here people live; love and death, birth and burial, weekdays and holidays roll on. For a moment you forget the wounds of this city, the cruelty of its tornness."[22]

YET GOURI did not really forget, and he was not alone.

He and Narkiss had been born in British Palestine and had reached adulthood in the years before partition. As poet and writer, Gouri often acted as witness, as Greek chorus, for a significant slice of the native-born—those who had grown up in socialist Zionist youth movements tied to the United Kibbutz, who had served in the Palmah and remained loyal to the party known as Ahdut Ha'avodah, the Unity of Labor.

A strange pamphlet called *In Your Covenant* bears testimony to the passions of their youth.[23] The booklet was produced in 1937 by older members of the youth movement called Hamahanot Ha'olim, the "Ascending Camps," who spent the summer together working at Kibbutz Gvat in the Jezreel Valley. Like other Zionist youth movements, Hamahanot Ha'olim was the creation of young people, not of adults trying to provide wholesome education. Youth itself, the newness offered by the young, was part of these movements' ideology, along with intense politics and a return to nature. Hamahanot Ha'olim stood out because it was founded in the Land of Israel, rather than among Jews abroad, and its members sought to demonstrate their credentials as children of the homeland through outdoing others in the romance with the countryside, exploring its contours and trekking for days through its hills and gorges.[24]

The event that shaped the summer was the Peel Commission's partition proposal. *In Your Covenant* is an answer, an adolescently anguished rejection. The word *Your* in the title, in feminine singular, refers to the Land of Israel. *Covenant* alludes both to marriage and to the covenant with God in traditional Judaism. The name itself conjures up the Freudian view of Zionism: The Jews have declared God the Father dead, and have married the motherland.[25] Hiking and working the land are the acts of physical love.

Maps in the booklet show the Land of Israel as including both sides of the Jordan River and stretching northward into Lebanon. A table explains that the total territory of the land including Transjordan and parts of southern Syria and Lebanon—identified by biblical names—is nearly 29,000 square miles, while the Jewish state proposed by the commission is less than 2,200 square miles.

There are texts praising physical labor, fitting the youth movement's proletarian ideology, but more of the booklet is devoted to the homeland. One section chronicles a hike through the northern tip of British Palestine and across the border into the Syrian heights, the area known as the Golan in Hebrew, overlooking the Jordan Valley. Another travelogue describes how movement members explored the Land of Israel by trekking into biblical Gilead, in Transjordan. A short essay on the Peel plan declares, "We have never accepted our unnatural border in the north. . . . We have always longed for the far bank of the Jordan . . . the one complete Land cannot be torn asunder." Another writer rejects the "fate of Nebo"—an allusion to Moses looking at the promised land but not being allowed to enter.

The next year a group of Hamahanot Ha'olim graduates founded Kibbutz Maoz Hayim, just west of the Jordan River, fifteen miles south of the Sea of Galilee. "May this house be the gate to Gilead. The lights of the labor of Hebrew settlements will yet glow in the Golan, Bashan and Horan . . . ," the commune's charter declared, using biblical Hebrew names for regions east of the Jordan, and in the next breath: "The working man will yet arise and build his home in a world of brotherhood and freedom."[26]

The contrapuntal music of socialism and nationalism was perfectly in tune with the positions of the United Kibbutz, whose leader—father figure, teacher, ideologue, secular equivalent of a Hasidic master—was Yitzhak Tabenkin. Raised in a religious family in Warsaw, Tabenkin gave up faith to become a student, in his own description, of Karl Marx and Zionist poet Haim Nahman Bialik. Early in his career, he referred to kibbutzim as "communist settlements," later giving up the term because he did not accept the Soviet approach to communism. Tabenkin thought poorly of the political concept of the state. Much closer to anarchism, he aimed at creating Jewish socialism from the bottom up, one commune at a time, but he also insisted that his utopia be built in what he called the Whole Land of Israel. At times his arguments had the veneer of scientific socialism: The land was by nature a single economic unit. At times he used arguments drawn from history and the Bible, which secular Zionism had transformed from scripture to national epic.

The tangle of nationalism and Marxism looks strange only from the anachronistic perspective of a much later European or American left-ism. A similar mix drove Ho Chi Minh and other Third World revolu-tionaries, not to mention Joseph Stalin. In Tabenkin's eyes, the Middle East's political borders—including the League of Nations' post–World War I grant of a mandate over Palestine to Britain—were the imposition of European imperialists. The Jews sought national liberation.[27]

Tabenkin belonged to Mapai in its early years, but he opposed the Peel plan and quit Mapai's central committee because the party did not take a strong enough position against the proposal. In 1944 his faction of the party, regarding Ben-Gurion as lukewarm on both proletarian and national issues, walked out and created Ahdut Ha'avodah.[28]

In the meantime, Tabenkin's United Kibbutz had become the spon-sor of the Palmah. The underground army drew many of its recruits from Hamahanot Ha'olim and similar youth movements, and itself re-sembled a youth movement with guns—disdainful of rules, rife with backslapping camaraderie, in which privates called their commanders by their first names. When Palestine descended into war in 1948, the Palmah formed the core of the Jewish forces and then the Israeli army. Yigal Allon, a kibbutz member and the Palmah commander, became a general, in command of the southern front at age thirty, and pushed the Egyptian army out of the Negev desert, securing that area for the new state. His chief of operations, another Palmah man, was the twenty-six-year-old Yitzhak Rabin.

Allon, "the armed prophet of the Whole Land" (in the description of Haim Gouri, who served under him),[29] argued for territorial maximal-ism, the military justifications of his generation supplanting Tabenkin's socialist reasoning. Late in March 1949, as Israel was on the verge of signing an armistice with Transjordan, Allon sent an urgent message to Prime Minister Ben-Gurion. Transjordan's army, the Arab Legion, re-mained the greatest Arab threat to Israel, he said. It continued to hold the hill country north and south of Jerusalem; it could slice Israel in half to gain access to the Mediterranean. "We must aspire to reasonable depth," Allon wrote, and argued, "One cannot describe a stronger border than the line of the Jordan the entire length of the land." Allon was certain his forces could quickly seize the West Bank, and he wanted Ben-Gurion's permission to do so. As for the Arab residents, he assumed most would flee, and proposed planning the operation to leave them escape routes.[30] Ben-Gurion refused, and earned yet another reason for Ahdut Ha'avodah's fury.

Later that year, Ben-Gurion invited a select group of writers and intellectuals to his Tel Aviv home for a discussion of the new state's direction. Haim Gouri, still in uniform, newly celebrated for his poetry, was the youngest. During a break in the discussion, he walked into the prime minister's study and asked why he hadn't allowed Allon to finish the job. "Tying ourselves up in hostile Arab territory would have imposed an unbearable choice," Ben-Gurion answered, "accepting hundreds of thousands of Arabs among us, or mass expulsion with the methods of Dir Yassin," a reference to the Arab village near Jerusalem where members of two right-wing Jewish organizations had committed a massacre in April 1948. Ben-Gurion wanted a state with a Jewish majority more than he wanted the entire homeland, and though he had no objections to Arabs fleeing, he believed they would no longer do so unless Israel used harsher methods than he could accept.[31]

Tabenkin and his followers, though, remained committed to the dream of possessing the Whole Land. Tabenkin regularly expressed his vision for the future as "the entire Jewish people, in its complete land, nearly all in communes, as part of a worldwide alliance of communist peoples."[32] The United Kibbutz's "Ideological Foundation," adopted in 1955, insisted on the complete homeland as the basis for a socialist state of "the Jewish people . . . and the Arabs living in the land"—phrasing that treated the Jews as a nation, and the Arabs as individuals without national rights.[33] After the 1956 Sinai war, the Ahdut Ha'avodah party opposed withdrawal. But by the 1960s, the hope of the Whole Land seemed distant, and the party ran for parliament as the junior partner in an alliance with Mapai.

Yet some continued to believe. In July 1966, Gouri wrote of

imagining "all of Jerusalem before me, Jerusalem of then, before the border, of our youth, the days of *In Your Covenant*," and of imagining, too, "a distant 1948, somewhere in the future."[34] As usual with revolutions, the reality had turned out smaller than the vision, and in this case the difference could be seen on a map. Ergo, the war of independence was not over. A 1948-to-come would complete the dream.

General Narkiss and Gouri finished their May 1967 tour of the border in Jerusalem by stopping at a café. There they found General Mordechai Hod, the commander of the Israel Air Force, who had come to Jerusalem to relax. A couple days before, Hod said, he had gone with Shlomo Goren, the chief rabbi of the Israel Defense Forces, to a spot nearby from which one could see the Western Wall in the Old City. The Wall forms one side of the Temple Mount, the thirty-five-acre plaza where the ancient Temple once stood. For centuries, a narrow courtyard next to the Wall's immense stones was the most sacred spot for Jewish prayer. Zionism turned it into a secular, nationalist symbol as well, again embracing the mythological energy of religion, sans the obligations and God. But in the years since the Arab Legion had conquered the Old City in 1948, Jews could not reach the site.

"You saw the Wall?"

"Yes, we saw it. General Goren's eyes filled with tears and I—don't quote me—I was also very moved."

Narkiss and Gouri left their tiny cups of Turkish coffee on the table. The lookout point was an abandoned position from 1948, shaded by a pine. The golden Dome of the Rock, the Muslim shrine at the center of the Mount, glowed in the last light of day. With his binoculars, Narkiss found the top three rows of stone, gazed silently, and said, "That must be the Wall." Gouri stood entranced by the Old City. "I think we'll get moving," Narkiss said at last, and Gouri felt he was waking up.[35]

SEVERAL DAYS LATER, Hanan Porat stood in a somber crowd of a hundred people at Mount Herzl, the military cemetery on the west of Jerusalem. The mass grave they faced held a crowd of similar size: over a hundred bodies. It was May 14, 1967. More important, it was the fourth day of the Hebrew month of Iyar—Israel's Memorial Day and the eve of its Independence Day, a sequence of holidays requiring that respect be paid to the fallen before celebration begins. Porat was twenty-three years old. Unlike many people his age in the crowd, he was not facing his father's grave.

In 1944, when Porat was six months old, his family moved to Kfar Etzion, a newly established kibbutz in the rocky hills between Bethlehem and Hebron.[36] *Kfar* is Hebrew for village; *Etzion* means "tree of Zion," a tribute to a Jewish farmer named Holzman—"timber man" in German—who had tried settling in the area earlier. He gave up when Palestine's Arabs rebelled against the British, and the Zionist presence, in 1936. It was an inauspicious portent. Surrounded by Arab villages, the kibbutz was isolated from other Jews. Jerusalem lay ten miles to the north.

Kfar Etzion was an Orthodox kibbutz, adding religion to the mix of socialism and nationalism. In Europe, Zionism and Orthodoxy usually battled each other. Like other nationalist movements welling up in Eastern Europe, secular Zionism elevated homeland, language, and ethnic identity to serve as its supreme values.[37] It regarded itself as the heir to Judaism, with the right to reinterpret the Bible, the Jewish past, and the Jews' destiny. The Orthodox did not see reason for inheritance procedures; Judaism was quite alive. Most rabbis rejected the replacement of religious values with national ones and regarded mass return to the homeland before the arrival of the messiah as a rebellion against God. Socialist Zionists were the most dedicated opponents of the "opium of the people."

But people are more complicated than ideological categories. Some of the Orthodox embraced Zionism as a practical solution to Jewish persecution; some found justification for socialism in the works of Moses rather than Marx. Still, religious Zionists were marginal everywhere, not doctrinaire enough for either the Orthodox or the Zionist mainstream.

Two more religious communes—Massu'ot Yitzhak and Ein Tzurim—were soon established near Kfar Etzion, in what became known as the Etzion Bloc. Moshe Moskovic, a founder of Massu'ot Yitzhak, explained that Orthodox Jews felt a special connection to the area, since "the real Land of Israel is between Hebron and Bethlehem," cities of the Bible, of Abraham and King David. He offered another explanation as well, reflecting the old resentments on which Israeli politics is built: Ben-Gurion's dominant Mapai party controlled land allocations and sent minority movements to the worst spots. The Etzion Bloc was not only dangerously placed, it lacked water and had poor soil.[38] A fourth kibbutz in the area, Revadim, belonged to Hashomer Hatza'ir, the "Young Guard," radical secular socialists who in those days revered Stalin, advocated a binational Jewish-Arab state, and were also outsiders.

In early 1948, as Palestine slid into Arab-Jewish violence, the Etzion Bloc went from isolated to besieged. Children and most women were evacuated to Jerusalem, itself besieged and battle-torn. Thirty-five Haganah fighters sent to reinforce the kibbutzim were killed on the way. Porat's father ended up in Jerusalem, organizing convoys. Only one group of reinforcements got through. A landing strip sufficient for two-man Pipers was the last link to the outside. Moshe Moskovic, who had been abroad on movement business, returned to Tel Aviv in April 1948 and wrangled a place on a Piper flight. At the airfield, he was told that guns and ammunition—and matzah for Passover—would take his place in the airplane. As it was, the pilot had to remove the doors and tie himself to his seat with rope so he could carry the load.[39]

The matzah saved Moskovic. Soon after, the kibbutzim received orders to block the road from Hebron to keep Arab fighters from reaching Jerusalem. That sparked the last battle. On May 13, 1948, the fourth of Iyar, the Etzion Bloc fell to a combined onslaught of Arab Legion regulars and armed men of the surrounding villages shouting, "Dir Yassin." In the final battle, 155 defenders died, men and women. The bloodshed was worst at Kfar Etzion, where villagers massacred almost all those who surrendered. Seventy-nine members of the kibbutz were killed. Bodies lay in the fields for a year and a half, until Transjordan allowed army rabbi Shlomo Goren to retrieve the corpses and bury them at Mount Herzl.[40]

Death was nothing unusual that year, and many more Arabs than Jews were torn from their homes. But the Etzion Bloc's hopeless battle turned it into a symbol in Israel, especially for religious Zionists: It was proof that they had fought and bled as well as anyone.

The survivors of Kfar Etzion moved to houses on the edge of Jaffa abandoned by Arabs who were now refugees someplace else—some, perhaps, living on the ruins of Massu'ot Yitzhak, where Arab refugees from the Jaffa area built a village.[41] Hanan Porat spent five years in a kibbutz with many women and few men, in which most of his friends shared the same anniversary for their fathers' deaths, the same day designated as the nation's Memorial Day. There was no line between personal and political; their tragedy belonged to the nation. The psychology of survival and guilt suggests that the sacrifice of the parents loomed as a demanding, unattainable standard, and that the boy who actually had a father would want all the more to show his mettle. Finally the commune unraveled, the families moved on, but the children still met regularly. They were raised on a constant diet of loss and longing for a place they knew mostly through photographs and secondhand memories of adult survivors. At gatherings for teens, parents told long stories of daily life in their lost Eden. The teens spun dreams of starting a new kibbutz together.[42]

Every year the survivors gathered on Mount Herzl. At a reception after the ceremony, those old enough to remember the lost kibbutzim traded memories, and someone would say wistfully, "Maybe we'll return someday." On May 14, 1967, such comments were regarded, as usual, as nostalgia and wishful thinking.[43]

INDEPENDENCE DAY would begin at sunset, like all Jewish festivals. Porat invited some friends from the Etzion clan to join him that night for the celebration at the yeshivah, or Talmudic academy, where he studied. Without meaning to, he was inviting them to be extras in an eerie historical drama.[44]

Yeshivah study is an ideal in Orthodox Judaism, but in 1967 nearly all of Israel's yeshivot kept their distance from Zionism. Merkaz Harav, Porat's school, was the exception.[45] Its late founder, Rabbi Avraham Yitzhak Hacohen Kook, had not exactly made peace with Zionism. Rather, he had audaciously transformed it into theology, absorbing the secular rebellion back into religion.

Born in what is today Latvia, Kook received a traditional rabbinic education in Talmud and religious law, to which he added a brew of Jewish mysticism and European philosophy. One influence on Kook was the sixteenth-century kabbalist Yitzhak Luria, who portrayed the cosmos as spiraling upward, through a process of destruction and renewal, toward perfection. Another was Johann Gottfried von Herder, the German thinker who virtually invented ethnic nationalism—the idea that every person belongs to a *Volk*, a nation defined by culture and language, with a unique role in history. For Kook, the Jews' role was to be the vessel that brings the "divine idea" into the world. The world's redemption depended on the Jews living in the Land of Israel, and therefore the return of Jews to their homeland was an expression of God's will. Secular Zionism was thus a stage in God's plan, which in turn made the secular Zionist pioneers "good sinners," "principled evildoers," and "the lights of chaos." They would awaken religious Jews to act for the sake of the nation, while the believers would spur them to return to faith.[46]

Kook was honored by religious Zionists, often quoted, rarely studied in depth.[47] After his death in 1935, the leadership of his yeshivah fell to his sole son, Rabbi Tzvi Yehudah Kook. Though the son lacked the breadth and the brilliance of his father, by the 1960s he had a circle of young disciples. One of the followers was Hanan Porat, who found that his private dream of returning to Kfar Etzion fit into a greater vision of the nation "returning to the expanses of the Land of Israel"—the personal and national merging again.

On the night of May 14, several hundred students, alumni, rabbis, and other guests sat down for a festive meal in the Merkaz Harav dining hall. Tzvi Yehudah Kook began his holiday sermon. Utterly out of character, and to the shock of his students, he began to shout, rocked by grief. Nineteen years earlier, he recalled, when the news came that the United Nations had voted to partition the land and create a Jewish state, "the entire nation flowed into the streets to celebrate together. I could not go out and join in the joy." Instead, he said, quoting Lamentations, " 'I sat alone and kept silence, because He had laid it upon me,' and in those first hours I could not accept what had been done, the terrible tidings, that the verse had been fulfilled, 'They have divided my land'!"[48]

"Yes, where is our Hebron? Have we forgotten it?! And where is our Shekhem?" he roared, using the biblical name for Nablus. "And our Jericho—will we forget them? And the far side of the Jordan—it is ours, every clod of soil . . . every region and bit of earth belonging to the Lord's land. Is it in our hands to give up even a millimeter?

"In that state, my entire body shaking, entirely wounded and cut to pieces, I could not celebrate."[49]

Kook's students would remember his speech as prophecy. Read carefully, however, his words contain no predictions, just pain: The land is torn, and the rabbi identifies so sharply with the land that he feels his own body torn. Much as the thought would offend his disciples, his experience echoes that of Christian stigmatics who experience Jesus' wounds—particularly since for Kook, possessing the land was the key to redemption.

And read carefully, that memory was only an introduction to his real point: After his shock, Kook said, he accepted that "this is the Lord's doing, it is beyond our understanding."[50] Despite the division of the land, the State of Israel represented the "beginning of redemption" and was "the state that prophets foresaw" when they spoke of the End of Days. In the end, Kook's argument was not with the secular Zionists who had accepted partition, but with the ultra-Orthodox Jews who failed to recognize the state's sanctity and the need to thank God on Independence Day.

Even the annual military parade—to take place the next day in Jerusalem—was a religious event, he said. "All of the weapons . . . all are holy," he proclaimed, because the state had fulfilled a divine commandment to conquer the land, and the military was the means. Hanging in that argument, perhaps, is an implication that the army must yet complete the work. But Kook did not call on it to do so. Rather, he referred in past and present tense to what had already been done, proof that the state was fulfilling its mission.

The speech contains two parts: a reasoned defense of his political theology and a cry of longing for the land beyond the armistice lines. The cry was what inspired awe and made his listeners into a fellowship sharing illumination. Only in light of events that began that night, Porat and others would insist, could they grasp what the rabbi had vouchsafed them.

CHIEF OF STAFF Yitzhak Rabin passed the first report to Prime Minister Levi Eshkol that evening. They and several other Israeli leaders had gathered with their wives at the Prime Minister's Office, which over-looked the stadium where the official Independence Day celebrations would begin with a dress review of troops. It was time to enjoy the cere-monial side of leadership, another chance for Eshkol to show off his wife, Miriam, thirty-four years his junior—except that Rabin had word of Egyptian troop movements through Cairo toward the Suez Canal.

By that time, in Washington, national security adviser Walt Rostow's morning staff meeting had already discussed Egyptian leader Gamel Ab-del Nasser's decision to mobilize his army. While Rabin's source was the teletyped bulletins of news agencies, Rostow had more direct informa-tion: thousands of Egyptian soldiers were marching past the U.S. em-bassy in Cairo. Rostow knew that the day before the Syrian Foreign Ministry had told its ambassadors of "the probability of a large Israeli offensive" against Syria. Only later did he learn that the Soviet Union was the source of the false warning. After the morning meeting a Na-tional Security Council staffer, Harold Saunders, suggested to the State Department that it inform Nasser that Israeli forces were not massing on the border. State declined; the United States would have looked fool-ish if Israel did launch a quick raid.[51]

That evening and the next day, more reports followed. Egyptian troops were pouring into the Sinai Peninsula, the desert staging ground for any attack on Israel. Publicly, Eshkol and Rabin maintained form, at-tending the military parade. When it ended, Colonel Gazit of Military Intelligence drove straight from Jerusalem to army headquarters in Tel Aviv, where he convened his research staff in late afternoon. For hours they tried to decipher Nasser's motives, predict his next movements.

Close to midnight, Gazit got in his car to head home. On the radio was the finale of the last Independence Day event, the Israel Song Festi-val in Jerusalem. As a special treat, at the invitation of Jerusalem mayor Teddy Kollek, popular songwriter Naomi Shemer had composed a new song in honor of the city, "Jerusalem of Gold." "The melody and the words captured my heart," Gazit later wrote. "From that moment, the IDF parade, the first research discussion and Naomi Shemer's prophetic song were for me the first act of the Six-Day War."[52]

Virtually the whole country would feel that way about Shemer's song, yet like Kook's speech, it intimates nothing of the future. Wildly mournful, suffused with romantic imagery borrowed from classical Jewish sources, "Jerusalem of Gold" is a ballad of two star-crossed lovers: the Jews and Jerusalem's Old City. The phrase "Jerusalem of gold" is an ancient Hebrew term for the tiara worn by a rich man's bride—hinting at the Talmud's romantic tale of a rabbi who married in poverty, lived for years apart from his wife to study Torah, and at last rewarded her faithfulness with the golden adornment.[53] The chorus's words, "To all your songs / I am a harp," are taken from a lament for Jerusalem by the twelfth-century Hebrew poet Rabbi Yehudah Halevi, known both for his love poetry and hymns, who in turn was reweaving the biblical lament, "By the rivers of Babylon," in which the exiled Judeans "hanged up our harps" rather than sing songs of Zion in a strange land.[54]

Unlike Kook (or her own sources), Shemer makes no mention of God or faith. The song is a younger sister of *In Your Covenant.* It is an example of how, in an age when many people find that God has gone missing, secular nationalism can declare itself the heir of religion. Instead of finding one's place by submerging oneself in the great religious community stretching across generations, one becomes a link in the chain of an ethnic community also stretching across eternity. No less than a religion, the national group needs grand stories to define itself, and often builds them by refashioning religious myths and images—while insisting that meaning comes out of the romance between a nation and its land, rather than between believers and their God. In the Talmudic tale that Shemer borrowed, a "Jerusalem of gold" is a symbol of love delayed and fulfilled, and the story intimates that Jerusalem itself is a tangible symbol of the marriage—often described in religious literature—between God and the Jewish people. In the song, Jerusalem is herself the lover.

Also missing from Shemer's song are the Arabs. She describes the Old City market and the Temple Mount as empty, along with the land beyond them: "None descend to the Dead Sea / by way of Jericho." The lost land, the lost lover, simply waits for the Jews to return.

Gazit was right, though, to link his intelligence branch staff meeting and the song. Together, they mark Israel's contradictory state of mind at that moment, which would shape its response to the crisis of 1967. Militarily, Nasser's moves were a shock, defying Israeli assumptions. War was not planned. It came as an avalanche, the ground of certainty sliding away. Tactically, the IDF could face the challenge. But beyond simple defense there was no agreed political goal for war, no end to be achieved by means other than diplomacy. The ruling party had reconciled itself to partitioning the land between Jews and Arabs, and to the permanency of temporary borders.

Yet there were also people for whom, quite consciously, the borders were a violation of their emotions and their ideology, and others who could resonate with that feeling. They would be ready to give meaning to what was about to happen.

THE MOST OBVIOUS lesson of the avalanche is that brinkmanship really can lead to the abyss. Rabin and Eshkol intended their threats to frighten Syria into reining in the Palestinian groups, not to announce a war. By giving Syria and Egypt the false information that Israel was massing troops on the border, Moscow may have hoped to put them on such obvious alert that Israel would not attack. The result, though, was that Nasser marched his army into Sinai. Nasser, it seems, aimed at facing Israel down and renewing his dog-eared credentials as the defender of the Arabs, not at starting a war. When he demanded on May 16 that U.N. secretary-general U Thant remove the U.N. Emergency Force from Sinai, he may have expected a simple "no," allowing Egypt to look strong and avoid battle. Two days later, when the U.N. chief made the stunning decision that the peacekeeping force would move aside, Nasser's public bravado virtually required him to close the Straits of Tiran. He did so on May 22.

For Israel, that meant war had begun, and it had a paper trail to prove that the United States was committed to the same view. In 1957, Israel had agreed to withdraw from Sharm al-Sheikh only after Eisenhower's secretary of state, John Foster Dulles, signed off on a deal: Using words approved by Dulles, Israeli foreign minister Golda Meir announced in the U.N. General Assembly that armed interference with Israeli shipping in the straits would be "an attack entitling [Israel] to exercise its inherent right of self-defense" under the U.N. Charter. Immediately afterward the American ambassador rose to the podium to confirm that the United States stood behind Meir's declaration.[55]

By May 25, Israel had called up its entire military reserves. Men up to the age of fifty-four disappeared from streets, homes, jobs. It was a nation interrupted, holding its breath, waiting for the explosion that with each day seemed certain to be more destructive. Nasser's gambit forced other Arab leaders to show they were as determined in their enmity to Israel. On May 30 King Hussein flew to Cairo and signed a defense pact with Nasser. On June 4, Iraq joined and began sending troops into Jordan. Arab radio stations broadcast calls for Israel's destruction.[56] Reasoned miscalculation had led quickly to contagious hysteria.

But there were more implications to the avalanche days, which would bend Israel's course of action long afterward. U Thant's instant surrender to Nasser delegitimized the United Nations and foreign peacekeeping efforts. In particular, it suggested to Israelis that they had been conned when they withdrew from the Sinai a decade before.

Once the U.N. vanished, it was up to the United States to fulfill its commitments from 1957. The Johnson administration's response would undermine Israeli trust in American guarantees as well, and would complete the proof that the Sinai deal was worthless.

At the start of the crisis, as NSC staffer Saunders wrote in a secret summary afterward, the administration "decided" to keep Israel from acting on its own militarily. The quotation marks are Saunders's own; the policy, he says, was assumed rather than discussed. War, in principle, was something to be avoided, and would "put off the day of Arab-Israeli reconciliation just that much further." But by Saunders's inside account, Johnson and his aides also felt "deep concern for our own position if Israel got in over its head and asked for help in the middle of the Vietnam war."[57] Johnson knew he could not convince Congress to let him send American soldiers to another strange part of the globe when he was already sinking in a quagmire elsewhere.[58]

Instead, the administration both reassured and cajoled Israel while seeking another solution. On May 23, Johnson went on TV and radio to voice "support of the political independence and territorial integrity of all the nations" of the Middle East, and to stress that the Straits of Tiran were international waters, open to all shipping.[59] Soon after, Israeli foreign minister Abba Eban arrived in Washington. The eloquent, Cambridge-educated diplomat knew the 1957 commitments well; he had helped negotiate them.

The climax of his visit was a Friday night meeting with Johnson. The president read from a text carefully prepared by his aides, his own emendations scrawled in, telling Eban: "The United States has its own constitutional processes which are basic to its actions on war and peace." In other words, he lacked Congress's backing for military action. "Israel would not be alone unless it decides to go alone," Johnson said, a warning that if the Israeli cabinet decided to go to war, the United States could not back it up. Instead, he urged waiting for America to "pursue vigorously" organizing an international naval force to open the straits.[60]

Eban himself wanted to avoid war. Returning quickly to Israel, he presented Johnson's comments to the cabinet as a promise of help, just barely convincing the ministers to postpone attacking Egypt.[61] But Johnson found it hard to enlist other countries in a naval force. Worse, America's own participation depended on congressional approval, which Congress was not ready to grant. Johnson's secretary of state, Dean Rusk, described the reluctance on the Hill as "Tonkin Gulfitis."[62] With Johnson straitjacketed by Vietnam, Israel would at last decide to go it alone.

BEFORE THAT, though, the crisis would warp Israeli politics, eroding Eshkol's power, forcing rivals into an unworkable partnership, and paralyzing policy for years to come.

By May 1967, Eshkol had ruled for four years, serving as defense minister as well as prime minister. He was seventy-one, born in a small town in the Ukraine, in the crumbling empire of the czars, raised in a Yiddish-speaking, religious family: an Everyman of Eastern European Jewry, except that instead of joining the much larger Jewish migration to America, he had left for Palestine at age nineteen. His father, who stayed behind, was murdered in a pogrom. In Palestine, Eshkol's path was again archetypical, this time for the "new Jew" that socialist Zionism sought to mold. He helped establish a kibbutz, Deganiah Bet on the Sea of

Galilee, became a dedicated farmer and a dedicated Mapai man.[63] Balding, round-faced, he was a master of the backroom meeting, and particularly of seeking and listening to opposing viewpoints. "I can talk for an hour in favor of anything, then for an hour against," he liked to say.[64] His public speeches were often tangled, the monotonal soliloquies of a man meandering through all possibilities without quite making up his mind.[65] His ascension to leadership in Ben-Gurion's place appeared as a victory of the party machine over dynamic personality and vision—a sign the party was growing up, or growing old.

Yet Eshkol did have his own appeal, crafted out of self-deprecatory jokes and constant use of Yiddish. That was a subversive combination, as hinted by his phrase for Israel, *Shimshon der nebechdikker*, "poor little Samson." Samson was the image of the new Jew to which secular Zionism aspired: a Hebrew-speaking Hercules, powerful and passionate, taken from the Bible but oblivious to piety. Not only is *nebechdikker* Yiddish, the language of exile, but the word encapsules the "old Jew"—powerless, ironic, deflecting insults with jokes. The contradiction defined Eshkol himself—a man of the earth, a womanizer, builder of a powerful army, whose use of Yiddish in policy discussions nonetheless contained a whispered jibe, as if to say to the "new Jews" around him, "Gentlemen, whom are we kidding?"

By the time the Straits were closed, though, the panicked Israeli public wanted a hero, without the irony. After the cabinet's vote to delay war, an exhausted Eshkol spoke to the nation by radio and stumbled over handwritten corrections in a text written for him at the last moment.

That was the breaking point. Newspaper ads, protesters outside his office, delegations of politicians demanded that Eshkol appoint an experienced defense minister. He could not ignore the pressure: An Israeli prime minister rules only at the pleasure of the coalition of parties that gives him a parliamentary majority, and is only the first among equals in his cabinet, which must approve his policies. Eshkol would not consider one popular candidate for the defense post, his predecessor and rival David Ben-Gurion, who accused him of having created the crisis. That left two candidates—the former generals Yigal Allon and Moshe Dayan.

The two men shared such a common past, and were such opposites, that they seem like a pair of forever-wrestling twin brothers. Both were born in Palestine and grew up in farming villages; both rose to leadership through the military. An early photo shows them at the founding of Hanita, a kibbutz on the northern edge of British Palestine, in 1938. Between them is their mentor Yitzhak Sadeh, a radical socialist and military pioneer. The two young men hold rifles. Dayan's face is angular, with high cheekbones and a sharp chin. The operation in Vichy-ruled Syria in which he will lose an eye is yet ahead of him; he does not yet wear the patch that he will despise for the stares it attracts, the attention it draws. But at age twenty-three he already leans back, away from the camera, self-conscious, barely smiling, an inch or two of air between him and Sadeh. Writing later of that period, Dayan would say of himself, "Emotional partnership, sociability, and absolute egalitarianism were not in my nature." Allon, three years younger, shorter, square-faced, his shoulder pressed warmly against Sadeh's, grins widely, seizing the foreground.[66] The stones marking the border with Lebanon originally cut across the hilltop chosen for the kibbutz, Allon recalled years later, and "it bothered me because it wasn't . . . symmetrical or aesthetic, so I rounded up my guys and we moved the border stones a few hundred meters northward."[67] As much as the picture, the story portrays Allon: carefree, in command, unconcerned with rules, happy to redraw an international border to fit his imagination.

When Sadeh later organized the underground Palmah fighting force, he chose Allon and Dayan as his first two company commanders. Allon was the star. By 1945 he took over as the Palmah's commander and its avatar: He was, says historian Anita Shapira, "the person who in the eyes of an entire generation symbolized . . . the image of the human being . . . conceived and educated in the Land of Israel in the era of struggle for a Jewish state."[68] A colleague would describe Allon as someone who could put his hand on your shoulder and convince you of anything; Dayan "didn't tend to put his hand on anyone's shoulder," Shapira says.[69] He had a reputation, however, for more extensive physical contact with numerous women.

Following the war of independence, Allon, a member of Tabenkin's United Kibbutz movement, belonged to the pro-Soviet, far-left opposition. In October 1949, Ben-Gurion gave orders to replace him as southern front commander—with Dayan. This led to two conversations with Ben-Gurion in which, Allon recalled, "it was made clear to me that my movement and ideological comrades were suspected of disloyalty to the state's security and independence." At age thirty-one, Allon left the army. Perhaps Ben-Gurion's fears made sense. Just a year and a half had passed since the pro-Soviet coup in Prague. And charismatic revolutionary generals have done worse after victory than Allon, who ended up neither in exile nor with an icepick in his skull. He spent two years at university in Oxford and London, and later studied international relations with Henry Kissinger at Harvard, but returned home to become a leader of the leftist Ahdut Ha'avodah party as it finally broke with Moscow. By the 1960s, his party joined the governing coalition and he was minister of labor: a man of moderate power, adored by his former soldiers but unable to electrify others.[70]

As for Dayan, Ben-Gurion promoted him to military chief of staff, so that he became the hero of 1956's quick victory in Sinai against Egypt. From the army, he went directly into Mapai as Ben-Gurion's protégé. Impulsive, individualistic, Dayan seemed naked of political philosophy—qualities that may have boosted his appeal to Israelis tired of ideological bombast. When Ben-Gurion broke with Mapai in 1965, Dayan followed him and found himself out of power. The crisis of May 1967 opened a way back.

On May 31, Eshkol was about to give in to pressure from his own Mapai and Ahdut Ha'avodah ministers, who sought to make Allon defense minister. But the National Religious Party (NRP), a pillar of Eshkol's coalition, insisted on Dayan as defense minister, and on bringing his Rafi party and Menachem Begin's right-wing Gahal bloc into a "national unity government" to shore up morale.[71] As Allon saw it, the NRP's preference for Dayan was simple: The religious Zionist party was dovish, and Allon himself was a known expansionist.[72] On the other hand Dayan's mentor, Ben-Gurion, opposed war. The next day, Eshkol agreed to Dayan.

The change allowed Dayan to stride onstage as a savior. But it left the prime minister weak, physically sick at heart, half deposed, distrustful of party comrades who betrayed him, with a political enemy in charge of his military. The government reassuringly included everyone, and therefore lacked any common ground. It was capable of deciding to go to war, but not of defining the war's purpose or deciding what goals to pursue after victory—issues that would permanently shape the Jewish state.

Besides, Dayan's appointment did not prevent expansionism. When the crisis erupted, Chief of Staff Rabin's first battle plan was limited: Israel would conquer the Gaza Strip, and use it as a bargaining chip to convince Egypt to reopen the Straits of Tiran. That was the plan that the cabinet had postponed when it agreed to give the United States time for a diplomatic solution.[73] Dayan, though, argued that Egypt would not want Gaza's refugees back. He sought a wider offense, aimed at destroying the Egyptian army and taking much of Sinai, though stopping short of the Suez Canal.[74] History cannot tell us if Rabin's plan would have worked, but it was tailored to the strategic purpose at hand: defending the country and reopening the straits. Whatever Dayan's military arguments, his plan had another obvious goal: repeating his previous victory, retaking the land he had conquered and lost to diplomacy.

At the same time, Jordan and Iraq joined the Arab alliance, and the fever of "liberating Palestine" rose in the Arab world. Syria appeared ready for an offensive. Now there was a risk of war on three fronts.

For some generals, that represented an opportunity. Uzi Narkiss, who had fought in Jerusalem in 1948, had his own unfinished business and wanted to exploit any Jordanian attack to take the West Bank. Dayan wanted to keep the war to one front, but he could not count on the choice being his. Each day, the avalanche widened the potential conflict.

In Israeli cities, high school students dug trenches in public parks, volunteers filled sandbags, citizens cleaned bomb shelters and taped windows as protection against bomb blasts: all statements of vast vulnerability.[75]

Memory magnified fear. Just five years had passed since the trial in Jerusalem of Adolf Eichmann, architect of Nazi Germany's genocide of six million Jews. The trial, in which over one hundred witnesses described the Holocaust, brought to the surface the horrors that survivors had held silently within, and from which native-born Israelis had been protected. The identity of nations, like that of individuals, is built out of stories—told in past tense but perceived as timeless, as "who we are," as scripts that will be reenacted in the future unless by an immense effort of will they can be rewritten with new endings. The Eichmann trial confirmed the old story of Jewish persecution, amplified its terror, scarred a new generation. Abba Eban would later recall that as Arab tanks gathered on the borders, "In many places . . . there was talk of Auschwitz and Maidenak."[76]

In the Negev, facing Egypt, reservists yanked from normal lives alternated between boredom and unnatural seriousness. "It's no longer a game that you do everything to avoid," a reservist tank commander named Kobi Rabinovich wrote to his girlfriend about his men's attitude toward their Centurion. "They've finally realized that without this machine, nothing will help them." Rabinovich, a broad-shouldered, gentle-faced twenty-two-year-old with thick wavy hair, wrote about his tank—"I gave this machine all my heart"—with the affection another young man might feel for a Harley-Davidson, or for a horse. A child of Kibbutz Na'an, southeast of Tel Aviv, he was the exemplar of a social experiment's second generation: disciplined, speaking in the slogans of his movement, devoid of the rebelliousness that had given birth to the kibbutz movement in the first place. After finishing his regular army service the year before, he had begun his prescribed year of "volunteer" service to the United Kibbutz, leading youth movement activities in Tel Aviv, but in front of children he felt like a bolt screwed into the wrong nut. The call-up notice had brought him back to work "that fits my inclinations and abilities," he admitted in his letters. "Expectations are high," he wrote on May 30, the day Hussein flew to Cairo, and in the next line, "The strong desire is that nothing will happen."[77]

Hanan Porat, back in his paratroop unit with some of his yeshivah friends, had no mixed feelings. Those who had been at the Independence Day dinner believed they had special information about what was coming. Kook's speech "echoed in us, as if . . . the spirit of prophecy had descended upon him," he recalled. On the Sabbath, they began to sing the traditional song, "Next Year in Jerusalem." Their commander, joking, answered in tune, "Next week in the Sinai." The student-soldiers responded, "Next *week* in Jerusalem."[78]

Haim Gouri's brigade of middle-aged reservists consisted entirely of Jerusalemites, men with children, with two wars or three behind them.

The unit he personally commanded was known as "the professors' company" for the four Hebrew University scholars who convinced the brigade commander to let them join though they had not received call-up notices. "Men feared they would be left out of the war that was approaching by the minute," Gouri wrote for his paper. His soldiers waited on the northeast edge of the city. Behind them was an ultra-Orthodox Jewish neighborhood, apartments crowded with children. In front, beyond "the barbed wire fences [that] we thought would rust till the end of all generations," stood a Jordanian police academy. A few dozen meters separated the houses and the heavily fortified academy. "Everything testifies that this time the fire will take hold of Jerusalem," Gouri wrote, without need for a prophet. "For now, no one knows D-Day or H-Hour."[79]

D-DAY WAS JUNE 5, set by the cabinet the morning before. Military Intelligence chief Aharon Yariv reported that the Arab buildup was continuing on all fronts, so each hour increased the danger. The United States was still focusing on reopening the straits, not on the potential for an Arab invasion—and the American effort to organize an international convoy was going nowhere. Johnson had sent another cable warning Israel not to "go it alone." In the cabinet, the National Religious Party's ministers were among the last holdouts wanting to wait. But at last they came around. Israel would announce that Egypt had attacked, and strike first.[80]

Nasser had succeeded in one thing—frightening Israel. The decision to attack rested on the principle that offense would be the best defense, and the hope that it would be necessary only to fight Egypt. What followed shows that even the most successful offensive is a return to primeval chaos. It is shaped by what military theoretician Carl von Clausewitz called "friction"—all the unpredictable events that shatter plans and yield unimagined results.[81]

The day of the decision, Eshkol sought to control one kind of friction, the will of individuals. In a letter to Dayan, he laid down rules for their relationship. "The defense minister will not act without the prime minister's approval in anything involving: beginning . . . warfare against a particular country; military action within war beyond the general guidelines set down. . . ."[82] Eshkol's concerns proved justified, his note ineffective.

H-hour was 7:10 A.M., set by the military high command. Waves of Israeli warplanes took off, swept beneath enemy radar, and struck Egypt's air bases. Before 8:00 the ground assault began in Sinai. Only then did the air-raid sirens begin wailing inside Israel, sending frightened civilians to bomb shelters.

At the Knesset, legislators met that day in the parliamentary bomb shelter to discuss a bill financing the war effort, as Jordanian artillery shells fell on West Jerusalem. "Our people faces a fateful war . . . as the Hitlerite-Nasserist barbarianism sets for itself the goal of exterminating us," said the Finance Committee chairman as he presented the legislation, still caught in the fear of a new Holocaust, unaware of the progress of the fighting.[83]

That morning the BBC correspondent in Israel, Michael Elkins, a personal friend of several Israeli leaders, got a scoop unknown even to the country's legislators: Israel had destroyed the Egyptian air force, virtually ensuring victory. The news coming over the BBC would have shocked King Hussein, who heard that morning from Nasser that Egypt was smashing Israel's military. But Elkins's item was held up for several hours by the Israeli military censor, then by disbelieving BBC editors, who broadcast it only that evening.[84] Israel broke its own news blackout on the battles only at 1:00 A.M. the next day, with a radio announcement by Rabin.[85]

No one can know if an early report on Egypt's debacle from the respected British network would have convinced the young Jordanian king to stay out of the war, saving half his kingdom. Through the war's first morning, Israel was sending Hussein warnings via third parties to keep his army out. Yet while Hussein feared Israel, he also feared the pro-Nasser frenzy in his own population. Jordanian artillery shells fell on Israel's narrow waist, on an air base near the northern edge of the West Bank, on West Jerusalem. In early afternoon, the ground assault began, as Jordanian troops took the U.N. headquarters on a hilltop in the no-man's-land between East and West Jerusalem. The battle for the West Bank had begun.

Initially, the Israeli counterattack was defensive. One goal was to seize a slice of the northern West Bank, around the town of Jenin, to end the fire at the northern air base. In Jerusalem, the army sought to take U.N. headquarters, and also to link up with Mount Scopus, a threatened Israeli enclave in northeast Jerusalem that had been surrounded by Jordanian land since 1948. The latter task was assigned in part to Colonel Mordechai Gur's paratroop brigade, quickly bused to the city from the southern front. Among the soldiers were Hanan Porat and his yeshivah friends. After midnight the paratroops moved past Haim Gouri's overage soldiers and began their assault on the police academy fortress.[86]

Yet once the troops crossed the Green Line, the logic of the avalanche took over. On the ground, commanders seized opportunities. In the cabinet, politicians renewed dreams unconnected to defense. By the war's first afternoon, Menachem Begin and Yigal Allon—rightist and leftist made partners by territorial desire—arrived at Eshkol's office and pressed the prime minister to take Jerusalem's Old City.[87] A cabinet meeting that night postponed a decision; Eshkol was nervous about diplomatic fallout and the walled city's symbolism to other faiths. The next morning, arriving on Mount Scopus via ground conquered by the paratroopers in bitter fighting, Defense Minister Dayan refused to give Uzi Narkiss permission to enter the Old City. Surround it, Dayan said, but keep out of "all that Vatican."[88] But by the predawn hours of June 7, with a U.N. cease-fire call expected, Eshkol gave the go-ahead to exploit opportunity, and Dayan ordered Colonel Gur's paratroopers to conquer Old Jerusalem.

Gur rode the lead half-track himself that morning, through the gunfire and smoke at St. Stephen's Gate on the east side of the Old City, through narrow alleyways and another gate onto the wide plaza in the shadow of the Dome of the Rock. At precisely 10:00 A.M. he radioed Narkiss, "The Temple Mount is in our hands." Narkiss's jeep pulled up moments later, followed by Rabbi Goren, who arrived on foot carrying a Torah scroll in one hand and a ram's horn in the other, recited biblical verses, and let loose with the horn's wild wail while the troops began singing "Jerusalem of Gold."[89] Hurrying on, some of the soldiers descended from the Mount into the alleyways and found the courtyard of the Western Wall.

On the army's advice, Eshkol delayed visiting the Wall that afternoon, leaving the stage to Dayan to appear at the holy spot as conqueror, with a brief speech hinting neither at his hesitations about conquering the Old City nor at military goals: "We have reunited the dismembered city. . . . We have returned to our most holy places, returned in order never to be separated from them again." Goren's speech at the spot, which appeared the next morning on the front page of the National Religious Party's daily paper, expressed more cosmic expectations, rooted in prophecies he believed were being fulfilled before his eyes. "This is the most exalted moment in the history of the [Jewish] people," he proclaimed, describing the conquest as "heralding redemption."[90]

For yeshivah student and paratrooper Hanan Porat, a very specific prophecy was coming true. When men from his unit sacked a kiosk in East Jerusalem, Porat stole postcards of West Bank towns and mailed them to his yeshivah, Merkaz Harav. "You remember, gentlemen, Rabbi Tzvi Yehudah's words—Shekhem, Hebron . . ." he wrote. "Here they are before you." At the yeshivah, the cards were posted prominently.[91]

Military advances were outpacing plans elsewhere as well. At the beginning of the West Bank offensive, Allon later recalled, Dayan sought only to "correct the line near Jenin to move the Jordanians out of artillery range." Allon, who by his own description "still held to the idea of the Whole Land of Israel," argued that with the same effort, the IDF could seize the entire West Bank.[92] Dayan, it seems, was easy to convince; he described the West Bank as "part of the flesh and bones—indeed the very spirit—of the Land of Israel," and instantly related each landmark to a biblical story.[93] Initially, the cabinet approved conquering only the high ground that forms the West Bank's spine, running south from Jenin, Nablus, and Ramallah through Jerusalem and on to Bethlehem and Hebron, but as the Jordanian army cracked, the IDF rolled forward all the way to the Dead Sea and the Jordan River, taking the entire West Bank.[94]

In Jerusalem, Haim Gouri's radio squawked orders from the battalion chief to head north, to newly conquered Ramallah. Gouri found himself in a long convoy of jeeps and trucks. In the northern Jerusalem suburb of Shuafat, home of the city's wealthy Arabs, white flags fluttered from the roofs of mansions. Stores along the high road gaped open, already looted. A new model Buick, bullet-perforated, stood before a stately two-story house, from whose grated window a face peeked, isolated testimony that the residents actually existed. And then on the road: a lone Arab woman, in her thirties, wearing a white head scarf and a black village dress embroidered with blue and crimson, "straightbacked and lovely and petrified," Gouri wrote, "lips tight, watching," as if posted there to remind the eternally conflicted poet that there were people in his beloved countryside.[95]

On the southern front, too, chaos shared command. Dayan had planned to stay out of the Gaza Strip, with its teeming refugee camps, but when Egyptian-sponsored Palestinian units opened fire on Israeli communities on the Gaza border, Chief of Staff Rabin ordered troops in. In the Sinai, field commanders ignored Dayan's orders to stop twelve miles short of the Suez Canal, reaching the waterway as they chased the shattered Egyptian army—and a share of glory equal to those who had taken Jerusalem.[96]

But tank commander Kobi Rabinovich wrote from the canal's bank that he had found horror there, rather than glory. "We turned this peninsula into a valley of slaughter, one big graveyard," the kibbutz reservist told his girlfriend. "Unarmed men, captives with raised hands, were killed in violation of orders. In war you destroy weapons and those who hold them, but I've seen too many murders even to cry," he said, begging her to believe that he had "remained a human being, unstained."[97]

That letter was written on Saturday morning, June 10. By then, the war's final unplanned campaign was under way on the northern front. Syria's artillery had begun pounding Israeli border communities the first afternoon of the war, but Dayan did not want the burden of opening a third front and feared attacking the Soviet Union's closest ally in the region. In the bomb shelters of kibbutzim along the border, though, members desperately wanted the IDF to push the Syrians back. They had an ally in General David (Dado) Elazar, an ex-Palmah man who headed the army's Northern Command—and another in his friend and former commander, Yigal Allon. Allon's own home, Kibbutz Ginnosar, looked across the Sea of Galilee at the Syrian heights. But beyond that, as he later explained, Allon harbored a dream of Israel redrawing the Mideast map by thrusting over fifty miles to the Syrian city of Suweida. Once there, it would help the Druse religious minority that dominated the area to secede from Syria and establish an Israeli-allied Druse republic, "constituting a buffer state between Syria, Jordan and Israel. . . . That was my obsession."[98]

When representatives of the border kibbutzim contacted Allon, he arranged for them to meet Eshkol on June 9, drilled them on what to say, and joined the session himself. Convinced of the need to seize the border area (even if he was not swept up in Allon's dream), Eshkol took the extraordinary step of bringing the kibbutz leaders to a meeting that night of his war cabinet. But Dayan spoke adamantly against attacking Syria, and the ministers postponed a decision.[99]

Yet early the next morning, ignoring the limits on his authority, the utterly erratic Dayan ordered General Elazar to invade Syria. Only after the troops were moving did Dayan inform Eshkol. For his part, Allon spoke directly to Elazar, urging him to rush forward. "I shouted at Dado, 'Why don't you grab the chain of hills?'" Allon would recount, referring to the approaches to the Syrian town of Quneitrah. "He said, 'Listen, I've already grabbed more than they allowed me to.'"[100] In the chain of command, all links were undone. Meanwhile, as the IDF broke Syrian defenses and rushed forward, Syrian civilians—except for the Druse minority—fled eastward.

IN THE MIDST of the fighting, the first proposals were born for the aftermath. At Military Intelligence's research department, Colonel Shlomo Gazit and his staff completed a document that called for a near-complete Israeli pullback to the prewar lines in return for full, formal peace agreements. Gazit's paper also proposed establishing a Palestinian state in the West Bank and Gaza Strip. The paper was sent to Dayan, Rabin, and other top military figures on June 9. None responded.[101]

The same day, two Israeli officers met in Ramallah with Aziz Shehadeh—an Arab refugee from Jaffa who was a prominent lawyer and opponent of King Hussein's regime. Shehadeh quickly formulated his own proposal for a Palestinian state that would sign a peace agreement with Israel and passed it on to the Israelis—and also got no response.

Shehadeh's sixteen-year-old son, Raja, raised on memories of the lost paradise of pre-1948 Arab Jaffa, with its beach and nightlife and affluence and scent of orange groves, typed the document for him. But what stuck in the teenager's memory that week was the shock of defeat, and his first sight on a Ramallah street of an Israeli soldier, barely older than himself, chest hair showing from his half-unbuttoned shirt, carrying a long rifle, someone "who had trained as a soldier and fought a war against us and won. And what had I been doing? A few marching exercises. . . . I felt more ashamed than I had ever felt in my life," he wrote years later, touching an issue beyond the reach of his father's paper. "But worse . . . I felt my manhood compromised."[102]

On that day as well, Allon shocked two of his old Palmah brigade commanders with his own gestating ideas. Allon picked up the two men, members of northern kibbutzim, for a jeep trip into the Syrian heights, following the advancing Israeli troops. Beforehand, by Allon's testimony, he had already toured the West Bank by helicopter and jeep, and what he saw defied his expectations: Though some of the residents were fleeing across the Jordan, "most were staying put . . . which hadn't happened in 1948." He saw that annexing the entire West Bank—as he and his party had long advocated—would shift the balance of Jews and Arabs in Israel and make it a binational state. He needed a compromise between old commitment and new facts.

So on the road into the heights, when one of his old comrades turned to him and said, "Nu, Yigal, the Whole Land of Israel at last!" Allon answered, "Right. But I have second thoughts about implementing that." Then he began describing a plan for holding much of the West Bank, what he saw as strategically essential, while giving up the mountain ridge where most of the Arabs lived. For Allon's friends, this was heresy from the prophet, at the very moment of fulfillment.[103]

ON SATURDAY, JUNE 10, as nightfall approached, the fighting guttered out in response to a United Nations call for a cease-fire. Quneitrah, now a ghost town, fell that day.

It was less than a week since Israelis had feared a new Holocaust. Measured by the original goal of defense, Israel's victory was complete.

The armies that had loomed on its borders were in ruins. Measured in tactical terms—battles won, land gained—the Israeli success was stunning, as was the Arab humiliation. It was in those terms that Israelis, Arabs, and the watching world responded.

Yet during the war, "friction" and appetite overwhelmed strategic plans. Accidentally, Israel had acquired an empire. It was a shirt-pocket empire, to be sure, less than 3 percent the size of France's recently relinquished Algerian lands or Belgium's former holdings in the Congo. But the territory conquered, 26,000 square miles, was still more than three times the size of Israel itself on June 4, 1967. With 2.7 million citizens, most of them Jews, Israel occupied land that was home to an estimated 1.1 million Arab noncitizens.[104] Now, after the fact, the purpose of conquest would have to be defined. A meaning needed to be found.

2

CREATING FACTS

As night fell, searchlights lit up a warren of buildings next to the Western Wall. The Jewish Sabbath was ending. In the north, on the Syrian front, the cease-fire was at last taking hold. In Jerusalem's Old City, the work of demolishing the Mughrabi Quarter was beginning.

A public lavatory that leaned up against the Wall came down first, by one version of events that night. A group of twenty or so gray-haired Jerusalem contractors, available because they were overage even for the Israeli military reserves, knocked it down with sledgehammers. Teddy Kollek, the Israeli mayor of West Jerusalem, who had no official jurisdiction in the east city, had recruited them to create a wide plaza in front of the Wall. The work went slowly, the army brought bulldozers, and the contractors proceeded to level the rest of the neighborhood, home to 135 Arab families. (By another account, army engineers operated the bulldozers.) When Colonel Shlomo Lahat, the military governor of East Jerusalem, showed up in the morning, he found most of the contractors drunk "on wine and joy."

The families were given a few minutes to leave their homes. By one telling, based largely on testimony from Lieutenant Colonel Ya'akov Salman, the deputy military governor, who commanded the operation, the hapless residents initially refused to leave. Salman ordered an Engineering Corps officer to begin the demolition. A bulldozer struck a house, which collapsed on its inhabitants. Medics rushed to treat the wounded, and residents poured out of the remaining buildings to waiting buses, which took them to abandoned homes elsewhere in East Jerusalem.

"The order to evacuate the neighborhood was one of the hardest in my life," Salman later said. "When you order, 'Fire!' [in battle], you're an automaton. Here you had to give an order knowing you are likely to hurt innocent people." A semiconscious old woman, Hajja Rasmia Tabaki, was pulled from one half-destroyed house and died in the course of the night.

One reason for multiple versions of what happened is that participants sought to avoid creating a paper trail. Ironically, that allowed key figures to make conflicting claims to what they regarded as credit for the operation.

One claimant is Lahat, who had been the deputy head of the Armored Corps until shortly before the war. German-born, impeccably groomed, Lahat stood out as a stickler for discipline among his relaxed fellow officers. In South America on a fund-raising tour for Israel when the fighting began, Lahat rushed to New York, boarded a flight with Israeli officers headed home, and reported for duty at the command center in Tel Aviv at 4 A.M. on June 7. "Where have you been?" Moshe Dayan greeted him. "We're about to conquer Jerusalem, and I need a tough military governor." The defense minister feared Israelis would take revenge on Arabs for the brutal fighting of 1948, and wanted "someone prepared to shoot Jews if need be."

After the conquest, in a meeting that included Dayan, Lahat, Mayor Kollek, and Central Command chief Narkiss, the decision was made to keep East Jerusalem closed off until the Jewish holiday of Shavuot the following week, when Israelis would be allowed to visit the Western Wall. In Lahat's telling, he pointed out that when crowds crushed into the constrained courtyard at the holy site, "we'll have more losses than in the war," and suggested widening the open area. Dayan, he says, approved.

Kollek, in his memoirs, says it was his idea: "Do it now; it may be impossible later, and it *must* be done." He, too, says Dayan agreed. At a city council session in the midst of the war, Kollek called for officially uniting East and West Jerusalem. In a meeting with Prime Minister Eshkol, he laid out an $80 million reconstruction plan for Jerusalem, including settling Jews in the Old City. But he did not wait for formal declarations to act. East Jerusalem was hooked to the west city's water pipes; Kollek's officials saw to burial of Arab corpses, and the mayor found contractors to erase a neighborhood.

Salman, a forty-year-old lieutenant colonel in the reserves, had also flown back from America hoping to fight. A battlefield commander in 1948 known for his daring, in civilian life he had become a deputy director-general at the Finance Ministry, one of the army of managers who wore their curly hair combed back and their white shirts open at the collar, the lack of a tie indicating membership in the socialist ruling class. In his telling, he was the one who pointed out the courtyard's limits to Dayan. The defense minister made it clear that it was up to Salman to solve the problem, and quickly.

When General Narkiss came to see the work on Sunday morning, June 11, he commented to Salman, "Yankele, the Wall has vanished." That was a trick of perspective. Before, visitors to the courtyard had to gaze upward to see the top of the stones. Now, seen at eye-level across a field of rubble, the Wall no longer pushed a person's gaze heavenward. But when Eshkol phoned the general to ask why and where houses were being demolished, Narkiss feigned ignorance, promising to "look into it." Afterward, he got orders to investigate who was responsible. Salman received a call from Dayan. "I don't need to tell you who's out to get me in the government and how much joy it will bring them if everything leads to me," the defense minister said. Salman, aware he could face legal trouble for violating the Fourth Geneva Convention on rule of occupied territory, had armed himself in advance with documents from East Jerusalem City Hall showing that the Mughrabi Quarter suffered from poor sanitary conditions and that the Arab municipality eventually wanted it evacuated. But the investigation led nowhere. When Shavuot came on June 14, an estimated 200,000 Israelis visited the Western Wall.[1]

The razing of the Mughrabi Quarter took place in a twilight time, between war and the first formal government discussions of postwar policy. It fit a wartime pattern: actions of great consequence, taken by Dayan or those beneath him, without authorization, improvised to fit the moment's demands as they saw them, borne on euphoria. Yet in this case, no battle had been fought. The military exploited its rule of occupied territory, to the clear benefit of Israeli citizens over the occupied population.

The bulldozers set a precedent. Top officers and officials joined with private citizens, acting not in line with government policy but in order to set it. The dusty plaza carved out before the Wall stated ownership over the Old City. The action fit the pre-state strategy of the Zionist left, which believed in speaking softly and "creating facts": using faits accomplis to determine the political future of disputed land. It fit as well what Israeli political scientist Ehud Sprinzak described as an ethic of "illegalism" rooted in the pre-state conflict between Zionists and foreign rulers: Laws were a weapon used against Jews, and breaking the law for the sake of ideals was proof of true dedication.[2] Israel's early years saw a painful passage, as rebels became leaders, from the old underground values toward the new authority of the state, of democratic decisions, and of the rule of law. Now, though, officials were defying the laws of the country they served, in the name of their duty to that country. In the process, they marked out the occupied land as a reserve belonging to a different time, before 1948—except that now Jews would play the role both of government and rebels. Before ministers sat down at the cabinet table, a paradigm had been created.

OTHER WALLS, too, were falling the morning after the war. "On way to Old City, I noted workmen with heavy equipment removing concrete baffles on side street adjoining Fast Hotel," the American consul-general in Jerusalem, Evan Wilson, cabled Washington, referring to the downtown alleyways that dead-ended in fortifications at the Green Line. Wilson, an old Mideast hand, was pleased: No longer would he have to detour through an inconvenient border crossing to get between his offices in East and West Jerusalem—run as a single consulate because the United States did not recognize Israeli or Jordanian claims, but only the

1947 U.N. designation of Jerusalem as an international city. Wilson was less happy to hear from a staffer that earth-moving gear was rolling into town from the Qalandiya airport to the north—equipment apparently left by American contractors working at the Jordanian airfield until war broke out. The spoils, it appeared, included a Caterpillar tractor he had seen at work, an inadvertent U.S. contribution to creating facts.[3]

While the tractors worked, the cabinet convened for its first discussion of the new realities. Regarding the newly conquered land, Eshkol was even more passionately conflicted than usual. At a Mapai meeting during the war, he expressed "great desire" to keep the Gaza Strip, "perhaps because of Samson and Delilah," but more so because it would remove the strategic danger of an "Egyptian finger" stuck into Israel. In the next breath he described the Strip as "a rose with lots of thorns," because of its large Arab population. "Who has counted the dust of Ishmael?" he said, playing ironically on a biblical verse about Israelite numbers.[4] Including the West Bank as well as Gaza, Israel had just gained over a million Arabs, and while the Jewish birthrate was low, the Arab rate was high. Yet he implied he also wanted to keep the West Bank. "We'll have to devote some thought to the question of how we'll live in this land without giving up what we've conquered and how we'll live with that number of non-Jews," Eshkol said.[5] With that, the prime minister succinctly introduced both sides of the debate that would henceforth define Israeli politics—but offered no solutions.

But Eshkol did know that he wanted to annex East Jerusalem and reunite the city. Before the cabinet session, he began lining up support among ministers, who shared his fear that Israel would very soon face international—most important, American—demands to pull back to the June 4 lines. Opposition to Israeli rule of the Old City would be particularly strong because of its Christian and Muslim holy places. Eshkol's answer was to act quickly, to make the east city part of Israel before anyone said not to—that is, to create a fact.

In the cabinet debate, several ministers objected. Two represented Mapam, the political party of the Hashomer Hatza'ir movement, at the left edge of Zionism. The party had given up advocating a binational state after Israel's establishment, and later ended its support for Moscow. But it remained determinedly dovish, and its leaders worried that annexation would block chances for peace. Education Minister Zalman Aran of Eshkol's own Mapai party reminded his colleagues that in 1956, Ben-Gurion had proclaimed that Israel would never retreat from Sinai, only to fold under U.S. pressure. "I'm concerned about a Knesset decision that 'we won't budge' and then there will be pressure and we'll give in," Aran warned. "A Knesset declaration annexing Jerusalem followed by a withdrawal will be a disaster."[6]

The majority, though, agreed with Eshkol and argued only over the method. Rightist leader Menachem Begin, who loved grand rhetoric, wanted a law proclaiming all of Jerusalem to be Israel's capital. He objected to "annexation" as implying that Israel was taking land to which it did not have rights. The National Religious Party's leader, Haim Moshe Shapira, on the other hand, suggested avoiding any legislation, which would attract world attention. As interior minister, responsible for local government, he would simply decree a change in Jerusalem's city limits.[7] The idea contained a contradiction: The very point of annexation was to tell the world that even if Israel had to retreat elsewhere, it would not give up East Jerusalem. Shapira proposed a ringing statement, issued in a whisper.

That fit the contradictory desires of most of his colleagues. The cabinet assigned a committee of its members, headed by the justice minister, to engineer the precise legal device for enlarging the city. Dayan, a panel member, turned over the job of drawing the new city limits to the army's deputy operations chief, General Rehavam Ze'evi, a flamboyant warrior whose thin face and eyeglasses had earned him the incongruous nickname "Gandhi." Though the impetus was the historic Jewish tie to the walled Old City and uniting the two halves of Jerusalem, no one considered annexing only the area within the walls, or the slightly larger territory within the Jordanian city limits.

Dayan's guidelines to Ze'evi called for taking the Qalandiya airfield and reclaiming real estate that Jews had owned before statehood. That included Neveh Ya'akov and Atarot, Jewish farming communities to the city's north, whose residents had fled during the 1948 fighting. As one Israeli researcher notes, there was an "almost mystical attraction to redeeming Jewish-owned land."[8] Victory brought with it not only the right but even the obligation of return. Ze'evi was also told to include Mount

Scopus, strategic ridges, sites with Jewish historical significance, and land for future urban development—and as far as possible to avoid adding Arab suburbs and villages.[9] Decisions about the contested city would be first political and military, and only afterward—if at all—a matter of urban planning.

Ze'evi worked hastily. Like others in the army's general staff and in the cabinet, he was also haunted by the Sinai war of 1956. Most drew the opposite lesson from Zalman Aran; by preemptive annexation, they believed, Israel could hold at least some land this time.[10] And if it had to pull back from the rest, it would insist on much more in return than American or U.N. assurances.

"There are constant references and comparisons to 1956," wrote White House special counsel Harry McPherson, in a cable from Tel Aviv. McPherson, a thirty-eight-year-old Texan jack-of-all-policy-trades for President Johnson, had arrived in Israel hours before the fighting began, and sent a detailed report just hours after it ended. "The Israelis do not intend to repeat the same scenario—to withdraw within their boundaries with only paper guarantees that fall apart at the touch of Arab hands," he warned. "We would have to push them back by military force, in my opinion, to accomplish a repeat of 1956; the cut-off of aid would not do it."

McPherson's cable also hinted at ideas he had brought with him from home. "Incidentally, Israel at war destroys the prototype of the pale, scrawny Jew," he wrote. "The soldiers I saw were tough, muscular, and sunburned."[11]

THE PROBLEM was deciding what to demand, what to concede. A special U.N. General Assembly session on the Mideast crisis, due to convene on June 19, added urgency to formulating a stand. Yet doing so was difficult: Political positions and the machinery of policy making had both suffered battlefield damage.

Jewish claims to land suddenly stood once more at the center of the national agenda. Irredentists such as Menachem Begin and some ideologues in the left-wing, maximalist Ahdut Ha'avodah party believed that the conquests presented an unexpected opportunity to realize their dreams. The hard choice made between nationalist goals two decades earlier—favoring statehood in part of the land over possession of the Whole Land, pragmatism over visions of restoring ancient grandeur—no longer seemed final or inescapable. One right-wing splinter party quickly began running newspaper ads saying, "No Soil of Liberated Territory of Our Land Will Be Returned!"[12]

Yet as Yigal Allon's case shows, even a dedicated dreamer could be shaken by seeing the actual land, with the actual people living there, and be pushed to heresy. "I consider myself a rationalist, even if I don't lack emotions and I'm not free of myths," Allon would say of his internal struggles after the war, proving that a person is best known by his contradictions.[13] The territory of myth was in hand, but Allon's reason told him that Israel could neither grant citizenship to over a million Arabs nor rule over them.

The pragmatists of Eshkol's dominant Mapai party were more confused: They had accepted the need for partition, yet the music of biblical names such as Hebron and Jericho aroused them as well. As Eshkol's ramble shows, even Gaza had ancient echoes. And victory did nothing to erase the trauma of the prewar days. King Hussein's decision to go to war made Israel's narrow waist seem more vulnerable. "Before June 1967, the West Bank, the Sinai Peninsula and the Golan Heights had not seemed to [cabinet ministers] to have vital security value," notes military historian Reuven Pedatzur, who describes the war's result as "the victory of confusion."[14] Now nothing was certain.

Meanwhile, Eshkol felt he had suffered half a putsch; his ejection from the Defense Ministry left him distrustful of colleagues and friends.[15] His position was further weakened by a rush to reunite his Mapai with the two other parties that had broken off from it, Ahdut Ha'avodah and Dayan's Rafi party. Israel's political system, in which a mere 1 percent of the national vote gave a party representation in parliament, encouraged creating small parties, splitting big ones, and ruling by coalition. That, in turn, fanned an eternal hope of putting together a single party strong enough to win an absolute majority in the Knesset, allowing it to rule on its own. That hope was particularly strong in the parties representing what was known as Labor Zionism. The splits in Mapai had divided kibbutzim, separated comrades-in-arm, set sons against fathers. Now Moshe Dayan and his colleagues in Rafi were pressing to rejoin the mother party, hoping Dayan's new popularity would complete their climb to power.

Unable to say no, key Mapai leaders, such as its aging secretary general, Golda Meir, sought a quick merger with Ahdut Ha'avodah as well, in order to reduce Dayan's influence. Reaching unity meant ignoring old disputes about the Land of Israel and partition, even if they were suddenly more relevant than ever. Living together required indecision.[16]

Dayan himself did not wait for policy decisions to put his position before the world. In an interview for *Meet the Press* on U.S. television, broadcast the day after the war, he asserted that Israel should keep both the Gaza Strip and the West Bank. Rather than receiving citizenship, the West Bank's Arabs "would have their own autonomy," he said. If the Arab countries wanted peace, they would have to negotiate directly with Israel, he added, warning, "If they don't want . . . to sit [with] us, then we shall stay where we are and there will be an absolutely new Israel."[17] In private, his preference was for staying put. Meeting with top generals, he suggested that Israel should "shut up and rule" Sinai.[18]

Forced to respond, Eshkol began a marathon of meetings—first a ministerial committee, then the full cabinet—that lasted nearly a week. What he lacked was a position worked out in advance by a few key ministers, the usual method of imposing a decision. As the debate came to a climax on June 18–19, the sharpest disagreements were on the future of the West Bank. Predictably, Menachem Begin proposed annexing it, while putting off the inconvenient decision on the status of its Arab residents.

Virtually the same position was suggested by Ahdut Ha'avodah's Yisrael Galili, a birdlike man considered a master of backroom politics. Galili, a leader of the United Kibbutz, had been the Haganah chief of staff until he had been purged by Ben-Gurion in 1948. Now he officially served as minister without portfolio, and unofficially as a top defense adviser, receiving the same intelligence reports as the prime minister.[19] Galili, who had never wavered from his party's advocacy of the Whole Land of Israel, based his argument in the cabinet on the need for strategic depth. "I am not raising the possibility now of giving citizenship to the residents of the West Bank. I know how serious that is, not only from a moral, abstract democratic perspective, but also because of the concrete [security] risks," he admitted, but a solution would have to be found later.

Dayan proposed an answer: Give the West Bank autonomy, with Israel keeping control over defense and foreign affairs. If King Hussein wanted peace, he would have to agree to the Jordan River as the border, giving up his claim to the West Bank.

Dayan's rival, Yigal Allon, laid out the plan that started taking form in his mind during the war: Israel should quickly establish a Palestinian Arab entity—perhaps an independent state—in an enclave along the mountain ridge of the West Bank north of Jerusalem. At the same time, it should annex the barely populated desert lowlands along the Jordan River and the shore of the Dead Sea, along with the Hebron hills south of Jerusalem. The tiny Palestinian state would be surrounded by Israel. In the annexed areas, he argued, Israelis should quickly build settlements. "We have never held territory," Allon argued, "without settling it."

But there were minimalists as well. Yaakov Shimshon Shapira, the Mapai minister of justice, blasted Dayan's proposal. "In a time of decolonialization in the whole world," he demanded, "can we really consider an area in which mainly Arabs live, and we control defense and foreign policy . . . ? Who's going to accept that?"[20]

Shapira was speaking in terms his colleagues understood—at least when applied to more distant lands. Israel had spent the past decade developing ties with the newly independent nations of Africa, and in 1966 Eshkol had made a high-profile tour of seven countries south of the Sahara. "Our policy is that every vestige of colonialism must be displaced by independence," he would later write to Zambian leader Kenneth Kaunda, pledging support against the white-minority regime in Rhodesia.[21] In 1959, when Dayan acolyte Shimon Peres—then deputy defense minister—proposed that Israel arrange with France to lease the resource-rich South American colony of French Guiana, Mapai leaders responded with horror. Pinhas Sapir, who would later become Eshkol's finance minister, told Peres that the idea was "a catastrophe, colonialism, imperialism."[22]

Justice Minister Shapira also rejected annexation, arguing that it meant turning Israel into a binational state, in which Jews would eventually become a minority. The necessary alternative was to return almost all of the West Bank to Jordan, "because otherwise we're done with the Zionist enterprise." Only four other ministers (including Sapir) backed his position.[23]

When Eshkol summed up the debate, he dismissed Allon's ideas as "formulating what's good for us . . . playing chess with ourselves." He said that Israel could ignore the United States for a few months, as the white government in Rhodesia was ignoring Britain—a loaded parallel—but would eventually have to provide proposals. With his warning that Israel could not negotiate with itself, Eshkol completed a remarkable process: Just a week and a half after the war, the ministers had outlined most of the key positions in an argument that would drag on for decades over the West Bank's future.

While worrying aloud about the size of the Arab population, Eshkol favored annexing Gaza and vaguely suggested "autonomy or something else" for the West Bank. Wanting to eat his cake and push it away, he articulated the spirit of the meeting.[24]

As for Egypt and Syria, a resolution to offer a return to the international borders in return for full peace and security arrangements passed the cabinet on the morning of June 19 by a 10–9 vote, a majority but not a mandate. Eshkol appointed a committee to word a compromise. That afternoon—by the grace of time zones, morning at the White House and at U.N. headquarters—a new resolution was in hand, and the cabinet unanimously adopted Israel's first diplomatic response to the Six-Day War. To Egypt and Syria, Israel offered "a full peace treaty on the basis of the international border and Israel's security needs." The international border meant the boundaries of Britain's Palestine mandate, not the armistice lines with their demilitarized zones. The cabinet decision also said explicitly that "the Gaza Strip falls within the territory of the State of Israel." Israel's requirements for peace included demilitarizing the Sinai Peninsula and "the Syrian heights,"[25] free passage in the Straits of Tiran and the Suez Canal, and a guarantee that the Jordan River headwaters would not be diverted. "Until the signing of a peace treaty," the statement read, ". . . Israel will continue holding the territories it now holds."[26]

With the June 19 decision, Israel offered to give up most of the land its army had conquered. Though ministers might interpret "Israel's security needs" in different ways, they were clearly offering Israel's two most hostile neighbors a near-total pullback. Even Begin voted for it, indicating that his map of the homeland did not include the Sinai or Syrian land. Allon later attributed his "yes" vote to the "psychological error" of believing that the Arab states would now make peace.[27] Others, such as Galili and Dayan, apparently read Arab intentions pessimistically—and so expected that Israel would be able to stay put.

For all, the crucial subtext was the experience of 1956–57. Israel's leaders expected to be pressured by the United States to pull out. They were willing to agree, but this time they asked a higher price. Egypt and Syria had to accept Israel and agree to peace. Full peace, rather than land, would guarantee Israeli security.

At the same time, Israel sought to keep Gaza, based on the hope that its Palestinian refugees could be resettled elsewhere.[28] And regarding the West Bank and the Kingdom of Jordan, the proposal said not a word. Were security the only issue, Israel could also have offered Jordan a pullback in return for peace, demilitarization, and border adjustments. But this piece of occupied territory was a lost, longed-for part of the Land of Israel.[29] Despite the anxiety about U.S. pressure, therefore, Eshkol could not lead; the government could not decide.

ISRAELI POLICYMAKERS actually had less to fear than they thought. The United States was not preparing an encore of its 1957 demand for full withdrawal. From the moment Washington woke up to news of the fighting on June 5, Lyndon Johnson's foreign policy team almost reflexively worked to avoid the Eisenhower administration's example.

After war broke out, "we 'decided' . . . to go for a full Arab-Israeli settlement and not just for another truce," NSC staffer Harold Saunders writes in his inside account—again noting that the decision was instinctive, that "the men around the President just started talking this way." One reason, Saunders says, was the hope of exploiting the crisis to reach peace. Another was that "we were convinced that we just could not move Israel against its will."[30]

By June 6, Johnson's national security adviser, Walt Rostow, wrote a note to the president suggesting that the United States should seek "to negotiate not a return to armistice lines, but a definitive peace in the Middle East."[31] The next day, in another note, Rostow added Cold War context: The U.S. interest was full peace, with Israel accepted by its neighbors—and with Arabs no longer needing Soviet support to fight Israel.[32]

Rostow, though, had his hands full with the war in Vietnam. Seeking reinforcements, Johnson called back Rostow's predecessor, McGeorge Bundy, who had left the White House the year before to head the Ford Foundation. For the next month, Bundy coordinated a special National Security Council committee on the Middle East. In Bundy's view, part of his task was to provide "a special balancing weight against the normal bias of Arab-minded State Department regulars" so that policy would match the White House's greater concern for the "rights and hopes of Israel."[33] Bundy regarded Johnson's inability to provide stronger backing to Israel before the war as "instructive to both sides as to the limits . . . of the executive assurances."[34] That is, the promises made by Eisenhower had proved hollow at the first test and had failed to prevent war.

There were domestic considerations as well. Johnson had close ties to the American Jewish community.[35] In April 1967, a paper on guaranteeing Jewish support for Johnson's reelection by Washington lawyer David Ginsburg circulated among the foreign policy team. It noted that Richard Nixon had lost Jewish support as the Republican presidential candidate in 1960 because he was identified with "what most Jewish voters regarded as the Eisenhower-Dulles double-standard policy against Israel during the Suez crisis."[36] Once war erupted, Johnson had further reason to be concerned about Jewish support. A State Department spokesman, responding to Arab accusations that America was fighting on Israel's side, declared that the United States was "neutral in thought, word and deed"—and provoked a storm of criticism from American Jews. Reporting to the boss, two Johnson aides said that Jewish leaders' major fear was that Israel "may be forced to lose the peace—again (as in 1956)."[37]

In the week after the cease-fire, Bundy led intensive discussions aimed at a presidential policy statement by the time of the U.N. General Assembly debate on June 19. But any hope of building a peaceful Middle East had to compete with Vietnam's gravitational pull on officials' time, energy, and emotions. "From the end of the war on, the top levels of the U.S. government were exhausted" with the Arab-Israeli conflict, Saunders recalled years later, adding, "You will remember that we had another problem on the other side of the world."[38]

There was also a dispute on whether the Israeli pullback had to be all the way to the prewar boundaries. The American line should be "let's have peace," Bundy said, in a call from U.N. headquarters to the White House on June 11, adding that he opposed State Department officers who wanted to stress the "territorial integrity" of all countries. That phrase, meant to protect Israel when Johnson used it before the war, now meant a full Israeli pullback. "Old boundaries cannot be restored," Bundy asserted.[39] In a White House meeting the following day, Johnson wondered, "How do we get out of this predicament?"

"We're in a heck of a bind on territorial integrity," Secretary of Defense Robert McNamara answered, hardly reassuringly.[40]

The opposite view came from Secretary of State Dean Rusk, who insisted that the armistice lines of 1949 would not endanger Israel if there were peace. "Israel's keeping territory," Rusk forecast, "would create a revanchism for the rest of the twentieth century."[41]

The solution, at Bundy's suggestion, was for Johnson to avoid proposing concrete solutions. Instead, the president would identify problems, and call on Israel and the Arabs to solve them.[42] That fit advice from Ambassador Walworth Barbour in Tel Aviv: Let the Israelis struggle with seeking direct negotiations, lower their expectations, and then seek U.S. help.[43] It also fit the lack of energy for a major American initiative. It evaded the need for precise positions, and for giving U.S. guarantees—which, to have value, would need approval from a skittish Senate.[44]

Drafting the speech took nearly a week. Bundy apparently framed the final version.[45] The core was what became known as Johnson's "Five Points": the right of every nation in the region to live and be accepted by its neighbors; a solution for refugees; respect for maritime rights; ending the Mideast arms race; and maintaining the "independence and territorial integrity of all states." Johnson's speech quickly added to that last crucial point that it could be achieved only through peace. Instead of "fragile and violated truce lines," he called for "recognized boundaries" and security arrangements. Troops must withdraw, but only with the realization of the other conditions. The main burden of peacemaking, he concluded, fell not on the U.N. or the United States, but on the sides to the conflict.

The result, on the crucial issue of territory, was finely tuned ambiguity. The United States had affirmed "territorial integrity," which meant that no Israeli soldier should stand on land belonging to an Arab country. Yet if "truce lines" must be replaced with agreed upon borders, then until such an agreement was reached, it was entirely unclear what land belonged to whom. America left that for the Arabs and Israel to negotiate. It clearly expected that process to begin quickly, but did not commit itself to deep involvement.[46]

Johnson spoke to the TV cameras at a State Department educators' conference, chosen for its convenient time on the morning of June 19, just before the U.N. General Assembly convened. At about the same time in Jerusalem, the Israeli cabinet adopted its decisions, which it kept secret even from military Chief of Staff Rabin. Foreign Minister Abba Eban, in New York for the U.N. gathering, received the proposals by cable and presented them to American officials, including Rusk and U.N. ambassador Arthur Goldberg. The Americans must have been relieved that Israel had chosen a "realistic" stance, as the diplomatic cables termed a readiness to pull back. Israel's leaders had every reason to be relieved as well. While Johnson's speech did not match Israel's policy, it was a far cry from 1957. In fact, they may have felt like someone who sets a high price for his house, then kicks himself for not asking for more when he hears the first interested buyer say "Okay."

The U.S. passed the Israeli proposals on to Egypt and Syria through diplomatic channels, according to Eban, and within a few days both governments rejected them.[47] The public behavior of both countries confirms Eban's testimony. Shell-shocked and humiliated, they were not ready to make peace. But they missed a moment of opportunity to regain their land. After that, Israel's price did rise. In the absence of decisions and diplomacy, "creating facts" took over.

THE FIRST U.S. POLITICIAN to arrive in the accidental empire held no office except has-been and want-to-be. Former vice president Richard Nixon, the defeated Republican presidential candidate of 1960, landed in Tel Aviv on June 21, 1967, at the end of months of globe-trotting intended to establish him as a foreign policy authority for his comeback run for the presidency.

Eshkol's expressed preference was to see Johnson reelected in 1968,[48] but both protocol and prudence ensured that Nixon received VIP handling, including meetings with ministers and generals. First, though, came a tour of a hospital to see wounded Israeli and Arab soldiers. Nixon devoted two dozen scrawled words in his legal pad to that look at the price of war. Of the wounded Israelis, he recorded nothing. The Arabs were "poor" and "frightened," he noted. What stood out for him was an Egyptian tank commander's comment. "Russia is to blame," Nixon recorded his words. "They furnished arms. We did the dying."[49]

Nixon repeated that quotation in his summary of what he had learned in Israel about the Soviets—or rather, of what he heard that confirmed the picture that he had brought with him. At his press conference on arrival, Nixon labeled Nasser as the aggressor, then stressed the Soviet Union's decisive role in arming and inciting the Arabs to fight. Israel should not withdraw, Nixon said—putting distance between himself and Eisenhower's policy a decade before—until peace was reached. But that, he said, would require a U.S.-Soviet guarantee.[50]

Nixon presented virtually the same formula to the U.S. press on his return home.[51] He had built his career as a cold warrior, a believer not only in confronting communism but in seeing conflicts around the world as the manifestations of a single Manichean struggle.

Beneath the chaos was seductive simplicity, the conceptual cleanness that can bewitch a person attracted to ideas. Even more than Walt Rostow, Nixon treated the Middle East as one corner of the Cold War chessboard, and the Egyptians and Syrians as knights and bishops moved by Moscow. Any real peace would require agreement with the Soviets, and that would be achieved only if the United States made sure its own rook—Israel—stood firm, without retreating. Nixon was partially correct; the war did fit into the U.S.-Soviet great game. But his calculus did not include the pieces themselves thinking, ignoring orders, or changing the shape of the board while one superpower waited for the other's will to weaken.

* * *

BACK HOME, Nixon received a packet of photographs of his trip from his Israeli Foreign Ministry escort officer, including one that showed him as "the first foreign dignitary" to land at "the airport of united Jerusalem"—presumably by helicopter from Tel Aviv.[52] The escort's effusive description contains an error: The city was officially unified four days after Nixon left, perhaps while the film was at the lab.

Balancing haste and caution, Eshkol had already delayed action. He had overwhelming public support—one opinion poll showed over 90 percent of Israelis in favor of keeping East Jerusalem permanently.[53] But at Eban's urging, the prime minister kept a low profile on Jerusalem as the U.N. General Assembly convened. Eban wanted to maintain a united front with the United States against Soviet demands for an immediate pullback. A meeting in New York with Dean Rusk deepened his concern; the secretary of state warned that a misstep in handling the Holy City could spark "strong anti-Israel feeling" in the American public.[54]

The next week, Eshkol ran out of patience. Ironically, one reason was the U.N. debate, in which British foreign secretary George Brown spoke emotionally against any move by Israel to unify Jerusalem. Eshkol feared an international demand to maintain the status quo. Better to be criticized after the fact, he thought, than to do something Israel had been told in advance not to do.[55]

By the time the cabinet met on June 27, it had agreed on the method recommended by Justice Ministry experts for uniting the city. The Knesset would pass amendments to two existing laws. One would allow the cabinet to extend Israeli law and jurisdiction to "any part of the Land of Israel" by administrative decree. The second would allow the interior minister to order changes in city limits at his discretion. In practical terms, land under Israeli jurisdiction was part of the state, but neither law mentioned "Jerusalem" or "annexation." The approach fit the hopes of cautious cabinet members to minimize the international reaction—while territorial maximalists believed it offered them an opening for further annexations in the future. At the same time, the Knesset would approve new legislation protecting freedom of access to the holy places of all religions and barring "anything likely to violate [believers'] feelings with regard to those places." A Foreign Ministry cable to Israeli envoys abroad urged them to emphasize Israel's protection of Christian and Muslim holy sites, and to play down the other two laws. Unification of the city should be described "not as annexation but as municipal fusion," a practical necessity for meeting local needs.[56]

Another key decision dealt with the city's new borders. Eshkol sought to include Rachel's Tomb, a site at the northern edge of Bethlehem traditionally identified as the grave of the biblical matriarch, which aroused adoration from secular Zionists as well as from religious Jews.[57] But the ministerial committee he appointed dropped that idea, in order to avoid taking part of another town that was sacred to Christians. The cabinet received two possible maps, both drawn by General Ze'evi. One extended the municipal limits—and therefore the State of Israel—much farther eastward than the other, to take in natural springs and guarantee the city's water supply.

Allon favored the maximalist plan, but Dayan opposed it, arguing that it would cut access between the northern half of the West Bank and the southern half—all of which he still hoped to turn into a single autonomous region. Another, unspoken consideration may have been that it would divide and reduce the territory under military rule, his personal domain as defense minister. Beyond that, he was demonstrating what would soon be recognized as a law in the quantum physics of Israeli politics: Dayan could not occupy the same position as Allon. Allon's stand usually proceeded from his grand conception, as a predictable instance of theory. In advance, Dayan's view could be predicted only as "elsewhere."

At the June 27 meeting, Dayan prevailed, and the cabinet approved the more limited map. Only months later did Eshkol discover that the matriarch's tomb had been left out.[58] But even the minimalist plan added over twenty-seven square miles to Israeli Jerusalem's area, nearly tripling the size of the city. To the Israeli population of 200,000 it added 66,000 Arabs. The additional territory went far beyond the Jordanian city limits, adding open countryside yet avoiding Arab villages and neighborhoods.[59] The expanded Jerusalem intentionally included room beyond the Green Line for major housing developments for Jews. The map testified against the term "municipal fusion." The Foreign Ministry cable on unification, sent before the cabinet met, brought no joy to Eban or the other Israeli representatives at U.N. headquarters on the East River. They cabled back, urging a delay of a week, until after the expected end of the General Assembly session. At the start of its June 27 meeting, the cabinet leaned toward accepting that advice. Eshkol left the room and phoned Eban, telling the foreign minister that word of Israel's plans had already leaked and that waiting would risk international pressure, citing the British foreign secretary's speech. Eban dropped his objections. Two days later, he cabled Eshkol, with words suggesting a slightly quivering diplomatic upper lip. "I cease to comprehend developments," Eban wrote, saying that on the phone, the prime minister had misled him to believe that the cabinet already overwhelmingly opposed postponement. Eshkol answered that the press was on to the story, public pressure was high, and "delay . . . would have made us a laughingstock." Eban's memoirs skip that exchange, instead suggesting dryly that "George Brown had more to do with Israeli unification of Jerusalem than he might have wished."[60]

On the afternoon of June 27, all three unification laws were submitted to the Knesset, sent to committee, returned to the plenum and passed, in defiance of normal procedure. Only the two small communist parties (pro-Moscow and anti-) objected.[61]

The next day, responding to the Knesset vote, the State Department cabled U.S. ambassador Barbour, instructing him to warn Israel against presenting the world with a fait accompli.[62] The seven-hour time difference with Israel rendered the warning irrelevant. By then, Interior Minister Haim Moshe Shapira and the cabinet secretary had issued decrees applying Israeli jurisdiction to an area specified by two and a half typed pages of map coordinates and adding it to the City of Jerusalem. Military orders were delivered by courier to commanders in Jerusalem: As of 1300 hours, June 29, Jerusalem City Hall would take over from the army, permits would no longer be needed to cross between the two sides of Jerusalem, blocked roads must be opened, minefields must be removed.[63]

On the day of unification, army Central Command chief Uzi Narkiss suddenly recalled that he had neglected to dissolve the Jordanian city government, which meant East Jerusalem had two mayors and two city councils. The general phoned Lieutenant Colonel Ya'akov Salman, the deputy military governor, and ordered him: Dissolve it, fast.

"But how?" said Salman, according to Israeli journalist Uzi Benziman's account.

"That's your business. Confirm orders carried out today."

"It has to involve some legal procedure. We need to cite some regulation."

"You figure the method," Narkiss told him. "You think I know how to do it?"

Salman sent military police to locate the Arab council members and bring them to the East Jerusalem City Hall. At 5:00 that afternoon, he found the mayor, Ruhi al-Khatib, with four of the other eleven councilors outside the building's locked doors. The group proceeded to the hotel next door, where Salman quickly drafted a four-sentence decree and read it out: "In the name of the Israel Defense Forces, I respectfully inform Mr. Ruhi al-Khatib and the members of the Jerusalem City Council that the Council is hereby dissolved." A liaison officer translated the statement into Arabic. When the deposed mayor asked for something in writing, the liaison officer found that the only paper in the meeting room was a napkin, on which he wrote out his translation. Uzi Benziman, describing the incident, notes that the decree had no basis in law. But Salman, who later wrote that the decision to annex was "made emotionally, without serious deliberation," had fulfilled his orders.[64]

That first day, a two-way pilgrimage flooded the city. At Mandelbaum Gate, the main crossing point between east and west, Haim Gouri found crowds streaming in both directions, and felt "a hundred megatons of expectation, a hundred megatons of curiosity, exploding before our eyes." On streets leading to the Old City, he wandered through an impromptu fair, painting with words a scene that should have called Brueghel back from the dead to grab his brushes:

> Thousands of Jews and Arabs mixed together . . . Arab village women in embroidered dresses, Jewish girls in tight pants and T-shirts— through the thin weave shout the delights of young, ambitious, conquering, arrogant Israel, heart-captivating in its fevered *sabra*-ness, rushing to see and buy—and next to them hundreds of soldiers carrying guns, and stunned tourists . . . and nuns and priests and Arab kids yelling and selling and wheedling . . . and cabbies shouting "Ramallah!" and Jewish women carrying baskets, rushing past the historic

moment into the dark alleyways of the Old City to buy cheap, who cares what! . . . the crowd growing like a wave, noisy, moving in the crazed brotherhood of the moment of removing barriers and breaking dividers, in megatonic curiosity bulldozing forward.[65]

Inside the walls, in the old covered markets, he passed through crazed commerce and heard one well-dressed young souvenir merchant shouting in English, "I will never take Israeli money!" Later, Gouri wrote, would come the time to understand the problems. For a moment, "Jerusalem of the Mandate," of his youth, had returned; Gouri imagined not a reunited city, but the city of innocence and nostalgia, never divided.[66]

Meanwhile, in the streets of Qatamon and Baqa—West Jerusalem neighborhoods whose mansions had been abandoned by wealthy Arabs in 1948 and subdivided among Jewish immigrants—packed cars with Jordanian plates rolled slowly by, as families from East Jerusalem and beyond looked at houses left behind nineteen years before.[67] One of the cars, that day or soon after, belonged to Ramallah teenager Raja Shehadeh's family. Earlier, Raja had bicycled from Ramallah to Jerusalem, noticing as he came over the last hill that this time, past the Arab neighborhood of Sheikh Jarrah, he could see the low houses of the west city, as if they had not been there all along but had suddenly appeared, as if some divider of fog had been pulled down. Now the family crossed into the Jewish city, where Raja's mother had gone to school. His mother, excited, pointed out places she knew; for her, he later wrote, "this was a true return to the past." For him, the second side of the city was stunningly foreign. "This Jerusalem had a majesty and anonymity that did not exist in the eastern side," he found, in a subtle variation on his melody of humiliation.[68]

"Topsy-turvy world department: All week we have been meeting Arab visitors at our New City premises and Jewish visitors at the Old City," read a cable from bemused American consul-general Evan Wilson in early July. "Arab owner of grand piano, which has been in living room of our New City residence for 19 years since he entrusted it for safekeeping to my predecessor . . . in 1948 when leaving in a hurry, has come to claim it back." Unification was "proceeding smoothly," he said, except for the traffic and pedestrians choking the streets and the army engineers' continued demolition of buildings just outside the Old City to reopen thoroughfares.[69]

Ambassador Barbour, offering advice on whether America should recognize Israel's "territorial acquisition," asked whether "we have any real alternatives to making the best of a potentially good situation." Israel's willingness to sacrifice troops to avoid damaging religious sites during the conquest, he cabled home, proved it could be trusted to protect the holy places. Ending the city's division was positive, and Israel had acquired the Old City "in a purely defensive action," which should mitigate American commitment to territorial integrity. Walt Rostow passed the cable to Johnson with a note that it expressed a "Tel Aviv perspective," a hint that the ambassador identified a bit much with the locals.[70]

The U.S. administration quickly adopted the position that while it rejected Israel's "administrative actions" in Jerusalem, no territorial acquisition had occurred or even could occur. At the State Department, Rostow's brother Eugene, the under secretary for political affairs, met with Israeli ambassador Avraham Harman, and took note of his insistence that Israel's "steps do not constitute annexation but only municipal fusion." In a memo afterward, Eugene Rostow asserted that creating "a unified municipal administration" did not mean annexation, since no country actually had the power to change Jerusalem's status as an international city. Israel, he noted, had affirmed that it had not annexed anything. Based on that view, the United States abstained twice in July on General Assembly resolutions demanding that Israel rescind any change in Jerusalem's status. The U.S. position was that Israel need not reverse what it had never done.[71]

By early July, Eshkol phoned Yehudah Tamir, a businessman and former director general of the Housing Ministry, and gave him the job of building Jewish neighborhoods in East Jerusalem as quickly as possible. Tamir would report directly to the prime minister. Eshkol's logic was simple, explains Benziman: Israeli control in Jerusalem depended on Jewish settlement. Eshkol's own files show that in the weeks and months to come, he personally oversaw the construction efforts, and urged others involved to avoid publicity.[72]

On paper, annexing land while claiming not to was absurd: The denials muted Israel's own insistence that it would not withdraw. Yet the move satisfied Israeli public opinion and its leaders' desires, while evading a clash with the United States, Israel's patron and diplomatic ally. Unification also prepared the ground for the moves that mattered: large-scale construction for Jews beyond the Green Line in expanded Jerusalem.

The bulldozers of the Mughrabi Quarter prefigured annexation: In the first case, the officers and civilians cast the government as British mandatory authorities, and created a fait accompli to set policy. In the second, the government itself took the role of the pre-independence Zionist movement, cast the United States and United Nations as British high commissioner, and sought to establish a fact that would only be fully appreciated once it was irreversible. Without noticing it, the country's leaders had immersed themselves in a fountain of youth that took them two decades into their past.

ON JUNE 19, the day that Israel offered to give up the Syrian heights for full peace, a staff officer in the IDF division holding those heights informed battalion commanders that the next day "a settlement survey team will began working in [our] sector, led by Meir Shamir of the Settlement Department."[73] Neither the officer nor Shamir could have known of the government's diplomatic initiative. Possibly no one in the cabinet knew of Shamir's work plans, whose purpose was to explore conditions establishing Jewish farming communities on the newly conquered land.

The Settlement Department belonged to the Jewish Agency—which, historically speaking, *was* the pre-independence Zionist movement. Established along with the British mandate after World War I, the Agency represented Palestine's Jews to the British authorities, served the Jews as a government-in-the-making, and funneled Jewish philanthropy from abroad to projects in Palestine. Its Siamese twin, with overlapping boards and shared officials, was the Zionist Organization, the international body created by Theodor Herzl in 1897 to promote Jewish nationalism.

In 1948, the Agency turned over most of its functions to the new state. Yet as if time were frozen, it continued to exist. That way, Diaspora Jews could keep up financial support, donating to a nongovernmental organization rather than to a foreign state. The Agency, though, was not precisely an independent philanthropy. A contract with the government laid out a division of functions. Along with the Jewish National Fund, which bought and managed land holdings in the name of the Jewish people, it was considered a "national institution." Israeli politicians filled the top roles at the Agency. Levi Eshkol himself had headed the Settlement Department from 1948 until assuming the premiership in 1963; for most of those fifteen years he was also finance minister.[74]

The Settlement Department was a bureaucratic shrine to an ethos from the revolutionary period: the ideal of settling on the land. The traditional Hebrew word for Jewish immigration to the Land of Israel, *aliyah*, literally "ascent," is better translated as "repatriation"—it connotes the return home of exiles, refugees adrift for generations. Beginning in the late nineteenth century, Zionism turned repatriation from a hope into a pressing obligation, and added a second stage: A Jew should return not only to the homeland, but to land itself, to the earth. True repatriation meant becoming a farmer and a person of nature. "The return to nature," as Israeli political philosopher Yaron Ezrahi has written, "was a commitment to the naturalization of an entire people as an act of collective emancipation from the 'culture of exile,' a deliberate attempt to leap over two thousand years of Jewish history and somehow retrieve the primordial universe that existed before expulsion from the land."[75] Modern Hebrew adopted the word *ascent* for this process as well: to settle on a new piece of land is "to ascend to the soil," as if arising from the depths.

The ideal has its roots in European thinkers who romanticized both nature and the peasantry, in socialism's beatifying the workingman—and in the inclination of a persecuted minority to accept the majority's caricature of it. Distaste for "the prototype of the pale, scrawny Jew" runs through Zionist writing as well.[76] Of course, there was also a practical side: In the struggle between the Jews and Arabs for one territory, each new piece of land acquired and settled by Jews was an additional stake in the whole of the land. Beginning in the 1880s, European Jewish immigrants established farming colonies in which they soon employed Arab fieldworkers. The next generation of immigrants, influenced by socialist ideology, insisted that Jews do the labor themselves, leading to the creation of the kibbutzim, communes on Jewish National Fund land.

Members of the first kibbutzim led an intensely ascetic life, following a philosophy known as the "religion of labor," in which the central sacrament of traditional Judaism, religious study, was replaced by the sacrament of physical labor and settlement on the land. Labor Zionism regarded itself as the successor to Judaism. The kibbutzim formed a secular monastic order (albeit without celibacy), a minority whose members treated the group as their true family, and whose greatest pride was to own nothing, to work entirely for others, to live in the fever of an ideal that the wider society admired but could not match.

Another wave of immigrants after World War I, inspired by the Russian Revolution, brought the dream of turning Jewish Palestine into a single commune. The United Kibbutz, born of this effort, sought to create large kibbutzim, often at the edge of towns, as with Ramat Rachel next to Jerusalem. Members worked not only in fields but at city labor, to prove—in the words of one pioneer—"that a [former] yeshivah student or Jewish gymnasiast could work harder than an Arab."[77] A member's status depended on the intensity of his toil. Children lived in separate houses, raised by the group. In some communes, their names were chosen by the membership.

At the same time, a second tier of labor settlements developed—cooperative villages, or *moshavim*, where members sold their produce together but had family fields and houses. The socialism was softer; the stress on "Hebrew labor" remained.

The outbreak of an Arab revolt in 1936, followed by the Peel recommendations to partition Palestine, brought a shift: The strategy was now to place settlements in new areas of Palestine, to prevent division of the land, or at least to make sure that as much as possible ended up in the Jewish share.[78] Labor Zionists, who dominated the growing Jewish community in Palestine, scorned grand political statements. Settlement, carried out quietly, would establish facts, conquer the land, set borders. The Jewish Agency and its Settlement Department coordinated the entire effort.

The settlements, particularly kibbutzim, now became military strongpoints. The creation of the Palmah as a kibbutz-based underground army sped the transformation. When the battle for the land exploded in full force in 1948, kibbutzim served as frontline fortresses. Settlement, Yigal Allon would write in a 1954 paean to the fallen kibbutzim of the Etzion Bloc, "served as the main source of independent [Jewish] military power," especially because of the "great resemblance between a kibbutz and a military unit"—both being built on volunteerism, discipline, and dedication to the group.[79] With no advance intent, the monastic orders had become military orders, adding machismo and tragedy to the romance of settlement.

After the 1948 war, kibbutzim were established in a rush along the armistice lines. In the state's first years, Levi Eshkol's Settlement Department filled whole new regions with moshavim, cooperative villages populated by new immigrants.

Yet at that very moment, the settlement ideal was yellowing into history. The socialist Zionist youth movements of Eastern Europe that once supplied legions of eager new kibbutz members had vanished in mass graves and crematoria ash. Few of the Jews who poured into newly independent Israel from other Mideast countries sought a secular replacement for Judaism—and many regarded the kibbutzim as an arrogant gentry, pampered by the ruling parties. Kibbutz members were disproportionately represented in the Knesset and officer corps. But the new country's modernizing economy offered new paths to success, opened by academic education—a subtler substitute for Talmud study.

To help the youth movements within Israel, the army allowed their graduates to serve together in a unit—Pioneering Fighting Youth, known by the Hebrew acronym Nahal—in which they split their time between combat duty and stretches at border kibbutzim or at outposts, half military, half agricultural, that in most cases eventually became new settlements. After Nahal, the next stage of movement-scripted life was supposed to be joining a settlement. Yet in the post-independence kibbutzim, new members joined and left, while most communes remained tiny.[80] The kibbutz movements were now monastic orders of an established faith that had gained power but lost its passion.

Worse, ideological battles ripped apart the kibbutz movements in the early 1950s. In the United Kibbutz, supporters of the far-left sage

Yitzhak Tabenkin and his radical Ahdut Ha'avodah party faced off against backers of Prime Minister Ben-Gurion and his political party, Mapai. A major issue was support for the Eastern Bloc or the West, North Korea or South. Another was Ben-Gurion's preference for the state over party and proletariat. It was a theological schism in the church of atheism. The movement split, as did individual communes, and sometimes families. The United Kibbutz remained the foundation of Ahdut Ha'avodah; a rival kibbutz organization aligned with Mapai was established. The third major kibbutz organization, linked to the radical-left Mapam party, was also roiled by ideological battles. Afterward, graduates of the youth movements within Israel were sent to strengthen the existing kibbutzim rather than establish new ones.[81]

Tabenkin and his disciples still spoke of the Whole Land of Israel and hated the armistice lines. They resembled the aging American wagon-train veterans painted by John Steinbeck in 1930s California: "a line of old men along the shore hating the ocean because it stopped them."[82] Pioneering was glorious and obsolete.

Since 1952, the United Kibbutz had managed to establish only one new commune. Between 1961 and early 1967, only ten new kibbutzim and moshavim "ascended to the soil."[83] Malaise set in at the Settlement Department. A committee recommended slashing the size of the department.[84] Building settlements to create facts belonged to the era of ethnic struggle, not to a time when a state existed, marked on the map, with an army on its borders.

YEHIEL ADMONI reported back for work at the Settlement Department on June 12. A forty-year-old Palmah veteran and agricultural adviser, Admoni had spent the last two years studying at Purdue University in Indiana. Through the old boys' network, he managed to get a flight home in mid-war. He found the department office ruled by euphoria and chaos. The decade of decline was over. "Within six days, the fullness of the land had become ours," he later wrote. A fever to work seized bored bureaucrats. Plans blossomed. "The golden opportunity had fallen into our hands to go out to the open expanses," says Admoni, who was particularly impressed by how quickly Meir Shamir, the head of the department's Galilee office, got to work on settling the high ground taken from Syria.[85]

Admoni, who took over as the department's number-two man, under Mapai politician Ra'anan Weitz, explains that after the war, settlement "was again needed, as in the '30s, to share in the political and defense effort by settling . . . regions that the state saw as essential to its security."[86] The comment is remarkable in two ways. First, it labels the years between 1948 and 1967, the years of state-building, as a moratorium, a parenthetical phrase. Zionism, as it were, had hibernated in those years. Now the glory days would resume. Yet the 1930s had been a time when two national groups wrestled, under foreign rule, for liberation at the price of the other. Now that struggle would also resume—except that one group had achieved political independence in part of the land, its army ruled the remaining territory, and settlement would be imposed by the powerful side in land inhabited by the weaker side. Second, the department leapt into this task before any government decision that it was needed. More was at work than a bureaucracy rushing to prove it still had a function. A generation sought to prove that its ideals were still relevant.

On June 13, before Eshkol began his cabinet consultations on the future of the occupied land, Ra'anan Weitz organized a trip into the hills south of Bethlehem, where the four kibbutzim of the Etzion Bloc had stood until the day before Israel's establishment. With him he brought a survivor of each of the communes.

At least one of Weitz's companions came to the exploratory visit with an intense commitment to resettle the area: Moshe Moskovic, the man from Massu'ot Yitzhak who had given up his seat on the Piper to the besieged settlements in April 1948. His kibbutz's survivors had rebuilt their community east of Ashkelon in southern Israel. Moskovic, a born politician, bubbling ideas, always smiling, had become head of the regional council—a kind of county government—in the area. To commemorate the lost land, he had started a yeshivah that combined a modern high school curriculum and traditional Talmud study, brought a charismatic disciple of Rabbi Tzvi Yehudah Kook to head it, and named it Or Etzion, the Light of Etzion. He was close to Eshkol and counted Allon as a longtime friend. In his journal, at the first news of the Etzion area's reconquest, he wrote plans for rebuilding, not just what had been there before, but more, bigger, an Etzion Bloc that could not fall again.

Weitz's delegation found the kibbutz buildings razed, the orchards uprooted, "shattering our dreams and expectations," Moskovic wrote afterward. A Jordanian army base, now abandoned, stood on Kfar Etzion's grounds. The next night, Moskovic got a call from the man from Revadim, the secular kibbutz originally located in the Etzion Bloc and linked to the left-wing Mapam party: His dovish movement rejected settling in the West Bank, for political reasons. It was groping toward the position that Israel should negotiate with King Hussein to trade the West Bank for peace. Moskovic did not let that dissuade him. He typed up his program for the bigger, better Etzion Bloc and sent it to Weitz. His plans could have been blueprints for rebuilding a community destroyed in a hurricane; they said nothing of strategic goals, Arabs, or the future of the West Bank. He was driven, he explained afterward, by the thought that "it's pure chance I'm here and not lying in the dust. Had I been in the bloc at the time, grass would be growing out of me."[87]

At Kibbutz Ne'ot Mordechai near the northern tip of Israel, on the other hand, strategic goals were explicitly on the mind of forty-six-year-old commune member Rafael Ben-Yehudah. Ben-Yehudah had left his native Vienna as a teenager in 1938, a month after the Nazis marched in, reached Palestine with a boatful of illegal immigrants who swam to shore, spent World War II in communes of landless workers, became a follower of Yitzhak Tabenkin, and helped found Ne'ot Mordechai on the Jordan River. On June 14, Ben-Yehudah sat down to talk with Dan Laner, a member of Ne'ot Mordechai and the chief of staff of the army's Northern Command. Ben-Yehudah had decided, even before the cease-fire, that he wanted to establish an Israeli settlement quickly in the occupied Syrian heights. The region's future was up in the air, and Ben-Yehudah wanted to make sure that the Syrians and their artillery would not return. Laner, also a Tabenkin disciple, promised his support. Sometime in the next few days, it appears, Ben-Yehudah brought in Meir Shamir from the Settlement Department.[88]

Ben-Yehudah would find another partner in Eytan Sat of Kibbutz Gadot—the kibbutz on the Jordan that was destroyed in Syrian shelling weeks before the war. Gadot was a United Kibbutz commune, and the thirty-one-year-old Sat had virtually no family but the movement: When he was seven his father died, and his mother sent him to grow up in a children's house at Kibbutz Gvat in the Jezreel Valley. When he was sixteen, "the age when your personality forms," by his own description, his kibbutz split in the great schism. He stuck with the United Kibbutz side and "the world of the revolution."

A few days after the war, Sat was released from his reserve unit to manage the rebuilding of Gadot. But he quickly turned his energies to a new project. In Sat's mind was the memory of the shellings, of having to carry a gun with him when he went to work at the kibbutz cowsheds next to the border, and of 1957, when Ben-Gurion had been pressured to withdraw from Sinai. The way to prevent that from happening now, he said, was to create a "settlement on the Syrian heights—a civilian presence, so that no one could just order a withdrawal. There'd have to be a debate in the Knesset."[89]

This was one more variation on creating facts: from the bottom up, the activists pulling in sympathetic officers and officials, intent on dragging the government after them. They would set policy, and draw the map of the country themselves.

3

SILENT COWBOYS

ON THE NEW FRONTIER

Look north or south, and you see low green fields, a prairie tamed, flocks of birds scooting above eucalyptus and pines planted by the farmers. Look east or west from Kibbutz Gadot, and mountains point toward the sky. To the west, across the valley, rise the Galilee hills. On the east, the stark climb of the land is even closer, right past the creek, neither deep nor wide, known as the Jordan River. In June, the air is hot, quiet, and heavy with the stink from the cowsheds. The river marks a geological border between two plates of the earth's crust, one bearing Africa, the other Asia, moving in opposite directions. The green valley is the bottom of a rip in the world.

The clubhouse at Gadot was also ripped when thirty or so representatives of the farming communities of the valley and the Galilee hills gathered there in mid-June 1967 at Eytan Sat's invitation. In normal days, a kibbutz clubhouse was the collective living room where members spent their evenings. At Gadot it was still torn by shells that had fallen during the war. There was no electricity. Were Sat a calculating politician, one might guess he chose the venue so that the reminder of the Syrian shelling would lend support to his proposal. Since he is gruffly practical, more bulldozer than calculator, it is likely he simply used the normal spot for a meeting. In either case, most of the people he called together were surprised by his idea of establishing a Jewish settlement on the newly conquered heights to the east. Some regarded it as "delusional," according to Yehudah Harel, who was there representing Kibbutz Manarah in the Galilee hills. Others were cautiously receptive. In the end, the group agreed he should check out the response from the relevant authorities, a nondecision providing him an entirely informal mandate for going ahead.

As the meeting's end, Harel told Sat, "Count me in." Harel, thirty-two years old, was the son of a Tabenkin disciple and had practically grown up on the knees of the United Kibbutz's spiritual master. In his youth, by his own testimony, he was "on the extreme left. You could say I was a communist," though of the anarchist leaning encouraged by Tabenkin, for whom the way to communism was by establishing communes rather than establishing a party or taking control of a state.

The day before the Gadot meeting, Harel and his father visited Tabenkin, who spoke of building settlements on the Syrian heights. Harel thought his white-bearded mentor "had gone nuts," he later recalled. "It was clear to us that Nablus and Gaza were the Land of Israel, but the Syrian heights? Only Tabenkin could say that, because he was out of touch with reality." Yet when he heard Sat propose the same thing, as a plan of action, he was primed. "It was an anarchist approach" that appealed to him. "You don't *talk* about the Whole Land. You start settlements." Harel also worried about the precedent of 1957, and about Syrian shells again falling on the kibbutzim of the valley. A way was needed "to keep the politicians from giving up the heights."[1] Distrust of politicians was part of what he had learned from his teacher. While settlement in the high ground would most often be justified by the need to protect the valley from Syrian guns, that concern was just one ingredient in the mix. Two others were as essential—the sense of a covenant with a homeland that stretched beyond political borders, and commitment to direct, anarchic action by a vanguard whose very willingness to act testified to its glowing truth. It required Tabenkinism.

In fact, Tabenkin was already wrestling with younger leaders over how his movement should respond to the conquests. At a meeting of the United Kibbutz secretariat, he rejected "any concession of [land] in our hands." He acknowledged that adding over a million Arabs to Israel's population created a problem—but said it could be solved through Jewish immigration. Israel's victory, he presumed, would arouse a vast awakening among Diaspora Jews, a great selling of homes and packing of bags. Unnoticed, he reversed the logic of maximalism: Before statehood, advocates of the Whole Land insisted on the need for territory to accommodate the desperate, threatened Jewish masses of Europe. Now the need to keep the land obligated the Jews of Leningrad, Los Angeles, and London to come to Israel, regardless of whether Soviet Jews could or Western Jews felt any need.[2] But that was a surface contradiction. With iron consistency, he believed in possessing the Whole Land, and in the primacy of principle over pragmatism.

Honored as the eighty-year-old ideologue was in his movement, by now he had competitors who—unlike him—had served in the military and in cabinets, who had considered strategy, compromises, and changes. Next to him, they were pragmatists. At the same secretariat meeting, Yigal Allon proposed quickly establishing settlements in "strategically important" areas in the West Bank—a hint that some territory was not essential—and at "problematic" spots along the international border with Syria. Crossing that line into the heights was not yet on his agenda. Yisrael Galili, the birdlike minister without portfolio, rejected "weak knees" and "talk of retreat"—yet urged avoiding any public statement on Israel's future borders. "It seems to me there are territories we won't be able to hold," he said.[3]

Given Galili's stance in the cabinet in favor of keeping the entire West Bank, it would appear he was referring to the Sinai and the Syrian heights as land that might have to be given up. From then on, though, Galili's views would remain a shimmering ambiguity, with as many interpretations as people who knew him. Did he want to keep every inch of territory, but silently, unnoticed? Or was he open to compromise, as long as he could avoid a split in the United Kibbutz movement? The mystery was a deliberate achievement. Galili wrote an incessant stream of letters, phrased countless resolutions and decisions, yet according to his closest aide, "he never wrote his true thoughts, because what's written can be revealed." In conversation, he told people he might deny everything he had said.[4] As his political power grew over the next decade, he would turn ambiguity into national policy.

Tabenkin had the upper hand. A movement resolution, adopted two weeks after the war, called for "action of major dimensions to settle areas of the Land that were cut off from us in the War of Independence and to consolidate our gains on the new borders" and for "the masses" of Diaspora Jewry to immigrate.[5] The old sage expected a great awakening within his movement as well. All the dreams of the 1930s were ripe for fulfillment. On June 23, kibbutz members from around the north came to Kibbutz Dafnah, at the very tip of Israel, in the valley below the heights, to hear Tabenkin lecture. He called for settling, quickly, throughout the newly conquered land, of establishing hundreds of new settlements—at a time when there just over 230 existing kibbutzim. Both Eytan Sat and Rafael Ben-Yehudah were there, and met, and decided to join forces.[6]

A week later they drove east together from Gadot, down the narrow country road to the one-lane bridge across the river, into the land that had lain beyond enemy lines, upward, the road rising steeply in switchbacks, until they could look back down at the valley, hundreds of feet below them, the fields and kibbutz buildings laid out, so the two practical men must have thought, like targets. Today's job was to find a spot for a bridgehead. The road, straighter now, kept rising. Cattle, left behind by vanished villagers, grazed in yellow grasslands and abandoned fields beneath the wide sky.

They checked the Syrian base next to the village of Naffakh, just a nine-mile drive from Gadot and 2,000 feet higher, where the land was poor for farming but the deserted buildings were in decent condition, and another Syrian base farther north, with better land but worse quarters. On the way back down they agreed that Ben-Yehudah would take care of technical arrangements, and Sat would find recruits to settle at Naffakh in two weeks.[7]

Very quickly, they found another ally from a northern kibbutz: Yigal Allon. According to Sat, Yehudah Harel made the connection; he was "born into the party's old-boys' club."[8] On July 3, Allon submitted a proposal to the cabinet to allow the Settlement Department to establish two or three temporary "work camps" in the heights, to house laborers from the Galilee who would farm the land. If the government preferred to disguise the camps as military rather than civilian, the workers could be reservists, the proposal said.[9] He had changed his mind about staying within the international border; the heights were now on his settlement map but, he later explained, "I thought it would be easier for me, politically or psychologically, to define it as an experimental farm and not necessarily as a permanent settlement."[10]

While the proposal lingered on the cabinet agenda, Allon pushed ahead. "The army needed . . . people to take care of the abandoned livestock on the Golan Heights—abandoned cows, wild horses that ran around," he later said. "There was no problem reaching an understanding that our guys would do the work." As for cash, "as labor minister I had a large budget . . . for work projects for the unemployed." The settlers, therefore, would be registered as needing jobs. He wrote to the Settlement Department. "Since I knew they didn't have much money, the misers, I said that when it comes to funding the people's work, I'll cover it."[11]

Ben-Yehudah's pocket calendar filled with details. Get food, mattresses, guns, flares, a pipe wrench, official permits from the army to be in occupied territory. Get maps, DDT, a generator. Explain to his own kibbutz why he wanted time off, that he did not intend to leave, only to get the project going. Meet representatives of the Upper Galilee regional council, explain that the settlers would gather the cattle, sheep, donkeys, harvest the abandoned crops, plant for next year. He marked down a promise from the council of 10,000 Israeli pounds ($3,300) and the loan of a jeep. He and Sat met General David Elazar of the Northern Command and Settlement Department chief Ra'anan Weitz.[12]

On July 13, Ben-Rafael and Sat came to the little town of Rosh Pinah, to meet Weitz's deputy, Yehiel Admoni, who drove up from Jerusalem, and his Galilee man, Meir Shamir, in Gittel's restaurant, the size of a living room, with shaky tables that Gittel waited on herself serving the food she cooked. There was a balcony looking out over the highway north, the place you went to sit to be seen in the Galilee. Admoni was impressed that Ben-Yehudah and Sat were serious, and the department agreed to help, knowing, as Admoni acknowledged, "that they weren't talking about gathering cattle . . . but about settling in the

Golan." The department agreed to kick in for supplies and a van, without telling or asking higher officials, and "disguised the action" as "arrangements with the regional council."[13] It was a congenial conspiracy, not of rebels but of well-connected people, who had fought together in the Palmah or who regretted being born too late to do so, who spoke in the same accent, had the same friends, and assumed they could bend the rules because their cause was so accepted, so absolutely assumed.

Eytan Sat went from kibbutz to kibbutz in the north, meeting with the secretary of each, asking for young volunteers. He did not find the great awakening imagined by Tabenkin. Young people did not enlist in droves. Though Yehudah Harel wanted to come, his kibbutz did not want to let him leave. The effort was a failure, Sat felt, but he signed up one here, two there. "In some cases, the kibbutz secretary said to me, this is a bachelor, maybe he'll meet someone," he would recall. In the back of his diary, Ben-Yehudah listed a dozen and a half candidates.[14]

One was twenty-four-year-old Carmel Bar, a shepherd at Kibbutz Mahanayim, westward across the valley from Gadot, just released from his reserve paratroop unit. Romanian-born, Bar had spent part of his early childhood in a Cyprus detention camp where the British kept Jews who tried to enter Palestine illegally. Immediately after independence, when he was five, his family reached Israel. Eventually he came to Mahanayim with a youth movement settlement group. It was a schoolbook Labor Zionist biography; if there were an Israeli Norman Rockwell, he would have painted pictures of Bar. After Sat's recruiting stop at Mahanayim, someone dropped by Bar's room and asked if he was interested. He agreed, though "for my sins, I can't say why," he later recalled. "I was a bachelor . . . educated in a youth movement, with hot blood," ready for an adventure.

Ben-Yehudah and Sat, meanwhile, made a small shift in plans. The water supply was poor at Naffakh. The destination became the Syrian base at nearby Aalleiqa. One day Bar got a phone call, telling him what time to be out on the road. It was a Sunday morning; his mother had come to visit the day before and complained that he was moving even farther from the Tel Aviv area. At the appointed time, an open jeep pulled up, driven by Rafael Ben-Yehudah. Bar dropped his sleeping bag in the jeep, climbed in, and introduced himself. Ben-Yehudah, supremely taciturn, answered, "Eh." They crossed the river and headed uphill. To each question Bar asked, Ben-Yehudah again answered, "Eh."

At Aalleiqa, Bar got out. There were Bedouin there from Israel, hired by the Agriculture Ministry to begin collecting the livestock, and Ben-Yehudah paid them in cash and cigarettes. One young member of Gadot had already arrived, but left the next day. For practical purposes, Carmel Bar was the first Israeli settler in occupied territory.

The date was July 16, 1967. It was five weeks after the end of the war, less than a month after the cabinet voted that Israel would withdraw from the heights for peace. Contrary to custom, there was no ceremony, no speeches by officials, to celebrate establishment of a new kibbutz. There was no news coverage. For a day Bar was alone, and then a handful of others came, and more in ones and threes, most even younger than him, men back from war, lost in what had been routine and looking for something new.[15]

AT AALLEIQA, Ben-Yehudah, Sat, and Allon were contravening government policy on the future of the heights, even if only Allon knew it. That summer, there was no policy at all on the future of the West Bank.

What the public heard of the government's plans for occupied land were comments such as Defense Minister Dayan's statement, "Until there are peace agreements, we'll hold on to all the territories the IDF conquered . . . with our fingernails."[16] Regarding Egypt and Syria, that fit the June 19 decisions—rejecting 1957-style pressures while suggesting that land could eventually be given up for peace. So did Dayan's public remark that "the Gaza Strip is Israel and I think it should become an integral part of the country," even if the Foreign Ministry reassured the United States that the government was not about to annex the area.[17] In fact, both Dayan and the ministry were expressing government policy: The political consensus was that Gaza would be annexed, but only after its refugees were somehow resettled elsewhere—in the Sinai, or the West Bank, or the East Bank.

The West Bank's future inspired no such certainty. Publicly, Eshkol spoke of Palestinian autonomy. "It's possible to think about a Palestinian unit, whose border is the Jordan and that will include the large urban centers such as Nablus, Jenin, Qalqilyah, and Jericho," he said in an early July interview.[18] That offered a way to keep the Jordanian army out, while keeping the residents off Israeli voting rolls. Eshkol's list included only cities in the northern West Bank. The subtle implication was that Bethlehem and Hebron, south of Jerusalem, would stay under direct Israeli rule. Those were the West Bank cities that most strongly conjured up the Bible, read as national epic.

Unknown to the public, Eshkol may also have been sending a message to Jordan's King Hussein to make concessions, quickly, if he wanted to regain the West Bank. At the end of June, Hussein had visited Washington and lunched at the White House with Lyndon Johnson and his aides. McGeorge Bundy and Under Secretary of State Nicholas Katzenbach told the king that the United States could not impose a solution. If he wanted the West Bank back—they warned him explicitly that he could not count on regaining every inch of it—he had to negotiate with Israel.[19]

Eager, but afraid of crossing Egypt's Nasser, the thirty-one-year-old king met secretly in London on July 2 with Eshkol's emissary, Yaacov Herzog, the director-general of the Prime Minister's Office. When asked if he was ready to sign a peace treaty, the king said, "Give us time," and that he had to work with the other Arabs.[20] It was a narrow opening, but it meant Eshkol had to decide which option he preferred.

To advise him, he had a committee of top officials, headed by Herzog, conducting feelers with public figures in the West Bank. That panel, and another representing the Foreign Ministry and intelligence services, sent him a flurry of evaluations, with contradictory advice to hurry up and wait. The West Bank's future needed to be arranged quickly, said a Foreign Ministry memo in mid-July, both because of its large population and because "internationally, the impression could be created . . . that Israel is maintaining a colonial regime." The authors, Shlomo Hillel and Mordechai Gazit, would be known as hawks in the years to come. Strikingly, as professional diplomats they were laying before Eshkol the two key arguments against keeping the West Bank that Israeli minimalists would cite in the decades ahead: the danger to Israel's Jewish majority, and the stain of colonialism.

In July 1967, though, colonialism was also the argument against establishing a Palestinian state that, the memo said, "would be regarded in the world as an Israeli puppet." As the least-worst option, Hillel and Gazit suggested that such a state be created, but seek confederation with Jordan to gain legitimacy as an Arab country.[21]

By the end of the month, the two retreated from that position. Summing up both committees' work on July 27, they again urged haste in deciding policy. But now that mainly meant choosing a position to present in talks with Hussein. Israel, they said, should drop the idea of Palestinian independence or autonomy, as local Palestinian leaders' initial openness to the idea was evaporating. An attached report on the contacts with those leaders said that they now believed Israel might withdraw, as it had from Gaza in 1957, and anyone who had cooperated with Israel would meet a "bitter fate." Failing an agreement with Jordan, therefore, Israel should "keep all possibilities open." That meant avoiding decisions and maintaining military rule indefinitely.

For Eshkol, given to delaying choices, it was appealing advice. Still, his experts had failed to address an issue that concerned him—the future of places to which Jews felt a bond. On a page of the memo dealing with how to administer the West Bank, the prime minister scrawled the words:

> *Etzion Bloc*
> *Beit Ha'aravah*
> *Our holy places in the enclave of the Bank.*

"Holy places" apparently referred to sites such as the Tomb of the Patriarchs in Hebron, the burial place of Abraham, Sarah, Isaac, Rebecca, Jacob, and Leah. Beit Ha'aravah was an isolated kibbutz near the northern tip of the Dead Sea that had been abandoned during the 1948 war. At the end of July, one question weighing on Eshkol, the former head of the Settlement Department, was what to do about the lost kibbutzim in what was now Israeli-occupied territory.[22]

Yigal Allon's advice, on the other hand, was to redraw Israel's borders, avoiding all delay. In late July, he submitted to the cabinet the first detailed version of what became known as the Allon Plan. Since discussing the idea with his friends while riding into the Syrian heights during the war, he had devoted days of driving the countryside with an aide, who was an ex-intelligence officer and "an excellent scout," and more hours of racing thoughts, suddenly "free of preconceptions like the Whole Land of Israel" and simultaneously in pain, by his own description, from shedding them. The love of a political idea was part of who he was, and now, like Pygmalion, he was falling in love with a political idea he had created himself. The plan would soon become the point of reference for Israeli debate on the future of occupied land, the concept that one accepted, amended, or rejected. For Allon, who thrived on people liking him, a good word about his plan became the equivalent of a warm slap on the shoulder.[23]

Israeli's eastern border, Allon wrote, should be the Jordan River and the line down the center of the Dead Sea. He proposed to his cabinet colleagues that they vote immediately to annex the barely populated strip six to nine miles wide along the Jordan. Farther south, he said with uncharacteristic ambivalence, Israel should annex all of "the Hebron hills"—meaning all of the West Bank south of Jerusalem—or perhaps only the desolate lowlands next to the Dead Sea. That is, he leaned toward annexing Bethlehem and Hebron, noting that Rachel's Tomb was in the former and the latter held the Tomb of the Patriarchs, sites "that are valuable to us nationally and traditionally." He was willing to pay the price of giving Israeli citizenship to what he estimated as the 80,000 Arab residents. But he also allowed for the option of leaving the two cities as an Arab enclave, like the larger enclave he would create north of Jerusalem, where most of the West Bank's Arabs lived. The enclaves, surrounded by Israeli land, would be given autonomy or, as he called it on another occasion, "home rule."[24] The result would be "the Whole Land strategically and a Jewish state demographically." On annexed land, he said, Israel should establish settlements "camouflaged as military strongpoints," if need be, until annexation was completed.

Allon's flamboyant contradictions shone from the plan. It let him renounce the Whole Land yet swear allegiance to it "strategically." He wanted immediate decisions, yet he could not make up his mind about Hebron: Reason said to give up large Arab populations, romance said to possess the biblical city. He called for clear decisions and clear borders, a strict, ordered reality—yet the borders could leap out of his unruly imagination. The plan was coauthored by a young rebel and an experienced politician, both of them Yigal Allon. In the months ahead, Allon began revising his plan, adding areas in the Sinai, and the Syrian heights, to his annexation map.

Only after submitting his plan to the cabinet did Allon discuss it with his "masters and teachers and the best of my comrades" in the United Kibbutz, a flagrant violation of convention in the disciplined movement. Though he was pushing annexation and settlement more actively than any other minister, he could not count on his movement's support. He would recall having "a long painful conversation, one of the most painful in all my life, with Yitzhak Tabenkin." His cabinet colleague Yisrael Galili not only disagreed with the plan, but was hurt because, Allon said, "perhaps for the first time in my life, I hadn't chosen to have a personal conversation with him before such a far-reaching step."[25] When he presented his proposals to the United Kibbutz central committee in August, he did not ask for a vote; he knew he would lose. His speech got brief coverage in the party press. A U.S. diplomat cabled home that Allon was seeking to appear as hard-line as Dayan, who now spoke of keeping the West Bank; the two were the presumed competitors to succeed Eshkol.[26]

In fact, Dayan had submitted his own secret plan. Predictably, it was the photo negative of Allon's. The mountain ridge—not the lowlands along the Jordan—was the strategic land Israel needed, Dayan asserted. Israel should therefore build five large army bases on the ridge. Each would be connected by roads to Israel proper, and next to each civilian settlements should be built.

The plan meant permanent Israeli rule over the West Bank's Arabs, who would nonetheless remain Jordanian citizens. In the West Bank, according to Dayan's conception, two nationalities would live, connected to different countries, with no border between them, but the Jews would retain control. More precisely, Dayan, as defense minister, would retain control. If there was a philosophy behind his proposal, it found expression in his later comment to the Palestinian poetess Fadwa Tuqan of Nablus: "The situation today resembles the complex relationship between a Bedouin man and the girl he kidnaps against her will. . . . You Palestinians, as a nation, don't want us today, but we'll change your attitude by forcing our presence on you."[27]

Dayan's cabinet colleagues approved putting army bases on the ridge, but rejected his settlement proposal, which implied permanence. They also debated Allon's proposal, which satisfied neither extreme, without making a decision. Repeatedly, the cabinet postponed formulating a policy on the West Bank's future. Or rather, postponement became policy. At one meeting of Mapai's "political committee," the party's inner circle, Foreign Minister Eban argued that any decision would only tie Israel's hands. This was not 1956, he said; now the diplomatic deadlock was working in favor of Israel, and it should wait to hear Arab proposals. Golda Meir, the chain-smoking Mapai secretary-general and former foreign minister, agreed. "Why should we talk?" she said. "Nothing's pressuring us. Let Hussein talk."[28]

The fear of pressure to withdraw immediately was fading. In that respect, Eban was correctly reading the signals from Washington. In a memo that might be called the Bundy Doctrine, written in early July, Johnson's emergency adviser laid out his view of future U.S. Mideast policy. His lesson from the war was that "if Israel were in imminent danger of defeat . . . the U.S. would confront extraordinarily painful and unattractive choices." To avoid needing to go to war on Israel's behalf, America had to ensure Israel's ability to defend itself. So the administration could not easily withhold arms as a means of pressure. The United States did need to maintain its ties with moderate Arab regimes, and did favor Israeli withdrawal—but the result had to be peace. The onus was therefore on the Arabs: Unless they offered peace, the United States would not lean heavily on Israel for concessions.[29] Later in the summer, Bundy wrote to Johnson, "We can't tell the Israelis to give things away to people who won't even bargain with them."[30] The position was logical, yet it had the unintended consequence of allowing Eshkol's government to avoid making choices.

EUPHORIA IS THE WORD most often used by Israelis describing the summer of 1967. The biblical verse cited most, in a season when the

Bible was quoted constantly, was from Psalms: "When the Lord brought back those who returned to Zion, we were like dreamers."[31]

In more modern terms, victory felt hallucinatory. The prewar fear of impending annihilation did not vanish. For many people, rather, it amplified the proportions of victory to miraculous. The old Jewish script that made sense of the new events was the one of redemption at the end of days, and a person did not have to be religious to allude to it. Chief of Staff Rabin, granted an honorary doctorate by Hebrew University, spoke of a "sense of salvation" and of soldiers "touching the very heart of Jewish history," experiences that broke "the shell of shame and toughness" and made paratroopers cry at the Western Wall.[32] Naomi Shemer's "Jerusalem of Gold" remained the unofficial national anthem, with a new verse proclaiming, "We've come back . . . / To the market and the square / A shofar calls on the Temple Mount," turning the hymn of longing into a song of consummated national love.[33]

Those weren't the only feelings that drove Israelis to visit the West Bank en masse, as the government steadily reduced restrictions on daytime travel in occupied land. There was curiosity, and the simple falling of barriers, and childhood memories, though some also came with Bibles in hand, to read verses about wars of kings and judges as they visited the places where ancient battles had been fought.[34]

An opinion poll in July showed that 91 percent of Israelis favored permanently keeping East Jerusalem, 85 percent were for keeping the Syrian heights, and 71 percent wanted to keep the West Bank. Just over half thought Israel should keep the Sinai.[35] Security concerns influenced those figures. Though one could have concluded from the victory that Israel's prewar sense of vulnerability was exaggerated, the opposite conclusion was more common: Keeping land was the key to safety. Tzvi Shiloah, a minor Mapai politician, became a prominent advocate of keeping everything. To eliminate the need to choose between land and peace, he argued that holding the land would convince Arabs they had no war option. "Our being on the Canal will end any thought of an Egyptian military contest with Israel. That will force Egypt to seek peace arrangements with us," he wrote in the Mapai-linked newspaper *Davar*.[36]

Were it up to the poets, policy would have been clear. Nathan Alterman, a legendary figure, declared that Israel must give up nothing, particularly not "the cradle of this nation," as he described the West Bank. Alterman's political column-in-verse had appeared for years in *Davar*. He was known as utterly loyal to David Ben-Gurion and to his stress on the state over movements, proletarian interests, or particular borders. He was a Tel Aviv poet, in love with his bright, modern, historyless Mediterranean city. In 1955, Haim Gouri had walked with Alterman down Jerusalem's main street to the midtown barbed-wire border, where they could look upon the Old City. Alterman told him, "From here to Shanghai is Asia, and from here to the beach in Tel Aviv is Israel."[37] Now, in prose, Alterman changed his view, criticizing Ben-Gurion's declared willingness to give up the West Bank. "The meaning of this victory is that it erased the difference between the state of Israel and the Land of Israel . . ." he wrote. "The state and the land are henceforth one essence." The remainder of the Jewish people was therefore obligated to immigrate, creating a "threefold thread that shall not be broken."[38]

Yet Alterman was also following Ben-Gurion's lead: The founding father was known for asserting that the Bible was the Jewish deed to the Land of Israel. Alterman now told Gouri, "I know you know every path in the land, that you love the villages and their orchards, even the stink of the smoke from wood ovens. . . . I am a Tel Aviv man. But anyone who returns these pieces of land will first have to write a different Bible."[39] Alterman's twist was that the Bible not only gave the Jews a right to the land; it also imposed an obligation on them to keep it.

A more radical transformation came over Moshe Shamir, a prominent novelist. For his colleagues in the far-left Mapam party, it seemed he had lost his mind.[40] In an essay ringing with poetic rhetoric, he compared the conquest of the Temple Mount to God's revelation at Mount Sinai; he described it as completing Zionism—and completing the efforts of Shabtai Tzvi, a seventeenth-century false messiah, transformed by Shamir into a proto-Zionist hero. Rhapsodically, he described the conquest as introducing the end of days, when "nation shall not lift up sword against nation." To reach redemption required only explaining to the world that Jerusalem was "the capital of peace—the temple of brotherhood, justice, morality."[41] All that he had formerly expected from Marx and Stalin was on the cusp of fulfillment.

Alterman, Shamir, and Shiloah joined forces and began signing up other intellectuals and public figures in support of permanent Israeli rule over the Whole Land of Israel, whose borders, for them, coincided with the new cease-fire lines. At an initial meeting in Tel Aviv, Alterman declared that the war was the "zenith of Jewish history," overshadowing not only the establishment of the state but the founding religious events recorded in the Bible.[42]

The group enlisted prominent members of the United Kibbutz and the Orthodox novelist S. Y. Agnon, the winner of the previous year's Nobel Prize for Literature, along with far-right poet Uri Zvi Greenberg and Yisrael Eldad, the ideologue of the pre-state, fascist-leaning Lehi (Stern Gang) underground. Greenberg and Eldad needed no conversion; both had long dreamed of a wide new kingdom of Israel. But their support meant that lifetime enemies, radical rightists and radical leftists, now found themselves together, a sign that the new issue of the territories would cast the old ideological definitions on history's ash heap.

There were voices, though fewer, opposing euphoria and the conclusions it produced. In *Davar*, the twenty-seven-year-old novelist Amos Oz warned, "Even occupiers who went much further in oppression, far beyond where Moshe Dayan is willing to go, sat in most places on thorns and scorpions until they were uprooted. Not to mention the total moral destruction that long occupation causes the occupier. Even unavoidable occupation corrupts."[43]

Soon after, Oz would describe arriving in Jerusalem, city of his birth, the day after the war, in uniform, straight from the Sinai Desert, and discovering that "Jerusalem is mine, yet a stranger to me," and that "the city is inhabited. People live there, strangers: I do not understand their language, they are living where they have always lived and I am the stranger. . . . Their eyes hate me. They wish me dead. Accursed stranger." As a child in Jerusalem, Oz had feared looming enemies beyond the border, ready to kill him; now he found himself "stalking its streets clutching a submachine gun, like a figure from one of my childhood nightmares: an alien man in an alien city."[44]

Oz's relative youth was paradigmatic; he had grown up after statehood. The youngest of Alterman's circle were a generation older, the messianic Shamir and the perpetually conflicted Gouri. For Oz, the newly conquered land was foreign territory—occupied, not liberated. He could empathize with the people there, know they were oppressed. Yet, mark this, too: They were different and terrifying, and he wanted to be able to turn his back on them, knowing that a fence safely kept them distant.

Oz was a member of Kibbutz Huldah, which belonged to Mapai's kibbutz movement. He and a dozen other members of various kibbutzim spent that summer holding long discussions at communes around the country, from his own movement and others, with men home from the war—people who had seen battle, had seen many friends and more enemy soldiers killed. Out of the transcripts, the organizers created a book called *Soldiers' Talk*.[45] Published independently by young people, made up of conversations in which the speakers were identified only by first names, it belonged to the genre of Israeli youth movement newsletters and pamphlets. It was the child of the ecstatic *In Your Covenant* of 1937, but the genre had turned dark.

Because *Soldiers' Talk* contains multiple voices and the speakers are struggling with conflicting thoughts, the book has been used to prove many points: that Israeli soldiers were morally sensitive or militaristic, eager for peace or despairing of it. The overwhelming tone, though, is of melancholy and shock, of mourning for comrades and for innocence. "We didn't return drunk with victory," says a brief preface. "Between the lines grows dissent from a society that tends to see a military achievement as compelling proof of the justice of its values."[46]

The word that seems to repeat most often in the book is *mu'akah*, which translates as "depression" or "angst." Another leitmotif is "filthy," as when a young officer named Dan, at Kibbutz Gvat, says, "The feeling of [being in] an occupying army is an extraordinarily filthy feeling." His unit conquered the city of Gaza. He describes rounding up men who would be expelled to Egypt, for reasons he does not give. A woman pulling small children came to the bus bearing the men and begged Dan to release her husband, lest her children starve, and Dan felt helpless, until a higher officer agreed to free the man. Then, Dan says, he begged his commander, "Get us out of here. This is a shitty job. . . . I'm a kibbutz member. We weren't brought up for this." Amnon, also of Kibbutz Gvat, says that when his unit rode into Gaza, he "recalled all the pictures of conquering armies, and the feeling was amazingly shitty."[47]

The memory of the Holocaust is woven through the conversations. At Na'an, Yisrael Galili's kibbutz, tank commander Kobi Rabinovich says, "In my behavior . . . I was constantly facing the Holocaust. They killed us, obliterated us. Because of that, it was all more intense. . . . There were sights that reminded me of things I'd seen in pictures. . . . You see a pile of corpses and a hand sticking out of it." In the space of a thought, the broad-shouldered young reservist bounces between Jewish victimhood and the implication that he is the victimizer. If the other side had won, he says, they would have behaved like animals, and then he adds, "All in all, war is a filthy thing."[48]

Elsewhere, Oz talks with members of Kibbutz Geva in the Jezreel Valley about territory. A man named Gili describes conquering Nablus, and says he would be willing to give it up for peace, but adds that the borders must be changed for security, that the Jordan River and the Syrian heights must remain in Israeli hands. He adds, "And the only reason for depression is that in a few years we'll have to fight again." Oz asserts that for peace, he would be willing "to visit the Western Wall as a tourist" in a foreign country. A friend of his died in the battle for the police academy in Jerusalem, he says, and "if blowing up the Western Wall with dynamite would raise him up from the dead, I'd say: Blow it up!"[49]

Let the camera roll back to compare Alterman's comrades and Oz's. One will look in vain in *Soldiers' Talk*, even in the conversations at United Kibbutz communes that it records, for Yitzhak Tabenkin's awakening, for novelist Moshe Shamir's epiphany, or for Yigal Allon's enthusiasm to annex and settle. Indeed, one will look in vain for enthusiasm for any action. Young veterans like Amnon and Dan do not speak of organizing to end the occupation. The gulf between the older generation and the younger is not political. It is between ecstasy and shell-shock.

Let the camera move back farther, for a much wider panorama. This was the summer of 1967. In France, America, Mexico, the fuse of student revolutions was burning toward the explosions of 1968. One of the mysteries of Israeli history is why it produced only the tiniest of New Lefts, the vaguest echo of student rebellion. Surely, one thinks, it should have been an epicenter of the upheaval. Elsewhere, as Paul Berman explains in his book *A Tale of Two Utopias*, the founders of the New Left were often children of Old Left activists. In France and America, a disproportionate number were Jews. Many French student radicals were children of partisans or Holocaust survivors. The children had grown up in comfort, knowing their parents were heroes. The heroic parents had sent them to communist youth groups or to Hashomer Hatza'ir, the left-Zionist youth movement linked to Mapam. In America, their parents had lived through the McCarthy repression. In Mexico, some were children of exiled Spanish Civil War veterans. The children longed to match the heroism of their parents; they feared becoming "veterans of the cinemathèque." As the New Left developed in each of those countries, it formulated a goal of "participatory democracy," socialism built from the bottom up by communes and workers' councils instead of Stalinist bureaucracies.[50]

By definition, young kibbutz members were children of Old Leftists, many of them Holocaust survivors or partisans, and even more of them veterans of what for them was the revolutionary war of 1948. But by the summer of 1967 the children had their own war stories, which they told in *Soldiers' Talk*. They had stopped an expected Holocaust, and found that war left you feeling filthy. As for participatory democracy, they had grown up in the closest thing to success at it. For them it was as prosaic as an extra weekend shift milking the cows or the Saturday night kibbutz general meeting. The revolution was a yawn, and heroism was shitty.

ONE CAN also look in vain in *Soldiers' Talk* for one more conversation, unlike the rest, from that summer. Somehow, among the editors, the idea arose that students from Rabbi Tzvi Yehudah Kook's Merkaz Harav yeshivah, who had also served in combat units alongside kibbutz men, would become allies against the "nationalistic intoxication that had engulfed the country." A meeting was soon arranged between six yeshivah students and two kibbutz interviewers. The discussion lasted five tense hours.[51]

Asked for his feelings about the war, one student, Yohanan Fried, spoke of a clash of emotion and reason. "Someone who longs for the Whole Land of Israel has the feeling of a person who's missing a limb . . . ," he said, then qualified: "That is . . . reason tells the emotions that, 'You must feel that you are not complete.'" What he labeled as "reason" was the theology of his yeshivah. He was describing the process of appropriating his teachers' belief as his own.

The war was part of a great, divinely directed process, explained Yoel Bin-Nun, another of the students, citing Avraham Yitzhak Hacohen Kook as speaking at the beginning of World War I of "the greatness of every war, and that the greater a war is, the greater the events one should expect as a result."

Yohanan added that the latest war followed earlier divine acts: the creation of the state, and before that the Holocaust: "Maybe this is too cruel a sentence, but the Holocaust was some sort of giant broom that sped immigration to the Land. . . . As if the Holy One, Blessed be He, said to us, 'Enough children, you've played what you wanted. . . . Now I'll move you to the Land.'" The question of where God had been in the Holocaust was thereby answered; He was arranging redemption, so that the fate of individual victims had to be put aside.[52]

Stunned, a kibbutz interviewer said, "None of us wanted, at all, for there to be a war." The enemy's defeat, the charred convoys in the desert, the refugees—all that only depressed them, he said.

"In my opinion, that's not such a healthy sign," said Naftali, another student, explaining at length why it was a commandment to kill those who fought against Israel.

"What of the love of humanity in Judaism?" asked the interviewer.

And Yohanan answered, again describing the process of convincing oneself, of putting doctrine over the gut sense of morality: "The educating side of a person must come and tell him, 'Yes there's sadness and depression and respect for the enemy and all the feelings of mercy, but after all we're talking here about big things.'"[53]

The interviewers left "perplexed and grieving," Amos Oz wrote later, for "all this was a language totally foreign to us." Excerpts from the exchange were published the following year in a kibbutz movement quarterly. Judging from Oz's later comments, the original transcript contained much more about the miraculous conquest of biblical land and how it heralded the coming of the messiah—material apparently so strange it was snipped out. The excerpts appeared under a note explaining that for "technical reasons" this conversation had not made it into *Soldiers' Talk*. Yet it seems that Oz, with his comrades, preferred to turn away from thoughts and people so foreign and threatening. Once again, it was safer to fence off those who were different.

Which was a shame, because far more people read the bestselling *Soldiers' Talk* than the kibbutz journal, and it would have been worth their knowing of the students' comments. They reflected a theology about to sweep religious Zionist society. For the few who were already Tzvi Yehudah Kook's disciples, the war was breathtaking, mind-boggling proof of the doctrine, equivalent to the heavens opening. For other religious Jews, the victory needed an explanation. The messianism of the Kook school provided answers.

Messianism, it should be said, appears more foreign to secular eyes than it should. The idea that our world is rushing toward a perfected age is well rooted in Western tradition. People who have never sat in a yeshivah study hall, or heard the sermons of Christian fundamentalists, have written of the "end of history" or sung of the coming "age of Aquarius" or—as the Internationale would have it—the "last fight" that will "end the age of cant" and "unite the human race." Messianists presume that history is a well-constructed story with a happy ending. They acknowledge that our world is terribly flawed, but assert that it will be fixed, by God or humanity or the two working together. This can be a long-distance expectation, but when part of the expectation is met, optimism can turn into a collective, infectious, energizing mania: *Look, it's happening, get on board.*[54]

The students were quoting their teachers well. The elder Rabbi Kook, reading history under the influence of both Yitzhak Luria's messianic kabbalism and Hegel's dialectics, indeed greeted World War I as signaling rebirth: "When there is a great war in the world, the power of the messiah awakens," he wrote.[55] Very much a nineteenth-century liberal nationalist, he anticipated the end of European tyrants, heralding a universal as well as Jewish rebirth. His son, Tzvi Yehudah Kook, did in fact explain the Holocaust as "a cruel divine operation in order to lift [the Jews] up to the Land of Israel against their wills."[56] The state of Israel, he asserted after independence, was "the fulfillment of the vision of redemption."[57]

The swift victory in June 1967 turned such hopes into fever. Rabbi Ya'akov Filber, a disciple of Tzvi Yehudah Kook, wrote soon after the war that "He Who Sits in Heaven did not accept that the Temple Mount and Jerusalem, Hebron and Shekhem, Bethlehem and Jericho . . . were outside the borders of Israel." God had simply forced Jews to liberate their homeland. It was God's will that Nasser sent his troops to Sinai, that diplomacy failed. God "hardened the heart of Hussein," just as he once hardened the heart of Pharaoh to redeem the children of Israel. Now, Filber asserted, Israelis were reawakening to the divine commandment "as important as all others combined: settling the land of Israel."[58]

Filber regarded the future, as well as the past, as an open book. Several weeks after the war a group of young rabbis met with the National Religious Party's cabinet ministers, still suspect as minimalists, to sway them from any thoughts of supporting withdrawal from the newly conquered land. Filber told them, "I believe with a perfect faith, that if the Holy One, Blessed Be He, gave us the land with overt miracles, he will not take it out of our hands. . . . The wholeness of the Land of Israel is not within the realm of the government of Israel's decision." Retreat was not only forbidden, but impossible, Filber said, and his only concern was that the ministers not confuse and embarrass young people by estranging themselves from the Whole Land.[59]

Those ideas spread beyond Merkaz Harav. They were used in Bnei Akiva, the youth movement of the National Religious Party, to make sense of the victory. The movement's monthly magazine, Seeds, was printed on the same newsprint before and after the war, with the same bylines, but there is a discontinuity in tone—not a change, but a rupture.

As a movement, Bnei Akiva resembled a thin kid with glasses running after several hefty ones, asking in a squeaky voice and misused slang to be included in the next adventure. Its mandate was to teach kids that they should grow up to live on Orthodox kibbutzim—to be just as good Israelis as the secular kids in left-wing movements, but continue to keep kosher, pray daily, and observe the Sabbath. It was not easy. The Israeli ruling class regarded religion as something of the past, and saw establishment of the state as proving the victory of secular Zionism. Bnei Akiva was trying to accept and reject that victory at the same time. Its members sang songs from the Palmah underground and learned of the heroism of the Etzion Bloc fighters, just as good as secular fighters, and meanwhile they bore a litany of insults and sometimes blows from members of the Labor Zionist movements. The simplest solution was to give up Orthodoxy. For those who stayed in the movement, the required goal was to serve in Nahal, the army unit that combined active duty and settlement training, and then move to a kibbutz—though, as with the secular movements, few actually stayed.[60]

Largely in response to their parents' desire to keep their sons Orthodox, a growing number of yeshivot were established that combined secular high school studies, an intense Talmud program, and dormitory living. In name, many of the yeshivot were linked to Bnei Akiva, but kibbutz members who ran the movement thought poorly of them. Eventually, the yeshivot set up their own, semi-independent organization, to reduce interference from the youth movement.[61] The last issue of *Seeds* before the war carried the text of a long speech by Ya'akov Drori of Kibbutz Sa'ad at a movement convention. He attacked yeshivah high schools for encouraging their students to continue on to higher yeshivot instead of to kibbutz, "that special creation unmatched by anything in the most enlightened of peoples." Some of the yeshivot, he said, regarded the Orthodox kibbutzim as insufficiently religious because of men and women "sitting together in the dining hall or singing Sabbath songs together or even dancing the *horah* together."[62] Overweening piety was not the movement's goal, he implied.[63]

The same Drori wrote in the following issue, immediately after the war, "We have merited to see the process of deliverance progress from 'the beginning of redemption' to more advanced stages." He congratulated the National Religious Party's ministers for seeking to avoid war—because God had used their efforts to bring greater conquests. "That delay was undoubtedly the result of Divine providence, for otherwise who knows if Jerusalem and the Temple Mount, Rachel's Tomb and the Tomb of the Patriarchs would now be in our hands," Drori wrote, adding a prayer that God would give the politicians strength to resist concessions. "A religious party more than any other . . . is commanded not to give up one inch of holy soil in the borders promised by God." He also had a practical proposal: reestablishing the kibbutzim of the Etzion Bloc. If the government had not yet decided on permanent settlement, he said, it could immediately create a Nahal paramilitary outpost.[64]

If someone was looking for a large group of young people in Israel who had grown up in the shadow of others' heroism, scared they had missed the chance at revolution, it was among the readers of those words.

IN THE SYRIAN HEIGHTS, the settlers at Aalleiqa slept in a eucalyptus grove, next to a stream, until they could clean up rooms in the base, in shacks made of cement blocks, without foundations, closer to being ruins than buildings. A member of Mahanayim came to spray pesticide, unsuccessfully, against the bedbugs. Northern Command chief David Elazar provided several soldiers to guard the unofficial settlement, and gave the settlers permission to eat the canned Chinese meat in the Syrian storerooms. It took a week to get a generator, two to set up a radio link with Kibbutz Gadot in the valley below.[65]

Eytan Sat drove up to Quneitrah, the Syrian ghost town at the edge of Israeli-held land, where the military governor had set up his office. The air was thick with flies, drawn by corpses left from the war. Sat asked for a written permit for civilians to be in occupied territory. The governor "didn't have much to do, because he didn't have anyone to govern," Sat would recall. "He sat whisking flies away from his face. A fat guy sitting in this Syrian armchair. I wait for the verdict . . . and he doesn't take it serious like me, and he writes a letter, 'I hereby approve for a group of farmers from the upper Galilee . . .'." With that note, the settlers gained the first toehold of approval—not to create a settlement but to stay overnight in the heights.[66]

Gershon Meinrat was twenty-one when he came to Aalleiqa with a friend from Kibbutz Beit Hashitah, one of the big communes founded in the 1930s, where he had grown up. He was done with his two years of regular army service and was now obligated to give another year of service to the United Kibbutz. One day a phone call came from movement headquarters in Tel Aviv: "Head up to Gadot, they're waiting to take you up to the heights." Eytan Sat had convinced the movement's youth director to send some of the "third-years" to help out. Meinrat was happy to go, less for politics than for what he called "the adventure shtick."

There was plenty of work—building corrals, gathering cattle and sheep, inoculating them, harvesting the barley and chickpeas in fields of a few acres surrounded by stone fences, whose owners had lived in village houses of stone stuck together with mud and who were gone now. The pay that the settlers received from the Agriculture Ministry went into a shared kitty. Haim Gvati, the Mapai agriculture minister, was in on the effort, though there was a dispute with the ministry over whether they could keep the herd they were gathering.

They all knew they were building a kibbutz. They wanted to create a new, better commune—which was, after all, a hope shared by other young people, in other countrysides, in that era. And yet, Carmel Bar noticed, "Everyone who came from a kibbutz wanted to do things exactly as at his kibbutz." It made sense because "it's impossible to draw an animal you don't know." A strange comment, because the founders of their own kibbutzim had conjured up a creature never seen before. But the settlers were second-generation revolutionaries, and the second generation of a revolution is likely to be an institution.[67]

Then again, adult solidity had not yet set in. Every kibbutz has a work director, in charge of drawing up a daily schedule of where members will work. When Yehudah Harel arrived at Aalleiqa on September 1, he found a notice on the bulletin board from the work director, asking everyone to let him know before taking vacation—which in kibbutz terms indicated mad individualism, people taking off when the mood hit them, without the collective's permission. It had taken him two and a half months to get his own kibbutz's permission to leave for the heights. The United Kibbutz, in his description, had a tradition of "Bolshevik" discipline. In the end his comrades gave in when he threatened to go anyway. At Aalleiqa, someone told Harel to grab a Syrian mattress from a storeroom and throw it wherever he wanted to sleep. Rafael Ben-Yehudah immediately made Harel secretary of the commune, at age thirty-two the house grown-up, in charge of creating order.

Harel had been thirteen when Israel was established, old enough to absorb the dream of the kibbutz revolution in its glory before statehood, just young enough to stand on the sidelines of the battles in 1948. "We thought we'd missed the war of independence. . . . The kibbutz movement was no longer what we'd thought it was," he would later say, describing his sense of the mood at Aalleiqa. Now it seemed history was offering a second chance. "We dreamed . . . that a new era was beginning, that we would be the first settlement of hundreds, that thousands of young [Jews] would immigrate from abroad, that everything we'd read in books about the kibbutz movement and the war of independence, we were doing."

Best yet, the decision to create a kibbutz had not come from bureaucrats. The atmosphere was anarchist. "On the first day I was there," Harel would recall, "in the middle of lunch, I got a real shock—there was a burst of gunfire, from an AK-47 from inside the dining hall. Someone stood by a window and shot a wild dog." When they were in the mood, they slaughtered a Syrian sheep to supplement the canned food. The women did the cooking. The men herded cattle on horseback, cowboys on a secret frontier. The base had a spring-fed swimming pool. "Every evening—these were young people—they sat and sang." At night, the only lights in the heights came from their encampment; the sky was wild with stars. It was a picnic, a celebration—the true evidence this was not in fact the 1930s. "In other kibbutzim, people generally tell how hard it was at first. Here, you've got to tell how *easy* it was at the start."[68]

There is no trace of celebration, though, in the letters Kobi Rabinovich sent from Aalleiqa. Along with several other "third-years," the young tank commander who had fought in the Sinai found it unbearable to go back to leading youth movement activities after the war. When the United Kibbutz suggested fulfilling their obligations in the heights, they took the offer. "It's sad now. . . . Time doesn't move, it lies down, still. . . . The people here mostly bore me," he said in his first letter to his girlfriend, Eilat. The one comfort was that he now had time to start sorting out what he had been through in the war, to begin what became a series of letters that read like repeating nightmares.

He tells Eilat of the desert, "the land of dust, without horizons, sunscorched, rotting its carcasses. What were we doing there? We had no choice, but woe to people who have no choice but to do that . . . to wipe out, wipe out creatures who don't even know what happened." He writes of nighttime: The tanks stopped, lights approached, an order came: "Fire! The sky is red with lead, the ground with blood, people fall twisted, seized by terror. A death trap, people running wildly about, like penned animals, their throats hoarse with shouting." At last, "only the explosions of burning trucks were heard." The dead "all lie, en masse, and we walk between them."

Finally he speaks of the present: "My Eilat, the heart aches to see, here in the heights, the signs of war even on animals. Wounded limping dogs, donkeys that hit land mines." The day before a woman from Aalleiqa had found a puppy. "She said a soldier shot the mother and [the woman] found the puppies crying next to the corpse. One was scared and shaking, so she brought it here. . . . It always cries, looks for a hiding place. Such a sweet lost little thing, and what about the other babies? Near here there was a training exercise, every time you heard a burst of gunfire, the puppy began to shake. [She] explained to me that it's because his mother was killed with a burst of fire before his eyes. Maybe? If puppies are so vulnerable, what about those who understand a bit more," he writes, and concludes, a man looking for refuge, "My Eilat, it's good I have you. Otherwise, how would I take all this?"[69]

ON AUGUST 27, the cabinet finally discussed Allon's proposal for "work camps" in the heights. "It's clear that you neither destroy orchards nor start permanent settlements," said Eshkol. "But if orchards exist, you have to maintain them. Certainly, we can permit the workers to use buildings there, and then we'll see."

The last words hint that, yes, this might become something permanent. But the cabinet did not discuss that possibility. It simply "approved working land in the Golan Heights"—testifying that the name of the region had shifted, become Hebrew, a hint of taking possession. The cabinet also ratified a proposal to operate an experimental agricultural station left behind by the Egyptians at Al-Arish in the northern Sinai. Dayan, Allon, and Agriculture Minister Gvati were assigned to work out the arrangements. The decision was considered so sensitive that it was left out of the cabinet minutes, even though those were supposed to be secret as well.

The three ministers met on September 1, with Chief of Staff Rabin and several other generals joining them. A summary of the session refers to the three ministers being "authorized by the cabinet to deal with settlement outposts"—the term in Hebrew was normally used for Nahal settlements of soldiers under military command—"in the administered territories." The cabinet had not authorized exactly that; the trio had seized a small opening and widened it. They proposed a Nahal outpost in the southern end of the heights, and another at the Banias springs, a source of the Jordan River, which could have meant locating it in Syrian land or in the old demilitarized zone at the northern tip of Israel. At the Al-Arish farm, they proposed a settlement, either military or civilian.

As for "the group consisting of residents of the Upper Galilee," they said, it could remain in the heights. The wording does not indicate a permanent settlement—but neither does it specify a temporary arrangement. For practical purposes, the first settlement in occupied land now had the government's approval.[70] Rafael Ben-Yehudah immediately recorded in his diary, "Decision on outposts in the heights"—in Hebrew, four terse words of success.[71]

On paper, the cabinet resolution of June 19, offering a pullback from Syrian land for peace, remained in force. Yet small decisions, made bit by bit, with authority stretched beyond its intent, were adding up to a new policy, neither articulated nor admitted.

4

SETTLING IN

Jerusalem, 13 Elul, 5727
September 18, 1967

Top Secret

To: Mr. Adi Yafeh, Political Secretary of the Prime Minister
From: Legal Counsel of the Foreign Ministry
Re: Settlement in the Administered Territories

As per your request . . . I hereby provide you a copy of my
memorandum of September 14, 1967, which I presented to the
Foreign Minister. My conclusion is that civilian settlement
in the administered territories contravenes the explicit
provisions of the Fourth Geneva Convention.

Sincerely,
T. Meron

THEODOR MERON'S NOTE and attached legal opinion, preserved in
Levi Eshkol's office files, testify to two things.[1] The first: As of mid-

September 1967, Eshkol knew that settling civilians in occupied land, including the West Bank, violated international law. The second: By early September, after nearly three months of weighing the West Bank's future, Eshkol was actively exploring settlement in the region.

As legal counsel to the Foreign Ministry, Meron was the Israeli government's authority on international law. He had achieved that position at a remarkably young age and with an even more remarkable biography. Born in Poland in 1930, he had spent four years of his youth in the Nazi labor camp at Czestochowa. For the entire war, "from age 9 to 15, I did not go to school at all," he told a *New York Times* interviewer decades later. "There were tremendous gaps in my education. It gave me a great hunger for learning, and I dreamed that one day I could go to school." After reaching Palestine as a teenager he voraciously made up for lost time—earning a law degree at Hebrew University, then a doctorate at Harvard, then studying international law at Cambridge. The boy who received his first education in war crimes as a victim was on his way to becoming one of the world's most prominent experts on the limits that nations put on the conduct of war.

Those who received his opinion could not know where Meron's career would later lead: Following another decade in Israeli foreign service, he would become a law professor at New York University—and later, in a new century, president of the U.N. tribunal on war crimes in the former Yugoslavia. That record, though, does add historical weight to what he wrote in September 1967. And even then, the legal mastery of the Foreign Ministry counsel must have been known in the inner circles of government.[2]

Meron's actual opinion, dated September 14, is addressed to Foreign Minister Eban, his superior. But he states that he is relating specifically to "what I heard from Mr. Adi Yafeh," Eshkol's aide, "concerning the possibility of Jewish settlement in the West Bank and the heights." Virtually at the same time, Eshkol received a report from the Jewish Agency Settlement Department on the potential for settling at the Etzion Bloc. The land available for farming was limited to a mere seventy-five acres, it said, and those were being worked by the Palestinian refugees living on the site where Kibbutz Massu'ot Yitzhak once stood. That ruled out field crops, the report said, but settlers could raise chickens, engage in manufacturing, and develop tourism.³ Triangulate the two answers, and they point back to Eshkol as the man asking the questions.

The key provision in international law that stood in the way of settlement, Meron wrote, was the Fourth Geneva Convention on protection of civilians in time of war, adopted in 1949, which stated that an "Occupying Power shall not deport or transfer parts of its own civilian population into the territory it occupies."⁴ The authoritative commentary, he added, stated, "This clause . . . is intended to prevent a practice adopted during the Second World War by certain Powers, which transferred portions of their own population to occupied territory for political and racial reasons or in order, as they claimed, to colonize those territories."⁵ Writing those words, Meron knew all too vividly who the "certain Powers" had been.

The prohibition, Meron stressed, is "categorical and is not conditioned on the motives or purposes of the transfer, and is aimed at preventing colonization of conquered territory by citizens of the conquering state." If Israel did decide to put its citizens in occupied land, therefore, "it is vital that [it] be done by military bodies and not civilian ones . . . in the framework of bases" clearly temporary in nature. Even for that purpose, Israel had to respect the 1907 Hague Convention on war, which stated, "Private property cannot be confiscated."⁶

Because the Golan Heights lay outside of mandatory Palestine, Meron said, they were "undoubtedly 'occupied territory' and the prohibition of settlement applies." Regarding the West Bank, he noted, Israel argued that the land was not occupied, since Palestine had been divided in 1949 by armistice lines that were explicitly military and temporary. Jordan's annexation of the West Bank was unilateral and, Israel asserted, the armistice had expired when Arab aggression set off war in June 1967.

But those claims, Meron told Eban and Eshkol, would not convince the court that mattered, the court of world diplomacy. The international community had rejected Israel's "argument that the West Bank is not 'normal' occupied territory, and certain countries (e.g., Britain in its U.N. speeches) have explicitly asserted that our status in the West Bank is that of an occupier."[7] Moreover, Israel's own actions showed recognition of that status. The army command in the West Bank had already issued a legal proclamation stating that "military courts will fulfill the Geneva provisions" and that when a military decree contradicted it, the Geneva convention took precedence.[8]

If Israel decided to send settlers to the Etzion Bloc, Meron said, it could argue they were returning to their homes, and he assumed property rights would not be a problem. Nonetheless, Israel would face objections based on the Geneva convention, and other countries "are likely to see our settling at the Etzion Bloc as evidence of intent to annex the West Bank." Were settlements to be built in the Jordan Rift—the part of the Jordan River valley in occupied territory—the problem would be worse, since the claim of returning to lost homes would not apply.

As the prime minister weighed the fateful issue of settlement in the West Bank, his own counsel's advice endorsed the key legal arguments that Israel's government would face afterward from foreign and domestic critics. Meron's opinion was kept secret, though the paper trail shows that Defense Minister Dayan and Justice Minister Shapira received it.[9]

The lawyer's last points provide further evidence that Eshkol was specifically interested in settling the Etzion area, and also had his eye on the Jordan Rift. Pressure from activists and other politicians played a part in the decision taking form. But so did a failure of Arab diplomacy, and Eshkol's own inclinations.

FIRST CAME PILGRIMAGES. The morning after the war ended, a soldier born in Kfar Etzion hitched a ride to the lost kibbutz in an army jeep heading south from Jerusalem. Told at a military roadblock that he could only enter occupied land on duty, he said it was his duty to "go home." His account of his trip is both intense and strangely impersonal, like the descriptions of other children of the Etzion Bloc who came after him. They speak as a chorus, using the same words, images, and biblical verses, quoting an unwritten catechism.

On the road, the soldier wrote afterward, he imagined seeing ancient heroes and war of independence battles—Ruth and Naomi and King David in Bethlehem, the Maccabees fighting in the hills, 1948 convoys ambushed at twists in the road. Of the actual town of Bethlehem he says only that it was draped in white flags; he makes no mention of seeing people there. At Kfar Etzion, he found the minaret of a Jordanian army mosque, surrounded by metal military sheds. "Everything I knew about Kfar Etzion rose in my mind, a confusion of facts, descriptions, stories . . . ," he said. "Suddenly before my eyes stood a picture of the mass grave at Mount Herzl in Jerusalem, surrounded by a crowd of people, and beyond the graves, this hill I'm facing, Kfar Etzion, destroyed, in ruins!"[10]

Hanan Porat came two weeks later with a large group—survivors, widows, young people evacuated as children. They argued over the location of the erased chickenhouse and cowshed. Women searched for the remains of their houses. One survivor found a hoe on the ground and "pounded crazily . . . on the roof of the bunker where the last defenders of the bloc had blown themselves up when all hope ran out, as if he wanted to signal to someone down there," Porat wrote, in an account he entitled "Homeward!" that he read aloud later at a celebration at Merkaz Harav yeshivah for students home from the war. "It's too late," said another survivor, touching the shoulder of the one with the hoe, "too late." The second man had just lost his own son in battle. He walked "with his mouth tight, a strange glint in his eyes." A memorial ceremony was held for the dead of 1948 and the dead of what Porat called "the war of redemption" that had just ended, and a speaker called on the government, "Please, let us come back and build our home here. Don't deliver this sacred mountain again into the impure hands of the murderers from Hebron." Porat's sister read a concluding poem by ultra-nationalist poet Uri Zvi Greenberg, which proclaimed, "The twilight of dawn is ahead of me / And the twilight of dusk is behind me."[11]

Other people were making pilgrimages that season as well. On a July afternoon, lawyer and refugee Aziz Shehadeh descended from his current home of Ramallah to his lost home, Jaffa, driven by a Jewish lawyer with whom he had worked before 1948. Shehadeh, in his son's telling, was also stunned by the gap between memory and reality, like a person "who makes a long and difficult trip to see a dying loved one" and discovers her ravaged by age. He found his mother-in-law's house, paint peeling from the front gate. A familiar barbershop remained, and the church where he was married, but the courthouse where he had argued cases had been demolished. It would have been easier, he thought, were everything gone. The son's telling says nothing of noticing the Arabs who had stayed in Jaffa and become Israeli citizens, or of the Jewish refugees from Europe and Arab countries living in the houses left behind by families such as Shehadeh's. From Jaffa, the Jewish lawyer drove his friend to Tel Aviv, which Shehadeh remembered as Arab Jaffa's Jewish suburb and which was now the real city, alive with traffic, "young people out for the evening, sidewalk cafés," countless lights that could be seen from Ramallah and that Shehadeh had believed were the lights of Jaffa. He grew furious with Palestinians who had spent nineteen years "bemoaning the lost country" instead of building their own lives, and even more insistent on creating a Palestinian state next to Israel.[12]

Another refugee, Sabri al-Banna, came to Jaffa from Nablus with his family, at least according to one of the contradictory stories of his life. Al-Banna was about thirty years old. From the street, he would have seen the mansion of his childhood, with its wide portico framed in classical columns. Now it was an Israeli military courthouse. Soon after, he left for Amman. Under the name Abu Nidal, "Father of the Struggle," he began a career of terrorism that would frighten the world.[13]

Presumably, refugees from the village where Massu'ot Yitzhak once stood also visited Jaffa. But the pilgrims making their opposed journeys were invisible to each other, and each side treated loss and longing as its own discovery.

Not all Etzion Bloc survivors wanted to rebuild. At the new Kibbutz Massu'ot Yitzhak in southern Israel, most of Moshe Moskovic's neighbors told him, "We were there, we fought, we fell, we came here and built a beautiful community. Don't bother us with memories." Some wanted to build a monument to the dead in the Etzion Bloc, but no more. The old Massu'ot Yitzhak had taken up three years of their youth, ending in a nightmare. At the new one they had invested nearly two decades of adulthood. Moskovic, though, still felt "a debt to the place, to the people, to the rocks"—perhaps, by his own pensive admission, because he had not been there when his kibbutz fell. His neighbors had no objection to him using his time and connections as regional council head to seek government permission for a new settlement. The opposite of activism was disinterest, not protests.[14]

Among Kfar Etzion's second generation, though, many agreed with Moskovic. The oldest among them were in their twenties, they had been raised on martyrdom, and they had built nothing of their own yet. In early July, dozens of them gathered at the military cemetery in Jerusalem, at the grave of one of their number who was killed the first night of the war a month before. Afterward, they regrouped at a yeshivah in town to discuss "going home." Hanan Porat and two others were chosen to coordinate the effort and get government approval.

Soon after, everyone received a mimeographed questionnaire. "Are you prepared to settle immediately, if it becomes possible?" said one question. Another asked for suggestions on how to deal with the "hostile Arab environment" at Kfar Etzion. No suggestions were sought on whether the Etzion Bloc should be annexed, or whether all of the West Bank should be, or what status the Arab residents should have. On paper, the effort seemed aimed at fulfilling a private right, or obligation, of return, divorced from politics.[15]

But the larger issues could not be evaded. Porat and his friends met with Defense Minister Dayan. In Porat's account, Dayan told them that he did not want Jewish settlers in the West Bank. The defense minister said, "Friends, I understand the sentiment, but we don't conduct policy according to sentiment."[16] Yigal Allon, on the other hand, was enthusiastic. By his testimony, he "never forgave Ben-Gurion for keeping us from retaking the Etzion Bloc" at the end of the war of independence, and he had kept up a personal connection with the survivors. The delegation that visited him snapped into his categories: people wanting to reestablish a kibbutz to hold a strategic spot.[17]

Porat, however, thought in different categories. In late July, he wrote a letter to a secular high school girl who had stumbled into the Merkaz Harav victory party, dragged along by friends from the religious Bnei Akiva youth movement. Fascinated by his "Homeward!" speech, she had written to ask for a copy. Sending it, he explained that he was brought up to believe in "fulfillment"—a term taken from secular Zionism, meaning that ideals are useless unless acted on, as by starting a kibbutz. He wanted to "fulfill" both Torah—meaning the teachings of Judaism—and "national desires, which also flow from the wellspring of Judaism." This was straight from the rabbis Kook: Judaism has swallowed nationalism whole, as if a snake had swallowed a mongoose and roughly taken its shape. Even when secular Zionists are certain they are rebelling against religion, they are fulfilling God's will—but the ideal is a religious pioneer, synthesis of yeshivah student and communal farmer, and Porat described himself in those terms.

The longings of the children of Kfar Etzion, "a handful of dreamweavers" for their lost home, he wrote, actually have cosmic significance. "Take [our feelings] and multiply them by ten, a hundred, a thousand, a million, and you'll get the longings of a whole nation for a whole land" during the 1,900 years of Jewish exile. Now, "before our eyes the curtain is rising on the 'twilight of dawn' . . . of the beginning of redemption." The believers alone understand the full drama, "the great process by which the Master of the Universe is leading all of us on the way upward, homeward: all of the Jewish people in all of the Land of Israel." Returning to Kfar Etzion would be a representation of that greater march of history.[18]

Clean-shaven, casually dressed, a paratrooper and a child of kibbutz, Porat could appear to the politicians and officials he met that summer as a blue-eyed poster boy for the Labor Zionist ideal, albeit one whose skullcap identified him as a member of the rather tame, running-to-keep-up Orthodox auxiliary rather than the secular mainstream. Yet his reason for wanting to rebuild Kfar Etzion was also a practical application of Rabbi Tzvi Yehudah Kook's radical messianism, the same doctrine that had stunned the kibbutz interviewers for *Soldiers' Talk* when they met his classmates. You needed to look at Porat twice to see him once. By supporting the first Porat, an Allon or Eshkol would inadvertently cultivate the second.

The man who knocked at Porat's yeshivah dorm-room door one night presented less ambiguity. Moshe Levinger was the rabbi of the Orthodox cooperative farming village of Nehalim, east of Tel Aviv. He was thirty-two, thin, with a scraggly black beard, a rumpled white shirt, and a curt manner. He was also an alumnus of Merkaz Harav, where in his words he had learned "the commandment . . . that the Land of Israel must be in the hands of the Jewish people—not just by having settlements, but that it's under Jewish *sovereignty*." The significance of sovereignty indeed existed in his master's teaching, but the fact that Levinger heard that part most loudly said something about the listener. Levinger measured the world on the vertical axis running from weak to strong, and so learned that power was a religious obligation. As one associate would explain his demonstrative lack of respect for those higher than him on the social or political ladder, "he regarded himself as small only before God"—an attitude that could awe young religious Zionists suffering a group inferiority complex. To follow Levinger was to feel strong, even when he was ordering you around.

Levinger's reaction to the war was that Jews should settle in the West Bank to ensure Israeli sovereignty. Some of Nehalim's residents were refugees from Neveh Ya'akov, the farming community north of Jerusalem abandoned in 1948. Levinger tried to convince them and others from the spot to return, with no luck. Again, it seems, those who had rebuilt their lives did not long for return. When Levinger heard of Porat's effort to revive Kfar Etzion, he headed for Jerusalem to suggest joining forces. As his first bit of assistance, he told Ben-Tzion Heineman, a Nehalim farmer who had become his disciple and who owned a truck, to show up at Porat's door the next morning. "I'm here at Rabbi Levinger's command," Heineman said when he arrived, and volunteered to act as Porat's driver.

For the next two months, Heineman chauffeured Porat around the country as he sought to build support.[19] Leaders of the religious kibbutz movement put them off; unlike the older generation of the United Kibbutz, they saw nothing pressing about settling occupied land. The group around Nathan Alterman, taking shape as the Movement for the Whole Land of Israel, was enthusiastic, but aging Tel Aviv poets could provide public relations help at most.

MOSKOVIC AND THREE other middle-aged survivors of the Etzion Bloc got a few minutes with Levi Eshkol in mid-August. The transcript reveals the pendulum of Eshkol's own feelings and the divisions between his guests. The prime minister asked about the availability of land for farming. When told it was limited, he answered, "At the moment it's possible to establish only one settlement."

Yet when Moskovic pressed for permission to "revive the place in whatever way possible," Eshkol retreated. "The government is still up in the air on the matter. Soon we'll decide what to do with the territories," he said.

"It's possible to annex the area without including any Arab communities," a Kfar Etzion survivor offered. The suggestion presumed that Arab-populated areas must be given up. The Etzion Bloc would be linked by a tendril of land to Israel, rather than becoming a bridgehead for keeping the entire West Bank. Moskovic, who favored keeping everything, proposed "settling the place without much noise" to avoid international protests, a "creating facts" approach. One member of the delegation proposed sending a Nahal unit "to hold the spot."

"The question," Eshkol answered, ". . . is whether it's worth holding it now and leaving afterward." Putting a paramilitary settlement on the ground made sense only if Israel intended to keep the area, and that was undecided.[20]

For Moskovic, and for Porat when he heard of the meeting, it could only have been evidence that they were getting nowhere. They could not know that Eshkol's notation on his experts' recommendation for the West Bank's future concerned kibbutzim lost in 1948, or that after meeting the delegation he raised the subject in the smoke-filled room of Mapai's political committee. Moshe Dayan now favored settling in the Etzion area, Eshkol noted, though experts said no land was available—a technical objection, not a strategic one.

But Eshkol made no recommendation.[21] The prime minister was playing with ideas, worrying his way through them out loud, tentative and engaged. The same day he found time for a conversation with the French Jewish philosopher Raymond Aron, telling him that "from Jordan we demand a security strip along the Jordan River," trying out the taste of Allon's map, reworked as a potential compromise with Hussein. "We have signs that King Hussein is willing to talk with us," he said. "It's said he's waiting for the Arab summit to fail."

What if the Arabs do not want to reach an agreement? Aron asked.

"Then we'll stay put."

And was he not worried about a rebellion in the West Bank?

"No. This isn't Algeria," Eshkol said, reading what would be on a Frenchman's mind. "We can strangle terror in the occupied territories."[22]

Though Eshkol was right that Hussein wanted talks, he nonetheless utterly misread the king. Hussein was the person most eager for a summit meeting of Arab leaders, which he hoped would recognize that, alas, there was no choice but negotiating with Israel. He hoped for permission to dicker for the return of half his kingdom, without fearing Arab intrigues to take away the other half. He won Nasser's support for a conference, and the radical leaders of Syria and Algeria chose to stay away, more good news for the king.[23]

Eight Arab leaders gathered in the Sudanese capital of Khartoum, and from Hussein's perspective, the summit was close to a complete success. Nasser agreed to let him negotiate. The conservative oil monarchies pledged financial aid to Jordan and Egypt—leaving Nasser beholden to the kings he once hoped to sweep away in a tide of Arab nationalism. The summit's closing resolution, on September 1, announced, "The Arab Heads of State have agreed to unite their political efforts at the international and diplomatic level to . . . ensure the withdrawal of the aggressive Israeli forces from the Arab lands . . . occupied since the aggression of June 5."

Decoded as its authors intended, that meant that these Arab countries were aiming only at getting back the land lost in the last war, not at erasing Israel from the map, and that they would use diplomatic means, not tanks and troops, to accomplish their goal, even though that meant accepting some kind of non-belligerency with the Jews. And, yes, to show that they were not selling out Arab principles, the resolution added that the leaders would keep to a framework of "no peace with Israel, no recognition of Israel, no negotiations with it, and insistence on the rights of the Palestinian people in their own country." One was supposed to understand that this allowed for indirect negotiations, for informal peace, for de facto recognition, all regarded as crucial concessions.[24]

It was a shining example of what Levi Eshkol had called "playing chess with oneself." The leaders at Khartoum negotiated a formula for what Israel should accept, then coded it in bellicose rhetoric. But face-to-face negotiations, formal peace, and explicit Arab recognition were Israel's conditions for a pullback. The reasoning was that only if an Arab leader could make the psychological shift and say, "We recognize you," would it be safe to make concessions. In Israel, the "three no's of Khartoum" were read as an Arab declaration of eternal hostility.

For the small circle of cabinet ministers and diplomats who knew of Israel's June 19 offer to pull back to the international border for peace or of the contacts with Hussein, the resolution was a public rejection of secret offers.[25] A U.S. diplomat explained to Washington that Israeli analysts believed that the summit had decided on a two-stage strategy. The Arabs would first "make marginal political concessions to get their land back. At the same time, military preparations continue for a future second stage—war against Israel."[26]

On an airborne tour of the northern Sinai with Dayan and the Settlement Department's Yehiel Admoni just after the Arab conference, Eshkol told journalists, "If Khartoum is the declared position, then our answer is, 'We stay here.'"[27] Politically, it made little sense to press for a decision on what Israel would keep or give up in the West Bank. Why strain the fragile ruling coalition when there was no Arab partner anyway?[28]

For Eshkol, Khartoum was the tipping point. Allon was asking him about Kfar Etzion, as was the religious affairs minister, Zorach Warhaftig of the National Religious Party, who felt a sentimental tie to a place where friends of his had died in 1948.[29] They had a receptive audience. The settlement ethos, in the words of Eshkol's official biographers, "had been the cornerstone of his worldview and public career for 53 years."[30] On the Sinai trip, he looked over the Egyptian experimental farm at Al-Arish and the abandoned fishing boats at Bardawil Lagoon on the northern coast. "Eshkol, in his vision of settlement, imagined Jewish farmers and fishermen making the desert blossom and pulling fish from the sea," Admoni wrote of the outing.[31] Settlement Department chief Ra'anan Weitz gave Eshkol a plan for the Jordan Rift that called for building thirty farming settlements and a town that together would have a population of 32,000 Israelis within a decade.[32]

In the cabinet on September 10, Eshkol mentioned the delegation of Etzion Bloc survivors. Justice Minister Shapira warned of the legal problems of settling in occupied territory. "We could do it," he said, "but we should know that we will be violating not only the Geneva conventions but also the [army] General Staff's standing orders." Not liking that legal opinion, it appears, Eshkol sought another from Theodor Meron.

HANAN PORAT was not privy to such discussions. The children of Kfar Etzion were not educated in the anarchistic leanings of Yitzhak Tabenkin; they wanted permission to start a settlement.[33] Levinger, on the other hand, was compelled by the idea of defying the government, as was his follower Heineman. "I don't expect them to give you approval," Heineman told Porat on one of their road trips. "Just get up and do it."[34]

Without telling his childhood friends, Porat pursued a second track. Levinger found a handful of people willing to move to the Kfar Etzion site without permission, including old yeshivah friends from Merkaz Harav, some already in their thirties, with families, men more suited for the study hall than the cowsheds. They did not actually "want so much personally" to live at Kfar Etzion, Levinger later said. "We wanted it to be there." At Nehalim, they began gathering equipment—beds, tents, a water pump. Also in on the plan, in Porat's telling, was an aspiring National Religious Party politician named Zevulun Hammer, the leader of the party's Young Guard.[35] Hammer's group was ready for rebellion against the party's moderate leaders. Seizing the standard of the Whole Land of Israel fit their postwar mood. It also conveniently satisfied their need to set themselves apart from the party's old men, and for a religious stand on a central national issue.[36]

In early September, Levinger met in Tel Aviv with intellectuals from the Movement for the Whole Land of Israel. Among them was Aharon Amir, a most unlikely partner for a rabbi. From his youth, Amir had belonged to the radical secular right. His fascist leanings extended to asking to be accepted for officer's training at a military academy in Mussolini's Italy in 1940.[37] Afterward he joined a circle of a few dozen writers who believed in creating a "Hebrew" nation, both new and ancient: It would return to Canaanite roots, before the Hebrews were corrupted with Judaism. Amir could not bear the Israel created in 1948, little and Jewish; he wrote around the time of independence of a vast Hebrew land, from the Mediterranean to Basra on the Persian Gulf, inhabited by a "mixture of bloods and a confusion of races," all Hebraicized. It was a wildly romantic nationalism, a vision of conquest and glory cooked up in Tel Aviv cafés.[38] If there was anyone less like Amir than Levinger it was Porat, part of the pious wing of a movement that preferred starting settlements to making statements and that regarded café dwellers as effete, rather like Diaspora Jews.

"Dear Hanan Porat," Amir wrote. "At a meeting on Monday evening between several activists in the 'movement' and a few of your people, such as Rabbi Levinger . . . it was agreed and decided that the deed *will be done*"—he drew a heavy line under the lovely verb—"and absolutely as soon as possible. The initial makeup will be about 35 people, and its purpose will be mainly as a demonstration, with about 20 Orthodox settlement people and youth and the rest city people, mostly secular, some of them writers and professors. . . . We decided to ask you (a) if you are ready to come with us, (b) if there are any other students from your yeshivah who would be willing to . . . spend at least a week at the place."[39] Soon after, September 25 was set as the day for defiantly establishing a settlement, or at least publicly acting like it for a week or so to break down Eshkol's presumed resistance.[40]

In the meantime, though, Porat found himself sitting in the prime minister's office, along with other Etzion young people, Moskovic, and Michael Chasani, a Knesset member from the National Religious Party, who was the prime mover in setting up religious farming settlements. It was Friday morning, September 22. In that day's newspapers, the Movement for the Whole Land of Israel made its public debut, with large advertisements declaring, "We are faithfully obligated to the wholeness of our land. . . . No government in Israel has the right to relinquish that completeness." Among the names at the bottom was Moshe Moskovic.[41]

No minutes were taken of the meeting. A summary in the prime minister's files says that the group pressed for permission to settle in the old Etzion Bloc. Eshkol explained that "no decision had been made on the future of the administered territories. . . . Nonetheless, the prime minister took on himself . . . to check the situation" and promised a quick answer.[42] As participants remembered the conversation, Eshkol's comments were pithier—but just as ambiguous.

"So, *kinderlach*," the prime minister said, using the Yiddish word for "little children," "you'd like to go up? Go ahead up!"

The verb suggested settlement, but left room for uncertainty. Porat pushed. "We're getting close to Rosh Hashanah," the Jewish religious new year. "Will we be able to pray there on Rosh Hashanah?"

"Nu, *kinderlach*, if you'd like to pray, go ahead and pray."

"When we say 'to pray,'" Porat said, "we mean to return . . . to this land, this home."

"You use big words," Eshkol answered. "I've said what I've said."[43]

When the story was passed down, Eshkol's comments were retold—depending on the storyteller's personality—as everything from warm approval to an absolute no, overcome only by the activists' defiance.[44] At the time, though, no one was sure what Eshkol meant. Members of the Kfar Etzion second generation spent that Friday night and the next day at Moskovic's yeshivah, debating what to do if the government said no.[45]

Eshkol solved that problem for them. "We're taking care of the matter of outposts," he told the weekly cabinet meeting that Sunday, using the word for Nahal paramilitary posts. "By 'we,' I mean the Agriculture Ministry, the Settlement Department, and I'm in on the business. Regarding the Etzion Bloc . . . within two weeks . . . they'll be entering the place."

Eshkol's wording fit an administrative decision, as if he were reporting in his old role of Settlement Department chief on developing a district within Israel. The announcement surprised his colleagues, who would have expected a cabinet debate on a strategic matter such as settlement in the West Bank.

Eshkol's explanation was that "the Etzion Bloc enters [the category] of one of the army bases" along the West Bank mountain ridge, approved the month before on Dayan's suggestion. He was not preempting a decision on the future of occupied land, he said, indicating that the Etzion area could be connected to Israel by a corridor. "The only question is how to do it so that we take as few Arabs as possible," he said, "and what will happen afterward with the whole West Bank."

When a minister from the dovish, left-wing Mapam party pointed out, correctly, that the cabinet had specifically resolved that the bases would be built without housing for families, Eshkol answered, "Right now we're only talking about the Etzion Bloc, and as for what we discussed, we said the opposite."

Actually, the Etzion Bloc was not the whole story. Eshkol said he was also checking into reestablishing Kibbutz Beit Ha'aravah, at the north end of the Dead Sea. A Nahal group was already setting up an outpost near Banias, on the border of the Golan Heights, he added. "I think someplace that was decided on," he said, vaguely. Agriculture Minister Gvati assured his colleagues that the Banias spot was "kosher," inside the borders of mandatory Palestine. "I'm not quite sure of that," Eshkol replied. Gvati was actually right that the spot was inside the mandatory borders—it lay within the former DMZ, on land that Syrian forces controlled de facto before June 1967 but over which Israel had claimed sovereignty. But Eshkol appears not to have been exercised about whether the outpost was on "kosher" land.[46]

Eshkol was as vague about what he had approved at the Etzion Bloc. He spoke of an "outpost," but added, "in the course of time, kids become goats." Everyone knew that outposts normally grew up to be civilian settlements. Using the word *outpost* was a way to impose a far-reaching decision with a wink. And by speaking of an outpost, Eshkol was also exploiting the loophole in Meron's legal opinion: Kfar Etzion would be labeled a military base.[47]

In the end, the cabinet adopted a strange "decision," saying that "the prime minister has announced that an outpost will be established soon at the Etzion Bloc."[48] It was a resolution to acquiesce. Or perhaps the official record of a decision was also a *fait accompli*: A U.S. diplomat in Tel Aviv reported a leak that some ministers were surprised after the meeting to see the minutes listing a decision they knew nothing about.[49] Either way, Eshkol's move was a front-page story the next morning in Israeli papers, and in the *New York Times*. The *Times* reporter, naturally knowing nothing of Aalleiqa, said this was the "first announcement . . . of concrete plans for settlement of the territories seized from the Arabs in June."[50]

As those newspapers were sold, Porat and two friends were called to the Settlement Department office in Jerusalem to get the news officially, drink a toast, and begin planning. It was September 25, the day Porat and Levinger had marked for illegal settlement, but there is no available evidence that Eshkol knew that.[51] Thirty sons and daughters of Kfar Etzion would return to the spot, a memo from the meeting says, beginning with fifteen to twenty who would set up camp two days hence. The memo says nothing of Nahal, or of the settlers being soldiers. Bizarrely, it states that "preparations around the founding should be kept to a minimum" as if, despite that day's headlines, the media might ignore the event.[52]

From there, according to Porat's later account, he headed to Tel Aviv to meet Levinger at National Religious Party headquarters and give him the good news.

Except Levinger was not pleased. "We decided to do it today," he insisted. The equipment was already on a truck at Nehalim.

"We have the good fortune of being able to do it through the state," Porat answered.

"But we prepared for today."

"Listen, circumstances changed," Porat said.

Waiting was out of the question, Levinger said. The tone rose. A moment before stepping onstage in the theater of defiance, Levinger found that he was losing his part. At last Porat said, "You know what, you go ahead on your own." With that, Levinger backed down. Without the returning children of Kfar Etzion, the drama would lose meaning.

The difference in approach remained between them, though, in the years to come. His view, Porat later said, was that "we have to be a vanguard, not separatists." The words are loaded. "Vanguard" in Hebrew also means "pioneers," the term used by Labor Zionists for themselves, meaning people who create facts instead of talking. "Separatists" meant the Zionist right, which split from the Mapai-controlled Zionist Organization in the 1930s, eventually developing into Menachem Begin's Herut party, and which the left dismissed as preferring proclamations and public posturing to actions. Arguing about how to carry Tzvi Yehudah Kook's vision of redemption through territory, the two disciples were reenacting an old argument, and Porat claimed the methods of the Zionist left.[53]

* * *

THEY MET AT eight in the morning, September 27, in a Jerusalem parking lot—the handful of young men and women who would move into the Jordanian army buildings, along with survivors, widows, Jewish Agency officials, and reporters. The national bus cooperative, Egged, provided a bus of 1948 vintage, complete with the sheets of steel plating that the Haganah had used to turn buses into ersatz armored vehicles for convoys through Arab-held territory—except the "armor" was plywood painted gray, with the words "Once We Traveled Like This" daubed on it. The driver was the one who had driven the last bus to Kfar Etzion before it fell. Newspaper descriptions of the event give the strange feeling of a historical pageant designed to ride down Main Street on an anniversary, except in this case the point was to leap back in history and make it come out right, with the children acting their parents' part.

They had another role to play as well: They were to present themselves to the press as Nahal settlers, in line with the official announcements. The flyer they had received from the organizing committee had not mentioned that story line. None of the actual characteristics of an outpost existed: The settlers were not soldiers, and therefore were not serving in Nahal, a branch of the army; there were no officers, no uniforms, no military tasks such as conducting patrols of the area. Nonetheless, the next morning's papers all dutifully reported the establishment of a Nahal security outpost.

The old bus led a small "convoy" through the hills. At Kfar Etzion, a member of the National Religious Party's Young Guard told a reporter that "without our determined decision, who knows if we'd be standing here." The morning before, he asserted, Knesset member Michael Chasani had told Eshkol that the trucks were ready at Nehalim to roll. Only because of that threat, he said, did Eshkol give permission to go ahead—a story that salvaged a fragment of the drama of defiance even if it did not jibe with the headlines two days earlier about Eshkol's cabinet announcement.

Chasani gave a speech about the Etzion Bloc's heroic defenders in 1948. As he spoke, "a number of women, widows of the fallen, stood to the side and wept bitterly—among them ones whose children have now come to settle here," the normally dry *Ha'aretz* reported. The writer did not know that the night before, Porat was called to an apartment of a survivor to meet five widows who, as Porat later described the scene, spoke as an angry chorus: "We were bereaved of our husbands at the Etzion Bloc . . . and we're not ready to be bereaved of our children too. . . . You can't go off for an adventure at the price of our children." Porat told them a new era of history was dawning, "and we can't stand on the sidelines," besides which they had the army to protect them.

Zorach Warhaftig spoke, too, praying that "this settlement will be forever and the sons will return for eternity," which in the *Jerusalem Post*'s English report, quoted in diplomatic cables, came out as a simple assertion by a cabinet member that the settlement was permanent. "Today," proclaimed Porat, "we have removed the shame of the term 'administered territories' and returned to the true and fitting term, 'redeemed territories.'" After the speeches, Levinger installed a Torah scroll in one of the Jordanian buildings, converting it into a synagogue, and the convoy left for Jerusalem, leaving Porat and a dozen or so friends to face the sudden, quiet loneliness of the windy hilltop.[54]

One invited dignitary refused to come. "This ascent to the soil and others like it in the administered territories and especially in the West Bank, I reject as a serious error," wrote Joseph Weitz, an unexpected critic, to Chasani. Weitz was the old man of settlement. He had served for decades as a top official of the Jewish National Fund, for much of that time responsible for acquiring real estate and assigning it to new farming communities. The head of the Settlement Department, Ra'anan Weitz, was his son.

But the elder Weitz saw settling in occupied land as a failure to understand that times had changed. A new settlement was not "a 'position' or 'weapon' as in the 'days of storm' of our struggle before the establishment of the state," he wrote to Chasani, with a carbon copy to Eshkol. The future of the West Bank would be determined in negotiations for peace, "which is vital to the future of the state." Returning to the Etzion Bloc would "anger our few friends and provide our many enemies with a stick to beat us." Besides, he said, "you know how few young people are willing to join rural settlements." Did it not make more sense to put them on Israeli soil, in places to which Israel's claim was clear, "not just in the view of Isaiah and Jeremiah but also in the view of the gentiles"?[55]

Weitz's typed words beg to be read aloud in the cold, high, angrily sober voice of an old man. He did not want to go back to the past; he had already been there. He did not share the euphoria of biblical verses. The old struggle for land and a state had been won; the new struggle for peace was to be fought by diplomats, not by young men with long locks swept across their foreheads in the old Palmah style, and most young men and women were no longer interested anyway. His friends read his letter and filed it.

Policy, it turned out, could be conducted according to sentiment. Eshkol knew he could not annex the West Bank. But the United States was not pushing him to withdraw before peace, and at Khartoum the Arabs had proclaimed "no peace." The Allon Plan fit Eshkol's own sense that the Jordan River must be Israel's line of defense.[56] But his divided government was incapable of choosing that or any other policy.

The Allon Plan's strategic logic dictated that Israel should give up the Hebron hills and their Arab population. But Allon himself felt tied to Hebron and even more so to the Etzion Bloc, which he had been unable to save in 1948. They represented another of the goals he had fallen short of reaching. Nostalgia for the lost kibbutzim moved Eshkol as well. His solution was to fall back on the method that Labor Zionism and his own past provided: to redraw the map one settlement at a time.

The myth of a reluctant Eshkol pushed by Orthodox settlers into reestablishing Kfar Etzion would later serve the purposes both of the Israeli left and of the young Orthodox rebels. But the evidence is stronger that after a characteristic argument with himself, Eshkol made a choice, knowingly evaded legal constraints, imposed his decision on the cabinet, and misrepresented his intentions abroad. From that point, he personally directed settlement in occupied territory.[57]

"NEW YORK TIMES has item on Eshkol declaration on need to settle territories in our hands. . . . Please cable urgently whether this actually said. . . . If it was not—we would like to publish immediate denial. We await your immediate reply," said the cable from an Israeli diplomat at U.N. headquarters.[58]

"There is no declaration," said the return cable, from Eshkol's aide Adi Yafeh, "rather, cabinet agreed on and publicized establishment of military settlement outposts repeat outposts in Etzion Bloc, and plans for establishing additional points. At Banias heights a first point in Golan was established yesterday."[59]

The exchange indicates how Israeli emissaries abroad—including Foreign Minister Abba Eban, who was then at the United Nations—heard of Eshkol's decision. A few nights before, over dinner with Arthur Goldberg, the U.S. ambassador to the U.N., Eban had elegantly explained why Israel would not annex the West Bank, but would return it to Jordan on condition of demilitarization and free access for Israelis.[60] For him, the headline of his morning *Times* was a mess that he and his staff again had to clean up.[61] "When we set up Kfar Etzion," Eshkol admitted two months later, "Eban was really boiling, angry, upset."[62]

The press was also the State Department's intelligence source for what looked like a major shift in Israeli policy. But State did receive some analysis: The embassy in Tel Aviv noted that according to a "usually well-informed" reporter, government policy "in settlement of occupied territories is to be based on establishing facts quietly rather than making noisy statements." Among the Mideast hands at State, the words *establishing facts* had no cultural resonance; they did not conjure up old ballads and legendary photos as they did for Israel's leaders, and the point was not seen as worth including in a message to Under Secretary of State Eugene Rostow, then traveling in Brazil.[63]

At his noon briefing the next day, the State Department spokesman said, "If accurately reported, the plans for establishment of permanent settlements would be inconsistent with the Israeli position as we understand it—that they regard occupied territories . . . to be matters for negotiation. We have not been officially informed of any change in that policy."[64] In diplomats' language, that was meant to be a biting rebuke.[65] At the U.N. General Assembly, British foreign secretary George Brown attacked the Israeli decision.[66] Back at the Etzion Bloc, Porat and his friends wrote in their founding-day flier, with the joy of college students holding a successful demonstration, "It turns out that the ascent to Kfar

Etzion has made lots of noise in the world. Those settling today have joked that each one has shocked five countries."[67]

The job of explaining Israeli policy fell to Foreign Ministry official Shlomo Argov, who told an American diplomat that since peace was not imminent, the army needed to establish "military positions in control of occupied territory . . . for [the] necessary length of time." The Nahal unit at Kfar Etzion would hold the southern approaches to Jerusalem only until Israel gave up the land. Argov did not have an easy time. "He could not deny attachment of Israelis to that particular piece of ground," the U.S. diplomat recorded. "Similarly, while claiming elements of coincidence was [sic] present in fact Nahal unit included sons of original . . . settlers, Argov admitted that governments [sic] had responded to pressure in permitting these individuals to take part in establishing position."[68]

In Saudi Arabia, a representative of King Faisal showed up at the U.S. ambassador's residence to say that Israel's settlement decision was undermining the "spirit of moderation which came out of Khartoum talks." An Amman paper's editorial blasted the Israeli use of "pioneer" for settlers, as if they were "explorers of African jungles paving the way for white settlers." Another Jordanian daily, though, "cast doubt Israel will seriously try to establish permanent settlements in occupied areas." Rather, it explained, Israel was trying to pressure the Arabs into direct negotiations and signing peace treaties. The article underlined what was to be feared most: negotiating openly with Israel.[69]

The diplomatic squall quickly blew over. The Johnson administration was "exhausted" with the Mideast crisis and "had another problem on the other side of the globe," as National Security Council staffer Harold Saunders would say many years later, referring to Vietnam.[70] Despite the awkward conversation with Argov, U.S. officials continued to refer to Kfar Etzion as a Nahal outpost. The next spring, commenting on the fact that the Israeli Tourism Ministry was providing assistance to build a restaurant there, an official at the U.S. consulate in Jerusalem reported, "the Government of Israel apparently has long-range plans for Kfar Etzion."[71]

THE ONLY ACTUAL connection to the military, according to Porat, was that "they sent us a wooden sign, saying 'Kfar Etzion Nahal Outpost.'" The fact that "this isn't an outpost, this is a civilian settlement" was obvious. So "we took the sign, put iron strips on it, and put it at the dining hall door, and everyone who came in cleaned their feet on it."[72]

The cabinet, meanwhile, tried to restore order after Eshkol's decision on Kfar Etzion. The ministers voted that future settlements would belong to Nahal, as would "outposts" already approved, including the one at Aalleiqa in the Golan Heights.[73] With that, the original status of short-term "work camp" was forgotten.

In mid-October, with the help of the army's Northern Command, the Golan kibbutz-in-the-making moved to a compound in the ghost town of Quneitrah, at the edge of Israeli-held land. The three-room houses, built for Syrian officers' families—or by other accounts, for Soviet advisers—were better suited than the ruins at Aalleiqa for winter in the heights. They came equipped with the beds and tables and chairs of those who had fled, even if they lacked electricity. The inside walls of a larger house were knocked down to create a communal dining hall for a group now numbering over eighty people.[74]

Soon after, the commander of Nahal appeared, accompanied by aides and secretaries. "I've received orders that you are to be a Nahal outpost," the officer told kibbutz secretary Yehudah Harel. "Tomorrow send people to headquarters in Jaffa to get uniforms, a flag and a sign."

"On Friday, I'll discuss it with the kibbutz secretariat," replied Harel, enjoying an anarchist moment.

"This is an order," said the stunned commander.

"We're civilians," answered Harel. "We don't take orders."

Still, Harel sought advice from Yigal Allon, who told him to agree. The idea was to make life easier for Eban, Allon said. "Once we built an army camouflaged as settlements," he said, referring to the Palmah in pre-state days. "Now we'll build settlements camouflaged as an army." Harel disliked that advice, but bent because the same order came from the always helpful Northern Command. He agreed to a sign saying "Quneitrah Nahal Outpost" and a flag from the unit, but no uniforms.

The sign and flag went up early one morning in a field in front of the compound. That morning a kibbutz member hooked a disk harrow to a tractor to clear the field of brush, knocked down both sign and flag, and harrowed them. By ten o'clock, the settlement's Nahal period was over.

Afterward, the kibbutz newsletter reprinted a rather desperate letter from a major, saying, "For the *last time* we request you call the settlement 'Quneitrah Outpost' and not 'Kibbutz Golan' or any other name."[75]

The kibbutz secretariat was soon corresponding with the committee in the Prime Minister's Office that assigned names to new communities. The committee said nothing of "Quneitrah Outpost," but politely explained that a settlement could not have the same name as a region, so "Golan" by itself was out.[76] The kibbutz eventually chose the name Merom Golan, "Peak of the Golan." A history of Nahal, co-published many years later by the Defense Ministry, describes each outpost established after June 1967. Neither Kfar Etzion nor Quneitrah—under that name or another—appears.[77]

At Quneitrah, the young kibbutz members rode herd on cattle, tended crops, and opened a lunch stop for tourists, using tables taken from the town's houses. On paper, thirty members were employed each day in Labor Ministry work projects for the jobless. The commune's bookkeeper, borrowed from an established kibbutz, had to fill out a form each day listing who had worked where, and instead quit and went home, because the jobs were "a complete fiction," in Harel's words, invented so Allon could provide the funding he had promised. Someone else filled out the forms, and the funds kept flowing. Allon, according to Harel, was "certainly" aware of the ruse.[78]

"The place is new, of top importance. But it seems that's not enough," reservist tank commander Kobi Rabinovich wrote to Eilat, his girlfriend, trying to make sense of why he did not enjoy his work at the kibbutz in Quneitrah. He missed the responsibility he had borne in the army. The letter flashes back to the first night of the war. He is in command of a tank, standing in the turret looking into darkness, in a long line of tanks on a road through the Sinai. The lights of the tank ahead of him vanish beyond a curtain of dust. Dust glues his eyelids shut. He finds himself falling as his knees give out, awakening, dozing, shouting the order, "Driver, stop!" a moment before crashing into the next tank. From the radio pleads the voice of a tank commander who has gone lost, who sees heavy vehicles moving in the dark and does not know if they belong to his side or the enemy. On the road Kobi sees "the smoking corpses of vehicles" and he smells burning rubber, the remains of "something that went on here between life and death." At last he sees a pale horizon emerging from night. The letter ends.[79]

"REGARDING THE GOLAN HEIGHTS," Levi Eshkol told the Knesset on October 30, "we will not allow a return to the status quo . . . which brought destruction and ruin to our settlements in the valley. The status quo ante in the Sinai . . . and the Suez Canal will also not return." The Gaza Strip and West Bank, he asserted, had been under Egyptian and Jordanian occupation. So, he said, "we must now seek to set agreed national boundaries based on peace accords." In Jerusalem, the Jewish Quarter of the Old City would be rebuilt. Besides that, a team was planning a new neighborhood to house 1,500 families on the north side of East Jerusalem. It was a major foreign policy address; for once Eshkol appeared to have a clear, decisive message.

Or did he? Outside of the specifics on Jerusalem, Eshkol's speech was a Rorschach test. Analyzing it, White House staffer Harold Saunders said headlines such as "Israel Digging In" had "badly mauled the meaning." Actually, he told national security adviser Walt Rostow, Israel had simply repeated its stand that it would stay put until negotiations succeeded, and that the starting point for talks was the postwar lines. The United States pointedly disagreed with that position, Saunders noted; it saw negotiations as necessarily beginning with the prewar boundaries. But in practical terms that did not matter "since we aren't about to press the Israelis to withdraw" before an agreement.[80]

At the opposite extreme are recent histories asserting that Israel was repudiating its June 19 offer to pull back to the international border for peace. After Eshkol's address, they note, the Knesset ratified a cabinet statement saying that, in light of the "three no's of Khartoum," Israel would "maintain the situation fixed by the cease-fire agreements and fortify its position."[81] Yet by themselves, those words imply only holding land until the Arabs were finally willing to talk. Rejecting the status quo ante, Eshkol did not say what would replace it.

Eshkol did not answer that question because his cabinet, with its rainbow of views, could not do so. In a more typical Eshkol talk, a zigzagging argument with himself before a convention of his party's kibbutz movement, he asserted that "any minister who has gone up to the heights" agreed that Israel must keep the Golan—yet he concluded that "we're not rushing to decide." Decisions would make life inconvenient for Eban, he said. Israel's "security border" had to be the Jordan, he added, but in the West Bank cities of "Nablus and Jenin, [the Arabs] are as numerous as olives" on the local trees. The solution was to keep the unpopulated land between the river and the Arab cities, he suggested, borrowing Allon's ideas.[82]

But while the cabinet debated Allon's plan, it never accepted or rejected it. Without winning approval for his new borders, Allon erased the old ones. On the same day that Eshkol spoke in the Knesset, but with none of the fanfare, he sent written instructions to the head of his ministry's cartography department, which produced virtually all of the country's maps. Henceforth, maps should bear the title, "Israel: Cease-fire Lines," he said, referring to the cease-fire at the end of the fighting in June. "The mandatory borders and the armistice lines will not be printed."[83] With that, Allon redrew Israelis' picture of their own country. If the generation that grew up after 1948 had learned to see the land beyond the armistice lines as foreign, the next generation would learn the opposite. Henceforth, bored schoolchildren staring at the classroom map would see Nablus and Gaza, Quneitrah and Al-Arish as part of Israel.

The redrawing of maps fit with changes in language. Already, the government had adopted "administered territories," suggested by the army's chief legal officer, as a compromise term between "liberated territories" and "occupied territories." By December, the biblical name "Judea and Samaria" replaced "West Bank" in official documents.[84]

Eventually, according to Allon, Eshkol phoned him, invited him for a tête-à-tête to discuss the Allon Plan, and told him, "If we call for a vote, there's no chance of a majority." Instead, Eshkol committed himself to following Allon's guidelines for where to build settlements in occupied land.[85] The real map of what Israel would keep would be drawn one fact at a time.

Allon took Eshkol for a field trip, two happy boys with aides and bodyguards riding in jeeps down from Jerusalem to the Jordan Rift, over 1,000 feet below sea level where it meets the Dead Sea, between hills that look like piles of sand poured out by a gargantuan child with a bucket. Then they drove north through the dust-heavy air along the river, really a twisting creek—which Allon regarded "not as a river but simply an anti-tank canal"—all the way north back into Israeli territory. Eshkol kept ordering the driver to stop, so he could jump out to look at a stream or have someone turn a shovel so he could examine the color of the soil, because, as Allon would admiringly describe him, "He was a man of the soil, a man of settlement in every sinew of his body."[86]

At the end of the year Eshkol met with Allon and Dayan, and they agreed to set up two Nahal outposts, real ones this time, one at the north end of the rift close to the old armistice line and another at the south end, close to the Dead Sea, in the furnace-hot region where Beit Ha'aravah had stood before 1948. That satisfied the longing to restore any lost spot settled in pre-state days, but putting the outposts at the ends of the rift was also meant to appease both Allon and Dayan, since the latter wanted to leave untouched what the former wanted to settle and so preferred to leave the rest of the rift empty.[87]

For the Golan Heights, the Settlement Department drew up plans for a score of farming settlements and a town that would together bring 50,000 Israelis to the region. As a modest start, two more civilian communes were established by January, and two military outposts. Actually, the department's aim was to build only civilian settlements in the Golan, but while the kibbutz movements were eager to sign up for land for new communes, they did not have prospective settlers for them. Eager as an older generation was to return to the golden age of settling the land, they lacked young people willing to sweat, plant new fields, and commit themselves to communal life.[88] Measured against the official policy that left the future of occupied land open, the new settlements loomed as a muscular statement. Measured against kibbutz sage Yitzhak Tabenkin's dreams of hundreds of new communes, against Allon's vision or the Settlement Department's plans, the effort to plant settlements in the newly conquered territories was anorexic. A new supply of settlers was needed.

LYNDON JOHNSON's foreign policy team had reason to feel satisfied after the Security Council's unanimous vote on November 22, 1967.

Five months of excruciating diplomacy since the war finally yielded a resolution by the United Nations' most powerful body on the Mideast conflict—and it was a restatement of Johnson's Five Points. Formally, the vote meant that the Soviet Union and the United States had found an agreed formula; tacitly, Israel, Jordan, and Egypt were grudgingly willing to live with it. Resolution 242 would become the point of reference for future diplomacy.

The resolution called for ending "all claims or states of belligerency," which was somewhat less than Israel's demand for formal peace agreements. At the same time, it required "withdrawal of Israeli armed forces from territories occupied in the recent conflict." In sharp contrast to 1956, Israel's pullback was conditioned on ending the state of war. The principle of reaching Arab-Israeli peace by trading land for peace became international policy.

As often happens in diplomacy, agreement was built on ambiguity. The reference to Israeli withdrawal "from territories" rather than "from the territories" was the key. For the Soviets and Arabs, that meant a full retreat to the prewar lines. In Israel's reading, the absent "the" indicated that it needed to give up some land, but not necessarily all.[89]

But the ambiguity also helped bridge the gap between the United States and Israel on the extent to which borders could be changed. It even papered over what White House staffer Saunders called the "wide gap within our ranks" in the Johnson team over what the United States meant when it called for the "territorial integrity" of Mideast states. Secretary of State Rusk, Saunders noted, was telling foreign ministers that America would like to restore the pre-June boundaries as part of peace. Other officials—left unnamed by Saunders—saw no reason to "go that far" in pushing Israel, in part because "we [in the administration] honestly feel that the Arabs asked for what they got by pulling the rug out from under our 1957 peace settlement." Johnson himself seemed to lean that way, telling Arab visitors that the United States was unable to force Israel to pull back completely.[90]

Without the crucial "the," Resolution 242 allowed for both positions. It also moved the burden of negotiating between Israelis and Arabs to a U.N. emissary. Swedish diplomat Gunnar Jarring, innocent of any Mideast experience, was appointed to the job.[91]

In January, Levi Eshkol flew to Texas to meet Lyndon Johnson at his ranch. Cold, bitter winds blew at the air base where Eshkol landed. The key subject on the agenda was Israel's desire to buy arms, particularly fifty advanced F-4 Phantom warplanes, to match Soviet rearming of the Arabs. Johnson joked with Rusk that "it shouldn't take the air that these people are here for the express purpose of buying bombs and threatening world security."[92]

The fat pads of briefing papers by Johnson's Mideast hands recommended delaying the sale of the Phantoms, lest the military buildup end all chance of peace. But Eshkol should get other planes, to make Israel feel secure enough to agree to concessions. Johnson's pre-summit reading described the danger of Israel sticking to a "narrow and rigid" insistence on face-to-face talks with the Arabs, but also cited Abba Eban's assurances that Israel sought only "minor border adjustments." The Israeli foreign minister remains an urbane mystery: Was he out of the loop in Jerusalem; or did he hope to lock his government into his own dovish stands with the promises he made abroad?

The briefing papers said nothing of settlements. The subject had come up briefly when Eban came to Washington and met Dean Rusk, but it was a technical problem, not one for the leaders of nations to discuss.[93]

But in the long conversations in the warm living room of Johnson's ranch, first Rusk and then Johnson asked Eshkol to describe "what kind of Israel we would be expected to support." The line seems rehearsed, a friendly push for a commitment to peace rather than land. Eshkol evaded answering.[94] Johnson posed the question yet again—"What kind of Israel do you want?"—in a one-on-one conversation with Eshkol. Afterward, Eshkol told Allon he had replied, "My government has decided not to decide."[95] The lack of an answer had no effect on the summit's outcome: Johnson held out the possibility of supplying Phantoms later and promised lighter Skyhawk warplanes immediately.[96] The Bundy Doctrine held sway; the United States would not use arms to pressure Israel.

Eshkol had stronger reasons than ever to avoid defining his goals. He was returning home to the ceremony merging his Mapai party with Allon's Ahdut Ha'avodah and Dayan's Rafi party, in a celebration of Labor

Zionism unity. Even as Israeli politics was redefined by the issue of territory, the new Labor Party contained nearly every possible view on the matter. The aging Golda Meir, appointed Labor's secretary general, urged avoiding "stormy debates" that might divide the party. When Eshkol held small meetings to set policy, he had to invite Dayan as well as Allon. Labor's symbol should have been a large red question mark.[97]

But facts could still be created. Replying to a right-wing legislator's question in the Knesset in late February 1968, Eshkol said there were already ten "outposts" in the "administered territories," with establishment of seven more approved. Eshkol's figures are taken from a summary apparently provided by the Settlement Department. It lists slightly more than eight hundred Israelis living in the "outposts" in occupied land.[98] In the Knesset, of course, Eshkol said nothing of Theodor Meron's inconvenient legal opinion.

5

THE "INVISIBLE" OCCUPATION

Yaakov Perry spent the winter studying from morning till after midnight, sometimes straight through the night. The course consisted of Palestinian Arabic—not as one language, but a Babel of dialects of towns and villages, so students could know where a suspect was from or change their own speech to fit a disguise—and local customs and the reading of handwriting, so they could read a half-educated informer's note in a second, and the art of "winning the heart of potential agents," as Perry wrote many years later, after a long career in the Shin Bet. That winter he was twenty-three years old, having spent less than two years in the security agency, a square-jawed young man whose hairline was just hinting at later baldness, who had expected to study music at Juilliard until, in a fit of frustration with drunken fellow musicians in a radio orchestra, he answered a cryptic ad offering "challenging work." The promising trumpet player sought to become an artist of secrecy.

The Shin Bet handled counterintelligence—catching spies, uncovering terror groups, preventing attacks. "Defends and Shall Not Be Seen" was inscribed on its seal. The full name of every employee, up to the agency's director, was classified. Until June 1967, it was a compact agency of a few hundred staffers. Suddenly it had to add the Palestinians of the Gaza Strip and West Bank to its watch, along with the Sinai's sparse population and the Syrian Druse who remained in the Golan Heights. By that winter, the agency was expanding like a company whose product has found a new market. It called back retired agents and borrowed from the Mossad, the service that spied on foreign countries, but also began wholesale recruitment of young people right out of the army.[1]

The Shin Bet buildup was one piece of the entrenchment of Israeli rule over the occupied territories—a piecemeal process, guided by no agreed government policy, based on no explicit decision except, perhaps, the ambiguous government response to the Khartoum summit. Left undefined was how long Israel would stay put, what outcome it sought, and—most important—what Israel's attitude and policy would be toward the people over whom it now ruled.

In the war, Levi Eshkol was fond of saying, "We got a lovely dowry. The trouble is that with dowry comes the wife."[2] His government was unable to give up the dowry of land or make up its mind about what to do about the bride, the people. It could not answer, even for itself, the question that Lyndon Johnson put to Eshkol: What kind of Israel do you want?

IN THE LONG MEANTIME, that meant the Palestinians lived under military rule, which meant they lived under the rule of Defense Minister Moshe Dayan. The military government was tossed together in a hurry after the unplanned conquests. In August 1967, needing help, Dayan told Colonel Shlomo Gazit, the outgoing head of Military Intelligence's research department, that he was canceling his leave for university study. "We've held the territories for over two months and we still can't see the end," Dayan told Gazit, as he appointed him to the new, half-undefined position of "coordinator of government activities in the territories," perhaps best translated as viceroy to Dayan. Gazit expected to fill the job for a few months, until the occupation ended.[3]

Dayan ruled the occupied land directly, personally, with minimal oversight from cabinet or parliament. That role became his central concern, filling his time. According to Gazit, Dayan's appointment book stayed virtually empty, except for the cabinet meeting at the start of each week and the military staff meeting at the end. He decided how to spend his day when he got up each morning, visiting Arab mayors and Israeli officers to see what was happening in the field, issuing verbal commands on the spot, to be translated by an officer at his elbow into formal orders. He cut the military general staff out of the loop.[4] Dayan transformed himself into the sultan of the occupied territories.

He regarded himself as a benevolent ruler. Soon after the war, officers began allowing West Bank trucks to ford the Jordan River to carry produce to the East Bank, giving farmers an outlet without undercutting the Israeli market. As winter rains approached, Bailey bridges were put up to replace those destroyed in the war. Dayan, artful improviser, enshrined the measure as his "open bridges" policy. West Bank and Gaza residents could cross into Jordan. De facto, they could also enter Israel and get jobs in manual labor.[5] By October, Dayan formulated a policy of "invisible" rule, with the goal that "a local Arab can live his life . . . without needing to see or speak with an Israeli representative." The army was to avoid unnecessary patrols in Arab towns, keep Israeli flags to a minimum, refrain from interfering in how Arab mayors ran their towns.[6]

Dayan presumed that as long as life improved economically for his subjects, as long as he was a stern but kind ruler, they would tolerate his rule indefinitely. In his memoirs, he expressed fascination with the West Bank's biblical history. Without pausing, he went on to portray the Arabs who lived there now, "the field hands behind a wooden plow and pair of oxen, the women moving sedately from well to village with a pitcher on their heads. . . . I did not think of them as being interposed between me and the land." He felt closest, he said, to the Bedouin of the southern Gaza Strip, who maintained their desert customs. Dayan, infatuated with the ancient past, unabashed about his decades of pilfering of antiquities from archaeological sites he obsessively sought out, did not see the Arabs as standing between him and the land because they were figures in his diorama of the romanticized Bible.[7] That they would step off his stage and seek to live by a script they wrote themselves was not on his mind.

Then again, military orders issued in the summer of 1967 forbade strikes, the celebration of Egyptian national holidays in Gaza, the publi-cation of political material without military government approval.[8] One needed an Israeli permit to cross the bridges, or to sell goods in Israel, or for other matters.[9] The raw material most easily exported to Israel was physical labor. "At the end of the sixties," Gazit would write with strik-ing honesty nearly three decades later, "the world was already watching the end of the era of colonialism, and precisely then Israel found itself marching in the opposite direction." That was all the more surprising, in Gazit's view, because Israel's leaders were themselves the veterans of a national liberation struggle against foreign rule.[10]

Colonialism is a loaded word today, but if we accept British scholar Stephen Howe's bid to restore its dry meaning—a system "of rule by one group over another, where the first claims the right . . . to exercise exclusive sovereignty over the second and to shape its destiny"—then Is-rael was indeed backing into colonialism in the occupied territories.[11] Colonialism, like the conquest itself, reflected a vacuum of strategy. It was born of a national evasion of choices.

PROTESTS IN DAYAN'S DOMAIN—a strike here, a petition elsewhere—were sporadic.[12] For most people in the towns, villages, and refugee camps, it appears, politics was something that happened else-where, in Arab capitals or perhaps the camps of the fragmented Palestin-ian organizations in neighboring Arab countries. But the organizations, especially Fatah, the nationalist group led by a militant named Yasser Arafat, did have local supporters, and the Jordan River was easily crossed by others. Entering Israel proper was even simpler. The Palestinian groups, dedicated to "armed struggle," did not acknowledge the Jewish presence as any more legitimate within the Green Line than in occupied territory, and civilian targets were more available inside Israel.

The first burst of attacks began toward summer's end of 1967. A bomb at a farmhouse killed a small boy and wounded his parents, a kib-butz factory blew up, a mine derailed a freight train. The Shin Bet was unready but lucky: The would-be revolutionaries all knew each other; organizations unraveled with the first arrests.

And soon reorganized. A bomb was discovered before it exploded in a movie theater in downtown Jerusalem, mortar shells fell on a Tel Aviv suburb.[13] The strategy of Fatah and its rival organizations was terrorism—another word that must be rescued from shouted use. Used quietly, as the political scientist David Rapoport has written, *terrorism* properly refers to a doctrine of revolution that dates back to nineteenth-century Russian anarchists. Its goal is to awaken an apathetic populace; its means is atrocity, beyond any conventional use of force. Terrorism, says Rapoport, was invented to "provoke government to respond indiscriminately, undermining . . . its own credibility and legitimacy."[14] Fatah cribbed the strategy from *The Wretched of the Earth*, psychiatrist and revolutionary Frantz Fanon's treatise on decolonization, which anointed "absolute violence" as the only means of ending colonial rule. By killing, rebels would spur rulers to slaughter, in turn provoking more of the oppressed to rise up.

Murder, wrote Fanon, is also therapeutic; it "frees the native from his inferiority complex . . . it makes him fearless and restores his self-respect."[15] Put bluntly, he prescribed killing to heal the injured masculinity of the colonized. In Ramallah, Aziz Shehadeh's son responded to the presence of Israeli soldiers with long guns and half-buttoned shirts by forlornly trying to get his father to notice he was shaving and by listening to the urgent masculine voices on Palestinian radio broadcasts. Some of his high school classmates left for training camps beyond the river.[16]

In February 1968, Yaakov Perry finished his retraining and was assigned to the Shin Bet's new bureau in Nablus. He was the third man in the office. He received a 9-mm pistol, a first-aid kit, an army uniform with captain's bars for when he needed that camouflage, and responsibility for dozens of villages and refugee camps in the hill country stretching south to Ramallah.

His first, pressing task was to recruit informers. People asking for permits or other favors from the military government were sent to talk to "Captain Yaakov," and Perry led the conversation to collaboration. In one case, an aging sheikh from a refugee camp sought permission for his wife to receive gynecological treatment at an Israeli hospital but refused to aid "infidels" and stormed out of Captain Yaakov's room. In his memoirs, Perry writes that he granted the permit anyway—and that later the old man came around, asking for a promise that his tips would be used only to prevent injury to women and children. His payment was an old truck that allowed him to drive from village to village, "selling clothes, granting spiritual comfort and gathering information" that he wrote up in hints spiced with Koranic verses. Payment to informers was always modest; sudden riches would look suspicious. But they had to be paid, Perry explains, so that they knew they were stained irreversibly, with no way home.

Perry, like other Shin Bet agents, drove a white Israeli-made sedan called a Carmel, with a fiberglass body and an extra roof antenna. Army officers drove the same car. Even when he wore civvies, the car and antenna identified him as a Shin Bet man. Eventually the antenna was removed, but a telltale scar remained in the fiberglass.

At times, Perry writes, the army and Shin Bet carried out "stranglehold ops" in the casbah, the crowded old town, of Nablus. Troops encircled the area, all men were ordered to gather at a central point, soldiers searched houses and rooftops for suspects and arms caches. Though terror did not ignite popular revolution or spur Israelis to slaughter, it did help ensure that the occupation was not invisible.

Nor was Perry invisible. When his first son was born, Fatah Radio announced the news, with the comment, "We know just where your wife takes walks with the baby." Perry gave her a loaded pistol, which she kept under a blanket in the baby carriage.[17]

UNLIKE DAYAN, Amos Oz refused to romanticize. In an essay published in *Davar*, the newspaper of the ruling Mapai party, the young kibbutz novelist scorned those who looked at Palestinian Arabs as "a colorful component of the biblical setting, or at best as natives who would drool with gratitude if we treated them kindly." Oz did not make policy suggestions, but he did argue for a very different way of seeing the relationship between Israelis and the Arabs of Palestine—bleakly.

Oz's essay reverses the roles of generations: An author in his twenties grimly rejects the naïveté and extravagant hopes of older leaders. Philosophically, Oz insists that Zionism aims for a Jewish state in part of the homeland, not at possessing the entire homeland. Subtly, he also engages in a literary dispute: Oz argues against politicians but also writers, like those of the Movement for the Whole Land of Israel, who cast history as epic poetry. History is a claustrophobic modern novel, he implies, whose characters refuse to be wholly heroes or victims, and whose conflict will not reach a resolution but, at best, an uncomfortable accommodation.

Zionism, Oz writes, is an escape from the nightmarish Jewish fate in Europe of being persecuted as a perpetual "symbol of something inhuman." Jews need a state to live as individuals, not as a character in someone else's myth. Yet neither that motive nor the Jews' historical tie to their land can matter to the country's Arabs. "The Zionist enterprise has no other objective justification than the right of a drowning man to grasp the only plank that can save him," he argues. That right justifies only grabbing a place on the plank, not pushing others off. It gives moral basis to partitioning the land, not taking it all.

The irony, Oz suggests, is that to evade this problem, many Jews have turned Arabs into characters in a Jewish myth: Canaanites to be embraced or driven out, primitives to be uplifted. The fact is that the Palestinians are a people, entitled to determine their own future. "The land is our land. It is also their land. Right conflicts with right," tragically. The only possible compromise, "burdened with bitterness," would be between "an inconsistent Zionist and an inconsistent Palestinian." For Israel to seek everything will confirm the Arab belief in the "Satanic power of Zionism." It will turn Jews into a symbol of something inhuman, in the land where they came to escape that fate.[18]

This was a calmer Oz than the one who described himself stalking East Jerusalem the day after the war as the shade from his own nightmares. Now he sought to unravel the nightmare, drawing conclusions that were as radical for the time as Copernicus's were for his. It was an accepted truth in Israel in 1967 that the "Arabs of the Land of Israel" were not a distinct community with the right to a distinct national future, subdivided from that of other Arabs. It was even more heretical among Palestinians to suggest that the Jews were a legitimate nationality with a claim to Palestine.

It is difficult to know how many Israelis, or how few, agreed with Oz. It was unusual for a person his age to have access to the pages of the ruling party's paper, but he was not the only person who believed Israel would have to give up most or all of the June conquests.

Minimalists, though, faced an essential asymmetry: They could not create facts. They could not carry out a wildcat withdrawal, or undo a settlement. The number of Israelis ready to settle in occupied territory in 1967 was also small, but they had power not matched by words in a newspaper. If any of the ministers who read Oz even half agreed with him, they would have needed a government decision to stop colonialism. Moshe Dayan needed only the inclination not to decide.

THOUGH LEVI ESHKOL wanted part of the dowry, he knew he had to find a way to avoid keeping the bride. As usual, he was not sure what it was. Eshkol, to be fair, was uncertain because he listened to competing voices, and because he saw the flaws in what they suggested. In a given day's conversation he was likely to state, as his own position, what he had heard in the previous day's meeting, and to tear it apart. He was a walking parliament. Even if he acted, he might only be testing an option.

In November 1967, Eshkol appointed Moshe Sasson, a Foreign Ministry Arabist, to conduct "contacts on matters of state" with leaders of "the Arabs of the administered territories." Explaining the appointment to Dayan, Eshkol said there was a need "to examine the possibilities of establishing a movement for an independent state in the territories." The phrasing suggested that Israel would support the Arabs creating such a movement and that their "independence" would be from Jordan, not Israel.[19]

The same month Eshkol's emissary Yaacov Herzog, director-general of the Prime Minister's Office, held two secret meetings with King Hussein to explore the possibility of a peace deal restoring part of the West Bank to Jordan. Hussein's proposal for getting around the Khartoum resolution was that a different Palestinian movement should "spontaneously" arise, asking him to negotiate on its behalf.

Exploring both paths, Eshkol's motive was to redraw the border and to make sure that no Arab army again entered the West Bank, without Israel having to annex the population. The talks on both fronts dragged on fitfully. When the cabinet discussed the contacts with Hussein, it could not agree on what to offer him.[20]

Eshkol was certain the Gaza Strip had to remain in Israel's hands; restoring it to Egypt was too much of a military risk. He had appointed a group of experts to suggest ways of solving the Palestinian refugee problem. But the committee's real job, as he discussed in December with the two professors who headed it, was to find ways to resettle the refugees packed into the Gaza Strip somewhere else. The professors proposed settling them in the West Bank, an idea Eshkol did not like. Unlike them, he was not sure Israel would be able to give up that land. At Khartoum, he said, "Nasser stuck a knife" in Hussein's back, so talks with the king would probably lead nowhere. Yigal Allon was still pushing the idea of an Arab "entity" with its defense and foreign affairs controlled by Israel, but Eshkol was skeptical. "Where do you have something like that in our day?" he demanded. He preferred to encourage the Arab refugees to emigrate. What would be immoral, he asked, if a hundred thousand went to Iraq? The question underlined his definition of them as generic Arabs, not as Palestinians.

In his ramble with the professors, Eshkol touched on another problem: whether to keep the Hebron area, with its Arab population. Besides the biblical allure of the city, the familiar factor of return to lost homes was at work: In pre-state days, several hundred Orthodox Jews had lived in Hebron. Many had come to the Holy Land to spend their lives in religious study. Others were Middle Eastern Jews who had lived in the area for generations. In 1929, when Arab opposition to Zionism exploded for the first time in countrywide violence, Arab rioters massacred sixty-seven Jews in Hebron. Most of the surviving Jews left; the Hebron Yeshivah moved to Jerusalem. The remaining Jews fled in 1936, with the start of the Arab revolt.[21]

Now Eshkol said he had received a letter from a rightist Knesset member on behalf of the Hebron Yeshivah, whose dean wanted to reestablish a branch in its home city. Eshkol told the professors he had met the rabbi, "and I asked him, 'Would you like a building or two?' " The rabbi wanted a whole street, Eshkol said, hinting the conversation had led nowhere. It was one more idea he was playing with, like a cat batting around a scrap of cloth.[22]

*　*　*

THE IDEA OF HEBRON had absolutely seized another mind, one less fertile with doubts. Rabbi Moshe Levinger heard about the Hebron Yeshivah dean's interest in returning to the city from Elyakim Ha'etzni, a firebrand ultranationalist Tel Aviv lawyer he had met during his abortive bid to lead the reestablishment of Kfar Etzion. Once again Levinger saw the sentiment of return as an opportunity. In his own accounts of the coming months, though, he makes no mention of contacting the Hebron Yeshivah. Instead, the curt young rabbi took the mythic role for himself: He would be the one to restore the Jews to Hebron.[23]

The National Religious Party's rebellious Young Guard began running newspaper ads: Anyone interested in "going up" to Hebron should contact Rabbi Moshe Levinger via a Tel Aviv post office box. Levinger also spread the word among former classmates from the Merkaz Harav yeshivah. At the end of 1967 a couple dozen people gathered at National Religious Party headquarters to lay plans. Beforehand, in Levinger's telling, his wife, Miriam, told him: "The government won't send you there. Go settle, and things will work out." At the meeting, he was alone in supporting his absent wife's approach. Everyone else wanted government approval. He embarked on a round of lobbying.

Levinger's activism left a meager paper trail. His testimony— sometimes corroborated or contradicted by other people's—must therefore be cited, but suspiciously. In Levinger's account, when Eshkol and Dayan refused to meet him, it was because they were at a loss before him, because "they didn't know how to answer us," and not because he was an unknown thirty-two-year-old rabbi. Levinger claims to have met Dayan's viceroy, Colonel Gazit, at the Defense Ministry. "You'll get an answer," Gazit told him, but no answer ever came. Gazit would recall no such meeting, nor a reason for one—dealing with Jewish settlement was not his bailiwick.[24]

Levinger did meet leaders of the Movement for the Whole Land of Israel. He stood as he spoke in the Tel Aviv office, clenched his fist, and blasted Dayan—the wrong move in front of the movement's poet-leader Nathan Alterman, who regarded Dayan as the avatar of Israeli courage. A young Orthodox journalist who was working with Alterman, Yisrael Harel, was both embarrassed and captivated by the rabbi's refusal to show respect to the secular elite of Israeli culture. Orthodox Zionists did not normally act that way; they showed deference.[25] Rudeness had unsettling charisma.

Despite the tense introduction, Alterman's movement decided to lend a hand, and raised Levinger's project with Yigal Allon. For Allon, it was a useful tool toward his own goals. In mid-January 1968, he submitted a proposal to the cabinet for building "a Jewish neighborhood in the immediate vicinity of Hebron." To back up the idea, he cited requests by Israeli citizens to settle in the town.

Allon's reasoning was historic, not strategic. "Jews lived in Hebron for hundreds of years under Ottoman rule and the British mandate," he said. They should be allowed to do so again, he asserted—regardless of who ultimately ended up ruling the city.[26] The last comment defies Allon's principle that settlement would determine the state's borders. It can be read as a ploy to lessen opposition from cabinet minimalists, or as a rationalization to himself. The claim of historic rights to Hebron, though, is consistent with his original presentation of the Allon Plan, where he raised the option of keeping the city despite its large Arab population.[27] Allon was still wavering between his old romance with the Whole Land and his new compromises, and could not resist asserting the right to return to Hebron.

Two months later, in mid-March, Allon reminded Eshkol of his proposal, and noted that among those who had sought his help in settling in Hebron was Levinger's group, comprising "23 families and several dozen young singles." The group, Allon indicated, would reestablish Jewish religious study in the town. On Levinger's stage, cabinet ministers were supporting actors. On Allon's stage, the rabbi and yeshivah students were extras needed for a crowd scene, in lieu of old-fashioned pioneers plowing kibbutz fields.

Attached to the memo was a cable to Allon signed by Levinger and Harel in the name of the Movement for the Whole Land of Israel: "Hebron settlers await green light."[28] No green light came. Levinger therefore assumed the right of way. He held another gathering of his recruits in Tel Aviv. This time the vote was to establish facts: to move to Hebron and hope for permission afterward.

On the last day of March, Levinger and several companions toured

Hebron with an aging survivor of the pre-1929 Jewish community. On the street they talked briefly with an Israeli Druse serving in the paramilitary Border Police, which kept order in occupied towns. The search for available apartments was fruitless. Levinger and friends agreed on an alternative—to rent hotel rooms for the upcoming week-long holiday of Passover, and see "what develops." The rabbi and a companion entered the town's small Park Hotel. In one of Levinger's accounts, they presented themselves to the owner as Swiss tourists, interested in renting the entire establishment for ten days, with an option to extend. The owner agreed, also giving permission to make the kitchen kosher for Passover. Levinger's account hints they were unsure where the escapade would lead. Like his plan the previous autumn to camp out at Kfar Etzion, it may have been intended simply to seize attention for the cause.[29]

Looking out from the next morning's newspaper was the face of the Border Policeman they had met the day before. Shortly after their meeting, he was shot dead in the Hebron casbah. It was the first such attack in Hebron since the war. Among Levinger's supporters, the murder was seen as a warning, a response to rumors racing about town that Jews were about to move in.

For the moment, they were probably overrating their own role. If the victim was not chosen simply for his uniform, he may have been targeted as a Druse. Israeli members of the Arabic-speaking religious minority emphasized their loyalty to the Jewish state, arousing particular antagonism among West Bank residents.[30]

But the would-be settlers' interpretation still matters. The possibility that they could ignite conflict, and endanger Israeli troops in Hebron, did not inspire hesitation.

Strictly speaking, shooting a uniformed, on-duty member of the occupying force was not terror, but it served the same purpose. Fifteen hundred Hebron men were detained and questioned, in a roundup that lasted till the next afternoon.[31] The occupation was quite visible that day.

THERE WERE THINGS Levi Eshkol had made up his mind about—such as moving many Jews to East Jerusalem, quickly. If foreign pressure ever gave cabinet members second thoughts about annexing the east city,

Israeli neighborhoods beyond the Green Line would strengthen their resolve.[32]

When his East Jerusalem planning chief, Yehudah Tamir, found that there was not enough publicly owned land in the east city for massive new housing developments,[33] the prime minister won approval for expropriating a swathe of over 800 acres that would reconnect West Jerusalem to Mount Scopus, the once and future campus of Hebrew University. The expropriation orders were issued in early January with a campaign of non-publicity planned by the secretive minister Yisrael Galili that included barring the item from state-owned radio, which had a monopoly on the airwaves, and pressuring newspaper editors to downplay the story.[34] When the move nonetheless ignited international protests, Eshkol instructed Tamir to move even faster on construction. An Eshkol aide sent a secret memo to other officials, including Mayor Teddy Kollek, saying that "since our desire is to develop the east city rather than talk about it," they should avoid publicity and keep working.[35]

In the same spirit, Kollek decided to squash the results of a survey City Hall had carried out among Jerusalem's Jews on how they saw unification and East Jerusalemites. The descriptions of Arabs with which respondents identified most were "a people with many hypocrites . . . a people of cowards . . . primitive . . . a people that does not tend to wash." More than 80 percent expected unification to increase crime in the city, while only half expected it would bring prosperity. The groom thought very little of the bride, results that would do nothing to promote a picture of coexistence. Kollek informed Eshkol he was destroying all copies of the survey in city hands, leaving the prime minister to decide what to do with his copy.[36]

Meanwhile maps were drawn up for the next round of expropriations—a thirty-acre piece of the Old City for restoring the Jewish Quarter and a larger area in the city's north, where a new neighborhood would take the place of the abandoned pre-state Jewish farm community of Neveh Ya'akov.[37]

Another effort was kept even quieter. "What I can tell you is to see and not be seen," Eshkol told the veteran intelligence operative Ada Sereni at a top-secret discussion of Palestinian refugees in February

1968. Sereni had worked for years in Europe on covert efforts to bring Jews from the Soviet Union to Israel. Now Eshkol wanted her to speed migration in another direction. "Find ways and paths that will help the Arabs to emigrate. What interests us now most is the Gaza Strip. The intent is to encourage them to emigrate, beyond what is now going on without our intervention," he told her. Perhaps they could be channeled to South America, Eshkol suggested. "It's possible to move people there that no one would even know about their existence in the world."[18] Sereni reported back on March 20 on efforts that included paying the fare for families who left by truck from Gaza to the Jordan River bridges and from there, "it seems, to the closest refugee camp, in Karameh," between the river and Amman. She sought funds for more agents to spread the idea in refugee camps.[39]

"How many Arabs did you send this week?" Eshkol asked, opening the next week's meeting.

"Last week there was a drop in the number leaving. It was unavoidable, because of the week's events," Sereni said. "The number fell to 800, from 1,200–1,500 in previous weeks."

The "events" were the Israeli army's massive attack on Karameh, where Fatah leader Yasser Arafat had his headquarters, on March 21. The proximate cause was a terror attack a few days before, in which an Israeli school bus hit a Palestinian-planted mine. To the IDF's surprise, the Palestinians at Karameh put up a strong fight and Jordanian troops joined the Palestinians in a fierce battle. Karameh became a symbol of valor for Fatah, and would draw thousands of young Palestinians to its training camps. By the cold logic of terror, killing two adults and wounding ten children on the school bus had indeed provoked Israel to lend a hand in recruiting apathetic Palestinians to armed struggle.

Turmoil in Jordan did not make life on the East Bank more attractive to inhabitants of the occupied Strip. Worse, Sereni pointed out, destitute refugees who did reach Jordan were likely to join Fatah simply to gain a livelihood. She wanted funds to offer a few hundred dollars per family so they could buy land or houses. A few days later Eshkol approved funding for that purpose and more agents to work the refugee camps.[40]

On the settlement front, Eshkol was still playing with the idea of Hebron. At the end of March, he gave a briefing to Hannah Zemer, editor of his party's *Davar* newspaper, whose pointed questions showed marked discomfort with entrenchment in the occupied territories. When she asked about "demands to settle in Hebron," Eshkol answered, "If there are those who suggest creating a settlement in Hebron without dispossessing anyone, I don't see a sin in that."

"And then our boys will have to serve an extra three months . . . to guard those yeshivah students," Zemer warned.[41]

Another warning on settlement came soon after, from the U.S. State Department. A message on April 8 to the U.S. embassy in Tel Aviv noted that Nahal settlements were "taking on aspects of permanent, civilian, kibbutz-like operations and some are, in fact, civilian kibbutzim with Nahal covers." Eshkol's Knesset comments about the number of "out-posts" added cause for concern. The embassy, said State, should remind Israel's government of America's "continuing opposition to any Israeli settlements in the occupied areas." Even when under military control, settlements violated Article 49 of the Geneva Convention. They indicated that Israel did not intend to reach a peace accord involving withdrawal. The sharp language makes clear that the United States saw settlements, including Nahal ones, as illegal under international law. But the message was drafted by the midlevel diplomats who handled technical issues, and was sent by diplomatic mail rather than cable, meaning it would take about a week to arrive.[42] By the time an embassy officer could meet a Foreign Ministry official of similar rank to pass on the protest, the next escalation in settlement almost certainly had begun.

PASSOVER BEGAN at sunset on Friday, April 12. That day the Park Hotel in Hebron filled with guests. It was a square, two-story stone building with small rooms, which had lost its clientele of Arab pilgrims to the city of the prophet Ibrahim and was now getting a rush of customers ostensibly coming only to conduct a Passover seder, the festive dinner celebrating the Israelites' exodus from Egypt, in the city of Abraham.[43]

By most accounts General Uzi Narkiss, head of the army's Central Command, granted Levinger permission for his group to stay overnight. Narkiss was convinced they were coming only for seder night. Approval was needed because Narkiss's most recent order permitting Israelis to visit the West Bank allowed them to enter and leave only during daylight hours.[44]

In another version, by the pro-Dayan writer Shabtai Teveth, they need not have bothered with permission, since the poorly worded order accidentally allowed entering occupied land during sunlight of one day and leaving during daylight of another. The order would have to be amended before the defense minister gained control over the presence of Levinger and company—providing an additional reason, in Teveth's view, for Dayan's slow response, beside the fact that on that Passover night he was lying in a hospital bed recovering from injuries to his vertebrae, ribs, and vocal cords sustained three weeks earlier (on the day before the Karameh operation), when he took time off from military planning to loot an archaeological site for Bronze Age relics, and a cave collapsed on him.[45]

Dayan, in any case, did not know in advance of Levinger's arrival. Yigal Allon did, or at least knew that Levinger was considering the Passover plan. "I'll tell you just what happened," Allon explained to an interviewer eleven years later, by which time he was eager to defend himself against the charge of supporting defiance of the government. "They . . . wanted to turn the seder at Park Hotel at the entrance to Hebron into the first toehold of settlement. They turned to me. Why? I don't know! Maybe because they knew I'd helped the Etzion Bloc people, I'd helped in the Jordan Rift and the Golan. . . . I said I'd help them under two conditions. First, that the seder would be held with the agreement of the military governor. Second, that if the government or the prime minister decides that there shouldn't be a settlement in Hebron or nearby—they talked about the city of Hebron—they'll accept the decision."[46]

Some guests at the Park were supporters who did not intend to stay. Moshe Shamir, the formerly far-left novelist from the Movement for the Whole Land of Israel, showed up. Journalist Yisrael Harel was there, interested but uncommitted to remaining. The dean of Moskovic's Or Etzion yeshivah, Rabbi Haim Druckman, came to conduct the seder. Even within Levinger's group of would-be settlers, some thought their stay was to be symbolic, and came with only a few days' clothes. Miriam and Moshe Levinger and their four children arrived in the afternoon—at Miriam's insistence, with a truck carrying their refrigerator, washing machine, and the rest of their household.

Before sunset, Levinger and a companion visited Hebron's military governor and demanded assistance with security for the seder. In Levinger's telling, the governor at first refused to have anything to do with them. Then he relented, tore off a long strip of paper from the margin of the newspaper he was reading, and scribbled, "To the police commander. Give the bearer of this note four rifles and two Uzis." At police headquarters, the commander honored the note. Soon after, Druse Border Police came to the hotel. Since they were not celebrating, they said, they would stand guard.[47]

How many people took part in the seder depends on the narrator. Yisrael Harel, who years later said it bothered him that he had failed to feel a "mythic experience" that night, estimated that there were forty to forty-five people present.[48] Levinger has given numbers as high as one hundred.[49] Druckman asked each participant to say something about the holiday. Moshe Shamir, by one account, commented on a piece of the seder liturgy known by its refrain, "It would be enough for us." Each of God's miracles in the course of the Exodus would have been sufficient, say the classic verses of thanksgiving; how much more so should He be praised for all of them. No, Shamir declared, the individual miracles were not enough! All were needed! It was a sign of weakness to be satisfied! The text was criticism, he insisted, of Jews willing to "settle for the achievements of the past," like those who a year earlier would have been willing to settle for a Jewish state without Hebron. Druckman gave a kiss on the forehead to the former Marxist who had seen the light—though the comment showed exactly what the old Shamir shared with the new: a revolutionary's disgust with halfway and compromise, a certainty that anything short of everything is nothing.[50]

When the seder ended after midnight, the participants went outside to dance with the Border Policemen in the streets of a town known among other Arabs as bleakly conservative. After a night's sleep, the group marched through town to the Tomb of the Patriarchs carrying Torah scrolls, singing and dancing.

The Tomb, sacred to Muslims as the Ibrahimi Mosque, was already a flash point. A stone complex dating back to King Herod's time two thousand years before, it had been converted to a church by the Byzantines, then to a mosque after the Muslim conquest. From the thirteenth century, Jews could come no closer than the seventh step of the wide stone stairway leading to the entrance. That rule vanished when Israeli troops rolled into the town. What remained was uncertainty and conflicting claims. Eventually Dayan flew to Hebron to meet the sheikh of the mosque and work out a modus vivendi for Muslims and Jews to share the holy place.[51] Now, on their first full day in town, the settlers were indicating that quiet compromise was not on their agenda.

In another corner of occupied territory, that Passover seder night was also the first that the settlers in the Syrian officers' quarter of Quneitrah celebrated together. The Golan kibbutz now had a population of 117, and was growing up: There were now a few married couples, and five children. Carmel Bar, the original settler, invited his parents from their Tel Aviv suburb, signaling that this was really home. The guest of honor, the living representative of kibbutz tradition, was the white-haired secular sage, Yitzhak Tabenkin.[52]

"Sometimes I have to look at others to see that we, we're actually happy," Golan settler Kobi Rabinovich, still haunted by Sinai battles, wrote to his girlfriend. "I can see that I have it so good. It's good, good for me that I have you, and I don't need any more. But why is the world like this, so much sadness and evil? I feel like I have no right to have this."[53] The words are an unintended gloss on "It would be enough." The man singed by war, lacking a grand idea that turns death into a detail, looks at normal life and says, "This is too much."

Shin Bet man Yaakov Perry did not get home for seder. At dusk in his office in Nablus, finishing a quiet day, he received an informant's urgent message that a group of armed Palestinians would cross the Jordan that night, on their way to a holiday attack in Israel. They would be led by a commander known only as Samir, who had repeatedly escaped capture. At midnight Perry waited in ambush with a squad of paratroopers above the river. Silhouettes rose from the darkness just when the informant said they would. But after the soldiers' first shots, the intruders escaped westward. Before dawn, troops caught up with them outside the village of Beit Furik, near Nablus. The firefight, Perry records in his memoirs, was tough. A paratroop sergeant was killed, several Palestinian gunmen also fell, and others surrendered.

The Palestinian commander escaped again, toward the cover of the houses. By now there was a drill for this, Perry writes: Jeeps with loudspeakers rolled through the village, ordering all men to the local school. In the first light of this spring morning, soldiers and Border Police searched houses and yards. In the schoolyard, Shin Bet agents questioned the men, one by one, through the day. At last, on a hunch, Perry records, he confronted one of the remaining men, and said, "I know you're Samir." He was right.[54]

For most Israelis that day, the occupation was unnoticeable, in part because of an informant's tip. At the Park Hotel, the occupied were half-visible, like the outlines of the seated people seen from a stage, the faceless and essential audience. In Beit Furik, the occupation was quite apparent.

AFTER NIGHTFALL Saturday, at the end of the Sabbath, the older fellow travelers left Hebron's Park Hotel. The group that remained was young, most in their twenties—several families and more singles, many of them yeshivah students, excited about getting away with their gambit, starting the de rigueur endless late night discussions of what to do next.[55]

Without knowing it, they had stumbled into a moment of weak authority: Colonel Gazit's father had died that Saturday morning, and the Jewish mourning customs observed even by secular Israelis pulled the officer in charge of occupied land away from his office for days to come.[56] Dayan, by his own testimony, returned to his office only that Sunday, still battered, drugged against pain.[57] The first weekend passed with the viceroy absent and the sultan dazed.

Expelling Jews from Hebron, Gazit later argued, was too loaded a decision for local commanders. It required cabinet-level action, quickly, before support built. Dayan played for time: When he got word of the group's presence, he ordered the army to guarantee its safety but not to assume formal responsibility for it.[58] More young Orthodox Jews began arriving, such as Benny Katzover, a Hebrew University freshman and ex-Merkaz Harav student who came to help with guard duty and stayed on. The mood, he would recall, was euphoric and tense; no one knew what the government would do.[59]

Sunday afternoon, a telegram was sent to Yigal Allon:

BLESSINGS FOR FESTIVAL OF OUR FREEDOM TO YOU FROM HEBRON CITY OF PATRIARCHS FROM FIRST OF THOSE RETURNING TO IT TO SETTLE IN IT IN THE NAME OF 30 FAMILIES RABBI MOSHE LEVINGER

Allon's office got the message Monday morning.[60] He responded immediately, heading south from Jerusalem along with the poet and activist Nathan Alterman and the head of the government's employment service.

A report the next day, in the newspaper of Allon's Ahdut Ha'avodah faction, begins as if Allon were fulfilling his normal duties: "Labor Minister Yigal Allon yesterday paid a holiday visit to the first settlers in Hebron. The settlers . . . raised the problems of employment and professional training in the place." The settlers' presence is taken as established fact. "The labor minister announced that . . . his ministry will supply work-projects employment to all settlers seeking work," the paper said. The sole hint that the settlers lacked government permission is Allon's concluding comment that "it is inconceivable that Jews would be barred from settling once more in this holy city."[61]

On his way back to Jerusalem, Allon stopped at Kfar Etzion to talk to Hanan Porat. "They're in danger," he said of the Hebron settlers. "You have to give them guns."

"That's not so simple," Porat replied. The kibbutz had guns from the army for guard duty, he acknowledged, "but we've signed for them personally."

Allon stared at what was clearly a well-behaved young man from Bnei Akiva. "In the time of the Palmah"—Allon held his arm down and jabbed the palm of his hand forward, as if pushing it under something, "we knew to do things like *this*." Porat, the eager student, sent the guns.[62]

* * *

MOSHE LEVINGER'S FIRST meeting with Hebron mayor Muhammad Ali al-Jabari went pleasantly, historian Shabtai Teveth writes, because there was no communication. Levinger and two companions, one of whom could stutter a bit in Arabic, were received by the mayor during their first week in town. Jabari spoke no Hebrew and thought he was hospitably greeting tourists. Levinger told journalists now flocking to cover the story that the sixty-seven-year-old mayor had welcomed Jewish settlement in the town.[63]

Sheikh Jabari, mayor since the last days of British rule, knew how to sail with the wind. After Transjordan conquered the West Bank, he headed a staged congress of prominent citizens that called for continued rule by Amman, paving the way for annexation to the renamed kingdom of Jordan. Three times Jabari served as a Jordanian cabinet minister. A secret Israeli report on the West Bank elite written a week after the cease-fire in June 1967 described him as "a cleric. Holds reactionary views. Avaricious and easily bribed. Hated in the West Bank for his corruption"—which does not contradict other portrayals of Jabari as a uniquely powerful mayor, his influence extending throughout the Hebron region. Jabari built ties with Dayan, and publicly criticized Palestinian attacks on Israelis.[64]

Still, he did not like reports of welcoming settlers. His letter of protest to Eshkol and Dayan was pitched precisely to Israeli fears. In principle, remnants of the old Jewish community, who knew Arabic and the Arab way of life, might return to Hebron, he wrote—as long as Arab refugees could also return to Jaffa. In practice, settlers would be targets for attacks by the Palestinian "self-sacrificers," and coexistence between the two peoples would be destroyed.

Jabari's comments, leaked to the Israeli press, brought Levinger back to the mayor's office, accompanied by fellow Merkaz Harav graduate Rabbi Eliezer Waldman and another settler. This time communication was more successful. Jabari phoned the military governor to say that the men were in his room, threatening him. The officer arrived in time to hear shouting. Levinger insisted that Hebron had always been Jewish and—as Jabari quoted him in a telegram that day to Eshkol—"we will settle the city whether you want friendly relations or not." When the governor tried to calm matters, Jabari demanded an apology from Levinger, whom he accused of "Hitler-like comments." The settlers stormed out.[65] The schematic of the scene was simple: Levinger claimed ultimate authority in Hebron, Jabari rejected the claim, and the military governor—ostensibly the agent of the ruling power—stood ineffectually between them.

By now it was May 7; Levinger's group had made itself at home for nearly a month in the Park Hotel, and in the news pages. Jabari's messages underlined the lack of an official response. Two cabinet ministers—Menachem Begin and the National Religious Party's Warhaftig—had followed Allon to Hebron to show support. The United Kibbutz's central committee passed a resolution sending "congratulations to the first settlers in the city of the patriarchs."[66] Allon received a proposal from a Jerusalem architect—prepared "at the request of Rabbi Levinger of Hebron," the architect said—for building a Jewish "Upper Hebron."[67]

In a discussion of the problem on April 20 in Labor's most important smoke-filled back room, the party's political committee, Eshkol complained about ministers acting on their own, about "our dear Allon showing up" in Hebron, and about Warhaftig "running [after him] like a dog two days later and giving his blessing. We're making a joke of ourselves." Allon's party colleague, Yisrael Galili, was also caustic.[68] Though he was a maximalist, a United Kibbutz man, Galili's most unambiguous commitments were to secrecy and top-down control—what a Leninist would call "democratic centralism"—and he found the spectacle in Hebron painful.

Minimalists in the cabinet—including Foreign Minister Abba Eban and the dovish Finance Minister Pinhas Sapir—opposed settlement in Hebron on principle.[69] Apparently for the first time, settlement sparked public objections, including an open letter from prominent academics and authors to the cabinet. The signatories objected to letting a small group set national policy, and to that policy being annexation.[70]

Eshkol was caught not only between opposing political pressures but between his own opposing inclinations. An orphaned scrap of minutes in his files, from an unidentified meeting of the time, has him asserting that in "the strip of Judea and Samaria"—apparently referring to the mountain ridge—"there's nothing for us" and that "I don't know what there is in Hebron besides the sentimental matter—the Tomb of the Patriarchs." Which was fine, but sentiment moved him.

Finally, on May 12, a ministerial committee approved a proposal to "authorize the defense minister to make the necessary arrangements to ensure the personal safety of the volunteers in Hebron, including moving them from the Park Hotel to other lodgings."[71] The wording evaded the issues of principle—should Israel keep Hebron, should Israelis settle in an Arab city—and even avoided recognizing that the "volunteers" were settlers.

When the news leaked out, settler Rabbi Waldman told the press that "God has shown us the way to redeem the Jewish nation," and noted that according to the Bible, King David ruled from Hebron before conquering Jerusalem.[72] The practical implication was that direct, defiant action was an effective means of holding the Whole Land, central to Rabbi Tzvi Yehudah Kook's vision. The theological implication was that settling in Hebron had cosmic significance, even beyond settling elsewhere: David's kingdom was a model for the messianic kingdom, David began in Hebron, so settling in Hebron would lead to final redemption.[73]

In Hebron, the military governor came to read the government's decision to the group. The settlers were told they would be allowed to establish a yeshivah, but that the government decision did not imply approval for a Jewish city next to Hebron or for Jewish businesses in the town. Only those connected to the yeshivah could stay—though in practice that meant the full group got the permits now needed to dwell in occupied territory. Any contacts with local Arab authorities would have to be through the military government. Dayan's solution to the security problem was that they would move from the hotel to the military government headquarters, a former British fortress at the edge of town. Dayan, settler Benny Katzover would recall, seemed antagonistic, since the group had come to Hebron without his knowledge; Gazit was downright hostile. The settlers debated all night whether to agree to the move and the conditions, and at last decided to accept it as government approval. On May 19, a group now numbering one hundred settlers crowded into the west wing of the fortress.[74] In ministerial-level meetings, meanwhile, the possibility of building a Jewish neighborhood regularly popped up, without any decision taken.[75]

In Levinger's view, the confrontation with Jabari brought the government concession.[76] By showing just who was in charge, he had won. That bends facts to fit his character. Yet Teveth's account lends some oblique confirmation: Dayan, he says, sought to "remove them . . . from the life of the city and distance them from the residents." Politically unable to evict the settlers, he minimized their contact with the mayor, and restricted them to a compound under his control.[77] Dayan thought he had made them invisible in his kingdom, yet confirmed to Levinger that abrasive visibility got him what he wanted.

"EVERY WEEK A THOUSAND to twelve hundred were leaving the Gaza Strip. In the last few weeks the numbers have shrunk," Eshkol complained to the director of his emigration effort for refugees, Ada Sereni, in mid-May. Sereni admitted she was getting nowhere with sending refugees to Brazil or Australia. Both countries wanted immigrants, she said, "but when they hear they're Arabs, they're not interested." The Australians could not even be bribed. "We're trying to bribe a Saudi to give them visas," she said.

The real problem lay in Jordan, Colonel Gazit explained. The authorities were confiscating cars used to drive refugees from the bridges. Just the day before, Gazit had heard of a new Jordanian law that forbid transporting refugees. Armed Fatah men roamed the streets in Jordan, which was no attraction for immigrants.[78]

The meeting is the last in Eshkol's files on the subject. The project unraveled. The idea that Gaza's refugees could be enticed en masse to go elsewhere died, Gazit later explained, because they had no elsewhere.[79] The policy of keeping the Gaza Strip remained.

Jordan, meanwhile, posed another problem for Eshkol: Hussein wanted to negotiate peace. In early May, Eban met the king secretly in London.[80] Lyndon Johnson was leaning on Israel to move forward.[81] For Eshkol, negotiating meant his party and government had to decide on a vision of the West Bank's future to offer the king.

Allon's answer was an updated version of his plan. He had realized, he later explained, that Palestinian autonomy under Israeli sovereignty "would be identified as . . . some kind of South African Bantustan."[82] Instead, he suggested offering the West Bank's populated areas to Hussein, and providing a narrow corridor from Ramallah to Jericho to link the enclave with the East Bank. Israel would still keep, and settle, the strip along the Jordan and the Dead Sea. Allon began promoting the plan publicly—beginning with the peculiar venue of a meeting with the professors who had protested against settlement in Hebron. His logic and his smile, he seemed to believe, could persuade anyone. A U.S. diplomatic cable, summing up press reports, said Allon told them to "bear in mind that in matters of security, he has never been wrong." They answered that his Zionism was out of date, that a sovereign country did not need to stake claims to land with armed settlements as Jews had done in Mandate days. But they faced the same limit as the dovish novelist Amos Oz—they could not undo settlement by wildcat action.[83]

To decide on a proposal for Hussein, Eshkol met at the end of May with Allon, Dayan, and Eban, assuming that any consensus among that awkward group could be imposed on his fractious party and cabinet. Nearly a year had passed since the war. "The truth is we don't know so clearly what we actually want," Eshkol said, which was why he was unhappy with ministers presenting negotiating positions publicly, or running to Hebron to support a settlement begun without government approval. He wanted agreement with Jordan; it would satisfy Johnson and let Israel avoid "swallowing another million Arabs," he said. "There have been imperialist countries larger than us, and they taught [the colonial subjects] their languages and created francophones and anglophones. . . . Then the people knew to say 'enough, we don't want you here,'" Eshkol warned.

Dayan's suggestion was that Israel should insist on keeping its army bases on the mountain ridge, and on the Jordanian army staying out of the West Bank. Militarily, Israel would rule the region. But the civilian administration would be Jordanian—except, perhaps, in the Etzion Bloc and the Jordan Rift, where Israel now had settlements. The Arab residents would be Jordanian citizens, voting for the Jordanian parliament. Israeli citizens would be free to go where they wanted up to the Jordan River, to live in Hebron or perhaps elsewhere in the West Bank, without need for visas, thereby expressing their "Jewish connection to the cradle of the homeland."

"So from the start you say, 'Yes, it's your country, but I'm a permanent resident here'?" Eshkol asked.

No, Dayan answered, "I don't say it's your country. You give the name, I say to them. Or to you. It doesn't interest me." Israel could claim the West Bank, and Jordan could claim it. "I don't say this is the classic, accepted structure of borders between two countries," Dayan admitted. Borders and formal ownership did not interest him in affairs of state—which fit the way the inveterate philanderer and antiquities raider behaved in private life. His offer to Hussein was that the West Bank could be the mistress of two countries. He was willing to make a similar offer to Palestinians, he said, relating to a new proposal by the Ramallah lawyer Aziz Shehadeh and Nablus mayor Hamdi Kanan to negotiate the establishment of a Palestinian state. But he did not actually expect talks to lead anywhere. As he saw it, Israel would rule the West Bank indefinitely, and should "integrate" the region with Israel proper and Gaza.

If Dayan's proposal was the only security solution, Eban answered, "then we may despair" of agreement with Hussein. Instead, endorsing Allon's approach, he pushed a "clean-cut" division of territory, with Israel retaining a strip along the Jordan River.

Suddenly, at the meeting's end, Dayan blurted out that he "was familiar with Yigal's conception" and could live with it. The comment backs up Gazit's description of Dayan as an outsider in the government, willing to present ideas but not to fight for them. In his own realm, he was the sole ruler; in the cabinet, a loner.[84]

The meeting ended with no formal decision, but implied support for Allon's position. Afterward, Labor's political committee debated the Allon Plan, and the leaks gave the proposal more headlines. The decision by Eshkol and the Labor Party's secretary-general Golda Meir to make Allon deputy prime minister and head of a new ministry for immigration—infuriating Dayan—could only increase interest in his plan.[85] But neither the party nor the government adopted the Allon Plan, allowing other politicians to continue pushing their views.

So when Dayan met Jabari and a delegation of local leaders in early June, he not only rejected their request to remove the Hebron settlers but also said that the government's policy in the occupied territories was to "function as if peace had come." The occupation, he implied, had become normalcy, an imposed but positive coexistence between Israelis and Arabs.

That contented view was seeping into the Israeli public as well. "This is peace. It is being created little by little, in the endless meetings happening constantly between them and us," Haim Gouri wrote in his paper, describing summer traffic across the Jordan River bridges. Gouri guessed that the Arabs waiting to cross were quietly cursing foreign rule, but also that many were saying that "a year has passed since the war and the way is open . . . and people come and go and it's possible to live and the Jews are not so bad."[86]

The contacts with Shehadeh and other moderates from the northern West Bank collapsed. Eshkol was slow to respond, then willing to offer only autonomy. In July, Jabari tried to sail with that breeze, suggesting that he be appointed governor of the West Bank, under the military government. Dayan favored the idea; it was a way to declare the occupation over, to proclaim normalcy, while Israel remained in control. But the other West Bank leaders were unwilling to accept Jabari, and the plan was trimmed to him becoming governor of the Hebron district. Before signing, Dayan said at a meeting with Eshkol and other ministers on July 23, "I suggest we exchange some words [with Jabari] on a Jewish settlement at Hebron." The cabinet was ready to examine building a Jewish neighborhood next to the city, he noted. Jabari should know in advance. "I have no doubt," Dayan said, "that he'll swallow that."

Eshkol mused aloud about where the neighborhood should be, but assumed it had to be close to the city's contested holy site. "I don't know exactly where the Tomb of the Patriarchs is there," he said.

"It's in the middle of the city," Dayan told him.

"Maybe we'll make a different tomb?" Eshkol joked, and adjourned the meeting.[87]

But the self-rule plan also fell apart. Jabari decided he would be satisfied only with the entire West Bank—or as Gazit has argued, he used that as an excuse, after Jordanian radio broadcast warnings against reaching separate agreements with the enemy.[88] It makes little difference. Ultimately, self-rule was not intended to end occupation but to make it less visible—to hide the bride and keep the dowry—while allowing settlement to continue.

West Bank Palestinians interested in statehood alongside Israel had more reason for discouragement, and fear. The Palestine Liberation Organization—set up by Arab governments but increasingly dominated by Fatah—declared in July that anyone trying to set up a "counterfeit Palestinian entity" in the land occupied since June 1967 was an "enemy of the Arab Palestinian people."[89] The PLO sought the Whole Land of Palestine, and rejected halfway measures. In 1968, the two-state option resembled Leonardo da Vinci's flying machine: It could be imagined, not built. But it was dangerous to imagine. At night, young Raja Shehadeh heard the radio station of the Syrian-backed Palestinian group Al-Saika warning his father, "We shall eliminate you. . . . Traitor. Collaborator. Quisling."[90]

THE KATZOVER WEDDING was set for August 7. Benny had met Binah while he was in the army. They announced their engagement after he moved to Hebron, and she joined the informal commune in the government headquarters building. Unmarried women shared a single room crowded with bunk beds. Families and singles ate together in a shared dining hall. In the kitchen next door stood the refrigerators that families had brought with them.

In the midst of a revolution, there is little room for private life. The settlers' first wedding would be a celebration of their presence, orchestrated by the collective. A thousand people were invited, including the entire cabinet. Buses were chartered to bring guests. The radical nationalist Shlomo Goren, who that year stepped down as chief army chaplain to become chief rabbi of Tel Aviv, would officiate at the ceremony.[91]

The Israelis in Hebron were either disturbingly dug in, or disturbingly denied their due, depending on who was commenting. In late July, U.S. deputy assistant secretary of state Roger Davies phoned Israeli diplomat Shlomo Argov to check on a media report that military authorities would soon begin building a yeshivah, synagogue, and nursery school in the government headquarters courtyard. Davies had been asked to convey that State was perturbed at "what seems to be the per-

manent civilian settlement in Hebron" and that "this could only compli-
cate Israeli efforts to obtain a peace settlement with Jordan." Davies
scrawled Argov's answers that, well, yes, Hebron was a "controversial issue within the cabinet" but there was a matter of "reestablishing Jews in
[the] City of Prophets," presumably Davies's mistranscription of "Patriarchs."[92]

Shortly afterward, the settlers sent a letter to Eshkol, demanding
construction of a yeshivah campus with housing for students, teachers,
and staff, along with approval for a Jewish neighborhood—a project
they justified both by the "deep historical tie to the city of our fathers"
and by Hebron's record as "a center of murderous activity" against
Zionism and Israel. They also complained that too few Jews were visiting the Tomb of the Patriarchs, a problem they ascribed to the authorities' refusal to let the settlers open a kosher restaurant next to the holy
place. "UNTIL WHEN WILL OUR BRETHREN BE PRE-
VENTED FROM EATING IN A JEWISH RESTAURANT AS IN
ANY CITY IN ISRAEL?" the letter shouted, with no intent of irony.
The subtext was the settlers' frustration with Dayan, who had put off requests to open businesses in town by telling them to get licenses from
city hall—that is, from Mayor Jabari.[93]

On the wedding day, assuming that guests would arrive early to visit
the tomb, the settler group set up a table outside the holy site to sell soft
drinks. They brought the supplies for the so-called kiosk in a van that
Allon had provided to the community. Military governor Ofer Ben-
David gave permission or turned a blind eye for the happy day. The
wedding meal was held in the government headquarters courtyard, with
disposable plates flying in the wind.

The next morning the kiosk was back, with a large sign reading "Hebron Settlers." Now Ben-David called Gazit, who did not intend to let
Levinger get away with overextending his welcome again. Gazit took off
by helicopter from Tel Aviv for Hebron, while on his orders the governor headed for the kiosk and told the three settlers behind the table to
remove it. Levinger, also on the scene, asked not to dismantle the kiosk
before the crowd of locals. The governor ordered his soldiers to take it
away. The settlers were incensed, they told reporters afterward, at being
humiliated in broad daylight "with Arabs standing and laughing at us."

The proper hierarchy of power, they felt, had been turned upside down. When Gazit landed, determined not to allow "wildcat creating of facts, as on Passover," he canceled the three settlers' permits to live in Hebron. They had until noon on Sunday, three days hence, to leave town.[94]

Sunday morning was when the cabinet met. It immediately became the court of appeals for Gazit's order, with settlers—including Katzover, the new groom—lobbying ministers and Knesset members. Allon, in Katzover's telling, promised them the order would be rescinded, and that they would get permission to open businesses. Reporters poured into Hebron. One of the Kiosk Three, a young woman named Hannah Meir, proclaimed, "Our settlement here is a supreme imperative that takes precedence even over orders and decisions of the government." That day the government decided only to give the threesome a week's extension. By bizarre coincidence, the settlers were again helped by a death, this time that of Moshe Dayan's father.[95] The defense minister was in mourning, and his colleagues politely awaited his return.

In the meantime, four political parties demanded a Knesset debate. From the podium, Eshkol sounded resolute. "The settlers entered the place [Hebron] as visitors and presented all of us with a fait accompli. . . . Turning that behavior into a system . . . will undermine the authority of the military government," if not of the state itself, he said. "No Israeli citizen who cares about national security can agree to be the party to such a thing."[96]

When Dayan returned to work, he met with a delegation of Hebron settlers. They, too, framed the issue as the rule of law—from the opposite direction. The group had held a general meeting, Levinger said, and resolved that there were "matters in which we think that we are not permitted to be subject to the laws of the military government." Among the "traditional Jewish laws" they cited as higher authority was the Law of Return—Israeli legislation that granted every Jew the right of repatriation to the State of Israel. In their reading, that became a principle entitling Jews to return to the entire Land of Israel, and to any place in the land they chose.[97]

Allon again acted as the settlers' patron when the cabinet finally debated Gazit's order. "I don't want to institute a system of exiling a Jew from his place of residence, even if he lives there under a permit from the military government," Allon argued. "Just as I would not be exiled from Ginossar, a Jew should not be exiled from Hebron."

"They're living in an area under military government, and they must have permits!" objected another Labor minister.

"They live there for security purposes," Allon answered, giving the wildcat settlement a role in national defense.[98]

The cabinet session again ended without a resolution. In Hebron, the settlers chose tactical retreat. "In a general meeting . . . we reached the conclusion that we must not break the law in dedication to our cause," said a note they sent to Dayan, "and we commit ourselves to obeying the military government's laws and orders in their entirety."[99] Dayan recommended renewing the settlers' permits to live in Hebron.[100] The following Sunday morning, August 25, the cabinet ratified that decision—and set up a committee on settlement in Hebron.[101] In practice, the committee's mandate was to choose a location for a Jewish neighborhood, a matter that Eshkol handled personally. Before the ministerial panel met, he had a report in hand from three top officials whom he had assigned to find possible locations.[102]

Allon kept his promise to help the settlers set up businesses inside Hebron. It was with his help, according to Katzover, that they were eventually able to lease a building owned by the Jordanian government, which under occupation rules was now controlled by an Israeli agency.[103]

Levinger and his followers won the skirmish and the battle—or so it appeared. In fact, Eshkol, Dayan, and other policymakers were drifting toward accepting Allon's proposal for planting an Israeli quarter on the edge of Hebron even before the strange street theater of the kiosk affair. For Levinger, though, the affair could only prove that confrontation and defiance worked wonders. For the Israeli public, it was evidence that the government was unwilling to enforce the law against those who broke it in the name of nationalism.

Eshkol's behavior, given his strong words in the Knesset and his warnings that Israel could not annex the West Bank's Arabs, seems particularly contradictory. An explanation can be found in his office file of outgoing mail, amid countless pro forma telegrams to couples who had invited the prime minister and his wife to their weddings. The telegram sent the day before the kiosk affair to "Katzover, Hebron settlers,

Hebron," is unusual; it is written in lyric language borrowed from Jewish liturgy:

BLESSED BE HE WHO HAS KEPT US ALIVE AND PRESERVED US
TO HEAR THE VOICE OF JOY AND HAPPINESS IN THE HILLS OF
JUDEA[104]

The concluding blessing recited in a Jewish wedding, looking forward to final redemption, asks God to let "the voice of joy and happiness, of bridegroom and bride be heard speedily . . . in the hills of Judea." The fact that Eshkol wrote, or signed, that telegram does not mean he had signed on to Levinger's messianic theology. Nor does it mean he was insincere when he told the Knesset that the government must assert its authority. It does suggest that the people defying him conjured up wild feelings of history and glory, that human beings are consistently inconsistent, and that Eshkol wore his oversized inconsistencies as a badge of honor.

In allowing settlement at Hebron, Israel's leaders were swayed by ancient and recent history—by the biblical power of the city's name and by their consistent impulse to return to places from which Jews had been pushed out in their own memory. More than deciding on settlement, the government drifted into permitting it. Doing so contradicted the efforts of the same months to negotiate with Jordan or to create limited self-rule in the West Bank. It defied the fears of territorial minimalists in the cabinet, and of Eshkol himself, about the dangers of annexation. It blatantly violated Dayan's declared intent of low-profile occupation. It resulted not from strategy, but from a lack of it.

More than anyone in the cabinet, Allon claimed to have a strategic concept, cleanly built out of analysis, goals, and means. In the weeks ahead, the ministerial panel decided to place the Jewish neighborhood on the east side of Hebron. Allon claimed this fit his plan: Israel would keep the strip of land from the Dead Sea all the way up to the edge of Hebron, but not the Arab city itself. But placing the settlement up against Hebron, and allowing settlers to open businesses in the city, would create an umbilical tie between the Jewish quarter and the Arab town. Though Allon tried to convince himself otherwise, within his own strategic calculus his actions in Hebron made no more sense than dividing by zero.[105]

Along with helping Levinger, Allon continued acting as patron to Hanan Porat and Moshe Moskovic, the leading advocates of settlement in the Etzion Bloc. Allon told Moskovic he was helping him in order to make up for the "failure of 1948"—the fall of the Etzion Bloc and Allon's inability to retake it, the youthful experience of falling short that haunted him in middle age. As soon as the kiosk affair was over, Allon sponsored cabinet approval for building a new settlement in the Etzion area. The center of the community would be a yeshivah. Until the new settlement was built, the yeshivah would be located at Kfar Etzion, creating what was then an unusual partnership of religious kibbutz and seminary.

The students would alternate between study and army service—just as Nahal soldiers alternated between farmwork and active duty. One such seminary had existed in Israel before 1967. After the war another was established in the Jewish Quarter of Jerusalem's Old City—Yeshivat Hakotel, the yeshivah of the Western Wall. Along with the institution in the Etzion Bloc, it created an unlikely synthesis: Yeshivot, dedicated to the ideal of the religious scholar, the quintessential "old Jew," would be used for creating settlements in places seen as the new frontier. For graduates of yeshivah high schools, caught between their rabbis' ideal of study and their youth movement's demand for pioneering, that synthesis was peculiarly attractive. "Why should you care whether they harvest tomatoes or study Torah?" Moskovic asked Allon, explaining this new version of Nahal. The theology of redemption through militant nationalism that would be taught in the new study halls was entirely outside Allon's concerns.[106]

"I WORSHIP MOSHE DAYAN. . . . I don't miss a public statement of his, a newspaper interview. I believe he's the man who can bring some sort of solution that will lead us to peace." So writes Yaakov Perry in his memoirs, putting the past in present tense as he describes his feelings in 1968. Emulating Dayan, Perry has made himself part of the social life of Nablus's upper crust, sometimes visiting nationalist poet Fadwa Tuqan, listening to her poems. His hosts all know he is a Shin Bet man. Dayan, he writes, stops to see Tuqan nearly every time he passes through town.

In September, Perry gets to meet his idol. His commander calls him, telling him to come alone at 7:30 the next Saturday morning to a junction at the edge of the West Bank. "You'll meet Moshe Dayan there and go with him wherever he wants," the voice on the phone says.

Dayan arrives at the set time, and knocks on the window of Perry's car. "Come meet my girlfriend," the defense minister says. They step over to Dayan's car, in which "sits a pretty blonde, who introduces herself as Rachel." The defense minister tells Perry to get in, and says, "I want to go to Iskaka." Perry blanches. Iskaka is a village of a few hundred people on the mountain ridge road between Nablus and Ramallah, in an area teeming with armed Palestinians. "Any trip to Iskaka without heavy military guard seems irresponsible," Perry writes, adding that Dayan is unarmed and that he himself has only his pistol. "What are we doing in Iskaka?" Perry asks.

"Excavations," Dayan answers.

Since it is Saturday, the day off from work in Israel, nearly everyone is home in Iskaka. Dayan tells Perry to get directions to the center of the village. Later Perry will learn that Dayan "has scouts searching the West Bank for archaeological sites, and they sent him to Iskaka." At the center of the village is a pit, an abandoned excavation. Dayan gets out, takes digging tools from the trunk, tells Perry, "Keep an eye on Rachel," and disappears into the pit. Villagers shout, "It's the *wazir*," the minister, and crowd around. Imagining how this can end, Perry takes Rachel's hand and leads her through the crowd into the dig. "I want to assume that they won't hurt a woman, or all of us together."

He finds Dayan digging slowly, carefully, as if the entire village were not watching. "Look at this!" Dayan says happily as he pulls pottery from the dust.

Perry watches, as if seeing himself in a surrealistic film, as villagers bring a stool for Rachel to sit on, then serve juice, coffee, and fruit. Without asking Dayan, Perry returns to the car and radios the Border Police. Minutes later Border Policeman pour into Iskaka. Perry urges them to stand back, stay polite, keep a watch.

In the pit, with his mistress watching, the minister of invisible occupation plunders antiquities.[107]

6

CHANGING OF THE GUARD

S top in London on your way home, said the message for Yigal Allon. "I love stopping in London," Allon would later describe his reaction, as if the point were to go to the theater or watch the changing of the guard at Buckingham Palace. In this case, though, his perpetual tone of excitement made sense: He would meet a king. And get to tell him about his plan, and perhaps prove that it could be the basis for peace.

In America, on his lecture tour that September of 1968, Allon had described the plan to McGeorge Bundy and to Henry Kissinger, Allon's old professor at Harvard, and both—according to Allon—praised it to the skies. He even presented it to President Johnson, who listened with absolute attention and did not reject it. Allon reminded Johnson about the Phantom warplanes that Israel needed, and that night, when Johnson spoke at a B'nai B'rith dinner, he sat Allon between himself and Lady Bird, and over the meal said, "I can tell you I've decided to approve the Phantom sale," though he waited a month to announce that publicly.[1]

In American records, the Allon-Johnson meeting—attended also by Yitzhak Rabin, now retired from the army and serving as Israel's ambassador in Washington—lasted sixteen minutes, was off the record, and took place on the recommendation of national security adviser

Walt Rostow, in order to give "one of the most influential Israeli leaders a firsthand picture of our reservations about current Israeli policy." The session included only a bare mention of the Allon Plan as something the visitor explained beforehand to Rostow, who urged Allon to base peace proposals on coexistence with Jordan, not on "topographical premises—a purely military boundary," a polite way of rejecting Allon's dearest axioms.[2]

The testimony gap is typical. A few weeks earlier, Assistant Secretary of State Joseph Sisco and George Ball, the U.S. representative to the U.N., toured the Middle East. A cable to Washington mentions in one sentence that Allon briefed them on his plan, and that Eban "stressed that this plan was not endorsed" by the Israeli government.[3] In Allon's telling, he was visiting Druse leaders in the Golan Heights when he received instructions via army radio link to fly by helicopter to Ginossar, his kibbutz, where he landed next to another Israeli army copter bearing Ball and Sisco, sent by Eshkol to hear about the plan. Over lunch, Sisco's compliments on Allon's ideas were "unrestrained," and Ball said, "It's an ingenious plan." Allon also told his guests that the Druse wanted Israel to annex the Golan Heights, and Sisco said that if that was what the residents wanted, there was no reason to say no. Afterward Allon wrote a memo to Eshkol proposing annexation, noting that Ball and Sisco "explicitly said they had no reservations about our settlements in the Golan Heights," but Eban managed to kill the idea as a diplomatic disaster.[4] Then again, the American cables also say nothing of lunch being at a wooden picnic table, as Sisco would recall many years later, or that "the first thing Allon did was ... put a bottle of bourbon on the table, and we each had a drink," a detail perhaps significant to the testimony gap. Nothing was said of the Golan, Sisco would insist, but Allon "made a tremendous impression ... he was a very engaging man."[5] People liked Yigal, and he was sure they liked his great idea.

Now, after all the delays, King Hussein wanted to meet secretly with senior Israelis who would present peace proposals. Labor's inner sanctum, the political committee, accepted Eshkol's suggestion that Eban and Allon raise Allon's plan as Allon's "own thoughts, his personal proposal," not as the government position.[6] The government did not actually have a position. If Hussein bought the idea, Eshkol would bring it to a cabinet vote.[7]

So Allon found himself on September 27, 1968, in a room in London with Eban, Yaacov Herzog, the thirty-two-year-old king of Jordan, and the king's even younger adviser Zaid al-Rifai, the son of a former Jordanian prime minister. Allon later described Rifai's job as being the tough guy in Hussein's good-cop, bad-cop routine, the one who posed hard questions and gave negative answers so that the elegant Anglified king could be relaxed and courtly. Eban, as elegant, said that if Hussein rejected the principles presented to him, Israel would be forced to seek an agreement with the Palestinians—an empty threat, as Hussein had shown by sabotaging the deal with Jabari. Eban's principles included a signed treaty, demilitarizing the West Bank, and Jerusalem remaining united under Israel, perhaps with a Jordanian-Muslim status for the Islamic holy sites. Then Allon, who by one account said this was the "happiest moment of his life," brought out the maps he carried with him of his plan, explaining that for defensive reasons Israel would have to annex part of the West Bank. Jordan had to take into account that it had lost the war, he said.

"Because of the war," interrupted Rifai, "we are now willing to agree to the June 4 lines, which we were unwilling to do before the war."

Surely, Hussein insisted, security depended on mutual trust, not topography, more graciously rejecting Allon's thinking. Allon and Eban asked to meet again, to keep trying. Two days later, after a call from Rifai, Herzog sat down again with the king's adviser. Rifai's purpose was to eliminate doubt. He brought a text of Jordan's own principles for peace, which stated that the king's ability to reach an agreement depended totally on being able to explain it to the Arab world. The most Jordan could accept in Jerusalem was Israel's right to Jewish holy places. Border changes would have to be mutual, a tit-for-tat trade of territory. The real security problem was Jordan's, which could not possibly protect the West Bank with Israeli bases and settlements there and with Jordanian areas tied to the East Bank via a corridor that Israel could cut. Allon's plan, the Jordanian paper said, was "wholly unacceptable."[8]

The dialogue mapped the gap, fifteen months after the war, between

Israel's most forthcoming, not-even-official offer and the stance of the Arab ruler most eager for an agreement. Rifai laid out what would be the conciliatory Arab position thenceforth: The June 1967 defeat meant that Arabs would have to do what they had refused to do from 1948 to 1967—accept Israel's existence within the original armistice lines. Allon and Eban's subtext was that after the threat of May 1967 and the joy of June, Israel could not return to the Green Line. It would keep what it saw as most essential militarily (the Jordan Rift) and emotionally (East Jerusalem, the Etzion Bloc). Compromise meant Israel was willing to split the conquered land. Each side, seeing itself as more threatened, thought it obvious that the other would have to accept its security demands. Allon had done a wonderful job of negotiating with an imagined Arab who understood Israel's needs. Hussein dickered as well with an imagined Jew. In London, facing real people, they failed.

Nonetheless, Allon's passion for his plan, and for Jordan as the partner who would accept it, only increased. Faced with evidence that his idea would not work, he redoubled his effort to show that it would. Allon later testified that his commitment to the "Jordanian option" solidified "after my first conversation with the king in London . . . when I felt that there was an address here for negotiations."[9] After the London meeting, Allon also launched a new push for settlement in the areas his plan marked as permanently Israeli—as if Israeli settlements in the Jordan Rift would convince his friend the king that he really had no choice but agree to the Allon Plan.[10]

Sporadically, contacts between Jordan and Israel continued, with no progress on peace. Hussein's demand that territorial changes be mutual did produce one innovation: the idea of giving Gaza to Jordan as payment for West Bank land. Allon would claim the proposal was his, and that it grew from recognition that the Palestinian refugees were not going to disappear from the Strip. His principle of giving up heavily populated Arab areas would have to be applied to Gaza—despite the government policy of keeping the Strip. According to Allon, he raised the proposal with Eshkol, who allowed him to float it in another meeting with Hussein—again, as his own thoughts, not as a government position.[11] Or perhaps the idea was originally American: Under Secretary of State Eugene Rostow suggested it to Eban over lunch in Washington in

October 1968—though a moment before, Rostow said that "Israelis should know that we considered [the] Allon Plan . . . a non-starter." Eban answered that if Jordan liked the idea of getting Gaza, it should suggest it to Israel.[12]

However the idea was born, the corollary for Allon was, once again, a need for settlements. To protect its southern flank, Allon reasoned, Israel would need a finger of territory separating Egypt and its army from Gaza. To mark out that buffer, it should start settlements at the southern end of the Gaza Strip and in the adjacent area of northeast Sinai, which Israel labeled the Rafiah Plain. Allon was enchanted by the king, but got nowhere negotiating. In the meantime, the Rafiah Plain showed up in his settlement proposals.[13]

THE EFFORTS to broker an Egyptian-Israeli accord were also frenetic and futile. Egypt fought with Israel on the Suez Canal line, and simultaneously offered non-belligerence in return for a full Israeli withdrawal. That fell far short of the direct negotiations and signed treaty that Israel demanded, Eban told Secretary of State Dean Rusk.[14]

Lyndon Johnson sent a letter to Eshkol—a rare gesture, whose meaning is *this matters*—leaning on him to resist pressure from those in his government "who find it easier to risk Israel's future on today's expanded boundaries than to reach out for real peace." To end on a softer note, Johnson added that he looked forward to Eshkol's next visit, planned for late November.[15] A follow-up message from State to Eban asked Israel to state clearly its position on withdrawal from the Sinai, and urged that the answer be willingness to pull back to the international boundary, with "special arrangements" for Gaza and Sharm al-Sheikh.[16] That was a code suggesting that some non-Israeli force would hold those spots—a solution Israel regularly dismissed, based on its experience with the U.N. pullout from Sinai in May 1967.

At least regarding Israel's position toward Egypt, deciding not to decide would no longer work. The cabinet met on October 31 at Eshkol's home. The prime minister was ailing, unable to reach his office; he had missed several previous cabinet sessions. The decision was to tell the United States that as part of a peace agreement, a secure border between Israel and Egypt requires changes in the former international border, including—as self-evident—retaining Gaza within the domain of Israel and continued Israeli control of Sharm al-Sheikh with territorial contiguity to Israel. . . . These conclusions of the government supersede the declaration of June 19, 1967.

The decision, as an official biography of Eshkol states, sealed "a steady process of cabinet members distancing themselves" from the original offer of a pullback to the international line in return for peace. Egypt and Syria had rejected that offer, and Israel's leaders had discovered that the trauma of 1956 was not repeating itself. The Labor-led government believed it could safely stay put until the Arab countries realized they would have to pay a higher price.[17]

The same day, army and Settlement Department representatives toured the Rafiah Plain to check the feasibility of the department's own ideas for settling northeast Sinai, an area that most certainly did not link Israel with Sharm al-Sheikh. Three spots that settlement planners had marked on their map for Israeli farm villages turned out to be "problematic, being occupied by Bedouin who claim rights" to the land.[18]

Eban and Ambassador Rabin delivered the cabinet's message to Rusk on Sunday, November 3.[19] Two days later, Richard Nixon defeated Johnson's vice president, Hubert Humphrey, in the presidential election, ensuring that not only Johnson but also his top officials would soon clean out their desks. Soon after, Rabin and Mordechai Hod, the commander of the Israel Air Force, met with Walt Rostow and NSC staffer Harold Saunders to wrap up the Phantom sale, in what Saunders described as "a highly spirited, heavily colloquial, amicable" conversation, apparently a diplomat's way of saying that the boys shouted, cursed, and enjoyed each other's company. Saunders's report has him and Rostow telling Rabin, "We've told you the U.S. position *ad nauseam*—you have to give the West Bank back, you have to give Hussein a role in Jerusalem, a 'Polish corridor' to Sharm al-Sheikh doesn't make sense. . . . If the Israelis aren't tired of hearing this, we'd be glad to say it again."[20] The Phantom deal went through anyway, showing that the Bundy Doctrine of not using arms supplies as a means of pressure still held. Eshkol, meanwhile, informed the White House he would have to cancel his visit "on advice of his doctors."²¹ The stage lights were fading, and not just on the Johnson era. The diplomacy of autumn served to show that the war's aftermath was not a "crisis" but a stalemate. Stalemate was the soil in which settlements grew.

WHAT A PERSON does on the Jewish New Year, says a traditional belief, is an omen for the coming year. If so, Rosh Hashanah, September 23, 1968, did not promise calm in Hebron, especially not at the Tomb of the Patriarchs, also known as the Ibrahimi Mosque.

Under an agreement between Dayan and the sheikh of the mosque, Jews were allowed to visit, except at times of Muslim prayer, including midday.²² Technically, the agreement said nothing about Jewish prayer, but in practice Jews did worship at the tomb during the allowed visiting hours. Before their first Rosh Hashanah in Hebron, the settlers asked permission from the military government to conduct the long services of that day, and the all-day worship of Yom Kippur soon after, at the tomb.²³ Their attraction to the building was a mix of spiritual and proprietary, like their attraction to Hebron. "We had . . . become visitors in our holy site," Chaim Simons, a British-born immigrant who had joined the settlement in the military government courtyard, later recalled. The Arabs "had unlimited access. . . . They had the sole manager, the sole keys."²⁴ It was not enough to *be* in sacred space, one had to own it—the impulse behind conflicts over holy places everywhere. To own a place where God is thought to be palpably present inspires a feeling perilously close to owning God.

The group got no answer from the military government and, true to form, stayed in the tomb on Rosh Hashanah through midday, violating the rules. A score of prominent Hebronites, including Mayor Jabari and the city's top clerics, sent a telegram that day to the military governor, complaining that "the Israeli occupation authority in Hebron committed an offense against the pure Ibrahimi Mosque, by giving permission to a group of Jews to pray within the pure mosque . . . and it was therefore not possible for Muslims to pray at noon in the blessed mosque." The site was strictly Islamic, they asserted, "and no one but Muslims may worship there." They thereby denied any Jewish connection to the place, a formula perfectly pitched to rally secular Israelis to the settlers' side. The answer—officially from the army commander in Hebron, but written by the justice minister and approved by Eshkol—criticized the telegram's "sharp and unjustified" language and described the holy site as "the eternal resting place, according to ancient belief and tradition . . . of the fathers and mothers of the Jewish people." The settlers got permission to spend all of Yom Kippur in the tomb, yet another success for Levinger's methods.[25]

Just after Yom Kippur comes the week-long Jewish festival of Sukkot, when many Israelis exploit the last blue days of the dry season for outings. On the holiday's third day, October 9, at four in the afternoon, 4,000 Israeli and foreign tourists filled the square in front of the tomb-mosque, waiting their turn to enter. Arab peddlers, many of them children, offered combs, dolls, and kaffiyehs for sale. From the crowd, a grenade sailed through the air, landing on the top step of the stairs to the entrance. Then came the roar and screaming and blood and running, the wounded lying on the steps, mothers shouting wildly for children, the peddlers fleeing, the sirens and thumping of helicopter blades. Forty-seven people, almost all Israelis and foreigners, were wounded. Some young men from among the visitors began beating up Arabs. Shop shutters began slamming closed.

The day after next, Israeli papers reported the arrest of an eleventh-grade Hebron boy suspected of throwing the grenade, along with other members of the cell that had sent him and that had carried out previous attacks in Jerusalem and Tel Aviv. The holiday crowd may merely have been a convenient target. Then again, the attackers may have seen the time and place as having added value, as a statement about ownership.[26]

Another letter came to the West Bank military commander in November, this one signed by the Hebron Settlers Secretariat. "Given that we are residents of Hebron and regularly walk in the city and to the Tomb of the Patriarchs," it said, "we hereby permit ourselves to express our opinion that the indulgence toward the Arabs, with all their acts of terror perpetrated here . . . endangers our residents and visitors." The settlers "expected and believed" that the army would reconsider its "lenient" policies, since "enough Jewish blood has already been spilled in Hebron."[27] The subtext was hierarchy: The army stood a notch below the town's rightful heirs; its job was to protect them by showing Arab "local residents" where power lay. Another letter, two weeks after, demanded quicker government action on establishing a Jewish neighborhood.[28]

Much more quietly, another Allon-sponsored settlement project turned from plan to fact. In November, two dozen or so young men moved into the youth hostel at Kfar Etzion to become the founding class at the Har Etzion *hesder* yeshivah—*hesder*, "arrangement," referring to the agreement to alternate between religious study and army service.

To head the institution, Etzion Bloc activists Hanan Porat and Moshe Moskovic recruited Yehudah Amital, a Transylvanian-born scholar who had arrived in Palestine in 1944 at the age of nineteen straight from a Nazi labor camp, the sole survivor in his family. Besides being a charismatic believer in the theology that made Zionism proof of impending redemption, Amital had a résumé that included army service in 1948, setting him apart from the usual cloistered yeshivah dean. The new students were told to bring plenty of blankets with them to the windy hilltop kibbutz, along with the volume of Talmud they would be studying and the biblical text of Joshua, Judges, Samuel, and Kings with rabbinic commentaries, those being the books recounting the Israelites' conquest of the land and the rise of the House of David. Porat would give lessons, as would Yoel Bin-Nun, the Merkaz Harav student who had quoted Avraham Yitzhak Hacohen Kook on war as part of God's plan and whose comments remained on the cutting-room floor of *Soldiers' Talk*.[29]

In the Golan Heights stood at least eight Israeli settlements by that fall, according to government documents, which included the Nahal outpost in the old demilitarized zone next to Banias in the count, and more were in the pipeline. The kibbutz in Quneitrah was no longer listed as Nahal, even in official papers.[30] Even the minimalist finance minister Pinhas Sapir supported settlement in the land taken from Syria.[31] Sapir's concern was over adding large numbers of Arabs to Israel's population, and the Heights did not present that problem. Only in the left-wing Mapam did debate burn about settling in the area, though the party's "right" faction—more or less the same faction that wanted to run for Knesset on a joint ticket with Labor—favored putting kibbutzim there.

Still, Merom Golan secretary Yehudah Harel admitted in his kibbutz newsletter, "A year has passed . . . and settlement activity is not taking place on the scale we see as essential." The dry words were his eulogy for the hope that he had held for a kibbutz renaissance, for hundreds of communes springing up in "liberated" land. No revival had swept the young generation.[32]

A third Nahal outpost, named Argaman, was established in the Jordan Rift nearly midway between the first two—Kalyah near the Dead Sea, and Meholah at the Rift's north end. The soldier-settlers arrived in November and quickly planted ten acres of peppers to take advantage of the winter sun. Symbolically, the Argaman pepper field and the settlers' tents suggested Israeli intent to claim the whole desert valley, though there was no declared policy of doing so. Dayan had once opposed settling the center of the rift, a move too visibly showing West Bank Arabs they were being cut off from the East Bank. He had since dropped his objections.[33]

"THE FUNDAMENTAL ASSUMPTION is that no peace with the king of Jordan is in sight, and we should see our presence in the territories as permanent," Dayan wrote in October, in a memo to fellow ministers. Diplomatic stalemate was a golden opportunity to push his own vision of the West Bank's future. "We must consolidate our hold so that over time we will succeed in 'digesting' Judea and Samaria and merging them with 'little' Israel."

He acknowledged that Israel could not come close to creating a Jewish majority in occupied land. But he again suggested building Israeli towns along the mountain ridge, near the major Arab cities of Hebron, Ramallah, Nablus, and Jenin—to show that Israel was staying, and to "dismember the territorial contiguity" of the West Bank and "enable regional interconnections between [each] Arab and Israeli community." What frightened Dayan was not ruling a large Arab population, but allowing the West Bank to remain a united Arab area that could demand independence.

He proposed abandoning the ideal of agricultural settlement, because with towns, less land would suffice for more people, and because construction and industry in the Israeli communities would provide jobs for local Arabs, "on condition that they continue to live in their existing communities." The towns would be built next to army bases, on land expropriated from Arab owners, "with it said that the step is necessary for military purposes"—a legal justification more acceptable under the laws of occupation.

"Settling Israelis in occupied territory contravenes, as is known, international conventions, but there is nothing essentially new in that," Dayan wrote, acknowledging and dismissing the problem. The legal challenge that would have to be solved, he said, was the status of the settlers—would they be subject to the Jordanian laws still in effect in the West Bank, or to Israeli law?[34] Dayan clearly did not like the first option; the subtext is that he sought extraterritorial status for settlers. He appears to have been the first Israeli politician to raise this issue, and not by accident. Allon sought to annex the areas he marked for settlement. Dayan's question underlined that he wanted the opposite. "Digesting" the West Bank meant that Israel would settle it, divide it so that it could not gain independence, employ its people as workers. Israelis living there would have the same legal status as those living in "metropolitan" Israel. Arabs would be subjects. Dayan enthusiastically sought to invest Israeli government funds on hospitals, waterworks, power lines, and other projects to improve Arabs' lives.[35] But they would not be citizens; they would not even be allowed to live in Israeli cities in the West Bank. Dayan wanted the West Bank as a benevolently run colony, one so close to home you could go there for lunch (or to steal antiquities) and be home for dinner.

While his settlement plan was marked "Secret," Dayan gave speeches promoting "an effort to bind the two economies"—of Israel and the West Bank—"so that it will be difficult to separate them again."[36] His most prominent opponent was Finance Minister Sapir, Mapai's master of backroom political and economic dealing, a gruff, bearlike man, often vulgar, strangely vulnerable. In the fall of 1968, Sapir was temporarily serving as the Labor Party secretary-general, after the apparently exhausted Golda Meir gave up the position. His unwritten mandate was to keep the fragile new party together—and to maintain the dominance of the Mapai machine, keeping both Dayan's wing and Allon's from taking over. That gave him even more reason to resist Dayan's program which, he argued, would add so many Arabs to Israel it would cease being a Jewish state. At the end of October, he spoke to an audience of seventy people in a Beersheba hall with seating for 1,200. Several days later Dayan packed the same hall, with 2,000 or more people standing outside to listen to his speech from loudspeakers. Dayan called for linking Beersheba economically with Hebron and Gaza, and attacked "party secretaries who know how to organize elections" but did not understand the Jewish tie to Hebron.[17]

In early December, when Eshkol was finally feeling well enough to take part, the cabinet devoted three sessions to Dayan's ideas and the future of the West Bank. Dayan said his proposed cities and the roads linking them to Israel would stay Israeli "till the end of all generations." The rest of the land could conceivably, in some indefinite future, be turned over to Jordan, he said, though the economic ties would remain. Explaining why Israel should spend money on social services for the territories, he recalled a visit to the West African country of Togo. People still had good memories there of German colonial rule before World War I, he said; the Germans "left orchards and culture." Israel, he argued, should follow the example of benevolent colonialism.

"I'm going to explode," Sapir interrupted, saying he cared more about poverty inside Israel than "the Bedouin woman in the Sinai you describe so emotionally," and insisting that Dayan's "integration" meant annexation.[18] Sapir had more support in the cabinet than in Beersheba, and Dayan's proposals were rejected. "I think there is much more diplomatic and defensive logic to the program that Minister Allon submitted," said one cabinet minimalist.[19] The debate sparked by Dayan defined Allon as a moderate. The Allon Plan was the "absolute minimum" to which most cabinet members would agree, an Eshkol aide told an American embassy staffer, though he added that officially adopting it would likely push Dayan, the rightist leader Menachem Begin, and three other ministers to resign.[40]

Yet even as Sapir objected to creating an economy of Arab "hewers of wood and drawers of water" and white-collar Jews, he did not try to block the powerful pressures for employing West Bank Arabs in Israel.[41]

Dayan's "integration" plan did not die. It remained as a blueprint of what would happen, bit by bit, in the absence of annexation or withdrawal.

APPEARING IN THE MIDST of the Dayan-Sapir spat, Labor politician Arie Eliav's articles in his party's newspaper in November 1968 may not have received proper attention at the time—like a historical landmark that a family drives right past while arguing where it is going.

"We must see the existence of the Palestinian people as a fact," Eliav asserted. It could be, he admitted, that Zionism's struggle with Arab nationalism had accidently begat the Palestinian nation, but the parentage was irrelevant. Israel needed to declare that "we will never repress the rights of the Palestinians to national self-determination, and we are willing to help them establish a state."[42]

Eliav was forty-seven, with a hint of a Russian accent from the country he left as a child, and a hint of pudgy Russian cheeks. Before independence he had served in the British army, then captained an illegal immigration boat running the British blockade on Palestine. After a stint of intelligence work and another as an Israeli naval officer, he became Levi Eshkol's assistant at the Settlement Department, build-ing farm villages and towns for Jewish refugees. It was a standard heroic CV. By the time of the 1967 war, he was deputy industry minister, a rising Mapai man. His next step was not standard: He asked Eshkol for six months off. His postwar euphoria had given way to hungry curiosity. He spent the months in Gaza and the West Bank, listening to refugees, engineers, lawyers, leaders, and a host of others late into the nights.

Afterward he returned to Eshkol. There is a Palestinian nation, he told his father figure. It was a pragmatic evaluation, not an ideology but a report, followed by a recommendation for what to do. Eliav wanted a new job, building towns and industry for the Palestinian refugees, immediately, where they were, "before the residents of the territories begin to flood our fields and cities with cheap labor." Eliav was an upbeat, technocratic rewrite of the bleak, dovish novelist Amos Oz.

Eshkol, tired and sick, sent him to talk to Golda Meir and Moshe

Dayan. Meir "looked at me with angry eyes: 'What Palestinian people? . . . What are you talking about?'" Eliav recalled. Dayan was uninterested in Eliav's plans for refugees, and when "tens of thousands of workers from the territories began arriving in Israel's fields and on its construction scaffolds, I understood why," Eliav would recall.

Eshkol appointed Eliav to be Allon's deputy in the new ministry for immigration. The ministry was like the airstrips built by cargo cults in Pacific islands, in the faith that clearing the land would bring planes laden with gifts. If the bureaucracy were built, the great wave of Jews would arrive from the Soviet Union and America, fulfilling the tragically frustrated dreams of the 1930s and solving the demographic problem. In office conversations, Allon showed Eliav his maps of what he wanted to settle and annex—a strip of land along the Jordan, and a strip at Rafiah and another stretching to Sharm al-Sheikh. "Why do you need all those Danzigs?" Eliav asked him.

Finally, Eliav wrote his ideas in the party newspaper. Along with recognizing Palestinian peoplehood, he declared allegiance to the old pragmatic Mapai stance on land: Until June 1967, Israel insisted it was able to realize its goals within the armistice lines. To prove it had spoken truth, it now needed to declare it was holding "the territories"—meaning all of them—only until peace.

Eliav's radicalism had limits. He believed Israel should keep East Jerusalem. His proposed Palestinian state was Jordan, including the East and West Banks; the Palestinians could decide whether they wanted to employ the king. He suggested that after peace, with Arab agreement, Jewish settlement "east and west of Jordan" might be possible, but those Jews would have to be Palestinian citizens, the mirror image of Israeli Arabs. The suggestion testifies to the hold that the settlement ethos had on him as well. He was not actually a radical; he was a prewar Mapai man.

Eliav had the articles printed as a pamphlet, mailed out to party leaders. He loved his ideas, and he was also a politician with ambition, and this was his calling card. His ambitions were probably helped by the fact that some who received the pamphlet—like Golda Meir—did not read it.[43]

* * *

FINANCE MINISTER SAPIR GOT TOGETHER that winter with a young Israeli friend named Yossi Sarid in Manhattan. Sarid had spent a year as Mapai's spokesman leading up to the 1965 election. He had been twenty-four at the time. Sapir, nearly sixty, the backroom man, had befriended the precocious spinmeister. After the election Sarid left for New York, to get a master's degree in political science at the New School for Social Research. When Sapir came through town, Sarid met him at the barbershop of his Midtown hotel, where the older man stopped for a daily shave of his face and pate.

First Sapir checked to make sure that the barber did not know Hebrew. Then he told his news: Eshkol was a goner. He did not have much longer.

Sarid asked if an heir had been picked.

"Golda," Sapir answered.

The young man was incredulous.[44] This was a whole different course in politics. The contenders of whom everyone spoke were Dayan and Allon. If Mapai wanted to keep the leadership for itself there was Abba Eban, the most senior Mapai minister after Eshkol, or Sapir himself, master of the party-run economy, "an artist of numbers" and of patronage, with the little black notebook in his pocket in which he recorded every interesting figure he heard. Golda Meir was seventy years old, the ex-labor minister, ex-foreign minister, ex-party secretary, in short, *ex*. Nor had years of intrigues made her popular. "She was known in her party as 'a woman of great loves and great hates.' One couldn't always notice the loves, but the hates were so strong she couldn't hide them if she wanted to," another politician said.[45]

Sapir, though, wanted to stop Dayan, the bandit prince who had rebelled against Mapai before the last election, then forced his way back in with the declared goal of taking over. Allon was likable, but if he were chosen, Dayan would leave Labor—and with his war charisma, probably defeat it in the next election, in the fall of 1969. Eban's erudite urbanity aroused suspicion in the party. As for himself, Sapir simply did not want the prime minister's responsibility for ultimate decisions.

Instead he picked Meir, the last member of the state-founding generation in the Mapai leadership, who had worked with him and Eshkol to depose Ben-Gurion. Sapir knew she was a hawk, had been one all the way back to the 1930s when she opposed the Peel Commission proposal to partition Palestine between Jews and Arabs. Though she now acknowledged the demographic problem, she lacked Sapir's own horror that keeping the occupied territories would bring disaster on Israel. But because she was a hawk, Dayan and Allon would accept her. Sapir told Eban that Golda was sick, and would only rule for a year. In the fall he had visited her at a Swiss sanatorium and told her the job was hers.[46] Sapir's choice did not jibe with his beliefs or his fears for the country. Its logic was loyalty to the party and old comrades, and perhaps his own hesitation before the peak.

A photograph from mid-January 1969 shows Meir, with what might be a smile, on a dais next to Eshkol and the wildly white-bearded Yitzhak Tabenkin of the United Kibbutz and Mapam leader Ya'akov Hazan, whose left-wing party was signing an alliance with Labor. As "the Alignment," they would run one electoral ticket and act as a partnership in parliament. The agreement was Meir's baby. It brought all the old Labor Zionist parties together, ending the socialist schisms, and gave the alliance 63 seats in the 120-member Knesset, the first time an Israeli party ever had an absolute majority. It also completed the process of creating a ruling party that stood for every possible policy and no policy on the country's most fateful issue, the future of the territories.[47]

"Eshkol will head the Labor Party list and *will continue as prime minister*," the labor attaché at the American embassy wrote to Washington a few days later, underlining the last words as she passed on the intelligence she gained by having her old friend Golda over for dinner. "The tone of her remarks suggested that any other possibility was too ridiculous even to discuss." Eshkol's health was "perfectly okay," she quoted Meir as saying, so the attaché concluded that his announced illnesses "are really diplomatic ones." As for Meir herself, she said she did not want to run for Knesset again, "*but* she had no choice—the Party leadership insisted." Asked about Israel's image problems, Meir said she had decided "other people just didn't like Jews except when they could pity them, and

Israel must pursue her policies without constantly wanting to be 'liked.' "[48] That comment, at least, appears to have been her real feeling.

IT WAS CLOSE to being the last decision Eshkol shepherded through. On January 26, the cabinet received a set of settlement proposals on the lines Allon was pushing—more outposts in the Jordan Rift and the Golan, and four in the Rafiah Plain of northeast Sinai. The discussion, notes historian Reuven Pedatzur, dealt not with peace and the future of the land, but with priorities: which places to settle first. Only the two dovish Mapam ministers tried, ritually and unsuccessfully, to block settlement in the Rift and the Rafiah Plain.

Dayan's preference was for Rafiah. He emphatically pushed aside his usual romantic feelings for the Bedouin and their timeless agriculture. "I want to say that first off, we've got to get the Bedouin out of that area, to take a bulldozer and uproot the almond groves and then reach a deal on the price," he said. Alluding to an outbreak of Palestinian attacks in the Gaza Strip, he added, "If we decide it's for military purposes, we have to say, 'We're putting up a military position.' We have to plow the ground, uproot the orchards, and help them find a place elsewhere. . . . I see the time as ripe for it, as long as there's terror there, grenades being thrown and land mines planted, and the Bedouin are involved."

Dayan's idea was not ratified. The cabinet made Rafiah its third priority, and asked for staff opinions on how to settle in the area, given the Bedouin presence.

But the ministers did approve settlement in all three areas. The decision did not use the term "Allon Plan." But Allon was already speaking of government actions in the occupied territories as implementing the "operative part" of his program, and later described the January 26 decision in the same way. So did press leaks at the time. The decision passed, Allon said, because hard-liners such as Menachem Begin backed settlement even if they wanted to keep more land than he did. In this case, Allon's spin appears close to accurate. The cabinet was not moving as quickly as he wanted, but it was approving settlements that staked a claim to the areas he said should remain Israeli.[49]

Eshkol had never passed a cabinet resolution on the West Bank's future. But he had presented the Allon Plan to King Hussein as a peace proposal. His message to the United States via his aide was that it was his government's most forthcoming offer. Now he had won approval for it as a settlement map. It was the closest thing to a policy that the postwar government had produced.

Perhaps that is why Eshkol virtually described Allon's map, without mentioning his name, when *Newsweek* journalists Arnaud de Borchgrave and Michael Elkins spent two hours in his office interviewing him on February 3. Israel would have to control Sharm al-Sheikh, and would never give up the Golan or Jerusalem, he said. "We don't want any part of the settled area of the West Bank—Nablus, Jenin and so on . . . our army shall be stationed only on the strip" along the Jordan.[50]

An hour after the interview, Eshkol had a heart attack. A week later, when the interview appeared and was quoted in Hebrew papers, he was at home, restricted to bed. Abroad, his words sounded intransigent. In Washington, the National Security Council's Harold Saunders wrote to his new boss, national security adviser Henry Kissinger, that Eshkol was "naturally taking a hard line publicly"—an optimistic evaluation allowing that the prime minister might be more flexible in real negotiations.[51] At home, a storm broke over Eshkol's declaration that Israel would give up part of the West Bank. Menachem Begin's Gahal alliance threatened to quit the unity government, and another right-wing party submitted a motion of no confidence. An hour before the Knesset convened the next day, Allon phoned *Newsweek*'s Elkins. He explained that Eshkol had assigned him to deny the story publicly and had asked that he call the newsman in advance to apologize. "He is too embarrassed to call you himself," Allon said. "He hopes you'll understand." In the Knesset, Allon said the offending sentence was not in the text of the interview that the magazine sent the prime minister's office for approval. Perhaps it was the reporters' impression from background comments.[52]

Allon's job that day was a peculiar indignity: He had to deny, in Eshkol's name, that the prime minister had endorsed his cherished plan as Israel's position. To have a government, Eshkol could not have a position.

Eshkol did not leave his house. According to Meron Medzini's scholarly Hebrew biography of Meir, "Friends recounted that . . . he muttered to himself in juicy Yiddish about the *klafte* [bitch] that was sitting waiting for him to die."[53] He said he wanted to be buried at Deganiah Bet, his kibbutz. He was a settlement man; he wanted to go home.

YEHIEL ADMONI of the Settlement Department and Agriculture Minister Haim Gvati left Jerusalem early in the morning, driving east, downhill into the desert. By eight o'clock they were walking through the fields at Kalyah, the Nahal settlement near the northern tip of the Dead Sea—a few acres planted in corn and winter tomatoes, and stretches of soil still too salty to grow anything unless washed with copious, expensive quantities of water. In the midst of business talk, someone brought word: Eshkol was dead of a heart attack. Gvati rushed back to Jerusalem, to the prime minister's house. It was February 26, 1969.[54]

Arie Eliav was sitting in Pinhas Sapir's office in Tel Aviv when they heard. They also drove up to the capital. At the residence, each new arrival ascended to the second floor, looked at Eshkol, and came down to the living room, which filled with dozens of people engaged in whispered argument—one more debate, but without Eshkol there to argue both sides—on whether to bury him at the national cemetery on Mount Herzl in Jerusalem or at his kibbutz on the shore of Lake Kinneret, the Sea of Galilee. Golda Meir arrived, paid her respects to the deceased, came downstairs, sat on a couch, and lit a cigarette. And then everyone—Allon, Dayan, Sapir, Begin—began sitting on either side of her, explaining the issue. She was the arbiter. "This is the prime minister," Eliav thought. The funeral, Meir ruled, would be in Jerusalem.[55]

Eshkol had ruled for a year and a half after the war. The fruits of victory were an empire he had not sought, and a political realignment that left him wounded. He did not have a ready strategic or ideological meaning to assign to the conquests. Around him were men—from the poet Alterman and kibbutz ideologue Tabenkin with their grandiose visions of the Whole Land, to Allon, to the dovish Eliav—aflame with ideas. Eshkol listened to everyone, and listened to himself argue the advantages of land and the impossibility of ruling another people.

But it is not true that he was simply dragged by events, or that the settlement enterprise was imposed on him. He spearheaded the decisions to annex East Jerusalem and build Jewish neighborhoods there. By the fall of 1967, he fell back on his personal experience in settlement as a response to the new situation. He created facts on the ground, and sometimes imposed faits accomplis on ministers in order to do so.

Wanting to improve Israel's defenses and worrying about demography, he essentially adopted the Allon Plan, without formal approval. Like Allon, he bent the logic to fit his feelings about Kfar Etzion and Hebron. In Admoni's insider description, Eshkol virtually returned to his role as Settlement Department chief. A shortage of settlers, Admoni writes, slowed the effort, as did technical problems, but the lack of an articulated settlement policy was not an impediment.[56] By Eshkol's death, there were ten settlements in the Golan, three in the Jordan Rift, along with Kfar Etzion and the Hebron settlement south of Jerusalem, and plans to settle in the Rafiah area.[57] The first Israeli neighborhood in East Jerusalem was reaching completion, and would be named for him.

By the time of Eshkol's death, Israel had dropped its initial willingness to withdraw to the international borders with Syria and Egypt. Diplomacy had reached a deadlock. Within the land under Israeli rule, the Green Line had been erased from the map, and was being blurred in daily life. Israel was still engaged in a conflict with its neighbors, a conflict between states. Inadvertently, though, an older conflict between two ethnic groups inside one land had been brought back from history, and with it the pre-state tactic of settlement as a way of determining future boundaries.

What must be said for Eshkol is that his willingness to weigh every idea projected pragmatism and compromise. Though he used Allon's approach, he treated it as the least-worst choice, not a new faith, and moved more slowly than Allon wished. Even with his body failing, Eshkol's mind remained open. Shortly before his death, he sent a note to Abba Eban and Yisrael Galili. He had received a letter, he said, from someone suggesting that Israel, as if with a magic wand, was creating a Palestinian people, a new enemy. What, he asked, did they think of this?[58] It was typical that he asked two people who could not bear each other, at nearly opposite poles of his party, for their views. Yet much as

Eshkol debated himself, he saw the government's indecision as a problem, not a long-term position. "We don't know so clearly what we actually want," was a complaint. His openness would be missed, and even his uncertainty.

BY COINCIDENCE, the big gregarious man from Deganiah left the stage five weeks after the big gregarious man from Texas left power. One of Eshkol's last acts was to send a letter to Lyndon Johnson's successor, Richard Nixon. Despite Eshkol's mistrust of the new American president and Eban's description of Nixon as picking appointees "even less impressive than himself,"[59] the letter was perfectly pitched for Nixon and his key foreign policy adviser, Henry Kissinger.

Preventing a new Mideast war, Eshkol's letter said, depended on keeping Israel strong enough to deter the Arabs, but also on making sure the Soviet Union knew that to "encourage the Arab states [toward war] . . . would gravely prejudice its relationship with the United States." The aim of Soviet diplomatic proposals was to "weaken and undermine Israel and thereby discredit America." Peace with Egypt was unlikely because "Nasser is the slave of rigid anti-Israel ideologies and of Soviet global strategy."[60]

In short, the Mideast was one corner of the Soviet-American arena and Cairo was a Soviet pawn. Just so, Nixon must have said. In his June 1967 visit to Israel, he had described the war in those terms. The secretive, suspicious man who had moved into the White House preferred to fit foreign affairs together into a grand pattern. Behind disparate events lay the same adversary. He and Kissinger shared the "general sense that internal or external power always flowed from the top," writes William Bundy in his history of Nixon's foreign policy. They focused on communism and underestimated nationalism. The Soviet Union could and did control its clients. The ultimate target of all policy was Moscow, to which the United States must demonstrate toughness, with which it must negotiate, to which it must deny victories.[61]

There were other people whom Nixon distrusted, though, including the bureaucrats of the State Department. Kissinger would recall Nixon's initial assessment this way: They "had no loyalty to him; the Foreign Service had disdained him as vice president and ignored him the moment he was out of office," comments demonstrating just how personal the political can be.[62] Nixon and Kissinger would handle the big issues. William Rogers, Nixon's secretary of state, a lawyer lacking foreign affairs experience, would get the rest. Then again, Nixon had to give something to Rogers, an old friend. "The areas he did not mind consigning were those where success seemed elusive . . . or those where the risks of domestic reaction were high. The Middle East met both of Nixon's criteria," writes Kissinger in his memoirs. Nixon also feared that Kissinger's "Jewish origins" would bias him toward Israel, and wanted him to steer clear of the region.[63]

Giving Rogers responsibility for the Middle East meant demoting it, postponing it. That suited Kissinger, who put the Arab-Israeli problem in the category of conflicts where "the opposing positions are simply irreconcilable." Besides, he preferred to wait on Middle East diplomatic efforts until "those who would benefit from it would be America's friends, not Soviet clients." If diplomacy stalled and Israel remained strong, eventually the Arabs would give up on Moscow and turn to Washington.[64] This was a long step beyond the Bundy Doctrine: On the White House chessboard, letting Israel stay put was a gambit for hurting the Soviets. Kissinger's writings make no mention of the possibility that on the ground, in the land held by Israel, conditions might change in the meantime.

GOLDA MEIR WAS just short of seventy-one years old when she became prime minister of Israel. Born in czarist Russia, she spent her early years in Kiev in Ukraine and Pinsk in White Russia, in the brutal poverty typical of Jewish life in Eastern Europe. Her childhood, according to her biographer Medzini, provided virtually no love or appreciation; constant family squabbling taught her to hate argument and seek compromises. Her memories included hiding in an upstairs room when rumors of a pogrom spread in Pinsk, an experience that scarred her with fear, and her older sister's participation in an illegal Zionist group, which taught her the sanctity of secrecy.

Before she turned eight, her family left for America, part of a flood of Jewish emigration. As a teenager in Milwaukee, she joined a left-wing Zionist group. At the age of twenty-two, she became a much more non-conformist emigrant, an American Jew moving to Palestine, pulling along her non-Zionist, book- and theater-loving husband, Morris Meyerson. Soon after, they joined Merhaviah, a kibbutz in the Jezreel Valley of northern Palestine.

Her political career was born when she represented the commune at a kibbutz movement convention at Deganiah, the first kibbutz. There she met Labor Zionist leaders including Levi Eshkol and David Remez, head of the recently founded Jewish labor union, the Histadrut, who became her patron and longtime lover, though that would later make him the jealous rival of Zalman Shazar, another prominent Labor Zionist. She eventually left both Merhaviah and Morris Meyerson as her movement career progressed. One of her early appointments, at Remez's initiative, was as co-secretary of a Histadrut body, the Council of Women Workers. She was picked because the incumbent secretary was too assertive on women's issues and, in Medzini's description, "It was possible to depend on Golda to carry out party directives and not pose a threat or challenge to the leadership."[65]

The Golda myth, in which she is both feminist and national Jewish mother, is a fiction. But she was an effective organizer and politician, who could be counted on to arbitrate disputes, represent the party or the Zionist movement, rally Diaspora Jews. She was known as a propagandist, not a strategist.[66]

With Eshkol's death, Allon became head of a caretaker government that would serve only until a new prime minister could put together a coalition and win Knesset approval. By March 7, Labor's central committee ratified Sapir's machinations and chose Meir as the candidate. Only the old Rafi faction, led by Dayan and Shimon Peres, abstained in protest that Dayan had not been chosen. Four days later, she was officially assigned to form a government by the country's symbolic, powerless head of state, her former lover, President Zalman Shazar. "Golda reached the summit when she was actually aged and tired . . . cautious, conservative and not open to new ideas, daring experiments in foreign or domestic policy," writes Medzini. "Because of her age she tended more than ever to see things as black and white."[67] Chosen to preserve the party, she represented the end of a revolution, the apparatchik as leader.

Her initial coalition and cabinet, until the autumn elections, were the same as Eshkol's. Nothing needed to change. No breakthroughs were needed or desired. The new government's official guidelines said that until peace treaties were reached, Israel would stay put at the cease-fire lines "and strengthen its position." Meir's acceptance speech before the Knesset was written by Yisrael Galili, the secretive, maximalist Ahdut Ha'avodah minister who immediately became her chief adviser. "The government," she declared, "will regard . . . the settlement . . . of our sons on the soil of the homeland as of vital importance for the country's security and survival."[68] Stalemate was no longer tentative but intentional. It was time to dig in.

7

THE REIGN OF HUBRIS

The visitor to Kalyah did not actually enter the desert settlement, just drove past. Pulling up to the gate with diplomatic plates and asking the female soldier on guard duty to let him in might have been too bald a declaration that the U.S. consulate in Jerusalem was curious about Israeli settlement activity. That put the quiet American at a disadvantage to *Time* correspondent Marlin Levin, whose recently published story he had come to check.

Levin had driven in (after noting that the guard who met him was a "shapely, smiling, blue-eyed blonde wearing fatigues and armed with a rifle and transistor radio"), looked over the corn sprouts and irrigation pipes, and found out that the Nahal soldiers spent eight hours a day farming along with four or five more hours on military training and guard duty. The men got fieldwork and night guard shifts; women guarded by day, worked in the kitchen, and cared for the commune's 450 ducks. While Kalyah was technically an army camp defending the frontier with Jordan and the highway from the river to Jerusalem, "No one would ever think of saluting; everyone is known and called by his or her first name," he wrote, in February 1969.[1]

In the Kalyah dining hall, Levin had lunched with Dani, a twenty-seven-year-old expert on desert farming, whom he called "the most important man at Kalyah." The agronomist complained good-naturedly about the high price of water from an Arab family's spring, and talked about the road being paved along the Dead Sea shore southward to Ein Gedi, a kibbutz just inside the Green Line. Gaza refugees were hired for the roadwork, to give them jobs. Overpaying for water and labor, Levin explained, fit a policy intended to show local Arabs "that living with Israelis can be good for everyone." Kalyah could do well on winter produce, Dani said; his challenge was how to farm in summer, when the heat hit 120 degrees Fahrenheit.

"If someone says we have taken land that does not belong to us, he is wrong. No one ever worked this land. No one ever lived here," Dani said, explaining, "We need three things. The road, water and peace. The one we're building. The second we'll find. And if we have those two, the third will come in good time." He was providing Cliff Notes for the 1969 edition of the settlement ethos: Settlers made worthless soil bloom; the land's political status was so irrelevant as not to merit mentioning; settlements would actually push the Arabs to make peace.

Levin did not speak to the Gazans on the road crew but did mention that Arabs might not agree with Dani. *Time's* introduction to his article explained that Kalyah was part of a string of fortified settlements that Israel intended to build along the Jordan, along with others in the Golan and Sinai, in line with the cabinet's secret approval of Allon's proposals. Somewhere in the American diplomatic hierarchy, the report provoked enough concern to send a consular officer down to the desert.

His report to Washington, after driving by, was all reassurance. Kalyah was hardly fortified, he wrote, and was too far from the river or the highway to guard either. As for the "string of fortified settlements," he wrote, Israel had only built two settlements in the Rift, though it had announced plans for a third. *Time*, his report concluded, "presented a somewhat distorted picture of actuality." Kalyah "has not made as much progress toward permanence as the article suggests."[2]

In short, his superiors could ignore media exaggerations and relax. The comments show that the diplomat did not know of the existence of Argaman, the settlement midway up the Rift established in November, and did not want to imagine that more settlements might follow. Even while looking at a settlement, he preferred not to see it as altering the map, closing diplomatic possibilities. While pointing out that Kalyah was no fortress, he did not draw the conclusion that it was the foundation for a permanent, civilian community.

In one respect, though, he touched a truth. The process of creating facts was going slowly. Standing in the path of Allon's dreams and the Settlement Department's grandiose proposals were dry soil, empty wells, and a shortage of young people dedicated to the Labor Zionism of the 1930s.

At the State Department, Assistant Secretary Joseph Sisco was not as complacent. When Foreign Minister Abba Eban arrived in Washington in March 1969 for his first talks with the Nixon administration, Sisco drew up talking points for his new bosses, William Rogers and Under Secretary Elliot Richardson. Some of Israel's actions, he said, "have conveyed the impression that Israel has already made up its mind to retain certain territories." Sisco wanted Eban to hear from the Americans that Israel must not "present the world with accomplished facts."[3]

Despite the change in administrations, the position at State remained that peace required a virtually complete Israeli pullback to the prewar lines. That said, Sisco's language both stressed and played down the question of settlements. He expected Richardson to be the one to raise the issue with Eban, since Rogers would be discussing "the broad themes of our policy," not details. Settlements merely "conveyed the impression" that Israel intended to stay put, as if that were an unintended implication Israel should be more careful to avoid—as if Israel in fact agreed with its patron on final borders.

Superpower relations stood at the center of the new administration's visible strategy for solving the Arab-Israeli problem. With Nixon's go-ahead, State was to engage in two-way talks with the Soviet Union and four-party talks that included Britain and France. The goal was a peace proposal, not an imposed solution. But the assumption was that the various client states would have a hard time refusing such a proposal. The effort gained urgency when Egypt's Nasser declared in March that the cease-fire was over and launched what became known as the War of Attrition: artillery barrages across the Suez Canal, intended to show Israel that holding the Sinai was too costly. The fighting quickly escalated into air battles. But Nixon did not expect the talks to go anywhere, and

Kissinger was happy to have them fail, lest the Soviets get credit for wringing concessions from Israel.[4] The operating assumption was also false: Clients were not puppets. Nasser, the nationalist, did not operate on a Soviet remote control. And even if Washington put aside the "impression" created by settlements, it still had the new prime minister's explicit statements that Israel intended to keep land.

"LINES THAT EXISTED before the fifth of June can never again be the boundaries of Israel," Golda Meir said, at a foreign press briefing on taking office. Though Israel sought signed treaties, she assumed they meant little—"Wars usually break out among countries that have peace agreements"—so new borders would have to eliminate any Arab military advantages. The Golan and Sharm al-Sheikh would remain Israeli. She refused to specify territorial goals in the West Bank. Israel would do "everything that is possible" for "the inhabitants"—Meir would never say Palestinians—who might find that "it is not so terrible to live together with us." If the Arabs chose to negotiate, the Israeli government would decide its position.[5]

"I rebel against someone saying there's no peace because we haven't decided on our map," she said afterward at a lunch for Hebrew journalists. The dispute with the Arabs was "over the very fact that we're alive, and it doesn't matter what territory we live in." On the other hand, she rejected annexing occupied land, "because I want a Jewish state . . . without me having to count the Jewish and non-Jewish population every morning, for fear the figures have changed. . . . A very dear friend told me that in that case, I'm not a Zionist. Well, I have an opinion of myself, which isn't always so good, but on the fact that I'm a good Zionist . . . you can't change my opinion."[6]

The music was insecurity: People wanted Jews dead, she did not think much of herself, she needed to stand up against more powerful views. The lyrics said the ideal choice was no choice. Concessions would endanger Israel, yet annexation meant an end to the Jewish state. Unstated was that defining territorial goals would fracture the party, whose unity was her achievement. The Arabs of the occupied territory would therefore have to accept Israeli rule, without citizenship.

That view put her close to Dayan. Indeed, Dayan and Yisrael Galili quickly became her chief confidants, especially on security. They were members of the real governing body, "Golda's kitchen," which actually met in her living room, usually on Saturday night, to decide what would be decided at Sunday morning's cabinet meeting. In one account, the other fixed members were Yigal Allon and Justice Minister Yaakov Shimshon Shapira, the group's sole Mapai moderate. In Shapira's telling, only Dayan and Galili were regulars. Either way, the kitchen was dominated by leaders of Labor's smaller, hawkish factions, Rafi and Ahdut Ha'avodah. The three central figures—Meir herself, Dayan, and Galili—were profoundly pessimistic about peace, an emotional stance that preceded and shaped analysis. They regarded Israel's new territorial depth as the best means to convince the Arabs they could not win a full-scale war, and so should not try.

Besides military experience, Dayan possessed political power: He could split the party again, run against it, form a government with the right. Galili shared Meir's suspicions and bent for secrecy, and as an added benefit, her distaste for the erudite Eban.[7] The view from the kitchen window was of a foreboding world. The key policy cooked up there was to sit tight, protected by the captured land.

But that did not mean sitting still. Settlement would continue, staking Israel's claim to pieces of occupied land. It followed Allon's map, whether because Meir personally agreed with his logic or because anything past his lines would split her government and her party. Settlement represented the real decision. Yet in the eyes of Labor settlement advocates, the effort moved all too slowly. And unnoticed by them, fertilized by their own actions, the seed of a new, radical settlement movement was growing.

"I WOULD SPEAK to the Arabs in Hebron in Hebrew. They wanted our business and they made jolly sure they would not lose it by not knowing Hebrew," writes Hebron settler Chaim Simons in a memoir of settler life in the West Bank city's military headquarters. Who spoke whose language set status: landlord and tolerated occupant. "I myself would not learn Arabic at all. Hebrew is the language of Eretz Yisrael," the Land of Israel. His ignorance occasionally caused problems. Once he did a favor for an Arab, who responded "*shukran.*" Simons wondered why the man was calling him a liar, *shakran* in Hebrew. Later he learned that *shukran* meant "thanks." At the military headquarters, the settlers managed to get a single phone line from the local provider. When the bill showed up in Arabic, they sent it back with a note that they did not know the language. "Soon after, we duly received it in Hebrew," Simons reports.[8]

Simons had grown up in London. At twenty-four, in the summer of 1966, with a fresh doctorate in chemistry, he moved to Israel to teach at Bar-Ilan University, an Orthodox institution that was the pride of religious Zionism, proof that faith and modernity could fruitfully coexist and that religious Jews could match secularists at academic pursuits. In June 1968, at a Movement for the Whole Land of Israel conference, he heard Moshe Levinger speak. Ironically, the rabbi was the poster boy of that secular movement: By helping him settle in Hebron, it had created a fact, rather than simply producing florid articles. Levinger hooked Simons. By summer's end, the young Englishman moved to Hebron and became a student at the yeshivah that officially justified the settlement's existence.[9]

Simons's personal cause was the Tomb of the Patriarchs. He founded a movement—a bank account, a post-office box, a rubber stamp—for "restoration of Jewish rights" at the holy site. He bombarded newspapers with letters, handed out leaflets to Jewish visitors. A chance to assert ownership of the shrine came in March 1969, on the holiday of Purim, which celebrates—with the help of costumes, copious liquor, and hilarity—the biblical Queen Esther's victory over the evil minister Haman in ancient Persia. On Purim morning the settlers headed for the Tomb for the required reading aloud of the Book of Esther. The same morning, Simons writes, a group of Arabs brought a coffin, following a Muslim custom of bringing bodies to Ibrahim's mosque before burial elsewhere. The mourners "wanted to carry it through the place we were praying. We were not prepared to tolerate such interference," he writes. The settlers "formed a long line . . . and started singing Purim songs, and thus prevented them from carrying their dead bodies in our place of prayer."[10] Soldiers on guard duty, watching carnival confront funeral, were "in a difficult situation," Simons concedes; they asked the settlers not to sing so loudly.

The soldiers were again caught in the middle on Israeli Independence Day. At morning services, Simons draped a "very large flag" over the stone cenotaph believed to mark Isaac's tomb in the building's main hall, and a string of small flags on a barrier separating Jews and Muslims. The military governor arrived and removed the flags. When Levinger heard, he told his followers to put up another flag. They sneaked one past soldiers at the entrance, and when the service ended, began dancing with it. A bizarre game of capture-the-flag began in the ancient hall, with Border Police chasing settlers to snatch the piece of cloth. A military government spokesman defensively explained afterward to Israeli reporters that the tomb "served . . . as a place for prayers alone." The settlers wrote to cabinet ministers, demanding that a Jewish director be appointed for the building, since it actually belonged to the Jews.[11]

The army and the settlers were like a couple that fights in public and goes home together. In the courtyard of the military headquarters, two three-story prefab apartment blocks were completed, six apartments each, along with two small dormitory buildings for single yeshivah students. In May 1969, settlers moved into the new space. The community expanded; yeshivah students married; couples took over dorm rooms, washed their dishes in lavatory sinks. A couple moved into the room that served as the settlement's office. Levinger matched Simons up with a single British woman who had been there from the original Passover incursion, and they soon announced their engagement. The army converted the British stables into a study hall for the yeshivah. Levinger taught, as did Eliezer Waldman. The yeshivah was an unofficial branch of Merkaz Harav, but without the main street of secular Jerusalem and its bookstores and coffee shops outside its doors, without nearby synagogues where Orthodox historians and philosophers and government officials prayed on workday mornings before their secular pursuits. Simons's journey from Bar-Ilan University to Hebron was a pilgrim's progress to an isolated, radical Judaism, further than its members imagined from Israel or from the Eastern European philosophical ferment that produced the elder Rabbi Kook with his alloy of kabbalah and modernity. The yeshivah manufactured a plethora of jobs to justify settlers' presence, Simons records: teachers, secretaries, clerks, kitchen staff, babysitters, and schoolteachers. Within the military compound, the second generation of Hebron settlers quickly increased.12

The group decided to make contact with other settlers in "liberated" territory. Simons and his fiancée, Dina, along with Rabbi Waldman and Benny Katzover and several others, set off in the van Allon had provided for a tour of settlements in March 1969. The Jordan Rift road was still unpaved in parts. A photo from the time shows Simons, in the black pants and rumpled white shirt of a yeshivah student, standing on the dirt track next to a sign saying "Nahal Argaman." In the background, a couple of prefab huts and a telephone pole stand in an empty expanse.

From there they reached Merom Golan in Quneitrah. Simons was unprepared for the fact that the kibbutz dining hall was not kosher, that "such kibbutzim who have a positive attitude to Eretz Yisrael" were distant from "other mitzvot," or religious commandments. The kibbutz newsletter recorded a pleasant conversation with the visitors. "The core group consists of students of Rabbi Kook of Jerusalem, who have been taught the abnormality of a partitioned Land of Israel, and that it must be made complete because it was given to the Jewish nation by Providence." Both Kook's name and his doctrine appear to have been new to the listeners. "We have no intent of pushing out our cousins," Waldman assured his hosts, using a common condescending term for Arabs, "cousins" of Jews by dint of their descent from Ishmael and thence from Abraham, the shared ancestor buried in the Hebron tomb. Only a lack of housing held back the settlement's growth, Katzover said, asserting that "we have a list of one hundred families who are interested in settling in Hebron." The first meeting between the socialist settlers and the religious ones, both clients of Allon, resembled contact between two tribes, each a curiosity to the other.13

BUT THE QUESTION OF SETTLEMENT growth may have touched a nerve, painfully. At a United Kibbutz conference in May, Yehudah Harel and other representatives of Merom Golan lobbied for the movement to invest more in "liberated territory," starting with a new commune in the Jordan Rift. Harel demanded that established kibbutzim make more members available to help new ones, and also insisted "that it is possible today to bring outsiders"—not just kibbutz-bred young people—to a new wave of settlements.[14]

The demands point to what was not happening. So did a speech by Galili, demanding allegiance to the movement's 1955 "Ideological Foundation" with its doctrine of the eternal indivisibility of the land. "No new reason has arisen to justify negating . . . our right to settle in the entire land," he insisted. "If someone stands and asks why I have raised these principles . . . the answer is that I'm not the only one who perceives new winds, expressing heresy."

It was not just that a few kibbutz representatives were ready to stand up and openly suggest that occupied territories could be given up for peace. Others asked whether the movement had the people to support new communes. Small kibbutzim did not want to give up members. Larger ones worried about losing their next generation—especially when only about half the children growing up on kibbutzim were staying on as adults. The war had not stopped the inner decline of the kibbutzim. Fewer young people were volunteering for a year of service to the movement. The government had extended military service for men to three years, since the army faced continual conflict on the new frontiers. After three years in uniform, giving another year was harder.[15] At the edges of the stated explanations, there are hints of an unstated one: Among the children of the kibbutzim, those who stayed on as adults were not usually the ones with the passion for something new. They were simply returning to the life they knew and did not expect to live the 1930s over again.

The United Kibbutz was not alone. Leaders of Mapai's rival kibbutz movement, though not committed to the Whole Land, still sought the chance to build new settlements. So did the various organizations of moshavim, the cooperative farm villages. The ethos of putting more Jews on the land was accepted truth. When the government approved new settlement locations in occupied territory, the movements pushed and shoved to get them. Then they searched for young people to settle them. One stopgap solution was to assign a spot to the army's Nahal settlement arm. Groups of soldiers, graduates of youth movements in the cities, could take turns developing a new settlement until the movement was confident it had people ready, in theory at least, to spend their lives there.

The moshav movements expected better luck, for an ancient reason: At the cooperative farm villages, only one son could inherit his parent's farm. Yet when movement officials went from village to village looking for land-hungry second sons, history's readiest colonists, they came back empty-handed. "The sons and daughters did not believe in the future of the new wave of settlement"—that is, in occupied land—"refused to move far from their families, and demanded to settle in their parents' communities," an official reported back to Yehiel Admoni at the Settlement Department. According to Admoni, responsible for carrying out the department's plans, "The most limiting factor was the human factor."[16]

"Eilat, you've got no idea how hard it is to establish a kibbutz, a new society, so that everything will be OK. . . . A million problems, organizational and social," wrote Kobi Rabinovich from Quneitrah to his girlfriend, then serving in the army. He was one of the recruits who had come and stayed—yet the letter gives another hint at why the generation of *Soldiers' Talk* was uninterested in settlement. For that was as much as he wrote of Merom Golan. Instead, he returns to the Sinai Desert, as if living eternally in June 1967. The heat pounds him, clouds of flies swarm in the air. Standing in his tank turret, he sees distant figures in the dunes. The deputy company commander leaves in a half-track, returns with Egyptian captives. Kobi swings the strap of his Uzi over his shoulder and hikes to the commander's tank, where curious soldiers are gathering to look. Two dark men, hands bound, sit on the earth, swatting away flies with their heads.

A few steps away, another captive lies, "moaning, wailing, groaning. A filthy rag is tied around his head, totally soaked in blood." Bullets have shattered his jaw.

> His breath gurgles, his face toward the ground, wailing. . . . People pass as if it's nothing, shout at him to be quiet. . . .
> Here is my enemy. War.
> One of ours wouldn't be left like this. . . . And still, I found myself turning back to my tank.
> The tank is far. . . . Hot, hot! The Uzi bangs my thighs like lead. Unlike the others, I made myself share his pain. . . . Now I've turned my back. . . . If only at least I hadn't seen. Eilat! Mom! Dad! I'm getting further! As if it's nothing.[17]

It is the last of the war letters Rabinovich left. Months later, after Eilat's discharge, she joined him at Merom Golan. Perhaps he told her the rest of the journey to the Suez Canal on cool late nights in Quneitrah. Or perhaps this is the last scene in the repeating nightmare, the place it took two years of letters to reach and that left everything afterward, including building a new kibbutz, naked of meaning.

THE SINAI DUNES were as hot at the end of May 1969, when the first Nahal soldiers came to establish their outpost in the region. A person's feet sank into the dry sand as if it were marshland. But there were no longer expanses of corpses to draw flies. Two miles north lay the Mediterranean coast. The old international boundary between Israel and Egypt, erased from Israeli maps, was eight miles to the east.[18]

Between the dunes, in spots where sparse rainfall flowed together, Bedouin farmers tended almond, peach, olive, and castor-oil trees and patches of wheat. Near the beach, where groundwater rose almost to the surface, they farmed a strip a few hundred meters wide that yielded richer crops. Herds of sheep and goats added to their livelihood. So did working for whoever ruled the area—Egyptians before, Israelis now. They were settled tribes; some lived in tents, but more in tin shacks and concrete houses.[19]

The Nahal unit consisted of seventy-three men and women, from the religious Bnei Akiva youth movement. On the way to the Sinai, they told a reporter, they sang over and over, "Who has kept us alive, and sustained us, and brought us to this day"—words of a blessing recited at celebrations. "When we got here, there was nothing. . . . The wind lifted the sand, which cut into our eyes, and in front of us stood two lonely structures in the desolation," the reporter quoted them.[20] The outpost was named Dekalim, "palms," then renamed Diklah, the singular form. By one account, the palm in question had grown from a date in the pocket of Avshalom Feingold, killed by Bedouin during World War I on his way from Turkish Palestine to deliver information from a Jewish spy ring to the British in Egypt. The prosaic name thereby gave the place a martyr and instant historical pathos.[21]

Immediately, a dispute began between Bnei Akiva and Beitar, the youth movement linked to Menahem Begin's right-wing Herut party, over who would turn Diklah into a civilian settlement. The rightist movement was a minor player in the settlement effort; the fact that it took part demonstrated the pervasive influence of the left's ethos of liberating land one field at a time. Beitar won, and sent the next groups of Nahal soldiers.[22]

Diklah was the easiest spot to begin settling in the area because farmland was available. It had 500 acres, according to Settlement Department documents—fields formerly cultivated by an Egyptian authority for desert development and taken over by the Israeli military government, which employed Bedouin to work them.[23] But the army apparently needed to establish its possession of the spot where the outpost's houses stood. A month after the Nahal soldiers' arrival, the military commander of the Gaza Strip and northern Sinai, Brigadier General Mordechai Gur—the officer who led the conquest of Jerusalem's Old City in 1967—issued two decrees. An attached map showed the Nahal outpost, with a line drawn around it, expanding its area. "I hereby declare that the area whose borders are marked on the diagram is seized for military purposes," said one decree. The second declared the land a "closed military area," off-limits to civilians. In theory, "seizing" land was less draconian than expropriation—it left legal ownership in the original hands, while giving the army use of the real estate for as long as military need existed. Practically, there was no measurable difference. The owners were to receive compensation, but lost their land. A prefatory sentence in the order seizing the land said the measure was "required for immediate and pressing military needs."

Another pair of decrees seized and closed some 4,000 acres, about six square miles, just to the east, where Settlement Department plans called for three moshavim to be established.[24] The orders, also citing "pressing military needs," took effect the next day. Later, top officers would argue that the seized land was clearly marked with barrels, but that in an "act of leniency," the army allowed local Bedouin to continue working plots inside the boundaries.[25] The decrees aroused no public notice. Settlement of the Rafiah Plain of northeastern Sinai had begun.

Incrementally, new "facts" appeared elsewhere. That summer, a second Orthodox kibbutz was established near Kfar Etzion, on the site of another of the fallen communes of 1948. No pretense was made that it belonged to Nahal.[26] In the Jordan Rift, soldiers arrived in autumn to establish two new outposts. One was earmarked for the United Kibbutz, meeting the demands of activists in the movement to start another commune in the dry land next to the river.[27] The outpost, called Gilgal, sat at the foot of a hill that looked like a sleeping dinosaur, its head down, its feet stretched toward the houses, creases visible between its toes. Meanwhile the first outpost at the Rift's north end, Meholah, was turned over to civilian settlers, an explicit statement that settlement in the region was intended as permanent.[28] Allon's map was slowly filling in.

ANY SUSPICIONS that Golda Meir was a caretaker prime minister, filling the office only until the October 1969 election, were soon swept away. She enjoyed power. She called back former aides to work for her, a sign she intended to stay on the job. She blasted the four-power talks on the Middle East, declaring that outside powers would not dictate to Israel. She ruled by reacting to events; taking the initiative, Medzini says in his biography, "would only arouse problems in her governing coalition and in the delicate fabric of her party."[29]

Dayan made particularly clear that the Labor Party could come unraveled unless the platform fit his hard-line views. "I'm not a devotee of the formula that we'll stay at these lines until peace comes," he told a party forum. He did not want to retreat, even for peace, and especially not in the West Bank. Labor's policy, he said, should be that "we will establish permanent facts with settlement and military consolidation."

Labor's nightmare was that Dayan would run on his own ticket. Besides, maximalism had support in the party. So language was found to satisfy Dayan. The 1969 Labor election platform did not say anything about what Israel would be willing to give up. It did say that Israel would not return to the prewar lines, and that it would establish settlements "in accordance with security considerations and the development of the state"—the vague last phrase meaning that security would not be the only consideration. A closed-door meeting adopted a secret "oral doctrine," the approved gloss on the platform, saying that if negotiations were ever to take place, Israel's position would be to retain the Golan and Sharm al-Sheikh, and to allow no Arab military in the West Bank.[30] The hawkish face of Labor matched Meir's own.[31]

A visit to Washington a month before the election appeared perfectly timed to show that she was successfully managing the country's most critical foreign relationship.[32] A cartoonist privy to U.S. administration discussions before the visit could have portrayed Nixon with Secretary of State Rogers and national security adviser Kissinger as imps perched on his shoulders, offering opposite advice. Rogers urged Nixon to tell Meir that "Israel's stand-pat policy is detrimental to both U.S. and Israeli interests." While asserting that "Israel is capable of maintaining the present military status quo for some years at least," Rogers argued that ongoing conflict increased Soviet influence. He advised Nixon to tell Meir that the United States had always operated on the assumption that Israel did not want Egyptian territory and sought only to "correct anomalies" in the prewar lines with Jordan, but to warn her that Israel was projecting "an expansionist image" by establishing settlements.[33] The phrasing continued the State Department approach of treating Israel's explicit statements on territory merely as clumsy public relations. Kissinger, meanwhile, argued that "a continuing deadlock was in our interest . . . it would demonstrate Soviet impotence," and show Egypt that it had to turn to the United States to achieve "progress." In Kissinger's account of the policy dispute with Rogers, settlements do not exist as an issue.[34]

Starkly anti-Soviet, Meir hit it off well with Nixon. Kissinger was swept away. In his memoirs, he lavishes praise on Meir, adding, "To me she acted as a benevolent aunt toward an especially favored nephew, so that even to admit the possibility of disagreement was a challenge to family hierarchy producing emotional outrage."[35] Nixon and Meir agreed to set up a back channel between them, via Kissinger and Ambassador Rabin, who were linked by a private phone line. Rogers and Eban were left out of the loop. Whatever the secretary of state said through normal channels, Kissinger could reassure Meir on the side.[36]

On October 28, elections were held not only for parliament but for local governments throughout the country. The Arabs of East Jerusalem could vote for city council but not the Knesset. At the time of unification they were granted the status of permanent residents of Israel but not citizenship. The reason, according to the Israeli journalist Uzi Benziman, is that a cabinet committee concluded that international law forbade imposing one country's citizenship on another's citizens.[37] On this legal issue, the ministers chose to be cautious. The city's Arabs were equal and not equal. Even their cars marked them as such: They carried Israeli license plates, but the numbers all began with the same three digits, for easy identification by security forces.[38] But the government wanted them to vote in city elections, to legitimate annexation.

Before election day, deposed Jordanian officials and underground Palestinian groups urged a boycott. In response, writes Benziman, Israeli officials "spread the warning in East Jerusalem that without a stamp in their identity papers showing they had voted, East Jerusalem residents would not receive essential services." Polling places were put near the Green Line, to be shared by Jews and Arabs, so that an Arab boycott would be less obvious. The Labor Party organized an operation to bus voters to the stations—which in the best tradition of Israeli machine politics, also helped ensure that they voted Labor. Seven thousand of 35,000 eligible voters—which for the first time in East Jerusalem, meant women as well as men—turned out, helping to reelect Kollek as mayor of the united city.[39]

The night before the election, Hebron settlers Chaim and Dina Simons stayed in Jerusalem. In the morning, heading to the east city to catch an Arab taxi back to Hebron, they watched the buses with Kollek's name on the side carrying Arab voters to West Jerusalem. The Simonses were hurrying to vote at the polling station set up for the settlers in the military headquarters in Hebron.[40] That ballot box marked another legal twist of occupation: By incremental bureaucratic decisions, settlers would retain the status of residents of Israel while living in land under military occupation, surrounded by people with no such rights.[41] Fitting the same trend, an Israeli court was established in Quneitrah, in the Golan Heights.[42]

At first glance, the Labor-Mapam Alignment won the election. It remained the largest party, with fifty-six Knesset seats, next to twenty-six for Menachem Begin's right-wing Gahal coalition. At second glance, the Alignment had lost over 10 percent of its parliamentary strength and its absolute majority.

Meir had led a retreat. Labor was entering the rigor mortis that precedes rather than follows a political movement's death. It won votes through patronage and old loyalties, not by presenting a vision. Kissinger's comment about Meir's attitude toward disagreement described Labor under her rule, except that its members were children, not nephews. New ideas signified disloyalty, if not matricide. "The policy for which there was least tolerance of criticism," comments the political scientist Myron Aronoff, was the assumption "that retention of the territories . . . would guarantee the nation's security from another war for at least a decade."[43] Nostalgia made it unthinkable to question the value of settlement. Meir's Labor was powerful and decaying.

Meir again chose to include Gahal in her coalition, giving Begin's rightist party six of the twenty-three cabinet posts. Dayan obtained reinforcements with the promotion of his loyalist Shimon Peres to the cabinet.[44] Another perennial coalition partner, the National Religious Party, was moving rightward. Its Young Guard had gained enough power to get its leader, thirty-three-year-old Zevulun Hammer, into the Knesset. While Labor suffered disaffection of the younger generation, the National Religious Party's aging, moderate leaders faced militant young people determined to show that nothing was off-limits for Orthodox Jews, that religion could set national policy. Their policy of choice was the Whole Land.[45]

Just as the new government was installed in December 1969, Meir faced what looked like a crisis with the United States. The appearance was misleading. Listening to the advice of one imp, Nixon gave Rogers permission to announce an outline for an Egypt-Israel accord. In a speech outlining what became known as the Rogers Plan, the secretary of state called for Israeli withdrawal to the international boundary as part of a formal peace agreement.[46] That was followed by a proposal for a Jordanian-Israeli agreement in which Rogers said the new border would "approximate" the prewar armistice line.[47]

Listening to the other imp, Nixon used another back channel—Leonard Garment, his adviser on Jewish affairs—to alert Meir that he did not intend to push the proposals.[48] Though the Rogers Plan signified nothing, Meir was politically obligated to respond with sound and fury. A statement by the freshly installed cabinet asserted that the U.S. proposals would be construed by Arab rulers "as an attempt to appease them," and declared, "Israel will not be sacrificed [to] any Power policy."[49] Egypt's Nasser also rejected the American proposals, and the Soviet Union followed suit. Only King Hussein was reportedly positive.[50]

From then, Kissinger's approach dominated Nixon's Mideast policy: The United States could comfortably sit tight until the Arab states were ready to switch sides in the Cold War. Like Meir, Kissinger believed that "Israel was too strong to succumb to Arab military pressure," and that time was on his side.[51] Hubris was in control.

THE SUCCESSION successfully navigated, Pinhas Sapir returned to the Finance Ministry. The deputy immigration minister, Arie Eliav, decided to do something considered almost barbaric: he openly ran for the vacant position of Labor secretary-general. Custom required that publicly "a party man wants nothing . . . but then the 'comrades' come and demand forcefully that he accept the 'party's will' and against his will he serves as minister or ambassador," in Eliav's description. But chutzpah paid off. In January 1970, he was chosen for the very post that Meir had used as a stepping-stone to the premiership.

Then he got a call from Marlin Levin, the *Time* correspondent, who remembered Eliav's radically dovish pamphlet of over a year earlier. Levin wanted an interview with the new party secretary. Besides Jerusalem, Eliav told Levin, "we should not annex any more territories." He repeated his call for recognizing the Palestinian national movement—a view, Levin wrote in his article, "in direct contradiction with that of Mrs. Meir, who is on record as saying that there is no such thing as . . . a Palestinian nation." The article was entitled "The Lion's Roar," playing on Eliav's first name— "Arie" means "lion" in Hebrew.

Eliav was not sure Meir had read his own articles, but he knew she read *Time*. The issue containing the interview took three days to reach Israel. He knew it had come, because his secretary told him Golda was on the phone. " 'Would you like to have a cup of tea with me?' she asked, with cold courtesy," Eliav later wrote. She invited him for five that afternoon, in her kitchen, the inner sanctum of power. When he knocked on her door, the prime minister answered herself, and sat him at the kitchen table while she fixed him tea and herself coffee and she sliced a cake. "On the table lay the *corpus delicti*, a copy of *Time* open to 'The Lion's Roar,' with several key sentences underlined in blazing red," Eliav writes. She served the drinks, lit one of her seventy daily cigarettes, and asked in a teacherly tone if he had read the article. Certainly, he said.

"And I assume you will deny several sentences in it?"

"Why deny? I think Levin did excellent work."

She read a sentence aloud to make sure.

"Yes, Golda," Eliav said. "He quoted me word for word."

So why, she asked, had she been unaware of his views?

"I really couldn't say," he answered. He had published the same things in *Davar*—the party paper!—and had mailed her a pamphlet, with a personal dedication.

"Really. . . . I can't remember getting it. Maybe the mail . . ." said the prime minister. Silence filled the kitchen. "So those are really your views?" she finally said.

"Those are my views."

"Nu, okay. . . . Another cup of tea?"

"No thank you," Eliav said.

"Maybe some more cake?"

"No thank you. The cake was very tasty."

Again, silence.

At last she proposed taking the matter to the party central committee. Fine, he said.

Her eyes stared into his. "I intend to say to the central committee," she said, "that they have an old stupid prime minister chosen by the party and the nation and a young, smart party secretary-general just chosen by the central committee, and I'll ask if they want to stay with a young smart secretary-general or an old stupid prime minister."

Fine, he said, convene the central committee. He did not intend to change his views or burn his articles. "I know my views are a minority position in the party, and that I'm bound by the majority position," he added. His agenda was building the party—conducting internal elections, holding a party congress. "So I suggest we agree to disagree, and work together as long as we can," he said.

"Fine. We'll agree to disagree."

"WE KNOW THIS IS THE BORDER": Israeli soldiers put barbed wire along the armistice line dividing Israel from the West Bank in early 1967. (GPO/Moshe Milner)

THE AVALANCHE: On June 7, 1967, Israeli troops reach the symbol of the unreachable—the Dome of the Rock. (GPO)

CREATING FACTS: Immediately after the war's end, a bulldozer demolishes the Mughrabi Quarter in Old Jerusalem. *(K. Weiss)*

RITE OF RETURN: Kfar Etzion survivors visit the kibbutz's ruins after the conquest of the West Bank. *(The Etzion Bloc Survivors Organization)*

SILENT COWBOYS: The first settlers, secular leftists, began rounding up abandoned Syrian cattle in the Golan Heights in July 1967. A corral at Kibbutz Merom Golan, 1968. *(GPO/Moshe Milner)*

SULTAN OF THE OCCUPIED
TERRITORIES: Defense
Minister Moshe Dayan
(photograph right) meets
Palestinians in Qalandiya
refugee camp in 1967. (©
Micha Bar Am/Magnum Photos)

"A MAN OF SETTLEMENT":
Prime Minister Levi Eshkol
(photograph below left)
examines an irrigation ditch
in the West Bank's Jordan
Rift on a late 1967 trip with
Yigal Allon *(at right in photograph)* to check settlement
options. *(GPO/Moshe Milner)*

"WHAT KIND OF ISRAEL
DO YOU WANT?": At Lyndon
Johnson's Texas ranch
(photograph below right),
Eshkol could not answer the
president's question on his
government's plans for
occupied land. *(GPO/David
Eldan)*

PASSOVER PLAN: Led by Rabbi Moshe Levinger, settlers celebrated Passover in Hebron and stayed on. *Above:* Settler quarters at Hebron military headquarters, 1968. *(GPO/Moshe Milner) Right:* Levinger—addressing a Hebron rally in 1976—was the most public and abrasive voice of the new religious radicalism. *(© Micha Bar Am/Magnum Photos) Below:* Palestinian workers build Jewish Kiryat Arba, 1971. *(GPO/Moshe Milner)*

VISIBLE OCCUPATION: Troops round up Palestinian suspects after a shooting incident, Gaza Strip, 1969. (© *Micha Bar Am/Magnum Photos*)

EXPELLED: Oded Lifshitz (*right*) and other Israeli activists meet a Bedouin next to the ruins of her house, northeast Sinai, early 1972. (*Oded Lifshitz*)

HIRED: Bedouin laborers with an Israeli farmer at Sadot, northeast Sinai. (*GPO/Moshe Milner*)

AFTER SHOCK: Henry Kissinger—with Prime Minister Golda Meir in February 1974—seized the war that he failed to foresee as America's opening to shape the Middle East. *(GPO/Moshe Milner)*

TORN SOUL: Poet Haim Gouri *(photograph above left)* feared Gush Emunim would provoke civil war. *(Courtesy of Haim Gouri)*

BRASH DOVE: Yossi Sarid *(photograph above middle)* promised to ensure that "nothing remains" at Gush Emunim's secret settlement, Ofrah. *(GPO/Ya'acov Sa'ar)*

INTO THE WILDERNESS: Rising Labor star Arie Eliav *(photograph above right)* proposed recognizing the Palestinians. *(GPO/Moshe Milner)*

TROIKA PLUS ONE: From 1974 to 1977, Yitzhak Rabin *(second from left)* ruled in dysfunctional partnership with Shimon Peres *(far left)*, Yigal Allon *(second from right)*, and settlement czar Yisrael Galili. *(GPO/Moshe Milner)*

CAMP DEFIANCE: Gush Emunim supporters await confrontation at Sebastia, December 1975. *(Israel Sun Ltd.)*

PLANNED ECSTASY: Celebrating
victory over the Rabin government, Gush
Emunim backers *(photograph above)* lift
leader Hanan Porat aloft and dance,
Sebastia, December 8, 1975. *(GPO/Moshe
Milner)*

THE BUILDER: Rabin *(photograph at left)*
pours the first trowel of mortar for a
building at the Sinai settlement of Yamit,
1976. *(GPO/Moshe Milner)*

"MANY MORE
ELON MOREHS":
Menachem Begin
(left) and Ariel
Sharon celebrate
the right's election
victory at Camp
Kaddum, May 1977.
(Israel Sun Ltd.)

They shook hands and he left. Two weeks after taking office, he had passed the pinnacle of his power in Labor. When Meir had been secretary-general, she was a regular, vocal member of the political committee, the small body that Eshkol used to cook up the most important decisions on foreign policy and national security. For discussion of those issues, Eliav was never invited again to Golda's kitchen.[52]

YIGAL ALLON, on the other hand, had evidence of his influence. In early February, the secretive cabinet committee on national security approved his proposal to build 250 housing units for Hebron's settlers. Professionals would get to work immediately on planning "Upper Hebron," the working name for the Jewish town right next to the Arab city.[53]

The move capped Allon's push for settlement at Hebron. His efforts within the government were the essential complement to the Hebron settlers' provocative lobbying from without. At one stage, Benny Katzover would later recount, Rabbi Moshe Levinger asked him to go through the office files and make a list of everyone "who ever approached us."

"Approached about what?" Katzover asked.

"It doesn't matter," Levinger said.

Katzover made a list of 110 names. Two days later, he opened a newspaper and, in his words, "passed out." The names appeared in an advertisement listing 110 families who "demanded from the government to settle in Hebron." Katzover shouted at Levinger: Some of the people had made donations or written letters of support, some had asked to join the settlement, but certainly had never given permission to use their names. "It'll work out," Levinger answered. The post soon brought letters of protest from some whose names had been used—and a wave of requests to join the settlement in the West Bank city. A month later, Levinger asked for the new names. The next ad listed 250 families. As Katzover saw it, the number of housing units in the government decision was taken directly from the advertisement.[54]

The Hebron decision was a milestone: The government was fully legitimizing Levinger's wildcat settlement in Hebron. It was establishing a settlement in the midst of a heavily populated Arab area. For the first time, it was creating an urban settlement, and one close enough to the Israeli cities of Jerusalem and Beersheba for residents to commute, so that "pioneering" would not require turning barren land into fields. About 140 settlers were living at the Hebron military headquarters—fifty families and some singles.[55] "Upper Hebron," funded by the government, would eventually draw thousands of Israelis into occupied territory.

The significance was only partly apparent at the time. After the decision became public, news reports said that Finance Minister Sapir and other cabinet moderates had opposed the step, arguing that it closed negotiating options. Meir and Dayan had reportedly supported Allon's position. In Hebron, pamphlets called on Arab residents to protest "Zionist expansion," and the army imposed a curfew.[56] Yet the move also demonstrated how petty political fights can blur monumental decisions. Allon wanted the Hebron project assigned to the new Settlement Coordinating Committee he headed, which was to direct government and Jewish Agency efforts.[57] The housing minister, Zeev Sherf, insisted he get responsibility. Town-building was his ministry's job. Sherf was known as a moderate, but was more interested in protecting his turf than in the impact of settling at Hebron.[58] As Allon once said, an Israeli government was more a "federation of ministers" than a single regime.[59] As the settlement enterprise progressed, even known doves could be recruited when a project gave their ministries more responsibility.

Announcing the decision in the Knesset, Allon also boasted of twenty-two settlements already established in occupied territory and another eight in the pipeline, not to mention the housing developments in East Jerusalem. Yet to mollify moderates, he denied any decision had been made about the Hebron region's political future.[60] Meir continued to declare that territory and borders were irrelevant, a distraction from the cause of conflict with Arab states. "They say we must be dead," she said on the American television program 60 Minutes, "and we are a very ruthless people, and we say that we want to be alive. Between life and death I don't know a compromise."[61]

Allon's claim that "Upper Hebron" served Israeli security needs could not convince those most familiar with settlement and sympathetic to his positions. "Settlement in Hebron is in my view an example showing that Allon deviated from his original plan," the Settlement Department's Admoni later wrote.[62] "Practically nothing was left of the strategic conception underlying the Allon Plan," Shlomo Gazit, the officer in charge of government activities in occupied territory, would later assert.[63] Despite Allon's strategic rationalizations, the driving force was the desire to claim a place that conjured memories of ancient glory and recent martyrdom, the very stuff of nationalism, including secular Zionism.

To accomplish his goal, though, he used Levinger's group, which belonged to a very different Zionism, in which Allon does not appear to have taken much interest. It was a different fabric from the prewar religious Zionism of Bnei Akiva, the National Religious Party, and Bar-Ilan University, which tried to let Orthodoxy and Zionism get along, to show that an Orthodox Jew could be *as good as:* as secular pioneers, politicians, or professors. Secular Israel was fine with such religious Zionists *as long as* its army was kosher, its businesses closed on the Sabbath, it had a chief rabbi and a religious party in government.

Levinger was at the moment the most public, abrasive, and radical representative of those, mostly young, who were done with *as good as, as long as.* The new school brought together the theology of the rabbis Kook, the apparent confirmation their beliefs received in the war, the resentments of young religious Zionists, their desire for heroism in secular Israeli terms, and their conflicting desire to show religious greatness. It created a new, nationalist religion that, like many radical religious innovations, claimed to be a return to old-time faith.[64] It turned sovereignty and settling conquered land into sacred commandments, and into part of the drama leading to redemption. Secular Zionists were not models for religious ones; they were incomplete, flawed. In 1970 it was not apparent that Allon was helping to build a community that sought to cast him on the ash heap of history.

IN CONTRAST TO LEVINGER'S group, Rabbi Yehudah Amital's Har Etzion yeshivah was not provocative. Still at Kfar Etzion, it was an intimate institution, the kind of post-family family, complete with charismatic father-scholar, that embraces young people freshly away from home. The students did not produce news stories about settlers vying with soldiers. Quietly, they simply served as soldiers. The seminary began producing a newsletter for those on active duty. Amital answered soldiers' questions about how to keep Jewish law under military conditions. One asked about the prohibition on eating before morning prayers, a rule difficult to keep when one's schedule was set by commanders. The rabbi cited sources saying the ban applied to eating for pleasure, not for necessity. But first he gave his own reasoning: "In my opinion . . . there is no doubt that military training is a religious obligation in our day." A person engaged in one sacred duty can be more lenient about others, and serving in Israel's army was sacred.[65]

Merkaz Harav graduates Hanan Porat and Yoel Bin-Nun, young teachers certain of coming redemption, contributed theological commentary. Bin-Nun glossed the verse in Deuteronomy warning Israelites against conquering Canaan and then saying in their hearts, "My power and the might of my hand hath gotten me this wealth."[66] Actually, Bin-Nun argued, that thought was not necessarily negative. It was good to take pride in strength, remembering, of course, that ultimately it came from God; good to emulate King David, the Israelite—or Israeli—ideal of strength, who prayed to "pursue my enemies and overtake them."[67] Having inserted the nationalist ideal of military glory into the heart of Judaism, Bin-Nun added that the kings after David were weaker, presaging the faintheartedness of the present day, but "the kingdom of Israel will rise again to the messianic heights, speedily and in our days."[68] Porat examined the Book of Esther, asking why it mentioned neither God nor the Land of Israel. It made no sense for a scriptural work to lack those two pillars. The book, he concluded, demonstrated how God worked secretly in history; its verses hinted at "the stages of redemption that lie ahead of us."[69] Every sacred text, opened to any page, shouted the same message for those with ears to hear: As signified by the state's existence and conquests, history was accelerating toward its glorious conclusion.

A mood—of expectation and defiance, of being called, of understanding what others were too deliberately blind to see—was spreading, in high school yeshivot and in the Bnei Akiva youth movement, among young rabbis and novice politicos, unevenly and unmeasurable, barely planting a thought in one mind, seizing another. It was the embryo of a rebellion.

Binyamin Hanani, a seventeen-year-old student at the Or Etzion high school yeshivah, earnestly wrote to a girl, quoting the verse from the Song of Songs that describes a lover outside his beloved's house, "Behold, he standeth behind the wall." The verse referred to God, he said, in line with the Orthodox reading of the sensual book as an allegory of divine love. "There's no other generation that has felt Him so clearly just behind the wall," he wrote, adding that the verse could refer to the Western Wall, liberated in the war. As for those who asked how the war could be a miracle, since that meant God had performed miracles via irreligious Jews, he found the answer in a recent book, *The Great Era*, which argued, "At a time when the Jews are in danger—God performs miracles for them even through evildoers."[70]

The Great Era was making the rounds. Written by Menachem Kasher, a respected encyclopedist of rabbinic literature, it set out to prove that the current era fulfilled all signs predicted for the messiah's coming. Those who refused to recognize that God had performed miracles during the 1967 war, Kasher argued, were denying faith. Kasher admitted that through history, most rabbis avoided speaking of the End, but he had gathered lost texts. One, *The Voice of the Turtledove*, printed for the first time in Kasher's volume, was by a student of the most renowned Talmudic scholar of Eastern Europe, known as the Vilna Gaon, and claimed to present the eighteenth-century master's doctrine. It proclaimed the beginning of the first stage of the last days, when God would work through human events to return the Jews to their land. For close to two hundred years, Kasher said, the manuscript was kept in the author's family.[71] Kasher was demonstrating what happens when messianic fervor seizes a religious community: Old texts gain radical new meaning, prophecies are matched with events, and esoteric ideas, previously considered too dangerous for the masses, become public, available to every neophyte.

Another tract of the time was *The Spark of the Light of the Messiah*, a collection of notes by Merkaz Harav students from lessons of Rabbi David Cohen, a close companion of the original Rabbi Kook who had survived him by decades. Cohen asserted that World War I had broken out on the ninth day of the Hebrew month of Av, the anniversary of the destruction of the Temple in Jerusalem. A traditional dialectic said the messiah would be born that day, the darkest moment heralding dawn. Cohen was bending history—in 1914, Austria-Hungary declared war four days before the anniversary—in order to anoint the Great War as a first act of deliverance, since it brought the British conquest of the Land of Israel. Cohen's next sentence described the conquest of Jerusalem in 1967, when his son-in-law, army chief rabbi Shlomo Goren, blew the shofar at the Western Wall. The fact that secular Israelis had come to the Wall, cried for joy, kissed the stones, was itself a sign of redemption, he argued.[72] That fit another standard symptom of a messianic outbreak: Mass enthusiasm serves as proof that dawn is breaking, for only if something is true could so many believe.[73]

Citing the wartime scene at the Western Wall as evidence that secularists would find their way home—and that their Zionism was actually God's work—was a standard in the culture of Orthodox resurgence. It pops up in another piece of youthful writing, by Daniel Orlik, a high school yeshivah student who would continue on to Amital's Har Etzion. In his school newspaper, Orlik blasted foreign influences on Israeli youth, plans to bring the musical *Hair* to Israel, the Marxism of Mapam's Hashomer Hatza'ir youth movement. Look back in Jewish history, he suggested, and you will find the Maccabees "putting a man dressed in strange clothes to death by the sword. . . . That is a Hellenist . . . and for that he has been punished." The sign of light was that even soldiers from Hashomer Hatza'ir had prayed at the Wall. Faith could blossom again.[74] Orthodoxy could overcome secularism.

The rebellion of the Orthodox youth was gestating in schools and youth movement clubhouses around the country. But the *hesder* yeshivot that mixed study and army duty had a special role, helping to create the elite cadres who served together and absorbed an intensely ideological education. At Har Etzion and at Yeshivat Hakotel in Jerusalem's Old City, they could also regard themselves as pioneers, like other Nahal soldiers.

In June 1970, Alon Shvut, the settlement built for Har Etzion yeshivah, was established.[75] The name meant "the oak of return," referring to a lone tree that had been visible from Israeli territory before the

THE REIGN OF HUBRIS | 211

war. Yigal Allon would claim that the name was chosen, "through no fault of mine" to honor him.[76] In pushing for its establishment, Allon had made another crucial contribution to a new settlement culture. Alon Shvut's settlers, those who did not work at the yeshivah, would commute to Jerusalem. The hills were green, at least in winter, and the Arab towns passed on the way to work were part of the scenery. New residents would need approval from an acceptance committee.[77] It would be a small community of like-minded people, like a kibbutz, but without the demands of a communal economy or physical labor. One could live in a homogeneous religious suburb, with state support, and take pride in being a pioneer. Eventually, that new model would be far more successful than the communes and cooperatives that Labor still sought to build.

DESPITE THE NAME, it was hard to regard the War of Attrition between Egypt and Israel as a low-level conflict in the first half of 1970. At the year's start, the Israeli government decided to answer the Egyptian artillery barrages on the Suez Canal with bombing raids deep into Egypt. Yitzhak Rabin, the ambassador in Washington, pushed the move. Foreign Minister Eban, who opposed it, says Rabin claimed that "some people in Washington" were sympathetic. Given Rabin's back channel, that was a hint at Kissinger, and probably Nixon.[78] Nasser flew to Moscow and got help: antiaircraft missiles and Soviet personnel to operate them. By spring, Soviet pilots were flying patrols over Cairo. By June, over ten thousand Soviet military advisers, missile crewmen, and pilots were in Egypt.[79] If Nixon and Kissinger approved the escalation, the result fulfilled their view of the Mideast as a place where superpowers boxed.

At the same time, the groups making up the Palestine Liberation Organization continued their attacks from Jordan and challenged Hussein's pro-Western regime. A Palestinian insurgency was also gaining strength in Gaza. Attacks on Israelis became more common, and the Palestinian organizations were gaining control of refugee camps.

By June 1970, the fighting between Egypt and Israel was dangerous enough to demand U.S. attention. Nixon let Rogers put forward a cease-fire proposal, much more limited than his previous try. The

Rogers Initiative, or "Rogers II," called for a three-month cease-fire and negotiations based on Security Council Resolution 242.[80] Meir, rejecting the plan, told the Knesset that Rogers II would allow Egypt to recover and attack again.[81] But after both Egypt and Jordan accepted the proposal, Israel acceded to U.S. pressure. At the end of July, the cabinet approved the cease-fire—and publicly agreed to the "framework of . . . Resolution 242,"[82] which meant a willingness to give up at least part of the 1967 conquests. In response, Menachem Begin led his rightist Gahal alliance out of the government. Even so, Meir retained power; her fear of splintering her party, and her belief that Israel was safer staying put than making concessions, prevented any noticeable change in direction.[83]

ON AUGUST 7, THE cease-fire took effect. Soon after, Yisrael Galili submitted a proposal to the cabinet for two more Nahal outposts in the Jordan Rift—and for establishing outposts, for the first time, in the Gaza Strip.

Diplomatic developments, Galili wrote, created the risk that the U.S. administration or the United Nations might now seek to prevent settlement efforts. "Any further delay could put us before unnecessary diplomatic difficulties," Galili said. It was essential to work fast to stake Israel's claim to the Strip, "to establish convincing facts." As always, he called for stealth: "The preparations and dates of establishment will be subject to [military] censorship."[84]

Galili, constant adviser behind the scenes, was now also the Meir government's settlement boss, having taken Allon's place as chair of the Settlement Committee.[85] The change made sense technically—Allon had become education minister, a consuming task, while Galili was minister without portfolio. But the handoff also put settlement under the control of a man who resonated with Meir's suspiciousness, secrecy, and obsession with unity.

Galili's views on territory remained encrypted. It is possible that he himself lacked the key to the code. Did he believe in the Whole Land, or in Allon's map? "Galili was suspected, overly so in my opinion, of not being at peace with the Allon Plan," Allon later said, insisting that Galili kept zealously to the plan—but Allon liked to believe that people agreed with him.[86] Galili's closest adviser, like him a United Kibbutz man, argues that Galili accepted the plan but avoided saying so, so that Yitzhak Tabenkin, the white-haired master, would not leave his own kibbutz movement in protest.[87] Yet Galili's ambiguity would live on, even after Tabenkin died in 1971.

Galili's proposal to settle in Gaza was not the first. The year before, as Palestinian attacks multiplied in the Strip, Brigadier General Gur, the commander in the area, asked at a General Staff meeting to examine setting up outposts. Afterward, Shlomo Gazit—Dayan's viceroy in occupied territory—wrote to the cabinet secretary that the military favored establishing two outposts "because of the political meaning that such a step will have for residents of the Strip."[88] A Settlement Department listing of potential settlement sites in January 1970 includes two in the Strip—one outside Gaza city; another near the Strip's southern end, next to the town of Dir al-Balah.[89]

Attending the Settlement Committee, Gazit admitted that the outposts had no tactical value. Indeed, he said, "From a security perspective, it's a catastrophe to put those two settlements in the heart of the Strip." But the step was needed, he argued, "to give an electric shock to the residents of the Strip." In June, under Galili, the committee again weighed the idea. "The two settlements don't come to solve a military problem, but almost to create one," Gazit explained. The purpose was "political-psychological. . . . For three years we've asserted that Gaza won't return to Egyptian rule. We've done practically nothing to back up those words." Settlement was expected to shatter Palestinian hopes, helping "to create a local [Arab] element willing to be integrated into Israel."

Gvati, the agriculture minister, said some top officers—such as Ariel Sharon, head of the army's Southern Command—thought putting Nahal soldiers in the area would in fact be beneficial militarily. But General Sharon also believed that settlements would "wean the Arabs of the Gaza Strip from the illusion that we will eventually get out of there."

Still, Gvati and settlement professionals thought the idea impractical. Little land was available, and no water. The meeting ended with only a decision to reexamine the options.[90]

The Rogers Initiative convinced Galili he had to act immediately.

Now he faced the risk of real diplomacy, with pressure to stop settlement and to give up land. On September 13, the cabinet approved establishing two Nahal outposts in Gaza.[91]

The first would be Kfar Darom, outside Dir al-Balah. The choice of location and name was loaded. The original Kfar Darom, "village of the south," had been a religious kibbutz established on the eve of Yom Kippur, 1946. It was an embodiment of the pre-state settlement ethos—one of eleven settlements established simultaneously in southern Palestine in a bid to ensure that the area would be included in a future Jewish state. The day after Israel declared its independence, the invading Egyptian army attacked the small commune. After a seige of nearly two months, the defenders escaped under cover of darkness. The commander of the Palmah brigade responsible for the area, Moshe Netzer, writes with pain in his memoirs of the decision to "shorten the lines" for lack of troops.[92]

Netzer, a kibbutz member, later became an activist in the Rafi party. In 1967, Dayan appointed him as the Defense Ministry official in charge of Nahal. Resettling Kfar Darom was "an idea that I personally raised, for sentimental reasons," Netzer asserted afterward.[93] As Allon put it, "Just as the Etzion Bloc people were crazy about going back to the Etzion Bloc . . . and the Beit Ha'aravah people dreamed of Beit Ha'aravah," Netzer agitated for the right to return to the place he had lost. The new Kfar Darom, next to the old site, lacked strategic value, Allon argued.[94] But the desire to erase the pain of youthful defeat won out. After cabinet approval, Netzer took just four weeks to set up the outpost, bringing some of the original defenders to the ceremony. Israeli settlement in the Gaza Strip began on October 11, 1970, the day after Yom Kippur, virtually the anniversary of Kfar Darom's original founding.[95]

Galili's rush to settle in Gaza fit a pattern: Diplomatic initiatives spurred settlement. Faced with the prospect of negotiations and pressures that would set borders, Israeli governments would speed efforts to establish facts. Foreign diplomats, concerned with the outcome of talks, paid scant attention to what was happening in occupied territory. If the diplomatic push dragged out or died, the settlements remained as monuments to it.

∗   ∗   ∗

THE ROGERS INITIATIVE provided another, more overt proof of the Law of Unintended Consequences. Hussein's assent to a cease-fire meant stopping PLO attacks against Israel from his country. The existing tensions between the king and the PLO exploded into civil war. Palestinian groups seized control of pieces of Jordan. On September 17, Hussein ordered his army to crush the rebellion. Syrian tanks rolled across the border to support the Palestinians.[96]

The United States saw an Arab ally on the verge of falling to a Soviet client. Israel faced the danger of Arab radicals ruling the East Bank. By coincidence, Meir was in Washington, leaving Allon as acting prime minister. Kissinger contacted Ambassador Rabin, asking that Israel launch air attacks against the Syrian forces, and approving use of ground forces if needed.[97] According to Allon, even before he heard from Washington, he ordered that tanks be moved—by daylight, as visibly as possible, for deterrent value—from southern Israel to a potential launching point in the north. Israeli warplanes flew reconaissance missions over the Syrians.[98] The threat was enough: A strengthened Hussein attacked, Syria withdrew, and the Palestinians caved in, asking for peace.

Seen from Washington, the crisis vindicated the Cold War picture of the Mideast and Kissinger's view of Israel as a strategic ally. The evaluation was not changed by Nasser's sudden death from a heart attack in late September, and his replacement by the little-known Anwar al-Sadat. The United States could keep Israel strong and wait for Egypt to come knocking for help.[99]

New diplomatic paths led to dead ends. Allon held another secret meeting with Hussein in the fall. In Allon's account, he suggested as an interim arrangement that Israel institute autonomy in the West Bank, run from Amman via pro-Jordanian local Arabs. In an arrangement explicitly short of full peace, Hussein could live with the Allon Plan lines, while asserting his influence and reducing the PLO's. The proposal was strictly Allon's own, without the advance backing he had received from Eshkol. In his telling, "in a short time, I received a positive answer" from Hussein. Meir convened several ministers—Dayan, Galili, a few others—to rule on the idea. "Everyone was against!" Allon would re-count. "It could be that Golda and Dayan and the others were afraid it would hasten discussion of the future of the territories." Allon faulted himself for not putting up a fight, but fights and discussion guttered out quickly in Meir's presence.[100]

In February 1971, U.N. Mideast emissary Gunnar Jarring made one more effort to bring peace between Egypt and Israel, asking each country for "parallel and simultaneous commitments": Egypt would agree to recognition of Israel and to full peace; Israel would agree to pull back to the international border, with arrangements guaranteeing free passage in the Suez Canal and Straits of Tiran. Sadat, who had made regaining the Sinai his paramount goal, agreed, while adding conditions including Israel's withdrawal from Gaza. Israel's answer, as proposed by Galili, welcomed Egypt's openness to peace but stated, "Israel will not with-draw to the pre-June 5, 1967, lines."[101]

Jarring's mission collapsed. So did a last effort by Rogers and Sisco to arrange an interim agreement that would include an Israeli pullback from the Suez Canal. The idea had originally come from Dayan, who saw it as a way to preserve the cease-fire while holding most of the Sinai. It was adopted by Sadat, who viewed it as the first step toward a full Is-raeli withdrawal.[102] Meir was steadfastly opposed: Any diplomatic ap-proach leading to a full pullback was unacceptable, even if the proffered payoff was full peace. Israel was strong enough to deter attack, and could wait for a better offer.

"Anyone who proposes Israeli agreement to opening the canal as an instrument for total Israeli withdrawal from Sinai and Gaza should not be surprised by Israel's absolute rejection," Meir explained, at the open-ing of the Labor Party congress in April. "We have a cease-fire. Let's hope it continues. But if not—have no fear." She warned Sadat that at-tacking "is not worth it, really not worth it for you. We say that when we see the IDF, the human material, the equipment, the efficiency, talent, ability, and dedication . . ."[103]

The congress was the grand spectacle of a ruling party. Guests came from around the world. Delegates sang Israel's national anthem and "The Internationale," the hymn of socialist revolution. Galili and Dayan gave speeches as hawkish as Meir's. Finance Minister Sapir, the dove, said nothing of foreign policy. Eliav, the party secretary-general, duty-bound to neutrality, later described his own speech as "lukewarm and insipid," hiding his "maelstrom of frustration and fury." The morning after the congress, he sat bleary in the party headquarters and wrote his resignation. To his colleagues, he explained that he wanted to write a book. They concluded, he knew, that he was a "strange man." Certainly, he was a stranger at Golda's party.[104]

WHEN RAJA SHEHADEH LEFT RAMALLAH to study in Beirut, he could not take the overland route through Jordan and Syria. His father was the best-known advocate of breaking ties with Amman and establishing a West Bank Palestinian state next to Israel, and he might be in danger in Jordan. The alternative was flying to Cyprus, then on to Lebanon.

He and some friends and his mother took a taxi to the Israeli airport near Tel Aviv. At the entrance, a soldier ordered them to open their bags for a security inspection. Young Palestinian men were automatic suspects. They had the everyday response of innocent suspects: discomfort, humiliation, anger, fury. The soldier was thorough. When she came across Shehadeh's electric razor, she ordered him to take it apart. The request would not have been remarkable for her, certainly not personal. Normal objects hide murderous ones. He broke down the razor, held out the parts in his hand, and hurled them at her. "Bitch," he said in Arabic, thinking it was under his breath. The word, a mere sound in English, still carried all its contempt in Arabic. He was arrested for insulting a soldier. His mother went with him to the police station, and slowly wore him down to apologizing so he could fly away.[105]

In Shehadeh's understated, poetic memoirs, a razor is always shorthand for being a grown man, for the respect due a man. A woman wearing a soldier's uniform could tell him to take his razor apart. The meaning of the confrontation would be understood by any African-American man ever called "boy." For the woman getting through another day of army service searching suitcases, his response could only prove the unreasonableness of people like him, allowed to use an Israeli airport, to live their lives with small adjustments for security.

★   ★   ★

THE CEASE-FIRE HELD. Despite Galili's fears, the pressure to negotiate faded. It was, Admoni commented, a "routine year" for settlement.
A landscape of wide fields, young orchards, and new homes was emerging in the Golan Heights, he noted proudly. At Merom Golan, the settlers were preparing to move out of the Quneitrah officers' quarters to a
permanent site two and a half miles westward. Elsewhere, too, the map
of settled areas grew. A cooperative farming village was established on
the southern Sinai coast between Eilat and Sharm al-Sheikh. At Sharm
al-Sheikh itself was already the start of a town, Ofirah.[106] They indeed
"conveyed the impression" that Israel intended to keep land.

In the barren hills above the Jordan Rift, along the road from Nablus
to the river, another moshav was set up. It was a statement that settlement would not merely describe a line along the river, but mark off the
whole rectangle that Allon wanted to keep. A familiar problem faced
planners: finding people who wanted to call the place home. The heat
was not as furious as at the Rift floor, but the isolation seemed even
greater. At last a small moshav organization claimed the spot and ran
newspaper ads—an individualist approach suggesting the bankruptcy of
the ideological movements. Twenty singles and two families, strangers
to one another, signed up to build a cooperative village.[107] "The lack of
available manpower for settlement in the territories," Admoni says in his
memoirs, "continued to disturb us the entire time."[108]

In the Rafiah Plain, on land seized in 1969, another farming cooperative began, with the generic name of Sadot, "fields." To find settlers—
so officials told the story, with the variations typical of legends about a
mysterious man who appears to solve a problem—a kibbutz member
traveled the country, searching out young people who had left communes but still wanted to farm.[109] Nearby, at Diklah, the original settlement in the area, civilian settlers took the place of Nahal soldiers, in a
modest ceremony intended to evade publicity.[110] Nahal was still being
used to stake out new points, but the pretense that settlements were
temporary military bases was history.

Officially, Admoni's Settlement Department was not actually working in the occupied territories any more, for fear of endangering the tax-

exempt status of donations to the Jewish Agency in the United States. Instead, a new "Settlement Division" of the World Zionist Organization would handle the job, using government money. In fact, the Division was a shell that contracted all services from the Jewish Agency. When Admoni or any of his staff worked over the Green Line, they were officially employed by the Settlement Division. The change kept the U.S. Jewish philanthropies clear of the occupied territories. On the ground, the same people continued the same efforts.[111]

The first apartments in the Jewish neighborhood next to Hebron were ready in September. Settlers from the Hebron military headquarters moved in immediately. "It was advisable to create facts without any delay whatsoever," Chaim Simons explained, since the "left-wing government" might spring "unpleasant surprises."[112] The Jewish neighborhood was named Kiryat Arba, a synonym for Hebron from the Book of Genesis, as if to make the place instantly ancient. By the end of the year, settlers were demanding that the "left-wing government" build at least two hundred more units.[113]

The Hebron settlers preferred to see themselves as rebels, but for the moment that was largely posturing. Hanan Porat, the believer in settlement as the path to redemption, would remember it as a quiet time. Even if the government did not know where it was going, the direction satisfied advocates of the Whole Land. "There was confidence in the leadership," he recalled. "There was a feeling things would grow. We didn't have a feeling of urgency."[114] Time was on their side.

8

ALL QUIET ON THE SUEZ FRONT

In the early morning hours of the 14th of January, 1972, Petitioner No. 1 was urgently alerted by members of his tribe that soldiers of the Israel Defense Forces had ordered them, orally, to leave their homes and their community.

Petitioner No. 1 proceeded to those IDF soldiers, addressed their commander, a second lieutenant, and asked that he explain the actions of his soldiers. The officer answered Petitioner No. 1 that, "This is a government order to expel you from here."

Petitioner No. 1—Suleiman Hussein Udah Abu Hilu, the sheikh, or leader, of a tribe of Bedouin in what Israel called the Rafiah Plain of northeast Sinai—drove eastward to the city of Khan Yunis, at the southern end of the Gaza Strip, to speak to the district commander, a lieutenant colonel named Nissim Kazaz. According to Abu Hilu's deposition to Israel's Supreme Court, Kazaz said he had no idea what was happening, but would check with headquarters.

The sheikh returned to his community and found soldiers engaged in knocking over tents. His deposition continues:

Petitioner No. 1 approached the soldiers and protested,
asking if it was humane to drive people from their
tents in the cold of winter.

As a result of said intervention of Petitioner No.
1, the commander . . . gave the members of the tribe
permission to take shelter under the sheets of the
tents that had been toppled. The commander added that
permission was granted until the following morning, and
if, "Tomorrow after sunrise you're still here, we'll
burn the tents." . . .

On the 15th of January, 1972, at 6 a.m., a unit of
IDF soldiers appeared. . . . Several of the soldiers
were equipped with bullhorns. Petitioner No. 1 heard
voices bursting from the bullhorns: "Everyone out!
Everyone out!"

Again, Abu Hilu drove from his home, near the settlement of Sadot,
to Khan Yunis. This time Kazaz said, "The order has come from the
government to expel all the Bedouin." According to the sheikh, he
begged Kazaz to prevent "the expulsion of thousands of farmers, with
their old people, women and children, from their soil." Kazaz, says the
deposition, "swore by his life and the life of his children" that he could
do nothing. In his own signed statement, while confirming much of the
sheikh's account, Kazaz curiously chose to dispute this particular point:
He did not, he told the court, swear by his life and his children's lives.

By now, the tents and their inhabitants were gone. Part of the tribe,
however, lived in concrete houses, including the sheikh. Their turn came
the next dawn, when soldiers again appeared. The soldiers who entered
Abu Hilu's house, his deposition states, "beat one of the wives of Petitioner No. 1; his children were likewise beaten," as were other tribes-
people. All fled, leaving their possessions and food behind, to the north,
outside the area being cleared by the troops. In the sheikh's account, it
was more than a week before they were allowed to reenter the area to remove their household goods—only to find that everything was buried
beneath the broken concrete.[1]

No one knows exactly how many men, women, and children were
driven from the Rafiah Plain in early 1972. In later court statements, the
army put the population of the nine tribes expelled from an area of

about eighteen square miles stretching south from the Mediterranean coast at 4,950. According to the tribes' sheikhs, 20,000 people were forced from their homes and land.[2]

The army would defend removing the Bedouin and fencing in the Rafiah Plain as an essential step for security, a means of cutting off smuggling routes to the Gaza Strip and stopping terror attacks. Yet General Ariel Sharon, head of the Southern Command, would also be censured for "exceeding authority" by ordering the expulsion—indicating that it was a rogue operation. Whether Sharon was in fact acting on instructions or hints from Defense Minister Moshe Dayan remains an open, perhaps unanswerable, question.

There is no question, though, that the land was used for Jewish settlement, whose most extravagant expression was aggressively promoted by Dayan. Settling northeastern Sinai, in turn, was a key piece of Dayan's push to tie occupied territory permanently to Israel. The land would protect Israel but not be annexed; the residents would accept Israeli rule because their living standard would rise—except when their land was needed for settlement.

AT FIRST, VERY few Israelis knew what was taking place in the Rafiah Plain. Nothing appeared in the press. The story emerged because the society was militarized, with the army continuing to call most men, well into middle age, for weeks of reserve duty every year.

Some reservists came home from duty in the Sinai to communes belonging to the left-wing Mapam party in the corner of southern Israel that faced the Gaza Strip on one side and the Sinai on another. It was classic kibbutz landscape, barely rolling countryside of fields and orchards farmed by people who grew up in youth movements dedicated to socialism and return to the soil and who aspired to be the patriotic elite, ready to live in dangerous borderlands. For those at the Mapam kibbutzim, the vision also included a utopian hope of Jewish-Arab solidarity. Now soldiers returned to the communal dining halls with rumors that the Bedouin were being driven out, houses demolished, wells destroyed, orchards uprooted, and the land fenced.

Activists went out to check the rumors, and returned with testimony and photographs.[3] In one picture, a man from Abu Hilu's tribe, wearing a long black Bedouin gown and a head scarf, stands next to a shattered structure—a concrete ceiling lying askew on hunks of gray rubble joined by the metal rods that once reinforced a house. Another photo shows the concrete cover of a well with a square metal door, lying on the sand.[4] The concrete and the photographic black-and-white were modern; the destroyed well, as an icon of one tribe driving out another, was as ancient as stories from Genesis, schoolbook myths for the Hebrew reader, of Philistines stopping up Abraham's and Isaac's wells.

Not only the public was in the dark. In mid-February, the head of the International Committee of the Red Cross delegation in Israel asked to see Shlomo Gazit, Dayan's viceroy in the territories, now a brigadier general. The ICRC was getting complaints of population transfer, he said, asking why Israel was forcing the Bedouin out. Gazit was stunned. "I had to put on a poker face," he would recount. "I couldn't tell him that I had no idea." Neither, in Gazit's telling, did David Elazar, the conqueror of the Golan who was now the IDF chief of staff. The next day Elazar flew by helicopter to the Rafiah Plain to see for himself, then appointed an inquiry commission to examine what Sharon had done.[5]

The activists at the Mapam communes had no doubt that the purpose of expulsion was to use the land for Jewish settlement. Yisrael Galili, the government's settlement czar, was lobbying Mapam to take part in settling the Gaza Strip and the Rafiah Plain. Even before the Rafiah rumors, opposition was strong in the kibbutzim close to Gaza.[6] One key activist was Oded Lifshitz of Kibbutz Nir Oz, a wiry thirty-one-year-old with a mustache, sixties-style muttonchops, and a farmer's muscular hands. Lifshitz was the dissident as loyal son: His mother had left Ahdut Ha'avodah in the 1950s in rejection of the party's then-theoretical claim to the Whole Land of Israel.[7] At the end of February 1972, Lifshitz and some comrades at Nir Oz sent a mimeographed letter to the secretaries of other Mapam kibbutzim, describing the destroyed huts of the Bedouin, and "plans . . . that speak of a Jewish port city in the Rafiah area" and more farming communities. "Such faits accomplis," it said, "will cause difficulties for any future efforts to reach peace."[8]

At the time, a high-level team in the Defense Ministry was indeed quietly developing plans for a city with a deep-water port in northeastern Sinai, close to the Gaza Strip.[9] Planning cities was not the Defense Ministry's bailiwick. It later became clear that the grandiose project had Dayan's passionate backing.

The kibbutz activists related to the Strip and northeastern Sinai as one region, as was common at the time. Their concerns could only grow with news reports on March 1 that another Nahal outpost had been established in the Strip, between the city of Gaza and the massive refugee camps of Al-Bureij and Nusseirat. The clump of fifteen tents, with its well-lighted perimeter fence, was called Netzarim.[10]

Placing the tiny outpost in the most densely populated stretch of occupied territory was deliberate. The army and Defense Ministry argued that it would "close off the spread of the city southward, cutting Gaza off from the southern [half of the] Strip," and help the army keep watch on the area.[11] A press report noted that it fit a "military-political" design to "send Jewish fingers from the Western Negev through the Strip to the sea."[12]

The "fingers" concept belonged to Ariel Sharon. For a year, Sharon had been conducting a campaign to catch, kill, or drive out the hundreds of Palestinian militants operating in the Strip and to retake control of the refugee camps. The offensive included intensive patrols, undercover units, and reliance on bulldozers: to unearth bunkers, to rip down hedges around orchards that provided cover, to destroy houses in refugee camps, creating roads that could be patrolled more easily. "Behind every commander's jeep," Sharon later declared, "I wanted to see a bulldozer."

In Sharon's autobiography, he recounts standing on a dune with cabinet ministers, explaining that along with military measures to control the Strip, he wanted "fingers" of settlement separating its cities, chopping the region in four. Another "finger" would thrust through the edge of Sinai, helping create "a Jewish buffer zone between Gaza and Sinai to cut off the flow of weapons" and divide the two regions in case the rest of Sinai was ever returned to Egypt.[13] By Sharon's account, it is worth noting, the Gaza campaign was virtually over, the militants defeated, by the time the Bedouin were expelled and Netzarim was set up.[14] But breaking up occupied territory and dividing the population fit Sharon's long-term strategic view, which was also a political view of the area's future. The purpose was to shatter the territorial contiguity of the Arab population, in the conviction that doing so would ease permanent Israeli control.[15] The son of a Labor Zionist cooperative farm village, Sharon adopted the idea of settlements holding the land to fit his own military conception.

On an evening in early March, three hundred people from Mapam communes in southern Israel packed Nir Oz's wooden dining hall. Moshe Epstein, a Nir Oz man, described recent events in northeastern Sinai. The army "drew lines on the map of the area and a bulldozer goes through, ignoring any natural or unnatural obstacle, and cuts a path several dozen meters wide," he said. "Fields, orchards, huts where Bedouin live and cisterns—nothing stops it. . . . In one section the bulldozer clearing the earth for the fence came to the cistern of a Bedouin family. The operator . . . figured, like the others working in the place, that it wouldn't be terrible if he made a small detour so he wouldn't destroy the cistern. . . . Two days later a high-ranking IDF officer came to the spot and gave the order to put up the fence and immediately cover the cistern." The crowd adopted a resolution demanding that Mapam fight "dispossession . . . and settlement" in the land past the old border.[16] Newspaper coverage of the gathering, followed by more stories in the following days quoting Lifshitz, Epstein, and others, finally put the expulsion in the public eye. Military censorship broke down.[17] Elazar announced his inquiry commission, as if freshly appointed.[18]

A subtler, social censorship remained: The people who lived in occupied territory—the ones who in this case were expelled from their homes—did not have a voice. In Israel's public debate, not to mention secret policy discussions, people spoke of "the residents," "Arabs of the Land of Israel," or even heretically of "Palestinian Arabs." They argued about the impact of "the population," which was often a dangerous feature of the landscape in minimalists' eyes and a harmless or enchanting one for maximalists. The debate, however, was not *with* "the population." The Rafiah affair broke when kibbutz activists, Israelis, spoke out about the Bedouin.

"In mid-March," Abu Hilu's deposition noted, "the petitioners, their families, and their tribes were permitted to resume cultivating their fields, but their presence . . . was allowed only in daytime, from 6 A.M. to 5 P.M." With nightfall, they had to return to their temporary encampments beyond the fence.

Meanwhile, perhaps jogged by the controversy, army commanders noticed—according to a military attorney's later court statement—that "the area closed and seized for military purposes in 1969 . . . was only part of the area . . . evacuated . . . at the beginning of 1972." That is, by the military's own legal standards, there was no basis for the expulsion. Five days after the Nir Oz gathering, the local commander issued a decree officially taking over the land from which the Bedouin had been driven, and stating that any actions already taken there "will be seen as if done for the purposes of this order and according to it."[19]

Yisrael Galili was aghast at the controversy. Public attention was his nightmare. According to Yehiel Admoni of the Settlement Department, Galili had known nothing of the expulsion. He had expected to negotiate quietly with the Bedouin for the land, paying them in cash or alternative real estate. His effort to recruit Mapam to help settle the area was in ruins. For the first time, settlement in occupied territory—old-fashioned Labor settlement, by farmers, plowing one new field at a time—was under wide attack, by people who could themselves appear in inspirational films on the glory of pioneering.[20]

It was small comfort that much public fury was aimed at the left-wing Mapam. Prominent Labor backers of the Whole Land, including Rachel Yana'it Ben-Tzvi, widow of the country's second president, published an ad attacking Mapam's "slander" against settlement.[21] Press reports said that slogans against Diklah, the right-wing moshav on the Rafiah Plain, had been painted on roads near the Mapam kibbutzim. The story sparked a blistering Knesset speech by a rightist legislator. (Later reports said the road graffiti were a year old and had been touched up by an enterprising photographer.) The right called a Knesset debate on "propaganda against settlement."[22]

The military inquiry, according to a laconic cabinet statement issued in late March, found that "several officers" had "exceeded their authority."[23] The inquiry report remains classified to this day. Gazit, Admoni, and other writers would later identify the most senior of those officers as Sharon, who received a reprimand for ordering the expulsion without

General Staff approval. Military Intelligence chief Aharon Yariv, who conducted the inquiry, also recommended "acquiescing in the reality that has been created," as Gazit put it, which meant not allowing the Bedouin to return. In protest, Gazit asked to be transferred from his post as coordinator of government activies in the occupied territories. In that case, Chief of Staff Elazar told him, he would also have to end his military career—in effect, a punishment more severe than Sharon's. Gazit backed down.[24]

The story of the Rafiah expulsion is absent from Sharon's autobiography. He does, however, note that in the early 1950s, Dayan explained to him why he was chosen to lead retaliation raids: "Do you know why you're the one who does all the operations? Because you never ask for written orders. Everyone else wants explicit clarifications. But you never need it in writing. You just do it." Likewise, Sharon attests, Dayan gave him no written instructions for the offensive in Gaza. Rather, "from him there was only a signal, the nod of a head. That meant, as it always had, 'Do what you want. If you succeed, fine. If it backfires, don't start looking to me for support.'"[25]

Gazit, for his part, comments, "I used to say that Dayan doesn't know how to write." Dayan allowed trusted aides to sign his name, but his own orders were oral. At the same time, he kept close track of what was happening among the people in occupied territory, had his own informers, and often knew of developments before anyone else in the military.[26]

So Dayan's role in Rafiah is an enigma. Did he give an oral order? A nod of the head? If not, did his informers tell him about the troops arriving at dawn?

"The Rafiah affair," Gazit would write, "is a striking example of the struggle between opposed interests in Moshe Dayan's policy." Dayan sought invisible occupation; "on the other hand stood strategic concerns that could not be realized without hurting innocent Arabs."[27] But Dayan, holding the strategist's pen to the map, wanted to keep half the Sinai Peninsula, with peace or without, and not only the small stretch of coastal dunes that would seal off the Gaza Strip.[28] Even by the logic that said land could be held only by establishing Jewish settlements, the settlements did not need to be on the land of the Rafiah Bedouin.

Dayan's declared view of the Rafiah Plain as the "new Jezreel Valley"[29] may better explain his passion for settlement there. The Jezreel Valley in northern Israel was the "land of splendor"—in the words of a Nathan Alterman poem turned popular anthem—of the 1920s and '30s, the heroic age of Labor Zionist pioneers.[30] It was also Dayan's childhood landscape, as a son of those pioneers. In the farm communities of the Rafiah Plain, it seems, he imagined repeating the splendor of the valley. In the beach city he would create a new Tel Aviv, urban counterpoint of the valley in early Zionism. Since the Bedouin were part of the landscape, they could be moved when the land was to be reshaped.

Perhaps Dayan merely expressed his interest in Rafiah before Sharon, as he had done before the cabinet, and the general with the bulldozers worked out what was expected of him. For what happened in northeast Sinai in January 1972 is strikingly similar to what Dayan proposed in January 1969 to his fellow ministers: The Bedouin were uprooted, and the justification given was fighting terror in Gaza.

EVERYTHING holds a spark of holiness, yeshivah student Dov Indig wrote. For example, there were "Hashomer Hatza'ir members who smear the roads of the Gaza Strip in order to defend 'victimized Arabs.'" One could disagree with them, mock the contradictions in their arguments. But still, they revealed "sincere desire to repair" the world, and that desire reinforced a believer's faith that the messiah would come, "the hope that all the positive desires . . . will become a mighty stream, sweeping away evil and falsehood."[31]

Indig was twenty years old in the spring of 1972 when he wrote that letter, splitting his time between yeshivah studies and service in the Armored Corps. One day at a base in the Golan Heights, a middle-aged secular kibbutz member on reserve duty quizzed him about religion. Afterward he received a letter from the man's daughter, packed with her own questions. Soon he was spending late nights corresponding with her, then with two other secular kibbutz girls as well, about faith, human purpose, and the meaning of Jewish history.[32]

Trying to convince one of the girls that true happiness could be achieved only through dedication to an ideal, and that religion held the highest ideal, he enlisted Molière and Victor Frankl as well as the Talmud.[33] His description of Hashomer Hatza'ir's defense of the Bedouin as both misdirected and showing a "spark of holiness" that would help bring redemption echoed the writing of Rabbi Avraham Yitzhak Hacohen Kook, who had described an earlier generation of socialist Zionist pioneers as "good sinners" and "the lights of chaos," bringing the messiah without knowing it.

But the theology also fit a mood among intent young religious Zionists—arguing to oneself, most of all, that faith was the best path, that it made sense to keep praying three times a day while in the army, and all the while feeling that the model to match or exceed was set by secular Zionists who had settled the land. Having grown up on a kibbutz, "you lack the principal thing we ask of life, true happiness," he wrote in another letter. Yet "to a certain extent I envy you," he wrote. He was studying "the Torah of the living God, and nothing is likely to be more satisfying." Nonetheless, "a person also needs the opportunity to realize his ideals," which he implied she was doing simply by living in a kibbutz. "That opportunity has not yet been given to me," Indig wrote, "though I hope to merit it one day."[34]

While serving in Quneitrah, he dropped by Kibbutz Merom Golan for a look. He found small houses surrounded by gardens and lawns, a green corner of paradise in the shadow of the black volcanic mountains. A kibbutz member grabbed him, he wrote. "'Why don't the Orthodox establish settlements in the Golan Heights?' he asked me. 'The Heights . . . cry out for more settlers. What happened to the commandment of settling the Land of Israel?' I was a little embarrassed, but it seems to me he's right. Thousands of settlers should be brought to the Golan, to fill the Heights with light and life."[35]

Yehudah Etzion, a tall redhead, also twenty years old, felt he was getting the chance to live his ideals. Etzion was born on a religious kibbutz, tying him to the side of religious Zionism that emulated secular pioneers, even if his family had left for the city when he was young. But his uncle was a veteran of the pre-state Lehi underground—the Stern Gang—the small, violent far-right group that dreamed of establishing the Jewish "Third Kingdom" in an expansive Land of Israel.[36] That education redoubled his feeling as a teenager, watching the conquests of 1967, that "the heavens opened."

Etzion was an early student at Har Etzion yeshivah. While there, he changed his original last name, Mintz, fitting the Israeli preference for exchanging names from "exile" for Hebrew ones. Naming oneself after the place one had settled was one way of doing that. When the yeshivah moved to Alon Shvut, Etzion discovered that outside the study hall, he could help put a new settlement together. "It got me out of the world of the book to the world of action. I built a temporary electric grid, as the son of an electrician. Partly I knew how, partly I had good hands." He caught "the settlement bug," but was disturbed at "slackness," lack of ambition. "I wondered why there weren't new settlements. There'd been a start at Kfar Etzion, at Kiryat Arba." Elsewhere the new land was "empty," meaning empty of Jewish settlement. He saw the West Bank hill country as "primeval," biblical, wanted to swallow it up, join himself to it, see "the entire people return to this landscape." His words are a lexicon of romantic nationalism. Settlement meant escaping the quotidian for the mythical. In 1972, he began organizing yeshivah students and others to settle at Susiya, in the southern West Bank, where archaeologists were excavating an ancient synagogue, showing that Jews had lived there 1,500 years before.[17]

In Kiryat Arba, settler Benny Katzover would recall, a question wove itself into meetings and conversations: When would another group of Jews, like the one that came to Hebron in the southern half of the West Bank, settle in Samaria, the northern half?

Occasionally, a dot appeared, very briefly, on the map. A group of rightists claiming thirty members arrived several times in the area near Nablus, the largest city in the northern West Bank, and each time was quickly evicted by the army.[18] The evictions, as much as the settlements established by the Labor government, underlined that the Allon Plan was de facto policy: The heavily populated hill country north of Jerusalem remained out of bounds.

The Nablus group—mostly secular, mostly students—sought advice from the Hebron settlers. Its members sought only to demonstrate in favor of settlement, an unimpressed Katzover concluded, not to do it themselves. Meanwhile, the question of Samaria kept "coming up with longing and pain. As the years passed, the pain and shame became stronger," Katzover recalled—shame that there was "empty territory," that "the whole world sees . . . Samaria is empty." In 1972 the idea still did not occur to Katzover that he would do something about it himself. But in his testimony, as in Etzion's, is the first scent of an intoxicating impatience.[39]

THE MOST impatient man in the Middle East, though, was Anwar al-Sadat. Egypt's leader wanted the Sinai Peninsula back. Recalling the lessons of his Nile Delta peasant childhood, speaking of neighbors who would fight for fifty years over a meter of land, he said in a *New York Times* interview after taking power that "our land . . . means our honor here . . . and one dies for this honor."

Sadat was willing to do almost anything to get the Sinai. That included war or even peace—though this is considerably more obvious in the lovely light of later events than it was in the present tense. In the *Times* interview, he said that "if you want to seek peace," all that was needed was fulfilling Resolution 242. By saying "peace," Sadat cast aside the "no peace" of Khartoum. But he also said he would "Never! Never! Never!" establish diplomatic relations with Israel, and that Israeli use of the Suez Canal would depend on first solving the Palestinian refugee problem.[40] He thereby effectively rejected two pieces of what Israel regarded as peace, while insisting he would not "surrender one inch" of Sinai.

Read in Golda's kitchen, Sadat's words proved he would remain hostile even after an agreement—and that he was still rejecting the obvious, that the price of peace was for him also to give up land.

At one point, Sadat tried asking *Newsweek* journalist Arnaud de Borchgrave to pass the message to Israel that he was ready to talk peace. De Borchgrave flew to Israel and called the precocious Labor politician Yossi Sarid, Pinhas Sapir's protégé, who had completed his graduate studies in New York and had returned to Israel. De Borchgrave knew Sarid as a source well connected to Labor leaders, and indeed, Sarid went to Meir the same day. "She gave me an icy look," he later wrote. "She told me . . . first, there is nothing new here; I've already heard about it. Second, do you have any idea what he wants from us, Sadat? He wants all of Sinai. And she then fell gloomily and angrily silent."[41]

Sadat also spoke publicly of regaining his land by force. Repeatedly, he had referred to 1971 as the "year of decision" leading to a political solution or war.[42] When the year ended with neither, he looked like a man speaking loudly and carrying a small stick. Arie Eliav would later describe the common perception of Sadat in Israel: "In Egypt ruled a president who appeared spineless and weak-kneed to Israeli policymakers and public opinion. This man . . . dared several times to threaten Israel that he would take up arms if it did not withdraw from all of Sinai, but who took him seriously? Particularly when each time he gave a target date for attacking Israel and afterward stammered and backed down."[43]

Israeli intelligence knew that Sadat was pressing the Soviet Union for better arms. According to a highly placed Israeli source in Egypt, Sadat would not go to war unless Egypt received Soviet fighter-bombers with the range to attack air bases inside Israel, and Scud missiles able to hit Israeli territory. An idea became accepted truth in the Israeli military: Since Moscow had not provided those arms, Egypt would not attack.[44] This was to be known as "the concept." It rested on the deeper assumption that American arms and Israeli territorial depth served as overwhelming deterrents to all-out war.

In May 1972, President Richard Nixon flew to Moscow for a summit with Soviet leader Leonid Brezhnev. The Mideast was left as a footnote to the talks. The agreed communiqué at the summit's end simply reaffirmed the superpowers' commitment to Security Council Resolution 242, leaving its meaning as uncertain as ever. Sadat felt sold out. The Soviets, more concerned with détente, were doing nothing to help him get his land back. In July, to the world's surprise, he evicted the Soviet Union's 15,000 military advisers. The move removed Soviet reins—diplomatically and militarily.[45]

In theory, Kissinger was waiting for this: the strongest Arab country moving away from the Soviet Union. In practice, he was distracted. His boss, Richard Nixon, was running for reelection, and did not want Mideast initiatives, with their potential for unpopular friction with Israel. Besides, Kissinger was consumed with a larger problem in Southeast Asia—as American foreign-policy officials had been since the Middle East blew up in 1967. "The seminal opportunity to bring about a reversal of alliances in the Arab world," he explains in his memoirs, "would have to wait until we had finally put the war in Vietnam behind us."[46]

The military threat implicit in Sadat's move was missed. Israeli leaders and generals saw the exit of Soviet advisers as evidence that Egypt had no war option.[47] It reinforced confidence that the government's policies were working. Staying put was keeping Israel safe.

EVEN THE MOST provocative dissident in the house of Labor, though, did not trust Sadat's talk of peace. "Egypt demands that we pull out of all of the Sinai Peninsula 'just like that,' " wrote Arie Eliav. Without making clear what he meant by peace, without negotiating, Sadat expected Israel to give up the "strongest and most sophisticated" military bulwark it had created against the threat of eradication. "The very fact that Egypt's rulers assume that such an act will take place on its own . . . testifies to the illusions under which the Egyptians are living. And what is much worse, to the secret intentions in their hearts."[48]

The words appeared in the book that Eliav had given up his post as party secretary-general to write. It was called *Land of the Hart*, a traditional term for the splendor of the Land of Israel. Eliav's thick tome argued that to reach splendor, Israel would eventually need to give up nearly all the land it took in 1967.

If Eliav did not differ with Prime Minister Meir on Sadat's intentions, he disagreed completely on how Israel should respond. It should challenge Egypt: "We are sitting on your territory, and we are willing to return it" for full peace. That meant demilitarizing the Sinai and exchanging ambassadors; it meant Israeli ships sailing down the Suez Canal, Israeli tourists on the pyramids, Egyptian businessmen in Tel Aviv, Israeli and Egyptian soccer teams playing each other—all of which Eliav described as being, for the moment, "dreams and mirages in the barren desert of our relations with Egypt."[49]

Whether the Sadat of 1972 would have accepted that challenge remains another of history's "what ifs." In Israel, *Land of the Hart* quickly sold close to 20,000 copies—equivalent to over a million in the United States. At the same time, Eliav reported, "women and men who had not read it were infuriated at its very appearance. . . . I began to taste the bitter flavor of defamatory articles, of anonymous threats. . . . Some of my former 'friends' began to vanish from my vicinity." In Eliav's accurately melodramatic description, the book helped transform him "from 'a promising young man' to a veteran wanderer in the wilderness, full of scars, burned by sun and wind."[50]

Eliav wrote that as part of any peace settlement Egypt would also have to drop any claim to Gaza, whose future would be negotiated between Israel and "the Palestinian Arabs." The question was whether Israel would give up "some, most, or all" of the Strip to a future Palestinian state.[51] That underlined his most controversial argument: that a Palestinian nation existed and deserved self-determination. By now Eliav had achieved enough prominence for that assertion to grab attention. Despite the Jews' historic claim to "the mountains of Judea and Samaria," he said, Israel must declare its willingness to return most of the West Bank to Arab rule, under a Palestinian state that would also include Gaza and the East Bank.[52]

Most, but not all. Eliav presumed that Israel would annex some West Bank settlements—"the Etzion Bloc, for instance." He mentioned, without irony, the "right of Jewish settlement in all of the Western Land of Israel"—a phrase hinting that the East Bank was also part of the Jews' historic homeland—and "the spirit of dedication and volunteerism" that drove "young settlers," for almost all settlers in occupied territory belonged to the young generation of Labor Zionism. The party-platform phrases, worn smooth by use, were not a sop to readers; they expressed Eliav himself, the product of his time and past, the ex-Settlement Department man—like any revolutionary, a part of the age he rejects.

For between those phrases, Eliav now rejected the idea of using settlements to hold land. Those brave young settlers, he wrote, must be told that they might end up as a Jewish minority in a Palestinian state. Israel must announce that "we do not want the territory of the West Bank and the Strip for Jewish settlement, for it is not there that we will settle the millions of Jews whom we intend to repatriate to Israel." Having announced that, Israel would "wait with infinite patience for a true partner [for peace] from among the Palestinian Arabs."[53]

Eliav acknowledged that his words would be seen as "heresy and apostasy."[54] In retrospect, they also bear witness to what was established belief. Ironically, the sharpest criticism that summer of what was happening in settlements was sparked by a writer far more mainstream than Arie Eliav.

"SADOT IS A WONDER—a mix of zealous patriotism and the spirit of the Wild West," wrote Haim Gouri, after a visit to the Sinai farming community in June 1972. Now writing for *Davar*, the Labor Party newspaper, he reported that Sadot's residents "were nearly all native-born, children of kibbutzim and moshavim, farmers born and bred"—the nobility, for youth movement graduates and *Davar* readers. "They export the produce of this good earth . . . and import good dollars"—the latter also considered patriotic, though subtly discordant, out of key with the original ascetic ethic of pioneering.

Gouri had driven to the Rafiah Plain with a colleague from *Davar*, who had a friend from reserve duty who lived at Sadot—a bearded young man brought up on a kibbutz. On his bookshelves, Gouri found the canon of Hebrew literature—fiction by S. Y. Agnon, poetry by Nathan Alterman. Outside was the young family's used car and their "personal Bedouin laborer, a member of the tribe that was evacuated."

Hiring workers had caused stormy debate in the community, as in the whole moshav movement, the young man said. Gouri did not need to explain to his readers that employing Arab workers violated the principles of both socialism and "Hebrew labor," Jews returning to manual labor. But Sadot's members had decided they could not harvest their crops alone.

"Does every farm have a Bedouin laborer?" Gouri asked.

"Yes—actually, yes."

"Just one?"

"One or two, or maybe a few."

"How much do they make?"

"Eight pounds a day," the farmer said—$1.90. The military government set the pay scale, he apologized, adding that his laborer "doesn't exactly get eight a day. Actually he gets more. He gets vegetables from me and if a turkey is about to die, I give it to him. So actually he gets more."

"And it doesn't matter to you, to start your lives here with a hired Bedouin in every farm?"

"What do you want? That they won't work, that they'll go hungry, that they'll be unemployed? Who works up north?" the farmer demanded, meaning inside Israel. Even Mapam kibbutzim had Arab laborers, he said. "And who's building Jerusalem and Tel Aviv? Did we invent Arab labor? What are we supposed to do? . . . Not develop? Not produce?"

The Bedouin lived several kilometers away, next to the main junction, in shanties and tents, the young man said.

"The ones living next to Rafiah junction," Gouri wrote, "lived here."[55]

The ironies in Gouri's article began with his byline.[56] He did feel more at home, among *his* tribe, with people who spoke in the accents of the native-born, in homes with those writers on the shelf. He still resonated with the *In Your Covenant* vision of soil, settlement, and socialism. But at Sadot, the vision cracked. People pushed off the land returned as laborers on the farms of others. The Bedouin ostensibly posed a security risk when they lived there, but were no longer dangerous as laborers in Jewish fields. Sadot's small farms were not plantations, and Gouri the poet did not use words like "settler colonialism," but he drew a picture that called up that term.

The new controversy over hired labor at Sadot burned for months. Another *Davar* commentator, in an article called "The Whole Country Is Sadot," attacked Gouri for having a "divided heart" and speaking quietly. "If this happened in a distant land . . ." he said, "our poets would raise an outcry."[57] Gouri's ambivalence, though, again rendered him a one-man Greek chorus for the Labor ruling class.

The reports on Sadot further damaged the prestige of settlement which "until then was sky-high," in the view of Yehiel Admoni of the Settlement Department. Outside of the left-wing Mapam party's refusal to build kibbutzim in the Sinai, though, the impact was minimal. Admoni would not enter Sadot, which made little difference. The farmers' quick economic success freed them of dependence on the Settlement Department. Two more farming communities were planned next to Sadot, on land from which Bedouin had been expelled. Government allocations of irrigation water were large enough to ensure that those settlements, too, would have crops that required employing Bedouin laborers.[58]

Gouri's host, in any case, was right: Laborers from the occupied territories were working on the building sites of Tel Aviv and Jerusalem. In that sense, the whole country was Sadot. The most prominent advocate of an open flow of workers was Dayan, who in the summer of 1972 pressed his demands for economic "integration" of the occupied territories with Israel. He also wanted to encourage Israeli investment in the land under military rule, to create manufacturing jobs there. Dayan's constituency included both ideological believers in keeping land and business interests able to profit from cheap labor.[59] The Arabs were expected to accept Israeli rule in return for higher income—as Israel's working class. In Dayan's view, the status quo of no war no peace, of occupation without annexation, could last indefinitely.

THE ISRAELI LEGAL SYSTEM has a fast track to the Supreme Court: An individual can petition the country's highest court directly against an alleged injustice by the executive branch. Following the war in 1967, the IDF's top legal authority, Advocate General Meir Shamgar, chose not to challenge petitions to the court by residents of occupied territory against the military government. Shamgar's step subjected the army's actions to judicial review. It also extended the court's authority beyond the borders of the state to occupied territory, in a hint at annexation.[60] Whether liberal or nationalist, Shamgar's decision stuck, in part because he went on to become the country's attorney general, on his way to a long, influential stint as a Supreme Court justice.

In July 1972, nine Bedouin sheikhs asked the Supreme Court to order the army to let them go home. Telling Petitioner No. 1's tale, the suit at last gave the Bedouin a voice.[61] Though collectively accused of helping terror groups, the Bedouin had fewer qualms than Palestinians in turning to the Israeli court, legitimizing its power. In a letter beforehand to Israeli leaders, Abu Hilu had protested that his tribe was wronged even as it "cooperated in living under the protection of the state in security and peace"—a declaration of fealty that Gaza militants would have regarded as outright collaboration.[62]

The sheikhs' lawyer—a Mapam man, Haim Holzman—argued that what happened in the Rafiah Plain had no legal or military basis, and violated the Geneva Convention's ban on the transfer of occupied populations. Days after filing the petition, Holzman asked the court to act quickly: The Rafiah district commander had called in his clients, told them their lawyer was a communist, and urged them to drop the suit. Meanwhile, "earthwork by agents of the authorities has begun in the petitioners' land, causing destruction of their orchards and crops."[63]

The court ordered the government and Southern Command chief Ariel Sharon to show cause for the expulsion.[64] The government's response, strikingly, did not include depositions by Sharon or by Dayan, the responsible minister. What they could truthfully declare, one must conclude, was deemed unhelpful to the state's case.

Instead, depositions by other officers explained that the Bedouin had not actually been driven from their land, because part of the land they were working had been seized under the 1969 orders. As for the rest, it was seized in that strange decree issued after the expulsion but effective beforehand.[65]

The most important argument, on the need for a buffer between Sinai and Gaza, came from General Yisrael Tal, a hero of the 1967 war whose record was not stained with "exceeding authority." Tal detailed attacks on Israelis and local residents in the Rafiah Plain or elsewhere by terrorists who had used it for shelter. Egyptian intelligence agents, he added, had passed through the area or had hidden there. To break that pattern, a fenced buffer zone was needed—without "the permanent presence of local residents," he said, and with "Jewish settlement and presence."[66]

"I grant all due respect to Moshav Sadot," Holzman responded, "but I will argue that establishing the moshav is not an 'imperative military reason'"—the only justification the Fourth Geneva Convention provides for the forcible transfer of an occupied population.

Besides citing international law, Holzman sought to pull apart the threads of Tal's argument for a buffer zone. Tal claimed that terror attacks increased toward the end of 1971. A map he submitted showing each attack proved the opposite: Attacks were already falling off before the expulsion—and most incidents had taken place outside the seized area. There was no escape, Holzman wrote, from concluding that the Bedouin were expelled "for reasons the respondents have concealed from this honorable court." Holzman's final arguments—the restrained lawyerly tone now giving way to sarcasm and passion—were presented by his law partner to the three justices who heard the case. Holzman had written them and died of a heart attack.[67]

In the meantime, Dayan's plans for a port on the northeastern Sinai coast leaked to the press. A booklet prepared in the Defense Ministry described a metropolis to be called Yamit, "Of the Sea." The booklet said it would become one of Israel's largest cities, home to a quarter-million people by the year 2000. With Finance Minister Sapir blasting the plan as an epic boondoggle that would come at the cost of Israel's poor, the cabinet officially shelved the idea.[68] As a side benefit, that absolved the government of the need to explain in court why a port city was needed in a military buffer zone.

"A FEW WEEKS AGO I visited friends of mine ... Holocaust survivors," said Arie Eliav, addressing Labor's secretariat. "A spectacularly beautiful farm in the south of the country. One son is a pilot in the air force, the other supposedly works on the farm, but he doesn't actually work there. The tractor by now is for driving to the beach, because at the edge of the moshav are a few 'Ahmeds.' That's a collective name. Not Palestinian Arabs, not Arabs of the Land of Israel. Now there's a concept of 'Ahmeds.' ... My friends' son says, 'Something really funny happened a few days ago with one of those Ahmeds. They live over with the horses and donkeys. ... Since the horses have ticks, one of the Ahmeds got ticks, and he just swelled up.'" The friend's son thought that was a laugh. "I'm not coming to say that fellow is to blame," Eliav said, implying that the blame lay with others, some of them in his audience.

Eliav was speaking in September 1972, before over 170 people including Prime Minister Golda Meir, at the first session of a party debate on what government policy should be in occupied territory—now the pressing question in party branches, kibbutzim, and the press. The party secretary-general, Aharon Yadlin, asked speakers not to deal with conditions for peace, Israel's future borders, or settlements meant to set those borders; the issue was the indefinite interim, "how to live together until a peace agreement." That really meant the economics of occupation, such as whether to let fewer or more West Bank and Gaza Arabs work inside Israel. The active labor force in those territories, Yadlin noted, was 160,000 people. As many as 50,000 were already working inside Israel, he said, though his comments indicate that more might be working for cash, off the books.[69]

Yadlin's framing of the question showed that the spark lighting the fire was Dayan's demand for economic "integration," and also that Yadlin did not want to cross Meir, who emphatically wanted no debate of borders. After another session, she reportedly tried to stop the debate.[70] For once given the floor, politicians would not stay off forbidden subjects.

As with Eliav. In principle, he said, it made sense that a developed country would draw outside workers—though the flood of cheap labor was actually *undeveloping* Israel, encouraging farmers and contractors to revert to hands in place of machines. But if Palestinians found jobs in Israel, he wanted them to come as citizens of their own state, with a consulate to defend them. The relation between the farmer's son and his "Ahmeds" was the predictable relation of employers with people who lacked rights, a consequence of occupation.

The debate demonstrated that four years after its founding, Israel's ruling party lacked a hint of a shared answer to Lyndon Johnson's question, "What kind of Israel do you want?" The clearest camps were Moshe Dayan's supporters and his opponents, a division putting Yigal Allon on the same side as Arie Eliav.

Allon had begun looking more moderate partly by staying put as others, particularly Dayan, staked out steadily more intransigent positions. But by now, Allon also embraced the heresy that there was such a thing as the Palestinian people. "What's certain is that a Palestinian population exists, whether or not one defines it as a nation; that a Palestinian public with its own unique lines exists, whether or not one recognizes it as such," Allon said in a November session. Besides sparking his found-a-new-toy enthusiasm for a new concept, the idea provided another argument for his plan: If the Palestinians were a nation, then Israel should give up the part of the West Bank where they lived—while retaining the land Allon saw as essential to security. The deal should be made with Jordan, since the East Bank was part of the Palestinian homeland, he argued, though he did not oppose negotiating with West Bank Palestinians as well. What he did oppose was Dayan's idea that only "under the aegis of Israel and the IDF," meaning permanent Israeli rule, could Jews and Arabs live together.[71]

The strongest barrage against Dayan came from Pinhas Sapir. The dovish finance minister lectured his party's leaders in the tone of a high school teacher harassing students flunking both math and social studies. The flood of Arab labor, he warned, was a "social, political and moral danger," creating "a class that does the clean work and those who do the dirty work"—akin "to Negroes in the United States." Whether Israel officially annexed the occupied territories or just drifted toward that de facto result, a million Arabs would be added to its population. Anyone who expected a rising standard of living to erase their national aspirations, he said, "hasn't learned the lesson of history." Denying them equal rights would put Israel in a class with "countries whose names I don't even want to say in the same breath."

Then he gave his math lesson, using birthrates and migration figures to predict how many Jews and Arabs would live in Israel, the West Bank, and the Gaza Strip when Israel celebrated its golden jubilee in 1998. Calculating population increases, he said, just meant figuring compound interest, and "there are teachers sitting here, they can tell us what grade in elementary school you learn compound interest." If Jewish immigration remained steady and Israel kept the occupied territories, Sapir said, in 1998 the Arabs would be 48.5 percent of the population. If immigration more than doubled, Arabs would still be over 40 percent. "Is this the Jewish state we aspired to?" he berated his students. (Sapir's predictions, checked against later reality, also taught that statistics can indeed be truthful. At the end of 1997, after unexpectedly high immigration, Arabs constituted approximately 44 percent of the population in Israel and the occupied territories.)[72]

Shimon Peres, speaking for the Dayan camp, accused Sapir of ideological weakness. Just as Zionists had had faith in pre-state days that immigration would create a Jewish majority, they should have confidence now that Jews would come from the Soviet Union, Europe, the United States. The Arabs of the occupied territories could then live as a minority with equal rights in an expanded Israel. Meanwhile, Peres said, the current situation was fine. Without need for treaties, there was de facto peace with Jordan, and "terror has almost stopped." In the West Bank, incomes were rising. "I'm proud that tens of thousands of laborers are working in Israel, in the professions they are capable of," Peres said. ". . . And all of this is when Jerusalem is united, a Jewish neighborhood has been established in Hebron, and settlements have been established in the Rift and the Rafiah Plain."[73]

ONE MORNING in early winter, Benny Katzover sat in his friend Menachem Felix's home in Kiryat Arba outside Hebron, parsing a page of Talmud with him. Katzover was frustrated. The night before, he had attended yet another gathering of rabbis and Orthodox activists on settling in Samaria, the northern West Bank. Government policy kept the area from Jerusalem north off-limits to Jewish settlement. The ideas raised at the meeting for action—lobbying the National Religious Party, demonstrating, holding a hunger strike—did not impress Katzover.

Felix, twenty-seven years old, had come to Hebron directly from Merkaz Harav, where he had spent several years absorbing Tzvi Yehudah Kook's messianic nationalist teachings. As he and Katzover studied, the conversation shifted to the previous night's meeting. Their books closed. If no one else would act, they decided, they would. Settling in Hebron had taught them how to do it.

First, they needed a group ready to settle—fifteen or twenty families, "strong enough," in Katzover's words, "that if you threw them on a mountain, without water or electricity or phones or kindergartens, they would hold on with their teeth and create a settlement." That day, in Katzover's account, they signed up two or three families from Kiryat Arba. Then they began contacting friends, asking for names of potential recruits, traveling the country, meeting people. Katzover and Felix were done with the quiet of living in an established settlement; they were back in action.

On Friday, February 2, 1973, fifteen young couples and several singles met in a Kiryat Arba apartment. They set their goal as settling near Nablus, the biblical city of Shekhem, just as Kiryat Arba neighbored Hebron.

Nablus was the major Arab city of the region, the "strongest city" in Katzover's description, and settling there would be "an answer to Arab power," breaking open the gates to the area. Shekhem was also where God had promised Abraham that his descendants would inherit the land, as told in Genesis. Katzover and his friends were Orthodox Jews, but his explanation for the choice of where to settle tapped two impulses of militant modern nationalism: the desire for power, as a value, especially power in the face of another, threatening group; and the desire to fulfill promises of the mythic past, to live the myth.

That fit the goals of yeshivah student Yehudah Etzion, who heard of the plan through friends. He dropped his own project of settling elsewhere in the West Bank, and joined the new group.

The activists began meeting politicians. If they could not get government approval, they hoped to gain influential support, so that "the government and the army couldn't run us over," in Katzover's words, if they tried settling anyway. The strategy, that is, was a repeat of Hebron in 1968, when a wildcat settlement gained the backing of Yigal Allon and other cabinet members. This time, though, Allon told them clearly that he was opposed. Samaria was outside his map. In the Labor Party, in Katzover's account, only two prominent figures expressed support— "Moshe Dayan, and especially Shimon Peres."[74]

AT LAST, Henry Kissinger was done with distractions. A peace agreement for Vietnam was signed; Nixon had won his landslide reelection. In February 1973, Anwar al-Sadat's national security adviser Hafiz Ismail came to Washington. Kissinger and Ismail retired to a private estate for two days of talks on how to get Mideast diplomacy moving.

Kissinger had ideas, but a central one was to wait. Nothing much could get done, he reasoned, until after the Israeli elections scheduled for the end of October. Less than a week after Ismail had left, Golda Meir came calling in Washington, and the U.S. press reported that

Nixon promised her more warplanes. The impatient man in Cairo did not feel encouraged.[75]

OFFICIALLY, the cabinet made no decision at its meeting on April 8. Unofficially, that meant Golda Meir had come down against Dayan's latest proposal: allowing Israeli individuals and companies to buy land from Arabs in the West Bank.

For two months, the idea had roiled domestic politics and set off a gale of diplomatic cables to Washington from U.S. envoys in the Mideast. It underlined another return to the thinking of pre-state days, when land-buying was a key tactic in the Jewish-Arab ethnic struggle for Palestine. The move seemed certain to create a new class of Israelis opposing withdrawal and would privatize settlement policy. Private developers would not keep to the Allon Plan's lines. The change also violated a fundamental Labor position: Land should not be private property; it should be owned by the Jewish National Fund in the name of the Jewish people, or by the state. Sapir, as usual using economic arguments for his dovish positions, said the Dayan proposal would set off a wave of land speculation—a term of moral contempt in the Labor lexicon.

From the U.S. embassy in Amman came reports of near-panic in Hussein's court in response to Dayan's proposal. West Bank Arabs would sell, attracted by easy money, pushed by fear that land might be expropriated anyway. A new wave of Palestinian emigrants would flood the East Bank, the king's constant nightmare, and any hope of getting Israel out of the West Bank would evaporate.

This time, advance publicity in Israel and distress warnings from Jordan led to U.S. pressure. On the eve of the crucial cabinet meeting, Under Secretary of State Sisco phoned the new Israeli ambassador in Washington, Simcha Dinitz, a Meir confidant. Meir, previously wavering, decided that Dayan's proposal would be "divisive." The defense minister, seemingly defeated, did not ask for a vote.[76]

Meir also found her party's debate on the occupied territories divisive, and put her foot down: one more session.[77] Dayan, finally, stood to present his positions. To speak early was to be lost in the crowd. To speak last was power. If the Arabs "have not dared, so far, to renew the shooting," Dayan said, a major reason was the land Israel held. That included the mountains of Samaria and of the Sinai, because radar stations there provided the air force with early warning of any Arab attack. Allon's idea of giving up the mountains, he implied, showed poor understanding of modern war.[78] But Dayan's military reasons were only his preamble. Explicitly, he rejected the view that Israel should settle and keep only land that it needed for security. "When we stop studying the Bible," he declared, "Jews will no longer feel that they are at home in Judea and Samaria."[79] That feeling, he argued, should drive a policy of maximum settlement, by all means possible. The Arabs were not offering peace, and it might take a generation before they did. If by then "the area that is up for discussion has been reduced and cut" by settlement, "I don't see that as such a grim possibility."[80] In the long term, Israel was seeking to turn "an Arab entity and essence" into a Jewish one, just as Jews had done in the Jezreel Valley of his youth before 1948. Inevitably, that required negating the "national and political rights" of the Arabs. Arabs would have to move to make way for Jews, Dayan said. Their compensation would be economic improvement.[81] It was a vision that mixed paternalism and dispossession, one that cited hard military calculations but ultimately rested on his passion for the romanticized past, the Bible as epic.

The very last word was reserved for Meir. Trying to decide what Israel's final borders should be, she said, would only cause "war among ourselves" and tension internationally. The prime minister feared discord most of all. She had not wanted the party's argument. Now, she summed up simply, "There is no need to make decisions."[82]

Dayan wanted the party to endorse his positions. Again, it seemed he was defeated.

"WE HAVE NO REASON to doubt," wrote Supreme Court Justice Moshe Landau, that the military justifications for creating a buffer zone in the Rafiah Plain "have been argued before us in complete good faith." Landau and his two fellow justices issued their ruling on the Sinai Bedouin in May 1973. They affirmed that the Supreme Court could oversee decisions of the military. On the other hand, "on such matters, certainly the opinion of army men is to be preferred to that of the petitioners' counsel." True, the expulsion order had been issued retroactively—but the reasons for it continued to hold true. While terrorism had dropped off in Gaza, it might "catch fire anew." The three justices agreed: The petition was rejected. The Bedouin could not go home.[83]

HOSTING SOVIET LEADER LEONID BREZHNEV at his San Clemente estate in June allowed Richard Nixon to show that détente was progressing, that he had a firm hand on foreign policy. That was useful, because messy questions concerning the break-in a year before to Democratic Party headquarters in Washington's Watergate complex were entangling him domestically.

On June 23, the summit's last night, with the final communiqué written, the leaders of the two superpowers went to bed early. Then something strange happened. At 10:00 P.M., Brezhnev demanded to wake Nixon to speak again. At the unscheduled midnight meeting, in Kissinger's description, Brezhnev delivered an hour-and-a-half monologue on the Middle East. He demanded that Nixon sign a Soviet proposal for principles for an accord: total Israeli withdrawal, in return for an end to belligerency, less than full peace. "I am categorically opposed to a resumption of the war," he said—but if America would not agree, at a minimum, to the principle of full withdrawal, he could not prevent it. Nixon told him, "We don't owe anything to the Israelis," but could only promise that "the Middle East will be our project this year."

In his memoirs, Kissinger writes that Brezhnev was trying to "exploit Nixon's presumed embarrassment over Watergate." The Soviet leader, he says, knew that war would result in Arab defeat.[84] His memoirs do not suggest that Kissinger regarded himself as having missed a critical warning.

IT WAS LATE JULY. With the elections just three months off, Dayan used his ultimate weapon. Because of the party's policy in the occupied territories, he said, he was not sure he could run on the Labor ticket.

"The territories are not a 'deposit'" to be held temporarily, he declared.[85] The government had to build cities beyond the Green Line. It had to allow private land purchases. He wanted to speed building at Yamit and to build a port; he wanted subsidies for Israeli businessmen to build factories in occupied land.

Dayan was national security incarnate, the man publicly regarded as the victor of 1967. If he split the party and ran separately, no one knew how many votes he might take. Worse, he might join the new alliance of right-wing parties that Ariel Sharon, now out of uniform, was putting together. The unthinkable could happen: Labor could lose power.[86]

Labor's top leaders—a dozen minus one, since Yigal Allon was in the hospital after a heart attack—met in three urgent, interminable, secret sessions to agree on a platform that would keep Dayan in the party and that Sapir could accept.[87] In the last meeting, responding to Sapir's attacks on the cost of a port, Dayan pointed at the northeastern Sinai coast on a map, and said that the area "is more or less empty today. I think there's a vital need to settle it. It's empty," he repeated, ". . . the area is empty, and it has water and sand and it has to be settled."[88]

Yisrael Galili was assigned to write the compromise. One consideration that the secretive, powerful adviser to prime ministers did not need to take into account was the alternative platform, based on *Land of the Hart*, on which Arie Eliav and a band of young volunteers were gathering signatures.[89] Rank-and-file independence meant mutiny in Labor, though the popularity of the petitions may explain why party leaders felt they could not drop Eliav from the Knesset ticket.

The Galili Document was brought to the party secretariat on September 3. Technically, Dayan received less than he wanted; his proposal for a port, for instance, would only be "examined." But as Labor's public face, the "compromise" represented victory for Dayan and the maximalists. The Galili Document promised that "new settlements will be built . . . the population will be increased." Towns would be established, not just farm villages. In the next four years, eight hundred homes would be built in Yamit. Without annexation, Labor's policy would be to dig in.

In response, Eliav delivered eight sentences from the podium, a record for bitter brevity, written in biblical fury. "This document has been brought to us by flailing the lash of time and the scourge of panic and haste. This document chastises with scorpions what I understand as the values of the Labor movement," he said. "In this hall and this land . . . are those whose souls weep in secret because of this document."[90]

The text was approved by a vote of 78–0, though the secretariat had 161 members.[91] Most opponents, in Eliav's account, "went to the beach" to avoid endangering their political futures.[92] Even he did not cast a vote against.

"ON THE BANKS of the Suez all is quiet," declared an entirely typical election ad in the press for the Labor-Mapam Alignment on September 20.

> Also in the Sinai desert, in the Gaza Strip, in the West Bank, in Judea and Samaria and the Golan.
> The lines are secure. . . . Settlements are rising, and our diplomatic position is secure.
> This is the result of considered, daring, and far-seeing policy. . . .
> We've come this far with your help. With you, we will continue."[93]

HENRY KISSINGER finally gained full control of American foreign policy, under a president whose power was fracturing. On September 22, taking over from Rogers, he was sworn in as secretary of state, while remaining national security adviser as well. Nixon was busy fighting to keep a Senate committee and a special prosecutor investigating the Watergate affair from getting the tapes of his office conversations. His vice president, Spiro Agnew, was under investigation for bribery. Kissinger, meeting with foreign ministers at the U.N. General Assembly, proposed that negotiations on the Egypt-Israel track should start in November, after the Israeli election. Both sides seemed willing.[94]

THREE DAYS BEFORE the holiday of Yom Kippur, Yehiel Admoni headed north to the Golan Heights for a work visit. Before he left, the

Settlement Department official got a request from Yisrael Galili: Check if the kibbutzim are "prepared for defense" and have reserves of food and water. "He warned me," Admoni later wrote, "to check the matter discreetly, so as not to raise suspicions. He said that and no more."[95]

9

MERE ANARCHY IS LOOSED

⌒

The order came at eleven o'clock Saturday morning: Women and children must immediately evacuate Merom Golan.

October 6, 1973, Yom Kippur, was a tranquil early-autumn day at the kibbutz resting in the mountain valley—though afterward one could remember low dark notes in the soundtrack of the days and hours before: rumors breathing through the kibbutz of Syrian troops building up across the cease-fire line; an air-raid siren a few days before; the army van that came early the same Saturday to take a member hastily to reserve duty; sonic booms waking those still sleeping at 9:30 that day.

Yehudah Harel drove downhill from the kibbutz to the big IDF base at Naffakh for explanations, and then the kibbutz secretariat met (three of the five members would be dead within three weeks) and agreed that the "noncombatant population" would leave for a kibbutz in the Jezreel Valley that quickly agreed to host them. The women rushed to empty their houses of everything packable, some joking that they should stay and the men take the children, and by 1:40 they were waiting for the army buses, except that ten minutes later someone spotted Syrian jets bombing the army observation post on the mountain two miles south and turned on the siren. Within seconds, while everyone rushed for the bomb shelters and rifles were being passed out, the shelling began, not a drizzle but a cloudburst of fire, as was falling all along the front, for now it was the front.

At dusk the pounding let up, so the buses left, some men leaving as well to report to reserve units, the remaining ones counting the minutes of quiet until they guessed that their families were out of range. As darkness fell, the roar of artillery and tank fire rose again, outgoing and incoming, ever closer. "We'd read a lot of the generation of 1948," one man wrote of that night, "but we never imagined we'd experience what they did," holding World War II–vintage Czech rifles and preparing to defend an isolated settlement against an onslaught.[1]

Along the length of the Golan line, 900 Syrian tanks were pouring forward against an Israeli armored force of fewer than 180 tanks; 40,000 infantrymen against a few hundred. At the Suez Canal, an even larger Egyptian force was crossing the waterway, by boats and then bridges, smashing down Israeli embankments with water cannon, overrunning or rolling past small Israeli forts of the front line—the Israeli forces in Sinai, as in the Golan, fighting without help of the reserves, the bulk of the army. Only that morning had Israel's leaders begun calling up reserves, because only then did they half-accept that war might break out.[2]

The Yom Kippur attack surprised Israel because Israel's generals and political leaders did not believe attack possible, and it demonstrated how tenaciously human beings can defend belief against evidence. Arabs could not fight, as 1967 taught. The subtle lessons of the six years since, of living in a society of Jews and "Ahmeds," added to the dangerous contempt. The Syrian troop buildup, the Syrian bombers being moved up to forward bases, the intelligence reports that the Egyptian "exercise" along the canal would turn into an invasion and that Egyptian soldiers had orders to break their Ramadan fasts—all were dismissed.[3] Israel's chief of Military Intelligence—General Eli Zeira, a Dayan favorite—stuck to "the concept" that Egypt would not attack without new weapons, and that Syria could not fight alone. Both Zeira's reasoning and his suppression of dissent fit the mood of the time that Arabs would not dare challenge Israel's power.

Zeira's superiors were equally able to deny evidence. On September 25, King Hussein secretly flew to Israel by helicopter to talk to Golda

Meir. The two met regularly but Hussein had asked for this conversation urgently. Syrian forces were "in position of pre-attack," he said, citing a high-level Jordanian mole. If Syria planned to fight, it would be in cooperation with Egypt. A worried Meir was reassured by Dayan, after he was reassured by military intelligence.[4]

The next morning, responding to the head of the Northern Command's concern about increased Syrian artillery facing the Golan, Chief of Staff David Elazar sent two tank companies to the Heights. If the Syrians were planning anything, the generals reasoned, it would be no more than an artillery barrage or a limited bid to overrun an Israeli settlement. Those hypotheses apparently lie behind Yisrael Galili's request of Yehiel Admoni to check if the kibbutzim were "prepared for defense."[5]

In the pre-dawn hours of Yom Kippur, the head of the Mossad intelligence agency called from Europe, where he had just met Israel's top Egyptian source: War would explode before nightfall on two fronts. At a sunrise meeting with Elazar, Dayan was doubtful. Military Intelligence chief Zeira reported that U.S. intelligence did not expect war. (A U.S. official explained afterward to Kissinger that "we were brainwashed by the Israelis, who brainwashed themselves.") Dayan wanted to call up 50,000 reservists, Elazar wanted 200,000. Without waiting for approval, Elazar had already ordered a call-up of key staff officers and commandos.

When Elazar and Dayan met Prime Minister Meir, Dayan wanted to wait till the afternoon to evacuate women and children from the Golan settlements. War, he believed, was still only a risk, of lesser weight than the political risk of panicking the country with a false alarm. He was the person responsible for the country's safety, the symbol of the calm his party promised; war would mean he had failed, and it is human to reach for the reading of reality that puts off such a danger. Meir, perhaps because she was less wedded to a military conception, ruled for evacuating the families immediately and a compromise of calling up 100,000 men.[6]

She agreed with Dayan, though, on rejecting a preemptive air strike. She had sent a message to the United States to pass to the Soviets for their clients: If you are planning war because you think *we* are about to attack, you are mistaken.[7] That ruled out preemption. Besides, this was not 1967; the world did not know a crisis existed; Israel would appear the aggressor, endangering U.S. support.

The lack of crisis headlines, of evening anchors in New York and Paris speaking rapidly of Mideast troop movements, was further indictment of failed conceptions. In 1967, Egyptian forces crossing the Sinai ignited the crisis. Now, with Israel holding the Sinai, that tripwire was gone. In 1967, Israel was frightened. In 1973, it did not see the danger and so did not sound an alarm. And for six years Israel had told the world that holding land guaranteed its defense. That argument left it naked of the rationale it needed internationally for preemption. Territory may have created defensive depth, but it also chained Israel in ways it had not foreseen.[8]

It had also not foreseen the kind of war Sadat meant to fight. Israel presumed that his military goal would be to reconquer all of Sinai, and he lacked the means to do that. But his actual plan was only to seize a narrow strip of land. That would be enough to awaken the United States, force it to intervene diplomatically, and begin the process that would get him his territory. War would be a continuation of diplomacy by murderous means.[9] It would demonstrate that Israel's "defensible borders" were the opposite of a deterrent.

HAIM GOURI went to a synagogue on Yom Kippur, not to pray, because he did not believe, but to visit a friend as he did every year, and "to hear the melody and the prayers." On Jerusalem's streets, the poet-journalist saw speeding jeeps, a strange sight because normally not a car moved on the sacred day. Couriers were out delivering call-up orders.

In the prime minister's Tel Aviv office, the cabinet met, listening to a shaken Moshe Dayan. At 2 P.M. came news of the attack, which had not waited for dusk. Sirens rose outside. The limits on calling up reserves evaporated. The army's plans presumed it would have forty-eight hours warning to mobilize its forces, but there was no time at all.

Yeshiva student Dov Indig returned to his Jerusalem home after the holiday ended at nightfall. He had not received orders, but he was reporting for duty anyway, along with a childhood friend, Chaim Sabbato. Though they studied at separate yeshivot, they had trained together, Sabbato as a tank gunner, Indig as a loader.

"War, war, what do you know of it?" Indig's mother said, packing cookies for him. She was from Romania, the sole survivor in her family of another conflict. "I know what war is, who knows when you'll return . . ."

"But Mom, we're not in Romania and this isn't a world war," he answered. "A little trip and we'll be home in a few days."

Close to midnight, Sabbato later wrote, they boarded the bus at the call-up point and rode north. At the tank base below the Golan, madness was in command. Indig and Sabbato were assigned to different tanks. A clerk refused to hand out rifles until he could find a pen to fill out the forms. An officer arrived, shouted, "Men are getting killed up there and you look for pens!" and kicked open a crate of guns. Sabbato grabbed an Uzi without a shoulder strap. He and two yeshivah comrades, Eli and Roni, found themselves in a tank under the command of a reservist, who when he heard them praying proclaimed, "I'm an atheist." At dawn, without adjusting the gun sights, they rolled down to the narrow bridge across the Jordan River and up the switchbacks toward the Heights, passing a tank coming down on which bandaged soldiers were crowded, shouting, "Where are you going? Have you gone nuts? Syrian tanks are here . . . Go back, quick!"[10]

At 3:30 A.M., orders reached Merom Golan for the men to leave. Yehudah Harel, displeased, drove down again to Naffakh and found soldiers desperately preparing to retreat. "You can evacuate or not," the commander told Harel. "I'm just telling you that between you and the Syrians I have no forces." Army engineers had orders to prepare to blow up the bridges over the Jordan River, so if the Golan fell it would be harder for the Syrians to advance into Israel proper. Harel returned to the settlement and whoever could fit into the kibbutz's own vehicles left, the rest going in trucks sent by the army, following retreating half-tracks down toward the Jordan.[11] One more preconception, the faith in settlements as fortresses, evaporated. Instead, border kibbutzim were another burden on an army holding off collapse.

Years afterward, Chaim Sabbato wrote a novel that was actually a strict, and thus nightmarish, autobiography of the war, called *Adjusting Sights*, which in Hebrew also means adjusting the intent of prayer. Sabbato's account testifies to the horror that Israel's soldiers, caught unready in battle, would bring home. More particularly, it gives voice to the new class of yeshivah-student soldiers, who faced the war as a spiritual test and who would become crucial actors in the internal Israeli conflict that followed.

Obsessively, Sabbato's story returns to the third day of combat, the morning after the Syrian tanks reached the fence of Naffakh base and were repulsed. Before sunrise, in a unit of survivors, Sabbato's tank rolls out for the counterattack and is caught in battle, his commander shouting, "Gunner, fire!" and Sabbato answering, "But my sights aren't adjusted," the commander telling him to fire anyway, enemy tanks so close they fill his sights, tanks carrying his friends getting hit around him, men who studied Talmud and went through basic training with him, and suddenly the commander shouts, "Gunner, pray!"

"You pray!"

"I don't know how!" the commander says, so Sabbato shouts ancient words from Psalms, "Please, O Lord, deliver us! Please!"[12] Their tank is hit, they manage to escape, Sabbato carrying his strapless Uzi, four men running through a tank battle, watching as soldiers leap from tanks, "aflame completely, like torches." When Sabbato and his comrades find cover, Eli announces he won't be taken captive, he has a grenade, and Chaim and Roni—arguing as if sitting in the yeshivah study hall reasoning out a passage of Talmud—quote rabbinic rulings against suicide and insist one cannot learn from the example of King Saul, who fell on his sword lest the Philistines capture him.

"What will be?" says Eli, wondering if the Syrians will cross the Jordan, if civilians will fight them in the streets of Tiberias. "Can it be we won't win? And what of the beginning of redemption? Can there be a retreat in redemption?"

No, Sabbato says, citing a rabbi who declared during World War II that Rommel's army would not reach Palestine because it had been promised that the Jews will not be forced into exile again.

That is one pole of Sabbato's story. The other is the question of how Dov Indig was killed, because he has heard only that that his friend has fallen. Months later he learns that Indig's phylacteries were found in their embroidered velvet bag in a scorched tank, hit the afternoon he reached the front.[13]

Binyamin Hanani, who as a teenage yeshivah student wrote that no other generation of Jews "has felt Him so clearly just behind the wall," also died in the Golan, on the second day, leading a hopeless bid to reach a besieged Israeli strongpoint.[14] Har Etzion student Daniel Orlik fell the next day in the Sinai. By the end of that day, 724 Israeli soldiers had been killed, more than in the entire war in 1967.[15] A simple explanation would have been that redemption was not beginning. Among the faithful, there would be other explanations.

"THE THIRD TEMPLE is in danger," Moshe Dayan said at sunrise Sunday, the second day of war—meaning that Israel itself faced destruction. He had come to the Northern Command's new headquarters, moved back from Naffakh to a mountain inside Israel, and learned the full consequences of refusal to see war approaching.[16] Dayan was on the edge of despair, or past the edge. Later that morning, a general who flew with him to the Sinai heard him mumbling nonstop about the fall of the Third Temple. As Dayan walked from the helicopter to the command post, an Egyptian MiG attacked the base; he apathetically ignored calls to take cover. That day he proposed retreating deep into the Sinai, which would have granted Egypt a greater victory than it imagined.[17] The next day, after an Israeli counterattack failed on the southern front, he spoke of drafting older men and teenagers, shocking his generals and Golda Meir.

The prime minister's first reaction to Dayan's talk of doom was, by various accounts, to consider suicide.[18] Instead, she applied her iron will to repressing panic, stopped listening to Dayan, and depended on Chief of Staff Elazar. Elazar "worked under the most difficult conditions, but there's no doubt he directed the battles," according to Tzvi Tzur, a former chief of staff who served as Dayan's adviser. "Dayan was fairly shattered." On October 9, Dayan gave an off-the-record briefing to the country's newspaper editors, and said he intended to go on TV that evening. An editor phoned Meir and urged her to stop his appearance; he would undermine the nation's morale. Meir put former intelligence chief Aharon Yariv, who had returned to uniform, to stand before the cameras in Dayan's place.[19]

Haim Gouri, now fifty years old, found himself on the Egyptian front. He was called up on Yom Kippur, told to report to the General Staff in Tel Aviv. He belonged to the army's education corps now. Other men his age were quickly sent home as it became clear there was nothing for them to do. The poet who earned his fame writing the war of independence was asked to stay and write the back-stiffening order of the day for the entire army. Afterward he got a request for another call to arms from a commander in Sinai, which Gouri said he could only compose from there. Another officer drove him to the front in a private car. Somewhere close to the canal he wrote a poem called "Poison," not intended for inspiration, in which the man with the strange ability to place a society inside himself, who had declared in a poem, "I am a civil war,"[20] foretold the desires to know and to deny that would sweep Israel.

> *In the expanses of my body, inquiry commissions*
> *day and night*
> *open hearings, within me taking testimony . . .*

he wrote, and then, as if answering,

> *Our true biographies are formed of all the things*
> *that we would forget, would hide.*[21]

THE PENDULUM swung back. The Syrian tanks, which could in fact have reached Tiberias had they found the empty hole in Israel's defense after their first assault, retreated to the prewar line in the face of battered, outnumbered Israelis fighting in the overnight-repaired tanks of slapped-together units, and then farther back, as an Israeli offensive seized a thumb-shaped piece of land pointing toward Damascus.[22] In the second week of war, Israeli forces in the Sinai broke through a gap between the Egyptian Second and Third Armies, crossed the canal, and began pushing south to cut off the Third Army from behind. A division under Ariel Sharon, who had returned to the army for the war, tried to batter its way northward, toward the city of Ismailiya, behind the Second Army.[23]

By then giant American planes carrying arms were landing in Israel, a step pushed by Kissinger, because the Soviets were airlifting supplies to Syria and Egypt, and the American client had to beat the Soviet one, especially after Vietnam. Nixon approved the move, thankfully distracted by a foreign crisis from Vice President Agnew's *nolo contendere* plea on corruption charges and resignation. Kissinger wanted Israel to take new Arab land on at least one front before a cease-fire. But he was pleased at Israel's dependence on the United States, particularly because Egypt's national security adviser Hafiz Ismail had contacted him barely after the war began, hinting that America could be the mediator afterward. In return, a week into the fighting, Kissinger sent a message to Egyptian president Sadat, promising, "The U.S. side will make a major effort as soon as hostilities are terminated to assist in bringing a just and lasting peace to the Middle East."[24]

The airlift would cement Nixon's pro-Israel reputation, soon to be nearly the only reputation he had left, and the negotiations to follow would mark Kissinger as Middle East peacemaker—and obscure any memory of the peacemaking opportunities he ignored before the war. A clever man climbs out of a hole into which a wise man does not fall, says a Hebrew proverb. Kissinger proved extraordinarily clever.

The cease-fire, voted by the U.N. Security Council, took effect on October 22, then fell apart as Israeli forces kept moving, with Kissinger's secret approval, and completed the siege of the Third Army.[25]

An hour before the cease-fire was to begin, reservist Kobi Rabinovich of Merom Golan—promoted on the battlefield to company commander—was leading his tank unit in the dash to surround the Third Army. As he stood in the turret, head out to see the battlefield, a bullet hit his neck. He died immediately. He was twenty-eight, now married and the father of an infant son.[26] War was his enemy, he had once written, but a strange enemy because he loved the big machines called tanks and the meaning that the army gave him. His enemy had defeated him.

Merom Golan lost four men, out of a hundred adult members. The proportion was unusually high, but it fit a wider logic: Kibbutzim were an elite; members of the elite went to combat units; in a young commune, more were on the front lines.

By the war's end, 2,656 Israeli soldiers had fallen, equivalent to the

United States losing 165,000 men in nineteen days.[27] Israel was a country of bereaved parents, widows, orphans too young to remember fathers. The number of Arab dead has been estimated as anywhere from 8,500 to 15,000. Chroniclers of war write that Israel achieved victory. Surprised, outnumbered, it avoided collapse, and ended with its troops near Damascus and besieging an Egyptian army.[28] Of that kind of triumph, Pyrrhus said 2,250 years before, "One more such victory and we are utterly undone."

The Israelis have suffered World War I–level losses, Kissinger told his State Department staff, "so it will take them a couple or three weeks to absorb the impact." He was summing up who had gained what in the war and was very happy with himself. The bottom line was that "we are in a very central position," that both sides were now dependent on the United States to work out solutions. The Arabs would have to negotiate with Israel. But they had forced "a realization on the part of the Israelis that this cockiness of supremacy is no longer possible—that like other countries in history, they now have to depend on a combination of security and diplomacy" for safety.[29]

That was October 23. The unraveled cease-fire would yet spark a Soviet threat of intervention and a U.S. nuclear alert, a brief moment when the superpowers approached war—a final frightening blast of brinkmanship handled by Kissinger because Nixon was lost in his Watergate battle, having just fired the special prosecutor and facing rising calls for his own impeachment. "They are doing it because of their desire to kill the President. . . . I may physically die," Nixon said of his domestic opponents, talking to Kissinger by phone as the secretary of state dealt with the Soviets.[30]

But Egypt agreed to negotiate directly with Israel on the Third Army's fate.[31] When an Egyptian general and an Israeli general sat down in a tent on the road to Cairo, it proved Kissinger right: Israel had gained direct talks, and had lost its hubris. The cease-fire left Israel with most of its men in uniform, unable to go home because war could reignite any moment. On the Egyptian front, the armies were dangerously tangled. Syria would not even reveal how many Israeli prisoners it held. Egypt was blockading the straits of Bab al-Mandeb at the Horn of Africa, blocking sea traffic to Eilat without need for Sharm al-Sheikh.

The illusion that Arabs could not fight was memory. Israeli generals now wanted an army so large that it would bankrupt the country. Israeli leaders knew that military strength was insufficient; they needed diplomatic compromise. Though his army was besieged, Sadat had achieved his political goal. By Clausewitz criteria, he had won.

"THE QUESTION ASKED in these days, which I hear whenever I meet with civilians or soldiers, is: What is the meaning of this war?" Rabbi Yehudah Amital said, speaking before students in the study hall of Har Etzion a month after the war.

The question "is asked against the backdrop of our certain faith that we live in the time of the beginning of redemption," he said. The Six-Day War, he said, "taught us that wars have a real purpose, which is conquering the land." So what, he asked, was the point of this one?[32]

The losses among the *hesder* yeshivah students proved that they had joined the elite. Har Etzion counted eight dead out of fewer than two hundred students.[33] The yeshivah's mourning was a microcosm of the national shock. Both the rabbi and his listening students had reason to feel that the world had been upended. "Is this a step backward, heaven forefend?" he asked. "Does not the very outbreak of the war . . . raise the possibility of a retreat in the divine process of the beginning of redemption?"[34]

The rhetorical question acknowledged that the war, in its senseless fury, was an assault on theological confidence, on the certainty rife since June 1967 that the actual footsteps of the messiah could be heard echoing in quiet hallways. History was supposed to move in one direction, but the war seemed to be disproof. The question also said: *That cannot be.*

The essential gloss on Amital's discourse had been written nearly two decades earlier, by the pioneering cognitive psychologist Leon Festinger and two colleagues. Their book, *When Prophecy Fails*, deals with dissonance, the conflict of belief and fact, based on study of messianic or millennial movements, groups that predict the world's transformation or end. History is littered with such movements, and each reaches a moment of "disconfirmation," when it becomes obvious that normal life will continue. At that point, some people drop out. But those who have invested themselves in the idea do not want to give it up. Instead, writes Festinger, "the introduction of contrary evidence can serve to increase the conviction and enthusiasm of a believer." Explanations will be found, prophecies reinterpreted or added. Indeed, the faithful will actually intensify their efforts to convince others, because the more that other people accept the idea, the easier it is to presume it true. To use the term of another scholar of messianism, the historian Albert Baumgarten, the movement will demand that its members "up the ante," to show their faith by devoting themselves more. "Upping the ante" can include selling possessions, provoking government authorities, or giving up one's current community for a new one. For surely an idea that produces such commitment must be correct.[35]

Amital's lecture is evidence of the war's impact on religious Zionists of the Kook school, which by now included not only rabbis and students at Merkaz Harav and a small number of Orthodox settlers, but also *hesder* yeshivah students, many members of the Bnei Akiva youth movement, and other young people who had read the doctrine in books, heard it in sermons, or picked up fragments of ideas from friends. The war had to be fit into the expectations it seemed to defy. In order not to lose faith, one had to redouble it.

So, Amital explained, the war was part of the messianic process. Any war over the Land of Israel was actually a war over Jerusalem, and so fulfilled the prophet Zechariah's vision of the battle for Jerusalem at the end of history.[36] When gentiles waged war against Jews, they were actually waging war against God. Attacking on Yom Kippur proved this. Their actual target was the "Jews of Yom Kippur," religious Jews, who represented God. Therefore, "The meaning of Israel's victory is: the victory of the divine idea."[37] Amital's portrayal removed the war from the context of politics and normal history, and put it in the mythological realm of darkness battling light: Gentiles attacked precisely because final redemption was beginning, and it threatened their existence "as gentiles, as the impure. Evil is fighting for its existence." Nonetheless, Israel experienced "great deliverance," a victory not yet appreciated.[38] Once the messianic process has begun, he reaffirmed, no retreat was possible. That faith, he told his students, must glow from them, so anyone meeting them would believe as well.[39] Amital's words were quickly published and widely distributed. Festinger would have written in the margins: Doubt would drive certainty, would ignite a new flame.

BEFORE THE CEASE-FIRE, as soon as the Syrians began retreating, a few men returned to Merom Golan.[40] As they farmed, wounded soldiers wandered into the fields. Trucks carrying harvested potatoes, heading down out of the Heights, passed ammunition trucks coming up. In the kibbutz orchards, hundreds of trees had been splintered by shells. When the fighting stopped, the women and children returned. The settlement was lucky; the Syrian high tide had not actually swept over it.[41] At Ramat Magshimim, an Orthodox settlement farther south in the Heights, Syrian soldiers had entered one gate as the last of the settlers left via another on the first night of war.[42]

This was proof, if anyone needed it, that evacuating the settlers had been essential—which did not lessen the fury and frustration some felt. The most ideological faced their own Festinger moment: Their belief said that settlements helped Israel to hold land; the war said otherwise. Settler representatives met in a Merom Golan bomb shelter near the end of October, and set an immediate goal of doubling the number of Israelis in the Golan, which—six years after the Settlement Department had drawn up plans for 50,000 Jews in the region—stood just above 1,700. There were seventeen Israeli farming communities in the Heights, some with only twenty families. A Merom Golan man proposed pushing the government to build a town, which he said "would prevent a repeat" of the evacuation—as if the presence of more civilians would have kept the army from retreating.[43]

The idea immediately gained political backing. Even Finance Minister Pinhas Sapir, touring the Heights that week, publicly endorsed it.[44] Like most doves, he had a short list of places he thought Israel needed to keep; his comprised East Jerusalem and the Golan.[45] When Kissinger met Syria's vice minister for foreign affairs, Mohammed Zakariya Ismail, in Washington on November 2—his first meeting with a Syrian official—Ismail quoted Sapir's words from that morning's *Washington*

Post. "Such declarations . . ." the Syrian official said, "do not give us encouragement regarding talks with Israel."

"Mr. Minister, one of our problems is that many people say many things for many reasons, particularly domestic reasons," Kissinger answered, with urbane sarcasm. Without an agreement, he added, Israel might build such a city.[46] The exchange did not merit mention in Kissinger's detailed memoirs; settlements still do not seem to have appeared yet on his agenda as a diplomatic difficulty.[47]

By January, though, diplomacy was at the top of the Golan settlers' agenda, as a threat to their future. Their hope that Israel would keep the newly conquered Syrian territory were now giving way to a fear that it would give up land occupied since 1967.

One reason was a change in tone within Labor. Because of the war, the elections scheduled for October were postponed to December 31. At a bitter, interminable central committee session in early December, the party essentially repudiated the Galili Document, the hawkish stance adopted before the war. Allon said he had only backed it originally to keep the party from adopting Dayan's even more extreme position. The new platform said that Israel would seek a peace agreement providing "defensible borders"—Allon's favorite phrase—"based on territorial compromise." That meant dividing the 1967 conquests, not returning to the Green Line, but this was the first time the party explicitly endorsed conceding land. The platform also declared that Israel would seek an agreement in which "Palestinian Arabs" would express their national identity in Jordan.[48] Another balancing act, this stance acknowledged that there were Palestinians and implied that Israel might give up West Bank land, while rejecting a separate Palestinian state. Again, as the party sought to project a more flexible image, it borrowed from Allon's lexicon. Allon, the expansionist, had become the voice of moderation mainly by being more moderate than Dayan.

In the small hours, speaking last, Golda Meir defended herself against charges she had passed up chances for peace, and said those in the party "who supposedly want peace more than me" were undermining Israel's negotiating position by proposing that it give up "everything." She blasted those who favored a Palestinian state, or who accepted the novelist Amos Oz's view that the conflict was tragic for both Jews and Arabs. Everyone in the hall was praying that the postwar negotiations would lead to peace, she said, but "maybe there are differences in realistic evaluation" of the chances. Her evaluation, she made clear, was not blessed with optimism.

Even if Meir had bent little, the speech suggests that her party was now home to some who believed the war was more than a failure of intelligence—one charge to which she pleaded guilty. And yes, she admitted, she might look too sad in her TV appearances, hurting morale. "At my age," she asked, with the self-denigration she used to cut off criticism, "should I start to use makeup?"[49]

Given only a yes-no choice, the committee voted—by an 85 percent majority—to keep her as its candidate for prime minister. In the election, Labor remained the largest party with fifty-one Knesset seats—five seats fewer than it had held before, twelve fewer than when Meir had taken the reins nearly five years earlier. The Likud, the new right-wing alliance put together by Ariel Sharon and led by Menachem Begin, won thirty-nine seats. It was the most available choice for protest, especially for anyone who believed that Labor had left Israel weak and would now give away too much. For the first time, Israel had two major parties, rather than one.

In mid-January, Kissinger introduced the technique of shuttle diplomacy, a marathon of flying back and forth between Mideast leaders to reach an initial accord between Israel and Egypt—not peace, but a small step toward it. Under the separation-of-forces agreement signed January 18, Israel withdrew to a line running ten to fifteen miles east of the Suez Canal. Egypt retained the narrow strip it had retaken, six miles wide, on the canal's east side. Both sides would reduce frontline forces, and between the armies would be a U.N. buffer zone. Egypt agreed to reopen the Bab al-Mandab straits and let ships carrying Israeli cargo pass through the canal, which would reopen. The danger of new war on the Egyptian front receded. The U.N. buffer, an idea discredited in 1967, regained meaning as a way to prevent a surprise attack. Israel could let the reservists sent to the Sinai front three months before go home. Kissinger brought a note from Sadat to a stunned Meir that said, "When I threatened war, I meant it. When I talk of peace now, I mean it."[50]

For the settlers in the Golan and the West Bank, and for other Israelis who believed the territory "liberated" in 1967 was part of a Whole Land that was Israel's by historical or theological right, the accord held a different message: Israel was giving up soil. Even before going home, Kissinger flew to Jordan to talk to King Hussein, then to Damascus to see Syrian leader Hafiz al-Asad, then hopped back to Israel, meeting Allon and Foreign Minister Eban in an airport lobby to report that both Arab leaders had ideas for disengagement agreements.[51] That meant Israeli pullbacks.

It did not mean that Kissinger endorsed all their demands. Already in December, after an earlier trip to Damascus, he told Meir and her top ministers his picture of where negotiating with Syria would lead: Asad would settle for Israel pulling back "from new territory you took, plus some symbolic step in withdrawing from the old territory."[52] That accurate evaluation of the endgame was not meant for the Israeli public, which knew only that Asad wanted the Golan.

Since the war, a Merom Golan member named Eli wrote in the commune's newsletter, too many people had taken a turn in the "negative direction" of thinking Israel could trade territory for peace. In Labor, even in the United Kibbutz, he worried, support was slipping for settlement beyond the Green Line. The world had grown strange.

"Leaving during the war had a terrible influence," a woman named Batsheva said at a kibbutz general meeting. "Today settlement appears in all the media as something unimportant that just gets in the way."

The answer, Eli replied, was that "security is not a sufficient reason [to give] for our existence here." No one would consider giving up the valley below, in pre-1967 Israel, for peace, and conceding the Golan was no different. A public campaign had to be launched, the kibbutz members decided. Allies had to be found.[53] The socialists of Merom Golan were ready for strange bedfellows.

"TRUE, THERE were mess-ups, but we won the war!" Hanan Porat thought, in a mix of frustration and his forced-march optimism, as he worked his way back to health. Called to his paratroop unit the evening after Yom Kippur, the passionate believer from Kfar Etzion had made it safely across the Canal. On the road to Ismailiyah, the shell with his name on it fell. His shoulder and five ribs were broken. A helicopter flew him out; the first, emergency operation to keep him alive was performed at a Sinai base and the second in a hospital outside Tel Aviv.

In the hospital and then the rehabilitation center, watching TV, reading, Porat confronted national depression. A kibbutz reservist named Arnon Lapid, who had served in Sinai, wrote a much-discussed article called "Invitation to Weep." He suggested that his readers join him to weep for their dead, and for "the dreams from which we've awakened . . . the gods that failed, the false prophets who rose to greatness . . . the powerful friendships cut off . . . the truths that turned out to be lies. . . . We will pity ourselves, because we deserve to be pitied, a lost generation like us of a tortured nation in a land that devours its inhabitants."[54]

Porat, utterly committed to the idea he was living in the messianic dawn, rejected such ideas. Israel had won, he thought, "and we should be declaring a day of thanksgiving and saying psalms of praise."[55] What was needed was "a revival movement" to change the mood. It had to come from the bottom up, because "there was a terrible crisis of leadership."

Porat's description of his goal bursts with contradictions: He rejects melancholy; he has lost faith in the nation's leaders; he wants to restore faith in the nation. A "revival movement"—an idea religious in essence—will answer the political crisis. Those tensions would be at the core of the movement he helped create, which became Israel's most successful or most dangerous (or both) grassroots rebellion: Gush Emunim. Add to that another irony, Festinger's irony: A movement confidently declaring that Israel was striding toward redemption was ignited not by the mania of 1967, but by the depression of 1973.[56]

In early January, finally at home, Porat got a call inviting him to a meeting at the home of Rabbi Haim Druckman, head of the Or Etzion yeshivah, in southern Israel. The election results had put some of Porat's friends in a more practical frame of mind. The ticket for which they voted reflexively, the National Religious Party, had shrunk from twelve seats to ten in the 120-member parliament. And yet, they realized, it held more power than ever. Without it, Meir's shrunken Alignment would find it nearly impossible to form a governing coalition. The ruling party was dependent on its former vassal.

Druckman and others from the militant wing of religious Zionism—the amorphous group gestating since 1967—decided on a gambit: They would pressure their party to insist on a coalition including Begin's right-wing Likud. That, Druckman explained at the January 8 meeting in his home, would express the "moral" value of national unity. It would also create a government in which advocates of the Whole Land and settlement had the upper hand.

Druckman's pitch hints at another tension between aspirations: Like Porat, the rabbi spoke of a wide agenda, of transforming the public's values. In practice, the issue that he and others could define and make operative was territory and settlement.[57]

A platform written by Porat for the movement illustrates the gap: It aims at turning religion into an all-encompassing political ideology. Its language is rich with calls for strength, for Israel's "absolute independence," and for self-sacrifice and struggle, along with attacks on Western individualism—all reminiscent of European reactionary politics fifty years before, and of the other politicized religious movements, loosely labeled "fundamentalist," that were springing up from Iran to the United States and attacking Western values.[58]

Porat's platform subsumes Zionism into messianism—so that "fulfillment of the Zionist vision" is the route to "complete redemption of the people of Israel and the entire world." Explaining the country's current mood of crisis, it avoids mention of the war and its graves, instead attacking people who put "personal ego above national destiny." It calls for immediate annexation of the land taken in 1967, and proposes that "alien minorities" choose between permanent disenfranchisement, swearing fealty to Israel, or emigrating. Israel, it says, should adopt "a resolute security doctrine, not deterred by 'moral' or political considerations"—a striking formulation in a religious context. Individuals, it asserts, should cease seeking personal satisfaction and see themselves as branches of a tree, part of the organism of the nation.

And, the document declares, the path to virtually every national goal is "settlement throughout the Land."[59] From its start, the group imagined itself as a movement of national salvation. Practically, it focused on virtually one concern: settling Jews in occupied territory. In doing so, it aspired to seize the mantle of pioneering from the secular left.

Many of those gathered in Druckman's living room that first stormy January night had already defined themselves by settlement—Porat; his patron Moshe Moskovic; Moshe Levinger; Eliezer Waldman, the rabbi who wove mystic significance into living in Hebron; Yoel Bin-Nun, the redemption-obsessed young teacher at Har Etzion. The plan to pressure the National Religious Party suited the leaders of its Young Guard, also present—Knesset members Zevulun Hammer and Yehuda Ben-Meir, a New York–born, thirty-four-year-old psychology professor and or-dained rabbi. They hoped to use the activists as a "front organization," in Ben-Meir's words, to impose their agenda on the party. In the end, Ben-Meir confessed years later, "the monster turned on its maker."[60]

A Young Guard meeting the next week in a Tel Aviv hall drew hun-dreds, and went down in the new group's memory as its founding con-vention. The name Gush Emunim, the Bloc of the Faithful, came out of a conclave of settlement representatives in the Kfar Etzion dining hall soon afterward—even if a Merom Golan member who drove down did not notice the formation of a new movement, only that religious settlers had passed a resolution backing settlers from the Golan Heights.[61] Gush Emunim had a way of absorbing partners, subsuming them into its manic energy.

THE MOMENT WAS ripe for protest movements. The war had knocked people loose from normal life. Reservists released from the Sinai front came home carrying anger and unanswered questions. Motti Ashkenazi, commander of the only strongpoint along the Suez that had not fallen, came alone to stand outside Prime Minister Meir's office, silently, bearing a placard attacking her and Dayan. A news photo brought another protester, then battalions of them.[62] Meir looked out her office window one day and saw a middle-aged man holding a sign: "My son didn't fall in battle. He was murdered, and the murderers sit in the Defense Ministry."[63] Young Labor activists lobbied ministers to press for Dayan's resignation.[64] A father wrote to the Speaker of the Knesset, demanding to testify before the state commission of inquiry investigat-ing the intelligence failures and lack of preparation for war. His son, he explained, had served at a training base and was sent unprepared to the front. "If until now I trusted the government with a full heart . . . today I see how blind I was. . . . My son's blood cries out to heaven," he wrote.[65] Meir, Dayan, and Chief of Staff Elazar met in mid-February with top army commanders to discuss the war. A colonel stood and said, "We learned in the Palmah and the IDF that someone is responsible for everything. The defense minister is responsible for the IDF, and thus for what happened. He should draw conclusions and leave."[66]

In the meantime Finance Minister Pinhas Sapir, in charge of lining up parties for a coalition, rejected bringing the Likud into the government. Instead the Alignment offered the National Religious Party a compromise: a commitment that before any decision to "retreat from Judea and Samaria," new elections or a referendum would be held. The religious party accepted. Gush Emunim regarded that as close to failure—and then again, as an accomplishment of its lobbying efforts. That appears to be a piece of the truth. The Orthodox party's dovish longtime leader, Haim Moshe Shapira, had died. Other leaders were drifting toward maximalism, particularly regarding the West Bank, with its biblical history. Gush Emunim's activism likely served as a warning that the National Religious Party could lose its younger generation to the Likud. The election commitment was a means to avoid taking heat for concessions. But to the extent that Gush Emunim was responsible for the compromise, it had succeeded in handcuffing the ruling Alignment more effectively than it realized.

Prime Minister Meir's greatest quandary was Dayan. As public fury grew, he announced he would not join the new government. Shimon Peres, loyal as a high school sidekick to the leader of the gang, said that without Dayan, he too would stay out. Dayan reminded his Rafi faction of the party that it could leave Labor and support the Likud— potentially putting Begin in power. Meir was at her breaking point. "I've sinned for the last forty-five years by allowing myself to paper things over," she told Labor leaders. "Under pressure from comrades and myself, I thought something needed to get done in this country and that the comrades thought that by putting Golda in charge, they'll overcome the internal conflicts. That's all over. The trick of Golda the Paperhanger doesn't help anymore." When she finally presented her government to parliament on March 10, 1974, Dayan was again defense minister. Arie Eliav, dissident but still in the party, abstained rather than vote for her as prime minister.[67]

The inquiry commission, led by Supreme Court Chief Justice Shimon Agranat, released its report at the beginning of April. It put the brunt of the blame on Military Intelligence, but also held Chief of Staff Elazar responsible. The panel avoided dealing with "ministerial responsibility," thereby freeing Dayan of culpability—and explicitly said Meir had behaved properly in the lead-up to war.

Elazar resigned, but the exoneration of Dayan only fed public anger. On April 10, 1974, Meir stood before a stormy session of the Labor Knesset delegation and said, "I resign. . . . I can't bear this yoke any longer. . . . I've reached the end of the road."[68] With her resignation, the government officially fell. In practice, she would serve, along with Dayan, until a new prime minister could sew together a parliamentary majority.

Seven years before, cries from the street brought Dayan to the Defense Ministry, and he became the face of unexpected victory. Now the street wanted Dayan to go. This time he was responsible for readiness for war, and had failed.

Before the 1973 war, Dayan had proposed a pullback from the Suez Canal and creating a buffer zone to reduce tension with Egypt. Whether that plan could have prevented war is unknowable. But when Meir rejected the idea, Dayan did not fight for it.[69] When he did threaten to split his party, it was over demands for building an Israeli city in the Sinai and for letting Israelis buy land for settlement.

For keeping the West Bank, he offered military justifications, but his ultimate reason was the tie to biblical land. Herein was another contradiction: He was passionately loyal to a collective past, but in his political behavior, loyalty mattered little. Part of his appeal, it has been suggested, is that he embodied individualism for a generation of Israelis tired of commitment to the group, the collective. His rival Allon later wrote that Dayan "symbolized the undermining of ethics and aesthetics in public life." But Allon was a man of collectives, an aging revolutionary.[70]

After the war that discredited him, Dayan seemed to undergo his own revolution, taking a central role in negotiations with Egypt and

Syria. High ground, good pilots, and more settlements, he realized, were not enough to provide safety. He was willing to improvise something else, at least regarding land that did not have biblical meaning for him.

Meir, who fell with Dayan, accurately described her political forte as papering over arguments. She had left Dayan to handle both the management of occupation and military preparedness, and Galili to build settlements. Reflexively, she repressed dissent and criticism as creating unnecessary conflict, and insisted decisions could be made later. Indecision meant that entrenchment in occupied territory continued. It continued even as she left the stage.

IN THE RAFIAH PLAIN, two miles from the Mediterranean coast, concrete was poured for foundations. It was March 1974. Prefab houses and apartment buildings would be put on the foundations. The Galili Document was no longer official policy, but a settlement was emerging where the town of Yamit had been drawn on planners' maps. Officially, it would be a small town serving the surrounding farm communities, to be called Avshalom Center, after the World War I Jewish spy who died in the area. On roads nearby, graffiti was painted, like repressed memory coming to the surface: "Have you murdered and also taken possession?" Handwriting appeared on the wall of a ruined Bedouin house: "It is good to die for Yamit"—a bitter, postwar twist on "It is good to die for our land," the last words attributed to an early Zionist pioneer.[71]

Two hundred miles to the south, along the road from Israel to Sharm al-Sheikh, another settlement grew. It was named Di-Zahav, after an unknown spot where the Children of Israel camped after the Exodus, and after a Bedouin village called Dahab nearby on the coast. The first settlers, with ties to the Labor Party, had come in 1971, illegally, after Dayan told them, "I won't give you permission, but if you settle, I won't give instructions to remove you." They made their living from tourists coming for sun, blue sea lapping the beach below stark gray mountains, and underwater jungles along the coral reefs. Now, after the war, the government was investing in houses for settlers and planning a hotel. The rule held: Every diplomatic action produced a settlement reaction. Postwar negotiations gave a sliver of Sinai back to Egypt and quickened creation of facts in the part of the peninsula that Israel intended to keep.[72]

THE RULING PARTY NEEDED to choose a leader. For the first time in the history of Mapai and Labor, a vote would be held in the central committee. That was a sign not of openness but of disarray, the political equivalent of an old landed family coming undone. The war had shaken the House of Labor, and the house was already rotting. No longer could the elders choose an heir who would be acclaimed unanimously by the appropriate obedient delegates.

The obvious candidate was Pinhas Sapir, the old kingmaker. Shimon Peres decided to run in order to carry the standard of Dayan's faction against Sapir—or so says an authorized biography of Peres, which follows the era's accepted plot line that a person would only seek power selflessly, because others want him to.[73] It is true, though, that Sapir represented both a party oligarchy and a dovish perspective that the Dayan camp despised.

Peres was fifty years old, part of a generation of aging *wunderkinder* who gained stunning responsibility barely into adulthood when the state was born and who then waited as deputies and almosts while the founders continued to run the country. He stood out among the prodigies because he was born abroad; his family came from Poland to Tel Aviv when he was ten. He tried very hard to fit in, and therefore did not. "Shimon's desire to prove himself seemed to border on masochism," his biographer says; the comment refers to his teenage efforts at physical labor, but applies equally to the rest of his career.[74] Before a podium, Peres sometimes sounded like a man desperately trying to make his lines convincing.

He also stood out because he never served as an officer, the almost universal path upward of that generation, though he had devoted most of his career to defense. By age thirty, he was director-general of the Defense Ministry, where he became the unqualified admirer and supporter of Dayan, a man naked of all of Peres's concern for being liked. Peres earned a reputation for big ideas and backhanded ways of achieving them. In the 1950s he sponsored the creation of Israel's own military aircraft industry, and cultivated France as Israel's source of arms and nuclear technology. In doing so he conducted a key foreign alliance out of the Defense Ministry, earning the enmity of Golda Meir, then the foreign minister. Siding with Ben-Gurion and Dayan in the great party split of 1965 completed his reputation for ambition and disloyalty among Mapai loyalists.[75]

The dovish Sapir again passed up leadership. "Between being prime minister and jumping from the tenth floor," he told Yitzhak Rabin, "I'd rather jump."[76] Foreign Minister Abba Eban, the most prominent younger Mapai man, wanted to run, but Sapir told him he had no chance.[77] Eban could have been elected by Diaspora Jews or foreign diplomats, not by his party colleagues. Though a dove, he endorsed Peres.

Yitzhak Rabin became Sapir's candidate. Rabin, fifty-two years old, also belonged to the waiting prodigies. At twenty-six, during the war of independence, he was deputy commander of the Palmah under Allon, the man who had taught him to be a soldier. Rabin was known for knowing all details, for analysis and reaching decisions. But he was shy, distant, outside the camaraderie that was the Palmah's essence.[78] Allon could not teach him charisma. Unlike Allon, he was not purged from the army, even though it was assumed his sympathies lay with Allon's Ahdut Ha'avodah party. At age forty-one, he became military chief of staff, serving in that post during the victory of 1967.

After leaving the army, Rabin spent five years in Washington, serving as Meir's conduit to Kissinger and Nixon. She had known him since his birth; she had worked with his mother, a pre-state socialist activist known as Red Rosa.[79] Social issues were not part of Rabin's own lexicon. He returned to Israel in the spring of 1973 having added statecraft to his military résumé, but with no experience in domestic politics. Not getting a job immediately served him well: He was not stained by the war.

Rabin's past contained an incident of surpassing symbolism. In June 1948, a ship called the *Altalena* arrived off the coast of newly independent Israel, bearing arms for the Irgun Tzva'i Le'umi, the rightist underground led by Menachem Begin. The Irgun represented the "separatists" who had broken with the Zionist leadership. With independence, Begin agreed to merge his fighters into the new Israeli army, as separate battalions. Now he wanted to keep the weapons for Irgun units. Prime Minister David Ben-Gurion regarded that as a bid to maintain a separate military, and ordered the weapons seized, the ship's commanders arrested. At the first spot where the ship reached shore, the army commander failed to carry out the orders. Afterward the *Altalena* ran ashore on the Tel Aviv beach, and another army commander evaded the task of confronting the Irgun. Allon got orders for the Palmah to do the job. Rabin, who happened to be at Palmah headquarters, took command of the battle on the beach. The ship was sunk; eighteen men died, most from the Irgun; the army patrolled Tel Aviv streets; and the Irgun never got its separate battalions. The *Altalena* crisis can properly be seen as the moment Israel actually became a state, when a single government overcame the chaos that threatens an emerging nation. Rabin's readiness to confront other Jews had been crucial.[80]

A mystery of Rabin's candidacy is why he seized the opportunity to succeed Meir, and Allon did not. Now Allon would become understudy to his protégé. In Rabin's account, one reason he ran was to stop Peres.[81] That comes in Rabin's bitter 1979 autobiography, colored by the experiences that followed, which pictures Peres as the root of all his failures.

The central committee voted on April 22. Rabin won, barely, by 298 to 254. In Rabin's telling, he wanted to make Allon his defense minister, but knew that the only way to avoid a walkout by the Dayan faction was to give the post to Peres. "I would yet pay the full price" for that appointment, Rabin writes.[82] Allon would therefore be foreign minister, under a prime minister who knew armies and world relations but nothing of brokering a political deal or creating a consensus. Rabin was the first former general to serve as prime minister, after a trauma that cracked faith in generals. He knew the country had not elected him, which weakened him. Call it war damage.

"FROM YOM KIPPUR our tanks were our home, and none could say when we would return to our own homes," yeshivah student and soldier Chaim Sabbato wrote of the winter and spring of 1974. His unit camped in the enclave pointing toward Damascus that Israel had taken the October before. "Some of our fellowship had left behind young wives, and not only had heaven not helped them fulfill the Torah's command, 'He shall be free for his house one year, and shall give joy to his wife,' but because of the Adversary, they were not granted even a month of joy. Some left pregnant wives, others left infants who missed them. Businessmen—their businesses collapsed, and students of Torah were far from the study hall."[83] War still smoldered, as if waiting for a gust of wind to goad it into flames. Syrian shells rained on the enclave and the Golan. Prisoners had not been exchanged. Men were still dying.

"You look at things more from the perspective of faith," another student-soldier, Private Avraham Steinmatz, wrote from the Golan to a yeshivah friend. "I'm in the army . . . and here it's really hard to feel such exalted thoughts—to believe that this terrible war . . . is simply 'the beginning of redemption.'" The previous October, Steinmatz was studying at Yeshivat Hakotel in Jerusalem's Old City, postponing his army service. When the war broke out, he joined up. Now he was a medic in the paratroops. He was writing to explain views that made him unorthodox among graduates of yeshivah high schools and the Bnei Akiva youth movment. The country needed quiet, he said, "and I'm not talking about 'every man under his vine and under his fig tree'" of messianic days. "Every soldier leaves after him many, many broken hearts. And for what? Let's give up territory, and we can build a country with better *values*, a country in which everything isn't sanctified to the military."[84] The letter is a dissenting gloss in the margins of the time, a reminder that no social movement is a monolith.

On Independence Day in late April, Rabbi Tzvi Yehudah Kook spoke again before guests and students at Merkaz Harav. "There are people who talk about 'the beginning of redemption' in our time," he said. They were mistaken. "We must see with open eyes that we are already in the middle of redemption. We are in the main hall, not the entryway." The arrival of the first Zionist pioneers had been the beginning. The State of Israel was a great leap forward beyond that. The state, he declared, was "entirely sacred and without blemish. It is an exalted heavenly manifestation" of God's return to Zion.[85] Kook, as the scholar Aviezer Ravitzky has highlighted, was sanctifying the state as concept, as platonic ideal. Historical mishaps, mistaken policies, the fact that most Israeli Jews were irreligious—all that was incidental.[86] His disciples could therefore glorify the state and denounce it: They glorified the abstract Israel, and would do battle with the actual political entity.

KISSINGER FLEW to the Middle East on April 28. He wanted an agreement between Israel and Syria to match the one between Israel and Egypt. It would give Sadat the legitimacy of another Arab country making a deal with the Jewish state. It would be another increment toward peace—with the Soviets on the sideline, with everyone dependent on America.[87]

Israel's offer, so far, was to pull back, but not all the way to the pre-October line, the so-called Purple Line. It would not reward Syria for attacking and losing.[88] Syrian leader Hafiz al-Asad wanted land past that line, to match Sadat's gain, and to show his own people that the deaths had some purpose.[89] Kissinger would shuttle between capitals, as if trying to pull them, inch by inch, toward each other. "I was in effect alone," he wrote of the effort.[90] He had barely left Washington when Nixon, responding to a congressional subpoena, released transcripts of his White House conversations on the Watergate affair, with their deleted expletives and undeleted discussion of raising a million dollars in hush money.[91] Behind Kissinger was a president imploding in slow motion. Awaiting him in Jerusalem was Golda Meir, still in office, as if she had walked off a cliff but not looked down and therefore had not fallen. She, Dayan, Allon, and Eban would negotiate, with Rabin and Peres added to the team, almost as extras, while Rabin tried to form a governing coalition.[92]

Among supporters of the Whole Land of Israel and Golan settlers, Kissinger's arrival was treated as the continuation of war by other means. They suspected the United States of pushing Israel for total withdrawal from the Golan.[93] Just before the shuttle, "we learned of the possibility that the government will agree to a serious move west of the Purple Line," said an unsigned report in the Merom Golan newsletter in early May.[94] "Serious" was undefined and frightening, a threat to the settlers' safety if not their homes. For some maximalists, conceding any land held by Israel before October 1973 was unthinkable; the 1967 ceasefire lines now defined the Land of Israel.[95]

Kissinger arrived in Israel to Likud-organized demonstrations and "signs spelling my name in Arabic—as if I were an Arab representative," he recalled.[96] Newspaper ads signed by "Citizens Against a Diplomatic Holocaust" welcomed "the high commissioner," suggesting that Kissinger, the Jew who fled Germany as a teenager, was both a Nazi and a reborn representative of British imperial rule.[97]

Ironically, Kissinger's account of the shuttle contains his first discussion of Israeli settlements as a diplomatic issue, and his position is simple: He "stressed to all the Arab leaders that Israel would not give up a single settlement for the disengagement and I had told Israeli leaders I would not press them to do so."[98] Transcripts of his conversations during the frenetic, interminable talks substantiate that. In a meeting with Meir, for instance, he reported on dickering with Asad about an Israeli proposal for the disengagement line. Kissinger told Meir, "He said, 'They don't want to give up settlements, Druse villages; all right. But why not a paralle[l] line with those two principles?' "[99] As that dialogue reflects, Asad himself had accepted that the disengagement would leave the settlements in place.[100] Instead, the talks revolved around Israeli return of the ghost town of Quneitrah, precisely because it would give Asad his symbolic gain without moving settlers.[101]

Outside Meir's house, a group of intellectuals held a hunger strike—among them Moshe Shamir and and Tzvi Shiloah, secular founders of the Movement for the Whole Land of Israel. The crowd grew—boosted by Golan settlers, and by Kiryat Arba residents who arrived in rented Arab buses, and Etzion settlers. Gush Emunim took a key role, stepping beyond party activism to street protests. Demonstrators slept on the street. In the morning, they held prayers there.[102]

By Friday, May 11, press leaks indicated that Israel would give up Quneitrah, and that the argument centered on nearby hills and on fields belonging to Merom Golan.[103] At the kibbutz itself, pounded by Syrian shells, members were living in bomb shelters. The way to hold the ghost town, Yehudah Harel decided, was the old and certain method: Put a settlement there. A place safe from shells was needed. He and another activist went looking. Under an abandoned Syrian military hospital, at the western edge of town, was a bunker. The pair stopped by Northern Command headquarters and spoke with the second in command about their plan. "First, you didn't ask me. . . . Second, if you're not already sitting there, you may be too late," the officer replied, or so Harel would tell the story.[104]

On Saturday night, at Merom Golan's weekly general meeting, Harel laid out his plan: The kibbutz and other Golan communities would loan members to set up the new commune. Permanent settlers would be recruited from Galilee kibbutzim. The proposal passed after midnight. At 1:00 A.M., in the clubhouse bomb shelter, a committee laid plans. By morning, people were moving into the bunker—cleaning, setting up the generator, bringing water, drawing up a work schedule for Merom Golan fields that would also be loaned to the instant settlement. Several days later the name Keshet was chosen, the Hebrew equivalent of *qantir*, "rainbow" in Arabic.

At the Jerusalem protests, a flyer appeared, urging people to "Stand Up and Go" to Quneitrah to bolster the settlement.[105] Gush Emunim volunteers began arriving, carrying sleeping bags and religious tomes. Harel had believed he was establishing a secular commune that would belong to the United Kibbutz. One night he came to the bunker and found rooms full of Orthodox Jews studying. He found the man from Merom Golan coordinating the settlement project. Pretty soon, Harel said, we will have a yeshivah here, and no one will work. "What's with you?" the man said. "These people work the hardest." In the meantime, the effort to recruit long-term settlers from the secular communes of the Galilee failed completely. Absolutely no young kibbutz members were interested.

Hanan Porat came to visit Harel. An all-night conversation ended with Porat agreeing to find Orthodox settlers. He turned the project over to a young student at Merkaz Harav. Five years before, when a van of Orthodox settlers from Hebron showed up at Merom Golan, kibbutz members had met them with almost anthropological curiosity, and learned that they were disciples of a certain "Rabbi Kook of Jerusalem." Now Harel drove with Porat to the yeshivah, to receive Kook's permission for his student to leave his books.

Negotiating with Kissinger, Meir paid no attention to Keshet. On May 29, before dawn, after a month of talks that verged perpetually on collapse, agreement was reached. As Kissinger had intended, Israel agreed to pull back to the Purple Line, the post–Six-Day War cease-fire line, and give a bit more, the bit being Quneitrah and a couple of hundred meters beyond. A corner of Merom Golan's fields would be in the demilitarized zone between the two armies. As in Sinai, both armies would thin their forward forces. A U.N. "observer force" would stand between them.

Harel was in a bind. He knew that Kook's followers would not voluntarily leave the bunker if it was to be handed over to Syria. After the disengagement accord was signed, a government-appointed geographer came to mark the line with barrels. Keshet was on the wrong side. Harel asked if he would bend the border a bit. The man refused; it would be unprofessional. "That night," Harel would recount, "we came and moved the barrels."

In the morning, according to Harel, a U.N. officer came and approved the line as marked by the barrels, not noticing the change. Afterward, the Keshet settlers agreed to turn the bunker over to the IDF, moving first to railroad cars placed in a nearby nursery, later to a permanent site.

On May 25, four days before Kissinger wrapped up his deal, Avraham Steinmatz, the yeshivah-student-turned-medic who wanted to give territory for peace, was hit by a Syrian shell while treating his wounded commander. He was one of the last fatalities before quiet came.[106]

IN BATTLE, THE tradition that settlements would stop an army had proved as obsolete as cavalry. Despite the small defeat in Quneitrah, diplomacy appeared to offer a different lesson—settlements could constrain the government, trump international pressure, keep land in Israeli hands.

"In the course of the struggle," Yehudah Harel wrote soon after, "we felt greatly the lack of a movement standing behind us."[107] The truth was slightly different. Another movement had taken the place of the United Kibbutz. Its teacher was not the socialist sage Yitzhak Tabenkin, but Rabbi Tzvi Yehudah Kook. Secular believers in the Whole Land were now supporting actors. The word *settler* would mean something new.

10

CONFRONTATION

A line of cars and trucks rolled out of the small village of Meholah. In Gush Emunim accounts, it would always be called a "convoy," a word with a whiff of struggles to cross hostile territory, an inference of glory.[1]

Meholah was picked as the launching point because it was a backwater. A community of religious farmers, it lay below sea level at the north end of the sauna-hot Jordan Rift, just outside the Green Line, the first settlement established in that part of occupied territory in 1968. Yehudah Etzion's father lived there, and the tall redheaded settlement activist enlisted his father in the group intending to defy government policy and settle near Nablus. The group had sent letters to Yitzhak Rabin and Shimon Peres, announcing its intent to "take the first practical step" and establish a settlement on its own, but did not want to be stopped by the army on the way.[2] No one would think of starting from Meholah. It was June 5, 1974, Rabin's third day as prime minister, and Peres's third day as defense minister. They were not getting a grace period.

The two dozen or so vehicles carried a hundred would-be settlers and supporters—men, women, and children—and tents, tools, kitchen gear, a library of religious books for study, even a seesaw and playground slide, "everything we would need for months," as one activist said afterward, the inventory indicating confidence that they were moving in to stay. From Meholah they headed up into the folds of the steep scorched West Bank hills on back paths till they reached the crest highway north of Nablus—or Shekhem, the biblical name used in Hebrew. Then they drove in a procession through the Palestinian city, past the military government headquarters, and on to the edge of a large army base near the Palestinian village of Hawarah, in a valley where the breeze rustled through tall purplish fierce-pointed thistles and grass. It was midmorning. The rush began, people putting up tents and a flag pole with an Israeli flag, pounding fence posts, stringing barbed wire around three sides of the instant settlement, the fourth side being the perimeter fence of an army base expected to provide security once the matter of defying military law by settling in occupied territory without permission was cleared up. The mood, organizer Benny Katzover would recall, was "extraordinary exaltation"—as one would expect of a group of mostly young people certain they have seized the ideals forgotten by the old people in power, and breaking the law to do so.

Ariel Sharon arrived along with another novice Likud Knesset member named Geula Cohen, who had earned her fame before statehood as the impassioned radio voice of the ultra-right Lehi (Stern Gang) underground, and with Rabbi Tzvi Yehudah Kook himself, wearing his rabbinic long black jacket and black hat in the June sun. Sharon, Cohen, and the white-bearded yeshivah head planted saplings while schoolgirls smiled next to them for a photographer.

The encampment was called Elon Moreh, a name chosen by Katzover and Menachem Felix during the months the two friends from Kiryat Arba had spent lobbying for approval to settle near Nablus. The name was an attempt, according to Katzover, to soften their image by not stressing "Shekhem," the West Bank's major town. "Elon Moreh" was an obscure synonym for the city used once in Genesis, referring to the place where God promised Abraham that his descendants would inherit the land of Canaan. The settlement would thereby relive the ancient past and carry out prophecy, while skipping the uncomfortable present. Katzover, in particular, tended to see himself as walking the Bible's landscape—ironically, an imitation of secular Zionists who stressed the Bible as a story of national birth, and who treated Jewish religious tradition as the unhappy product of exile, best erased. It was a tension typical of his peers, and indeed of the other militant religious movements emerging in the world in ostensible rejection of Western values. What looked and felt like a return to old-time religion actually represented a radical synthesis in which believers absorbed a modern political ideology and converted it into principles of religious faith.

Their meetings with Labor politicians had not won them official sanction. Active support came from political rebels such as Cohen and especially Sharon, who promised financial and organizational help and told them they were doing "the most important thing for Zionism. I'm at your service."[3]

The Yom Kippur War had interrupted their efforts. Afterward, their patience vanished. The interim agreements made members of the group "feel the ground quaking beneath us." Everyone knew that King Hussein was standing in line to negotiate next. Labor's small, hard-fought concessions made it the party of weakness in the eyes of Whole Land advocates, for whom weakness was a cardinal sin.[4] For some in the group, the war posed a theological demand. "When the Jewish people doesn't perform its task, it receives blows to chastise it, and to return us to the correct path," believed Yehudah Etzion, who possessed particular confidence concerning God's intent for history.[5] The war was not a retreat in redemption, he was sure, but rather was punishment of Israel for not marching forward.

So in the spring of 1974, the Elon Moreh group had begun talking of a wildcat settlement, a fait accompli that the government would be forced to accept. The idea got a cool reception from veteran activist Hanan Porat, who had joined in a capacity best termed "outside agitator," since he did not intend to move to Elon Moreh. Porat saw acting illegally as the last option. His misperception of Kfar Etzion's founding was that an unwilling Eshkol had given in at the final moment to political pressure, and he hoped the same would happen now. Likud leader Menachem Begin, with whom the group consulted, also opposed a wildcat attempt. The *Altalena* affair, Katzover felt, still weighed on him. Sharon, on the other hand, was in favor.

Katzover and Felix decided to consult their rabbi, the response of traditional yeshivah students. In Katzover's account Tzvi Yehudah Kook, also uncertain, asked to speak with Begin, who told him the attempt could cause civil war. The rabbi said no. Try again, the group's members said. The young men went to the old rabbi's Jerusalem house and "preached Zionism," telling him the Land of Israel was in danger. Kook asked to consult Shlomo Goren, the shofar-blasting army chaplain of 1967, now chief rabbi of Israel. But Goren, despite his militant messianism, also rejected confrontation.

Soon after, the two organizers showed up again at Kook's Jerusalem house. We're going to do it, they informed him. This was not how yeshivah students spoke to their rabbi. Chaos was creeping into the world.

"What do you want of me?" he demanded.

"Your blessing."

The old man smiled—so Katzover would remember—and blessed them. The day-and-night planning began, the writing of lists, the gathering of equipment, the exuberant free fall of organizing after the decision to act and before meeting reality. Sharon, famous for his love of maps, chose the spot for them, picking land on which he said there were no private claims and that was next to a base. In building an instant settlement, they were reenacting the story every Israeli schoolchild learned of pre-state pioneers braving Arab and British antagonism, but this time the antagonism came from the state that was expected to protect them. The date was set for June 4.[6]

ON JUNE 3, Rabin's government barely won parliament's approval. His coalition leaned unsteadily on two splinter parties, without the National Religious Party. Seeking to pull the Orthodox party back into the government, Rabin repeated Meir's pledge: He would negotiate with Jordan, but would call new elections before any "territorial concessions involving parts of Judea and Samaria."[7] He thereby entered office wearing diplomatic handcuffs he had locked on himself.

That evening the would-be settlers of Elon Moreh gathered at out-of-the-way Meholah and loaded their trucks. Then the phone rang: Tzvi Yehudah Kook wanted them to wait twenty-four hours. Hanan Porat would later say that he had gone to the rabbi, warning of a blow-up—and suggesting that Peres, newly installed as defense minister, might arrange official approval. Kook sent his secretary to Peres, asking to meet him urgently. According to a press report, it was Begin, not Porat, who pushed for the meeting. Either way, maximalists believed that Peres was on their side.[8]

On June 4, therefore, Peres sandwiched a meeting at the rabbi's home into his first full day in office. According to the press report, he told Kook he "identified with goals of the group's members," but he personally did not have the power to approve their settlement.[9] Attempting to convince Peres ended Kook's own ambivalence. He reportedly told the defense minister that the settlement bid involved a religious obligation that one must "die rather than disobey," and announced that he would take part.[10] When Sharon brought the rabbi to the encampment the next day, it was a sign that escalation had begun.

Soldiers arrived, followed by generals who tried to convince the would-be settlers to leave voluntarily. Finally, the soldiers were told to pull down the barbed-wire fence. The settlers spread out, holding on to the posts. "The order was given not to use force," a newspaper reported afterward, "and new efforts at reaching an agreement began." The depiction is tense and comic: The army does not know how to cope with a hundred civilians camped in a field, because facing Israeli civilians was outside military experience, especially civilians engaged in the patriotic act of settling the land.

The generals phoned Prime Minister Rabin. They passed the phone to Sharon, the prime minister's old military comrade, who suggested a compromise: The settlers would move to a nearby army base, and stay until the cabinet discussed their request to settle in the area.[11] After talking to his unhappy generals, Rabin agreed. The Elon Moreh activists leaned toward accepting. This could be a repeat of Hebron; the temporary would turn permanent.

Then they told Kook. "Is anything wrong with this spot?" the rabbi asked. We want to be near Shekhem, someone explained, we never were dead-set on this place precisely. "Is anything wrong with this spot?" Kook repeated. "If not, the demand that you leave is wrong. It is forbidden to leave." He turned to the officers and said, "Bring out the machine guns"—as if, it appeared to Katzover, "he were standing on the *Altalena*."

Night fell. The generals walked away. Soldiers rushed forward, ripped up the fence, began pulling the male settlers toward two waiting buses. They had orders to avoid violence, but found themselves dragging men who kicked, pushed, and shouted, lying on the ground, holding on to rocks. Women struck the struggling soldiers. Through the melee stormed Sharon, "seized by immense fury," and roaring, "Refuse orders! Refuse orders!" Spotting a tangle around Hanan Porat, he rushed over. "This guy was wounded in the Yom Kippur War!" Sharon shouted. "How dare you?" A soldier trying to lift Yehudah Etzion found himself flung away by the stocky ex-general, who himself remained immune, protected by the force field of celebrity.

"Arik," a captain told him, "when you gave the order to cross the canal during the war, I knew it was suicide, but I went anyway, because it was an order. Now you tell us to disobey our commanders' orders?"

"This is an immoral order and you have to disobey that kind of order. I wouldn't follow an order like that!"

Eventually, when all the men had been dragged from the field, Kook, too, agreed to board one of the buses, which took the men south to the police station in Jerusalem. They were released that night. The women and children got on waiting buses without resistance and were taken home. Troops took down their tents.

"I do not know if we fully get what happened at Elon Moreh south of Nablus," Haim Gouri wrote the next day, after reading his newspaper in his small Jerusalem apartment. The poet-columnist stressed that he wrote as "someone who supports the Galili Document," as a Labor maximalist. But the affair, he felt, "takes us back to the very beginning of the state, to the dispute we thought was over the day the Knesset was established and one army was set up that followed the orders of a government enjoying the legislature's confidence."[12] He, too, had a whiff of a sea breeze carrying smoke from the *Altalena*.

LET THE camera linger on the uniformed men dragging protesters through the dark to buses. Leave the shouts too distant for words to be clear. Without a subtitle to identify the location, the scene could be a campus quad, outside an administration building occupied for a day. There is nothing intrinsically left or right, it turns out, in "liberating" space, in defiance or in going limp as you are carried away.

Around the world, founders of the 1960s New Left had suffered an "illegitimacy complex" in the words of the social critic Paul Berman; raised comfortably on stories of their Old Left parents' heroism, they felt moral failure. Some solved their problem by rallying to the support of distant liberation movements—Latin American Marxists, Algerian or Palestinian nationalists—romanticizing their extremism and imagining away their victims.[13]

By the twists of history, those who suffered an illegitimacy complex in Israel were not children of the Old Left, but its stepchildren, young religious Zionists. They accepted secular Zionism's demand that Jews shed Jewish weakness and return to a half-imagined age of physical labor and military strength. But in Israel's schoolbook legends, the heroes were secularists who settled the land, defied the British, fought in the war of independence. A counter-tradition of heroes belonged to the separatist right-wing undergrounds of the 1940s. Packed with anger at the left's perfidy, that tale led to the *Altalena*. But it was also secular, someone else's story. To make matters worse, Orthodox Zionists suffered a second illegitimacy complex: Next to the ultra-Orthodox, they felt like religious amateurs.

Now it seemed the secularists had mostly gone weak. At Hawarah, a hundred religious Zionists cast themselves as the new heroes of Jewish national liberation, starring in a remake of building an instant settlement, as Labor Zionists used to do, and of defying the Labor Zionists, as right-wing "separatist" Zionists once did—with the excitement, without the risks. They had their own celebration of resistance, and discovered the joy of feeling righteous by breaking rules.[14] Unlike New Leftists, they claimed to act for their own liberation rather than that of someone elsewhere. Their demand for liberated land meant erasing the rights of another group, which was not unusual, except they could see the people they hoped to disinherit. It was the small difference between a city meat-eater and a farm one who has seen the blood. In the Israeli looking-glass, the place for the New Left was filled by the New Right.

The first attempt to establish Elon Moreh failed—but in a terribly encouraging way: Peres refused them permission in the tone of a parent who does not believe his own reasons. Rabin negotiated. The police let them go home. Allies initially doubtful of confrontation joyfully joined in. Next time, surely, they would win, or at least bring more people and feel even more extraordinarily exalted.

With a new prime minister just installed, with Nixon and Kissinger about to arrive in Israel, Hawarah seemed like a one-day incident. It was an incident like a spark in summer thistles and tall grass.

NIXON HAD good reason in June 1974 to prefer to be in the Middle East rather than in Washington, where the House Judiciary Committee was weighing impeachment. In Cairo, obedient crowds cheered the American president. In Damascus, Hafiz al-Asad kissed him on both cheeks and renewed diplomatic relations, cut off since 1967. In Nixon's spare time, he nervously listened to Watergate tapes. Former prime minister Golda Meir, who met Nixon in Israel, commented to Kissinger that Israel still had not received a visit from a U.S. president—Nixon's thoughts, she realized, were elsewhere.[15]

Kissinger, though, talked business. He wanted to push for another incremental Israeli-Arab agreement. The danger of war remained.[16] But reaching a full peace agreement between the Arab countries and Israel was impossible; what the Arabs wanted was beyond what an Israel government could give. Step-by-step diplomacy was best; it kept all sides dependent on the United States and sidelined the Soviets.[17]

Kissinger may also have suspected that a grand final success would render the United States irrelevant. "I'm a firm believer . . . that expectation of benefits to come is a greater bond than having received the benefits," he told Foreign Minister Yigal Allon professorially that summer. "Gratitude is not a governing principle in international affairs."[18]

He was therefore engaged in what could be called bicycle diplomacy: If you stopped, you fell off. During Nixon's visit, Kissinger told Rabin: "You can't say no movement with Egypt because of the military situation and no movement with Jordan because of the domestic situation and no movement with Syria because of settlements and no movement with the

Palestinians because they're terrorists." The options were trading more of the Sinai for something closer to peace with Egypt, or seeking an interim agreement with Jordan. Kissinger urged the latter path, because "the way to avoid dealing with the Palestinians is to deal with Jordan."[19]

The Palestine Liberation Organization was in fact looking for a way to enter diplomacy, to lay claim to the West Bank and push Jordan aside. The first obstacle was its own ideology, which insisted that Palestine was indivisible and could be liberated only by "armed struggle"—the "absolute violence" of Frantz Fanon's *Wretched of the Earth*. Just before Nixon's visit, the PLO's Palestine National Council leapt those hurdles by adopting the so-called phased strategy. The PLO would establish an "independent combatant national authority" on "every part of Palestinian territory that is liberated," as a step toward taking the rest. To do so, it would use "all means, and first and foremost armed struggle"— implying diplomacy could also be tolerated. Explicitly, the PNC resolution rejected peace or recognition of Israel. The PLO's nationalism remained total; it rejected anyone else having a claim on the land. Considering a two-state solution remained in an as yet unimagined future. The phased strategy may have been the first small shift toward that future—but it would also provide evidence for any Israeli opposed to talking to the PLO that the organization used diplomacy only as a ruse.[20]

The resolution was an extreme version of negotiation with oneself. Nonetheless, momentum was growing among Arab leaders to give the PLO the mandate to represent the people of the West Bank. Letting Jordan regain a piece of territory, Kissinger was arguing, would head that trend off by showing that Hussein could deliver the goods.

But Israel's new government was ill suited to choose. Kissinger had to negotiate with the "troika running overall strategy," as he called it, of Rabin, Peres, and Allon, a trio afflicted by intrigue and suspicion. "Rabin trusted Allon's character far more than his intelligence; his estimate of Peres was the precise opposite," Kissinger found.[21] The novice prime minister could neither crush dissent, as Meir had done, nor rally his ministers to work together, nor even schmooze endlessly with them, as Eshkol did.

Nor did Rabin trust his ability to win an election. Despite Kissinger's warning, therefore, he feared any deal that involved giving up West

Bank land. On that point, Peres agreed. Like Dayan, he was willing to offer Hussein only "functional compromise," in which the West Bank would belong to both sides and neither: Jordan would run civil affairs while Israel's army stayed put. Since Hussein would not accept that, Peres preferred negotiating with Egypt. Only Allon agreed with Kissinger. Seeking agreement with Jordan was a new chance to show that the Allon Plan could be the basis for peace as well as settlement.[22]

Allon, like the map of his grand conception, was a figure-ground problem: You could focus on what he wanted to keep, or what he wanted to give up. In the summer of 1967, the first U.S. diplomatic report from Tel Aviv on the Allon Plan had labeled it "Allon's hardline."[23] When Allon came to Washington a year later, a State Department memo termed him "moderately 'hawkish.' "[24] In June 1974, Kissinger left Israel with no Israeli commitment except that Allon would come soon to the United States. A briefing paper before that visit would label him simply "a moderate."[25] In the new government, he was the compromiser, the diplomatic activist. In the intrigues of the troika, he would complain, Peres used that against him, leaking to the press that "I'm about to turn over the whole West Bank and Gaza Strip to the Jordanians."[26]

The "troika," though, had a fourth member. Yisrael Galili, surviving the postwar Labor purge, remained as fixer and adviser to the new prime minister. The secretive, birdlike man was still in charge of settlement, which was still the way the government wrote its real intentions on the landscape. Under Rabin, Galili increased the pace of his work—spurred, it appears, by the new diplomacy to create more facts, to mark off what could not be conceded. In mid-July, Galili's Settlement Committee met for the first time under the new government and approved the plan for a town of 5,000 families in the Golan. There were too few Israelis in the Heights, Galili said. Earthworks would begin within weeks. A day later, from the Knesset podium, he answered a demand from Menachem Begin for more settlements. The government was boosting the pace, he said amid Likud heckling. But it would not allow private, "provocative" efforts. Begin's subtext was support for the Elon Moreh group. Galili's was that the right talked loudly while Labor acted.[27]

The U.S. ambassador, Kenneth Keating, got a cable from the State Department. "Israeli statements of intent to expand . . . settlements in occupied territories have prompted mounting expressions of concern from Saudis," it said, complaining of the "difficulties such publicity generates in U.S.-Arab relations." The administration had asked the year before that the Israeli government tamp down such reports, but unfortunately the "effort was hampered by absence of press censorship in Israel on any but purely military matters."

Still, the embassy was asked to find out what was actually being built—and for its views on how the government "might be induced to turn off public comments on expanding settlements."[28] Keating cabled back two days later. He had already raised the problem with Foreign Minister Allon, who was "quite sympathetic." Allon would be meeting Israel's newspaper editors to ask them to play down "sensitive issues" connected to peace negotiations, and "volunteered to add settlement to his list," the ambassador reported.[29] The secretary could rest easy.

Allon, though, had reasons to be edgy. With his U.S. trip approaching, the cabinet had for the first time discussed the Palestinian issue— in itself, a reminder the Meir era was past. To Allon's satisfaction, the cabinet decision said Palestinian aspirations would have to be met in a "Jordanian-Palestinian" state. The majority rejected a proposal by dovish ministers to announce readiness to talk with any Palestinian group ready to recognize Israel—a position that would have dangled a major reward before the PLO for a dramatic shift in its own stance. On the other hand, the cabinet said that Israel would seek "negotiations for a peace agreement with Jordan," a final accord resolving all issues. As at least some of Allon's colleagues read that decision, it meant he had no mandate to discuss the interim deal he favored with Jordan.[30]

THE NOTE to Allon had a Levinger touch: The tiny signals acknowledging hierarchy were missing. It presumed young activists could demand a meeting immediately with the foreign minister and get it, to discuss Gush Emunim's fresh plan for a dozen settlements the length of "Judea and Samaria" and "to find a way for settling in the Shekhem area by the Elon Moreh group without need for confrontation with the authorities." The note was signed by Moshe Levinger, along with Hanan Porat and Ben-Tzion Heinemann, the rabbi's disciple now living in the

Golan—which, like Hebron and Kfar Etzion, was a place where Allon had pushed settlement. Allon's recent past was writing to him.

In the mimeographed manifestos attached to the note, Gush Emunim described itself as being "above political parties." A month and a half after the Hawarah bid, it had cut loose from the National Religious Party and was intent on becoming a mass movement. Though its core members were Orthodox, it sought to reach out to the wider public—meaning the Orthodox would now be the vanguard, the secularists fellow travelers. It would promote "the goals of redemption," by stressing "attachment to the land and expansion of settlement." The settlement ethos had been swallowed whole and turned into the means of messianism.

Gush Emunim now spoke for the Elon Moreh group and four other groups that had picked places where they intended to settle. One marked the map at Shilo, where the Israelites offered their sacrifices in the time of the prophet Samuel. In the modern West Bank, it lay between Ramallah and Nablus, in the densely populated Palestinian area that Allon's map marked for returning to Arab rule. Another group, claiming thirty members, wanted to settle near Jericho—designated by Allon as part of the corridor that would link the East Bank with Ramallah.

To set a meeting, the note said, Allon could contact Porat or Yohanan Fried—the Merkaz Harav student whose explanation of God's purpose in the Holocaust had not made it into *Soldier's' Talk* seven years before. Allon did not answer.[31] Porat and Levinger's goals no longer fit his.

Rabin, though, agreed to meet Elon Moreh organizers Benny Katzover and Menachem Felix immediately after their settlement bid at Hawarah. In Katzover's description, the prime minister stressed authority: The government would set priorities where to settle. The conversation ended, as Katzover remembered it, with Rabin saying bluntly, "If you think the government is going to follow any lunacy of a few dozen Jews, you're mistaken," and with Felix getting the last word, "In that case, you'll meet hundreds of Jews."[32]

The perceived challenge added adrenaline. The Elon Moreh settlement group worked with Gush Emunim. A campaign of parlor meetings began, two hundred sessions that summer, to enlist grassroots support. A young religious Zionist named Meir Harnoy, invited to a neighbor's house one evening in a staid Tel Aviv suburb, was awed to find Ariel

Sharon lecturing. "I tell you that if we don't begin settling in Judea and Samaria, Jordanian artillery will come to us," Sharon warned. No one needed convincing, Harnoy felt, but they liked hearing the ex-general confirm their beliefs. Afterward, as Sharon enjoyed "the gastronomic part of the evening," Yehudah Etzion collected donations.

Two weeks later, Harnoy attended another meeting, in the lunch-room of a public school used as a synagogue by young Orthodox Jews, graduates of yeshivah high schools and Bnei Akiva. Hanan Porat, now one of Gush Emunim's chief spokesmen, spoke of settling with permission or without, calling up ideas Harnoy had regarded as belonging to pre-state history. The age of heroes was not over, it seemed. At the end of services on a Sabbath morning, a member of the congregation stood to announce what Gush Emunim was planning next. "This is a synagogue," someone shouted. "Here we don't make political announcements." The activist took a chair outside and stood on it as a crowd gathered. The synagogue became a base of Gush Emunim support.[33] The same happened elsewhere. At houses of worship, politicized faith had its audience gathered in advance.

Sharon helped pick a new spot for establishing Elon Moreh.[34] In a valley northeast of Nablus, near Sebastia, a village of a thousand or so Palestinians, stood a country train station used only by memory. An embankment for the track curved through the valley; a small stone bridge crossed the dry creek bed. The stone station stood on a slight rise. From a distance, it looked like a once-handsome farmhouse, with cypresses and pines lining the driveway that led to the main road. Once the train had come here from the coast and run on eastward across the Jordan River, linking to a line that carried travelers north to Damascus or south toward Mecca. It stopped running in 1938. The glen had room for crowds.

Hanan Porat and other activists met Shimon Peres. The defense minister set appointments easily with the young settler. Peres suggested he might win cabinet approval for the Elon Moreh group to settle at an army base on the slopes rising from the Jordan River toward Nablus.[35] The spot would widen the Jordan Rift strip of settlements, bringing it a step closer to the mountain ridge. Peres was offering to co-opt the group, to let it help him make policy incrementally more maximalist. The Elon Moreh group rejected increments.[36]

The next day—Thursday, July 25—the Elon Moreh settlers and supporters set out again, this time from a town near Tel Aviv, on dirt roads up toward Sebastia, evading army roadblocks set up to stop them. A second group, led by Ariel Sharon, took main roads. Sharon, by a Gush Emunim account, "broke through" the first roadblock he hit, and led pursuing soldiers on a wild chase through the West Bank roads, pulling them away from the settlers' actual destination. Other supporters walked in, or succeeded in driving in by not traveling in groups: Soldiers at roadblocks were not stopping Israelis on innocent outings. The settlement bid became a game of tag that grown-ups could join. Both sides agreed the issue was authority, maintaining it or joyously flouting it.[37]

"The mountains of Samaria are ours and we will no longer leave them in the hands of any other nation . . ." said a flier for participants. "The government has no right to prevent individuals and groups from living in any place on the soil of the homeland, as individuals . . . have done throughout the generations."[38] The second part of that statement equated the settlers to Jews through history who had come to live in the Holy Land for religious reasons, with no political expectations beyond hoping the current emperor would not disturb them. The first part made clear that settlement was a tool in a modern struggle between ethnic groups for sovereignty. It asserted a right to rule the land, not just to live in it. Blurred perception defined the new movement: It did not distinguish between individual rights and national ones, or between the faith of the past and faith-based nationalism. The strand of nationalism it transmuted into theology was exclusive: One nation's claims negated another's. Compromise became equivalent to blasphemy.

At Sebastia that afternoon, the tents went up again. Fifteen Knesset members arrived, allowed through the roadblocks on Peres's instructions, whether to avoid stoking the political fire or to maintain his personal ties with the right. Among them was Menachem Begin, who two months before opposed illegal settlement. Novelist Moshe Shamir, the onetime Marxist ideologue turned Whole Land of Israel apostle, drove in, spent the night without sleeping bag or jacket, and woke at dawn to find young men praying at the train station. "Have you seen an idea come true? Have you witnessed, tangibly, actually, the moment of a vision of redemption turning into reality?" he wrote in another of his rhapsodies, published in a major newspaper.[39] He had found young people with whom he resonated.

Rabin and Peres flew above the valley in a helicopter, looking down at a crowd they estimated at 400 to 500 people and that organizers described as 2,000.[40] The cabinet met in special session on Friday afternoon to confront a national crisis. Dovish ministers blasted the army's failure to stop the settlers. Peres was quoted by an admiring journalist as arguing that "this is an illegal, unacceptable act, but these guys are not professional criminals or lawbreakers. They're moved by national motives"[41]—concisely articulating the ethic of illegalism, which valued patriotic purpose over the rule of law. The cabinet authorized Rabin and Peres to remove the settlers, with the understanding that the evacuation would not occur on the Sabbath or the next day, the ninth day of the Hebrew month of Av, anniversary of the destruction of the ancient Temple in Jerusalem, when Orthodox Jews would be fasting.[42]

The crowd shrank before the Sabbath and grew again Sunday, as supporters hiked in through the hills under the July sun. Among them were Merkaz Harav students, acting on instructions of Tzvi Yehudah Kook, who permitted them to break the fast by drinking water. The obligation to settle the Land of Israel took precedence, he ruled.[43] In the symbolic lexicon of Judaism, the ruling intimated approaching redemption, when the fast would be replaced by a feast. Peres met a delegation from "Elon Moreh." Despite the cabinet's decision not to negotiate until the settlers left Sebastia, he offered them a Jordan Rift settlement nearly deserted the year before.[44] The government's project of settling the Rift was ailing and could use new energy.

At midnight Mordechai Gur—the paratroop commander who took the Old City in 1967 and now the new military chief of staff—came to the train station and unsuccessfully urged the group to leave. Early Monday, after waiting for the settlers to finish morning prayers, soldiers began carrying them to thirty-one waiting buses—all in good spirits, with troops and settlers apologizing to each other, according to news reports on the end of the carnival.[45] It was the first attempt to settle at Sebastia; it would not be the last.

Attorney General Meir Shamgar decided not to file charges. Shamgar said he wanted to avoid giving them the chance to exploit a trial as a political stage.⁴⁶ Yet his decision hinted at what Peres had said aloud: Offenses committed out of nationalist zeal would be forgiven. "After all, this isn't an enemy that has come to conquer the country," Peres said at a post-crisis meeting of Labor's Knesset delegation, answering angry doves such as Arie Eliav and Yossi Sarid who blasted him for indulging the settlers. A legislator from Peres's Rafi faction of the party—a kibbutz man who had signed the original manifesto of the Movement for the Whole Land of Israel—insisted no law was broken at Sebastia, and called for settlement in the area. In the Knesset plenum, Moshe Dayan criticized putting any limits on where Jews could settle on the West Bank, asserting that "our visa to Judea and Samaria is that they are Judea and Samaria and we are the people of Israel." Though the doves were more vocal now, Labor still represented nearly the entire range of Israeli views on the West Bank's future. The party mainstream supported settlement in occupied territory and had never officially adopted a map of where it would be allowed or barred or endorsed a rationale for such distinctions.

"This is a government of settlement, but it has an earlier and a later," Peres asserted.⁴⁷ It was an invitation to a pressure group to make the "later" happen sooner, especially after a success in mobilizing supporters that exceeded expectations. The Elon Moreh group merged with Gush Emunim, and a joint leadership met to plan the next steps of a quickly growing movement.⁴⁸

YIGAL ALLON conveniently missed the Labor catfight over Sebastia. He favored "removing the squatters," as he told Kissinger.⁴⁹ But speaking too strongly against "squatters" could have provoked questions from colleagues with memories of Hebron.

Then again, he did face Kissinger's rather undiplomatic quip, at a dinner at the Israeli embassy in Washington: "What are you doing, being merely a 'deputy' prime minister?" The professor, like a demanding father, expected complete success of his former students. The small talk between courses that night between senators and congressmen was about trying Richard Nixon in the Senate.⁵⁰ The House Judiciary Committee was already approving articles of impeachment. "He is listening to tapes and climb[ing] the walls," Kissinger said afterward at Camp David, where he and Allon went to talk privately.[51]

Despite the president's implosion, Kissinger was pressing ahead with his Mideast efforts, pushing for an interim agreement between Israel and Jordan. He did not need to push Allon hard. The foreign minister rejected the proposal from Zaid al-Rifai, now King Hussein's prime minister, for a deal based on Israel pulling back six miles from the Jordan River along the length of the West Bank. That would mean giving up the Rift. Instead, Allon suggested returning Jericho to Jordanian rule, as a first step toward realizing the Allon Plan—although, he admitted, he had no mandate to concede land. He and Kissinger agreed on tactics: Kissinger would suggest Jericho and a bit more to Rifai and Hussein, as an American idea, something that perhaps could be sold to Israel. Allon said he was "very happy" they had found a way to get talks rolling.[52]

When Rabin heard, he was less pleased. Three days later, before Allon left Washington, he gave a message to Ambassador Simcha Dinitz to pass to Kissinger. "As already explained to you, any territorial concession by Israel on the West Bank requires new elections," Kissinger was now told. "The cabinet is not prepared to call an election involving territorial concessions within the context of an interim agreement."[53]

Nonetheless, when Jordanian prime minister Rifai arrived in Washington immediately afterward, Kissinger did suggest an Israeli pullback from "Jericho, a corridor and part of the West Bank," stressing, "I've never discussed [this] with the Israelis." Rifai was willing to start from there, saying, "We can improve on that in actual negotiations."[54]

By then, the secretary of state was truly flying solo. Nixon had just been forced to release the final, incriminating Watergate transcripts. Two days after Rifai's visit, he resigned. When King Hussein himself arrived in mid-August, Kissinger was secretary of state to a new president, Gerald Ford. Hussein, though afraid of Arab reactions to a corridor running through Israeli-held land, accepted Kissinger's pledge to press forward on a disengagement agreement. Kissinger argued that it did not matter if Israel's opening offer was "outrageous"; what mattered was that Israel agreed "to disengage over the Jordan," to pull back in some way. From there, negotiations would take on their own life.[55]

Instead, progress ended. Rabin came to Washington, but the meeting of the unelected prime minister and unelected president was "close to a disaster," the epitome of bad chemistry, in Kissinger's telling.[56] Rabin insisted the Israeli public would only accept West Bank concessions for a full peace treaty. Ford found Rabin dour, tough, and inflexible.[57] Tremendously insecure, shy, and politically besieged would have been more accurate.

Allon later claimed that he held back from an all-out political fight over the need to negotiate with Jordan because of Hussein's hesitations. A summit of Arab leaders was scheduled for Rabat, Morocco, at the end of October. On the agenda was whether to allow Hussein to negotiate for the West Bank or to give that mandate to the PLO. Allon wanted a commitment from Hussein that he would stick with an interim deal no matter what happened in Rabat. Otherwise, Labor could find itself facing elections over a nonexistent accord. "We'd have been like the kid relieving himself behind a bus and the bus moves," he said.[58] Hussein was unwilling to give any such promise, and preferred to wait till after the summit.[59]

THE LAND lay on dry slopes leading up from Jericho to Jerusalem. In Hebrew it was called the Red Ascent, Ma'aleh Adumim, after the color of the rock. The Arabic name meant the Blood Ascent, supposedly for the blood of travelers spilled by bandits.

In August 1974, settlement czar Yisrael Galili wanted to build at Ma'aleh Adumim. For several years an idea had floated through officialdom of putting an industrial park for Jerusalem there, outside the territory Israel had annexed. Even inside the city on annexed land, though, construction did not keep up with plans, and apartments built for political purposes sometimes stood empty.

Now, facing diplomacy and the potential for a pullback, Galili sought to ring the metropolis with settlements. If new borders were drawn, they would not be next to the city. If Jericho were given up, a settlement between there and East Jerusalem would keep the Jordanians away from the Holy City. Once again, slow diplomacy spurred settlement efforts. There were doves in Labor who questioned such plans, but Rabin and Allon supported the policy. The more hawkish Peres did all the more so.

Intent on accelerating settlement, the defense minister had just appointed Moshe Netzer—the kibbutz member and former Palmah officer responsible for reestablishing Kfar Darom in the Gaza Strip—as his settlement coordinator. Unencumbered by the romance of farming and enamored of the defense industry, Peres put another old friend in charge of moving defense factories to settlements. Building a wide ring around Jerusalem fit their plans.[60]

With Rabin's approval, Galili put the head of the Jewish National Fund in charge of a panel to develop Ma'aleh Adumim.[61] As the Settlement Department's Yehiel Admoni read the map, the Red Ascent broke the Allon Plan's boundaries and opened the way to further eating away at the land available for returning to Arab rule.[62] Allon himself insisted that building at the site east of Jerusalem fit his intent and claimed credit for the idea of settling there.[63] Even among those involved in Labor's settlement project, there was no agreed line of what the Allon Plan allowed. Instead there was a rough concept, and as time passed the concept appears to have shimmered, shifted, and grown.

Galili reported to the Settlement Committee that land east of Jerusalem had been declared closed, officially for military use, in fact available for the industrial park. There were groups of citizens interested in settling in the Ma'aleh Adumim area, he added, which meant that more was planned than factories. Apparently Galili did not mention that those groups, though organized earlier, had now taken Gush Emunim as their sponsor. He did say that he and Rabin had met several days before with the Sebastia settlers, and offered them Ma'aleh Adumim. They rejected all compromises.[64]

In the month after the Sebastia bid, the settlers' representatives were actually treated to two meetings with Rabin and Galili, and at least one with Peres. The country's leaders did not want another face-off, and hoped to recruit the young, fervent activists for their own settlement plans. Peres again proposed that they take over a Jordan Rift site that had been nearly deserted by Likud-linked settlers. The Arabs were actually most interested in getting the Rift back, he said, hinting at the contacts with Jordan, and the Rift settlements were in danger of collapse.[65]

Seven years after the Settlement Department's plan for putting 32,000 Israelis in the Rift in a decade, there were a few hundred Jews there. The spirit was willing among officials with receding hairlines who sat at conference tables, wearing the Labor uniform of white shirts open at the collar, remembering the slogans of their youth. But the money was lacking, especially after the war. A greater problem was that few young Israelis were ready to put down roots in the Rift. Many passed through; few stayed.[66]

North of Jericho, below the ridge that looked like a sleeping dinosaur, the small concrete houses and vegetable fields of Gilgal now belonged to a young kibbutz. The former Nahal outpost had been turned over to the United Kibbutz the year before. For the moment, it consisted mainly of people who would have been college freshmen in another country. To hold the spot, the movement sent children of veteran communes who volunteered for a year of service after high school and before going to the army. None expected to spend their lives there. In September 1974 the kibbutz newsletter greeted "our replacements, our heirs, our hope"—the second round of teenagers, fourteen so far and four or more expected, replacing the first group, who described themselves as "elders in every respect, gushing with experience," and who would soon leave for boot camp.[67]

A seventeen-year-old named Vered, from a kibbutz north of Tel Aviv, arrived on the un-air-conditioned bus through the desert, got off at "nowhere," and walked from the main road to the patch of green in the midst of the yellow countryside. There was a lawn, and prefab buildings the size of mobile homes that slept eight people each, and heat "like an oven, impossible to breathe." The size of the rooms did not matter, because no one spent waking time in them. People rose at four in the morning to work in fields of eggplants, peppers, and onions until midmorning when the sun became monstrous, slept again until afternoon, worked into the dark, spent their evenings excitedly together in the clubhouse or on the lawn in front of the dining hall, clasped by the emptiness and the shadow of the ridge, and then slept a couple of hours before returning to labor. No one skipped work. You were judged by how you worked, and how you got along.[68]

There was no TV. Everyone ate together. If one person put on a record, everyone could hear it. The tiny apartments had sinks but no refrigerators; a refrigerator would have been private property. "We were fulfilling part of our education, the dream of our founding fathers," one of the volunteers from a veteran kibbutz later explained. "We were their dream." To spend a season or a year at Gilgal was to treat the kibbutz ideal as still young, still vital—with a hint of self-consciousness that something was being reenacted. "We behaved," Vered would recall, "like children playing kibbutz." The pre-army volunteers were joined by city-raised graduates of youth movements serving in Nahal, alternating between active duty and stretches at Gilgal, where they were expected to settle after military service. "I loved the *firstness* of it, that we were starting something new," another early settler explained Gilgal's attraction. The kibbutz was part of a government plan, uncontroversial, expected to last. Sometimes a Labor politician came to sit on the lawn and talk.

"It wasn't a commune at night," in one early member's words, meaning that free love was not part of the experience. But couples formed quickly. Nothing was simpler than getting a room together. Gilgal was "a matchmaking business," as Vered put it, eventually the meeting place of "thousands of couples around Israel." Few stayed to live there. In the memories of early settlers, Gilgal was a "train station," a confusion of arrivals and departures. Every week, it seemed, there was a going-away party. More people were on the track to university campuses, fitting bourgeois parents' dreams, than to the youth movement vision of kibbutz life. A new beginning of a fading idea, Gilgal would grow slowly and stay small.[69]

Against that gray backdrop Gush Emunim appeared, sudden and pyrotechnic, producing gasps from ex-pioneers of Yisrael Galili's generation. Gush Emunim was a magnet for people who wanted to settle in occupied territory, but not according to government maps, and not in the kind of collective farming communities that Laborites expected. Galili feared the new movement's energy and wished he could harness it. "There are those in whom I detect a sort of dangerous flame that is likely to burn . . . the tissues of the democratic experience," he wrote to a fellow kibbutz man, a supporter of the Whole Land of Israel enthralled by the new would-be settlers. Galili admitted nostalgia for such enthusiasm. But the settlers refused to follow democratic decisions—in practice, the choices of Galili's committee. If Gush Emunim accepted discipline, "they could be a positive factor in carrying out the existing settlement [map] which is still weak . . . and needs to be strengthened quickly."[70] To his comrade, Galili did not try to justify that map. Galili believed in the right and responsibility of elected representatives to make secret decisions, and he believed in settlement. If he could direct the new movement to the places he chose, he would be satisfied.

THE "OPERATION" was supposed to be secret and involve thousands of people, a contradiction in terms. The word *operation*, with its scent of military daring, hinted at the romantic picture that Gush Emunim's activists were drawing of themselves. This time they would move at night. They would start from points all along the Green Line. They would head for two separate targets, an abandoned police station among the Palestinian villages northwest of Ramallah and Jericho, to show both the government and Kissinger what they thought of reports that Israel might give up that town to Jordan. Since Hawarah, "settling" had morphed into a form of mass protest.

An order passed through the chain of activists to move on the evening of October 8. The religious holiday of Simhat Torah ended at nightfall, so synagogues could be used to get word out, and a school vacation made teenagers available. The "secret" reached the police and army with equal speed. Checkpoints went up on West Bank roads. Police showed up at Bar-Ilan University outside Tel Aviv, where crowds were gathering, and told drivers of chartered vehicles to go home. From the nearby Orthodox farm community of Nehalim, a line of "two hundred vehicles," according to an activist's account, rolled out with headlights off, led by Meir Har-Tzion, an ex-commando who had fought under Ariel Sharon in the 1950s and was legendary either for his bravery or his cold-bloodedness, depending on whom you asked. For Gush Emunim, recruiting this secular icon of machismo was another confirmation of being the new vanguard. Har-Tzion pushed through one roadblock, got stopped at another, and led his charges on foot twelve miles through the dark to the abandoned police station. Across the West Bank, in a vast game of hide and seek, groups broke up, got lost, headed for hilltops. When day came, soldiers began pulling protesters to buses. A party led by Levinger spent two days in a canyon near Jericho before being dragged out. For the next week, new groups kept heading out and getting caught. By one press estimate sympathetic to Gush Emunim, 15,000 people took part all together.[71]

A spoof diary of a "settler for half a night," printed in handwriting with childish drawings, appeared in the monthly magazine of Bnei Akiva. The narrator describes hearing from "the gang" at synagogue about the "operation," and tags along because "why not? It's not a bad trip for school vacation." He rides on the roof of a packed car that evades "an army of one soldier" at a roadblock. "Maybe it's illegal, but they explained to me that the ends sanctify the means," he writes. They reach their destination, which "doesn't seem like the best spot for a picnic, especially at night, but I kept quiet, because 'the ends sanctify etc.'" Stranger yet, he is asked to put up a fence around the picnic grounds. When two soldiers pick him up "like a stretcher . . . I saw that one of them was Kirshenpluk, our neighbors' son," who promptly drops him in surprise. Home at last, he gets a visit from friends who want to sign him up for a "real" settlement, but he needs to prepare for college entrance exams. "Who's got time to settle?" he concludes.[72]

The satire constituted a certificate of success for Gush Emunim. Not only had it brought out religious teenagers, it had reached the critical mass where people came without needing to understand or believe. "Settling" for a day was now the way to rebel and conform at the same time. In the year since the war, the Bloc of the Faithful had been born as a lobbying group within a middle-rank party, reinvented itself as settlement organization and protest group, and metamorphosed to subculture—a mood, the next happening thing.

Despite the spoof's gentle jabs, Bnei Akiva's magazine both reflected and shaped the Orthodox youth movement's own transformation into a support auxiliary for Gush Emunim. Articles by rabbis of the Kook school appeared as the proper religious commentary on current events. In the autumn of 1973, Rabbi Shlomo Aviner not only proclaimed the just-ended war to be "a stunning victory unlike any we have known since we returned to our land," but he also asserted that Jewish heroism in battle was "a manifestation of the sacred" and heralded the messiah's coming.[73] To mark the seventieth anniversary of the death of Zionism's founding father Theodor Herzl, the magazine published an essay by Har Etzion yeshivah head Yehudah Amital proclaiming the death of Herzl's secular nationalism. Herzl expected that the Jews' return to their land would make them a normal nation, accepted among other nation-states, Amital explained, but diplomatic and military threats to Israel proved that "the Jewish problem" was unsolved. Herzl—and secular Israelis—were mistaken. "But there exists a different Zionism," Amital said, "the Zionism of redemption," to take the place of Herzl's ideas.[74] Rather than secular Zionism being the heir of Judaism, religious Zionism would be the rightful successor of secular nationalism, free to take possession of its myths and rituals and assign them new meaning.

A columnist answering teenagers' questions of belief wrote that "in our generation, the generation of redemption," the Land of Israel was the primary value, which "comes before anything else."[75] A teenage girl identified only by her first name, Osnat, described a trip by her Bnei Akiva chapter to Samaria—the northern West Bank—and quickly segued to amazement at "talk of 'peace or territories' from Jews." Her movement's pressing task was "to support the hawks' position."[76] Dissenting voices did appear on occasion, as in a pro-and-con debate on the Sebastia bid. The "con" writer dutifully affirmed that "the Land of Israel . . . belongs to us and no other nation," but objected to putting greater stress on land than on the search for religious meaning.[77] Osnat answered him, in the joyous righteousness of youth, with hope that "you too will soon be privileged to see the light."[78] The dissenters looked as painfully out of place as a bow tie at a rock concert. Not that every member read the ideological debates. It was possible to tag along on a settlement "operation" because everyone else was going, be evacuated by the neighbor's son, and move later to a settlement—citing your Bnei Akiva upbringing, and insisting you had never read Tzvi Yehudah Kook's messianic writings.

GATHERING IN RABAT on October 28, 1974, the leaders of the Arab countries recognized the Palestine Liberation Organization as the "sole legitimate representative of the Palestinian people in any Palestinian territory that is liberated." King Hussein, utterly isolated, gave his assent.[79] Until now, the PLO's base of support was mainly Palestinian refugees living outside the land once labeled Palestine on maps. Young people from the occupied territories crossed into Arab countries to join. Inside occupied land, the PLO's influence was weak, though Israel's perceived defeat in 1973 boosted backing for the nationalists. The Rabat decision speeded the trend. Rather than recognizing West Bank support for the PLO, Rabat created it.[80]

If there had been an opening for an Israeli-Jordanian agreement, Rabin had feared to step through it. By the end, Hussein had as well. Now it was shut. The commitment by Golda Meir and then Rabin to hold new elections before ceding West Bank land, at least partially a product of Gush Emunim's pressure on the National Religious Party the previous spring, was a key factor in the setback.

By coincidence, Rabin succeeded in bringing the Orthodox party into his coalition virtually at the same time as the Rabat summit.[81] That gave him a stronger parliamentary majority, along with a more maximalist cabinet. On paper, the "Jordanian option" remained Labor's policy for the future of the West Bank's Palestinians. In practice, the political changes both in Israel and among the Arabs made that option a dead letter. "I tried to convince them to go ahead with you anyway, and we would protect them," Kissinger told the Israeli troika, describing his meeting with Hussein just after Rabat. "He wouldn't hear of it."[82]

Two weeks after Rabat, PLO leader Yasser Arafat, wearing a holster and treated as a head of state, spoke before the U.N. General Assembly, invited by an overwhelming majority of the member nations. He declared diplomacy an "enhancement" of armed struggle, rejected the idea that the Palestinians' struggle with Zionism was a conflict between "two nationalisms," and called for a "democratic Palestine" in place of Israel.[83]

Arafat was asserting a claim to a whole land that—to quote another movement of radical nationalists—"belongs to us and no other nation." Providing an extreme example of ends justifying means, he proclaimed that one who "fights for the freedom and liberation of his land . . . cannot possibly be called terrorist."[84] The Rabat decision, the U.N. invitation, the iconic image of Arafat on the General Assembly dais were intended to advance Palestinian interests. In fact, they also served Israeli hard-liners, giving evidence that there were two irreconcilable claims to one indivisible land, and reinforcing the association of Palestinian nationalism with terror. Those who proposed mutual Israeli-Palestinian recognition and negotiations were left more isolated.

Kissinger would spend much of the next year in the nerve-wracking pursuit of another agreement between Egypt and Israel. When he came to Israel he was greeted by ever more raucous protests organized by Gush Emunim. Diplomacy left the West Bank and Gaza Strip for another time, and in the meantime settlement continued.

YISRAEL GALILI MET representatives of the would-be settlers at Ma'aleh Adumim in late October. Their link with Gush Emunim did not seem to have been an obstacle. His talking points for the meeting, though, included the warning that "it is essential to avoid advance publicity." To work with him, they would have to learn the art of silence. No minutes were taken of the meeting itself.[85]

A month later, the cabinet approved Galili's proposal for the site. On his instructions, the ministers did not receive briefing materials in advance, "to prevent leaks and so we can discuss the subject . . . without sensationalist reports." For the moment, Ma'aleh Adumim would be an industrial area, with living quarters for employees—"until a further decision."[86] The move was later described in the press as a compromise between ministers who favored a settlement and those who opposed it.[87] But the allusion to a future decision meant that the cabinet was actually agreeing to the ruse of factory housing in order to create a full-fledged settlement later. In early December, Galili informed Rabin that a "work camp" would be set up within days. The only reason for delay was that Allon was about to land in Washington to talk with Kissinger, and a report on a new settlement would be inconvenient. Galili agreed to establish the "camp" right after Allon's meeting, when Kissinger would be in transit to Brussels.[88]

After that, the project hit a hitch. Galili's memos to the prime minister continued to refer to it in future tense.[89] By early January 1975, he was complaining of intrigues by doves within the Labor Party and its left-wing junior partner, Mapam, to foil the plan. Secrecy was crumbling. Someone had leaked financial objections raised in the cabinet. The precocious, dovish Labor politician Yossi Sarid, now a freshman Knesset member, was "spreading reports of plotting against" poor towns inside Israel. Galili, it appears, still feared pressure to pull back in the West Bank. Reasons of state, he told Rabin, made it essential to build at Ma'aleh Adumim, but the expectant settlers and their Gush Emunim sponsors were left waiting.[90]

Galili was not alone in concocting ruses. Sometime in late 1974, Gush Emunim leader Hanan Porat gave a tour of Samaria to Rachel Yana'it Ben-Tzvi, the widow of Israel's second president. Nearly ninety years old, still politically active in the Labor Party, she was an outspoken advocate of the Whole Land. Northeast of Ramallah, at an imposing peak called Ba'al Hatzor, they saw an army base under construction. They stopped the car and got out. "In our day," she said, referring to pre-independence Zionist pioneers half a century before, "we started settlements as work camps." Find out if construction laborers are needed, she suggested, create a camp, and simply stay. A voice from the faraway past, she was recommending to children who wanted to relive the legends to use the old method: create facts, quietly.

Porat's Gush Emunim colleagues were doubtful—except for Yehudah Etzion, then living in the movement's office in downtown Jerusalem, the agitator's agitator. He and Porat found the contractor building the base and subcontracted as a "work brigade" to put up the fence. Shimon Peres's settlement adviser, Moshe Netzer, gave them a permit to work in the area.[91] The "brigade" consisted of Etzion and three friends who commuted daily from Jerusalem to their project, and volunteers they rounded up—yeshivah students, Bnei Akiva teenagers, anyone willing to work for a day. They worked through the winter.[92] The army got used to their presence between the Palestinian villages. Etzion brought his fiancée, Hayah, to the steps of a building on a deserted Jordanian base nearby and said, "This will be our home."[93]

They married in January. Among religious Jews, it is traditional to follow a wedding with a week of smaller celebrations, reciting the seven blessings of marriage each time. On a surprisingly sunny afternoon, the Elon Moreh group showed up at the Sebastia train station to celebrate.

A newspaper headline described the visit as "nostalgic," as if their settlement attempt at the spot was a long-ago escapade of youth. The article, though, quoted Gush Emunim leaders as saying this was "a demonstrative act, intended to warn . . . the government what to expect." The army did not disturb the romantic event.[94]

11

LAST TRAIN TO SEBASTIA

March 1975 was the season for the sport of settling, as the Bloc of the Faithful played that increasingly unforgiving game. As the challenger, the Faithful chose the time and venue of matches, which the Rabin government and the army were bound to accept, lest they lose by default. Losing, for the government, would mean an end to its control over where and when Jews could settle in occupied territory. It would mean yielding command over defense and diplomatic strategy, which even a government divided is loath to surrender.

Gush Emunim's goal, short of a knockout, was to wear down government resistance and to pull public opinion to its state of mind: Settle everywhere, keep everything, reject all compromises as products of outside pressure and inner weakness. The timing of its new campaign had partly to do with Henry Kissinger's latest round of shuttle diplomacy. Kissinger was seeking a second Israel-Egypt accord, in which Israel would pull back farther from the Suez Canal for arrangements a step closer to peace. In a newsletter for supporters, Gush Emunim attacked the proposal that Israel would cede a Sinai oil field, since that would make the country more dependent on foreign supplies, and thus more vulnerable. Nationalist values of pride and militant self-sufficiency had become religious principles.

"More than ever, we are certain today that a 'phased withdrawal' beginning in Sinai will be prevented by settlement in Judea and Samaria, the Golan and Sinai," the newsletter said.[1] The logic is emotional: Settling in the West Bank would keep Sinai oil by showing that Jews do not yield. It would "heal the county's spirit."[2]

The timing also reflected tension within Gush Emunim. Hanan Porat, as ever wanting to be the "vanguard," not a "separatist," believed repeated clashes with the army cost the movement support. By March, the Elon Moreh group and other advocates of direct action tired of waiting. They decided to move, without asking the movement to bring out thousands of supporters again.[3] Ultimately, their logic was that defiance would bring admiration.

So forty would-be settlers cast off Yisrael Galili's admonishments of silence and showed up early one March day at Ma'aleh Adumim, set up a water tower and a prefab concrete building, and by afternoon were removed by troops, four soldiers carrying each settler, the drill now practiced. Galili's government project would henceforth be linked in public consciousness with the government's foes.[4] The Elon Moreh activists, announcing their willingness to "give our lives" for "redemption of the land,"[5] returned by night to Sebastia and were discovered in the morning, the men barricading themselves in a second-story room of the crumbling station, struggling and shouting insults and demands to disobey orders as they were extracted through the windows by soldiers balancing precariously on ladders balanced against the pink rough-cut stone walls. A watching journalist reported "intense hostility" between settlers and soldiers, "unlike anything during previous settlement attempts." Still, the incident "did not get the media coverage we expected," an activist later complained, because the same night eight Fatah men landed on the Tel Aviv beach and took over a seaside hotel, in the Palestinian organization's own effort to scuttle Kissinger's mission, and by dawn three Israeli soldiers and eight civilians and seven terrorists were dead, the hotel was recaptured, and the country was in mourning.[6]

The setback did not stop Gush Emunim. A hundred people briefly locked themselves into a Jordanian bunker cut into the mountainside at Ba'al Hatzor, the peak northeast of Ramallah.[7] Forty others managed to spend a Sabbath in abandoned houses near Jericho before the ritual removal by troops.[8]

"Friends tell us we are banging our heads against a wall. . . . But we're convinced that the wall's foundations are crumbling, and in the end we'll succeed," Elon Moreh organizer Menachem Felix said at an evening press conference—after which his group gathered in a quiet Tel Aviv suburb to set out for Sebastia, got arrested and released, regrouped in an orchard, dodged roadblocks to reach the ruined station, staged a repeat of barricading themselves in, and were pulled out, kicking, shouting, clawing. "Settler Yehudah Etzion prostrates himself on the ground, crying bitterly and kissing the soil," a photo caption read the following day, showing the tall curly-haired activist stretched flat out. This time they got the press they wanted, especially since after being booked and released in Jerusalem they burst into the Prime Minister's Office in giddy fury, sat in, and were dragged out and arrested the third time in twenty-four hours—which to their dismay, still did not earn them the trial for which they now begged.[9]

The settlers could take comfort, though, in the collapse of Kissinger's shuttle effort. Kissinger blamed the Rabin government's insistence that Egypt declare "non-belligerence," virtually agreeing to peace, while Israel kept most of the Sinai. Kissinger's approach was for Sadat to sign on conditions that added up to non-belligerence, without using that term. Nor were Israel's leaders ready to give up the strategic Mitla and Giddi passes in the Sinai. On his last day in Israel, Kissinger got a tour of the ancient desert fortress of Masada with Yigal Yadin, the archaeologist and ex-military chief of staff who had excavated the site. At Masada nineteen centuries earlier, the Jewish rebellion against Rome ended with the last rebels committing suicide to avoid capture. Kissinger's memoirs give no hint that Yadin mentioned his own thoughts of political rebellion, nor that Kissinger might have had associations of the reports he was getting from Saigon and Phnom Penh as America's anti-communist allies in Southeast Asia collapsed. That evening, Kissinger told the Israeli troika that "our strategy was designed to protect you" from international demands for a full withdrawal. "I see pressure building up to force you back to the 1967 borders—compared to that, ten kilometers is trivial. I'm not angry at you. . . . It's tragic to see people dooming themselves to a course of unbelievable peril."[10]

But he was angry. According to Harold Saunders, a member of the U.S. negotiating team, it was the only time in the Mideast shuttles that Kissinger "showed personal emotion . . . deep but controlled emotion."[11] Yitzhak Rabin could not bend, Saunders writes, because Shimon Peres threatened to quit the government if he did.[12] It was Dayan's old tactic: If Peres's faction split with Labor, it could bring down the government, forcing elections or bringing the right-wing Likud to power.

Then again, Kissinger may well have overreached that spring, seeking an agreement before it was ripe in order to compensate for other setbacks. While he negotiated in the Middle East, "the disintegration of Vietnam was bringing American foreign policy to its nadir," he mentions as an aside, petulantly adding that Rabin had other concerns. For years, America's troubles in Indochina had protected Israel from pressure. Now Vietnam was the source of U.S. pressure.[13] Ford announced a "reassessment" of U.S. policy toward Israel, which threatened a rethinking of the alliance.[14]

In his memoirs, Kissinger says that Ford "interpreted the stalling tactics of the Israeli troika . . . as reflecting their assessment that he was too weak" to fight Israel's supporters in Congress.[15] Read that as Ford's own insecurity: As an unelected president, he believed he had to show he had a backbone. He had more in common with Rabin than he realized.

AT THE END of March, as far as the Israeli public could see, Gush Emunim's settlement campaign had burned itself out. The Rabin government's wall had not fallen.

The public did not, however, see Yehudah Etzion's "work brigade" building a fence around the military base on the peak of Ba'al Hatzor northeast of Ramallah. Etzion made contact with the Gush Emunim group that wanted to settle at the biblical site of Shilo—several dozen singles from around Israel, many of them students, and a dozen or more young married professionals with children[16]—and suggested they settle instead at his imagined "work camp," seven miles to the south. To

Etzion's dismay, the group's leaders were not enticed by Zionist nostalgia to join in pounding fence posts while winter wind lashed the hills, but the opening for settlement did attract them.[17]

By January, a letter to members had announced the possibility of establishing a community at Ba'al Hatzor, to be called Ofrah.[18] The name belonged to a town mentioned in the Book of Joshua that once stood in the area, providing a requisite biblical aura.[19] A flier later passed out among Gush Emunim supporters, aimed at recruiting more people to work or to settle, noted that the brigade was also open to women, who could perform service jobs, and asserted: "It is possible . . . to create the fabric of a de facto settlement . . . and eventually receive some form or another of government approval."[20] The organizers wanted a low profile, but within a circle that included dozens, perhaps hundreds, of people, their goal was known.

That circle included some officials. The Shilo group's letter said, "We are in the midst of discussions with political and defense elements" on setting up the settlement.[21] Beyond that, Porat was a prominent Gush Emunim leader, and Etzion a known militant. Anyone who had contact with them could figure out their interest in the area. Moshe Netzer, the defense minister's settlement adviser, could see that the ideology-driven members of the work battalion he had approved were not looking for "a solution to the problem of making a living."[22] Both Netzer and Peres favored Jewish settlement on the mountain ridge and were at odds with Rabin and Galili on the issue.[23] When Netzer let the project develop, he was serving his boss's purpose, whether or not the boss knew the details.

But Peres almost certainly knew the intent. A Gush Emunim document from early 1975 claims that agreement had been reached with Peres on establishing a camp for civilian employees of the army at Ba'al Hatzor, but that the cabinet had delayed the plan.[24] Even if the report is an example of the movement's inclination to interpret a minister's evasive grunt as effusive assent, it indicates that the group was already in touch with the defense minister, who did nothing to put a stop to the work brigade. If their reading of Peres's stance is accurate, they had his full support, but he wanted cabinet ratification.

The activists took their next step on tiptoe, holding their breath. In mid-April, a few people gathered in Gush Emunim's office and divided up assignments. Etzion gave one a long handwritten list of equipment to buy: "30 beds, gas/kerosene lanterns, mattresses, food for a day or two, 15 jerry cans, generator, wire, lights . . . cooking gas, kitchen implements, weapons, polyethylene [sheeting] . . . sleeping bags."[25] The plastic sheeting was for covering the empty windows and doorways in concrete shells the Jordanian army had left when it abandoned its half-built base near the village of Ein Yabrud. The date that Etzion and his friends picked for moving in was Sunday, April 20, a normal workday, with no high-schoolers or other hangers-on available to draw attention.[26]

A dozen people working on the fence came at the day's end to the ghost base at Ein Yabrud. A similar number from the Shilo group arrived at the same time, packed into the minimum of cars. The watchman—a Palestinian from a nearby village who worked for the Israeli army and who lived at the base with his herd of goats—looked on as the cars came down the dirt driveway and people began to unpack. "It's okay," someone said, but the guard mounted his donkey and rode into the dusk toward Ramallah military headquarters.[27]

As night fell, the settlers set up camp. Now and then, a straggler arrived. One was Yoram Rasis-Tal, a young Orthodox Jew who had ended up on the Shilo settlement group's phone list almost by accident. Settling, in Rasis-Tal's mind, meant that "a group of people gets together in the evening . . . goes up to some hilltop, and in the morning the army brings them home," and he wanted to take part. When a stranger called him at two that Sunday afternoon and told him to come to the movement office in Jerusalem by four, he informed his boss he was leaving early, his wife that he was coming home late. By the time he reached Jerusalem, the group had left. The secretary pointed vaguely at a spot on a large-scale map, and Rasis-Tal hitchhiked north—a ride in an Arab car, another in a donkey cart, another with a Jew who let him off somewhere past Ramallah. On foot on the mountain road, wearing a thin sweater in the cold of the hills, he continued until he saw flashlights flickering in the dark. At Ein Yabrud, in an improvised kitchen, two "girls" were cooking vegetable soup in an industrial-sized can, formerly full of pickles, that served in place of a forgotten pot. The first person who tasted it turned red and said nothing. "Look friends," suggested the second, "since this is the first, historic soup, let's keep it to display in the museum when it's built."[28]

The army commander from Ramallah, Moshe Feldman, drove in an hour and a half after the watchman rode out. All right, Feldman said, looking around at a familiar scene, pack up and go home. "This isn't what you're used to," Etzion answered. "It's coordinated with the Defense Ministry." Feldman drove back to Ramallah to make phone calls.

In the most common account of the evening, this much was coordinated: Porat had gotten himself on Peres's appointment schedule for that night. When word arrived of the settlement bid, or soon after, he was sitting with the defense minister. You can see there's a big constituency that doesn't want to see that area empty of Jews, Porat would recall telling Peres. You're a smart guy, he said, create a safety valve before there's an explosion, and let them stay as a work camp.

Despite government policy, Peres acceded. Don't help them, he told the officers awaiting his word, and don't bother them.[29] When the news reached Ein Yabrud that night, a bottle magically appeared, and people began to dance.[30]

There are variations on this telling: that the army originally let them stay just for the night, that contacts with Peres began the next day, that delicate negotiations lasted two days before Peres gave backhanded instructions that "the workers will not be prevented from lodging at the site."[31] The result is clear: With Peres's consent, the "work camp" remained.

An unhappy Rabin asked Galili to look into the affair.[32] At the end of April, Galili sent Rabin's office a draft for what to tell Peres—that "the prime minister . . . reiterates that there is no cabinet decision to establish a settlement at Ba'al Hatzor," but also that "the number of workers lodging at Ein Yabrud will not exceed twenty men and four women."[33]

The note makes most sense as another of Galili's compromises: Rabin would not have to risk confronting Peres and ordering the "workers" evicted. At the same time, Peres would be on notice that the camp was really, truly temporary.

As always with a Galili compromise, that leaves the enigma of what Galili himself wanted. Months later, he was still cautioning Peres's settlement adviser, Netzer, that "he and the defense minister must take care, because I do not believe the cabinet will approve establishing a settlement at Ofrah."[34] When a dovish minister confronted Galili with evidence that Ofrah was not temporary lodging for twenty-four laborers, but a growing community, Galili wrote back, thanking him for "information of which I was not at all aware," and then added that since the place had never formally been approved, it was outside his bailiwick.[35] The unofficial minister of settlement only dealt with official settlements.

Galili, it seems, had negotiated a compromise with himself, between the passions of his youth and the caution of his maturity. The disciple of Yitzhak Tabenkin believed in settling the Whole Land—even if he resented the fact that only a movement not his own had the passionate cadres to do it. The sixty-four-year-old cabinet minister, who peppered his letters with the term "state authority" and who carefully orchestrated committee meetings to ensure political consensus on each new settlement, more or less stuck to the Allon Plan and would not accept open rebellion.[36] He therefore agreed with himself that Ofrah was not really there. As long as the settlers did not publicly demand approval, as long as their challenge to government authority stayed low-key, he satisfied himself with warnings aimed at Peres not to flout the cabinet in which he served.

Galili's suspicions that Peres was actively supporting Ofrah had a basis. Ofrah, according to settlement adviser Netzer, "fit our conception in the defense establishment—a work camp created a fact on the ground without closing options for the future."[37] Since the purpose of "creating facts" is to close options, this is a claim to have eaten a cake while leaving it untouched. Ofrah's location fit Peres's views on settlement. Labeling it as a temporary camp, only serving those working at putting up a fence, helped him reduce friction with others in the government.

At Ein Yabrud, the settlers heard neither of Galili's acquiescence nor of his stipulation of "twenty men and four women." People drifted in.[38] At first, Yehudah and Hayah Etzion were the only couple. Despite her fear that they could be evicted any moment, he brought their refrigerator and furniture from the apartment in Jerusalem they had barely lived in. One of the other settlers had come alone but quickly brought his wife.[39] Yoram Rasis-Tal returned home that Thursday. When his wife regained her voice, she shouted, "Is that you or a ghost?"

"Yes, it's me," he said.

"I was sure the children wouldn't have a father!" she answered, but she agreed to leave them with the grandparents and come with him to spend the Sabbath in the former Jordanian base, which now had a sign labeling it "Ofrah Work Camp." Despite his description of her as a Tel Aviv princess, despite sleeping on a mattress on the floor of a room from which goat excrement had just been removed and using an improvised outhouse, when Rasis-Tal said, "So?" on Saturday night, she answered, "So when do we move?" It helped, he would recall, that an Orthodox kibbutz donated fifty Sabbath meals.[40] Ofrah grew on the kindness of fellow travelers, among them some of Peres's staffers. With the defense minister's knowledge and support, Netzer writes, "we helped the 'camp' in various ways."[41] One form of help was a permit that Peres's settlement adviser provided for wives and children to reside at Ofrah.[42]

Besides the fence project, the settlers had the job of making the camp livable. One concrete shell had four rooms around a larger hall. A family got each room, with a blanket over the opening in place of a door. An outdoor faucet was the sole source of water. Out of necessity, not ideology, the settlers ate in a communal dining hall. It took three weeks to install the first toilets. As rumors spread of the place's existence, volunteers showed up to work; supportive contractors donated supplies. Hanan Porat stayed for a month to help and supervise. The Gush Emunim leader was the old man at age thirty-one, the counselor at a summer camp for barely-grown-ups. Early each morning before work, in his voice of constant warm spiritual wonder, he taught a class in "The Voice of the Turtledove," the esoteric text explaining the role of human efforts in the oncoming messianic redemption. After that, one could go on to fence-building or to cleaning rooms with bare-dirt floors, or whitewashing or putting in windows, with a foundation of faith that the labor had cosmic implications—even if everyone still wondered if they would be able to stay. The mood was a mix of apprehension and euphoria.[43]

Around the end of May, a Gush Emunim newsletter told supporters of Ofrah's existence. Eight families and eighteen singles were living in

Ofrah, it reported, with thirty-five more families interested in coming. Since the initial permission to stay, it said, "we intentionally have not held additional . . . contacts" aimed at official approval, since "precisely because of the decisive political . . . importance of the site in the midst of Arab villages . . . and controlling the Ramallah-Jericho road, the current government is not yet capable of officially recognizing the settlement."[44]

Knesset Member Yossi Sarid drove into Ofrah one day in early June with a reporter. Someone alerted Yehudah Etzion, at work on the fence project on the mountain, who rushed back to find Labor's dovish gadfly sitting on the wide steps of a building, brashly holding forth, "What chutzpah . . . ! We'll make sure nothing remains!"[45]

Sarid was overconfident. Answering questions in the Knesset, Peres described Ofrah as temporary housing for army employees—and at the same time, as part of the effort to keep the Jerusalem area Jewish. Arabs were building more houses around the city, he argued, so Jews needed to do the same. Each new house, in Peres's portrayal, was a position claimed, as two nationalities competed. The Knesset debate was pure chaos, with opposition rightists defending Peres, Sarid blasting him, hecklers shouting nonstop. "I don't believe you!" roared the dovish dissident Arie Eliav—who at last had left Labor for the wilderness of tiny feuding left-wing factions—at the defense minister.[46]

Neither, for that matter, did Yehiel Admoni of the Settlement Department believe Peres. Ofrah was outside any plan for widening Jerusalem, he would note.[47] If Ofrah were part of greater Jerusalem, then so was Ramallah and much of the West Bank's Palestinian population. As Gush Emunim writers justly asserted, the settlement shredded the Allon Plan.[48] Not only did it lie in the midst of Palestinian villages, it stood in the way of Allon's proposed corridor from Jericho to the northern West Bank.

Rachel Yana'it Ben-Tzvi, the wizened pioneer who had visited Ba'al Hatzor with Hanan Porat, had been right. Labor could be defeated with its own methods, drawn from the pre-state struggle that, for the party's leaders, still glowed with heroism and lost youth—claiming land one fait accompli at a time, without public declarations. It helped that many of those leaders had divided souls, and had a much easier time praising the ideal of settlement than explaining their reasoning for keeping some areas out of bounds. It helped that the ruling party was fractured, its hold on power fragile, its leaders feuding.

Still, Ofrah was only a partial victory for Gush Emunim. Its activists wanted a change of policy, publicly acknowledged—so they could establish more settlements, and also because they regarded Labor's restrictions as a mark of national shame, of "wavering faith in the redemption," as Porat said that summer in a movement journal. The correct response to the "question of whether or not to give up Judea and Samaria," he said, depended on a "proper attitude toward the question of the honor of the Jewish nation."[49] The romantic nationalist's pursuit of glory, in that formulation, became another religious obligation.

RABIN DECIDED that June to add a new adviser to his staff: Ariel Sharon. After a year as a Likud Knesset member, Sharon had quit parliament, sick of "smiling and talking and backslapping," as he put it.[50] Like many a general, like the prime minister, he had discovered that civilian politics was a difficult profession. His new appointment looked doubly strange: Not only had Sharon constantly, loudly criticized Rabin's government, Rabin was now making made him an adviser on defense affairs, a field the prime minister obviously knew well.[51] But old generals in politics often want the company of other men missing the weight of a gun on the shoulder, and Rabin and Sharon belonged to the same "clan," in Haim Gouri's words, a clique of old military friends whose personal ties preceded politics.[52] And—as Peres and many others saw it—by appointing a defense adviser, Rabin was proclaiming he had no confidence in his defense minister. "The move was designed to oust me," Peres told another Labor politician.[53] More likely, it was a sign of Rabin's frustration that he could not get rid of Peres. The feud was now very open.

"LARGELY DISCONNECTED" from the headlines of illegal settlement bids, Yehiel Admoni writes, the official settlement bureaucracy "got on with routine activity."[54] Gush Emunim succeeded in making settlement more controversial than ever before, and also diverted attention from the progress of government-backed building.

Keshet, the Gush Emunim–linked settlement that began in Quneitrah, got approval from Galili's Settlement Committee for a permanent site near the Golan Heights frontier. Galili, cautious, had wanted to put it farther back from the line, to leave a bit of land to give the Syrians in any new accord. But he folded under pressure from "militant members of the Golan kibbutzim."[55] In the Heights, the alliance held between the original socialist settlers and the later Orthodox ones.

On the red rock slopes east of Jerusalem, the first prospective residents of Ma'aleh Adumim were granted keys at a September ceremony.[56] Their prefab concrete apartments—listed as 410 square feet, or perhaps 250, depending on which Gush Emunim complaint one reads—were not ready yet.[57] Officially, the settlement was still a "temporary laborers' camp" for the industrial park being built.[58] "Ma'aleh Adumim wasn't built by Gush Emunim. It was my initiative. It was part of my plan," Yigal Allon insisted afterward, perturbed by the public's impression that the settlement was imposed on the government from without. The militant movement "adopted it and did damage to the status of that settlement," Allon complained.[59]

At the town of Avshalom Center on the north Sinai coast, 350 apartments were nearly ready, a Housing Ministry official reported to Galili's Settlement Committee in May 1975. The first settlers were ready to move in—a handful of immigrant families from the United States and the Soviet Union. When Galili suggested building another 500 homes, a dovish minister named Moshe Kol objected. The cabinet decided on a small town, he said, "not a city!" The objection got lost in the talk. The committee officially noted that the place's name would revert to Yamit—as per Moshe Dayan's original proposal—and that the Housing Ministry had already built the infrastructure for 1,000 families. With that, Admoni notes, Galili provided a stamp of approval, after the fact, for construction that exceeded the cabinet's original limit.[60]

In October, building at Yamit was back on the committee's agenda. Demand was high for the first batch of houses—not surprising for a town near the Mediterranean beach, with government-subsidized loans for buyers. Housing Minister Avraham Ofer, generally known as an outspoken dove, wanted to build the next 1,000. Wait, said the hapless Kol, wondering if Dayan's original idea of dredging a port was also on the agenda. Construction had to fit official decisions, he insisted. "I don't want to see private arrangements on this matter, like what the defense minister did with the work camp at Ofrah," he said.

Kol was outnumbered by colleagues who wanted to build, and to avoid bringing attention to the project with public debate. The Housing Ministry needed no further approval to build the next stage, Galili said, summing up the discussion. "Making a racket will only do us damage," he said. "The idea of Yamit was born as a city of a quarter million people." It was a typical Galili maneuver, Admoni comments. What looked like an innocent summation reinstated the idea that Israel was building a metropolis in the Sinai.[61]

By that time, Galili no longer had to contend with one particular critic of the Yamit plan. Pinhas Sapir, the former finance minister and Labor boss, had died in August at age sixty-eight, barely a year after he last passed up the chance to be prime minister.[62] Sapir could serve as an icon for the political ineffectuality of Labor's doves. Gruffly pragmatic, he believed in developing the State of Israel within its pre-1967 boundaries. "If we keep holding the territories," he often warned, "in the end the territories will hold us."

Yet once the decision was made to establish a settlement, Sapir believed in funding it properly, rather than using his power as Labor's economic master to stall. His deference to generals, his unwillingness to take responsibility for matters of state, left policy in the occupied territories to the hawks. And like other doves, he had his list of "kosher" areas for settlement. To oppose settlement completely in the Labor Party of those days, his young friend Yossi Sarid would comment, was equivalent to "denying a principle of faith and removing oneself from the congregation." The religious metaphor is appropriate: A sacrament can live long after its original purpose has vanished. Its very lack of practical meaning can deepen its sanctity as a sign of belonging to the community.[63]

Yet opposition existed. As settlement grew in northern Sinai, activists in the left-wing Mapam continued to fight for compensation for the expelled Bedouin. There was also a danger that more would be driven from their homes. Hundreds still lived along the coast, where fresh groundwater rose to the surface and fed crops. The plans for Yamit and its harbor posed a constant threat to them. Oded Lifshitz of Kibbutz Nir-Oz and Latif Dori, a Baghdad-born Jew who handled party contacts with Arabs, ran what they called "Rafiah Tours," bringing Israelis to see what had been destroyed, and to counteract the public image of Bedouin as nomads with no homes to lose.

Once they brought Knesset member Meir Talmi, Mapam's secretary-general, for over forty years a member of a farming commune in the Jezreel Valley. They found themselves on a hilltop in the area from which the Bedouin had been driven. On another hillock a few hundred meters away stood the tents of a Nahal outpost called Sukkot, designated to become a kibbutz. In the valley between the hills grew a Bedouin orchard of almonds and peaches. Despite the expulsion, the owners had informally been allowed to come and tend their trees—until now.

As Lifshitz and his companions watched, a bulldozer grunted below them, uprooting a row of trees, turning back, uprooting another row, leaving broken branches and sand scarred with tread marks, clearing ground for the kibbutz. Talmi, in his sixties, with deep wrinkles that at other times could emphasize a smile, stood and cried. The next day, he stayed in his room at his kibbutz, unable to go to work at party headquarters in Tel Aviv.

That added another name to the list of Knesset members who could be phoned late at night when word came that the Bedouin on the beach would be expelled, when army markings were found on houses designated for destruction. The next expulsion never happened. But it was a rearguard fight. At Sukkot, houses were built in place of tents.[64]

MAKING NOISE ABOUT Yamit would indeed have been inconvenient in the fall of 1975—embarrassing both Israel and Egypt just as they implemented a new diplomatic agreement.

The American reassessment of Mideast policy that spring had brought Ford and Kissinger back to where they began: conducting step-by-step talks aimed at interim agreements. Kissinger believed a comprehensive Middle East peace was out of reach, and made a "private pact" with himself that if the United States decided to dictate an agreement, "I would resign. . . . Two years ago, my colleagues and I had more or less imposed a settlement in Vietnam. . . . That settlement was now coming apart, and I had to manage the disaster. I would not be able to bear the responsibility for another such tragedy," he wrote, "especially vis-à-vis an ally so closely linked with my family's fate in the Holocaust."[65]

By summer, he resumed work as intermediary. A compromise took form for Israel to pull out of the Sinai passes, which would become part of a U.N.-controlled buffer zone with separate Israeli, Egyptian, and American early-warning stations. Instead of promising "non-belligerence," the agreement specified that "the parties . . . undertake not to resort to the threat or use of force or military blockade against each other."[66]

In August, Kissinger held another shuttle to wrap up the deal. The protests that greeted him in Israel, spearheaded by Gush Emunim, were a festival of anarchic ferocity, remembered afterward by those who took part with the nostalgia reserved for utter release. A crowd surrounded Kissinger's motorcade and tried to overturn the cars. Demonstrators lay down on the Tel Aviv-Jerusalem highway. Sound trucks rolled through the capital at four in the morning, barking "Kissinger, go home!" The epithets shouted at rallies included "Jewboy" and "Kapo." "Hitler spared you so you could finish the job," read a placard that Kissinger recorded in his memoirs as "hurtful." The Jewish secretary of state stood charged explicitly with being a turncoat, implicitly with being the caricatured Diaspora Jew, clever and lacking self-respect, that believers in national honor wanted to excise from family memory. "The violence," Gush Emunim recruit Meir Harnoy wrote years later, "was very intense, close to nine on the Richter Scale of demonstrations."[67]

Nonetheless, Israel and Egypt agreed on terms, initialing the Sinai II agreement on September 1. In Israel, even supporters greeted it more with exhaustion than joy. Viewed unemotionally, the accord committed Israel's most powerful neighbor to a peaceful resolution of the conflict, and left Syria without a partner for renewed fighting. Even if Egypt wanted to break its commitment, it would be unable to launch another surprise attack. Emotionally, though, the agreement registered as defeat. Despite Kissinger's proclaimed dislike of imposing terms, Sinai II was born of American pressure and payoffs, underlining Israel's dependence on the United States.

Among the payoffs were an American commitment to new financial aid, and a promise not to negotiate with the PLO unless the organization recognized Israel. The U.S. memorandum of understanding with Israel also ruled out another interim agreement with Egypt, or with Jordan. The next stage would be full peace.[68] Since Sadat's requirement for peace was to receive the whole of Sinai and Israel's was to keep part of it, Israel's leaders regarded creating facts in the peninsula, and keeping quiet about them, as necessities.

The agreement had strange ramifications. Dropping the idea of an interim deal with Jordan can be read as an American promise to Rabin to forget the gambit favored by Allon. A final peace with Jordan was clearly beyond reach—if Hussein agreed to negotiate at all after the Rabat decision, he was not going to sign on to Israel keeping East Jerusalem and the Jordan Rift, which was Israel's minimum. For Rabin, trying simply to keep his coalition together, deadlock was a relief: He would not be asked any time soon to give up West Bank land, and would not have to call elections.

But the government's declared policy remained the "Jordanian option": the solution to the Palestinian issue lay in a "Jordanian-Palestinian" state. The logic for its choice of where to establish settlements was Allon's plan, which rested on giving up the most populated parts of the West Bank—to Jordan.

Without being able to claim he was pursuing that option, Rabin's justification for settling in some parts of the West Bank but not others was government authority, the monopoly of democratically elected officials on setting national policy. The principle was correct. But for authority to appear legitimate, it needs a rationale beyond "because I said so." Rabin had left himself without a rationale for his settlement policy. In the face of Gush Emunim's public challenge, that made his political position even more fragile.

SINAI II also did nothing to reduce Israel's diplomatic isolation. Perhaps the opposite: As the talks took place, Arab hard-liners began pushing for

Israel's expulsion from the U.N. When that proposal failed to win support, a substitute was born.[69]

"The General Assembly . . . determines that Zionism is a form of racism and racial discrimination," proclaimed the resolution passed November 10. Seventy-two of the United Nations members voted in favor, thirty-five against, and thirty-two abstained.[70] Third World diplomats attributed their vote both to pressure from Arab oil states and to "resentment against the Yankees" and colonialism, with Israel as proxy for the United States.[71]

The resolution gave its Arab sponsors the satisfaction of a rhetorical victory. It had effects, though, beyond what they expected or saw. In Israel, the vote completed the process of delegitimizing the United Nations. It amplified anger at another General Assembly decision that day, calling for a PLO role in all Mideast diplomatic efforts, and further isolated the Israeli minority looking for a way to reach accommodation with the Palestinians.[72] It strengthened the right's argument that "the world is against us," and that both pride and pragmatism therefore required rejecting outside criticism.

Yisrael Galili convened the Settlement Committee to discuss a "fitting response" to the U.N. decision. The obvious, reflexive reaction was to affirm faith in Zionism, using means hallowed by tradition. All plans for new settlements should be speeded up, Galili proposed. That meant establishing another thirty settlements within the next year and a half, most of which would be in occupied territory—within areas set by the government, he stressed. He was not suggesting that the "camp" that "the defense minister approved" at Ofrah become a permanent settlement.

Most of the panel's members were swept up in the mood, though Moshe Kol—like the kid in the back seat asking his friend yet again about the speed limit—wondered aloud why some of the existing settlements seemed depressingly short of people. Galili's proposal was ratified, along with a suggestion that several new settlements should be established in early December during the Jewish Solidarity Conference that Rabin had announced, a gathering of Diaspora leaders in Jerusalem to show support for Israel and rejection of the U.N. resolution.[73]

Galili was not alone in thinking of settlement as an answer. On the morning of November 25, 150 men, women, and children set out for the

Sebastia train station. For months, Gush Emunim had put off a new settlement bid for reasons of "timing and public atmosphere," as one of its own accounts explained the delay. Illegal settlement efforts and violent demonstrations galvanized the movement's base but risked alienating the wider public, perhaps even giving the Rabin government some needed support. But a movement that is not visible becomes irrelevant, and despite all the noise Gush Emunim had made, it lacked a public victory. Its young supporters' excitement could evaporate. The General Assembly decision offered a moment when public sympathy could rise, when elected officials might find it harder to say no. The opening was so irresistible that for the first time, the movement's leaders took the chance of acting in winter, the Mediterranean season of wind, storm, and rain.

The new Sebastia "operation," activists told a reporter, was intended to "take the government's pulse." The government's pulse, and reflexes, appeared healthy. As usual, army roadblocks stopped some of the participants. Those who reached Sebastia began cleaning the station and put up signs declaring, "The proper answer to the U.N. and all Israel-haters is settling in all parts of the Whole Land of Israel." Within a few hours, soldiers arrived and perfunctorily removed them, which required chasing down thirty or so who ran into the hills.[74]

That was the rehearsal.

SATURDAY, NOVEMBER 29, was the start of the eight-day holiday of Hanukkah. Schools would be closed, teenagers free and bored. In hundreds of synagogues, fliers announced the next day's Gush Emunim event. Action was needed, the text explained, because the "organizations of murderers" trying to destroy Israel sought to reach it "via the areas still empty of Jewish settlement . . . being kept for them as an 'option' "—implying that the Rabin government was about to turn the West Bank and Sinai over to the PLO, lending a hand to the phased strategy. "Remember! We are following the path, rich in deeds, of the fathers of the Zionist movement," it declared. Under that came instructions to bring "especially warm clothes . . . long underwear . . . toilet paper . . . high spirits and love of the land." Friday's papers, Israel's fat weekend editions, had carried ads announcing the settlement bid.[75] The goal this time was not secrecy, but bringing masses. It would be a set-piece confrontation.

On Sunday morning, thousands gathered at the meeting points. Some, perhaps most, turned back at army roadblocks. The main group of supporters drove out of Netanyah, a coastal town at Israel's narrow waist. Ten miles to the east they entered occupied territory. Stopped by soldiers, they parked on the outskirts of the Palestinian town of Tul Karm, and began hiking up through the foothills, a long undulating line, half Scout outing, half protest march. The winter sun shone, the hills were green, and no soldiers appeared to stop the hikers. A high school girl told a reporter afterward of the joy of walking with "the entire Jewish people"—the familiar illusion of a mass happening, when "many" appears to be "everyone," when it becomes impossible to believe that anyone reasonable is not here.

Conflicting reports indicate that a few dozen or few hundred people reached the Sebastia train station that afternoon, on foot or driving back roads that inexplicably remained open. They found a company of soldiers already camped there, tents pitched, the Israeli flag and the standard of the Armored Corps waving.

Nightfall caught another 1,500 young people on hillsides outside the Palestinian village of Ramin. A woman named Hannah Levy from an Orthodox farm village, identified by a reporter only as "mother of one," dozed in exhaustion. When she opened her eyes, she saw hundreds of Hanukkah candles dotting the darkness. Cold rain began to pour down, soaking through clothes and sleeping bags. At Monday's first gray light, the march of the drenched pushed on to the muddy field before the train station. Most quickly left, on buses provided by the army or hitchhiking with Arab drivers. The crowd shrank. The army did not seize the chance to evacuate the remaining few hundred. As evening approached, a fresh wave of Gush Emunim supporters began arriving.[76]

"The defense minister's instructions to the IDF to stop the settlers on their way were given halfheartedly or carried out negligently," Yitzhak Rabin wrote in his memoirs, giving an explanation for how Gush Emunim's throngs got past the army: Peres's perfidy.[77] For his part, Peres argues in his memoirs—after attacking Rabin's appointment of

Sharon as his adviser—"During the Sebastia standoff . . . someone set up a pseudo-military headquarters in Tel Aviv, from which he transmitted advice and guidance to the settlers on how to dodge the army patrols. . . . Clearly, the man who did this was in possession of firsthand and fully updated information."[78] Both accusations are plausible, though as often the case in human affairs the most likely explanation is not conspiracy but incompetence: The army did not have a defensive line separating Israel from the West Bank, and despite Gush Emunim's repeated settlement efforts had not created means for keeping Israelis out of occupied territory. Rabin's and Peres's accusations do, however, testify to the pathology of distrust that paralyzed their government.

The army did know how to evacuate settlers. No one—Rabin, Peres, or the full cabinet—gave orders to do so. The political opening was turning out to be even wider than Gush Emunim expected. On Sunday, as the settlement bid began, the U.N. Security Council voted to invite the PLO to a full debate on the Middle East. The United States declined to veto the resolution.[79]

Each diplomatic setback abroad made the government more queasy about confronting domestic rivals who spoke in the name of patriotism. Ideologically, Gush Emunim regarded Labor's brand of secular Jewish nationalism as obsolete. The Faithful aimed not at a Jewish state achieving normal status among other nation-states in the practical business of history, but at redemption from history. Rhetorically, though, the radical movement used the slogans and symbols of its secular opponents—the appeal to Zionism, the act of settling. Labor's leaders failed to articulate an answer. By the third day of the settlement bid, government sources were telling reporters that the evacuation would take place only after Hanukkah vacation ended, or after the Jewish leaders' conference— either way, not until the following week. News reports of soldiers evacuating settlers would be embarrassing in the midst of a gathering dedicated to Jewish solidarity.[80]

THE SETTLEMENT COMMITTEE met on December 2. Galili's plan for quickly establishing thirty settlements in government-approved areas was no longer on the agenda. "Little by little," Settlement Department official Admoni records, "the enthusiasm [had] died out," for lack of funds and willing settlers. Galili scaled back his proposals to approving four new outposts in the Golan Heights, and asking the Jewish leaders from abroad to approve a resolution backing settlement. "I was shocked," Admoni writes, that in Galili's resolution he "refused to state how many settlements he proposed to set up or make any other concrete commitment. . . . The declaration was toothless, lacking any practical value."[81]

THE FIRST TWO dozen families moved into their rooms at Ma'aleh Adumim east of Jerusalem that Hanukkah week. The timing was an encouraging coincidence for Gush Emunim: It was getting somewhere.[82]

At Ofrah, meanwhile, Yehudah Etzion reported in the settlement newsletter that "after 2,000 years of exile we have renewed Jewish agriculture in the mountains north of Jerusalem"—a plot of less than a quarter acre had been planted in narcissus bulbs. Another ten acres, he said, were being readied for an orchard, though the Agriculture Ministry refused to extend the aid it usually gave new settlements.[83]

Other state agencies were more forthcoming. A letter arrived from Peres's settlement adviser, informing Ofrah's secretariat that "Ofrah Camp . . . has been recognized by the defense minister . . . for purposes of the home guard," meaning that the army would treat the place like any other settlement, eligible for army supplies to defend itself, even if it still lacked government approval to exist. Ofrah, said the letter, could also hook up to the local electricity grid, and the Defense Ministry would pay for floodlights around the settlement.[84] The decisions may have been made before anyone showed up at Sebastia that week. But it was a reminder of Peres's sentiments.

BEFORE THE TRAIN STATION, next to the army's tents, the settlers erected their own tent encampment. The rabbi who headed Bnei Akiva's high school yeshivot drove in, with an official pass that got him through roadblocks, and brought a Torah scroll. Hundreds of young men danced around him in circles, singing, hands on one another's shoulders, as he installed the scroll in a structure the settlers had managed to put up and dedicate as the synagogue of Elon Moreh. Naomi Shemer—the secular songwriter who had composed "Jerusalem of Gold"—showed up too, bearing boxes of jelly doughnuts, the standard Israeli Hanukkah treat, and handed them out by the hundreds. When a truck carrying parts for a prefab shed got stopped at a roadblock, hundreds of supporters hiked from the train station and carried the pieces back, putting it up next to others smuggled in earlier. The main path in front of the tents was dedicated as Zionism Avenue, and the tents got street addresses. A shed was dedicated as a yeshivah study hall. An icy wind blew through the encampment but no one stayed inside. A shop opened, selling cigarettes, batteries, and postcards. Business did not slow after midnight. No one seemed to sleep. The place "resembles a town in the Wild West," said a reporter, looking at the tents below the tall cypresses and pines. Rabbi Moshe Levinger's disciple Ben-Tzion Heinemann, "the camp commander" according to the press, walked about with an AK-47 slung on his shoulder. Army buses waited behind the tents. Rumors spread: The evacuation order would come once the conference ended; there would be no evacuation; the cabinet would approve the settlement as an answer to the Security Council.[85] The more people came, the more the stage set of a town grew, the more it seemed *real* this time.

A Knesset debate that week may have fed the settlers' hopes. Peres, as the minister responsible for the occupied territories, got the task of explaining the government's stand. Peres explained that the government itself was busy building settlements, that it had just approved new ones in the Golan and had more coming. But settlers had to obey the law, and he advised those at Sebastia to leave voluntarily. He did not explain, as a parliamentary reporter wrote in pointed bewilderment, what would happen if they refused his advice. "I did not come today to propose solutions," he stated. A Likud Knesset member, defending illegal settlement, recalled that Kibbutz Hanita had been established on the Lebanese border in 1938 in defiance of British authorities. The logic either equated Israel's government with the foreign ruler, or suggested that once Jews had their own state, they should be more tolerant of lawbreaking. A legislator from the dovish Mapam party called for uniting behind settlement within the Green Line; the pro–Gush Emunim Knesset member

Yehudah Ben-Meir shouted sarcastically, "Let's unite behind a Palestinian state, as you'd have it."[86]

Ben-Meir's response paralleled Gush Emunim's statements that "removal of settlers by the IDF will only serve the PLO."[87] In fact, the PLO had unintentionally aided the young, uncompromising nationalists of Gush Emunim, who returned the favor to the uncompromising nationalists of the Palestinian side.

The PLO was trying to establish itself as a popular force within the West Bank, superseding the older, conservative, often pro-Jordanian leaders. The Rabat decision helped, as did U.N. decisions recognizing the PLO: The world appeared to be pushing Israel to end the occupation. For young people in particular, the PLO seemed to be the best means of achieving that end. For West Bank high school students of 1975, Jordanian rule was a childhood memory, stamped "irrelevant" at Rabat. Even so, igniting anything that looked like mass protest proved difficult. The U.N. resolutions of November 1975 finally provided a spark, setting off school strikes, violent demonstrations—mostly by teenagers—and commercial strikes. The Sebastia settlement bid made the flame burn hotter and longer.[88] It may be that PLO organizers were paying more attention to settlement than in the past because they were now concerned with the West Bank in particular, as distinct from the whole of Palestine: It mattered now if Jews moved across the Green Line. But the real difference between Sebastia and previous settlement activity is that the Gush Emunim bid was terribly public: advertised, televised, next to the West Bank's biggest city. Only in Hebron had settlement been nearly as obvious before.

A group of a hundred Gush Emunim reinforcements in a bus and cars, taking back roads to dodge army roadblocks on the way to Sebastia, drove through the small Palestinian town of Anabta, and hit a different kind of roadblock: stones spread across the pavement. They stopped, and rocks started raining on them, hurled by boys standing on rooftops. The leader of the Gush Emunim party, an Ofrah settler, got out of his car and and fired a few bursts from his AK-47 into the air. The boys scattered. The gun was of a kind only available from the army, apparently one of those issued to settlers for self-defense. When soldiers showed up and asked the group bound for Sebastia to refrain from gunfire, a newspaper reported, "the settlers demanded to remove the [army] roadblocks" so they could drive freely to the settlement.[89] In Nablus, students at the town's three high schools skipped class to demonstrate and run from troops. Teenagers from the Palestinian village of Sebastia gathered in the village square and tried to march to the train station a mile and a half away. Soldiers stopped them, preventing a melee at the illegal encampment.[90] Even Mazuz al-Masri, the conservative mayor of Nablus, who had run for the office in a 1972 election only under Israeli pressure,[91] went to the military governor to protest against the settlement. Don't worry, he was promised, the army would remove the settlers as soon as Hanukkah was over.[92]

AT THE STONE TRAIN STATION in the mountains, on the railway line to nowhere or to redemption, and at the apartment in Netanyah serving as Gush Emunim's rear headquarters—where typewriters clacked madly, spitting press statements, where phones rang and doors burst open with people coming and going—fear of what waited after the weekend mixed with adrenalinated hope: The troops would come; if they had not come yet, they were not coming; if they came, this time they would not succeed.[93] The Sebastia controversy already divided the nation; the government, as usual, appeared too split to act.[94] Gush Emunim ran newspaper ads calling for reinforcements, listing meeting places for a Saturday-night journey to Sebastia.[95] A press release that sought to deter the government from confrontation declared, "We will defend our settlement as a man defends his home!" The precise means were left unstated.[96]

A number estimated, or overestimated, by organizers as 3,000 spent the Sabbath in the tent city. Ariel Sharon showed up unannounced on Friday night and "shut himself up with the settler leaders for a long meeting in the 'command bunker'" in the station. No one would comment afterward on the discussion. Whether Sharon was advising the prime minister or the settlers, or both, was a mystery, perhaps even to the participants.[97] The head of the army's Central Command, General Yonah Efrat, who would be in charge of any evacuation, brought his family, said the Sabbath blessing over wine, and ate food from the communal kitchen.⁹⁸ On Saturday night, a thousand people gathered in Netanyah for the trip to Sebastia. Naomi Shemer and ex-commando Meir Har-Tzion led the procession. Before setting out, Shemer read out lyrics to a new song, about strange, beautiful people she had met who sang, "The Land of Israel belongs to the People of Israel," meaning to Jews and no one else, and that ended, "Strange people, let my portion be with you."⁹⁹ The army let them drive to Sebastia village and walk only the last mile and a half.

HAIM GOURI drove out of Jerusalem on Sunday morning, heading north through the Arab suburbs where he had seen white sheets of surrender hanging from shuttered windows eight and a half years before, when he led his platoon this way in June 1967. He remembered the woman he had seen on the road, in her black embroidered village dress, "the stunned ambassador of a different nation hiding behind the stone walls and watching through the cracks in fear and astonishment and shame and eternal enmity and helpless fury. . . ." It was the same land, with its tall cypresses on the ridges undulating like Jews at prayer, with the "sky bright above the biblical landscape, the stone fences, the minarets of the mosques."¹⁰⁰ By December 1975, by his account, he had painfully accepted "Yigal's plan" as the only political possibility, though his heart belonged to the Whole Land.¹⁰¹ Driving, he thought of Nathan Alterman, the secular poet who had said that "anyone who gives up Samaria will have to change the prayer book, because the history of nations has never heard of a nation giving up its homeland."¹⁰² Gouri also saw the land through the translucent parchment of an ancient book, but he saw the minaret and the Arab woman as well. Sometimes, he wrote that week in an article about his journey, reasons of state required "unfair compromise."

He drove his small Fiat past Ramallah, toward Sebastia. Gush Emunim's tents had stood for a week. As a journalist, he could no longer ignore the story. In Nablus, he smelled the stink of burning tires. Rocks thrown by demonstrators lay on the road. Curiosity or a wrong turn took him toward Sebastia village. Soldiers said it was dangerous to drive onward. He got out and followed the squad. A crowd of female protesters in embroidered dresses stood beyond olive trees, for the moment not throwing rocks.[103]

Gouri turned and headed toward the encampment. Hundreds of people were still hiking in, through the orchards and vegetable fields of Arab farmers. The trampling upset him. So did the claim that the tent city itself was on unowned land. There is no unowned land around the train station, he wrote afterward, quoting a tough old expert who had been Ben-Gurion's Arab affairs expert a generation before. "Land is life," and every acre belonged to someone. The settlers "hadn't bothered to think that someone else existed here."[104]

At the station, he wandered about. The scene was jagged, did not fit together. In an Israel sick with materialism and status seeking, a post-revolutionary Israel, the fervent hundreds around Gouri reminded him of the barefoot youth movement idealists of another era. And yet they did not at all. This was a copy, a stage production, farce in place of tragedy. A man stood giving a political sermon to an entranced gathering of teenagers. The speaker quoted the words of Joseph from Genesis, "It is my brothers I seek," as an injunction to seek all Jews, their support, their unity, and Gouri felt he was watching the country being torn in two, all the ground rules of politics shredded.[105] People carried guns, playing the role of Jewish pioneers defending themselves in the days of Turkish and British rule; the man before the crowd defiantly attacked the "obtuse, idiotic government," yet the soldiers "supposedly threatening evacuation were actually guarding the festive happening." The idealists ignored the Arabs around them, and other Israelis who believed that "citizens must respect the laws of a young state . . . because otherwise this anarchist nation will demolish itself and its country," he wrote.[106] Gouri understood infatuation with the Whole Land, it was his young self; but he was middle-aged, and even if the state with its rules did not arouse passion, it was where he raised his children and he did not want it torn apart.

Just after two o'clock, a military helicopter set down next to the station.[107] Word had come to expect it only half an hour before. Out stepped Defense Minister Shimon Peres and an adviser, along with two generals. Circles of men surrounded them, dancing, as if greeting the groom at an ecstatic wedding. The defense minister's willingness to come, to talk, was a victory, after a week in which any contacts with top ministers had been through worried intermediaries. Organizer Benny Katzover, apparently not alone, thought the sympathetic defense minister was about to announce they could stay. The visitors entered the station with Gush Emunim's leaders, including Hanan Porat, Rabbi Moshe Levinger, and Katzover, and sat down around a table. Apparently it took a few minutes of formalities to get down to business. Then people outside heard voices turn to shouts.[108]

Peres's visit did show how much he and Rabin and those around them wanted to avoid sending troops in. The defense minister was the one to come because the occupied territories were his bailiwick, but he did not choose his message on his own. As he explained two days afterward to party colleagues, four men—himself, Rabin, Galili, and Justice Minister Haim Zadok—had worked out the ultimatum.[109] "If you don't clear the area within one day, the government will evacuate you by force," Peres told the activists. If they went voluntarily, he promised, the cabinet would hold a formal policy debate on settlement in the area within three months.[110]

Levinger burst out of the room to the expectant crowd. "This is expulsion of Jews. This is destruction," he shouted. The words were charged with history and martyrdom. "Expulsion" called up the banishment of Jews from Spain in 1492; "destruction" meant the razing of the ancient Temple in Jerusalem—archetypical moments of Jewish suffering at gentile hands. "We must rend our garments!" Levinger cried, and ripped his shirt in mourning. Some in the crowd followed his example. People sat on the ground and began chanting Lamentations, the biblical dirge for Jerusalem destroyed. A military vehicle pulled up next to the station, ready to extricate Peres if need be.[111]

Inside the room, a tense discussion continued. At some point, Porat stepped outside, saw Gouri, and urged him to come in. Gouri was a renowned poet in a country where poets were celebrities, if not oracles, and was known as a maximalist; perhaps he would imagine a way out. Porat later described Gouri as having been sent by divine providence. Gouri would remember entering the room as "the worst mistake of my life."[112] Inside, Peres motioned to Gouri to sit down next to him. Peres, a pale man, had gone even paler, Gouri would remember. The defense minister repeated his demand that the settlers leave quietly. "Shimon, where will we go from here?" shouted Katzover. "This is the Land of Israel."[113] For the young thin man with the dark trimmed beard and overwhelming confidence, the choice was absolute: Sebastia station or exile.

At last, Gouri the journalist reached for the forbidden fruit hanging in front of him: He entered the conversation, became actor instead of observer. He warned Peres against the scars that a forced evacuation would leave, and told the settlers they had to accept the rule of law. Then he tossed out a proposal: Some members of the Elon Moreh group would move to a nearby army base, where they would wait for the cabinet to discuss their request to settle in the area. It was a recycled compromise, the same one that Rabin had approved offering the Elon Moreh group a year and a half before, during its first settlement bid. According to Gouri's accounts, then and later, he hoped that by entering an agreement, Gush Emunim would be obligating itself to accept authority and rules.[114] There is no evidence that his listeners regarded the idea as accepting such an obligation; it was simply an alternative to confrontation.

According to Gouri, he asked Peres if the government would agree to the compromise; Peres turned the question to the Gush Emunim men. They, in turn, answered that they would consider the idea, if it came from the government.[115]

Close to four o'clock, Peres and his party left the station—the crowd now grim but letting him pass—and his helicopter rose into the dimming winter sky. The cabinet met late in the day. Peres reported that the settlers were unwilling to leave voluntarily, and that evacuation might mean spilled blood. He also described Gouri's idea, but did not endorse it. Only the National Religious Party's ministers backed the compromise, a hint that it was seen as giving in to Gush Emunim. Leftist ministers demanded strong action against the settlers.[116] The cabinet did not quite decide. Its closing resolution affirmed that settlement was allowed only by government decision, authorized the use of the army if needed, and stated a preference to avoid "the distressing results involved in confrontation."[117]

Rabin, by his own account, had made up his mind to send in troops, and called in the military chief of staff, Mordechai Gur. It will take 5,000 soldiers, and several days, Gur told the prime minister. Gur did not want this job. "The chief of staff did not bother to hide that he was not excited to carry out the action, and though he did not say so explicitly, my impression was that he would order the IDF to remove the settlers only against his own will," Rabin wrote in his memoirs.[118] Other accounts confirm Gur's dissatisfaction, perhaps insubordination.[119] "I choked with rage," Rabin would write.

The rage makes sense. Gur was avoiding the order that Yitzhak Rabin had accepted and carried out twenty-seven years before on the beach at Tel Aviv during the *Altalena* affair: to establish that there was a state, that there was one government, even if establishing this fact required fighting other Jews. But choking was also part of the story. Rabin himself did not follow the example of Ben-Gurion; he did not order another officer in and give him the job. Here is the tragedy of Yitzhak Rabin: for the second time in his life he faced the *Altalena* test, and unlike the first time, he failed it.

HAIM GOURI left Sebastia and drove through demonstration-torn Nablus and along the mountain ridge road south to Jerusalem in the dark, asking himself, "How did I get into this?" It was eight o'clock by the time he reached his apartment. His wife, Aliza, said, "What do you need this for?" He phoned Yisrael Galili, a friend since his Palmah days, someone with whom he could get together for a meal, though Galili was a dozen years older than he was. Gouri told him about Sebastia, the risk of bloodshed, the compromise proposal, Gush Emunim's willingness to consider it.

"Who asked you to get involved?" Galili answered. He was angrier than Gouri had ever heard him.

"The ball is in your court," Gouri said. He was very tired, had driven too far and been pulled in too many directions.

"You'll see, they'll trick you," said Galili's voice on the phone. The next day Gouri wrote that "to the best of my knowledge he supported a hard line against those gathered at the train station . . . and was far from supporting what I did."[120] Nonetheless, Galili said he would talk to his colleagues and get back to him.

Gouri drank coffee, and waited, and wrote an item for the next morning's paper. Just as Gouri's article describes Peres's arrival in Sebastia, it stops abruptly, like a phone conversation interrupted by a knock on the door, with the words, "I am going back to Elon Moreh. Later I will know more details."

Gouri had gotten a call from Galili, and then a messenger had arrived with a handwritten note from him, cautiously phrased. It summarized Gouri's proposal to the settlers as "to evacuate voluntarily; to place thirty individuals in a military installation under military authority; to await a new discussion in the cabinet concerning settlement." To that Galili added, "Such a proposal, if it comes *from them*, has a chance, but I have stressed: so far there is no such proposal from them."[121] With that, Gouri was to return to Sebastia. In his own files, Galili added to the text, "I stressed to Gouri that I have no proposals from the government."[122] The negotiating logic was that the government could not be turned down; it had offered nothing.

Gouri was not sure who had discussed the idea besides Galili and Rabin. At most, it appears, Justice Minister Zadok was also consulted. Peres had flown to the northern town of Nahariyah for a speaking engagement. Other ministers were surprised afterward to learn that a compromise was approved without the cabinet discussing it.[123]

Gouri got another call: Rabin said he must not return alone. The army would take him. Aliza said she was against the whole business, and that she would go with him. At a base north of the city, a jeep waited: A driver, another soldier riding shotgun, and Haim and Aliza Gouri rode north. The moon was down. Past Nablus, they turned down the dirt road next to the cypresses, tall silhouettes the shape of candle flames. It was 1:30 A.M. The valley was full of campfires. People walked about, awake, anxious, and expectant. Most were Orthodox, a few were wrapped for warmth in the wool prayer shawls they had brought for morning prayer, but there were secular kibbutz members as well, supporters of the Whole Land, of Tabenkin's old vision, the dream from *In Your Covenant*, which included neither a government nor Palestinians.

The settler leaders were waiting for Gouri. He handed them Galili's note. Porat, Levinger, Katzover, Felix, and three others entered the train station to decide. Gouri and his wife waited outside, freezing.[124]

Inside, Levinger argued against compromise. The government had to declare, in principle, that it permitted settling in Samaria, that no area was out of bounds, he said. Porat said that in a showdown, the government would have no choice but to defeat them. The compromise would open the door to what they wanted, if they could amend it somewhat. "That's weakness," Levinger answered. He did not like weakness. Even so, before dawn they voted, five to two, for Porat's position.[125]

They went out and told Gouri: We will accept, if we can speak first to Peres directly. Gouri passed the message via an army radio link and got an okay. Then he and Aliza got in the jeep. The settlers, he would always remember, had agreed with "gritted teeth."

When he got home, he wrote again, overwhelmed, and then slept through the day. In the afternoon, he turned on the television. On the news was a scene from Sebastia: crowds dancing, Levinger and Porat carried on men's shoulders, Porat with his trademark smile, too broad for his face, bottles being passed about. It made no sense, Gouri thought, he had thought the settler leaders "understood that they too must obeys the laws of the state" and wanted an honorable way out. Now, he saw, he had been tricked. "The compromise was not intended to prevent tragedy but to serve as a gambit in a struggle to which I am no partner."[126]

THIS HAPPENED while Gouri slept: In late morning, the foursome of Porat, Levinger, Katzover, and Felix sat down with Peres at the Defense Ministry in Tel Aviv.[127]

The meeting yielded a rephrased agreement, in Peres's handwriting. It said the settlers would leave Sebastia. Thirty families from the Elon Moreh group would move to a military base in the area, where "they will enjoy freedom of movement and the army will provide employment, with no commitment that the base will become a settlement." Within "two-three months," the government would debate settlement policy.[128]

Despite the words "no commitment," Peres's version made significant new concessions. It replaced the original "thirty individuals" with thirty families. The promise of jobs fit Peres's policy of using military employment to boost settlement. Instead of a group awaiting a decision, there would be a community with livelihoods. The promise of a cabinet debate implied at least a possibility of a change in policy, fitting Peres's own goals. Before the meeting's end, Peres left the room to call Rabin for his agreement.[129] Perhaps Rabin had fallen victim to bait and switch: Having agreed to compromise, knowing the army was not with him, he could not now oppose a more costly deal than he had accepted the night before. Or perhaps the differences are irrelevant: The experience of Hebron and Ofrah showed that any "temporary" presence was likely to become permanent.

On the way back to Sebastia, the Gush Emunim men discussed how to present the agreement: as a necessity to avoid a showdown, or as victory. They decided on victory. The crowd was told it had won. The celebrating began, Porat and Levinger and other leaders were lifted onto shoulders, Levinger waving an Israeli flag above hundreds of men wearing skullcaps, who danced in circles that turned into a crushing, ecstatic mass.[130] The news photos provided a large part of what Levinger wanted: proof to the country that the government was weak, the movement strong, the old policy overthrown.

RABIN SENT a memo to cabinet members on the deal. Peres had consulted him on everything, he wrote, and "the policy of the government has been upheld while avoiding a confrontation we did not want."[131] He, too, wanted to claim victory, but had less success.

At the demand of Sarid and other doves, the Knesset delegation of the Labor-Mapam Alignment convened. Backbenchers and ministers assailed the agreement. Among the critics was Yigal Allon, who demanded to know how the army failed to stop the settlers before they reached Sebastia.

"With instructions from the defense minister there should have been no difficulty—" Allon said, and Peres tried to interrupt, and Allon shouted, "Let me speak! You won't keep me from speaking. . . . I won't be silent any more!" Then he insisted there should be no settlement "in areas on which we might have to compromise." His plan was being violated, he had not been consulted, and he blamed Peres. That may have been easier than blaming Porat, to whom Allon had once explained how things were done in the Palmah, or blaming Levinger, his client in settling at Hebron.

Rabin spoke last. If the delegation asked to change the compromise, he said, he would resign. He had been pushed into a decision, and now he had to stand behind it.[132]

THE WALL HAD FALLEN. The foundations had indeed been weak. In facing Gush Emunim, Rabin's greatest problem was not the number of people gathered at Sebastia. It was the weakness of the case he could present—to the army, but more important to the country as a whole—to explain the painful need for confrontation.

He could not point to the Green Line on the map as the limit of Israeli sovereignty, nor argue that settlement in occupied land violated international law. He could not argue that settlement had become an obsolete means of showing patriotism, nor that it would entrench Israeli rule over people denied democratic rights considered basic within Israel itself. He could not point to another kind of border, between legal and illegal, and insist that breaking the law for political purposes was no longer allowable. At Merom Golan, Hebron, Keshet, and Ofrah, the government had condoned the old ethic of illegalism, as it had in the destruction of the Mughrabi Quarter and in the expulsion of the Bedouin from the Rafiah Plain. Insisting now on the rule of law looked like hypocrisy. In his memoirs, Rabin labeled Gush Emunim "a cancer in the body of Jewish democracy," but it was a secondary malignancy.[133] The cancer had been metastasizing for some time.

Nor could Rabin point to the government's clear policy on the future of the West Bank, because in the interests of holding together a party and a coalition, Israeli governments had evaded deciding on such a policy since June 1967. As a party, Labor could not decide on what "territorial compromise" and "defensible borders" meant without risking a split, and the ruling coalition was even more fragile than the party.

Without a case that he could cogently, sorrowfully present before the Knesset, or before television cameras, Rabin stepped back from the brink, and the precedence of political dedication over the rule of law won public victory.

*   *   *

IN DRIVING RAIN, on a field of mud, the tents were folded. It was Tuesday, December 9, 1975. The books in the study hall were packed. Hundreds of supporters drove away, some after nine nights in the valley before the train station. At two in the afternoon, the last settlers left in a procession of vehicles, headed for Camp Kaddum, just east of Nablus, where "they will begin their way as an independent settlement," a sympathetic reporter wrote. Gush Emunim would establish more settlements, Levinger told journalists. At Kaddum, the gate was shut. No one had informed the camp commander. While they waited for word to arrive, the settlers got out and began, once more, to sing and dance; bottles and glasses appeared, people shouted, "*Lehaim*"—"To life." The gate opened, and they entered.[114]

12

THE FALL OF THE HOUSE OF LABOR

Next to Camp Kaddum, bulldozers clawed a hillside, cutting out space for thirty mobile homes. A new road would loop to the compound, so the civilian residents could reach their homes without stopping at the gate of the military base, Defense Minister Peres promised when he visited the Elon Moreh settlers. The new mobile homes would join a dozen trailers already in the base, allowing more families to move in, a Gush Emunim newsletter said, the original limit of thirty families forgotten.[1]

At Bir Zeit College outside Ramallah on an early March day, Israeli soldiers broke up a demonstration by the college's Palestinian students. A foreign correspondent arrived after the noise and fury and inventoried the debris. In the men's dormitory, he saw "shattered windows, mirrors, picture frames and bookcases, overturned beds and, on one floor, dried blood." An army spokesman said that students had showered the soldiers with stones, and that they may have broken up the dorm themselves to manipulate media coverage.[2]

Across the West Bank, through the winter and spring of 1976, confrontations flared and smoldered out and caught flame again. One cause of protests was the settlers' presence at the base near Nablus, coupled with escalating antagonism between the Jews of Kiryat Arba—now home to nearly 1,500 Israeli settlers—and the Arabs of Hebron. West Bank municipal elections, set by Peres for April in hopes of showing how Israel encouraged self-rule, instead forced aging Arab mayors seeking reelection to talk like young nationalists—though real nationalists would defeat them anyway. For days in late March, Ramallah was under twenty-four-hour military curfew. The town of Abu Dis, just east of Jerusalem, seethed after troops shot a ten-year-old boy during a protest and he died of his wounds.[3]

In Hebron, by one Israeli press account, the troubles began when Palestinian high school students demonstrated against conservative Mayor Muhammad Ali al-Jabari, and Kiryat Arba settlers decided to restore order, using clubs and chains. The mayor's son, clearly not one of the protesters, was dragged from his car by settlers and badly beaten. In the most provocative incident, settlers stopped the leading cleric of the conservative Muslim town and forced him at gunpoint to remove stones with which young demonstrators blocked a road.[4] As usual, Hebron's contested holy site—the Tomb of the Patriarchs, or Ibrahimi Mosque— was a flash point. On the carnival holiday of Purim, Palestinians greeted settlers on their way to celebrate at the tomb-mosque with a rain of rocks. Moshe Levinger, rabbi and moving spirit of Kiryat Arba, was interviewed on Israel's evening TV news, watched by virtually the whole country. He stressed hierarchy. Rather than avoiding Hebron, he said, settlers should go there armed, and if need be, respond to stones with gunfire. "We want to live with the Arabs in peace and friendship, but we have put them in their place," Levinger said. "There won't be demonstrations."[5]

On March 23 at Camp Kaddum, families began moving into the new mobile homes.[6] That day, it happened, the U.S. representative to the United Nations, William Scranton, addressed an emergency Security Council meeting on Israel's occupation. "Clearly . . . substantial resettlement of the Israeli civilian population in occupied territories, including in East Jerusalem, is illegal" under the Fourth Geneva Convention, he declared, and "the presence of these settlements is seen by my government as an obstacle to the success of the negotiations for a just and final peace."[7]

American diplomats had been saying as much to Israeli officials since they first noticed that the original settlements were civilian communities, not military outposts.[8] But Scranton's condemnation was particularly public, the wording—*illegal, obstacle*—unusually sharp, and the venue one where Israel felt terribly vulnerable, especially with a PLO representative present. Nearly nine years after the 1967 war, Washington had moved from dealing with settlement as a technical issue for midlevel diplomats to openly declaring Israeli behavior an obstacle to American goals.

Though the U.S. afterward vetoed as "unbalanced" a resolution condemning settlement, and the Ford administration soon smoothed its rhetoric on Israel for the U.S. election campaign, the American dressing down left Israeli officials nervous.[9] Foreign Minister Yigal Allon blamed the Sebastia controversy. As long as Israel created facts quietly, he said in a meeting of Galili's Settlement Committee, the United States said nothing. Now, "the Americans . . . don't miss a chance to express their opposition."[10] In the cabinet he urged quicker settlement in the areas "where we want to settle," meaning those marked on his map. "Silence and resoluteness are our assets," he said.[11]

The words fit Allon's Palmah days: He cast the United States as a half-sympathetic Mandatory ruler who could tolerate Jewish settlement as long as it did not cause public embarrassment. With stealth, settlers could redraw the borders of a future Jewish state—though the state existed and Allon served as its foreign minister.

At the same time, Allon was writing a story about the present: Labor settlement, discreetly carried out, was pragmatic and internationally tolerated. Gush Emunim settlement was demonstrative, uncontrolled, and damaging. That presentation was half-true.

Gush Emunim's settlement efforts did draw international attention, and the Faithful saw government attempts to get along with the United States as shameful. "The true struggle is against Ford and Kissinger, while the Israeli government stands with its hands tied. . . . The government is simply not sovereign," wrote Yoel Bin-Nun, who had graduated from writing on redemption in Har Etzion's yeshivah newsletter to serving as one of Gush Emunim's main ideologues. By using pre-state methods, Gush Emunim was defying not Israel's government, but America's,

Bin-Nun wrote in a movement magazine that spring. Defiance, in his description, was the essence of independence.[12]

Moreover, the United States had chastised Israel because of a series of events that could be traced back to Sebastia. The high-profile settlement bid fueled Palestinian protests, which sparked Israel's attempts at suppression, which led to the Security Council debate.

But Kiryat Arba, Allon's own project, also stoked the protests. And Palestinian anger over settlements tapped a deeper frustration with Israeli rule, which no longer felt temporary and was not invisible. The pressure of occupation and the PLO's proselytizing were changing young people, teaching them the hot, exciting rhetoric of Palestinian nationalism. Sebastia seized Palestinian and American attention in a way that Galili's secretive activities did not. But it was not the only reason for dissatisfaction with settlement or occupation.

As for the PLO, its success came at a high price. For the first time, it swept young crowds to the streets in occupied territory—the premonition of rebellion, if not rebellion itself. But it could do so in part because November's U.N. resolutions against Israel had brought the settlers to Sebastia and Kaddum. After Palestinian protests guttered out that spring, a new wave of settlement would continue, tying Israel more tightly to occupied territory.

An ethnic struggle burned in the West Bank, and stories were being created about it. Gush Emunim's memory would not include the role it played in rallying Palestinian nationalism; the PLO's memory would not preserve the organization's part in the settlers' success. Allon, avatar of government settlement efforts, described himself as an unhappy spectator, erasing his own role in the drama.

THE CABINET debate on Israel's settlement policy was scheduled at last for early May—five months after the compromise with Gush Emunim, rather than the "two or three" promised in that agreement. By late April, 150 civilians were living in Camp Kaddum—twenty-eight families plus forty singles.[13] The Defense Ministry—according to Peres's settlement aide, Moshe Netzer—had "made the camp suitable for the group to inhabit, and helped its members refit buildings for public use. Soon there was a synagogue, a dining hall, and classrooms. . . . All this was done on the instructions of and with the blessing of the defense minister."[14] A visiting reporter found workmen laying water and sewer lines for the mobile homes.[15] Small children played tag among army jeeps. The place was not quite solid yet, but it was coming into focus. The Interior Ministry approved settler organizer Menachem Felix's request for a change of address in his identity papers to "Elon Moreh—Camp Kaddum."[16] Other government agencies were less cooperative. The Education Ministry ignored letters asking to accredit and assist the settlers' school.[17] Without a policy, each official did what was right in his eyes.

Defense Minister Peres, interviewed in Labor's daily newspaper, said if settlement was permissible, it should be allowed everywhere: "I don't understand why it's okay to settle in the [Jordan] Rift and not in the Samaria mountains. . . . I don't understand why settling in the Golan Heights is considered something left wing and settling at Ofrah next to Jerusalem is a right-wing act."[18] The comments were barbs aimed at Rabin and Allon, and aligned Peres with the National Religious Party and Gush Emunim.

The night before the cabinet met, demonstrators marched through downtown Tel Aviv, carrying signs such as "The Law Comes Before Kaddum." The left-wing Mapam party called the protest, aimed at the government in which it served. Party organizer Latif Dori expected "a couple thousand" people, a bit more than he had managed to bring out four years earlier to protest the expulsion of the Sinai Bedouin. Instead, he watched with disbelief as between 15,000 and 30,000 strode behind the party's Knesset members. Sebastia had also awakened Israeli opposition to settlement—at least in the West Bank—as never before.

Most of the protesters came from Mapam's kibbutzim and youth movement. While the party rejected West Bank settlement, it was divided on settling in the Rafiah Plain of Sinai. After sharp debate, it had just approved establishing a kibbutz in the Golan. Dori, a city activist in a kibbutz-dominated party, commented later that many members resented Gush Emunim's claim to the mantle of Zionist pioneering; they felt that the Faithful were "entering our Western Wall," the sacrament of settling the land.[19]

A distinction was emerging. Hebrew has two words for settling—a simple one for daily speech; and another, with a formal, biblical tinge, which literally means to take possession of an inheritance. Gush Emunim, following the Hebron settlers, made heavy use of "inheriting." Now the formal term was increasingly used in wider society to refer only to what Gush Emunim did. It called up a man wearing a crocheted skullcap, a woman wearing a long skirt tailored to Orthodox modesty. The simpler word could be reserved for settlement that fit the Israeli consensus—for building kibbutzim in the Jezreel Valley before independence, for instance, or within Israel afterward. It carried a scent of plowed fields and chickenhouses, and a distant echo of Palmah melodies. But there was an ambiguity: The simple word could also be used for government-backed settlements in the Golan Heights, the Jordan Rift, and Sinai. A supporter of the Allon Plan could reject "inheriting." Public opposition after Sebastia focused on Gush Emunim's very visible efforts. Ironically, it helped place earlier settlement activity at the blurred edge of perception, barely seen if not forgotten altogether.

The crucial cabinet meeting, on the other hand, opened with the Settlement Department's Yehiel Admoni reporting that a total of sixty-nine settlements had been built in occupied territory since June 1967.[20] The Golan Heights had twenty-five, including the new town of Katzrin, and had become Israel's chief source of beef. There were seventeen settlements in the Jordan Rift and along the Dead Sea Coast, five more south of Jerusalem, fifteen including Yamit in the Gaza Strip and northeast Sinai, and the rest scattered elsewhere. Admoni's figures included Ma'aleh Adumim on the red slopes east of Jerusalem as a settlement. They did not include Ofrah or Kaddum. Nor did they include the new neighborhoods in East Jerusalem, officially part of the capital.

There were plans, he said, for building a town in the Etzion area south of Jerusalem, to be called Efratah, a biblical synonym for Bethlehem, and for expanding a clump of settlements in the southern Gaza Strip. Admoni listed 6,500 Israelis as living in rural settlements. A partial figure, this left out the towns—including Kiryat Arba, the largest single settlement—and soldiers at Nahal outposts.[21] Even if no new settlements were started, existing ones would grow. Housing Minister Ofer said nearly as many homes were under construction as had already been completed.[22]

The debate that followed on settlement—in fact, a full-dress debate on the future of the occupied territories—showed that since 1967, the only consensus that had emerged within the small class eligible to sit around the cabinet table was that one must approve settling someplace in occupied land to be taken seriously. A Mapam minister, for instance, stressed that his party supported settlement in the Golan, as preamble to rejecting further settlement in the West Bank. "Settling in all parts of the Land of Israel is saying no to territorial compromise," he asserted, to which Peres impatiently interjected, "I'm against territorial compromise without peace, and I don't see peace"—meaning he saw no reason to restrict settlement anywhere.[23]

Galili, the settlement czar, was in a bind. On one hand, he sought to maintain his own freedom of action. In the past, he said, the government had decided only where settlement would take place, not where it would not. Henceforth, too, the cabinet should not "make decisions that exclude regions from settlement." That would allow him to seek agreement on each new site, unencumbered by explicit rules. He could show fealty to the ideas of his comrade, Allon, and also stretch the Allon Plan's limits. Perhaps, too, the white-haired maximalist, the longtime defender of United Kibbutz's Ideological Foundation, could live with limitations only if he did not have to state them loudly, did not have to declare the romance with the Whole Land to be over. To that end, Galili asked his colleagues to refrain, again, from a sharp stand on Israel's future map.

But Galili also insisted that no settlement be set up without government approval, which meant his committee's okay. He could not bear Gush Emunim's anarchy. The settlers had to leave Kaddum, he said, because planning professionals "believe the place does not have appropriate conditions for settlement."[24] The technical difficulty would allow him to maintain authority.

Allon, however, did want a clear stand, a set of principles on what to keep and what to concede. He had a strategic doctrine, which—he could argue with the same untired enthusiasm that had swept over him nine years before when he came up with it—adjudicated his own conflicts. "I want secure borders, I want a Jewish state, I want a democracy," he said. As for the Arabs accepting his plan, "A compromise always has a better chance than a lack of compromise," and at the least the rest of the world would know "that we looked for a way, we considered the Arab factor."

For Allon, Kaddum was an affront. "The subject is not just a geostrategic concept," he said, ". . . but a test of Israeli democracy." Every previous attempt to settle in that area had been stopped. "In the end, no settlement has ever been established without approval," he said. "I could reconstruct what happened in the establishment of Merom Golan, Kfar Etzion, and Kiryat Arba. Things aren't as they're described."[25] It was a confession that his past argued against him.

The National Religious Party's Zevulun Hammer, who had helped create Gush Emunim, saw no problem in unauthorized settling. After one year, he said, Ofrah had 150 residents. "Isolated, they are building their home by their own efforts," which showed "true pioneering." Kaddum, too, was "a serious settlement with ideology and vision," he said, implying that sincerity trumped legal niceties. The Hebron settlers had originally acted on their own, Hammer argued; ministers supported them, and "helped them . . . including with the problem of guns."

"If it weren't for Kiryat Arba, there'd be no issue of Kaddum," Peres interjected, blaming Allon for the current problem.

"How is it that ten times before a decision was made to evict" illegal settlements in Samaria "and one time it was decided not to evict?" demanded Allon, blaming Peres.

"Because they decided that Zionism is racism, and that changed our decisions," Peres answered.[26]

The dispute between Allon and Peres was the drama that mattered, an angry personal catfight that stood for the war of attrition within the ruling party. Peres filled Dayan's role as spokesman for continued Israeli domination of the West Bank. Unlike Dayan, he did not speak of the Bible, but stuck to security arguments. He proposed a settlement east of Tel Aviv to widen Israel's narrow waist—and more settlements east of that, creating a strip slicing across the West Bank, "for defensive purposes." More building near Jerusalem would create another such strip, breaking occupied territory into fragments. Besides that, he said, "there's a line of army bases in Samaria . . . I'd put a small civilian settlement next to each one," including Camp Kaddum. "I don't see how we can keep an Israeli passport holder from settling where he desires,"

Peres argued. Peres's plan fit Dayan's concept that if peace came it would require "functional compromise," joint Israeli-Arab rule of the West Bank, with the settlers staying put. It also fit the political tactic of maintaining power inside the party by showing that one had the option of bolting and bringing the right to power.[27]

"I don't understand," Rabin said, how a strip across the West Bank could be a defensive line. The intent was: Peres does not understand defense. The prime minister said he was willing to talk about settlements meant to fatten the waist, a break with the Allon Plan, but the government could not accept Kaddum.[28]

The debate, held only because Gush Emunim forced it on the government, ended in a Galili compromise. The government would "increase settlement on both sides of the Green Line" and "prevent attempts . . . to settle without its approval." The word for *settle* in the second clause was the formal one, "to inherit." "No settlement will be established at Kaddum," it said; the settlers would instead be offered a spot that fit "the government's approved plan."

The decision did not describe that plan. It said nothing of what would happen if the Kaddum settlers refused the government's offer.[29] Rabin and the Labor party wanted to avoid a political split. Challenged to define their stand on the country's future borders and on the rule of law, they again chose to avoid a choice.

"We cannot accept the cabinet's decision," Hanan Porat declared the next day, reading Gush Emunim's response at a press conference in the Kaddum dining hall. "We cannot acquiesce in any decision that means dismantling the settlement." On a bare knoll above the mobile homes, three Defense Ministry contractors looked over plans for Elon Moreh's electricity grid.[30]

GALILI ASSIGNED Yehiel Admoni to dicker with the Elon Moreh group. "Be careful to take exact notes," Galili advised in a memo (marked, habitually, "top secret"), so Gush Emunim could not twist media coverage, and "avoid discussing ideology or politics."[31] A messenger whom Admoni sent to Camp Kaddum to arrange a meeting found "construction work continues there, most obviously a large (prefab) structure for a metalwork plant," Galili reported to Rabin. "This fact . . . will not make the contacts easier."[32]

In late June, Admoni met with representatives from Kaddum and Gush Emunim's secretariat. He offered four alternative settlement spots—three on the hills rising from the Jordan Rift, barely below the line where desert gave way to Palestinian fields, and one east of Tel Aviv, in the foothills on that side of the West Bank mountains. The Faithful, its representatives replied, had groups ready to take three of the proposed sites, but "the Elon Moreh group does not regard those locations as appropriate for itself, as it sees itself as the vanguard of those . . . who will settle the Samaria ridge."[33] In a singularly firm voice, they replied to the demand to move: We would prefer not to.

The places that Galili offered, though, mapped the government's own plans. Widening the waist was now policy. Admoni favored the move: It demonstrated that the Green Line was history. Moreover, the underground aquifers that provided much of Israel's water lay under the West Bank foothills, and relatively few Palestinians lived there.[34] The principle remained of not settling Jews in heavily populated Arab areas, not sketching borders that would annex hundreds of thousands of Palestinians. But from both east and west, settlements narrowed the strip of territory that Israel designated for future Arab rule, and reduced resources such as water and empty land. Palestinians, ruled by Israel but not part of its polity, did not have a voice in those decisions.

With Gush Emunim's response, according to Admoni, negotiations ceased.[35] In the months afterward, Allon and other cabinet members wondered publicly when the settlers would be evicted from Kaddum. Rabin's answer was, "I have patience." The archaeologist and ex-general Yigal Yadin, who had announced that he would run for prime minister on an independent ticket aimed at government reform, said on the radio, "The Kaddum settlement affair is part of the widespread anarchy in Israel." At Elon Moreh, the metalwork plant got Defense Ministry business.[36]

AFTER nearly two years, the fence around the base at Baal Hatzor was completed.[37] The "work camp" at Ofrah kept growing. A small cherry orchard had been planted. Apartments for more families were being built. A synagogue was dedicated, built by the Religious Affairs Ministry.[38]

Since the settlement did not officially exist, it did not need to fit the categories for rural life—commune or cooperative farm village—set by officials faithful to Labor's settlement tradition. Ofrah's settlers quickly decided they did not want a socialist economy. But the idea of a village where people privately farmed or ran businesses or commuted to city jobs was new and needed definition. A maverick planner working with Gush Emunim provided it: Ofrah would be a "community settlement."[39]

In practice, that term meant a small, closed residential community, managed by an association responsible for "preserving the character of the settlement," as a Gush Emunim report explained. New residents would have to be accepted as members, so that all would share an "ideological-social background." They would enjoy "single-family homes, quiet streets, fresh air," a dream beyond the reach of most Israelis. The community would grow no larger than a few hundred families, attracting educated professionals to an "island" of a "selected population," deliberately "homogenous."[40]

The plan took what had developed de facto in Alon Shvut, the settlement dominated by the Har Etzion yeshivah that Yigal Allon had sponsored, and made the concept explicit. The "community settlement" would be an exclusive exurb, in which the shade of one's religious commitment could be a criterion for entry. Ofrah became the model, to be applied by other Gush Emunim communities.

Here is another irony. Gush Emunim began with hopes of transforming Israeli society, igniting a revival of faith. Yet by setting settlement as its strategy, it drew its supporters out of Israel to occupied territory. Young Orthodox Jews who had grown up in the cities, contending with a cacophony of political and cultural argument, moved to small communities of people like themselves, comfortable colonies with Palestinian towns and villages as scenery, a barely noticed backdrop. In their new homes, they did not need to face the secular Israelis who had mocked them on their way home from Bnei Akiva meetings. They became a sect, apart from the Israel they sought to lead.

* * *

IN DECEMBER 1976, two hundred settlers were living in Camp Kaddum—thirty-five families with eighty children, and sundry singles. "Intensive construction activity is under way," in coordination with the Defense Ministry, the daily *Ha'aretz* reported. Extensions had been added to the mobile homes. Classrooms and a grocery had been built.[41] Despite the cabinet's decision, Elon Moreh was flourishing.

Yitzhak Rabin's government was not. Rabin and Peres continued to feud on the front pages, like a celebrity couple on the way to divorce. Rabin accused Peres of campaigning from within the cabinet to replace him as Labor's candidate for prime minister in the elections scheduled for the following fall.

Inflation, meanwhile, approached 40 percent. The government had never managed to heal an economy wounded by the 1973 war. Nor had Rabin, the ex-general without party experience, done anything to reform Labor's despised political machine and its reign of patronage. The issues were knotted together, because the party controlled much of the economy—through state and union-owned companies created years before to build the country, and through government financial help to favored entrepreneurs.

In the fall, Rabin had nominated a Labor loyalist to be the next governor of the Bank of Israel, the country's top professional economic post. Asher Yadlin was head of the union-run HMO that provided health care to most Israelis. He was also under police investigation, it quickly emerged, for bribe-taking. The nomination was dropped. Next the news broke that Housing Minister Avraham Ofer was suspected of embezzling funds for party use during his tenure as head of a giant union-owned construction firm. These were the latest scandals, not the first ones.

Junior coalition parties were eager to quit, so they could run untainted by incumbency. Meanwhile, Yigal Yadin, the archaeologist-general, created the Democratic Movement for Change, a collection of rebels—intellectual reformers, businessmen certain they could run things better, Laborites frustrated by the machine, Likud dissidents—

united mostly by unhappiness with the existing parties. The new ticket generated instant enthusiasm. Yadin hoped to ride to the premiership.

Rabin's ruling coalition unraveled in late December. The pretext was a Friday afternoon military ceremony, greeting the arrival of Israel's first F-15 warplanes from the United States, which stretched into the Sabbath. The National Religious Party's ministers abstained in a vote of confidence; Rabin dismissed them, resigned, and called early elections. He may have hoped a shortened campaign would give his opponents less time to hurt him. It was a mistake.

Two weeks later, on January 3, Ofer shot himself, leaving a note that he was innocent but could not bear the charges in the media. Soon after, Rabin's onetime nominee for central bank chief was sentenced to five years in jail.[42]

In February, a Labor Party convention narrowly chose Rabin over Peres as its candidate for prime minister. By an equally narrow vote, it adopted a platform promising to settle Israelis in areas matching the Allon Plan—rejecting Dayan's demand for settlement throughout the West Bank. The party had a position, barely.[43]

The next scandal followed Rabin's trip to Washington to meet the newly elected American president, Jimmy Carter, and discuss resuming peace efforts. On his return in mid-March, *Ha'aretz* reported that Rabin and his wife, Leah, had kept a bank account in the United States after he served as ambassador—a violation of Israel's foreign-currency laws.[44] The offense was technical, but it completed the picture of a leadership that treated itself as above the law.

The attorney general decided to charge Leah Rabin, who had managed the account, while imposing an administrative fine on the prime minister. Rabin wanted to find "any way possible to bear responsibility equally" with his wife. The gruff, lonely man who had struggled for three years at consensus rule found a decision he could make entirely himself. On April 7, he declared on television that he was no longer a candidate for reelection. He also wanted to give up the premiership, but could not: He had already resigned. By law, he led a caretaker government until the May 17 elections and could not leave the post.

On April 10, Labor's central committee unanimously chose Peres as its new candidate for prime minister. Rabin announced that he was taking a vacation, leaving Peres as "chairman" of the cabinet. To get away from "political intrigues and gloating," Yitzhak and Leah Rabin left for the southern Sinai. At Ofirah, a settlement near Sharm al-Sheikh developing as a tropical beach resort, he would be the guest at a ceremony dedicating a new water pipeline that would let the town grow.[45] Before he left, Galili gave him a note that began, "I don't want to weigh upon you," and then provided talking points on settlement in the area.[46]

The political crisis did not slow Galili's work. In April, he completed arrangements for the first settlement east of Tel Aviv, two and a half miles outside the Green Line. A Gush Emunim group would receive the site, which would become a suburb known as Elkanah. Difficulties acquiring land had held up the project, and the Faithful's public demands to receive the site obscured the fact that it fit the government's new plans. Eager to avoid another fight with Gush Emunim before the election, Galili decided that land could be expropriated from its Palestinian owners if need be.[47]

Earlier, just before Rabin's resignation, Galili and Peres signed off on buying 250 acres at another spot five miles farther east of Elkanah, amid Palestinian villages. The Arab owner was eager to sell quickly and the opportunity would not last, said the memo they received.[48] The purchase did not yet mean approval for Israelis to move in. But it did fit Peres's proposal to create a strip of settlements cutting across the West Bank. By some accounts, in the spring of 1977 the Defense Ministry under Peres was already planning the town that would later be established in the area, to be called Ariel.[49] Building settlements did not bear an obvious political cost; refraining did. The land considered out of bounds steadily shrank.

THE RABINS returned after a few days for Leah's trial. She was convicted and fined $26,500. At her request, he stayed in his office during the brief court session.[50]

Shimon Peres was, at last, heir to the house of Labor. Two days before the election, he faced Likud leader Menachem Begin in the country's first televised debate. The event confirmed that Begin, once chief of the "separatists," far-right firebrand and political pariah, was a legitimate contender. Begin's alliance of the right rejected foreign rule over any part of the Gaza Strip or West Bank. On camera, he quoted Peres's own comments on the need to "maintain the width of the country." The Likud, by implication, was not extreme, merely clearer in its message. Demanding all of the homeland was no longer radicalism. Peres himself stressed that Labor had put settlers "in the Jordan Rift, the Jerusalem area, Ma'aleh Adumim and on the mountain ridge."[51]

The National Religious Party declared its independence from Labor. It promised to prefer a coalition with the Likud, and added to its ticket Haim Druckman—the rabbi who had presided over the seder at Hebron's Park Hotel and in whose living room Gush Emunim was founded.[52] The party that sought to avoid war in 1967 now wanted to attract young people who had camped at Sebastia, or who wished they had.

Yigal Yadin, the ex-general promising reform, finally stated his stand on peace and borders: West Bank settlements would be kept to the Jordan Rift; land would be conceded for peace, but not to the PLO.[53] The ideas could have been cribbed from Allon—the former "armed prophet of the Whole Land" now on the dovish side of his own Labor Party's candidate. Right-wingers wanting a general could vote for Ariel Sharon, running on his own ticket. A farmer and son of a cooperative village, Sharon may have had particular attraction for Labor believers in the Whole Land.

Still, experts and polls predicted a Labor victory. The party always ruled. But the exit polls on the night of May 17 heralded an overturning of the given order. Begin's party won forty-three Knesset seats. The Labor-Mapam Alignment took just thirty-two, half what it had at its founding eight years earlier. Yadin's list, mostly supported by former Laborites, had fifteen. With the help of the Orthodox parties and Sharon, whose ticket won two seats in parliament, Begin would be the next prime minister.

The reasons included scandals, mismanagement, and festering fury over the debacle of October 1973. They included the anger of Jews who had come from other Middle Eastern countries after independence and had been treated as outsiders by Labor, the party of the European founders. They included, too, the queasy feeling in the gut experienced by Labor loyalists who had watched Rabin and Peres feud, the government unable to clear out Sebastia or Kaddum, the party finally nominating Gush Emunim's patron as its leader. "How many voted Likud because of the Land of Israel and how many because of Yadlin in jail and Rabin resigning . . . and 'we're sick of it' and strikes and 'we feel shafted' and 'let's try something else' and all the rest of the causes?" wrote a bitter Haim Gouri in Labor's newspaper.[54] The reasons were tangled. The result was that a coalition unambiguously dedicated to the Whole Land would now rule.

TEN YEARS HAD passed since Haim Gouri and General Uzi Narkiss stood in the shade of Ramat Rachel's pines, looking out at what seemed to be the unreachable landscape of nostalgia.

The battles of June 1967 put that land in reach. An overwhelming and unexpected victory brought Israel sudden glory and accidental empire. By 1977, maps in Hebrew that showed the Green Line were pictures of another age, stuffed in drawers, torn at the folds. Young men and women of draft age remembered the smaller Israel vaguely, from the time in their childhood before places beyond one's neighborhood become solid.

The conquests came at a crucial moment in Israel's development. The settlement ethos had been fading. New settlements were hardly being built. The country now faced the challenges of consolidation that came with independence: integrating its founders and latecomers, learning to treat its laws and institutions as its own, defining the relations between the government and pre-state institutions such as parties and unions.

The victory of 1967 suddenly imposed new challenges: the future of the land, and of Israel's relation to the people who found themselves living under its rule. Yet the war also created political paralysis and a diplomatic stalemate. Pushed together by the crisis of June 1967, the rival parties of Labor Zionism merged, creating a single party that represented the entire range of views on the future of the land.

Asked by Lyndon Johnson, "What kind of Israel do you want?" Levi Eshkol could not answer. Johnson, the leader of Israel's essential ally, did not press the point because he did not want to repeat America's error in the 1956 Suez Crisis, and because his attention was elsewhere. Internally and internationally, it was easier to avoid decisions, or to keep them as vague as possible.

Instead, Israel's founding generation discovered that the accidental empire gave them the chance to return to the methods of their own younger days, when Jewish independence was a dream rather than a constrained and complicated reality. The partition of Palestine and the 1949 armistice lines were erased, or so it seemed both to those who had accepted them and to those who despised them. Once again, borders might be drawn by quietly creating facts. The glory days of Labor Zionism would return. Young people would again build kibbutzim, and the cause would trump laws and formalities. A solution would appear for dealing with the Palestinians: A new wave of immigrants would maintain Israel's Jewish majority, or Gaza's refugees would emigrate, or improved living standards would convince Palestinians to accept unobtrusive Israeli rule, or populated parts of occupied land would be given up for peace while unpopulated areas would be settled.

The most extravagant hopes of early settlement proponents were not fulfilled. Despite the dreams of Yitzhak Tabenkin, the white-bearded sage of the United Kibbutz, hundreds of new kibbutzim did not rise from the earth. Despite the plans of the Settlement Department, tens of thousands of Israelis did not move to the Jordan Rift or the Golan Heights.

By May 17, 1977, though, there were nearly eighty Israeli settlements in occupied territory.[55] Their population has been estimated at 11,000 or more.[56] Most of the Israelis living beyond the Green Line were in several towns. In the farm communities of the Jordan Rift, so central to the Allon Plan, about 1,800 lived. These figures do not include annexed East Jerusalem, which Israel treated as part of the state. The new neighborhoods there had drawn 40,000 or more Israelis across the pre-1967 armistice lines.[57]

The numbers, though, are just one part of the story. The first decade, under Labor rule, broke boundaries, established methods, and opened the way to continued settlement building that followed under governments of the right.

Not only was the Green Line erased from maps, the boundary between legal and illegal action was blurred. Levi Eshkol chose to use the cover of Nahal paramilitary outposts to circumvent international law. Yigal Allon, who would later decry Gush Emunim's anti-democratic behavior, lent political and logistic support to the first wildcat settlers in the Golan Heights and Hebron, setting a precedent for Shimon Peres's assistance to Ofrah and Elon Moreh—and for officials afterward who would continue to lend a hand to unauthorized settlements.

Limits were set and ignored. Kiryat Arba, backed by Allon, broke the logic of his own plan. In its last months, the Rabin government yielded to the temptation of building settlements near the Green Line along Israel's narrow waist, next to Israel's major cities. Labor was set to accelerate settlement-building if it retained power. At the same time, Gush Emunim had established its footholds next to Palestinian cities, with the help of some officials and the acquiescence of others. The government was just one body among others determining where Israelis would settle.

The Orthodox movement that became the best known face of settlement was a child of that decade. The triumph of 1967 turned messianism into mainstream belief among religious Zionists, particularly young ones. Paradoxically, the shock of 1973 gave birth to Gush Emunim, an organized movement dedicated to overcoming doubt through feverish action. Its activists took settlement as their method, and set out to prove they were the rightful heirs of secular Zionism. Initially, at Kfar Etzion and Hebron, the religious settlers received support from Laborites, especially Allon. Later, politicians of the right lent a hand to their rebellion. Neither the secularists of the left or the right understood the theology of their partners or the energy they were helping to unleash.

By 1977, new types of communities were ready to draw larger numbers of Israelis into occupied territory—"community settlements" and the seeds of larger suburbs near Israeli cities. The Jordan Rift's kibbutzim would remain small and struggling, but commuter communities between Palestinian towns would grow.

In practice, a policy of postponed choices also emerged on the Palestinian question: Since the land remained under Israeli rule, so did the people who lived on it. Yet they were not made citizens, since that would create a binational state. Palestinians remained subject to military rule, without political rights. They became part of Israel's economy, mainly as providers of cheap labor and buyers of Israeli goods. Meanwhile, the settlers who lived next to them had the rights of Israeli citizens.

The two-tier legal and political system in occupied land made it distinct from pre-1967 Israel. Yet as an expression of Israeli desire to erase the Green Line, the settlements also represented a return to ethnic conflict over the whole land. Looked at from one angle, the settlements were the colonial project of a sovereign state; seen from another, they represented a return to the struggle before statehood. In both aspects the settlement effort spurred Palestinian nationalism—and was also spurred by it.

Arab leaders, prisoners of their own past, also played a key role in settlement. Whatever the intent of the Khartoum decisions, their bellicose language convinced Israel's government that peace was out of reach. Direct negotiations, recognition, and peace—what Khartoum rejected—were precisely the tools that Arab leaders had in their hands to sway Israeli opinion. Waiting to use them allowed and encouraged the growth of the settlements.

The American role consisted mainly of being distracted and taking time to respond. The Johnson and Nixon administrations were burdened with the Vietnam War. Nixon and Kissinger in particular treated the Arab-Israeli conflict as one arena of the Cold War, and waited to become involved until the crisis of October 1973 forced them to. Only gradually did the importance of settlements as a diplomatic issue emerge, once they had already altered the map of occupied territory.

Strangely, though, both the 1967 war and Israeli efforts afterward to erase the old boundary had an opposite effect in the international arena: They changed the perception of the Green Line from the marker of an armistice to Israel's legitimate borders. The implication of demanding Israel's withdrawal or condemning settlements beyond the line was to confirm that everything within the line was rightfully Israel's.

Perhaps the greatest irony of the settlements is that they frayed the Jewish state. The process began in the summer of 1967 and reached a climax at Sebastia in the last month of 1975. The process of consolidation, essential to a new state, was reversed. A generation that built the state began unintentionally removing stones from its structure. The attempt to relive the bright anarchy of youth undid their accomplishments.

A decade after Labor's fall, the Israeli author Meir Shalev wrote a novel called *The Blue Mountain* about a village in the Jezreel Valley created by early Zionist pioneers who drained swampland and turned it into fields. One of their children is obsessed with commemorating their heroism. At last, he smashes an irrigation pipe; as water floods a field, he proclaims, "Here will be established a swamp!"[58] The story can serve as a parable for the settlement enterprise.

ON THE afternoon of May 19, 1977, Menachem Begin drove his small car up into the hills of the northern West Bank, accompanied by two paramilitary Border Police jeeps. The final election results were not yet in—the counting of soldiers' ballots continued—but Begin's victory was certain. At Camp Kaddum, the prime minister–elect would be the guest of honor at a ceremony installing a new Torah scroll in the settlement's synagogue. There he was joined by Ariel Sharon and the National Religious Party's Zevulun Hammer and other politicians who had shared in the glow of Gush Emunim's settlement bids and would serve in the new government.

Begin, with a ring of thin black hair and heavy black glasses that magnified his eyes, looked exhausted. His two bodyguards could not hold off the crowd. People kissed him, embraced him. Yeshivah students danced around him. After a brief tour, he stood in the square between the mobile homes and took the velvet-covered scroll in one arm, putting the other around Ariel Sharon's shoulder. Four men took the corners of prayer shawl and held it over his head; a band prepared to play. Before the ceremony, Begin made a statement to the crowd. "Soon," he said, "there will be many more Elon Morehs."[59]

EPILOGUE: EPHEMERAL,

FOR THE FOURTH DECADE

> In the course of the years, Israeli settlements have been established in the Gaza District and the area of Judea and Samaria. . . . The status of these settlements derives from the status of the territory, which is held in "belligerent occupation". . . .
>
> When the petitioners settled in the Gaza Strip and northern Samaria, they did so in full knowledge that they were settling in territory held by Israel in belligerent occupation. . . .

So argued the government of Israel before the country's Supreme Court in the spring of 2005, defending its decision to dismantle all Israeli settlements in the Gaza Strip and four in the northern West Bank. The state's lawyers said that the settlers who had gone to court to challenge the legality of that decision should have been fully aware from the start that "the government and/or Knesset have the authority to evacuate said settlements and end said occupation of the territory."[1]

Rarely has a legal argument been so fraught with irony. The state argued that while it had ruled the West Bank and Gaza Strip for thirty-eight years, the character of its rule was inherently temporary. Israel held those territories only in the meantime, until the status of the land was resolved in a diplomatic agreement or until Israel chose unilaterally to leave. Settling Israelis on occupied land was permissible—so the government said, repeating a stance it had first taken before the Court in 1978—because the settlements, too, were potentially ephemeral, always capable of being erased.[2]

Yet the purpose of settlement, since the day in July 1967 when the first Israeli settler climbed out of a jeep in the Syrian heights, had been to create facts that would determine the final status of the land, to sculpt the political reality before negotiations ever got under way. By the summer of 2005, nearly four decades after the project began, the facts included nearly 250,000 Israelis living in 125 officially recognized West Bank settlements.[3] Another 180,000 lived in the annexed areas of East Jerusalem—land regarded by Israel as part of the state but by other countries as being under occupation.[4] In the Golan Heights, which Israel annexed in 1981, 16,000 Israelis lived in 32 settlements.[5] Until August of 2005, 9,000 Israeli settlers resided in the Gaza Strip in 21 settlements.[6]

Numbers alone cannot express how the landscape of occupied territory has changed. East of Jerusalem, the apartment buildings of Ma'aleh Adumim rise starkly from the desolate slopes leading down toward the Dead Sea. The settlement that Yisrael Galili sought to establish surreptitiously as a "work camp" has grown into a bedroom community of thirty-one thousand people, the single largest Israeli community in the West Bank (excluding East Jerusalem).[7] North of Jerusalem, a highway built to serve the settlements runs through the hill country, bypassing Ramallah and other Palestinian towns and villages. On the way to Ofrah, now a gated exurb of over two thousand people, the road passes settlement after settlement—Adam, Kokhav Ya'akov, Psagot—carpets of houses with red-tile roofs on the hilltops overlooking Palestinian towns and villages.[8] On other hills stand "outposts," the newest wave of settlements, clumps of mobile homes lacking official approval but established with the active assistance of government agencies, often on privately owned Palestinian land.[9]

Indeed, the overall settlement effort reflects a vast investment of state effort and funding, though the full extent of Israeli government investment is unknown, even to cabinet ministers and Knesset members.

The national budget contains no chapter entitled "settlements." Subsidized mortgages for settlers are buried in the housing budget, extra outlays on settlement schools are woven into the education budget, the costs of guarding settlements are submerged in the defense budget. Asked for the cost of settlement activity in 2003, a Finance Ministry spokesman said, "We don't have any way of making an estimation."[10]

In effect, the settlements have been integrated into the legal and governmental structure of Israel proper, though they lie outside its internationally recognized territory and most lie outside what Israel itself regards as its boundaries. The problem that Moshe Dayan raised in 1968, the status of Israelis living in occupied territory, has been answered with legislation, regulations, and orders of the military government that grant settlers the status of Israeli residents. Municipal governments and regional councils—the equivalent of counties—have been set up to administer them. Meanwhile, neighboring Palestinian communities remain under military law or, since the 1990s, under a complex mix of Israeli military and Palestinian Authority administration. Under the two-tier legal system, Israel holds what Levi Eshkol called the dowry—the land—without consummating the marriage by integrating the people who live on that land into its polity.

On one level, the settlement effort may be seen as falling far short of its advocates' expectations. In the West Bank, excluding East Jerusalem, Israelis remain a small minority of the population. Even in the Golan Heights, the Israeli population is outnumbered by the Druse, the only Syrian residents who remained at the time of the Israeli conquest.[11] In East Jerusalem as well, Arabs continue to outnumber Jews in the land annexed in 1967.[12]

On another level, settlement has undone partition of the contested land. The two rival ethnic groups live intermixed in the same territory—an artificially created Bosnia. The problems raised by the opponents of annexation since 1967 have become steadily more acute. Pinhas Sapir's demographic projections of 1972 have been borne out: Even after massive emigration from the former Soviet Union in the 1990s, the Arab population in Israel and the occupied territories has moved steadily toward parity with the Jewish population.[13] Formal annexation of the West Bank would mean the creation of a binational state.

Yet the endless interim of occupation has come at high cost—to use Yisrael Galili's words from June 19, 1967, both "from a moral, abstract democratic perspective" and "because of the concrete [security] risks."[14] Twice—in the late 1980s and again at the start of the twenty-first century—Palestinian opposition to occupation has erupted into violent uprisings, including waves of terror attacks against Israeli citizens. Defending settlements has become an ever-greater burden on the Israeli military. And while the settlements are not the only reason that diplomatic efforts to resolve the Israeli-Palestinian conflict have been frustrated, they have complicated the task of drawing new partition lines as part of such a resolution.

IN ISRAELI MEMORY, the right's rise to power in 1977 is often seen as heralding a revolution in settlement. A more accurate description would be an escalation of existing trends. The shrinking enclave in the northern West Bank from which Labor had unsuccessfully sought to bar settlers was now opened to them. The Golan Heights were declared part of Israel. In the West Bank and the Gaza Strip, legal changes were made to ensure settlers extraterritorial status. Gush Emunim found the Likud-led government more willing to cooperate with its efforts. Still, the religious radicals reverted to confrontation when coalition politics or diplomatic pressures led the government to go slow or even dismantle settlements.

Indeed, the Begin government's most revolutionary step may have been its decision to evacuate settlements under the 1979 peace agreement with Egypt. Anwar al-Sadat achieved his goal of regaining the entirety of the Sinai by putting aside all the taboos of Khartoum. Moshe Dayan, who had finally bolted Labor to become Menachem Begin's foreign minister, played a key role in reaching an agreement that required Israel to pull back all the way to the international border and remove its settlements—including Yamit, his personal project—from Sinai. With that, an Israeli taboo was also shattered.

One critic of the agreement was Yigal Allon, who claimed that Sadat could have been convinced to make peace while leaving the northeastern part of the Sinai in Israel's hands.[15] Allon died of a heart attack at age sixty-one in February 1980, cutting short his fight to replace Shimon

Peres as head of the Labor Party. The man who believed he would re-draw borders therefore did not live to see the evacuation of the Rafiah Plain farm communities. Allon's lifelong rival, Dayan, died soon after, in October 1981, and therefore saw neither the bulldozing of Yamit by the Israeli army nor the return of Sinai Bedouin to their land.

For secular believers in the Whole Land, the Sinai withdrawal was a political disaster. For the Bloc of the Faithful, it represented the theo-logically unthinkable, a reversal of the messianic process. While Sinai settlers accepted generous compensation and left peacefully, thousands of withdrawal opponents—most identified with Gush Emunim—filled Yamit. Rabbis promised divine intervention. In the final, three-day showdown in April 1982, Israeli troops had to struggle hand-to-hand with protesters, pulling the last ones from rooftops.

Prominent Gush Emunim activists had planned to stop the pullout by far more extreme means: blowing up the Dome of the Rock, the Is-lamic shrine at the center of the Temple Mount in Jerusalem. Yehudah Etzion, the founder of Ofrah, was a leader of the conspiracy. The with-drawal, he believed, was a sign that God was again chastising Israel for not pursuing redemption. Only the fact that the group's bomb expert came down with hepatitis just before the withdrawal scuttled the plan. In 1984, the Shin Bet arrested members of a settler underground that had carried out terror attacks against West Bank Palestinians—and dis-covered during the interrogation that they originally came together for the Temple Mount plot. Among those arrested were Rabbi Moshe Levinger's longtime disciple Ben-Tzion Heineman and settlers from Ofrah, Keshet, and Kiryat Arba. Levinger's son-in-law was convicted of murder in a terror attack on a Hebron college that left three students dead.[16]

At first, the underground case appeared to give warning of how far the mix of messianism and nationalism could take people beyond law or the moral constraints of their own religion. Yet the sentences in the case were remarkably lenient, as if to reinforce the culture of illegalism. Gush Emunim fragmented between supporters and critics of the under-ground, but when the conspirators left prison some assumed leadership positions among settlers who were rapidly expanding their hold on the West Bank.[17]

Though the Sinai pullout taught that settlements had not determined the outcome of diplomacy, the Begin government responded by redoubling its efforts to create facts elsewhere. Ariel Sharon, serving as agriculture minister, replaced Yisrael Galili as head of the Settlement Committee. Working with Gush Emunim, Sharon applied to the West Bank the same logic that had driven his plan for "fingers" running through the Gaza Strip: Settlements would control the high ground, separate Palestinian towns, and fragment occupied territory to prevent the creation of a Palestinian state. Sharon would eventually propose granting the Palestinians limited self-rule in "autonomy enclaves" left between his settlement fingers. Sharon's approach to settlement was an extreme version of Allon's—holding land he considered essential for security—while lacking Allon's conclusion that Palestinian autonomy under permanent Israeli control would be regarded internationally as colonialism.[18]

Not constrained by Labor's old commitments to creating villages based on socialism, Likud officials endorsed the "community settlement"— small, closed Israeli exurbs, dominated by religious nationalists of the Gush Emunim camp, which soon sprouted along the West Bank's mountain ridge. Closer to the Green Line, large suburban settlements grew rapidly. Here, so-called "quality of life" settlers—many secular, many unconcerned with politics—were attracted by subsidized homes and easy commuting to Jerusalem or Tel Aviv.

The Likud also devoted attention to Gaza, where Labor had already established five settlements—three in the southern corner of the Strip, an area labeled the Katif Bloc. With the loss of the Rafiah Plain, the government developed the Katif Bloc as the buffer that would separate Egypt from the Strip's burgeoning Palestinian cities and refugee camps.[19] By 1987 just 2,500 settlers would control 28 percent of the Gaza Strip's land.[20]

Meanwhile, graduates of *hesder* yeshivot and other educators who identified with Gush Emunim's nationalist faith assumed a dominant role in the state-run religious school system. A new generation of Orthodox Israelis absorbed the paramount value of the Whole Land as an assumed truth. That ethic, combined with government subsidies, attracted Orthodox young people to settlements and sealed the public image of "settlers" as men wearing crocheted skullcaps and women in the long skirts of the Orthodox—though in fact the followers of Gush Emunim's ideology were outnumbered by "quality of life" suburbanites.[21]

Begin resigned in 1983, succeeded as Likud leader and prime minister by Yitzhak Shamir. In the next year's election, Shamir faced Shimon Peres, who was reinventing himself as a dove. At first, say Labor insiders, the change was tactical—as leader of the opposition, Peres could establish a distinct political identity only by placing himself left of the Likud. With time, the tactic turned into principle.

Israel approached the 1984 election while suffering hyperinflation and mired militarily in a quagmire in Lebanon. Yet the vote was a dead heat, forcing Labor and the Likud to share power. Peres and Shamir traded the role of prime minister; Yitzhak Rabin became defense minister. The arrangement slowed the establishment of new settlements but not the growth of existing ones. The number of Israelis living in West Bank settlements, beyond annexed East Jerusalem, rose 80 percent over the next four years.[22]

By 1988, what looked like slow-motion annexation helped ignite the first intifada, or uprising, in the West Bank and Gaza. Nightly TV footage of crowds of young Palestinians hurling stones at troops made the occupation starkly visible to Israelis, but it did not break the political deadlock on the future of occupied territory. Another near-tie in the 1988 election left the national unity government in power.

But with the collapse of power-sharing in 1990 and Labor's return to opposition, Yitzhak Rabin began a comeback that returned him to his party's leadership. In February 1992, he defeated Peres in Labor's first party-wide primary election. While Shamir's government brought busloads of couples to shop for homes at close-out prices in West Bank settlements, Rabin campaigned for prime minister on the promise to cut spending on settlements.

That June, Rabin at last became an elected prime minister. Determined to correct the errors of his first term, he stressed his personal control of government business. He gave his old opponent, Shimon Peres, the Foreign Ministry rather than Defense, and sought to limit his authority. He pursued a peace deal with the Palestinians, which would inevitably mean giving up West Bank land. Still, he was loyal to the

Allon approach, distinguishing between "security settlements" and "political settlements." The former fit Labor's old map and were acceptable; the latter were unnecessary.

The announcement of the secretly negotiated Oslo Accord in September 1993 seemed to mean that the Israeli-Palestinian conflict was near resolution, and that the contested land would be divided, at last, by mutual consent. Israel and the PLO recognized each other. The Palestinians would gain autonomy, first in the Gaza Strip and Jericho, then in larger parts of the West Bank, for a five-year interim period, to be followed by a final peace agreement.

Yet the agreement was less than it appeared. It left all major issues— the future of Jerusalem and its holy sites, the Palestinian refugees, the settlements, borders—for final-status negotiations. Left in place, the settlements determined the map of the interim agreement; Sharon's fingers indeed fragmented Palestinian territory. New roads bypassing Palestinian towns actually made travel to settlements faster and safer, drawing more settlers. Though Rabin remained loyal to Yigal Allon's concept of territorial compromise, the Oslo Accord and subsequent agreements showed the influence of Moshe Dayan's idea of functional compromise, as passed down to Peres: In large pieces of the West Bank, Israel was responsible for security and the newly established Palestinian Authority for civil administration.[23] According to knowledgeable sources at the time, the old clash of concepts made it difficult for Rabin and Peres to agree on goals for final-status talks.

Radical Palestinian groups—notably Hamas, which merged Islam and Palestinian nationalism—sought to foil the Oslo Accord with terror attacks, particularly against settlers. The Israeli right, meanwhile, saw the agreement as a mortal threat to the dream of the Whole Land. "Visionaries have seen their vision torn asunder before their eyes," wrote one ideologue of "redemptive Zionism" in the settler journal *Nekuda*.[24] The comment was intended to make sense of a Jewish settler's massacre of twenty-nine Palestinian worshippers during Ramadan prayers in the Tomb of the Patriarchs, the Ibrahimi Mosque. The American-born assailant, Kiryat Arba settler Baruch Goldstein, had told friends he had a plan for stopping the peace process. His plan also used the brutal logic of terror—atrocity causes escalation, thus enlisting new supporters.

Hamas responded to the massacre by initiating a campaign of suicide bombings in Israeli cities, which in turn intensified opposition in Israel to the Oslo process.[25]

Several prominent settler rabbis wrote to dozens of colleagues, asking their view on whether Rabin was a *moser*—a Jew who turns over other Jews, or their property, to oppressors, and who is theoretically subject to death under religious law—or a *rodef*, a person about to commit murder who may be killed to prevent the crime.[26] At protest rallies of mounting intensity, the crowds came almost entirely from the religious settlement movement and its supporters, though Likud politicians were often featured speakers. In October 1995, after the signing of the Oslo II accord, which laid out Israel's withdrawal from the West Bank's cities, Ariel Sharon spoke before tens of thousands of protesters in Jerusalem, accusing the government of "collaborating" with a terror group. "There is no memory in history of a nation willingly turning over part of its historic homeland," Sharon said.[27] Rabin, the focus of the right's fury, was dismissive of the protests and of the talk of threats to his life.

On November 4, 1995, a radical young supporter of the Whole Land, Yigal Amir, assassinated Israel's prime minister. It was the final, horrifying act of the tragedy of Yitzhak Rabin: The forces of chaos he had suppressed on the Tel Aviv shore in 1948, and to which he had yielded at Sebastia in 1975, now swept him away.

Rabin's murder marked the start of unprecedented instability in Israel. The young and politically inexperienced new Likud leader, Benjamin Netanyahu, narrowly defeated Shimon Peres in the next election. Unable to reconcile his hardline nationalism and his public promise to honor Israel's signed commitments to Oslo, Netanyahu could not provide direction.

In October 1998, Netanyahu and Sharon, now the foreign minister, attended a summit conference with Palestinian leader Yasser Arafat and U.S. president Bill Clinton at the Wye River Plantation in Maryland. Under pressure from Clinton, Netanyahu signed an agreement to continue implementing the Oslo accords by turning over another 13 percent of the West Bank's land to the control of the Palestinian Authority.

Afterward, speaking on Israel Radio, Sharon urged settlers to "grab more hills, expand the territory. Everything that's grabbed, will be in our

hands. Everything we don't grab will be in their hands."[28] That acceler-
ated a new kind of settlement drive, the rapid establishment of the improvised mobile-home "outposts" on the hills of the West Bank, without
official authorization. The outpost settlers, many of them young people
who had grown up in the ideological settlements, were few in number,
but their presence staked a claim to more land, filling in Sharon's fingers.
Government funding came via the World Zionist Organization's Settlement Division; the Housing Ministry built roads; the Defense Ministry
provided additional aid. Again, officials put a cause regarded as patriotic
above the rule of law.[29] And again, slow-motion diplomacy encouraged
rapid settlement.

Nonetheless, the Wye accord led to the collapse of Netanyahu's government. Promising a push for peace, Labor's new leader, Ehud Barak,
swept to a landslide election victory. In July 2000, seeking to reach the
overdue final-status accord, Barak, Arafat, and Clinton met for an ill-
fated summit at Camp David.

Amid accusations and self-justifications, the debate on the causes of
Camp David's failure will last many years. Two factors, though, deserve
mention here. First, the Oslo process, meant to build trust, did the opposite. Palestinian terror groups continued their attacks in Israeli cities,
undercutting the belief among Israelis that an agreement could bring
peace, or that the Palestinian Authority was interested in ending the
conflict. Meanwhile, between 1993 and 2000, the population of Israel's
settlements in the Gaza Strip and the West Bank (again, excluding East
Jerusalem) rose from 116,000 to 198,000. The spread of red rooftops on
the hills undermined Palestinian confidence that Israel would, indeed,
leave the occupied territories.

Second, the summit revealed the gap in the two sides' understanding
of the entire process. Palestinian negotiators insisted on the Green Line
as the basis for peace; they regarded their recognition of Israel within
the pre-1967 boundaries as conceding most of historic Palestine, and
saw no reason for further concessions. Israel saw the land up for division
as the West Bank and Gaza Strip, and insisted that the new border would
run through occupied territory, leaving key settlements and strategic
ground in its hands. It was the same disagreement that Yigal Allon and
King Hussein had confronted in 1968, though without the urbanity of

that meeting. "The Palestinian perspective was that Oslo was a compromise and that it was the last compromise. We were not aware of this," Shlomo Ben-Ami, Israel's foreign minister at the Camp David summit, said later. "We . . . thought that somewhere down the road there would be another compromise."[30] The statement is striking, because throughout the Oslo years, Palestinian and Israeli leaders had stated their goals publicly. Each side, though, assumed that the other's statements were bluff. Once again, they had been playing chess with themselves, believing that at the moment of truth, the people across the negotiating table would accept the inevitable.

Instead, the process collapsed. By the fall, a new and more brutal intifada began. The political pendulum soon swung yet again. Ariel Sharon, now head of the Likud, seventy-three years old, became prime minister, determined to put down the uprising with military force. Though he now spoke of agreeing to a Palestinian state, he said it would control just 42 percent of the West Bank's area—the size of the divided territory that was already administered by the Palestinian Authority.[31] In fact, the proposed state was an updated version of Sharon's idea of self-ruling enclaves separated by Israeli fingers.

Then came an unexpected turnabout. At the end of 2003, Sharon announced his intent to carry out a "disengagement" from the Palestinians, a "redeployment of IDF forces . . . and a change in the deployment of settlements . . . [to] reduce . . . the number of Israelis located in the heart of the Palestinian population."[32] Soon after, he explained his meaning: Israel would pull out of the Gaza Strip, evacuating all its settlements there, along with a handful of small settlements in the northern West Bank.[33] The longtime architect of settlement now intended to remove settlers—albeit as a unilateral action, a new way to create facts, to impose the lines he regarded as most defensible.

Sharon's goals remained veiled. One of his closest confidants, Deputy Prime Minister Ehud Olmert, spoke of unilateral withdrawal as a way to preserve Israel's Jewish majority—an acceptance of the argument against the Whole Land that dated back to Ben-Gurion's decision not to conquer the West Bank in 1949.[34] Another confidant, Sharon's chief of staff Dov Weissglas, described the pullout as "formaldehyde" for the peace process—in effect, a diplomatic shortening of the lines, a way to reduce international pressure for greater concessions.[35] The pull-out could be read as a response to Palestinian violence, Palestinian numbers, or U.S. concerns, or perhaps all three.

Sharon's determination, however, was unquestionable. Surviving the fury of hard-liners in the Likud and other right-wing parties, ignoring protests and rulings by some pro-settlement rabbis that soldiers should disobey orders to evacuate settlements, the prime minister pressed ahead, winning Knesset approval and Supreme Court affirmation of the legality of his plan. Among the general public, he maintained the support of a solid, if unenthusiastic, majority for the pullout.[36] One subtext was exhaustion with Gaza. Another was that settlement, once a secular sacrament, was now firmly identified with Orthodoxy in the long-running Israeli *Kulturkampf*.

While some settlers left Gaza quietly, others convinced themselves that with sufficient prayer and protest, the withdrawal would not take place. Young protesters, many from West Bank settlements and outposts, dodged roadblocks to reach Gaza. One of the journalists who went to see the settlement of Kfar Darom in its last days was eighty-two-year-old Haim Gouri. "It was a journey of one day in my life, just one. Yet my whole life was in it . . . all my memories and soul-searching," he wrote. He looked at settlers who "really believed it was possible to continue to live like this next to the urgent poverty of the Arabs." Yet when settlement had begun in the Katif Bloc and Kfar Darom, he recorded, "I cannot recall that I expressed doubts." He met "the grandchildren and great-grandchildren of religious Zionism, which in days long past was so different," and heard "the sacred mantra: 'There will be no disengagement!' because 'The soldiers will refuse to carry out the orders' and because 'The Holy One will perform miracles for us.' " A settler invited him to return at the summer's end, after the miracle, to lecture on literature. Politely, he accepted.[37]

Twice, Jewish extremists tried to stop the pullout with terror against Arabs. An army deserter opened fire on a bus in an Israeli Arab town, murdering four people before he was lynched by the crowd. In a factory at the settlement of Shilo in the West Bank, a settler turned on his Palestinian coworkers, murdering four. This time, terror did not produce immediate conflagration, and the withdrawal went ahead.

On Wednesday, August 17, 2005, columns of uniformed men and women entered the first settlements to begin removing settlers. Only a handful of soldiers refused orders. The heavens did not open. In a scene played again and again on Israel television, a father pushed his young daughter at soldiers, screaming a challenge, "Expel her! Expel her!" Soldiers and police who had trained at taking insults listened with haunting calm. A few families stepped out of their homes wearing yellow stars, equating the pullout with a Nazi deportation. The next day, hundreds of young infiltrators chose the synagogue at Kfar Darom as the arena for their final struggle. As troops climbed ladders to reach the synagogue roof, protesters hurled lye in their faces. That was the worst confrontation. The evacuation lasted but a week, much less time than anticipated. The struggle postponed at Sebastia thirty years before at last played itself out.

The meaning of the denouement in Gaza would be determined only by its yet-to-be-written sequel. It could later be interpreted as the moment showing that the cost in tears and fury of dismantling settlements was too high to be paid again, on a grander scale, for evacuating the larger Israeli communities in the West Bank—or as the proof that settlements are indeed potentially temporary, and that the settlers had lost the support of the Israeli mainstream. It may be recorded as the act that revived peace efforts, or as the intermezzo before a new battle over the torn land. It did not yet answer the question posed to Israelis when the unexpected conquests of 1967 were fresh: What kind of Israel do you want? That answer still lay in the future.

Notes

Abbreviations

Ad. MS   Yehiel Admoni, *Asor Shel Shikul Da'at: Hahityashvut Me'ever Lakav Ha-*
          yarok 1967–1977, author's manuscript, listed by year and page
BAGATZ   Beit-din Gavo'ah Letzedek (Israel High Court of Justice)
DC   Demant Collection, early Gush Emunim documents collected by Peter
          Robert Demant
DK   Divrei Haknesset (Knesset Record), listed by date and page number
FRUS   *Foreign Relations of the United States* series, Johnson Administration sub-
          series, listed by volume and document number
GA   Golan Archive
GEA   Gush Etzion Archive
HATZAV   Israel Defense Forces Intelligence Corps, Arab media translations
HHA   Hashomer Hatza'ir Archive
ISA   Israel State Archives
JMA   Jerusalem Municipal Archive
KMA   Hakibbutz Hame'uhad Archive
LBJ   Lyndon Baines Johnson Library
LPS   Labor Party Secretariat minutes, listed by date and page number
Memcon   Memorandum of conversation
MEI-MR   Midreshet Eretz Yisrael, Makhon Reshit (Eretz Yisrael Academy)
MER   *Middle East Record*, listed by volume and page number
MGA   Merom Golan Archive
NARA   National Archives and Records Administration

NPMP   Nixon Presidential Materials Project
OA   Ofrah Archive
PS   Protected source, material provided on condition of anonymity
RNyl PPS   Richard Nixon Library, Yorba Linda, pre-presidential series
YAOH   Yigal Allon oral history, listed by interview and page number
YLE   Yad Levi Eshkol
YRC   Yitzhak Rabin Center for Israel Studies
YTA   Yad Tabenkin Archive

Note: Israeli press coverage listed by newspaper and date, with further details on articles of particular significance. Article and book titles are in the original language, with English translations as provided by the publisher.

December 1975: North from Jerusalem

1. Gila Gouri, *Derekh Umikdash* (Tel Aviv: Hakibbutz Hame'uhad, 1976), 67; Haim Gouri, interview.

2. Haim Gouri, "Yom Valailah Bashomron," *Yediot Aharonot*, Dec. 12, 1975; Gouri, interview; *Ma'ariv*, Dec. 8, 1975, 1.

3. Haim Gouri, *Dapim Yerushalmiyim* (Tel Aviv: Hakibbutz Hame'uhad, 1968), 284-86; Gouri, "Yom Valailah"; Gouri, interview.

4. Gouri, "Yom Valailah."

5. Gouri, "Yom Valailah"; Gouri, interview.

6. Gouri, "Yom Valailah."

7. E.g., William B. Quandt, *Peace Process: American Diplomacy and the Arab Israeli Conflict Since 1967* (Washington, DC: Brookings Institution/Berkeley: University of California Press, 1993), 207; Henry Kissinger, *Years of Upheaval* (Boston: Little, Brown, 1982), 1043; William Bundy, *A Tangled Web: The Making of Foreign Policy in the Nixon Presidency* (New York: Hill and Wang, 1998).

8. Gouri, interview.

1. The Avalanche

1. Gouri, *Dapim*, 258-64.

2. Jordanian-Israeli General Armistice Agreement, April 3, 1949, www.yale.edu/lawweb/avalon/mideast/armo3.htm; Benny Morris, *Milhamot Hagvul Shel Yisrael 1949-1956* (Israel's Border Wars, 1949-1956: Arab Infiltration, Israeli Retaliation, and the Countdown to the Suez War) (Tel Aviv: Am Oved, 1996), 15ff.

3. Anita Shapira, *Yigal Allon: Aviv Heldo* (Igal Allon: Spring of His Life) (Tel Aviv: Hasifriah Hahadashah, 2004), 220.

4. Shlomo Gazit, *Peta'im Bemalkodet* (Trapped) (Tel Aviv: Zmora-Bitan, 1999), 15; Eitan Haber, *Hayom Tifrotz Milhamah* (Today War Will Break Out: The Reminiscences of Brig. Gen. Israel Lior) (Tel Aviv: Edanim/Yediot Aharonot, 1987), 147; Arnan (Sini) Azaryahu, interview.

5. Shlomo Lahat, interview; Benny Morris, *Righteous Victims: A History of the Zionist-Arab Conflict 1881–1999* (New York: Alfred A. Knopf, 1999), 302.

6. Morris, *Victims*, 304.

7. Morris, *Victims*, 304; Michael B. Oren, *Six Days of War: June 1967 and the Making of the Modern Middle East* (New York: Oxford University Press, 2002), 22ff; Avi Shlaim, *The Iron Wall: Israel and the Arab World* (New York, London: W. W. Norton and Company, 2001), 222ff.

8. Shlaim, 235ff; Oren, 45–46.

9. Oren, 46–47; Shlaim 234–35; Morris, *Victims* 304; Gazit, *Peta'im*, 20; Eytan Sat, interview.

10. Gazit, *Peta'im*, 20.

11. Shlaim, 221; Shlomo Lahat, interview.

12. Yossi Beilin, *Mehiro Shel Ihud: Mifleget Ha'avodah Ad Milhemet Yom Hakippurim* (Tel Aviv: Revivim, 1985), 44–45.

13. Morris, *Milhamot*, 16–23; Morris, *Victims* 192; Central Bureau of Statistics, *Statistical Abstract of Israel 2004 No. 55*, www1.cbs.gov.il/shnaton55/st02_01.pdf.

14. Moshe Dayan, *Story of My Life: An Autobiography* (New York: William Morrow, 1976), 188–90, 200–201; Morris, *Victims*, 289–90.

15. Morris, *Victims*, 291–301; Meron Medzini, *Hayehudiah Hageah: Golda Meir Vahazon Yisrael, Biografiah Politit* (The Proud Jewess: Golda Meir and the Vision of Israel. A Political Biography) (Jerusalem: Edanim, 1990), 250–57; LBJ, NSC histories, Middle East Crisis, vol. 2, document 40.

16. Shlaim, 222.

17. Beilin, 45.

18. Moshe Halbertal, interview.

19. Yonathan Shapira, *Leshilton Behartanu* (Chosen to Command: The Road to Power of the Herut Party—A Sociopolitical Interpretation) (Tel Aviv: Am Oved, 1989), 9–10.

20. Arye Naor, *Eretz Yisrael Hashlemah: Emunah Umdiniyut* (Greater Israel: Theology and Policy) (Haifa: University of Haifa Press/Zmora-Bitan, 2001), 99–100; Shlaim, 224.

21. Anita Shapira, "From the Palmach Generation to the Candle Children: Changing Patterns in Israeli Identity," *Partisan Review* 67, no. 4 (2000).

22. Gouri, *Dapim*, 259–62.

23. *Bivritekh* (Tel Aviv: Hamahanot Ha'olim, 5688 [1937–38]).

24. Shapira, *Yigal Allon*, 10.

25. See Jay Y. Gonen, *A Psychohistory of Zionism* (New York: Mason/Charter, 1975), 3–19.

26. Haim Gouri, "Hashivah Le'Abu Dis," *Ha'aretz*, May 25, 2004.

27. Naor, 104–22; Zeev Tsur, *Mipulmus Hahalukah Ad Tokhnit Allon* (From the Partition Dispute to the Allon Plan), 24–25, 72 (Ramat Efal: Tabenkin Institute, 1982); Yehudah Harel, interview; Yehuda Harell, *Tabenkin's View of Socialism*, trans. Hanna Lash (Ramat Efal: Yad Tabenkin, 1988).

28. Tsur, *Mipulmus*, 31; Beilin, 22–24.

29. Gouri, interview.

30. Tsur, *Mipulmus*, 73–74; Shapira, *Yigal Allon*, 444–48; YAOH, VII:10.

31. Gouri, interview.

32. Naor, 117.

33. Ibid., 120.

34. Gouri, *Dapim*, 254.

35. Ibid., 262–64.

36. Porat, interview.

37. Jacob Katz, "The Jewish National Movement: A Sociological Analysis," *Jewish Society Through the Ages*, ed. H.H. Ben-Sasson and S. Ettinger (New York: Schocken, 1971), 267.

38. Moshe Moskovic, interview.

39. Moskovic, interview; Porat, interview.

40. Larry Collins and Dominique Lapierre, *O Jerusalem* (London: Pan, 1973), 349–52, 365–69, 393; Morris, *Victims*, 214; Yohanan Ben-Yaakov, ed., *Gush Etzion: Hamishim Shnot Ma'avak Viytzirah* (Alon Shvut: Yad Shapira, 1983), 316ff; Hanan Porat, interview.

41. Ben-Yaakov, 336; YLE, 5/31, Settlement Department memo to Levi Eshkol, Sept. 12, 1967.

42. Hanan Porat, interview; Ben-Yaakov, 323–36.

43. Porat, interview; Moskovic, interview; Ben-Yaakov, 335.

44. Porat, interview.

45. Eliezer Don Yehiya, "The Book and the Sword: the Nationalist Yeshivot and Political Radicalism in Israel," *Accounting for Fundamentalisms: The Dynamic Character of Movements*, ed. Martin E. Marty and R. Scott Appleby (Chicago: The Fundamentalism Project, University of Chicago Press, 1994), 67–68.

46. Avraham Yitzhak Hacohen Kook, *Orot* (Jerusalem: Mossad Harav Kook, 5753 [1992–93]), 9, 83–85, 102–4, 121–23; Johann Gottfried von Herder, *Reflections on the Philosophy of the History of Mankind*, ed. Frank E. Manuel (Chicago: University of Chicago, 1968); Aviezer Ravitzky, *Haketz Hamguleh Umdinat Hayehudim* (Messianism, Zionism, and Jewish Religious Radicalism) (Tel Aviv: Am Oved, 1993), chap. 3. Kook scholar Yehudah Mirsky (interview) notes that Kook absorbed European philosophy through the rich Hebrew and Yiddish periodical press of his time and philosophical works in Hebrew, including the translation of Moshe Hess's *Rome and Jerusalem* and particularly Nahman Krochmal's *Guide to the Perplexed of the Time*, which itself shows the strong influence of both Hegel and Herder.

47. Ravitzky, 170.

48. Lamentations 3:28, in third person in the original; Joel 4:2.

49. Kook's speech, transcribed by students, was published as "Mizmor Yod-Tet Shel Medinat Yisrael," in various formats, including A. Ben-Ami, ed., *Hakol: Gvulot Hashalom Shel Eretz Yisrael* (Hakol: The Peace Frontiers of Israel) (Tel Aviv: Madaf, 1967), 65–75.

50. Psalms 118:23.

51. LBJ, NSC histories, Middle East Crisis, vol. 1, document 2a; Haber 147–49; Morris, *Victims*, 302–5.

52. Gazit, *Peta'im*, 20. In some accounts of the war, the first performance of the song is incorrectly dated to the previous night, May 14. The correct time appears in schedules of holiday events in the daily *Davar*, May 14, 1967.

53. Naomi Shemer, "Jerusalem of Gold," www.mfa.gov.il/mfa/templates/

BigPicture.aspx?GifsSrcEnding=&PageTitle=50%20Years%20of%20Hebrew%20S ong&ImgSource=/NR/rdonlyres/BEC65C24-4D3-47BF-AE0A-EAFFDD1E94BA/38043/MFAG005e0.gif; Babylonian Talmud, Tractate Nedarim 50a; Tractate Shabbat 59a.

54. Rabbi Yehudah Halevi, "Tzion Halo Tishali," benyehuda.org/rihal/ Rihal1_4.html; Psalm 137.

55. LBJ, NSC histories, Middle East Crisis, vol. 2, document 40.

56. Jehuda Wallach, *Atlas Carta Letoldot Medinat Yisrael: Asor Sheni* (Carta's Atlas of Israel: The Second Decade, 1961–1971) (Jerusalem: Carta, 1980), 53; Oren, 129–32; Morris, *Victims*, 310.

57. LBJ, NSC histories, Middle East Crisis, vol. 1, document 2a.

58. The problem of convincing Congress came up repeatedly in top-level administration meetings. See LBJ, NSC histories, Middle East Crisis, vol 2, tab 42, document 32.

59. FRUS XIX:49.

60. LBJ, NSC histories, Middle East Crisis, vol. 2, document 33; FRUS XIX:77.

61. Arnon Lammfromm and Hagai Tsoref, eds., *Levi Eshkol: Rosh Hamemshelah Hashlishi* (Levi Eshkol: The Third Prime Minister) (Jerusalem: Israel State Archives, 2002), 540.

62. Oren, 140.

63. Lammfromm, xviii–xix.

64. Arie (Lova) Eliav, interview.

65. E.g., ISA 153.8/7920/7A, Eshkol speech to Ihud Hakvutzot Vehakibbutzim, November 22, 1967.

66. Shapira, *Yigal Allon*, photo inset after 384; Dayan, 40.

67. YAOH IV:11.

68. Shapira, *Yigal Allon*, 9.

69. Ibid., 477.

70. Ibid., 464–69; Henry Kissinger, *White House Years* (Boston and Toronto: Little, Brown, 1979), 341.

71. Zorach Warhaftig, *Hamishim Shanah Veshanah: Pirkei Zikhronot* (Fifty Years, From Year to Year: Memories) (Jerusalem: Yad Shapira, 1998), 185–86.

72. YAOH II:5.

73. Oren, 81, 90.

74. Oren, 153; Dayan, 330.

75. Lammfromm, 532–33.

76. Abba Eban, *An Autobiography* (New York: Random House, 1977), 400; cf. Naor, 33–34.

77. Rina Kalinov, ed., *Kobi Rabinovich: Na'an, Merom Golan* (Israel: Hakibbutz Hame'uhad, 1981), 17–21.

78. Porat, interview.

79. Gouri, *Dapim*, 264–67.

80. Lammfromm, 550; LBJ, NSC histories, Middle East Crisis, vol. 1, document 2b; Oren 156–57.

81. Carl von Clausewitz, *On War*, trans. J. J. Graham (London, 1877), chap. 7, www.clausewitz.com/CWZHOME/On_War/ONWARTOC.html.

82. Lammfromm, 555.

83. Naor, 33.

84. "From the Editors," *The Jerusalem Report*, June 18, 1992, 3; "Michael Elkins 1917–2001," *The Jerusalem Report*, April 9, 2001, 10.

85. Oren, 213.

86. Motta [Mordechai] Gur, *Har Habayit Beyadenu* (Ma'arakhot, 1973), 13–15; Gouri, *Dapim*, 275–76; Dayan, 356.

87. Uzi Benziman, *Yerushalayim: Ir Lelo Homah* (Jerusalem and Tel Aviv: Schocken, 1973), 11.

88. Uzi Narkiss, *Ahat Yerushalayim* (The Liberation of Jerusalem) (Tel Aviv: Am Oved, 1975), 215.

89. Gur, 315–17; Narkiss, 247–50.

90. Haber, 234–35; *Ha'aretz*, June 8, 1967, 1; *Hatzofeh*, June 8, 1967, 1. Dayan repeated that Israel had returned to Jerusalem "never to be parted" at a press conference that evening. NARA, RG59 Central Files 1967–69, POL 28 Jerusalem, Tel Aviv cable 4019.

91. Hanan Porat, interview.

92. YAOH II:13.

93. Dayan, 356.

94. Lammfromm, 558.

95. Gouri, *Dapim*, 284–86.

96. Oren, 202, 259; NARA, RG 59 Central Files 1967–69, POL 28 Jerusalem, Tel Aviv cable 4019.

97. Kalinov, 23–24.

98. YAOH II:16, IV:13; Oren, 195; Lammfromm, 558; cf. NARA, RG59 Records of Henry Kissinger 1973–77, Box 9, Memcon Kissinger-Allon, August 1, 1974.

99. Lammfromm, 559; YAOH II:15, 25–26, IV:13.

100. Lammfromm, 559; YAOH II:22.

101. Gazit, *Peta'im*, 138–39.

102. Dan Bavly, *Halomot Vehizdamnuyot Shehuhmetzu 1967–1973* (Dreams and Missed Opportunities 1967–1973) (Jerusalem: Carmel, 2002), 125–37; Raja Shehadeh, *Strangers in the House: Coming of Age in Occupied Palestine* (New York: Penguin, 2003), 3–4, 48–52, 54.

103. YAOH II:14–16, III:1–3; YTA 15Allon/15/4, "Second Working Draft on the historical background of the Allon Plan."

104. Israeli population from the Central Bureau of Statistics, www1.cbs.gov.il/shnaton54/st02_01.pdf. Note that 1967 numbers include Arab noncitizen residents of annexed East Jerusalem. Postwar Israeli estimates of the population of occupied territories went as high as 1.5 million (ISA, 153.8/7921/2A, document 331). Later documents (ISA 153.8/7921/3A), including October 1967 census figures for West Bank and Gaza, lead to an approximate total of 1.1 million. The discrepancy is due in part to refugees fleeing the West Bank during and after the war.

2. Creating Facts

1. Shlomo Lahat, interview; Benziman, 35–46; Amnon Barzilai, "Kakh Nehersah Shekhunat Hamughrabim," *Ha'aretz*, May 13, 1999, B2; Teddy Kollek, *For Jerusalem* (New York: Random House, 1978), 197; minutes of (West) Jerusalem City Council meeting, June 8, 1967; Lammfromm, 568; "200 Elef Bikru Behag Hashavuot Leyad Hakotel Hama'aravi," *Hatzofeh*, June 15, 1967, 1.

2. Ehud Sprinzak, *Ish Hayashar Be'einav: Illegalism Bahevrah Hayisre'elit* (Every Man Whatsoever Is Right in His Own Eyes: Illegalism in Israeli Society) (Tel Aviv: Sifriat Poalim, 1986), chaps. 2–4.

3. NARA, RG59, Central Files 1967–69, POL 28 Jerusalem, Jerusalem cable 1123.

4. Numbers 23:10.

5. Lammfromm, 566–69.

6. Benziman, 47–49; Reuven Pedatzur, *Nitzhon Hamevukhah* (The Triumph of Embarrassment: Israel and the Territories After the Six-Day War) (Tel Aviv: Bitan/Yad Tabenkin, 1996), 117.

7. Benziman, 48, 51–52; David E. Eisenstadt, *Hatmurot Bagvulot Ha'ironiyim (Municipaliyim) shel Yerushalayim 1863–1967* (The Evolution of Jerusalem's Municipal Boundaries, 1863–1967), unpublished master's thesis, Bar Ilan University, Ramat Gan, 1998, 131–32.

8. David Eisenstadt, interview.

9. Eisenstadt, 133–34; Eisenstadt, interview; Benziman, 54–56.

10. Eisenstadt, 130–31.

11. LBJ, NSC histories, Middle East Crisis, vol 1, document 2b and vol. 4, tab 144; cf. Pedatzur, 30.

12. For example, *Ha'aretz*, June 15, 1967.

13. YAOH III:2.

14. Pedatzur, 27–28.

15. Pedatzur, 32.

16. Beilin, 9; LBJ, NSC histories, Middle East Crisis, vol 15, appendix S, Tel Aviv cable 4149.

17. J. Y. Smith, "Dayan Would Keep Major Conquests," *Washington Post*, June 12, 1967, A15.

18. Pedatzur, 39–41.

19. Azaryahu, interview.

20. Lammfromm, 573–75; Pedatzur, 47–54.

21. Lammfromm, 505–6; ISA 43/7231/3A, document 34.

22. Matti Golan, *Shimon Peres: A Biography* (London: Weidenfeld and Nicolson, 1982), 77–78; ISA 153.8/7921/2A, minutes of July 27, 1967 political committee.

23. Pedatzur, 53–55.

24. Lammfromm, 579–83.

25. Neither the Israeli government nor the Hebrew media were yet using the Hebrew term "Golan Heights" for the area.

26. Pedatzur, 55–56; YTA 15Galili/2/3/115.

27. Naor, 80; YAOH VII:8.

28. Lammfromm, 580–82; YAOH VII:15–16.

29. A reductionist military approach in accounts of Israeli history treats the deadlock on the future of the West Bank as strictly one of conflicting strategic conceptions. Eban, 436, properly rejects this, noting that the West Bank "raised problems that transcended strategic interest."

30. LBJ, NSC histories, Middle East Crisis, vol. 1, document 2.

31. LBJ, NSC histories, Middle East Crisis, vol. 4, document 41.

32. LBJ, NSC histories, Middle East Crisis, vol. 4, document 53.

33. FRUS XIX:325.

34. FRUS XIX:343.

35. Harry McPherson Oral History, LBJ Library Oral History Collection, Interview VII, Sept. 19, 1985, by Michael L. Gillette; www.lbjlib.utexas.edu/johnson/archives.hom/oralhistory.hom/mcpherson/mcpher07.pdf, 1–4.

36. LBJ, National Security Files, Country File, Israel Box 140.

37. LBJ, NSC histories, Middle East Crisis, vol. 3, documents 5, 15. Parentheses in the original.

38. Harold Saunders, interview.

39. LBJ, NSC histories, Middle East Crisis, vol. 4, document 112.

40. FRUS XIX:269.

41. FRUS XIX:287.

42. FRUS XIX:280.

43. FRUS XIX:290.

44. FRUS XIX:280.

45. FRUS XIX:325, paragraph 5(1). Drafts of the speech: LBJ, NSC histories, Middle East Crisis, tab 171.

46. U.S. National Archives and Records Administration, *Public Papers of the Presidents of the United States: Lyndon Baines Johnson, 1967*, vol. 1 (Washington, DC: United States Government Printing Office, 1968), 630–34.

47. Eban, 436.

48. ISA 153.8/7920/7A, document 6–70.

49. RNyl PPS, 347.13.19.

50. RNyl PPS, 347.13.17, 347.13.19.

51. Nixon's notes for New York press conference at RNyl PPS, 347.13.19.

52. RNyl PPS, 347.13.17.

53. LBJ, country files, Israel vol. 5, cables, folder 2, airgram A-934.

54. Benziman, 49–50; Eban, 437; FRUS XIX:314.

55. Eban, 437.

56. ISA 153.8/7920/8A document 4; Eisenstadt, 131–33; Protection of Holy Places Law 5727 (1967), www.knesset.gov.il/laws/special/eng/HolyPlaces.htm; Benziman, 53–54.

57. Susan Starr Sered, "Rachel's Tomb: The Development of a Cult," *Jewish Studies Quarterly* 2 (1995), 103–44.

58. Eisenstadt, 134–35; Benziman, 54–56; Pedatzur, 118–19; Lammfromm, 573.

59. Eisenstadt, 121, 130, 136–51.

60. Benziman, 51; Eban, 438; ISA 153.8/7920/8A, document 7.

61. Benziman, 51.

62. NARA, RG59, Central Files 1967–69, POL 27 Arab-Isr, Cable 218573.

63. JMA box 398.

64. Benziman, 61–64; NARA, RG 59, Central Files 1967–69, POL 27 Arab-Isr, Jerusalem cable 00600. Dissolution order: JMA box 398; Salman quotation: Nadav Shragai, "26 Beyuni 1967: Hamemshalah Mevakeshet Shehatikshoret Lo Ta'aseh Inyan Misipuah Mizrah Yerushalayim," *Ha'aretz*, November 3, 1967, B3.

65. Gouri, *Dapim*, 289–90.

66. Ibid., 290–91.

67. Uzi Benziman, "'Plishah Hadadit' Biyrushalayim," *Ha'aretz*, June 30, 1967.

68. Shehadeh, 55–56.

69. NARA, RG 59, Central Files 1967–69, POL 27 Arab-Isr, Jerusalem cable 00600.

70. LBJ, NSC country file, Middle East crisis, vol. 7, document 32.

71. FRUS XIX:333, 340; LBJ, Office Files of Harry McPherson, documents 7, 7b, 8.

72. Benziman, 253–54; ISA 153.8/7920/8A; ISA 153.8/7234/7A document 243.

73. Pedatzur, 167.

74. Yehiel Admoni, interview; Lammfromm, xvii–xix.

75. Yaron Ezrahi, *Rubber Bullets: Power and Conscience in Modern Israel* (New York: Farrar, Straus and Giroux, 1997), 49.

76. E.g., Theodore Herzl, *Altneuland*, Book II, www.wzo.org.il/en/resources/view.asp?id=1600, describes Jewish children in Europe as "pale, weak, timid." Cf. Arthur Hertzberg, ed., *The Zionist Idea: A Historical Analysis and Reader* (New York: Atheneum, 1973), Part 5.

77. Gershom Gorenberg, "Club Red," *The New Republic*, October 14, 1996, 10–12.

78. Tsur, *Mipulmus*, 31; Yehiel Admoni, *Asor Shel Shikul Da'at: Hahityashvut Me'ever Lakav Hayarok 1967–1977* (Decade of discretion: Settlement policy in the territories 1967–1977) (Makhon Yisrael Galili Leheker Hakoah Hamagen/Yad Tabenkin/Hakibbutz Hame'uhad: 1992), 17.

79. Yigal Allon, "Hahityashvut Bekibbush Ha'aretz,"*Gush Etzion Bemilhamto*, Dov Knohl, ed. (Jerusalem: Religious Division of the Youth and Hehalutz Department of the World Zionist Organization, 1954), 17–23.

80. Zeev Tsur, *Hakibbutz Hame'uhad Beyishuvah shel Ha'aretz* (The Hakibbutz Hameuchad in the Settlement of Eretz Yisrael), vol. IV, 1960–1980 (Yad Tabenkin/Hakibbutz Hame'uhad, 1986), 10, 52–53; Yehudah Harel, interview.

81. Yehudah Harel, interview; Sat, interview.

82. John Steinbeck, "The Red Pony," *The Short Novels of John Steinbeck* (New York: Viking, 1953), 199.

83. Tsur, *Hakibbutz Hame'uhad*, 53.

84. Admoni, *Asor*, 18.

85. Admoni, *Asor*, 11, 18–19; Admoni, interview.

86. Admoni, *Asor*, 19. Weitz was head, or chairman, of the department; Admoni was initially acting director, then director, the top administrative post under the department head.

87. Moshe Moskovic, interview and private papers; Refael Bashan, "Hamassu'ah Al Hehar Hudlakah Shuv," *Ma'ariv*, September 29, 1967; ISA 153.8/7920/7A.

88. MGA 502-10-01-01, Rafael Ben-Yehudah's diary; *Alei Golan*, no. 32, July 16, 1968, 2–4; Admoni, *Asor*, 23–24.

89. Eytan Sat, interview; Yehudah Harel, interview; Admoni, *Asor*, 23.

3. Silent Cowboys on the New Frontier

1. Yehudah Harel, interview; Yehudah Harel, "Meharamah Hasurit Leramat Hagolan," author's ms.

2. KMA, Mazkirut Hakibbutz Hame'uhad, box 15, book 90; Tsur, *Mipulmus*, 85; Beilin, 35; Naor, 43.

3. YTA, Mazkirut Hakibbutz Hame'uhad, box 15, book 90.

4. Azaryahu, interview.

5. KMA 5/26/1, Mo'etzet Hakibbutz Hame'uhad decisions, June 23-24, 1967.

6. *Alei Golan*, no. 32, July 16, 1968, 2-4; Yehudah Harel, interview; Yehudah Harel, "Meharamah Hasurit." Cf. Tabenkin's comments in KMA 5/26/1, Mo'etzet Hakibbutz Hame'uhad, June 23, 1967. At the end of 1966, there were 232 kibbutzim; see *Statistical Abstract of Israel*, no. 18, 1967 (Jerusalem: Central Bureau of Statistics, 1968).

7. *Alei Golan*, no. 185, June 30, 1972.

8. Eytan Sat, interview.

9. Admoni, *Asor*, 22; Pedatzur, 177-79.

10. YAOH VI:11-12. Allon's proposal to the cabinet actually refers to "work camps."

11. YAOH VI:11-12.

12. MGA, Rafael Ben-Yehudah diary.

13. Admoni, interview; *Merom Golan: Reshit* (Merom Golan, 1977), 9.

14. MGA, Rafael Ben-Yehudah diary; Sat, interview.

15. Carmel Bar, interview; *Merom Golan: Reshit* 8; MGA, Rafael Ben-Yehudah diary; Vardina Shnurman, "Esrim Vehamesh Shanim Le'ahar Quneitrah," *Eretz Hagolan*, May 15, 1997, 12-14. There are minor variations in accounts of the settlement at Aalleiqa, most based on later memories of participants, regarding dates, the order of settlers' arrival, and other details. The account here is based on the few contemporary documentary sources and winnowing of later oral testimony.

16. *Ha'aretz*, June 30, 1967, 1.

17. NARA, RG 59, Central Files 1967-69, POL 27 Arab-Isr, Cable 3985, July 6, 1967.

18. *Davar*, July 9, 1967, 1, based on the original interview with *Le Monde*.

19. FRUS XIX: 331.

20. Moshe Zak, *Hussein Oseh Shalom* (King Hussein Makes Peace) (Ramat Gan: Bar Ilan University, 1996), 151; Lammfromm, 575.

21. ISA 153.8/7921/2A, document 331.

22. ISA 153.8/7921/2A, documents 323, 321, 317.

23. Original text of the plan: ISA 153.8/7921/2A, document 192. The detailed explanation is dated July 13, the proposed cabinet resolution July 26, and the cover note to Eshkol's bureau chief, July 27, resulting in conflicting accounts of when it was submitted. Allon on developing the plan: YAOH III:3, XVII:3. YAOH contains numerous accounts of responses to the plan.

24. "Autonomy" appears in the written proposal; "home rule" in Allon's description in YAOH VII:22.

25. YAOH III:9.

26. YAOH III:9–10; Tsur, *Hakibbutz*, 125–26; NARA RG 59, Central Files 1967–69, Pol 28 Jordan, airgram A-113.

27. Pedatzur, 145–49; Gazit, *Peta'im*, 218.

28. ISA 153.8/7921/2A, minutes of Va'adah Mdinit, July 27, 1967.

29. LBJ, NSC country files, Middle East crisis, vol. 7, 189a.

30. FRUS XIX:399.

31. Psalms 126:1.

32. Yitzhak Rabin, *Pinkas Sherut* (Tel Aviv: Sifriat Ma'ariv, 1979), 590; Naor, 30ff.

33. Shemer, "Jerusalem of Gold."

34. On travel rules: see MER III:285. The Israeli press carried plentiful reports of touring occupied territories, e.g., *Ha'aretz*, June 18, 1967, 9; *Lamerhav*, July 28, 1967, 4; *Ha'aretz*, September 1, 1967, 4; *Hatzofeh*, Sabbath supplement, September 15, 1967, 4.

35. LBJ country files, Israel, vol. 5, cables, folder 2, airgram A-934. Polling at the time was generally of the Jewish population, excluding the Arab minority.

36. Tzvi Shiloah, "Hashuv Mah Ya'asu Hayehudim," *Davar*, July 3, 1967, reprinted in Ben-Ami, 147.

37. Gouri, "Hashivah Le'Abu Dis."

38. Nathan Alterman, "Hagadah Hama'aravit—Eretz Be'illum Shem," *Davar*, June 23, 1967, reprinted in Ben-Ami, 57ff. "Threefold cord" alludes to Ecclesiastes 4:12.

39. Gouri, "Hashivah Le'Abu Dis."

40. Amnon Barzilai, "Uve'itzumah shel Hamilhamah Tikhnenu Be'aman et Hamedinah Hapalestinit," *Ha'aretz*, June 5, 2002, B3.

41. Moshe Shamir, "Min Haplishtiut—El Hahar," *Ma'ariv*, July 14, 1967, reprinted in Ben-Ami, 24ff.

42. Naor, 61; Gershon Shafat with Tzviah Granot, *Gush Emunim: Hasipur Me'ahorei Hakla'im* (Gush Emunim: The Story Behind the Scenes) (Sifriat Beit El: 1995), 36.

43. Quoted in Barzilai, "Uve'itzumah shel Hamilhamah."

44. Amos Oz, "Ir Zarah," *Siah Lohamim: Pirkei Hakshavah Vehitbonenut*, Avraham Shapira, ed. (Tel Aviv: Haverim Tze'irim Mehatnu'ah Hakibbutzit, October 1967). I have used the translation of the essay by Nicholas de Lange in Amos Oz, *Under This Blazing Light: Essays* (Cambridge University Press, 1995), 175–81.

45. Shapira, ed., *Siah Lohamim*.

46. Ibid., 5.

47. Ibid., 118.

48. Ibid., 191.

49. Ibid., 134–34, 142.

50. Paul Berman, *A Tale of Two Utopias: The Political Journey of the Generation of 1968* (New York: W. W. Norton, 1996), 30–56.

51. "Sihah Biyshivat Harav Kook," *Shdemot: Bamah Lehinukh Tnu'ati*, no. 29, (Spring 1968), 15–27; Amos Oz, *In the Land of Israel*, trans. Maurice Goldberg-Bartura (London: Chatto & Windus/The Hogworth Press, 1983), 132–33; Amnon Barzilai, "Kakh Nignaz 'Siah Lohamim' Shel Merkaz Harav," *Ha'aretz*, June 16, 2002, 3B.

52. "Sihah Biyshivat Harav Kook," 15–16.

53. Ibid., 19–20.

54. For a fuller discussion of messianism, see Gershom Gorenberg, *The End of Days: Fundamentalism and the Struggle for the Temple Mount* (New York: The Free Press, 2000).

55. Avraham Yitzhak Hacohen Kook, 13ff.

56. Ravitzky, 176.

57. Tzvi Yehudah Hacohen Kook, *Lintivot Yisrael* (Jerusalem: Menorah, 5727), 188ff.

58. Filber, 31–33; cf. David Hakohen, *Hitnotzetzut Oro Shel Mashiah*, 2nd ed. (Jerusalem: Ariel/Nezer David, 5749), 17.

59. Ravitzky, 183–84.

60. Danny Rubinstein, *Mi Lashem Elai: Gush Emunim* (On the Lord's Side: Gush Emunim) (Tel Aviv: Hakibbutz Hame'uhad), 1982; Yisrael Harel, interview; and off-the-record interviews.

61. Menachem Klein, *Bar-Ilan: Akademiah, Dat Upolitikah* (Bar-Ilan University Between Religion and Politics) (Jerusalem: Magnes, 1998), 141–42.

62. *Zra'im*, Iyar 5727 (May–June 1967), 9–12.

63. Eliezer Don Yehiya, "The Book and the Sword: The Nationalist Yeshivot and Political Radicalism in Israel," *Accounting for Fundamentalisms: The Dynamic Character of Movements*, ed. Martin E. Marty and R. Scott Appleby (Chicago: The Fundamentalism Project, University of Chicago Press, 1994), 264–70.

64. *Zra'im*, Sivan-Tamuz 5727 (June–August 1967), 3ff.

65. *Merom Golan: Reshit*, 2–10; Bar, interview; Gershon Meinrat, interview.

66. Sat, interview; Yehudah Harel, "Meharamah."

67. *Merom Golan: Reshit*, 2–10; Bar, interview; Meinrat, interview; Sat, interview.

68. Yehudah Harel, interview.

69. Kalinov, 26–31.

70. Pedatzur, 180; ISA 153.8/1/7920/7A, document 288.

71. MGA, Rafael Ben-Yehudah diary.

4. Settling In

1. ISA 153.8/7921/3A. Legal opinion numbered as document 289–291, with unnumbered cover notes.

2. "Faculty Profile—Professor Theodor Meron," www.law.nyu.edu/faculty/profiles/bios/meront_bio.html; Marlise Simons, "Weaving the Threads of Law, War and Shakespeare," *New York Times*, January 3, 2004.

3. YLE 5/31.

4. Full text: "Convention (IV) relative to the Protection of Civilian Persons in Time of War. Geneva, 12 August 1949," www.icrc.org/ihl.nsf/o/6756482d86146898c125641e004aa3c5?OpenDocument.

5. Full text: "Commentary Art. 49 Convention (IV) Relative to the Protection of Civilian Persons in Time of War. Geneva, 12 August 1949," www.icrc.org/ihl.nsf/b466ed681ddfcfd241256739003e6368/523ba38706c71588c12563cd0042c407?Open Document.

6. Article 46 of "Laws of War: Laws and Customs of War on Land (Hague IV)," October 18, 1907. Full text at www.yale.edu/lawweb/avalon/lawofwar/hague04.htm.

7. Parentheses in the original.

8. Cf. Moshe Negbi, *Kevalim Shel Tzedek: Bagatz Mul Hamemshal Hayisre'eli Bashtahim* (Justice Under Occupation: The Israeli Supreme Court versus the Military Administration in the Occupied Territories) (Jerusalem: Cana, 1981), 22-24.

9. ISA 153.8/7921/3A, cover note to document 289-291, and document 227.

10. Ben-Yaakov, 338-39.

11. Hann Porat, *Et Ahai Anokhi Mevakesh* (Beit El: Sifriat Beit El, 5752), 12-14.

12. Shehadeh, 57-66.

13. Yossi Melman, *The Master Terrorist : The True Story of Abu-Nidal* (New York : Adama Books, 1986), 62-64; Gershom Gorenberg, "The Detonator," *The New York Times Magazine*, Dec. 29, 2003, 48-49.

14. Moshe Moskovic, interview; Hanan Porat, interview; Moshe Levinger, interview.

15. GEA 23IVf; Ben-Yaakov, 343-44; Avraham Shvut, ed., *Ha'aliyah El Hahar: Hahityashvut Hayehudit Hamithadeshet Biyhudah Veshomron* (Ascent to the Mountains: Renewal of Jewish Settlement in Judea and Samaria) (Jerusalem: Sifriat Beit El, 2002), 31-33; Porat, interview.

16. Porat, interview; cf. Pedatzur, 190.

17. YAOH VI:16, VII:1.

18. Porat, 9-11.

19. Shvut, 33; Haggai Segal, *Dear Brothers: The West Bank Jewish Underground* (Woodmere, NY: Beit-Shammai, 1988), 9-10; Porat, interview; Moshe Levinger, interview; Yisrael Harel, interview.

20. ISA 153.8/7920/7A. Moskovic was a signator of the Movement for the Whole Land of Israel's founding statement, *Davar*, Sept. 22, 1967.

21. Pedatzur, 33, 190.

22. ISA 153.8/7921/2A.

23. FRUS XIX:405, 418, 421; Fred J. Khouri, *The Arab-Israeli Dilemma* (Syracuse, NY: Syracuse University Press, 1968), 310-12.

24. Yoram Meital, "The Khartoum Conference and Egyptian Policy After the 1967 War: A Reexamination," *Middle East Journal* 54, no. 1 (Winter 2000); Khouri, 312-14; Shlaim, 258-59; William Quandt, interview. Text of the resolution: www.mideastweb.org/khartoum.htm.

25. Lammfromm, 576; Gazit, *Peta'im*, 143-44; Shlomo Hillel, interview.

26. FRUS XX:7.

27. *Lemerhav*, Sept. 7, 1967, 1; Admoni, *Asor*, 33-34.

28. Gazit, *Peta'im*, 143.

29. Pedatzur, 190-91; YAOH VII:1; Warhaftig, 294-95. Descriptions of the National Religious Party ministers as being advocates of the Whole Land of Israel in the summer of 1967 are anachronistic, based on the party's later positions. Warhaftig opposed settlement in the Golan Heights and Sinai; party leader Haim Moshe Shapira was known in the cabinet and party as an outspoken territorial minimalist. Warhaftig, 241-264; Yehuda Ben-Meir, interview.

30. Lammfromm, 576.

31. Admoni, *Asor*, 34.

32. YLE 5/31.

33. Ben-Yaakov, 345.

34. Shvut, 33.

35. Hanan Porat, interview; Moshe Levinger, interview.

36. Yehuda Ben-Meir, interview. Eshkol described the NRP leaders' interest in reestablishing Kfar Etzion as a glaring exception to their usual meekness; see ISA 153.8/7920/7A, Eshkol speech to Ihud Hakvutzot Vehakibbutzim, Nov. 22, 1967.

37. Aharon Amir, "Hakinor Vehaherev," *Keshet* (Tel Aviv) 18 (Fall 1975), 25-26.

38. Gouri, "Hashivah Le'Abu Dis."

39. GEA 23IVf.

40. Hanan Porat, interview.

41. *Davar*, Sept. 22, 1967.

42. YLE 5/31.

43. Hanan Porat, interview.

44. Shvut, 35; Shafat, 27; Naftali Greenspan, "The Story of Our Return to Gush Etzion," ms. at GEA 23IVg. Shafat's account of settlement consistently portrays a far sharper conflict between settlers and politicians than reflected in documents and accounts of other settlers. Note that the chronology in Shvut contains contradictions and does not line up with the calendar of September 1967/Elul 5727.

45. Shvut, 35.

46. Moshe Brawer, interview. Brawer, emeritus professor of geography, Tel Aviv University, surveyed the area in late June–early July 1967 and mapped the location of prewar Syrian and Israeli positions to determine the de facto June 4, 1967, lines. Cf. Frederic C. Hof, "The Line of June 4, 1967," *Middle East Insight*, Sept.–Oct. 1999. The site, afterward known as Kibbutz Snir, was settled by members of the dovish Hashomer Hatza'ir movement, which at that stage rejected settling in occupied land but did not see former DMZ land as belonging to that category. Moshe Netzer, *Netzer Mishorashav: Sippur Haim* (Life Story) (Ministry of Defense, 2002), 250-51.

47. Cabinet discussion: Admoni, *Asor*, 51-53; Pedatzur, 186, 193-94; Lammfromm, 576-77. Minutes of the meeting with Hamahanot Ha'olim representatives concerning Beit Ha'aravah, Sept. 19, 1967: ISA 153.8/7920/7A, document 5-69.

48. Pedatzur, 193.

49. NARA, RG59, Central Files 1967-69, POL 27 Arab-Isr, Dale-Atherton letter, Sept. 29, 1967.

50. E.g., "Rosh Hamemshalah Hodia Biyshivat Hamemshalah: He'ahzut Nahal Takum Bekarov Begush Etzion," *Davar*, Sept. 25, 1967, 1; Terrence Smith, "Israelis to Live in 2 Seized Areas," *New York Times*, Sept. 25, 1967, 1.

51. Earlier published accounts of the establishment of Kfar Etzion contain discrepancies in dating and other details, and create an impression of Eshkol approving the settlement under threat that the settlers would go ahead illegally, in line with the portrayal publicly promoted at the time by the National Religious Party's Young Guard. Pedatzur, 193, gives Sept. 25 as the date Kfar Etzion was established. Admoni, *Asor*, 53, has Porat et al. meeting Eshkol on the Hebrew date 20 Elul (Sept. 25). Eshkol's office diary at YLE shows no meeting between the prime minister and the Etzion group on that day, and the description of the conversation in Admoni fits

the meeting that in fact took place on Sept. 22. Eshkol's office diary does show that Eshkol met Settlement Department head Ra'anan Weitz at 8:50 A.M., Sept. 25. This fits the account of Settlement Department official Yehudah Dekel ("Kakh Alinu Mehadash Legush Etzion," *Ha'aretz*, Oct. 23, 1984, Letters to the Editor) that the Kfar Etzion group received official notice of the prime minister's approval in their meeting that morning at the Settlement Department. The correct chronology therefore is Sept. 22: Etzion group meets Eshkol; receives ambiguous reply. Sept. 22–23: Etzion young people meet for Sabbath. Sept. 24: Eshkol announces his decision to the cabinet. Sept. 25: Eshkol meets Weitz, who afterward meets Porat et al. to prepare for founding. Porat then meets Levinger. Sept. 27: Kfar Etzion established.

52. GEA 23IVf: Memo regarding meeting of Sept. 25, 1967; Yehudah Dekel, "Kakh Alinu"; Porat, interview.

53. Porat, interview.

54. *Davar, Hatzofeh, Ha'aretz, Hayom, Jerusalem Post, Lamerhav, Ma'ariv, Yediot Aharonot*, Sept. 28, 1967; Shvut, 35; Porat, interview; NARA RG59, Central Files 1967–69, POL 27 Arab-Isr, Jerusalem telegram 579. Organizing committee's flyer at GEA 23IVf notes that Nahal groups may later be assigned to the new kibbutz, as they sometimes were to civilian settlements, but says nothing of the settlement being defined as a Nahal outpost.

55. YLE 5/31.

56. See, for instance, ISA 153.8/7920/7A, Eshkol speech to Ihud Hakvutzot Vehakibbutzim, Nov. 22, 1967.

57. Eshkol's personal role in directing settlement is summed by Admoni, *Asor*, 68–72.

58. YLE 5/31, cable 461.

59. YLE 5/31, cable 676.

60. NARA, RG59, Central Files 1967–69, POL 27 Arab-Isr, cable 950.

61. NARA, RG59, Central Files 1967–69, POL 27 Arab-Isr, Dale-Atheron letter, Sept. 29, 1967.

62. ISA 153.8/7920/7A, Eshkol speech to Ihud Hakvutzot Vehakibbutzim, Nov. 22, 1967.

63. NARA, RG 59, Central Files 1967–69, POL 27 Arab-Isr, cables 921, 43163.

64. NARA, RG 59, Central Files 1967–69, POL 27 Arab-Isr, cable 44390.

65. Hedrick Smith, "U.S. Chides Israelis . . . ," *New York Times*, Sept. 27, 1967, 1.

66. Drew Middleton, "Brown Supports U.S. Peace Effort . . . ," *New York Times*, Sept. 27, 1967, 1.

67. GEA 23IVf.

68. NARA, RG59, Central Files 1967–69, POL 27 Arab-Isr, cable 972. Eban himself, at a press conference in Strasbourg on Sept. 27, described Kfar Etzion as being settled by a "youth military organization" and said the Israeli government regarded neither it nor "cultivation" under way in the Syrian heights "as in any sense excluding the free discussion of the territorial problem in the peace negotiation." LBJ, NSF country file Israel, vol. 7, memos, document 84b.

69. NARA, RG59, Central Files 1967–69, POL 27 Arab-Isr, cables 1283, 2533, 1620, 1666; *Al-Dastur* (Amman), Sept. 30, 1967, via HATZAV.

70. Saunders, interview.

71. NARA, RG59, Central Files 1967–69, POL 27 Arab-Isr, airgram A-226.
72. Hanan Porat, interview.
73. Pedatzur, 200–201.
74. *Merom Golan: Reshit*, 14; *Alei Golan*, no. 3, Nov. 10, 1967, and no. 32, July 17, 1968; Yehudah Harel, interview; Meinrat, interview.
75. Yehudah Harel, interview; *Merom Golan: Reshit*, 19, emphasis in the original.
76. *Merom Golan: Reshit*, 20.
77. Yair Douer, *Lanu Hamaggal Hu Herev II* (Our Sickle Is Our Sword: Nahal Settlements from 1967 until 1992) (Ministry of Defense and Yad Tabenkin, 1997).
78. *Merom Golan: Reshit*, 17; Yehudah Harel, interview.
79. Kalinov, 50–54.
80. LBJ, NSF country files, Israel Vol. VII, memos, document 57.
81. Pedatzur, 112–13; Shlaim, 259.
82. ISA 153.8/7920/7A, Eshkol speech to Ihud Hakvutzot Vehakibbutzim, Nov. 22, 1967.
83. YTA 15Allon/17/4, Oct. 30, 1967.
84. Gazit, *Peta'im*, 23n. 1; Shlomo Gazit, *Hamakel Vehagezer: Hamemshal Hayisre'eli Biyhudah Veshomrom* (The Stick and the Carrot: The Israeli Administration in Judea and Samaria) (Tel Aviv: Zmora, Bitan, 1985), 12. The Hebrew term *shtahim muhzakim* literally means "held territories" but has standardly been translated "administered territories," which properly conveys the bureaucratic blandness of the Hebrew.
85. YAOH III:13–23.
86. YAOH III:21, VI:18, VII:20. A photograph of Eshkol on that trip, no. D685-074 in the Israel Government Press Office archive, is dated November 12, 1967.
87. ISA 153.8/7920/7A, document 240; Moshe Netzer, 253; Netzer, interview.
88. Yehudah Harel, "Meharamah Hasurit"; Admoni, *Asor*, 28–31.
89. Quandt, 56; Meital, 81–82; Oren, 325–27. Text of Resolution 242: www.yale.edu/lawweb/avalon/un/un242.htm.
90. FRUS XIX:476.
91. Quandt, 56.
92. LBJ, President's Daily Diary, Box 14.
93. NARA, RG59, Central Files 1967–69, POL 7 Isr 1-1-68; LBJ NSF country files, Israel, Eshkol visit, briefing book; Saunders, interview.
94. FRUS XX:39, 40.
95. YAOH III:20–21.
96. FRUS XX:41.
97. Beilin, 49–50; Pedatzur, 33–34; Medzini, 347–49.
98. ISA 153.8/7920/7A.

5. The "Invisible" Occupation

1. Yaakov Perry, *Habba Lehorgekha* (Strike First) (Tel Aviv: Keshet, 1999), 14–48.
2. E.g., ISA 153.8/7920/7A, Eshkol speech to Ihud Hakvutzot Vehakibbutzim, Nov. 22, 1967.
3. Gazit, *Peta'im*, 20–22, 47; Shlomo Gazit, interview.

4. Gazit, *Hamakel*, 83–87; Gazit, *Peta'im*, 35–41; Gazit, interview.

5. MER III:284–85; Lev Luis Grinberg, *Hahistadrut Me'al Lakol* (The Histadrut Above All) (Jerusalem: Nevo, 1993), 188–91; Dayan, 397–401.

6. Gazit, *Peta'im*, 61–62.

7. Dayan, 393–94, 405; on Dayan's archaeological looting, see Raz Kletter, "A Very General Archaeologist—Moshe Dayan and Israeli Archaeology," *Journal of Hebrew Scriptures* 4 (2002–2003), www.arts.ualberta.ca/JHS/Articles/article_27.htm.

8. MER III:285.

9. Perry, 49–51.

10. Gazit, *Peta'im*, 33. On defining colonialism, see Stephen Howe, *Empire: A Very Short Introduction* (Oxford: Oxford University Press, 2002), 26–31.

11. Howe, *Empire*, 30–31.

12. MER III:282–83.

13. MER III:285–87; Gazit, *Peta'im*, 63–64; Wallach, 118.

14. David C. Rapoport, "The Fourth Wave: September 11 and the History of Terrorism," *Current History*, Dec. 2001, 419–25.

15. Frantz Fanon, *The Wretched of the Earth*, trans. Constance Farrington, (Harmondsworth, England: Penguin, 1985), 29, 56–70, 74; Ely Karmon, "Fatah and the Popular Front for the Liberation of Palestine: International Terrorism Strategies (1968–1990)," www.ict.org.il/articles/fatah-pflhtm.

16. Shehadeh, 54, 67–74; on "resistance movements" as a response to feelings of passivity, see also Hilary Kilpatrick's introduction to Ghassan Kanafani, *Men in the Sun and Other Palestinian Stories*, trans. Hilary Kilpatrick (London: Heinemann, 1982), 3–4.

17. Perry, 47–58.

18. Amos Oz, "Eretz Moledet," published in three parts in *Davar*, November 10, 15, and 17, 1967. Translation from Oz, *Under This Blazing Light*, 79–101.

19. ISA 153.8/7921/4A, memo of Nov. 12, 1967.

20. Zak, 152–53.

21. Gorenberg, *End of Days*, 82, and sources cited there.

22. ISA 153.8/7921/3, Dec. 7, 1967.

23. Moshe Levinger, "Kakh Zeh Hit'hil," www.hebron.co.il/agdot/ag29.html; Levinger, interview; cf. Segal, 13–14. Segal's version does not cite sources, but closely follows Levinger's accounts.

24. Levinger, "Kakh Zeh Hit'hil"; Gazit, interview.

25. Yisrael Harel, interview.

26. Pedatzur, 230–31.

27. See the original text of the Allon Plan, ISA 153.8/7921/2A, document 192.

28. YLE 5/31.

29. Levinger, "Kakh Zeh Hit'hil"; Levinger, interview; cf. Segal, 13–14.

30. Segal, 13–14; NARA, RG59, Central Files 1967–69, POL 27 Arab-Isr, Tel Aviv Airgram A-218, Apr. 17, 1968; NARA, RG 59, Central Files 1967–69, POL 27 Arab-Isr, Amman cable 0076, July 5, 1967. Warhaftig, 300, incorrectly puts the murder on the day that Levinger's group entered the hotel, but also describes it as a possible warning.

31. NARA, RG59, Central Files 1967–69, POL 27 Arab-Isr, Tel Aviv Airgram A-218, Apr. 17, 1968.

32. Benziman, 253–54.

33. ISA 153.8/7920/8A, document 51–52, Sept. 17, 1967.

34. Benziman, 259.

35. Benziman, 259–61; LBJ NSF country files Israel, vol. 8, documents 61, 3; ISA 153.8/7920/8A, document 243, Feb. 29, 1968; cf. ISA 153.8/7920/8A, document 102–27.

36. ISA 153.8/7920/8A document 160 (28), Mar. 11, 1968.

37. Benziman, 261–62.

38. ISA 153.8/7921/4A document 201–13, Feb. 19, 1968; Hagar Sereni, interview.

39. ISA 153.8/7921/4A document 206–18, Mar. 20, 1968.

40. ISA 153.8/7921/4A document 208–20, Mar. 27, 1968; ISA 153.8/7921/4A, document 252, Apr. 2, 1968; on Karameh battle, Morris, *Victims*, 368–370.

41. ISA 153.8/7931/1A, document 107–119.

42. FRUS XX:137.

43. Benjamin Katzover, interview; Levinger, interview. Shvut, 39, says the settlers arrived Apr. 11; Shabtai Teveth, *Klalat Habrakhah* (Tel Aviv: Schocken, 1973), 229, gives the date as Apr. 10. Levinger and other interviewees, however, speak of arriving only hours before the holiday on Apr. 12.

44. Gazit, *Peta'im*, 225; MER III:285; Shvut, 39.

45. Teveth 231, 236–37; Dayan, 415–17. While Dayan acknowledges that he was out of action during the Karameh operation, neither he nor Teveth mentions that he was digging illegally. Kletter, "General Archaeologist," shows that Dayan had already been warned that his activities at the site were illegal, and had continued his looting.

46. YAOH IV:17.

47. Levinger, "Kakh Zeh Hit'hil"; Levinger, interview; Segal, 14–15.

48. Yisrael Harel, interview.

49. Levinger, interview.

50. Segal, 16.

51. NARA, RG 59, Central Files 1967–69, POL 28 Jerusalem, Jerusalem Airgram A-131, January 31, 1968.

52. Bar, interview; Yehudah Harel, interview; *Merom Golan: Reshit*, 38.

53. Kalinov, 57–58.

54. Perry, 9–14.

55. Levinger, interview; Katzover, interview.

56. Gazit, interview.

57. Dayan, 417–19.

58. Teveth, 236.

59. Katzover, interview.

60. YTA 15Allon/18/4. The telegram states that it was sent at 1710 hours, Apr. 14; Apr. 15 is marked in hand by Allon's staff.

61. *Lamerhav*, Apr. 16, 1968.

62. Porat, interview. Admoni, in Ad. MS 76:36 describes Zevulun Hammer citing the incident in the cabinet meeting of May 9, 1975. Admoni, treating the incident as well-known, comments that moving army-issue guns from Kfar Etzion to Hebron

"violated all instructions and directions concerning use of weapons provided to settlements." In YAOH VI:18, Allon justifies his action by saying that on returning to Jerusalem, he asked Eshkol's aide-de-camp to inform Dayan that the guns had been sent. By the time of the interview, Allon was defensive about his ties to Levinger and Porat, and about his role in encouraging wildcat settlement. His defense of his actions, however, confirms that the incident took place.

63. Teveth, 233.

64. Moshe Ma'oz, *Palestinian Leadership on the West Bank: The Changing Role of Arab Mayors Under Jordan and Israel* (London: Frank Cass, 1984), 8–9, 24–25, 32, 50, 95ff; Bavly, 258; YTA 15Allon/18/3.

65. Teveth, 233–234; YLE 5/31 telegram of May 7, 1968; *Lamerhav*, May 9, 1968; Levinger, interview.

66. *Lemerhav*, April 18, 1968, 1.

67. YTA 15Allon/18/4, Apr. 18, 1968, received Apr. 26, 1968.

68. Pedatzur, 233.

69. Teveth, 235.

70. YLE 5/31, May 12, 1968.

71. Pedatzur, 235.

72. James Feron, "Hebron Settlers May Stay in Town," *New York Times*, May 16, 1968, 13.

73. Waldman continued to develop this idea; see Eliezer Waldman, *Al Da'at Hamakom Vehazman* (Kiryat Arba, 5743), 18ff.

74. Katzover, interview; Shvut, 41; Segal, 18; cf. ISA 153.8/7921/4A, meeting of May 29, 1968, in which Dayan refers to the "yeshivah in Hebron"; YLE 5/31, Hebron settlers' letter to Levi Eshkol, received Aug. 11, 1968, which cites the government's commitment to allow a yeshivah.

75. E.g., ISA 153.8/7921/4A, meeting of May 29, 1968.

76. Levinger, interview.

77. Teveth, 237.

78. ISA 153.8/7921/4A, document 203–25.

79. Gazit, interview; Sereni, interview.

80. FRUS XX:186,187; Zak 156.

81. See FRUS XX:134.

82. YAOH VII:22; cf. Pedatzur, 78–79.

83. NARA, RG59, Central Files 1967–69, POL 27 Arab-Isr, Tel Aviv cable 4099.

84. ISA 153.8/7921/4A, meeting of May 29, 1968. On contacts with Shehadeh and Kanan, Gazit, *Peta'im*, 178ff. On Dayan's political behavior, Gazit, *Peta'im*, 148 and Gazit, interview.

85. Terence Smith, "Eshkol Plan Stirs Political Storm," *New York Times*, June 15, 1968, 7.

86. Haim Gouri, "Leyad Hagesher," *Lamerhav*, July 5, 1968.

87. Gazit, *Peta'im*, 178–85; ISA 153.8/7921/4A, documents 216–28; ISA 153.8/7921/8A, meeting of July 12, 1968; ISA 153.8/7921/5A, documents 230–42, 239–51, 60. Dayan-Eshkol dialogue is in document 60.

88. Gazit, *Peta'im*, 185.

89. MER IV:431.

90. Shehadeh, 68.

91. Katzover, interview; on living conditions in Hebron, Chaim Simons, *Three Years in a Military Compound: Reminiscences of a Hebron Settler*, ms.

92. NARA, RG59, Central Files 1967–69, POL 28 Jordan, memorandum of July 23, 1968.

93. YLE 5/31. Eshkol's office received the letter on August 11, but it was sent the previous week. The precise date is unclear due to a typographical error. Capital letters have been used to translate the extra-large letters provided on Hebrew typewriters of the time for emphasis. On Dayan's tactic, Teveth, 239.

94. Gazit, *Peta'im*, 226; Gazit, interview; Katzover, interview; "Shloshah Mitnahalei Hevron . . . ," *Hatzofeh*, Aug. 9, 1968, 8; Micha Limor, "Mitnahalei Hevron . . . ," *Yediot Aharonot*, Aug. 12, 1968, 3. Press reports at the time all indicate that the kiosk was set up the day of the wedding, but that the confrontation took place only the next day, indicating that the settlers had at least tacit approval the first day.

95. Limor, "Mitnahalei Hevron . . ."; "Ukav Hagerush . . . ," *Hatzofeh*, Aug. 12, 1968, 1; Katzover, interview.

96. Lammfromm, 641–42.

97. Pedatzur, 237.

98. Pedatzur, 238–39.

99. YLE 5/31, 27 Av, 5728 (Aug. 21, 1968).

100. YLE 5/31, Aug. 22, 1968.

101. ISA 153.8/7931/3A, document 117.

102. ISA 153.8/7920/7A, memo of Sept. 25, 1968, signed by Eshkol's liaison with West Bank Arabs, Moshe Sasson; his East Jerusalem development director, Yehudah Tamir; and Col. Aharon Harsinah.

103. Katzover, interview.

104. ISA 43/7231/4A, document 98.

105. Admoni, *Asor*, 59; YAOH VI:18–19.

106. Moshe Moskovic private papers, July 7, 1968, letter from Col. Dan Hiram to commander of Judea and Samaria Area; ISA 153.8/7920/7A, documents 216–217; YLE 5/31, Sept. 3, 1968; Moskovic, interview; M. Menahem, "Hayshivah El Mul Hakotel," *Zra'im*, Nisan, 5728 (Mar.–Apr. 1968) 6–7; Klein, 141–42.

107. Perry, 59–61.

6. Changing of the Guard

1. YAOH V:1–4; VI:1–2. Official announcement of the Phantom deal was Oct. 9, 1968, see Quandt, 58.

2. FRUS XX:247; LBJ, President's Daily Diary, September 9, 1968; LBJ NSF country files, Israel, vol. 10, Memos, document 227a; NARA RG59, Central Files 1967–69, POL Israel-US 1968, Memo 12241, Sept. 9, 1968.

3. FRUS XX:217.

4. YAOH II:29–30; ISA 153.8/7921/5A, documents 253–65, 256–68.

5. Joseph Sisco, interview.

6. ISA 153.8/7921/13A, political committee, Sept. 20, 1969.

7. YAOH VI:3.

8. YAOH VI:1–3; Zak, 157ff; Pedatzur, 141–43.

9. YAOH XVII:8.

10. Pedatzur, 221; Zak, 160.

11. YAOH IV:1–6, VIII:2–4.

12. LBJ NSF country files Israel, vol 10, cables, document 46. On American officials' consistent dismissal of the Allon Plan see also NARA, RG59, Central Files 1967–69, POL ISR-US, Memcon of Nov. 18, 1968.

13. YAOH IV:1–6, VIII:2.

14. FRUS XX:287.

15. NARA, RG59, Central Files 1967–69, POL ISR-US, W. Rostow memo of Oct. 24, 1968, and attached W. Rostow note to Johnson, Oct. 23, 1968; FRUS XX:285.

16. FRUS XX:289.

17. ISA 43/7234/7A, document 287; Lammfromm, 643–45, 649.

18. Pedatzur, 247. Ad. MS 68:26 cites the same source document and dates it as Oct. 31, 1969, but brings it in material for 1968. Since the issue of the Bedouin was raised by Dayan in the cabinet meeting of Jan. 26, 1969, "1969" can be presumed to be a typo, and the date given in the published edition of Admoni, *Asor*, 63 (Oct. 1, 1969) is a compound error.

19. FRUS XX:303.

20. NARA, RG59, Central Files 1967–69, POL ISR-US, Memcon of Nov. 18, 1968.

21. LBJ NSF country files, vol. 10, memos.

22. NARA, RG59, Central Files 1967–69, POL 28 Jerusalem, Jerusalem Airgram A-131, Jan. 31, 1968.

23. NARA, RG 59, Central Files 1967–69, POL 28 Jordan, Jerusalem cable 1696, Sept. 27, 1968.

24. Simons, 118.

25. YLE 5/31, correspondence of Sept. 24–Oct. 16, 1968; NARA RG59, Central Files 1967–69, POL 28 Jordan, Jerusalem cable 1696, Sept. 27, 1968, Jerusalem airgram A-358, Oct. 10, 1968.

26. *Ma'ariv* and *Ha'aretz*, Oct. 10–11, 1968.

27. YLE 5/31, Bet Rosh Hodesh Kislev, 5728 (Nov. 22, 1968).

28. YLE 5/31, Kislev 14, 5728 (Dec. 5, 1968).

29. Moshe Moskovic private papers, Har Etzion yeshivah letters of Nov. 12, 1968; Porat, interview; Moskovic, interview; "Harav Yehuda Amital," www.vbm-torah.org/rya.htm.

30. ISA 153.8/7920/7A, budget document of May 15, 1968; ISA 153.8/7921/5A document 201.

31. ISA 153.8/7231/1A, document 155.

32. *Merom Golan: Reshit*, 50.

33. Douer, 47–49; Pedatzur, 219–20.

34. ISA 153.8/7920/7A, document 60, Oct. 15, 1968; cf. Dayan's letter of Sept. 4, 1968, to Eshkol, cited in Admoni, *Asor*, 44–45.

35. E.g., YLE 5/31, Aug. 9, 1968, Dayan proposal to cabinet on raising standard of living and services in occupied territories.

36. NARA, RG 59, Central Files 1967–69, POL 27 ARAB-ISR, Tel Aviv Airgram A-1233, Oct. 5, 1968.

37. NARA, RG 59, Central Files 1967–69, POL 27 ARAB-ISR, Tel Aviv Airgram A-1302, Nov. 9, 1968; Grinberg, 192–95; Admoni, interview.

38. Ad. MS 68:17–20.

39. Pedatzur, 145–55.

40. LBJ NSF country files, vol. 10, cables, document 89.

41. Lammfromm, 645; Grinberg, 193–94.

42. Arie Lova Eliav, *Ye'adim Hadashim Leyisrael* (Tel Aviv: Betzalel Cherikover, Feb. 1969), 7–8, 11.

43. Eliav, *Ye'adim*; Eliav, *Tabe'ot Edut* (Rings of Faith) (Tel Aviv: Am Oved, 1984), 288–92; Eliav, interview.

44. Yossi Sarid, interview; Amnon Barzilai, "Mibrerat Mehdal Ve'ad Lamehdal," *Ha'aretz*, Oct. 10, 2003, B4.

45. Victor Shemtov, *Ehad Mehem* (Kibbutz Daliah: Ma'arekhet, 1997), 41.

46. Medzini, 350–51; Beilin, 52–53; description of Sapir based in part on Admoni, interview.

47. Lammfromm, 654.

48. NARA, RG59, Central Files 1967–69, POL 12 ISR, Tel Aviv airgram A-54, Jan. 26, 1969.

49. Pedatzur, 221–25; MER IV: 743; YAOH VIII:18–19; "Israel's Decision: Security Without Peace," *Time*, Feb. 7, 1969. The cover date is a week after the publication date of Jan. 31, 1969. The article presents the government as approving more of Allon's proposals than it did at the time, possibly indicating that the source is Allon himself or a crony.

50. "Eshkol: A Reply to Nasser," *Newsweek*, Feb. 17, 1969, 28–29. Actual publication date was Feb. 10, 1969.

51. NARA, Nixon NSC Country Files, Middle East, Israel, vol. 1, Feb. 12, 1969.

52. Lammfromm, 655; Michael Elkins, "Notebook of an Irreverent Correspondent," *Jerusalem Report*, May 14, 1998, 68.

53. Medzini, 352.

54. Admoni, 68. On Kalya: NARA, RG 59, Central Files 1967–69, POL 27 ARAB-ISR, Jerusalem airgrams A-35, February 25, 1969 and A-38, March 4, 1969; "Israel Settling in to Stay," *Time*, February 28, 1969. On the discrepancies between descriptions of the site in the airgrams and *Time*, see page 188.

55. Eliav, February 8, 2004.

56. Admoni, 68–69.

57. ISA 153.8/7920/7A, document 202.

58. YLE 5/31, Dec. 16, 1968.

59. Eshkol expressed trepidation about Nixon as president on various occasions. E.g., Eshkol in ISA 153.8/7921/13A, political committee meeting, Sept. 20, 1968; and cf. Eban's comments in ISA 153.8/7921/13A, political committee meeting, Dec. 27, 1968, "Regarding putting together a cabinet the impression is that he has taken the approach of appointing people even less impressive than himself. Some say it is not so easy to find such people."

60. ISA 153.8/7931/3A, document 166, January 31, 1969.

61. William Bundy, *A Tangled Web: The Making of Foreign Policy in the Nixon Presidency* (New York: Hill and Wang, 1998), 56–57, 76–77.

62. Kissinger, *White House Years*, 11.

63. Kissinger, *White House Years*, 348; Bundy, 54–57, 126.

64. Kissinger, *White House Years*, 349–51; Quandt, 69–70.

65. Medzini, 21–60.

66. Ibid., 123–24.

67. Ibid., 355.

68. MER V:745; Medzini, 356.

7. The Reign of Hubris

1. "Israel Settling in to Stay," *Time*, Feb. 28, 1969.

2. NARA, RG59, Central Files 1967–69, POL 27 ARAB-ISR, Jerusalem airgram A-38, Mar. 4, 1969.

3. NARA, RG59, Central Files 1967–69, POL ISR-US, memos of Mar. 12, 1969.

4. Quandt, 74–80; Bundy, 126–27; Kissinger, *White House Years*, 368–69; Morris, *Victims*, 349ff.

5. ISA 106/2993/1P, Mar. 18, 1969.

6. ISA 106/2993/1P, Apr. 18, 1969.

7. Beilin, 53, who cites Shapira on the kitchen's composition; Medzini, 380–81.

8. Simons, 14, 17.

9. Ibid., 4–5.

10. Ibid., 69, 117–19.

11. Ibid., 120; MER V:357; Benjamin Katzover, Feb. 10, 2004.

12. MER V:358; Simons, 13, 31, 36, 91.

13. Simons, 22, 28–29.

14. *Merom Golan: Reshit*, 60.

15. *Merom Golan: Reshit*, 60; Tsur, *Hakibbutz Hame'uhad*, 140–41, 146, 154–55, 162.

16. Admoni, *Asor*, 31; Ad. MS 69:29, 70:44; Admoni, interview; Peter Robert Demant, *Ploughshares into Swords: Israeli Settlement Policy in the Occupied Territories, 1967–1977* (doctoral dissertation, Universiteit van Amsterdam, 1988), 209–12, 217.

17. Kalinov, 60–62.

18. Douer, 99–103. An initial group of Nahal soldiers arrived May 27, the rest on June 2. The founding ceremony was held July 13, leading to conflicting accounts in other sources on when the settlement was established.

19. Oded Lifshitz, interview; ISA 153.8/7920/7A, document 202 (85–21).

20. Douer, 100.

21. Demant, 237 n. 105.

22. Douer, 100–103.

23. ISA 153.8/7920/7A, document 202 (85–21); Ad. MS 68:26.

24. BAGATZ 302/72, attached to affidavit of Lt. Col. Dov Shefi; cf. affidavit of Col. Ofer Ben-David, and ISA 153.8/7920/7A, document 202 (85–21). The map attached to the latter document is not to scale. Ben-David states that the settlement of Sadot—the first of the three planned for the area—was located in the land that was

seized. The area of Diklah marked in the map attached to the 1969 orders is approximately 60 acres; the seized area is approximately 120 acres.

25. BAGATZ 302/72, affidavits of Col. Ofer Ben-David and Lt. Col. Yosef Cohen. On the distinction between expropriating and seizing land: Moshe Negbi, interview.

26. Netzer, 260; Archive of the Institute for the Research of Religious Zionism, division for religious settlement, file 44, invitation to founding of Rosh Tzurim, July 30, 1969.

27. *Merom Golan: Reshit*, 71; Douer, 87ff.

28. Douer, 87–90, 166–69, 192–95; Ad. MS 69:37.

29. Medzini, 357–58.

30. Beilin, 54–58. Oral doctrine text: YTA 15Galili/32/4/3.

31. See Meir's comments on page 190. Meir's hawkish record is consistent. On June 25, 1969, she instructed Eban and Rabin to again inform the U.S. administration of the Oct. 31, 1968, decision that Israel would keep Sharm al-Sheikh and a territorial link to it; ISA 43/7234/7A, document 287; cf. NARA RG59, Central Files 1967–69, POL ISR-US, Saunders memos of June 25 and July 1, 1969. In April 1968, Meir wrote to Yehudah Harel to express support for permanent civilian settlement in the Golan Heights. *Merom Golan: Reshit*, 38.

32. Medzini, 364.

33. NARA, RG59, Central Files 1967–69, POL 7 ISR, Rogers memo of Sept. 18, 1969.

34. Kissinger, *White House Years*, 368–69.

35. Ibid., 370.

36. Quandt, 80; cf. Kissinger, *White House Years*, 359.

37. Benziman, 203–5.

38. ISA 153.8/7920/8A, document 302, Dec. 23, 1968.

39. Benziman, 234–37.

40. Simons, 17.

41. On allowing settlers to vote, MER V:345ff.

42. *Merom Golan: Reshit*, 67.

43. Howard R. Penniman, ed. *Israel at the Polls: The Knesset Elections of 1977* (Washington, DC: American Enterprise Institute, 1979), 123–24.

44. Beilin, 86–87.

45. Ben-Meir, interview.

46. "Statement by Secretary of State Rogers—9 December 1969," www.mfa .gov.il/MFA/Foreign%20Relations/Israels%20Foreign%20Relations%20since%201 947/1947-1974/9%20Statement%20by%20Secretary%20of%20State%20Rogers% 209%20Decemb.

47. Quandt, 82.

48. Kissinger, *White House Years*, 376.

49. "Israel Rejects the Rogers Plan, Cabinet Statement, 22 December 1969," www.mfa.gov.il/MFA/Foreign%20Relations/Israels%20Foreign%20Relations%20si nce%201947/1947-1974/10%20Israel%20Rejects%20the%20Rogers%20Plan% 20Cabinet%20Stateme.

50. Quandt, 81–82; Bundy, 128.

51. Kissinger, *White House Years*, 376–79.

52. Eliav, *Tabe'ot Edut*, 293–97; "The Lion's Roar," *Time*, Jan. 26, 1970.

53. Pedatzur, 242–42; Admoni, 60–61; Ad. MS 70:3–4 describes the decision as taking place in two stages, a cabinet debate on Jan. 18, 1970, and a meeting of the Cabinet Security Committee on Feb. 5.

54. Katzover, interview.

55. Demant, 224.

56. MER V:358–59.

57. The committee's Hebrew name was *Va'adah Bein-mosadit Le'inyanei Hityashvut*. It could be more literally, and even more bureaucratically, translated as "Inter-Institutional Committee for Settlement Affairs." In some documents the same committee is referred to as the Ministerial Committee on Settlement. For brevity, it is referred to hereafter as the Settlement Committee.

58. Admoni, *Asor*, 60–61; Ad. MS 70:3–4. Beilin, 53, includes Sherf in a list of Mapai moderates sidelined by Meir.

59. YAOH IV:27.

60. Demant, 223–24.

61. ISA 106/2993/1P, Mar. 24, 1970.

62. Admoni, 59.

63. Gazit, *Peta'im*, 226.

64. The insight that the new approach was nationalist religion, rather than religious nationalism—that the core was religious—is from Gideon Aran, "From Religious Zionism to Zionist Religion: The Roots of Gush Emunim," *Studies in Contemporary Jewry* (Bloomington: Indiana University Press, 1986), 116–35.

65. *Alon Shvut*, vol. I, no. 2, 8.

66. Deuteronomy 8:17.

67. Psalms 18:38.

68. *Alon Shvut*, vol. I, no. 6, 2–3.

69. *Alon Shvut*, vol. I, no. 3, 2–3.

70. *Gvilei Esh*, vol. 6, book 1 (Parchments of Fire: Representative selection of literary works of those who fell while serving in the Israel Defense Forces, Oct. 1973–Dec. 1980) (Ministry of Defense, 1986), 96; Menachem M. Kasher, *Hatekufah Hagedolah* (The Great Era: A Comprehensive Study in the Position of the Jewish People, the Holy Land, and the Stages of Redemption at This Time, Based on Talmudic and Rabbinic Sources) (Jerusalem: Torah Shlemah Institute, 1968), 22–23.

71. Kasher, viii–xvi, 2–4, 14–15, 28–29.

72. Hakohen, 11–13.

73. Cf. Leon Festinger et al., *When Prophecy Fails* (New York: Harper & Row, 1964), 28; Gorenberg, *End of Days*, 47–49.

74. Benjamin Ish Shalom, *Tahat Hupat Barzel: Masekhet Hayyav Shel Daniel Orlik* (Under a Canopy of Iron: The Story of Daniel Orlik) (Jerusalem: Moriah, 5735), 100–106.

75. Demant, 226–27. Settlers moved in on June 25, 1970, according to Moskovic, interview, citing settlement records. The official founding ceremony was held on July 5, 1970.

76. YAOH VI:16.

77. Moskovic, interview.

78. Eban, 465; Bundy, 129.

79. Morris, *Victims*, 355–56; Eban, 465–66; Bundy, 131–32.

80. "The Second United States initiative, 19 June 1970," Israel Ministry of Foreign Affairs, www.mfa.gov.il/MFA/Foreign%20Relations/Israels%20Foreign%20Relations%20since%201947/1947-1974/16%20The%20Second%20United%20States%20Initiative%2019%20June%2019.

81. "Statement to the Knesset by Prime Minister Meir, 29 June 1970," Israel Ministry of Foreign Affairs, www.mfa.gov.il/MFA/Foreign%20Relations/Israels%20Foreign%20Relations%20since%201947/1947-1974/17%20Statement%20to%20the%20Knesset%20by%20Prime%20Minister%20Meir.

82. "Israel Accepts the United States initiative, Government Statement, 31 July 1970," Israel Ministry of Foreign Affairs, www.mfa.gov.il/MFA/Foreign%20Relations/Israels%20Foreign%20Relations%20since%201947/1947-1974/18%20Israel%20Accepts%20the%20United%20States%20Initiative-%20Go.

83. Beilin, 16.

84. YTA 15Galili/40/1/30, Sept. 8, 1970.

85. Admoni, *Asor*, 68; YAOH VII:12.

86. YAOH VI:16.

87. Azaryahu, interview.

88. Admoni, *Asor*, 64–65.

89. YTA 15Galili/40/1/2, Jan. 1970.

90. Admoni, *Asor*, 65–68.

91. Netzer, 265; Ad. MS 70:50. Ad. MS 71:15 suggests that the decision may have been made in the Settlement Committee, rather than in the cabinet.

92. Netzer, 94, 105–6, 112–15, 264–65.

93. Douer, 145.

94. YAOH VII:14–15.

95. Netzer, 264–65.

96. Bundy, 184–86; Morris, *Victims*, 373–75.

97. Kissinger, *White House Years*, 622–25; Bundy, 186–87; Quandt, 104–7.

98. YAOH V:14–16.

99. Quandt, 111–12.

100. YAOH V:16–20.

101. Quandt, 116–22; Beilin, 119–20.

102. Quandt, 122–29; Kenneth W. Stein, *Heroic Diplomacy: Sadat, Kissinger, Carter, Begin and the Quest for Arab-Israeli Peace* (New York: Routledge, 1999), 60–61.

103. Beilin, 124.

104. Beilin, 124–25; Moshe Meisels, "Hamismakh Hasodi Shel Pinhas Sapir," *Ma'ariv*, Apr. 15, 1971; Eliav, *Tabe'ot*, 298–301.

105. Shehadeh, 85–86.

106. Ad. MS 69:37, 71:43: *Merom Golan: Reshit*, 57–58, 64, 92–94. The Sinai coast settlement was Nevi'ot, near the Bedouin village of Nu'eibah.

107. Demant, 220, cf. Admoni, *Asor*, 98–99. The settlement was initially called Atarot, then renamed Hamrah.

108. Admoni, *Asor*, 95. The problem is also cited on 69, 94, 159. On 188–89,

summing up the years 1967–1977, Admoni states that manpower "was not a particular problem"—and then immediately discusses the lack of available settlers.

109. Ad. MS 69:30; Demant, 238.

110. Douer, 102.

111. Admoni, interview; Demant, 205.

112. Simons, 134.

113. Demant, 225.

114. Porat, interview.

8. *All Quiet on the Suez Front*

1. BAGATZ 302/72, petition of Sheikh Suleiman Hussein Udah Abu Hilu et al.; deposition of Lt. Col. Nissim Kazaz; IDF map of expulsion area.

2. BAGATZ 302/72, Justice Landau's opinion. Admoni, *Asor*, 108, gives a figure of "1,540 families" and an area of over 31 square miles. International Committee of the Red Cross, *Annual Report: 1972* (Geneva, ICRC, 1973), 73, states that "around 10,000," belonging to 14 tribes, were affected.

3. Oded Lifshitz, interview.

4. Lifshitz, private papers.

5. Gazit, *Peta'im*, 74; Gazit, interview. International Committee of the Red Cross, 73, states that the delegation first received complaints in early February. *Ma'ariv, Yediot Aharonot*, Mar. 28, 1972, reported that Elazar was informed on Feb. 15. The meeting with Gazit presumably took place that day or immediately before.

6. A flyer issued by activists at Nir-Oz in Nov. 1971, for instance, called on Mapam to lead the struggle against settlement in the Strip. Oded Lifshitz, private papers.

7. Lifshitz, interview.

8. Lifshitz, private papers.

9. Ad. MS 72:14–15.

10. Douer, 218–20.

11. Ad. MS 71:29.

12. Douer, 220.

13. Ariel Sharon, with David Chanoff, *Warrior: An Autobiography* (New York: Touchstone, 2001), 251–58; Morris, *Victims*, 370–71.

14. Sharon, 260. BAGATZ 302/72, Map of Movements of Terror Attack Perpetrators, shows that attacks had also dropped off in the northeast Sinai by the start of 1972.

15. Cf. Gershom Gorenberg, "A Belief in Force," *The American Prospect*, Apr. 8, 2002.

16. Lifshitz, private papers, "Summary of the Gathering Against Dispossession and Settlement in the Gaza Strip"; "Kenes Neged Nishul . . . ," *Al Hamishmar*, Mar. 9, 1972; "Al Ma Ragshu Haruhot Benir Oz," *Al Hamishmar*, Mar. 10, 1972; "Haverim Bakibbutz Ha'artzi Mesaprim . . . ," *Ma'ariv*, Mar. 14, 1972; Lifshitz, interview.

17. Admoni, *Asor*, 108–12; *Ma'ariv, Al Hamishmar*, Mar. 14–16, 1972; *Ha'aretz*, Mar. 21, 1972.

18. *Al Hamishmar*, Mar. 16, 1972.

19. BAGATZ 302/72, petition of Sheikh Suleiman Hussein Udah Abu Hilu et al.; deposition of Lt. Col. Dov Shefi.

20. Admoni, *Asor*, 108–12; Admoni, interview.

21. *Ma'ariv*, Mar. 17, 1972.

22. DK, Mar. 20, 1972, 1914; Mar. 27, 1972, 2099–106.

23. YTA 15Galili/69/1/11.

24. Gazit, *Peta'im*, 73–74, 310–12; Negbi, 30; Admoni, 108; *Ma'ariv, Yediot Aharonot*, Mar. 28, 1972.

25. Sharon, 250–51. The connection between this and the Rafiah affair is suggested by Gazit, *Peta'im*, 78.

26. Gazit, *Peta'im*, 75; Gazit, interview.

27. Gazit, *Peta'im*, 74.

28. Allon, another avid advocate of settling the Rafiah Plain, criticized Dayan for seeking too much of the Sinai. YAOH VIII:11.

29. Negbi, 29.

30. Nathan Alterman, "Shir Ha'emek" www.mp3music.co.il/lyrics/8513.html.

31. *Gvilei Esh*, 46.

32. Dov Indig, *Mikhtavim Letalyah* (Letters to Talia), ed. Hagi Ben-Artzi (Tel Aviv: Yediot Aharonot Books, 2005), 7–10; "Indig, Dov," www.izkor.gov.il/izkor86.asp?t=95484; Hagi Ben Artzi, interview. While the letters in *Gvilei Esh* are presented as correspondence with one girl, "Gadia," they were actually written to three, according to Ben-Artzi, who selected them. The names "Gadia" and "Talia" are both pseudonyms.

33. *Gvilei Esh*, 45.

34. Ibid.

35. Indig, 40–41.

36. After Israeli independence, Lehi's veterans revised their 18 principles of Jewish national renaissance, replacing "Third Kingdom," with the goal of "total redemption," to avoid the association with "Third Reich." See Gorenberg, *End of Days*, 92.

37. Yehudah Etzion, interview.

38. YTA 15Galili/40/1/9, settlers' letter to Galili, May 27, 1970; MER V:356; Admoni, *Asor*, 92.

39. Katzover, interview.

40. James Reston, "Egyptian Leader Gives Conditions for Peace Accord," *New York Times*, Dec. 28, 1970, 1; "Excerpts from the Interview with President Sadat of Egypt," *New York Times*, Dec. 28, 1970, 15.

41. Yossi Sarid, "The Spirit of Golda," *Ha'aretz*, Dec. 28, 2003; Amnon Barzilai, "Mibrerat Mehdal Ve'ad Lamehdal," *Ha'aretz*, Oct. 10, 2003; Sarid, interview.

42. "Interview with President Sadat of Egypt"; Morris, *Victims*, 390.

43. Eliav, *Taba'ot*, 314.

44. Abraham Rabinovich, *The Yom Kippur War: The Epic Encounter that Transformed the Middle East* (New York: Schocken, 2004), 22.

45. Uri Bar-Joseph, *Hatzofeh Shenirdam* (The Watchman Fell Asleep: The Surprise of Yom Kippur and Its Sources) (Lod: Zmora-Beitan, 2001), 91–92; Quandt, 135–37; Bundy, 338.

46. Kissinger, *White House Years*, 1296, 1300; Quandt, 132, 136.

47. Rabinovich, 14–15.

48. Arie (Lova) Eliav, *Eretz Hatzvi* (Land of the Hart) (Tel Aviv: Am Oved, 1972/eighth edition, 1983), 200.

49. Eliav, *Eretz Hatzvi*, 200–201.

50. Ibid., preface to the sixth edition (unnumbered pages).

51. Ibid., 195.

52. Ibid., 150–60.

53. Ibid., 163–67.

54. Ibid., 164.

55. Haim Gouri, "Hako'ah Vehapetza," *Davar*, June 9, 1972, 2.

56. The actual byline was "Hagur," his well-known pen name.

57. Aharon Geva, "Kol Ha'aretz Sadot," *Davar*, June 19, 1972, 7.

58. Admoni, *Asor*, 111–13; Admoni, interview.

59. Demant, 248–51.

60. Negbi, 12–18.

61. BAGATZ 302/72 and 306/72.

62. BAGATZ 302/72, Abu Hilu letter of June 12, 1972.

63. BAGATZ 302/72, Holzman letter of Aug. 7, 1972.

64. A third respondent was the commander of the northern Sinai and Gaza Strip, Brigadier General Yitzhak Pundak.

65. BAGATZ 302/72, affidavits of Lt. Col. Dov Shefi and Col. Ofer Ben-David.

66. BAGATZ 302/72, affidavit of Maj. Gen. Yisrael Tal.

67. BAGATZ 302/72, key arguments and summary of the petitioners; Negbi, 31–33.

68. Ad. MS 72:15; LPS Nov. 9, 1972, 41–42; Demant, 240–41; Negbi, 3–33.

69. LPS Sept. 21, 1972, 2–3.

70. Demant, 245–47; NARA, RG59 Central Files 1970–73, POL 28 Jordan, Tel Aviv cable 7411, Nov. 11, 1972.

71. LPS Nov. 9, 1972, 3–5, 12–15; cf. YAOH III:29.

72. According to Israel's Central Bureau of Statistics (www.cbs.gov.il), the population of Israel at the end of 1997 comprised 4.83 million Jews and 1.07 million Arabs. A Palestinian census the same year (www.pcbs.org) found 2.9 million Palestinians in the Gaza Strip and West Bank. Both sets of numbers include East Jerusalem Arabs, so an adjusted figure for the total Arab population in Israel, the West Bank, and the Gaza Strip is approximately 3.8 million, alongside 4.8 million Jews.

73. LPS Nov. 9, 1972, 54–57, 59–62, 66.

74. Katzover, interview; Menachem Felix, interview; Etzion, interview. DC 21, an early handwritten draft of reasons for settling near Shekhem begins with the passage in Genesis, followed by other biblical references to the city. DC 39, "Daf Divuah," a report to members of the settlement group, describes meetings with Galili, who said "the time is not right" for seeking cabinet approval for settling near Nablus, and with Peres and Deputy Transportation Minister Gad Yaacobi of Rafi, who promised to contact Dayan for them.

75. Quandt, 138–140; Marilyn Berger, "Nixon Assures Mrs. Meir of Aid," *Washington Post*, Mar. 2, 1973, A1; William Beecher, "Israelis Will Buy More Jets in U.S.; Total Is Put at 48," *New York Times*, Mar. 14, 1973, 1; Bundy, 433.

76. NARA, RG59 Central Files 1970–73, POL 28 Jordan: Tel Aviv cables 1282, 2534, 2768, 2770, 2784, 3398, Jerusalem cables 345, 367, 368, Amman cables 1793, 1837, 1851, 1891, 1926, 1944, U.N. cable 1285, Washington cable 67073; Demant, 253–257; Gazit, *Peta'im*, 228.

77. NARA, RG59 Central Files 1970–73, POL 28 Jordan, Tel Aviv cable 2768.

78. LPS, Apr. 12, 1973, 18–22.

79. LPS, Apr. 12, 1973, 22–25, 27.

80. LPS, Apr. 12, 1973, 26.

81. LPS, Apr. 12, 1973, 37–41.

82. LPS, Apr. 12, 1973, 42–45, 58.

83. BAGATZ 302/72, Justice Landau's ruling.

84. NARA, NPMP Henry Kissinger office files, "President's Meeting with General Secretary Leonid Brezhnev on Saturday, June 23, 1973, at 10:30 p.m. at the Western White House, San Clemente, California" via www.gwu.edu/~nsarchiv/NSAEBB/NSAEBB98/index.htm, document 3; Henry Kissinger, *Years of Upheaval* (Boston and Toronto: Little, Brown, 1982), 296–99; Bundy, 412–13.

85. Gazit, *Peta'im*, 228.

86. Ibid., 227–29.

87. Meetings of Labor ministers regarding the electoral platform, July 26, Aug. 2, Aug. 10, 1973; YAOH, IX:11.

88. Meeting of Labor ministers regarding the electoral platform, Aug. 10, 1973, 11.

89. Eliav, *Eretz Hatzvi*, preface to the sixth edition (unnumbered pages).

90. LPS, Sept. 3, 1973, 36.

91. *Ma'ariv*, Sept. 4, 1973.

92. Eliav, interview.

93. *Davar*, Sept. 20, 1973.

94. Kissinger, *Years of Upheaval*, 431–32, 462–66; Quandt, 145.

95. Admoni, *Asor*, 118; Ad. MS 73:25.

9. Mere Anarchy Is Loosed

1. *Alei Golan*, No. 250, Oct. 8, 1973; Yehudah Harel, interview.

2. Rabinovich, 87–89, 101–12, 142–44.

3. Rabinovich, 47, 59–61, 77–78.

4. Ahron Bregman, *Israel's Wars: A History Since 1947* (New York: Routledge, 2000), 119–20; Bar-Yosef, 243–45.

5. NARA, Transcripts of Secretary of State Henry A. Kissinger Staff Meetings, 1973–1977, Secretary's Staff Meeting, Oct. 23, 1973, via www.gwu.edu/~nsarchiv/NSAEBB/NSAEBB98/index.htm.

6. Medzini, 428–29; Rabinovich, 87–89.

7. NARA, RG59 Records of Henry Kissinger, Box 1.

8. Medzini, 428–29; Rabinovich, 21.

9. NARA, NPMP National Security Council Files, Box 638, Arab Republic of Egypt IX, Cairo cable 3023, via www.gwu.edu/~nsarchiv/NSAEBB/NSAEBB98/index.htm, and see notes there at Document 24; Stein, 4, 72; Kissinger, *Years of Upheaval*, 481–82; Rabinovich, 22, 26.

10. www.izkor.gov.il/izkor86.asp?t=95484; Chaim Sabbato, *Te'um Kavvanot* (Adjusting Sights) (Tel Aviv: Yediot Aharonot, 1999), 9–12, 34–35, 41–42, 88–90. Answering a question from my son in Feb. 2005, Sabbato stated that book is strictly autobiographical.

11. *Alei Golan*, No. 250, Oct. 8, 1973; Yehudah Harel, interview; Bar Yosef, 373.

12. Psalms 118:25.

13. Sabbato, 84–98, 150–51.

14. www.izkor.gov.il/izkor86.asp?t=93817.

15. www.izkor.gov.il/izkor86.asp?t=96540.

16. Bar Yosef, 373–76.

17. Ibid., 389–91.

18. Ibid., 394; Medzini, 437.

19. Medzini, 437–39.

20. Haim Gouri, *Shirim* (Collected Poems) (Jerusalem: Bialik Institute/Hakibbutz Hame'uhad, 1998), vol. 1, 238.

21. Gouri, *Shirim* II, 105; Gouri, interview.

22. Rabinovich, 301, 307ff; Morris, *Victims*, 407–11.

23. Rabinovich, 417ff; Morris, *Victims*, 423–33.

24. Kissinger, *Years of Upheaval*, 481–83, 498–99, 522–23, 561; NARA Transcripts of Secretary of State Henry A. Kissinger Staff Meetings, 1973–1977, Secretary's Staff Meeting, Oct. 23, 1973, via www.gwu.edu/~nsarchiv/NSAEBB/NSAEBB98/index.htm.

25. Rabinovich, 476. Kissinger's approval for Israel's continued advance is clear in both NPMP, HAKO, Box 39, HAK Trip—Moscow, Tel Aviv, London—Oct. 20–23, 1973, Moscow cable 13148, Oct. 21, 1973, and NARA RG59, SN 70–73, POL 7 US/Kissinger, Kissinger-Meir Memcon, Oct. 23, 1973, both via www.gwu.edu/~nsarchiv/NSAEBB/NSAEBB98/index.htm.

26. Kalinov, 6.

27. Rabinovich, 497.

28. Rabinovich, 497.

29. NARA, Transcripts of Secretary of State Henry A. Kissinger Staff Meetings, 1973–1977, Secretary's Staff Meeting, Oct. 23, 1973, via www.gwu.edu/~nsarchiv/NSAEBB/NSAEBB98/index.htm.

30. Kissinger, *Years of Upheaval*, 581.

31. Rabinovich, 478–88.

32. Yehudah Amital, *Hama'alot Mima'amakim* (Jerusalem/Alon Shvut, 5734), 11–12.

33. *Alon Shvut*, 27 Marheshvan 5736 (Nov. 12, 1974), lists what it refers to as "most" of the students after the war, totaling 148 Israeli students and 26 foreign ones.

34. Amital, 12.

35. Festinger et al.; Albert I. Baumgarten, ed., *Apocalyptic Time* (Leiden, Boston, Koln: Brill, 2000), x–xiii.

36. Amital, 12, 26–27.

37. Amital, 18–19. The words can also be translated as "the meaning of the Jewish people's victory."

38. Amital, 22–23.

39. Ibid., 31–32.

40. Returnees included men whose military task had been to defend the settlement, and others who were between units when war erupted.

41. *Alei Golan*, No. 250, Oct. 8, 1973, No. 253, Nov. 2, 1973; Bar, interview; Yehudah Harel, interview; Meinrat, interview.

42. Admoni, *Asor*, 119.

43. *Alie Golan*, No. 253, Nov. 2, 1973; Yehudah Harel, interview; Admoni, *Asor*, 123; Ad. MS 73:44.

44. "Arabs Hold 6-Hour Summit in Kuwait," *Washington Post*, Nov. 2, 1973, A20.

45. Ad. MS 74:36.

46. NARA, RG59 Central Files 1970–73, Pol 27 Arab-ISR, Kissinger-Ismail memcon Nov. 2, 1973; "Arabs Hold . . . ," *Washington Post*.

47. Kissinger, *Years of Upheaval*, 760–61.

48. Beilin, 141–42.

49. ISA 106/810/2P, Labor Party Central Committee, Dec. 5, 1973; Penniman, 135.

50. "Separation of Forces Agreement Between Israel and Egypt January 18, 1974," www.mfa.gov.il/MFA/Peace+Process/Guide+to+the+Peace+Process/Israel-Egypt+Separation+of+Forces+Agreement+–+1974.htm; Quandt, 199–200; Morris, *Victims*, 438; Rabinovich, 494.

51. Bernard Gwertzman, "Kissinger Is Given Syrian Proposals On Opening Talks," *New York Times*, Jan. 21, 1974, 1; Kissinger, *Years of Upheaval*, 851.

52. NARA, RG59 Central Files 1970–73, POL ISR-US, Memcon Kissinger-Meir et al., Dec. 16, 1973.

53. *Merom Golan: Reshit*, 151–53.

54. Arnon Lapid, "Hazmanah Levekhi," originally published in *Shdemot*, no. 53 (Winter 5754) (1974): 50, via www.notes.co.il/tirza/7754.asp.

55. The Hebrew term used by Porat, *hallel*, refers specifically to Psalms 113–18, part of the liturgy for holidays commemorating miraculous redemption, such as Passover.

56. Hanan Porat, Oct. 30, 2003.

57. Shafat, 11–17.

58. There is continuing scholarly debate on the meaning of "fundamentalism" outside of the term's original Christian context and on whether Gush Emunim fits into the category. See Laurence J. Silberstein, ed., *Jewish Fundamentalism in Comparative Perspective* (New York and London: New York University Press, 1993).

59. MEI-MR, unnumbered file, "Gush Emunim—Nispah Mispar 1," undated; Porat, interview.

60. Shafat, 14–18; Shvut, 47–48; Yehuda Ben-Meir, interview.

61. Shafat, 18, 22–24, 27; MEI-MR, unnumbered file, Gush Emunim flyer of Adar 9, 5754 (Mar. 3, 1974); *Merom Golan: Reshit*, 155.

62. Rabinovich, 499–501.

63. Medzini, 471.

64. YTA 15Galili/3/9/71.

65. YTA 15Allon/25/3.

66. Medzini, 472.

67. Medzini, 472–73; MEI-MR, unnumbered file, Gush Emunim flyer of Adar 9, 5754 (Mar. 3, 1974); cf. Golan, *Shimon Peres*, 142–43.

68. Medzini, 474–75.

69. See Rabinovich, 503–4, and Shapira, *Yigal Allon*, 486, for conflicting evaluations of the significance of Dayan's proposal.

70. Shapira, *Yigal Allon*, 492.

71. Ad. MS 74:11.

72. Ad. MS 74:11–13.

73. Golan, *Shimon Peres*, 143.

74. Ibid., 5.

75. Ibid. 19–88; Medzini, 476–77.

76. Rabin, 418.

77. Golan, *Shimon Peres*, 145–47; Medzini, 477.

78. The Jerusalem Report staff, *Shalom, Friend: The Life and Legacy of Yitzhak Rabin*, ed. David Horovitz (New York: Newmarket Press, 1996), 28–30, 37–39, 46–47.

79. Medzini, 477.

80. Shapira, *Yigal Allon*, 344–47; Morris, *Victims*, 236–37.

81. Rabin, 417–18.

82. Medzini, 477; Rabin, 421.

83. Sabato, 153–57.

84. *Gvilei Esh*, 554; www.izkor.gov.il/izkor86.asp?t=96801.

85. Ravitzky, 188–89.

86. Ibid., 189–90.

87. Kissinger's description of his goals comes at the beginning of his detailed description of the shuttle in *Years of Upheaval*, 1032–1110. Additional material on the shuttle comes from NARA RG59, records of Henry Kissinger, 1973–77, Box 8.

88. Kissinger, *Years of Upheaval*, 1042–43, 1052.

89. Ibid., 1044–46.

90. Ibid., 1071, cf. 1052.

91. Haynes Johnson, "President Hands Over Transcripts," *Washington Post*, May 1, 1974, A1.

92. Medzini, 477; Matti Golan, *The Secret Conversations of Henry Kissinger: Step-by-Step Diplomacy in the Middle East* (New York: Quadrangle/New York Times Book Co., 1976), 188.

93. Porat, for instance, later claimed that "If it were up to America, we would have retreated from the Golan Heights." Porat, interview.

94. *Merom Golan: Reshit*, 163–64. According to Golan, *Secret Conversations*, 211, Meir and Dayan decided before Kissinger arrived to give up all of Quneitrah, but doled out the concession in small bits. It is possible Merom Golan settlers received an intimation of this decision. Yehudah Harel enjoyed close ties with Yisrael Galili.

95. See, for instance, Shafat, 56–58; Terence Smith, "Israelis Protest Yielding to

Syria," *New York Times*, May 7, 1974, 7; B. Ehrlich, "Keshet: Hamered Hakadosh," *Nekuda*, No. 100, July 11, 1986, 12.

96. Kissinger, *Years of Upheaval*, 1052.

97. Shafat, 56.

98. Kissinger, *Years of Upheaval*, 1043.

99. NARA, RG59, records of Henry Kissinger, 1973–1977, Box 8, Memcon of Kissinger-Meir meeting, May 17, 1974, 10:35–11:35 A.M.

100. Kissinger, *Years of Upheaval*, 1082.

101. Ibid., 1052.

102. Terence Smith, "Israelis Protest Yielding to Syria," *New York Times*, May 7, 1974, 7; Shafat, 59–60; Porat, interview.

103. Bernard Gwertzman, "Kissinger Believes Syrian-Israeli Decision Is Near," *New York Times*, May 11, 1974, 2.

104. The description here of Keshet's founding draws on Yehudah Harel, "Ledatah Shel Keshet," GA, 055/039/01; Ehrlich, "Keshet"; Yehudah Harel, interview; Ad. MS 74:17–18; Porat, interview.

105. MEI-MR, unnumbered file.

106. Kissinger, *Years of Upheaval*, 1094–110; Quandt, 212–14; Jehuda Wallach, *Atlas Carta Letoldot Medinat Yisrael: Asor Shlishi* (Carta's Atlas of Israel: The Third Decade 1971–1981) (Jerusalem: Carta, 1983), 112; www.izkor.gov.il/izkor86.asp?t= 96801.

107. *Merom Golan: Reshit*, 166.

10. Confrontation

1. Gush Emunim–linked sources on the Hawarah settlement bid include: *Elon Moreh: Hiddush Hayishuv Hayhudi Beshomron* (Jerusalem: Gush Emunim, 5736); Shafat, 67ff; Shvut, 49–50, supplemented by interviews with Katzover and Etzion. Outside sources include: Yosef Walter, " 'Yom Krav Arokh' Leyad Shekhem," *Ma'ariv*, June 6, 1974; "Mefanim Bekhoah Hamitnahalim Mishekhem," *Davar*, June 6, 1974; Demant, 312ff; Gazit, *Peta'im*, 231. There are factual discrepancies between accounts; for instance, Shvut describes the encampment as lasting two days and Gazit as three, but contemporary press reports show it was set up and evacuated on June 5.

2. DC 67, letter to Rabin, May 31, 1974; DC 6, draft of letter to Peres.

3. DC 5, minutes of a meeting of the group's representatives with prime minister Meir; DC 95, "Duah Al Pe'ilut Hakvutzah," report to members, early 1974; DC 43, "Daf Divuah Lahaverim," report to members, Apr. 15, 1974; Demant, 306–9; Katzover, interview.

4. A striking example of such thinking is Gershon Shafat's *Gush Emunim*. Shafat, a founder of Gush Emunim, consistently uses strength and weakness as his standard for judging politicians and activists, and consistently finds Laborites weak. The Gush Emunim platform written by Porat (see page 267), shows the same mind-set.

5. Etzion, interview.

6. DC 43, "Daf Divuah Lahaverim," Apr. 15, 1974; Shvut, 48; Katzover, interview; Porat, interview.

7. "Statement to the Knesset by Prime Minister Rabin, 3 June 1974," www.mfa. gov.il/MFA/Foreign%20Relations/Israels%20Foreign%20Relations%20since% 201947/1947–1974/31%20Statement%20to%20the%20Knesset%20by%20Prime%20 Minister%20Rabi; *Davar,* June 3–4, 1974.

8. Porat, interview; Katzover, interview; Walter, " 'Yom Krav,' " *Ma'ariv,* June 6, 1974. Where not otherwise cited, the rest of my account of the Hawarah incident is based on the sources in note 1 above.

9. Walter, " 'Yom Krav' "; Shvut, 49, gives a similar account, citing Porat as present at the meeting. Porat have been Walter's source as well. The account, in any case, is consistent with Peres's known views at the time. Peres's memoir—Shimon Peres, *Battling for Peace: Memoirs,* ed. David Landau (London: Weidenfeld & Nicolson, 1995)—does not mention this meeting.

10. Walter, " 'Yom Krav' "; Shvut, 49, citing Porat.

11. Gazit, *Peta'im,* 233, citing internal army reports, says the base offered was Kaddum, west of Nablus; Demant, 316, says it was Yosef, close to the Jordan Rift area that was part of the government's settlement map.

12. *Davar,* June 7, 1974, 2.

13. Berman, 32.

14. Cf. Berman, 59–62, on student-left organizations of the late 1960s that created an "atmosphere of confrontation, which turned giddy and hot, which created a festival atmosphere, which got hotter."

15. Kissinger, *Years of Upheaval,* 1123–43; Quandt, 215–17; Bundy, 464.

16. The risk of renewed war is a motif running through Kissinger's talks in this period. NARA, RG59, Records of Henry Kissinger 1973–1977, Box 8.

17. Kissinger, *Years of Renewal,* 360–61.

18. NARA, RG59, Records of Henry Kissinger, 1973–1977, Box 8, Kissinger-Allon Memcon, July 31, 1974.

19. NARA, RG59, Records of Henry Kissinger, 1973–1977, Box 8, Kissinger-Rabin Memcon, June 17, 1974.

20. "Political Program Adopted at the 12th Session of the Palestine National Council," www.palestine-un.org/plo/doc_one.html.

21. Kissinger, *Years of Renewal,* 375–76; cf. Shapira, *Aviv Heldo,* 487–88, on Rabin's impatience with his former mentor.

22. Kissinger, *Years of Renewal,* 364. Peres, 164–65, 301, describes his views on "functional compromise." Cf. NARA National Security Council files, Box 612, Israel, vol. 16, State Department briefing paper, July 1974, describing three possible outlines of an interim agreement with Jordan. Though unattributed, the first is Hussein's, the second roughly fits Allon's, and the third is apparently Peres's.

23. NARA, RG 59, Central Files, 1967–69, Pol 28 Jordan, airgram A-113.

24. NARA, RG 59, Central Files, 1967–69, POL Israel-US, Memo 12241, Sept. 9, 1968.

25. NARA, National Security Council files, Box 612, Israel, vol. 16, memo 3229.

26. YAOH XVII:13.

27. Admoni, *Asor,* 128; Ad. MS 74:25; *Davar,* July 18, 1974, 1.

28. NARA, National Security Council files, Box 612, Israel, vol. 16, State Department cable 159161, July 23, 1974.

29. NARA, National Security Council files, Box 612, Israel, vol. 16, Tel Aviv cable 4185, July 25, 1974.

30. YTA 15Galili/4/10/1; Shemtov, 97–100; YAOH XVII:21; "Israelis Affirm Ban on Any Talks With Palestinians," *New York Times*, July 22, 1974, 3. Reflecting Peres's views, Golan, *Secret Conversations*, 220, interprets the decision as barring an interim agreement. Rabin's later actions indicate that he, too, took this position.

31. YTA 15Allon/25/7, 29 Tamuz 5734 (July 19, 1974). A second Gush Emunim letter, YTA 15Allon/25/8, 19 Av 5734 (Aug. 7, 1974) complains that Allon has not responded to the original request. A notation indicates that a meeting may have been set for Aug. 14.

32. Katzover, interview; Demant, 317–18; cf. Admoni, *Asor*, 144.

33. Meir Harnoy, *Hamitnahalim* (The Settlers) (Or Yehudah: Maariv, 1994), 10–15. Harnoy's memoir does not date the events, but his description fits the early months of Gush Emunim's public campaign.

34. Katzover, interview.

35. Yeshayahu Ben-Porat, "Beshevah Hahitapkut Vehametinut," *Yediot Aharanot*, July 31, 1974; Demant, 320.

36. *Jerusalem Post*, July 26, 1974, says Porat was open to the compromise but the Elon Moreh group rejected it.

37. Account of Sharon's "diversion" from Shafat, 78–79. Other sources on the first Sebastia bid include *Elon Moreh: Hiddush*; Demant, 320–26; Katzover, interview; *Davar, Ma'ariv, Yediot Aharonot*, July 26–31, 1974.

38. *Elon Moreh: Hiddush*.

39. Moshe Shamir, "Pitom, Ba'emtza Dibra Hatzionut," *Ma'ariv*, Aug. 2, 1974, 2.

40. *Ma'ariv*, July 30, 1974, 3; Demant, 320; Katzover, interview.

41. Ben-Porat, "Beshevah Hahitapkut."

42. *Davar*, July 28, 1974, 1.

43. Shafat, 83.

44. *Ma'ariv*, July 30, 1974, 3.

45. *Davar*, July 30, 1974, 3; *Ma'ariv*, July 30, 1974, 13.

46. Negbi, 36.

47. *Ma'ariv*, July 30, 1974, 3; *Davar*, July 30, 1974, 1; DK, July 31, 1974, 2569. Peres's dovish critics included Yossi Sarid and Yitzhak Ben-Aharon; the supporter of the Sebastia settlers was David Coren.

48. Shafat, 98.

49. NARA, RG59, Records of Henry Kissinger, 1973–1977, Box 8, Kissinger-Allon Memcon, July 31, 1974.

50. Dorothy McCardle, "17 Years After the Seminar," *Washington Post*, July 31, 1974, B1.

51. YAOH XX:16.

52. NARA, RG59, Records of Henry Kissinger, 1973–1977, Box 9, Kissinger-Allon Memcon, Aug. 1, 1974.

53. YTA 15Allon/25/8. The text is in English, with a handwritten annotation in Hebrew, "Oral message transmitted at my request to Kissinger by Dinitz before I left U.S. Aug. 4, 1974."

54. NARA, RG59, Records of Henry Kissinger, 1973–1977, Box 9, Kissinger-Rifai Memcon, Aug. 6, 1974.

55. NARA, RG59, Records of Henry Kissinger, 1973–1977, Box 9, Kissinger-Hussein Memcon, Aug. 16, 1974. Cf. Kissinger, *Years of Renewal*, 368–70. Stein, 170; and Zak, 164–166, assert that in a secret meeting with the Israeli troika on August 29, Hussein and Rifai rejected the Jericho plan and insisted on a pullback all along the Jordan. It is unclear, though, whether Israel offered as much in direct talks as Kissinger had in his own name. In any case, it appears that the decisive obstacle was not the differences in maps, but Rabin's opposition to holding elections over an interim accord, and Hussein's uncertain position before the Rabat summit.

56. Kissinger, *Years of Renewal*, 374–81.

57. Harold H. Saunders and Cecilia Albin, *Sinai II: The Politics of International Mediation, 1974–1975 (FPI Case Studies Number 17)* (Washington, DC: Foreign Policy Institute, John Hopkins University, 1993), 30.

58. YAOH VIII:16–17.

59. Saunders and Albin, 36.

60. Demant, 356–57, 503–8; Netzer, 283–84; Golan, *Shimon Peres*, 149.

61. YTA 15Galili/4/6/1.

62. Admoni, *Asor*, 102.

63. YAOH IV:25, VI:17, XIX:32–34.

64. Admoni, *Asor*, 101–2; Netzer, 287–88; Demant, 357, states that the area was declared closed in 1972.

65. Demant, 327; *Ma'ariv*, Aug. 5, 1974.

66. Demant, 481–85. Demant gives a Jewish population of 1,200 in 1976, after some growth in the intervening two years.

67. Vered Dror, interview; Amia Lieblich, *Gilgulo Shel Makom* (Tel Aviv: Schocken, 2000), 30–31; *Gilgalon*, Sept. 30, 1974.

68. Lieblich, 35–36; Dror, interview. Buildings from this period still stood at the time of my visit.

69. Lieblich, 30–44; Hedva Ben-Tzedek, interview; Dror, interview. At its peak in 1984, the kibbutz had nearly 100 adult members. In 2004 it had about 50. Lieblich, 27; Dror, interview.

70. YTA 15Galili/2/2/35, letter of Sept. 19, 1974, to Benny, apparently Benny Marshak.

71. *Elon Moreh: Hiddush*; Shafat, 105–18.

72. *Zra'im*, Adar, 5735 (Feb.–Mar. 1975).

73. Shlomo Aviner, "Veyatza Hashem Venilham Bagoyim," *Zra'im*, Heshvan-Kislev 5734 (Oct.–Dec. 1973), 4.

74. Yehudah Amital, "Tzionut Shel Ge'ulah . . . ," *Zra'im*, Tamuz-Av 5734 (June–Aug. 1974), 3.

75. Avraham Rekanti, "Kol Eretz Yisrael Lekhol Am Yisrael," *Zra'im*, Sivan 5734 (May–June 1974).

76. Osnat, "Ha'aretz Hazot Einah Stam Od Ahat," *Zra'im*, Sivan 5734 (May–June 1974).

77. David Zohar, "Lo Zo Haderekh," *Zra'im*, Elul 5734 (Aug.–Sept. 1974).

78. Osnat, "Emunah Be'at'haltah Dige'ulah . . . ," *Zra'im*, Tishrei 5735 (Sept.–Oct. 1974).

79. Saunders and Albin, 36–37; Kissinger, *Years of Upheaval*, 382–83; "Seventh

Arab League Summit Conference, Resolution on Palestine," mondediplo.com/focus/mideast/a2287.

80. Ma'oz, 111–116.

81. The party joined the government on Oct. 30, 1974. www.knesset.gov.il/history/eng/eng_hist8_s.htm.

82. NARA, RG59, Records of Henry Kissinger, 1973–1977 Box 25, Memcon, Nov. 7, 1974.

83. "Speech by PLO Chairman Yasser Arafat, United Nations General Assembly, New York 13 Nov. 1974," www.jmcc.org/documents/arfatun74.htm; Paul Hofmann, "Palestinians Win Right to Appear in U.N. Assembly," *New York Times*, Oct. 15, 1974, 1; Marilyn Berger, "Arafat Offers 'Olive Branch, Gun' at U.N.," *Washington Post*, Nov. 14, 1974, A1.

84. "Speech by PLO Chairman Yasser Arafat."

85. YTA 15Galili/4/10/3, Galili memo to Rabin, Oct. 20, 1974, with handwritten notation on meeting of Oct. 21.

86. YTA 15Galili/4/10/4, Galili-Rabin memo, Nov. 1, 1974; YTA 15Galili/4/10/10, Galili-Rabin memo, Dec. 16, 1974; Ad. MS 74:49.

87. Demant, 358.

88. YTA 15Galili/4/10/8, Galili-Rabin memo, Dec. 8, 1974; 15Galili/4/10/9, Galili-Rabin memo, Dec. 9, 1974.

89. E.g., 15Galili/4/10/10, Galili-Rabin memo, Dec. 16, 1974.

90. YTA 15Galili/4/10/13, Galili-Rabin memo, Jan. 7, 1975; DC 96, "Din Veheshbon Al Matzav Hagarinim" (Report on the status of settlement groups), n.d. Content places the report in Jan.–Feb. 1975.

91. Demant, 362, citing an interview by Demant with Netzer.

92. The exact date when the work began is unclear. The best estimate, in Hemdat Shani, "Mekimei Hagader—Hasipur Hamale," *Et Ofrah*, Sivan 5765 (June 2005), is that it started just before or after Rosh Hashanah in mid-September 1974.

93. Porat, interview; Etzion, interview.

94. *Ma'ariv*, Jan. 6, 1975; *Davar*, Jan. 7, 1975.

11. Last Train to Sebastia

1. *Gush Emunim—Dapei Meda*, No. 2, Adar 5735 (Feb.–Mar. 1975), 1; cf. Yehudah Litani, "Hitnahalut Besebastia," *Ha'aretz*, Mar. 6, 1975.

2. *Gush Emunim—Dapei Meda*, No. 1, Tevet 5735 (Dec. 1974–Jan. 1975), 2. The Elon Moreh group's March settlement bids were code-named "Operation Dedication" and "Operation Stubbornness," indicating the message the group wished to convey. Shafat, 148, 152. Shafat also links the settlement attempts with the Kissinger shuttles, 142–43.

3. Demant, 352–53. Citing other activists but not Levinger himself, Demant asserts that Levinger backed Porat. If so, it was a step back from the stance he took earlier regarding Kfar Etzion and later during the final Sebastia bid.

4. Demant, 361; Shafat, 143–49.

5. DC, 139. The Hebrew phrase, *"limsor et nafshenu,"* can figuratively connote

intense dedication, but literally means readiness to die, especially in a religious context.

6. *Ha'aretz, Davar, Yediot Aharonot,* Mar. 7, 1975; Shafat, 152; Henry Kamm, "Israelis Report Capturing Ship Used by Guerrillas," *New York Times,* Mar. 7, 1975, 1; John M. Goshko, "Hotel Raid Aimed at Egypt," *Washington Post,* Mar. 9, 1975, 25.

7. *Ma'ariv,* Mar. 11, 1975. The group arrived on the night of March 10.

8. The group arrived on March 14 and was evicted March 15. *Yediot Aharonot, Ha'aretz,* Mar. 16, 1975.

9. *Ma'ariv, Yediot Aharonot, Hatzofeh, Ha'aretz,* Mar. 19-21, 1975; DC 16.

10. Quandt, 235.

11. Saunders, interview.

12. Saunders and Albin, 46.

13. Kissinger, *Years of Upheaval,* 397, 416; cf. Saunders and Albin, 46-47, 62-65.

14. Kissinger, *Years of Upheaval,* 412-24; Saunders and Albin, 55-59.

15. Kissinger, *Years of Upheaval,* 388; cf. 416, where Kissinger himself attributes that view to Israel's leaders.

16. OA 2, Garin Shilo membership list, dated "1974." Membership may have grown by winter 1975.

17. Etzion, interview.

18. OA 2, Tevet 5735 (Dec. 1974–Jan. 1975).

19. Joshua 18:23.

20. OA 2. A handwritten notation dates the flyer as Adar 5735 (Feb.–Mar. 1975).

21. OA 2, Tevet 5735 (Dec. 1974–Jan. 1975).

22. Netzer, 290.

23. Netzer, interview; Admoni, *Asor,* 144.

24. DC 96, "Din Veheshbon Al Matzav Hagarinim" (Report on the status of settlement groups), n.d. Content places the report in Jan.–Feb. 1975.

25. OA 2.

26. Yehudah Etzion, Feb. 10 and Mar. 2, 2004; Admoni, 151.

27. Etzion, interview.

28. Yoram Rasis-Tal, "Mitel Aviv Hama'atirah El Mahaneh Ein Yabrud," *Et Ofrah,* Iyar 17, 5743 (Apr. 30, 1983).

29. Netzer, 290; Etzion, interview; Porat, interview.

30. Rasis-Tal, "Mitel Aviv."

31. Yosef Tzuriel, "Ba'u Kefo'alim—Vetaku Yated Shel Keva," *Ma'ariv,* June 5, 1975, records conflicting accounts from residents six weeks after the incident. Demant, 372-73, describes Porat as driving to the Defense Ministry on April 20 and interrupting Peres in the midst of another meeting. Netzer 290 describes a memo he wrote to Peres on April 21 stating that "approval of establishing a civilian 'work camp' next to the the IDF camps at Ba'al Hatzor" was in progress. *Gush Emunim—Dapei Meda,* No. 3, Sivan 5735 (May–June 1975), refers to two days of negotiations. DC 122, "Ofrah—Gader Shehekimah Yishuv," an early pamphlet produced at the settlement, describes Porat as meeting "a high-ranking military man" the first night, who in turn spoke to Peres and received permission for the group to stay.

32. Netzer, 290.

33. YTA 15Galili/2/2/52, Apr. 29, 1975.

34. YTA 15Galili/2/2/107, handwritten note to Rabin's military secretary, Oct. 1975, regarding a conversation with Netzer.

35. Ad MS 75:22, citing the full text of a note from Galili to Moshe Kol, July 8, 1975. Kol had sent Galili a copy of *Gush Emunim—Dapei Meda*, No. 3, describing Ofrah.

36. The picture of Galili's younger and older selves at war is based on Demant, 461–65.

37. Netzer, 290.

38. DC 30, "Elon Moreh—Pnimi Lehavrei Hagarin Bilvad," late April 1975, states that "about a week" after the group's arrival at Ein Yabrud, residents included three families.

39. Etzion, interview.

40. Rasis-Tal, "Mitel Aviv."

41. Netzer, 291. Admoni, *Asor*, 146, 150–54, also cites assistance that Peres and his aides gave to Gush Emunim settlement efforts, particularly Ofrah.

42. Demant, 364.

43. Shafat, 160–61; OA, minutes of general meeting, Sivan 17, 5735 (May 27, 1975); *Gush Emunim—Dapei Meda* No. 3; Etzion, interview; Porat, interview. The general meeting minutes show a consensus that the settlement would not be a commune.

44. *Dapei Meda*, No. 3. The content indicates it was written after the May 27, 1975, general meeting and before Yossi Sarid's early June visit.

45. Ran Kislev, "Hitnahalut Emunim Hukmah Mizrahit Leramallah Behashai—Lifnei Hodesh Vahetzi," *Ha'aretz*, June 4, 1975; Sarid, interview; Etzion, interview.

46. *Yediot Aharonot*, *Ma'ariv*, June 18, 1975; Netzer, 291, Ad. MS 75:22.

47. Ad. MS 75:22.

48. Shafat, 160; *Dapei Meda*, No. 3. Admoni, *Asor*, 150, comes to the same conclusion.

49. MEI-MR, Hanan Porat, "Ki Ayin Be'ayin Yiru Beshuv Hashem Tzion," *Emunim*, no. 1.

50. Sharon, 341, 346–47.

51. Golan, *Shimon Peres*, 166–69. Officially Sharon was to be a "general adviser," but his areas of responsibilities were well known. Cf. YRC shomarc 2 0014, Mapam political committee meeting June 4, 1975.

52. Gouri, interview.

53. Golan, *Shimon Peres*, 169; Demant, 375–76.

54. Ad. MS 75:24.

55. Ad. MS 75:28–29.

56. Demant, 361–62.

57. MEI-MR *Emunim*, No. 1, 15, says 38 square meters; OA 6/5 "Du'ah Tzevet Hahityashvut Shel Gush Emunim" (Gush Emunim settlement team report), autumn 1975, 4, says 23 sq. mi.

58. Demant, 508.

59. YAOH VI:17.

60. Ad. MS 75:28–29.

61. Ad. MS 75:42-44.

62. Admoni, *Asor*, 160-61.

63. Admoni, interview; Sarid, interview.

64. Oded Lifshitz, private papers, Rafiah journal, Feb. 9, 1975, and photographs of Sukkot demolition work from "Leket Itonut Benose: Pithat Rafiah" (Hashomer Hatza'ir: 1975); Douer, 225-27; Lifshitz, interview.

65. Kissinger, *Years of Upheaval*, 428.

66. Quandt, 238-41; Saunders and Albin, 73-84, 91-98.

67. Shafat, 168-71; Harnoy, 16-17; Henry Kamm, "Israelis Are Found Anxious . . . ," *New York Times*, Aug. 25, 1975, 1; Kissinger, *Years of Upheaval*, 452. Harnoy's description relates to protests during various Kissinger visits.

68. Saunders and Albin, 78-84; Quandt, 242-43.

69. Paul Hofmann, "Why and How Anti-Zionism Move Won," *New York Times*, Nov. 12, 1975, 17.

70. "General Assembly Resolution 3379. Elimination of all forms of racial discrimination," domino.un.org/UNISPAL.NSF/0/761c1063530766a7052566a2005b74 d1?OpenDocument.

71. Hofmann, "Why and How."

72. "General Assembly Resolution 3375, Invitation to the Palestine Liberation Organization," domino.un.org/UNISPAL.NSF/0/7e0524b7ead4a9e4852560de004 efdc7?OpenDocument.

73. YTA 15Galili/4/10/32, Galili to Rabin, Nov. 24, 1975; Ad. MS 75:45-48.

74. *Ma'ariv*, Nov. 26, 1975; Demant, 380-81; *Elon Moreh: Hiddush*.

75. MEI-MR, unnumbered files and OA 6/5; *Ma'ariv*, Nov. 30, 1975.

76. *Yediot Aharonot, Ma'ariv, Hatzofeh*, Dec. 1-2, 1975; Yosef Walter, "Kol Haderakhim Holikhu Lesebastia," *Ma'ariv*, Dec. 5, 1975; Shafat, 180-83.

77. Rabin, 550.

78. Peres, 169-70.

79. Terence Smith, "In Israel After U.N. Vote, Feelings of Isolation and Frustration," *New York Times*, Dec. 3, 1975, 2.

80. *Ha'aretz, Ma'ariv*, Dec. 3, 1975. Rabin, 550, cites the conference as reason for delay.

81. Ad. MS 75:50; cf. Netzer, 293.

82. Shafat, 189; *Gush Emunim*, Adar Bet 5736 (Mar. 1976), 6.

83. *Alon Ofrah*, Hanukkah 5736 (Dec. 1975).

84. Ad. MS 75:23; Netzer, 292.

85. *Ma'ariv, Ha'aretz, Yediot Aharonot, Hatzofeh*, Dec. 3-7, 1975.

86. *Ma'ariv*, Dec. 4, 1975.

87. MEI-MR, unnumbered files of newspaper advertisements and press releases. The quotation is from an ad published during the Sebastia confrontation. The idea repeats itself in various formulations in other advertisements and statements that week, e.g., DC 111, Dec. 3, 1975.

88. Ma'oz, 115-18, 124-25; Menachem Klein, interview.

89. *Ma'ariv*, Dec. 5, 1975.

90. *Ma'ariv*, Dec. 7, 1975.

91. Ma'oz, 104.

92. *Ha'aretz*, Dec. 3, 1975.

93. Shafat, 191, 202. Shafat says Gush Emunim deliberately cultivated fear of civil war in case of evacuation, while claiming the movement did not actually intend to engage in violence.

94. *Ma'ariv*, Dec. 5, 1975.

95. Original text in MEI-MR, unnumbered file of press releases.

96. MEI-MR, unnumbered file, handwritten text designated for distribution Tevet 3 (Dec. 7, 1975); cf. Yosef Walter, "Kol Haderakhim . . . ," in which settler leaders make the same threat; Shafat, 202; Demant, 398, quotes Porat that "as a man defends his home" was the public line, and "Everyone could understand what he wanted."

97. *Ma'ariv*, Dec. 7, 1975. No minutes would have been taken at a meeting on the Sabbath including Orthodox Jews.

98. *Ma'ariv*, Dec. 7, 1975; Shafat, 197.

99. *Ma'ariv*, Dec. 7, 1975; Shvut, frontispiece.

100. Haim Gouri, "Yom Valailah Bashomron," *Yediot Aharonot*, Dec. 12, 1975.

101. Gouri, interview. In columns relatively soon after the Sebastia confrontation, Gouri defended the Allon plan, e.g., Haim Gouri, "Bamarbolet," *Davar*, June 10, 1977, 2.

102. Gouri, "Yom Valailah."

103. Ibid.

104. Ibid.; Gouri, interview.

105. Genesis 37:16.

106. Gouri, "Yom Valailah."

107. A number of conflicting—and sometimes internally inconsistent—accounts have been published on the dénouement of the Sebastia confrontation. I have treated the small number of contemporary notes by participants as primary sources, followed by contemporary reportage and memos written soon after. Even early sources are affected by the desire of key figures to defend their roles or take credit for perceived achievements. In using memoirs, my own interviews with participants, and other work depending on oral testimony, I have sought verification of details by independent sources. Demant includes valuable interview material with several figures who were no longer alive at the time of my research. Another valuable source is Reuven Pedatzur, "Het Kaddum," *Ha'aretz*, Oct. 3, 1990, B2. The brief account in Peres's memoirs (Peres, 169–70) does not jibe with documentary evidence, and the chronology in Golan, *Shimon Peres*, 173–74, is distorted, unfortunately making both accounts questionable. More details of the events of Dec. 7–8, 1975, may emerge if and when currently classified material is released.

108. *Yediot Aharonot*, Dec. 8, 1975; Demant, 393.

109. *Davar*, Dec. 10, 1975. Peres also claimed, in the meeting of the Alignment Knesset delegation, that if settlers offered to move to a nearby army base, he had been authorized to tell them that their proposal would be discussed. It is possible he added this possibility to the committee of four's decisions after the fact, in order to provide a justification for the senior ministers' actions.

110. *Yediot Aharonot*, Dec. 8, 1975; Demant, 393.

111. *Yediot Aharonot*, *Ma'ariv*, Dec. 8, 1975.

112. Porat, interview; Gouri, interview.

113. Demant, 394; Gouri, interview.

114. Haim Gouri, "Hakera," *Davar*, Dec. 8, 1975; Pedatzur, "Het Kaddum"; Demant, 395-96; Gouri, interview; *Ma'ariv*, Dec. 8, 1975, 1. Gouri's first account in *Davar* does not specify a number of settlers or the base in which they would stay.

115. Gouri, interview; Pedatzur, "Het Kaddum"; *Ma'ariv, Yediot Aharonot*, Dec. 8, 1975; Demant, 398.

116. Pedatzur, "Het Kaddum"; Demant, 399; *Ma'ariv*, Dec. 8, 1975, 1.

117. YTA 15Galili/95/70/50.

118. Rabin, 550.

119. Demant, 400-401. Pedatzur, "Het Kaddum," quotes Gur confirming the conversation took place, while claiming Rabin was also hesitant to act. Demant cites Galili's top aide Arnan Azaryahu as saying Peres also threatened to resign rather than "order shooting."

120. Gouri, interview; Haim Gouri, "Be'od Hodshayim-Shloshah," *Davar*, Dec. 9, 1975; Pedatzur, "Het Kaddum." *Ma'ariv*, Dec. 8, 1975, reported that in a ministerial consultation earlier in the day, Galili spoke harshly against Gush Emunim, saying, "They won't run this country."

121. Haim Gouri, personal papers. Emphasis in the original.

122. YTA 15Galili/2/2/21. Except for the last line, the text is identical with the handwritten text in Gouri's possession.

123. Another note Gouri received that evening from Galili states, "I've spoken with Yitzhak." Haim Gouri, personal papers. Cf. Pedatzur, "Het Kaddum," on ministerial reactions, and Demant, 403. Rabin's note of the next day to the cabinet members, YTA 15Galili/95/7/50, lends weight to the claim they lacked advance knowledge. However, in a note to Gouri dated May 2, 1976, summarizing the affair, Galili wrote that he and Gouri had spoken while the cabinet was still meeting.

124. Gouri, "Yom Valailah"; Gouri, interview.

125. Both have described the discussion in these terms. Demant, 405-6; Shvut, 55-56; Porat, interview.

126. Gouri, "Be'od Hodshayim-Shloshah"; Pedatzur, "Het Kaddum"; Gouri, interview.

127. Demant, 408.

128. Haim Gouri, private papers. A copy of the same document appears in Shvut, 56. Peres's former aide Moshe Netzer confirmed to me that the writing was Peres's. The same wording appears in Rabin's notice to ministers of the agreement, YTA 15Galili/95/7/50, from the same day.

129. Shafat, 216; Demant, 410. Rabin's note to cabinet ministers, YTA 15Galili/95/7/50, says Peres "was in constant contact with me" during the negotiations.

130. Shvut, 56.

131. YTA 15Galili/95/7/50.

132. "Rabin Iyem Lehitpater Bediyun So'er Shel Si'at Hama'arakh al Sebastia," *Davar*, Dec. 10, 1975.

133. Rabin, 249-50.

134. *Ma'ariv, Al Hamishmar*, Dec. 10, 1975.

12. *The Fall of the House of Labor*

1. *Gush Emunim*, Adar Bet 5736 (Mar.–Apr. 1976), 6; Guga Kogen, "Kaddum. Eikh Bonim Uvdah," *Hotam—Al Hamishmar*, Feb. 20, 1976.

2. William Drummond, "Anti-Israeli Outbreak Spreads on West Bank," *Washington Post*, Mar. 12, 1976, A22.

3. Ma'oz, 124–26; Thomas W. Lippman, "Settlers, Funeral Raise West Bank Tensions," *Washington Post*, Mar. 24, 1976, A10; *Gush Emunim—Daf Kesher*, Shvat 5736 (Jan.–Feb. 1976), lists the population of Kiryat Arba as 1,444, including students at a *hesder* yeshivah.

4. Mordechai Artzieli, "Ma Era Behevron," *Ha'aretz*, Mar. 24, 1976, 11.

5. *Hatzofeh*, Mar. 18, 1976; *Ha'aretz*, Mar. 19–24, 1976; Lippman, "Settlers, Funeral."

6. *Ha'aretz*, Mar. 24, 1975; Yehudah Litani, "Kaddum: Shanah Aharei," *Ha'aretz*, Dec. 8, 1976.

7. "Excerpts From Scranton's U.N. Speech," *New York Times*, Mar. 25, 1976, 4.

8. See page 143.

9. Paul Hofmann, "U.S. Veto Blocks a U.N. Resolution Criticizing Israel," *New York Times*, Mar. 26, 1976, 1; Quandt, 246.

10. Ad. MS 76:48.

11. Ad. MS 76:3.

12. *Gush Emunim*, Adar Bet 5736 (Mar.–Apr. 1976), 14.

13. Yosef Walter, "Menachem Felix Shalaf Te'udat Zehut . . . ," *Ma'ariv*, Apr. 27, 1976.

14. Netzer, 294.

15. Terence Smith, "120 Israelis in the West Bank Dig In to Hold New Settlement," *New York Times*, Apr. 3, 1976. Visiting several weeks before Walter (n. 10), Smith gave a lower number of settlers.

16. Walter, "Menachem Felix Shalaf Te'udat Zehut."

17. DC 47, 63.

18. *Davar*, Apr. 30, 1976.

19. *Ma'ariv*, May 9, 1976; Latif Dori, interview.

20. The sources for the May 9, 1976, cabinet meeting are Admoni's transcript at Ad. MS 76:7–39, and Reuven Pedatzur, "Vekaddum Le'olam Tisha'er," *Ha'aretz*, Oct. 10, 1990. The former is apparently Admoni's own notes, and may not be word for word. There are variations in official settlement figures. In a secret memo of Aug. 19, 1976, YTA 15Galili/2/3/74, Galili's office listed 68.

21. Ad. MS 76:7–16

22. Ad. MS 76:20. Ofer said 7,000 units had been completed or were under construction in settlements in occupied territory and within the Green Line, 6,000 of them in occupied territory. Out of the 7,000 total, 3,000 were still being built. He did not specify how many of those under construction were over the Green Line.

23. Ad. MS 76:29–30.

24. Ad. MS 76:21–22.

25. Ad. MS 76:23–24.

26. Ad. MS 76:33–34.

27. Ad. MS 76:24–27; Pedatzur, "Kaddum Le'olam." Likud leader Menachem

Begin publicly spoke of taking power with a coalition of 62 Knesset members if Peres's Rafi faction left Labor and joined with the Likud and National Religious Party. Amnon Rubinstein, "Kaddum, Brooklyn, Ushar Ti'unav Hamuzarim Shel Sar Habitahon, Ha'aretz," May 15, 1976.

28. Ad. MS 76:38.

29. YTA 15Galili/4/3/32.

30. Ma'ariv, May 11, 1976.

31. YTA 15Galili/4/3/32, May 31, 1976.

32. YTA 15Galili/4/10/49, June 15, 1976. Parentheses in the original.

33. YTA 15Galili/4/10/52, July 1, 1976.

34. Admoni, Asor, 178.

35. Ad. MS 76:44–45.

36. Litani, "Kaddum: Shanah Aharei"; Aryeh Avneri, "Sarei Mapam Lerabin: Matai Tefuneh Kaddum?" Yediot Ahronot, July 27, 1976; "Yadin: Hitnahalut Bekaddum—Helek Meha'anarkhia," Al Hamishmar, Aug. 6, 1976; Penniman, 151.

37. MEI-MR, unnumbered file, report on Ofrah, early 1976, sets Iyar 9, 5736, the first anniversary of Ofrah on the Hebrew calendar (May 9, 1976), as target date for completing the fence. Shani, "Mekimei Hagader," says the work began around September 1974 and took "nearly two years."

38. OA 4, "Ofrah," undated report, early to mid 1976, signed "Pinhas Wallerstein."

39. OA 6/5 "Du'ah Tzevet Hahityashvut Shel Gush Emunim" (Gush Emunim settlement team report), autumn 1975, 12, identifies Ofrah as a community settlement (yishuv kehilati), before other Gush Emunim settlements were established. The same document (7–11) introduces the community settlement concept. David Newman and Leviah Applebaum, "Hakfar Vehayishuv Hakehilati Mera'ayon Limtzi'ut," in Shvut, 157–58, states that the concept was developed that year by planner Uzi Gdor, in part to define Alon Shvut. According to DC 74, "Du'ah Hatzevet Lekiddum Hahityashvut Shel Gush Emunim" (Gush Emunim settlement team report), Sivan 5735 (May–June 1975), Gdor was working with Gush Emunim by spring 1975. Hemdat Shani, "Ofrah Agush— Hatargum Hamale," Et Ofrah, Iyar 18, 5761 (May 11, 2001), notes that Gdor was also consulting directly with Ofrah. Gdor's concept provided a definition for Ofrah and for Alon Shvut, and a direction for Gush Emunim.

40. OA 6/5 "Du'ah Tzevet Hahityashvut Shel Gush Emunim" (Gush Emunim settlement team report), autumn 1975, 7–11.

41. Litani, "Kaddum: Shanah Aharei."

42. Penniman, 138–43, 150–54, 178–79, 187; Jerusalem Report, Shalom Friend, 92–95; William E. Farrell, "Rabin's Position Is Precarious . . . ," New York Times, Nov. 21, 1976, 4; Sprinzak, 93–119, on Labor's patronage system.

43. Jerusalem Report, Shalom, Friend, 94; Beilin, 161–62.

44. Rabin, 559–60. Jerusalem Report, Shalom, Friend, 94.

45. Rabin, 560–63.

46. YTA 15Galili/4/10/70, Apr. 12, 1977.

47. YTA 15 Galili/2/3/108, Nov. 8, 1976; YTA 15Galili/2/2/117, Jan. 16, 1977; YTA 15Galili/2/3/138, Mar. 1, 1977; YTA 15/Galili/4/9A/13, Apr. 14, 1977.

48. PS, memo of Mar. 29, 1977, requesting permission for purchase, signed by Peres, Galili, and Agriculture Minister Aharon Uzan.

49. Demant, 500.
50. Rabin, 563.
51. *Ma'ariv*, May 16, 1977, 3.
52. Penniman, 179.
53. Penniman, 161.
54. Haim Gouri, "Bamarbolet," *Davar,* June 10, 1977, 2.
55. As noted above, for technical reasons there are slight discrepancies in listings of settlement numbers. As of June 20, 1977, when the Rabin government left office, there were 79 settlements. The number is based on the listing at Admoni, *Asor,* 202–6, and Admoni, interview. From the list I have subtracted settlements that did not become permanent or that were established after June 20, 1977, and have added Ofrah, Kaddum/Elon Moreh, and Kfar Ruth, located in what had been no-man's-land between Jordan and Israel before 1967. This number includes Snir, located in a pre-1967 DMZ, on land that had been claimed by Israel but de facto controlled by Syria on June 4, 1967. Note that Galili (YTA 15Galili/2/3/77) gives the number of settlements "beyond the Green Line" as 68 on Aug. 9, 1976, of which 24 were established under the Rabin government. Admoni, Ad. MS 77:40, lists a total of 33 settlements during the Rabin government, indicating that nine more were established by the end of Rabin's term than appear in Galili's count. The total would therefore be 77. That figure does not include Kaddum/Elon Moreh or Ofrah, so the actual total, again, is 79.
56. Galili, YTA 15Galili/4/7/9, gives a population of 8,090 as of Feb. 18, 1976. Demant, 524, cites an estimate of 11,000–13,000 by the end of Rabin's term. I have used the lower figure, since an increase of over 50 percent in 15 months appears unlikely, even given the wide construction of new housing.
57. Demant, 524, cites an estimate of 45,000, noting this is "generous" and based on a count of 10,300 housing units.
58. Meir Shalev, *Roman Russi* (Tel Aviv: Am Oved, 1988), 343–44, published in English as *The Blue Mountain,* trans. Hillel Halkin (Jerusalem: Domino, 1991). The translation here is mine.
59. *Ma'ariv, Yediot Aharonot,* May 20, 1977.

Epilogue: Ephemeral, for the Fourth Decade

1. BAGATZ 1661/05, statement of the respondents.
2. Negbi 44. The position was originally put forward by Attorney General Gavriel Bach during a Supreme Court hearing in BAGATZ 606/78 in which Palestinian landowners challenged expropriation of their property for the settlement of Beit El.
3. According to tables provided by the Population Administration of the Interior Ministry, 247,378 Israelis listed their legal addresses in West Bank settlements on July 31, 2005. According to the Peace Now Settlement Watch, 101 unauthorized outposts also existed at that time in the West Bank. "The West Bank—Facts and Figures—August 2005," www.peacenow.org.il/site/en/peace.asp?pi=203&docid=1430&pos=0. Settlement Watch director Dror Etkes (interview) estimated the total population of the outposts as 1,500–2,000. Most outpost residents were probably registered as residing in recognized settlements, so their number does not increase the West Bank total.

4. As of Dec. 31, 2003, 179,600 Jews lived in Jerusalem neighborhoods outside the Green Line. *Statistical Yearbook of Jerusalem 2004* (Jerusalem: Jerusalem Institute for Israel Studies, in preparation), chap. 3.

5. As of Dec. 31, 2004, 16,100 Jews were resident in the Golan. Central Bureau of Statistics, spokesperson's office, provisional figures. The Interior Ministry's Population Administration does not tabulate separate figures for the Golan.

6. As of July 31, 2005, 9,053 Israelis lived in seventeen recognized settlements, according to the Population Administration of the Interior Ministry. An estimated 174 lived in four unauthorized outposts, according to the Peace Now Settlement Watch. See "Disengagement: Profiling the Settlements—July 2005," www.peacenow. org.il/site/en/peace.asp?pi=203&docid=1369&pos=2. It is likely that most outpost residents were registered as living in the authorized Gaza settlements, so their number does not increase the total for the Gaza Strip.

7. Population Administration, Interior Ministry: 31,106 registered residents on July 31, 2005.

8. Ofrah: 2,443 residents, July 31, 2005. Population Administration, Interior Ministry.

9. Talya Sason, "Havat Da'at Beinayim Benose Ma'ahazim Bilti Murshim," legal opinion presented to Prime Minister Ariel Sharon, 2005.

10. Gershom Gorenberg, "At What Price?" *Mother Jones*, July–Aug. 2003; Dror Tzaban, "Omdan Helki Shel Taktzivei Memshalah Hamufnim Lehitnahaluyot Bagadah Hama'aravit Uvirtzu'at Azah Veshel Hatiktzuv Ha'odef Bishnat 2001," report prepared for Peace Now, January 2003; Yehezkel Lein, "Land Grab: Israel's Settlement Policy in the West Bank," trans. Shaul Vardi and Zvi Shulman (Jerusalem: B'Tselem, 2002).

11. As of Dec. 31, 2004, 21,800 non-Jews were resident in the Golan. Central Bureau of Statistics, spokesperson's office, provisional figures.

12. As of Dec. 31, 2003, 228,700 Arabs lived within the Jerusalem city limits, 98% in the land annexed in June 1967. *Statistical Yearbook of Jerusalem 2004* (Jerusalem: Jerusalem Institute for Israel Studies, in preparation), chap. 3.

13. Official figures of the Israeli Central Bureau of Statistics and its Palestinian counterpart showed that on the eve of Israel's withdrawal from Gaza, 49.3% of the population in Israel, the Gaza Strip, the West Bank, and the Golan Heights was Jewish; another 2.7% were non-Jewish immigrants from the former Soviet Union; 46.2% were Arabs. The remainder were foreign workers in Israel. Amiram Bareket, "Larishonah: Shi'ur Heyehudim Bashetahim Shebishlitat Yisrael—Pahot Me-50%," *Ha'aretz*, Aug. 11, 2005: A1.

14. See pages 50–51.

15. YAOH VI: 13.

16. Gorenberg, *End of Days*, 117–18, 132–37; Ehud Sprinzak, *Brother Against Brother: Violence and Extremism in Israeli Politics from Altalena to the Rabin Assassination* (New York: Free Press, 1999), 155–72; Segal, *Dear Brothers*, passim.

17. While the name "Gush Emunim" continued to be used loosely to describe the religious settler movement, the organization ceased functioning. Amana, the settlement organization it had established, continued the work of planning and establishing new settlements, while the Council of Settlements in Judea, Samaria, and the Gaza District represented the settlers publicly and politically.

18. Jim Hoagland, "Sharon Sees Time Ripe to Regain Defense Post," *Washington Post*, Nov. 7, 1988; Gershom Gorenberg, "A Belief in Force," *American Prospect*, Apr. 8, 2002; Gershom Gorenberg, "Road Map to Grand Apartheid?" *American Prospect*, July 3, 2003.

19. *Yishuvei Gush Katif: Hagevul Hehadash—Etgar Lehityashvut* (Sept. 1982).

20. Morris, *Victims*, 565.

21. In 1995 the political scientist Ehud Sprinzak would estimate members of what he termed the "Gush Emunim culture" as comprising about a fourth of all West Bank settlers. The proportion is much smaller if Jewish residents of East Jerusalem are included.

22. At the end of 1984, there were 102 settlements in the West Bank, with 35,300 residents, and 10 in Gaza, with 1,600 residents. At the end of 1988, there were 110 West Bank settlements with 63,700 residents, and 12 Gaza Strip settlements, with 2,700 residents. Central Bureau of Statistics, spokesperson's office.

23. See "Israeli-Palestinian Interim Agreement on the West Bank and the Gaza Strip," Sept. 28, 1995, www.mfa.gov.il/MFA/Peace%20Process/Guide%20to%20the%20Peace%20Process/THE%20ISRAELI-PALESTINIAN%20INTERIM%20AGREEMENT.

24. Dan Be'eri, "Shuv Ha'Saison' Bapetah," *Nekuda*, Mar. 1994: 22–26.

25. See Gorenberg, *End of Days*, 203–8. The Hamas campaign of suicide attacks began at the end of the customary forty days of mourning after the Hebron massacre.

26. Sprinzak, *Brother Against Brother*, 253–55.

27. *Ha'aretz*, Oct. 6, 1995.

28. Morris, *Victims*, 646–48; "Provocative Words Raise Mideast Tensions," CNN, Nov. 16, 1998, www.cnn.com/WORLD/meast/9811/15/mideast.wrap/.

29. See Sason, "Havat Da'at."

30. Leslie Susser and Isabel Kershner, "The Tragedy of Errors," *Jerusalem Report*, July 16, 2001: 10–16.

31. Ari Shavit, "Oto Sharon," *Ha'aretz* Weekend Magazine, Apr. 13, 2001: 19–22.

32. "Address by Prime Minister Ariel Sharon at the Fourth Herzliya Conference, December 18, 2003," Ministry of Foreign Affairs, www.mfa.gov.il/MFA/Government/Speeches+by+Israeli+leaders/2003/Address+by+PM+Ariel+Sharon+at+the+Fourth+Herzliya.htm.

33. Yoel Marcus, "Hapinui Hamtukhnan: Esrim Hitnahaluyot Birtzu'at Azah Uvagadah Betokh Shanah-Shenatayim," *Ha'aretz*, Feb. 3, 2004.

34. Olmert floated the trial balloon for unilateral withdrawal before Sharon's first speech on the subject, quoting Ben-Gurion on preferring a Jewish state to the Whole Land. *Yediot Aharonot*, Dec. 5, 2003: B2.

35. Ari Shavit, "Beshem Marsho," *Ha'aretz*, Oct. 8, 2004.

36. Ephraim Yaar and Tamar Hermann, "Peace Index: July 2005: The Disengagement as a Done Deal," spirit.tau.ac.il/socant/peace/peaceindex/2005/files/july2005e.doc.

37. Haim Gouri, "Predah," *Yediot Aharonot* Shabbat magazine, Aug. 12, 2005: 14–15.

Bibliography

Archives

Gush Etzion Archive (Kfar Etzion)
Hakibbutz Hame'uhad Archive (at Yad Tabenkin Archive, Ramat Efal)
Hashomer Hatza'ir Archive (Givat Havivah)
Israel Labor Party Archives (Beit Berl)
Israel State Archive (Jerusalem)
Jerusalem Municipal Archive
Kibbutz Gilgal Archive (Kibbutz Gilgal)
Lyndon Baines Johnson Library (Austin, Texas)
Merom Golan Archive (Merom Golan)
Midreshet Eretz Yisrael—Makhon Reshit (Eretz Yisrael Academy—Keddumim)
National Archives and Records Administration (College Park, Maryland)
Ofrah Archive (Ofrah)
Richard Nixon Library (Yorba Linda, California)
Yad Levi Eskhol (Jerusalem)
Yad Tabenkin Archive (Ramat Efal)
Yitzhak Rabin Center for Israel Studies (Tel Aviv)

Private Papers

Admoni, Yehiel
Demant, Prof. Peter Robert
Gouri, Haim

Lifshitz, Oded
Mintz, Avraham
Moskovic, Moshe

Oral Histories

Allon, Yigal: Israel State Archives 154.0/1-19/5001/19-22A. 23 interviews, conducted in 1979 by the Davis Institute of Hebrew University.
McPherson, Harry: LBJ Library Oral History Collection, Interview VII, Sept. 19, 1985, by Michael L. Gillette.
Rostow, Eugene V.: LBJ Library Oral History Collection, Dec. 2, 1968, by Paige E. Mulhollan.

Books and Articles

Article and book titles are in the original language, with English translations as provided by the publisher. Date citation is by the Hebrew calendar if only the Hebrew year is given. For conversion to Gregorian date, the Hebrew year 5700 began in September 1939.

Abdul-Hadi, Mahdi. *Al-Mustawtanat Al-Israiliyyah Fi Al-Quds Waddifah Al-Gharbiyyah Al-Muhtallah 1967–1977* (Israeli Settlements in Occupied Jerusalem and the West Bank 1967–1977). Jerusalem: Jamiat Al-Multaqa Al-Fikri Al-Arabi Al-Quds, 1978.
Admoni, Yehiel. *Asor Shel Shikul Da'at: Hahityashvut Me'ever Lakav Hayarok 1967–1977* (Decade of Discretion: Settlement Policy in the Territories 1967–1977). Makhon Yisrael Galili Leheker Hakoah Hamagen/Yad Tabenkin/Hakibbutz Hame'uhad: 1992.
———. *Asor Shel Shikul Da'at: Hahityashvut Me'ever Lakav Hayarok 1967–1977*. Author's ms.
Amir, Aharon. "Hakinor Vehaherev." *Keshet* (Fall 1975): 5–43.
Amital, Yehudah. *Hama'alot Mima'amakim*. Jerusalem, 5734.
Aran, Gideon. "From Religious Zionism to Zionist Religion: The Roots of Gush Emunim." *Studies in Contemporary Jewry* (1986): 116–43.
Bar-Joseph, Uri. *Hatzofeh Shenirdam* (The Watchman Fell Asleep: The Surprise of Yom Kippur and Its Sources). Lod: Zmora-Beitan, 2001.
Barzilai, Amnon. "Hatardemah Ha'arukah Shel Hamishmeret Hatze'irah," *Ha'aretz*, June 9, 2002, B3.
———. "Kakh Nehersah Shekhunat Hamughrabim." *Ha'aretz*, May 13, 1999, B2.
———. "Kakh Nignaz 'Siah Lohamim' Shel Merkaz Harav." *Ha'aretz*, June 16, 2002: B3.
———. "Mibrerat Mehdal Ve'ad Lamehdal." *Ha'aretz*, Oct. 10, 2003: B4.
———. "Uvitzumah shel Hamilhamah Tikhnenu Be'aman et Hamedinah Hapalestinit," *Ha'aretz*, June 5, 2002: B3.
Baumgarten, Albert I., ed. *Apocalyptic Time*. Leiden: Brill, 2000.
Bavly, Dan. *Halomot Vehizdamnuyot Shehuhmetzu 1967–1973* (Dreams and Missed Opportunities 1967–1973). Jerusalem: Carmel, 2002.

Beilin, Yossi. *Mehiro Shel Ihud: Mifleget Ha'avodah Ad Milhemet Yom Hakippurim.* Tel Aviv: Revivim, 1985.

Ben-Ami, A., ed. *Hakol: Gvulot Hashalom Shel Eretz Yisrael* (Hakol: The Peace Frontiers of Israel). Tel Aviv: Madaf, 1967.

Ben-Yaakov, Yohanan, ed. *Gush Etzion: Hamishim Shnot Ma'avak Viytzirah.* Alon Shvut: Yad Shapira, 1983.

Benziman, Uzi. *Yerushalayim: Ir Lelo Homah* (Jerusalem: City Without a Wall). Tel Aviv: Schocken, 1973.

Berman, Paul. *A Tale of Two Utopias: The Political Journey of the Generation of 1968.* New York: W.W. Norton, 1996.

Bettelheim, Bruno. *The Children of the Dream.* London: Collier-Macmillan, 1969.

Bivritekh. Tel Aviv: Hamahanot Ha'olim, 1938.

Bundy, William. *A Tangled Web: The Making of Foreign Policy in the Nixon Presidency.* New York: Hill and Wang, 1998.

Cohen, Yeruham. *Tokhnit Allon.* Hakibbutz Heme'uhad, 1972.

Collins, Larry, and Dominique Lapierre. *O Jerusalem.* London: Pan, 1973.

Dayan, Moshe. *Story of My Life: An Autobiography.* New York: William Morrow, 1976.

Demant, Peter Robert. *Ploughshares Into Swords: Israeli Settlement Policy in the Occupied Territories, 1967–1977.* Diss., Universiteit van Amsterdam, 1988.

Don Yehiya, Eliezer. "The Book and the Sword: The Nationalist Yeshivot and Political Radicalism in Israel," in *Accounting for Fundamentalisms: The Dynamic Character of Movements,* ed. Martin E. Marty and R. Scott Appleby. Chicago: The Fundamentalism Project, University of Chicago Press, 1994: 264–302.

Douer, Yair. *Lanu Hamaggal Hu Herev II* (Our Sickle Is Our Sword: Nahal Settlements From 1967 until 1992). Ministry of Defense and Yad Tabenkin, 1997.

Eban, Abba. *An Autobiography.* New York: Random House, 1977.

Ehrlich, B. "Keshet: Hamered Hakadosh." *Nekuda,* July 11, 1986, 10–19.

Eisenstadt, David E. *Hatmurot Bagvulot Ha'ironiyim (Municipaliyim) Shel Yerushalayim 1863–1967* (The Evolution of Jerusalem's Municipal Boundaries, 1863–1967). Master's thesis, Bar Ilan University, 1998.

Eldar, Akiva, and Idith Zertal. *Adonei Ha'aretz: Hamitnahalim Umedinat Yisrael 1967–2004* (Lords of the Land: The Settlers and the State of Israel 1967–2004). Kinneret: Zmora-Bitan, 2004.

Eliav, Arie Lova. *Ye'adim Hadashim Leyisrael.* Tel Aviv: Betzalel Cherikover, Feb. 1969.

———. *Tabe'ot Edut* (Rings of Faith). Tel Aviv: Am Oved, 1984.

———. *Eretz Hatzvi* (Land of the Hart). Tel Aviv: Am Oved, 1972; 8th ed., 1983.

Elkins, Michael. "Notebook of an Irreverent Correspondent." *The Jerusalem Report,* May 14, 1998, 60.

Elon Moreh: Hiddush Hayishuv Hayhudi Beshomron. Jerusalem: Gush Emunim, 5736.

Ezrahi, Yaron. *Rubber Bullets: Power and Conscience in Modern Israel.* New York: Farrar, Straus and Giroux, 1997.

Fanon, Frantz. *The Wretched of the Earth,* trans. Constance Farrington. Harmondsworth, England: Penguin, 1985.

Festinger, Leon, et al. *When Prophecy Fails.* University of Michigan, 1956; New York: Harper & Row, 1964.

Filber, Ya'akov Halevi. *Ayelet Hashahar.* Jerusalem: Haskel, 5728.

Gazit, Shlomo. *Hamakel Vehagezer: Hamemshal Hayisre'eli Biyhudah Veshomrom* (The

Stick and the Carrot: The Israeli Administration in Judea and Samaria). Tel Aviv: Zmora, Bitan, 1985.

———. *Peta'im Bemalkodet* (Trapped). Tel Aviv: Zmora-Bitan, 1999.

Golan, Matti. *The Secret Conversations of Henry Kissinger: Step-by-Step Diplomacy in the Middle East.* New York: Quadrangle/The New York Times, 1976.

———. *Shimon Peres: A Biography*, trans. Ina Friedman. London: Weidenfeld and Nicolson, 1982.

Gonen, Jay Y. *A Psychohistory of Zionism.* New York: Mason/Charter, 1975.

Gorenberg, Gershom. "Club Red." *The New Republic*, Oct. 14, 1996, 10–12.

———. *The End of Days: Fundamentalism and the Struggle for the Temple Mount.* New York: The Free Press, 2000.

———. "The Detonator." *The New York Times Magazine*, Dec. 29, 2003, 48–49.

———. "Requiem for a Dream?" *The Jerusalem Report*, Aug. 12, 2002, 18–21.

———. "The Terror Trap." *The American Prospect*, Jan. 1, 2004, 13–15.

Gouri, Gila. *Derekh Umikdash.* Hakibbutz Hame'uhad, 1976.

Gouri, Haim. *Ad Alot Hashar* (Until the Breaking of the Day). Tel Aviv: Hakibbutz Hame'uhad, 1950; 2000.

———. *Dapim Yerushalmiyim.* Tel Aviv: Hakibbutz Hame'uhad, 1968.

———. "Hashivah Le'Abu Dis." *Ha'aretz*, May 25, 2004.

———. *Shirim* (Collected Poems). Jerusalem: Bialik Institute/Hakibbutz Hame'uhad, 1998.

Grinberg, Lev Luis. *Hahistadrut Me'al Lakol* (The Histadrut Above All). Jerusalem: Nevo, 1993.

Gur, Motta [Mordechai]. *Har Habayit Beyadenu*, ed. Gershon Rivlin. Ma'arakhot, 1973.

Gvilei Esh, vol. 6, book 1 (Parchments of Fire: Representative Selection of Literary Works of Those Who Fell While Serving in the Israel Defense Forces, October 1973–December 1980). Ministry of Defense, 1986.

Haber, Eitan. *Hayom Tifrotz Milhamah* (Today War Will Break Out: The Reminiscenses of Brig. Gen. Israel Lior, Aide-de-Camp to Prime Ministers Levi Eshkol and Golda Meir). Tel Aviv: Edanim/Yediot Aharonot, 1987.

Hakohen [Cohen], David. *Hitnotzetzut Oro Shel Mashiah*, comp. his students at Merkaz Harav yeshivah. Jerusalem: 5728; Jerusalem: Ariel/Nezer David, 5749.

Hadari, Yona. *Mashiah Rakhuv Al Tank* (Messiah Rides a Tank: Public Thought Between the Sinai Campaign and the Yom Kippur War 1955–1975). Jerusalem: Shalom Hartman Institute, 2002.

Harel, Yehudah. "Meharamah Hasurit Leramat Hagolan." ms.

Harell, Yehuda. *Tabenkin's View of Socialism*, trans. Hanna Lash. Ramat Efal: Yad Tabenkin, 1988.

Harel, Yisrael, and Motta [Mordechai] Gur, eds. *Sha'ar Ha'arayot: Hakrav Al Yerushalayim Bahavayat Lohamei Hativat Hatzanhanim.* Ma'arakhot, n.d.

Harnoy, Meir. *Hamitnahalim* (The Settlers). Or Yehudah: Maariv, 1994.

Herder, Johann Gottfried von. *Reflections on the Philosophy of the History of Mankind*, abridged and with an introduction by Frank E. Manuel. Chicago: University of Chicago, 1968.

Hertzberg, Arthur. *The Zionist Idea: A Historical Analysis and Reader.* New York: Atheneum, 1973.

Hof, Frederic C. "The Line of June 4, 1967." *Middle East Insight*, Sept.–Oct. 1999, 17–23.

Howe, Stephen. *Empire: A Very Short Introduction*. Oxford: Oxford University Press, 2002.

Indig, Dov. *Mikhtavim Letalyah* (Letters to Talia), ed. Hagi Ben-Artzi. Tel Aviv: Yediot Aharonot, 2005.

Ish Shalom, Benjamin. *Tahat Hupat Barzel: Masekhet Hayyav Shel Daniel Orlik* (Under a Canopy of Iron: The Story of Daniel Orlik). Jerusalem: Moriah, 5735.

Jerusalem Report staff. *Shalom, Friend: The Life and Legacy of Yitzhak Rabin*, ed. David Horovitz. New York: Newmarket Press, 1996.

Judah Halevi [Yehudah Halevi]. *The Kuzari: An Argument for the Faith of Israel*, introduction H. Slonimsky. New York: Schocken, 1964.

Kalinov, Rina, ed. *Kobi Rabinovich: Na'an, Merom Golan*. Hakibbutz Hame'uhad, 1981.

Kasher, Menachem M. *Hatekufah Hagedolah: Pirkei Hitbonenut Bematzav Ha'umah Ve'artzenu Hakedoshah Besha'ah Zo Uverur Makif Al Darkhei Hage'ulah Vesimaneha Al Yesod Divrei Hazal, Sifrei Harishonim Veha'aharonim* (The Great Era: A Comprehensive Study in the Position of the Jewish People, the Holy Land, and the Stages of Redemption at This Time, Based on Talmudic and Rabbinic Sources). Jerusalem: Torah Shlemah Institute, 1968.

Katz, Jacob. "The Jewish National Movement: A Sociological Analysis." *Jewish Society Through the Ages*, ed. H. H. Ben-Sasson and S. Ettinger. New York: Schocken, 1971, 267–83.

Khouri, Fred J. *The Arab-Israeli Dilemma*. Syracuse: Syracuse University Press, 1968.

Kissinger, Henry. *White House Years*. Boston: Little, Brown, 1979.

———. *Years of Renewal*. New York: Touchstone, 2000.

———. *Years of Upheaval*. Boston: Little, Brown, 1982.

Klein, Menachem. *Bar-Ilan: Akademiah, Dat Upolitikah* (Bar-Ilan University Between Religion and Politics). Jerusalem: Magnes, 1998.

Knohl, Dov, ed. *Gush Etzion Bemilhamto*. Jerusalem: Religious Division of the Youth and Hehalutz Department of the World Zionist Organization, 1954.

Kollek, Teddy, with Amos Kollek. *For Jerusalem*. New York: Random House, 1978.

Kook, Avraham Yitzhak Hacohen. *Orot*. Jerusalem: Mossad Harav Kook, 5753.

Kook, Tzvi Yehudah Hacohen. *Lintivot Yisrael*. Jerusalem: Menorah, 5727.

Lammfromm, Arnon, and Hagai Tsoref, eds. *Levi Eshkol: Rosh Hamemshelah Hashlishi* (Levi Eshkol: The Third Prime Minister—Selected Documents 1895–1969). Jerusalem: Israel State Archives, 2002.

Lieblich, Amia. *Gilgulo Shel Makom*. Tel Aviv: Schocken, 2000.

Ma'oz, Moshe. *Palestinian Leadership on the West Bank: The Changing Role of Arab Mayors Under Jordan and Israel*. London: Frank Cass, 1984.

Marx, Karl. "On the Jewish Question." *The Marx-Engels Reader*, ed. Robert C. Tucker. New York: W. W. Norton, 1972, 24–51.

Medzini, Meron. *Hayehudiah Hageah: Golda Meir Vahazon Yisrael, Biografiah Politit* (The Proud Jewess: Golda Meir and the Vision of Israel. A Political Biography). Jerusalem: Edanim, 1990.

Meital, Yoram. "The Khartoum Conference and Egyptian Policy After the 1967 War: A Reexamination." *Middle East Journal* (Winter 2000): 64–82.

Melman, Yossi. *The Master Terrorist: The True Story of Abu-Nidal.* New York: Adama, 1986.

Merom Golan: Reshit. Merom Golan, 1977.

Middle East Record, vol. 3–5, 1967–1969. Tel Aviv: Israel Oriental Society, Reuven Shiloah Research Center.

Morris, Benny. *Milhamot Hagvul Shel Yisrael 1949–1956* (Israel's Border Wars, 1949–1956: Arab Infiltration, Israeli Retaliation, and the Countdown to the Suez War). Tel Aviv: Am Oved, 1996.

———. *Righteous Victims: A History of the Zionist-Arab Conflict 1881–1999.* New York: Alfred A. Knopf, 1999.

Naor, Arye. *Eretz Yisrael Hashlemah: Emunah Umdiniyut* (Greater Israel: Theology and Policy). Haifa: University of Haifa/Zmora-Bitan, 2001.

Narkiss, Uzi. *Ahat Yerushalayim* (The Liberation of Jerusalem). Tel Aviv: Am Oved, 1975.

Negbi, Moshe. *Kevalim Shel Tzedek: Bagatz Mul Hamemshal Hayisre'eli Bashtahim* (Justice Under Occupation: The Israeli Supreme Court versus the Military Administration in the Occupied Territories). Jerusalem: Cana, 1981.

Netzer, Moshe. *Netzer Mishorashav: Sippur Haim* (Life Story). Ministry of Defense, 2002.

Oren, Michael B. *Six Days of War: June 1967 and the Making of the Modern Middle East.* New York: Oxford University Press, 2002.

Oz, Amos. *In the Land of Israel,* trans. Maurice Goldberg-Bartura. London: Chatto & Windus/The Hogworth Press, 1983.

———. *Under This Blazing Light: Essays,* trans. Nicholas de Lange. Cambridge: Cambridge University Press, 1995.

Pedatzur, Reuven. "Het Kaddum." *Ha'aretz,* Oct. 3, 1990, B2.

———. *Nitzhon Hamevukhah* (The Triumph of Embarrassment: Israel and the Territories After the Six-Day War). Tel Aviv: Bitan/Yad Tabenkin, 1996.

———. "Vekaddum Le'olam Tisha'er." *Ha'aretz,* Oct. 10, 1990.

Penniman, Howard R., ed. *Israel at the Polls: The Knesset Elections of 1977.* Washington, DC: American Enterprise Institute, 1979.

Peres, Shimon. *Battling for Peace: Memoirs,* ed. David Landau. London: Weidenfeld & Nicolson, 1995.

Perry, Yaakov. *Habba Lehorgekha* (Strike First). Tel Aviv: Keshet, 1999.

Porat, Hanan. *Et Ahai Anokhi Mevakesh.* Beit El: Sifriat Beit El, 5752.

Quandt, William B. *Peace Process: American Diplomacy and the Arab Israeli Conflict Since 1967.* Washington, DC: The Brookings Institution/University of California, 1993.

Rabin, Yitzhak. *Pinkas Sherut.* Tel Aviv: Sifriat Ma'ariv, 1979.

Rabinovich, Abraham. *The Yom Kippur War: The Epic Encounter That Transformed the Middle East.* New York: Schocken, 2004.

Rapoport, David C. "The Fourth Wave: September 11 and the History of Terrorism." *Current History* (Dec. 2001): 419–24.

Ravitzky, Aviezer. *Haketz Hamguleh Umdinat Hayehudim* (Messianism, Zionism, and Jewish Religious Radicalism). Tel Aviv: Am Oved, 1993.

Rubinstein, Danny. *Mi Lashem Elai: Gush Emunim* (On the Lord's Side: Gush Emunim). Tel Aviv: Hakibbutz Hame'uhad, 1982.

Sabbato, Chaim. *Te'um Kavvanot* (Adjusting Sights). Tel Aviv: Yediot Aharonot, 1999.

Sachar, Howard M. *A History of Israel: From the Rise of Zionism to Our Time*. New York: Alfred A. Knopf, 1979.

Sarid, Yossi. "The Spirit of Golda." *Ha'aretz* (English edition), Dec. 28, 2003.

Saunders, Harold H., and Cecilia Albin. *Sinai II: The Politics of International Mediation, 1974–1975 (FPI Case Studies Number 17)*. Washington, DC: Foreign Policy Institute, John Hopkins University, 1993.

Schwar, Harriet Dashiell, ed. *Arab-Israeli Crisis and War, 1967*, vol. 19 of *Foreign Relations, 1964–1968*. Washington, DC: United States Government, 2004.

Segal, Haggai. *Dear Brothers: The West Bank Jewish Underground*. Woodmere, NY: Beit-Shammai, 1988.

Shafat, Gershon, with Tzviah Granot. *Gush Emunim: Hasipur Me'ahorei Hakla'im* (Gush Emunim: The Story Behind the Scenes). Jerusalem: Sifriat Beit El: 1995.

Shani, Hemdat. "Mekimei Hagader—Hasipur Hamale." *Et Ofrah*, Sivan 5765 (June 2005), 10–16.

———. "Ofrah Agush—Hatargum Hamale." *Et Ofrah*, Iyar 18, 5761 (May 11, 2001).

Shapira, Anita. *Yigal Allon: Aviv Heldo* (Igal Allon: Spring of His Life). Tel Aviv: Hasifriah Hahadashah, 2004.

———. "From the Palmach Generation to the Candle Children: Changing Patterns in Israeli Identity." *Partisan Review*, Oct. 23, 2000.

Shapira, Avraham, ed. *Siah Lohamim: Pirkei Hakshavah Vehitbonenut*. Tel Aviv: Haverim Tze'irim Mehatnu'ah Hakibbutzit, Oct. 1967.

Shapira, Yonathan. *Leshilton Behartanu* (Chosen to Command: The Road to Power of the Herut Party—A Sociopolitical Interpretation). Tel Aviv: Am Oved, 1989.

Sharon, Ariel, with David Chanoff. *Warrior: An Autobiography*. New York: Touchstone, 2001.

Shehadeh, Raja. *Strangers in the House: Coming of Age in Occupied Palestine*. New York: Penguin, 2003.

Shemtov, Victor. *Ehad Mehem*. Kibbutz Daliah: Ma'arekhet, 1997.

Shlaim, Avi. *The Iron Wall: Israel and the Arab World*. New York: W. W. Norton and Company, 2001.

Shnurman, Vardina. "Esrim Vehamesh Shanim Le'ahar Quneitrah." *Eretz Hagolan*, May 15, 1997, 12–14.

Shragai, Nadav. "26 Beyuni 1967: Hamemshalah Mevakeshet Shehatikshoret Lo Ta'aseh Inyan Misipuah Mizrah Yerushalayim." *Ha'aretz*, Nov. 3, 1967, B3.

Shvut, Avraham, ed. *Ha'aliyah El Hahar: Hahityashvut Hayehudit Hamithadeshet Biyhudah Veshomron* (Ascent to the Mountains: Renewal of Jewish Settlement in Judea and Samaria). Jerusalem: Sifriat Beit El, 2002.

"Sihah Biyshivat Harav Kook." *Shdemot: Bamah Lehinukh Tnu'ati* (Spring 1968): 15–27.

Silberstein, Laurence J., ed. *Jewish Fundamentalism in Comparative Perspective: Religion, Ideology and the Crisis of Modernity*. New York: New York University, 1993.

Simons, Chaim. *Three Years in a Military Compound: Reminiscences of a Hebron Settler*, ms., 2003.

Simons, Marlise. "Weaving the Threads of Law, War and Shakespeare," *New York Times*, Jan. 3, 2004.

Smith, Louis J., ed., *Arab-Israeli Dispute, 1967–1968*, vol. 20 of *Foreign Relations, 1964–1968*. Washington, DC: United States Government, 2001.

Sprinzak, Ehud. *The Ascendance of Israel's Radical Right*. New York: Oxford University Press, 1991.

————. *Bein Meha'ah Hutz Parliamentarit Leterror: Alimut Politit Beyisrael* (Political Violence in Israel). Jerusalem: Jerusalem Institute for Israel Studies, 1995.

————. *Brother Against Brother: Violence and Extremism in Israeli Politics from Altalena to the Rabin Assassination*. New York: The Free Press, 1999.

————. *Ish Hayashar Be'einav: Illegalism Bahevrah Hayisre'elit* (Every Man Whatsoever Is Right in His Own Eyes: Illegalism in Israeli Society). Tel Aviv: Sifriat Poalim, 1986.

Starr Sered, Susan. "Rachel's Tomb: The Development of a Cult." *Jewish Studies Quarterly* (1995): 103–48.

Stein, Kenneth W. *Heroic Diplomacy: Sadat, Kissinger, Carter, Begin and the Quest for Arab-Israeli Peace*. New York: Routledge, 1999.

Sternhall, Zeev. *Binyan Umah O Tikkun Hevrah?* (Nation-Building or a New Society: The Zionist Labor Movement 1904–1940 and the Origins of Israel). Tel Aviv: Am Oved, 1995.

Teveth, Shabtai. *Klalat Habrakhah*. Tel Aviv: Schocken, 1973.

Tsur, Zeev. *Hakibbutz Hame'uhad Beyishuvah shel Ha'aretz* (The Hakibbutz Hameuchad in the Settlement of Eretz Yisrael), vol. 4, 1960–1980. Yad Tabenkin/Hakibbutz Hame'uhad, 1986.

————. *Mipulmus Hahalukah Ad Tokhnit Allon* (From the Partition Dispute to the Allon Plan). Ramat Efal: Tabenkin Institute, 1982.

U.S. National Archives and Records Administration. *Public Papers of the Presidents of the United States: Lyndon Baines Johnson, 1967*, vol. 1. Washington, DC: United States Government, 1968.

Wallach, Jehuda. *Atlas Carta Letoldot Eretz Yisrael Mereshit Habityashvut Ve'ad Kom Hamedinah* (Carta's Atlas of Palestine from Zionism to Statehood). Jerusalem: Carta, 1972; 1974.

————. *Atlas Carta Letoldot Medinat Yisrael: Asor Sheni* (Carta's Atlas of Israel: The Second Decade 1961–1971). Jerusalem: Carta, 1980.

Warhaftig, Zorach. *Hamishim Shanah Veshanah: Pirkei Zikhronot* (Fifty Years, From Year to Year: Memories). Jerusalem: Yad Shapira, 1998.

Zak, Moshe. *Hussein Oseh Shalom* (King Hussein Makes Peace). Ramat Gan: Bar Ilan University, 1996.

Internet

Alterman, Nathan. "Shir Ha'emek." www.mp3music.co.il/lyrics/8513.html.

"Biography, Yigal Allon." Beit Yigal Allon. www.bet-alon.co.il/museum/alon_01.php.

Burr, William, ed. "The October War and U.S. Policy." The National Security Archive, www.gwu.edu/nsarchiv/NSAEBB/NSAEBB98/index.htm.

Central Bureau of Statistics [Israel]. www.cbs.gov.il.

Clausewitz, Carl von. *On War*, trans. J. J. Graham. www.clausewitz.com/cwzhome/on_war/onwartoc.html.

"Commentary Art. 49 Convention (IV) relative to the Protection of Civilian Persons in Time of War. Geneva, 12 August 1949." ICRC, www.icrc.org/ihl.nsf/

b466ed681ddfcfd241256739003e6368/523ba38706c71588c12563cd0042c407? OpenDocument.

"Convention (IV) relative to the Protection of Civilian Persons in Time of War. Geneva, 12 August 1949." ICRC, www.icrc.org/ihl.nsf/0/6756482d86146898c12 5641e004aa3c5?OpenDocument.

"Egyptian-Israeli General Armistice Agreement, February 24, 1949." The Avalon Project at Yale Law School, www.yale.edu/lawweb/avalon/mideast/armo1.htm.

"General Assembly Resolution 3375, Invitation to the Palestine Liberation Organization to participate in the efforts for peace in the Middle East." UNISPAL, domino.un.org/UNISPAL.NSF/0/7e0524b7ead4a9e4852560de004efdc7?Open-Document.

"General Assembly Resolution 3379. Elimination of all forms of racial discrimination." UNISPAL, domino.un.org/UNISPAL.NSF/0/761c1063530766a7052566a 2005b74d1?OpenDocument.

"Hanita." Ha'arkhion Al Saf Beitkha. www.sifriya.org.il:4444/hanita.htm.

"Harav Yehuda Amital." Yeshivat Har Etzion. www.vbm-torah.org/rya.htm.

Herzl, Theodore. Altneuland. WZO, www.wzo.org.il/en/resources/view.asp?id=1600.

"Israeli-Syrian General Armistice Agreement, July 20, 1949." The Avalon Project at Yale Law School, www.yale.edu/lawweb/avalon/mideast/armo4.htm.

"Israel's Foreign Relations, Selected Documents, vols. 1–2, 1947–1974." Israel Ministry of Foreign Affairs, www.mfa.gov.il/MFA/Foreign%20Relations/Israels% 20Foreign%20Relations%20since%201947/1947-1974/.

"Jordanian-Israeli General Armistice Agreement, April 3, 1949." The Avalon Project at Yale Law School, www.yale.edu/lawweb/avalon/mideast/armo3.htm.

Karmon, Ely. "Fatah and the Popular Front for the Liberation of Palestine: International Terrorism Strategies (1968–1990)." Interdisciplinary Center Herzliya, www.ict.org.il/articles/fatah-pflp.htm.

"Khartoum Resolutions September 1967." Mideast Web, www.mideastweb.org/khartoum.htm.

Klein, Menachem. "The Negotiations for the Settlement of the 1948 Refugee Problem." www.tau.ac.il/law/cegla/11-07-03/Menachem%20Klein.doc.

The Knesset. www.knesset.gov.il/index.html.

Lapid, Arnon. "Hazmanah Levekhi." www.notes.co.il/tirza/7754.asp.

"Laws of War: Laws and Customs of War on Land (Hague IV); October 18, 1907." The Avalon Project at Yale Law School, www.yale.edu/lawweb/avalon/lawofwar/hague04.htm.

"Lebanese-Israeli General Armistice Agreement, March 23, 1949." The Avalon Project at Yale Law School, www.yale.edu/lawweb/avalon/mideast/armo2.htm.

Levinger, Moshe. "Kakh Zeh Hit'hil." Mehadshei Hayishuv Hayehudi Behevron, www.hebron.co.il/agdot/ag29.html.

Kletter, Raz. "A Very General Archaeologist—Moshe Dayan and Israeli Archaeology." Journal of Hebrew Scriptures 4 (2002–2003). www.arts.ualberta.ca/JHS/Articles/article_27.htm.

Palestinian Central Bureau of Statistics, www.pcbs.org.

"Political Program Adopted at the 12th Session of the Palestine National Council." Permanent Observer Mission of Palestine to the United Nations, www.palestine-un.org/plo/doc_one.html.

"Protection of Holy Places Law 5727 (1967)." The Knesset, www.knesset.gov.il/laws/special/eng/HolyPlaces.htm.

"The Second United States Initiative, 19 June 1970." Israel Ministry of Foreign Affairs, www.mfa.gov.il/MFA/Foreign%20Relations/Israels%20Foreign%20Relations%20since%201947/1947-1974/16%20The%20Second%20United%20States%20Initiative-%2019%20June%2019.

"Separation of Forces Agreement Between Israel and Egypt January 18, 1974." Israel Ministry of Foreign Affairs, www.mfa.gov.il/MFA/Peace+Process/Guide+to+the+Peace+Process/Israel-Egypt+Separation+of+Forces+Agreement+-+1974.htm.

"Seventh Arab League Summit Conference, Resolution on Palestine." Le Monde Diplomatique, mondediplo.com/focus/mideast/a2287.

Shemer, Naomi. "Jerusalem of Gold." Israel Ministry of Foreign Affairs, www.mfa.gov.il/mfa/templates/BigPicture.aspx?GifsSrcEnding=&PageTitle=50%20Years%20of%20Hebrew%20Song&ImgSource=/NR/rdonlyres/BEC65C2414D3-47BF-AE0A-EAFFDD1E94BA/38043/MFAG005e0.gif.

"Speech by PLO Chairman Yasser Arafat, United Nations General Assembly, New York 13 November 1974." Jerusalem Media and Communications Centre, www.jmcc.org/documents/arfatun74.htm.

"Statement by Secretary of State Rogers—9 December 1969." Israel Ministry of Foreign Affairs, www.mfa.gov.il/MFA/Foreign%20Relations/Israels%20Foreign%20Relations%20since%201947/1947-1974/9%20Statement%20by%20Secretary%20of%20State%20Rogers-%209%20Decemb.

"Theodor Meron." Faculty profiles, New York University School of Law, www.law.nyu.edu/faculty/profiles/bios/meront_bio.html.

Tolstoy, Lev Nikolayevich. "How Much Land Does a Man Need?" www.ccel.org/t/tolstoy/23_tales/htm/vii.iii.htm.

"United Nations Security Council Resolution 242." The Avalon Project at Yale Law School, www.yale.edu/lawweb/avalon/un/un242.htm.

Yehudah Halevi. "Tzion Halo Tishali." Proyekt Ben-Yehuda, benyehuda.org/rihal/Rihal1_4.html.

Yehoshua, A. B. "The Literature of the Generation of the State." Israeli Ministry of Foreign Affairs, www.mfa.gov.il/MFA/MFAArchive/1990_1999/1999/1/A%20B%20Yehoshua%20-%20The%20Literature%20of%20the%20Generation%20of.

Hebrew Newspapers and Periodicals

Al Hamishmar
Davar
Ha'aretz
Hatzofeh
Hayom
Lamerhav
Ma'ariv
Nekuda
Yediot Aharonot

Hebrew Internal Newsletters

Alei Golan (Kibbutz Merom Golan)
Alon Shvut (Yeshivat Har Etzion)
Emunim (Gush Emunim)
Et Ofrah (Ofrah)
Gilgalon (Kibbutz Gilgal)
Gush Emunim
Gush Emunim—Daf Kesher
Gush Emunim—Dapei Meda
Zra'im (Bnei Akiva)

English Newspapers and Periodicals

Newsweek
New York Times
Time
Washington Post

Interviews

Admoni, Yehiel. December 12, 2003.
Azaryahu, Arnan (Sini). November 5, 2003.
Bar, Carmel. November 3, 2003.
Ben Artzi, Hagi. February 24, 2005.
Ben-Meir, Yehuda. March 24, 2004.
Ben-Tzedek, Hedva. June 14, 2004.
Brawer, Moshe. April 17, 2005.
Dori, Latif. June 30, 2004.
Dror, Vered. June 14, 2004.
Eisenstadt, David. January 21, 2003.
Eliav, Arie (Lova). July 27, 2003; February 8, 2004.
Eshkol, Miriam. March 9, 2004.
Etzion, Yehudah. February 10, 2004; March 2, 2004.
Ezrahi, Yaron. May 31, 2005.
Felix, Menachem. February 10, 2004.
Gazit, Shlomo. December 10, 2003.
Gouri, Haim. August 6, 2003; September 12, 2003; October 28, 2003; July 9, 2004.
Halbertal, Moshe. June 16, 2004.
Harel, Yehudah. November 4, 2003.
Harel, Yisrael. March 23, 2004; May 27, 2004.
Hillel, Shlomo. December 1, 2003.
Katzover, Benjamin. February 10, 2004.
Klein, Menachem. April 25, 2005.

Lahat, Shlomo. August 26, 2003.
Lavie, Naftali. December 30, 2002.
Levinger, Moshe. March 18, 2004.
Lifshitz, Oded. March 3, 2004; May 18, 2005.
Meinrat, Gershon. November 4, 2003.
Moskovic, Moshe. December 24, 2003; December 31, 2003; January 12, 2004.
Negbi, Moshe. February 2, 2005.
Netzer, Moshe. February 11, 2004.
Parker, Richard. May 11, 2004.
Porat, Hanan. September 3, 2003; October 30, 2003; May 27, 2004.
Quandt, William. May 19, 2004.
Rosenblau, Shmuel. June 14, 2004.
Sarid, Yossi. February 22, 2004.
Sat, Eytan. November 5, 2003.
Saunders, Harold. May 10, 2004.
Sereni, Hagar. December 20, 2004.
Shemtov, Victor. July 23, 2003.
Sisco, Joseph. June 15, 2004.
Walker, Edward. May 10, 2004.
Yisraeli, Chaim. April 19, 2004.

Acknowledgments

Writing a book looks, from the outside, like a peculiarly lonely calling. From the inside, it is a celebration, a long intellectual feast shared with many friends.

In planning my research, I was able to benefit from the expertise of Michael Oren, Benny Morris, Yossi Heller, Menachem Klein, and Lev Grinberg, friends whose very different perspectives on Israel's past have enriched me. Yaron Ezrahi shared his insights into Israel's politics and culture. Yehudah Mirsky and Moshe Halbertal helped me explore the philosophical and cultural development of Gush Emunim. David Eisenstadt shared with me his research on Jerusalem's changing boundaries, and Moshe Negbi has regularly lent his knowledge of legal history. Asher Arian, Gad Barzilai, Warren Bass, Robert Caro, Eliezer Don Yehiya, Louise Fischer, Yossi Goldstein, David Greenberg, Ron Kuzar, Arnon Lammfromm, Peter Medding, Avi Raz, Tom Segev, and others gave of their time and knowledge. Naturally, I am solely responsible for how I chose to interpret their ideas.

My discerning research assistants, Joel Zisenwine and Amir Engel, helped find the treasures buried in archaeological mounds of paper.

Through the good graces of the Middle East Institute, Nora Achrati assisted in my research at the National Archives, doubling the worth of my time there. Ata Qaymari ably translated Mahdi Abdul Hadi's pioneering Arabic study on settlements.

The hunt for contemporary documents took me to archives ranging from one-room collections in individual settlements to major repositories in Israel and the United States. I am grateful for a grant from the Lyndon B. Johnson Foundation that made it possible for me to work at the LBJ Library in Austin, Texas, where archivist Regina Greenwell and others helped me explore sources on U.S. Mideast policy in the critical period during and after the Six-Day War. I also owe special thanks to Yehoshua Freundlich at the Israel State Archives for bringing to my attention the extensive oral history interviews with Yigal Allon, a free-flowing autobiography of a central figure in the settlement story, and to Michal Saft and the ISA reading room staff. At the Yad Tabenkin Archive, Maurice Kantor virtually became a partner in my work. Vardina Schnurmann at Merom Golan, Hemdat Shani at Ofrah, Ora Routtenberg at the Gush Etzion Archive, and Zvi Slonim at Midreshet Eretz Yisrael in Keddumim helped me with settlement collections. At the Israel Defense Force's memorial library for fallen soldiers, Smadar Spector-Danon assisted in finding writing by young Israelis—who, tragically, never grew old—that testifies to the mood and ideas that shaped the settlement movement. Israel Courts Administration spokeswoman Tamar Paul-Cohen and staffers Efrat Farkash and Hanit Haroosh outdid themselves in providing access to Supreme Court materials on the expulsion of the Sinai Bedouin. At National Archives in Maryland, the Richard Nixon Library, the Yitzhak Rabin Center for Israel Studies, and elsewhere, other generous staffers provided a hand.

Unfortunately, documentation on settlement in the IDF Archive, including the papers of defense ministers Moshe Dayan and Shimon Peres and the inquiry commission report on the expulsion of the Sinai Bedouin, remained classified—according to officials, on grounds that settlement is "a very delicate, very problematic" subject and that information on the expulsion of the Bedouin "could damage the foreign relations" of Israel. Such political justifications for secrecy are unworthy of Israeli democracy. The Association for Civil Rights in Israel and its dedicated attorney, Avner Pinchuk, have earned my thanks and admiration in their effort to open access to this material.

On the other hand, papers provided by individuals have filled in more of the settlement story. Yehiel Admoni, former director of the Jewish Agency Settlement Department, allowed me use of the manuscript of his book, *Asor Shel Shikul Da'at* (Decade of Discretion), more extensive than the published version and an archive in itself. Peter Demant was kind enough to share the valuable collection of early Gush Emunim documents he gathered during his doctoral research. Haim Gouri, Oded Lifshitz, Avraham Mintz, and Moshe Moskovic added material on key incidents.

To complement the documentary material and published research, I interviewed participants in the original events and experts, as listed in the bibliography. My experience as a journalist is that interviews, properly evaluated and weighed against other sources, are an essential resource. I am grateful to all those who shared their time—sometimes many hours—with me. I felt especially enriched by conversations with people in their eighth and ninth decades, who showed why "elder" connotes someone of knowledge and insight.

Dror Etkes of Peace Now's Settlement Watch project generously gave me a tour of early settlement sites. Esteban Alterman, photo editor of the *Jerusalem Report*, lent invaluable assistance in finding historical photographs. Sharon Ashley and Ronnie Hope, my editorial colleagues at the *Report*, read the manuscript chapter by chapter as I wrote. Sometimes I was sensible enough to take their suggestions.

As always, I am thankful to Anne Roiphe and Sid Bernstein for their support, to my agent Lisa Bankoff, and especially to my editor at Times Books, Paul Golob, whose encouragement and collaboration have been essential.

Last, but far from least, this book would not have been possible without the patience of my children, Yehonatan, Elisheva, and Shir-Raz—and most of all, without the help, involvement, suggestions, and love of my wife, Myra Noveck.

Index

About the Author

GERSHOM GORENBERG is the author of *The End of Days: Fundamentalism and the Struggle for the Temple Mount* and coauthor of *Shalom, Friend: The Life and Legacy of Yitzhak Rabin*. For many years a columnist and associate editor at *The Jerusalem Report*, he has also written for *The New York Times Magazine*, *The Washington Post*, *The New Republic*, *The American Prospect*, *Mother Jones*, *Ha'aretz*, and *Ma'ariv*. Born in America and educated at the University of California and Hebrew University, Gorenberg lives in Jerusalem with his wife and three children.

17390503R00293

Made in the USA
Middletown, DE
21 January 2015